Assembly Illinois. General

Official Directory of the Fortieth General Assembly of Illinois

Assembly Illinois. General

Official Directory of the Fortieth General Assembly of Illinois

ISBN/EAN: 9783744692441

Printed in Europe, USA, Canada, Australia, Japan

Cover: Foto ©ninafisch / pixelio.de

More available books at **www.hansebooks.com**

CLOTH, $5

OFFICIAL DIRECTORY

OF THE

FORTIETH GENERAL ASSEMBLY OF ILLINOIS

SESSION OF 1897

PORTRAITS AND BIOGRAPHICAL SKETCHES

OF THE MEMBERS AND PRESS

APPENDIX A

A COMPREHENSIVE AND ACCURATE STATISTICAL HISTORY OF ILLINOIS FROM 1809 TO 1897; ALSO, PORTRAITS AND SKETCHES OF ALL ILLINOIS GOVERNORS, PRESENT U. S. SENATORS, STATE OFFICERS, PRINCIPAL APPOINTEES OF THE GOVERNOR, TRUSTEES, COMMISSIONS, ETC.; PORTRAITS OF STATE INSTITUTIONS, APPORTIONMENT MAPS, UNITED STATES CENSUS BY DECADES FROM 1800, ETC., ETC., ETC.

APPENDIX B

OFFICIAL VOTE OF ILLINOIS, ELECTION OF NOVEMBER, 1896, FOR ALL OFFICES (ABOVE COUNTY), BY COUNTIES

SPRINGFIELD
PRESS OF THE ILLINOIS STATE REGISTER
MDCCCXCVII

Is not debatable, but the compiler of the Legislative Directory for 1897 begs leave to exercise his privilege under the rules and close the debate. The edition of 1895 was so well received by persons interested in Illinois and the men who have made Illinois the greatest and most influential among the galaxy of American states, that I have been to considerable expense in time and money to verify the data published in 1895. Not exceeding half a dozen errors were discovered, and the present edition is presented as being accurate.

Where so many men of many minds meet in an assembly it is impossible to bring all of them to a common center, viz: To realize the value of a work of this kind. This is the only excuse I offer for failing to secure portraits of every member of the Fortieth General Assembly. However, seventy-five per cent of the members are represented by portraits, and an epitome of the life of every one is given.

Thanking my friends for valuable assistance,

Sincerely,

J. L. Pickering,

Springfield, Ill., March, 1897.

FROM A FLASH-LIGHT PHOTO TAKEN IN EXECUTIVE OFFICE.

THE GOVERNOR.

John Riley Tanner was born April 4, 1844, in Warrick Co., Ind., the particular site of his birth being a log house three miles from Boonville. He attended the common school of his neighborhood and worked on the farm of his father, acquiring the rudiments of a pioneer education. There were five males in the family, father and four sons, and every one offered his life for his country in the civil war. The mother died at Carbondale, Ill., in 1863. The father enlisted in the 14th Ill. Cav., was captured and ended his life in a rebel prison pen in Columbus, Miss. Albert Tanner volunteered in the 26th Ky. Inf., was severely wounded in battle, and died in Nashville, Tenn., in 1863. Frederick enlisted in the 13th Ill. Cav., and died in a hospital in Pine Bluff, Ark., in 1864. J. M. Tanner was also a member of the 13th Ill. Cav., served with distinction through the war, and was mustered out a lieutenant in rank in 1865.

John R. Tanner entered Co. A, 98th Ill. Inf., in 1863, and served until June, 1865, when he was transferred to Co. B., 61st Inf., and was mustered out in September, 1865. He served in Kentucky, Tennessee, Alabama and Georgia. It is the united testimony of the comrades who marched and fought with John R. Tanner that a better and braver soldier never wore the Union blue. He never shirked a duty or avoided a danger. Generous to a fault, he shared his blanket and crust with a needy comrade, and under the deadly fire of rebel guns, where men became iron with nerves of steel, John R. Tanner never flinched nor showed his back to an enemy.

Returning to Illinois, Gov. Tanner purchased sixty acres of land in Clay county, for which he paid $600. Taking for a wife Miss Lauretta Ingraham, he began farming. This was his occupation in 1870, when he was elected sheriff of Clay county. This was followed by a term as circuit clerk, at the close of which he again engaged in farming and in the real estate business. In 1880 he was elected to the state senate from the 44th district, redeeming both his own county of Clay and the senatorial district from the democracy. During his senatorial term he engaged in sawing lumber in partnership with his brother, J. M. Tanner, continuing in this business until 1886, when he was elected state treasurer, receiving 276,-680 votes to 240,864 for Henry F. J. Ricker, democrat. It was one of the largest majorities ever given a state officer in Illinois, being exceeded, however, by the phenomenal majorities for the state candidates in 1894, which, in part, at least, were due to Gov. Tanner, then chairman of the republican state committee, and manager of the campaign.

For about a year Gov. Tanner was U. S. marshal for the Southern District of Illinois by appointment of President Arthur, and for about the same time member of the Railroad and Warehouse Commission, by appointment of Gov. Fifer. Resigning the latter office he was shortly thereafter made by President Harrison, Assistant United States Treasurer at Chicago, which responsible and important office he held until the democratic appointee succeeded him.

In the many responsible and honorable positions held by Gov. Tanner prior to his election as governor, he demonstrated his business capacity and his faithful attention to details. He ably and honestly discharged every trust reposed in him by the people. He is a prodigious worker. He knows that a sluggard cannot succeed in business or politics any more than a lazy general can win battles. Hence, he never saved himself, and labored early and late, giving minute attention to the details of his business or the duties of the office he held.

Reluctant to enter upon the race for governor in 1896, and becoming a candidate only upon the earnest solicitation of many prominent and influential republicans, once in he was in to win, and not to lose. The spring campaign in 1896 preceding the republican state convention was marked by an almost unanimous desire for Gov. Tanner to head the ticket in Illinois. County after county instructed its delegates to the state convention for him, and long before the convention met it was absolutely certain that he would be named for governor on the first ballot. Early in the contest, which was good-natured from start to finish, there were no less than six avowed candidates for governor, and a score more were hoping for an opening in the convention. Gov. Tanner was named on the first ballot by an overwhelming majority over all in the largest convention of republicans that ever gathered in Illinois.

He made a magnificent canvass of the state, but received a set-back by an accident at Quincy early in the campaign, when the horses attached to his carriage ran away. Almost every county was visited, and he was elected by an enormous majority, receiving 587,637 votes to 474,256 for John P. Altgeld, the candidate of the democrats and populists, who combined on ex-Gov. Altgeld.

In 1887 Gov. Tanner lost his wife by death, leaving to his care a son and daughter. December, 1896, Gov. Tanner married Miss Cora Edith English, an accomplished and highly connected lady of Springfield.

LIEUTENANT-GOVERNOR.

William A. Northcott, Lieutenant-Governor and President of the Senate, was born in Murphysboro, Tennessee. At the breaking out of the war his father, Gen. R. S. Northcott, was compelled to leave his home on account of his Union sentiments, and went to West Virginia, where he accepted a commission as colonel and served during the entire war, nine months of which he spent in Libby prison.

William A. Northcott received his education in the public schools and at the United States naval academy at Annapolis. He taught school for a time, meantime reading law, and was admitted to the bar in 1877, continuing his practice after he removed to Illinois in 1879. In 1880 President Hayes appointed him Supervisor of Census for the Seventh Illinois District. In 1882 he was elected state's attorney of Bond county by a majority of 252; was reëlected in 1884 by a majority of 383; and was again elected to the same office in 1888 by a majority of 513. In 1890 President Harrison appointed him a member of the Board of Visitors to the United States Naval Academy at Annapolis, and he was selected by the Board to deliver the oration to the graduating class. In November, 1890, he was elected Head Consul of the Modern Woodmen of America, a fraternal insurance society which has a membership in the northwestern states of 230,000—70,000 of the number being in the state of Illinois. To this same position which he now holds, he has been twice unanimously reëlected. In 1892 Mr. Northcott was the republican candidate for congress in the old Eighteenth congressional district of Illinois, commonly called "Morrison's District," and which contained the cities of Belleville, East St. Louis and Alton. While Mr. Northcott was defeated in the democratic landslide of that year, yet he conducted his campaign in such manner as to gain him a state reputation. He received the nomination for lieutenant-governor from the republican state convention in June, 1896, and at the election following received a majority of over 137,000 votes—being credited with a total of 601,829 to 464,475 for M C. Crawford, democrat-populist. Governor Northcott made a magnificent campaign in 1896, speaking in nearly every county in the state.

LIEUTENANT-GOVERNOR NORTHCOTT

March 31, 1880, Gov. Northcott married the daughter of Senator Dresser, of the present senate. Mrs. Northcott died in about a year, leaving a son, Nathaniel Dresser Northcott. Gov. Northcott's present wife was Miss Ada Stoutzenberg, of Marine, Madison county, and they have one child—Amy.

THE SENATE CHAMBER

THE GENERAL ASSEMBLY.

The General Assembly for the State of Illinois operates under a constitution adopted by the people in 1870—the fourth instrument of the kind that has been submitted to the people, and the third that has been ratified and adopted—the constitution of 1862 having been rejected at the polls. The general assembly meets biennially at noon on the first Wednesday after the first Monday in January in odd-numbered years. It consists of a senate and a house of representatives numbering on joint ballot, 204. This is the Fortieth General Assembly.

THE SENATE.

The Senate consists of 51 members, who are elected for four years, or two regular sessions. Senators from the odd-numbered districts are elected at the same time as state treasurer and superintendent of public instruction—1886, 1890, 1894, etc. Senators from even-numbered districts are elected in presidential years, 1888, 1892, 1896, etc. Until the present session of 1897 senators received $5 per diem during the session, $50 for stationery and 10 cents a mile for the actual distance from their homes to the state capital. By a law enacted in 1895 senators receive $1,000 for each regular session, stationery and mileage extra, and $5 per diem for special sessions. The new law does not apply to senators elected in 1894. The districts represented in the present General Assembly were organized in 1893 by the democrats. The senate of 1895 consisted of 18 democrats and 33 republicans. The senate of 1897 consists of 39 republicans, 11 democrats and 1 populist.

THE HOUSE.

The House of Representatives consists of 153 representatives, elected from 51 districts, every two years in November. They receive $1,000 for every regular session, and $50 for stationery and 10 cents a mile for the actual distance from their homes to the state capital. The system of minority representation maintains in Illinois. A voter is entitled to 3 votes for representative, and he can vote one for each of three candidates, 1½ votes for two candidates, or he can plump his three votes for one candidate. The present house was elected in 1896 and consists of 88 republicans, 61 democrats and 4 populists. The house in 1895 consisted of 92 republicans and 61 democrats. The democrats and populists combined their votes in many districts in 1896.

Biographies preceded by an * are not accompanied by portraits.

HOLD-OVER SENATORS.

The following state senators elected in 1896 hold over for the session of 1899:

2. Solon H. Case, rep.
4. Daniel F. Curley, dem.
6. William Sullivan, rep.
8. Flavel K. Granger, rep.
10. Delos W. Baxter, rep.
12. Homer F. Aspinwall, rep.
14. Henry H. Evans, rep.
16. Isaac Miller Hamilton, rep.
18. Charles Bogardus, rep.
20. Robert B. Fort, rep.
22. Geo. W. Stubblefield, rep.
24. James D. Putnam, rep.
26. W. Scott Edwards, rep.
28. Orville F. Berry, rep.
30. Henry M. Dunlap, rep.
32. Arthur A. Leeper, dem.
34. Edward McConnel, dem.
36. William L. Mounts, dem.
38. Nathaniel Dresser, peo.
40. Stanton C. Pemberton, rep.
42. Charles E. Hull, dem.
44. John Landrigan, dem.
46. Joseph T. Payne, dem.
48. Albert C. Bollinger, rep.
50. Walter Warder, rep.

Republicans, 17; democrats, 7; populist, 1.

MEMBERS RETURNED.

The following senators were reëlected in 1896:

Aspinwall, Evans, Bogardus, Berry, Dunlap and Leeper. Senators Curley, Mounts and McConnel were members of the house in '95. Senator Granger was a member of the house in '73-5-7-9. Senator Landrigan was a member of the house in '69 and '75, and the senate in '71. Senator Sparks was a member of the house in '89. Senator Warder was a member of the house in '93.

The following members of the house were reëlected in November, 1896:

Miller, Buckner, Boyd, Thiemann, Shanahan, Walleck, Noling, Bovey, Schubert, Schwab, Stoskopf, Cavanaugh, Novak, Bryan, Curtis, Morris, Glade, Brignadello, Bailey, Hammers, Fred Busse, McGuire, Revell, Barricklow, Sharrock, Cochran, Needles, Farrell, George Murray, O'Donnell, Kilcourse, Payne, Olson, Huffman, Daugherty, Merrill, Murdock, Steen, Kincheloe, Merriam, Perry, J. W. Johnson, Selby, Wylie, McLauchlan, Wilson, Guffin, Ely, Branen, Barnes, and Perrottet.

Mr. Nohe was a member in '93; Mr. Bartling was in the senate in '93-5. Mr. O'Shea was a member in '83. Mr. Craig was a member of the house in '89-91 senate '93-95. Mr. C. C. Johnson was a member of the house '85-87. Mr. Anderson was a member of the house '89-91-93. Mr. Allen was a member of the house '85-7-9-91.

HALL OF THE HOUSE

HENDRICK V. FISHER—*Senate.*

Col. Hendrick V. Fisher (rep.), of Geneseo, 33d district, president pro tempore of the senate, and in event of death or resignation of the lieutenant-governor, the successor of the latter under the constitution, is now serving his third term. He was born in Wilkesbarre, Pa., October 15, 1846, and received a good education at Wyoming Seminary, Pennsylvania. After his school days he entered the general offices of the D., L. & W. R. R., as clerk. In '68 he came west to Aurora, Illinois, where he engaged in the business of general merchandise. Later he embarked in the manufacture of stoves and hardware and moved to Geneseo in 1869.

SENATOR FISHER, PRESIDENT PRO TEMPORE.

In 1890 Mr. Fisher married Miss Abbie F. Steele, of Geneseo, and they have three handsome little girls.

Mr. Fisher was a member of the house in '87, and though it was his first experience in the legislature he was given charge of the important committee of Canal and River Improvement. At that time there was strong talk of making a ship waterway between the Mississippi river and Lake Michigan. Mainly through his efforts the General Assembly passed a bill ceding to the federal government all the locks and dams on the Illinois and Michigan canal, for the purposes indicated. Work has begun on the Hennepin canal, and it is possible that the original intentions may yet be carried out. In 1889 he was chairman of the Committee on Railroads, one of the most important in the house. He made a strong plea for a western hospital for the insane to be located in northwestern Illinois. The bill died on third reading. However, the measure became a law during the session of 1895, Senator Fisher's first year in the state senate. The hospital is located near Rock Island, in his district. He was, '89-'93, appointed by Gov. Fifer colonel and aide-de-camp on his staff.

Senator Fisher has been one of the leaders on his side of the chamber at every session of which he has been a member. He has always been a stalwart republican, and has been a prominent figure in state politics for many years. He was elected to the senate in 1894 by the large majority of 8,174 over his democratic opponent, although President Harrison carried the district by only 3,000 in 1892. He was chosen president pro tempore in the republican caucus in January, 1897, by acclamation. In the chair Senator Fisher is entirely fair and impartial. He has thus far made a most excellent impression on all senators.

Senator Fisher's great-grandfather was a Hollander, came to America in 1720, was President of the first Provincial Congress of New Jersey and chairman of the Committee of Safety. He was one of the founders of the Dutch Reformed church of America, and prominent in establishing Rutgers College, New Jersey.

SPEAKER ED. C. CURTIS.

Edward C. Curtis (rep.), of Grant Park, Speaker of the house, is probably the youngest man ever chosen to the position of speaker in this state. He was born in Yellowhead township, Kankakee county, August 12, 1865. He is a son of Alonzo and Elizabeth (Campbell) Curtis. The Curtis family has nearly two centuries of honorable history in America, and were among the early settlers at the head of Lake Champlain. The Battle of Bennington was fought on the old Curtis homestead. Alonzo Curtis came to Illinois in 1852 and engaged in farming. About 1870 he removed to Grant Park and entered the mercantile business.

After completing his studies in the village, Ed Curtis spent some years at DuPauw University, Greencastle, Ind., and Northwestern University, Evanston, Ill. In vacations he clerked in his father's store, and after college he took charge of this branch of his father's business. A banking department was soon afterwards added, and the Grant Park Banking Co. organized, of which Ed C. Curtis became cashier, a position he now holds.

Although active in politics Mr. Curtis never held an office until 1895, when, as a member of the house, he took a pronounced stand in favor of economy in public expenditures and in opposition to legislative corruption. The record he made during that session was endorsed by his people, and he was returned to the present house by an increased majority, receiving the nomination in convention by acclamation. He made a thorough campaign in his district for the republican ticket and spoke at many places outside of the district. He was made a candidate for speaker by his friends last January, the morning of the republican house caucus. Before night all the other candidates had withdrawn in his favor, and he was accorded the unusual distinction of being nominated by acclamation. Mr. Curtis is a member of the Methodist Episcopal church, a Knight Templar, Odd Fellow, Modern Woodman, and other societies. He is not married.

As a speaker he is as fair as it is possible for a partisan to be when confronted by able political opponents. His thorough knowledge of parliamentary law and practice has been demonstrated on more than one occasion. In order to facilitate business and close the labors of the session, Speaker Curtis instituted a much-needed reform in the Illinois house on April 7. The democratic side refused to vote, thus breaking a quorum, and Speaker Curtis noted on the journal the names of eighteen democrats who were present and not voting. He has surprised political friend and foe by exhibiting a thorough knowledge of parliamentary law and practice. He is a member of the Delta Kappa Epsilon fraternity.

SPEAKER CURTIS.

HENRY H. EVANS—Senate.

Henry H. Evans (rep.), of Aurora, 14th district, is the oldest member of the General Assembly in consecutive service. He was elected to the house of representatives in 1876, and in 1880 was promoted to the senate. His reëlection followed regularly in 1884, 1888, 1892, and 1896, and when Senator Evans completes his present term he will have served continuously for twenty years in the state senate. Only once during all that time was there serious opposition to his reëlection by democrats or republicans, and that was in 1888, when an independent republican ran against him. Senator Evans' majority, however, was about the usual size. His majority in 1896 was almost 10,000.

Senator Evans took a prominent part. The senatorial contest between Gen. John A. Logan and Col. Wm. R. Morrison in 1885 was one of the most prolonged battles of its kind, and several members died before the deadlock was finally settled. The General Assembly was a tie on joint ballot. At that time Senator Evans' advice was sought and heeded on many occasions. The battle of 1891 when the three farmers held the balance of power in the General Assembly between the two great parties tried the stalwart republicanism of Senator Evans. Many of the republican leaders, eager to defeat a democrat for United States senator, were so anxious to accomplish that end that they attempted to force republicans to vote for A. J. Streeter, populist. But Senator Evans, at the head of a

SENATOR EVANS, DEAN OF THE GENERAL ASSEMBLY.

Senator Evans was born in Toronto, Canada, March 9, 1836, and in 1841 his parents moved to Aurora, taking him with them.

His record in the Illinois legislature is a long and honorable one. At every session he was not only prominent but one of the leaders who made and unmade laws for the people of Illinois. At every session excepting one, he was the leader of the controlling element in the senate. Some of the greatest legislative battles ever fought have been witnessed in Springfield, and in every one of them

determined old guard, declared he never would vote for Streeter, even if the caucus decided for him. At the same time he was willing to vote for any republican the caucus might select. His constituents endorsed his action by returning him to the senate the next year by an increased majority. Senator Evans is financially interested in real estate and corporate property in Kane and Cook counties to a large extent. He is very influential in the senate, and his long experience in state affairs has given him a wide acquaintance with public men.

COL. CHAS. BOGARDUS—Senate.

Col. Charles Bogardus (rep.), of Paxton, 18th district, one of the oldest members in point of consecutive service, was born in Cayuga county, New York, March 28, 1841, and at the age of six was left an orphan. In a "catch-as-catch-can" way he obtained a fair common school education and began working in a country store at the age of twelve. For nine years he practiced industry and frugality, meantime learning from school books and the wider school, the world, practical lessons. In 1862 he enlisted as a private in the 151st New York infantry; was elected first lieutenant of his company, and his conduct was such that he was soon promoted to a captaincy. Later on he was promoted to the lieutenant-coloneley of his regiment, and was brevetted to a coloneley, "for gallant and meritorious services before Petersburg." He was once severely wounded, and captured by the enemy. Colonel Bogardus participated in some of the fiercest battles of the war—among which are the Wilderness, Spottslyvania, Cold Harbor, Petersburg and Appomattox. In 1872 he came to Illinois, to Ford county, which has since been his home. In 1885 he was appointed colonel and aide-de-camp by Gov. Oglesby, and was reappointed in 1889 by Gov. Fifer. He has dealt extensively in farm lands as buyer and seller, and himself owns and operates many magnificent farms in the fertile prairies of eastern-central and northern Illinois. Col. Bogardus is a practical farmer; the latest improvements in machinery and modern methods are employed on his property.

In 1862 Col. Bogardus married Miss Hannah W. Pells, of Orleans county, N. Y. They have but one child living.

Senator Bogardus has a long and honorable record in Illinois politics beginning with his first session in the Illinois house in 1885, an experience that tried every member as with fire. It was the famous session when Gen. Logan and Col. Morrison so long fought for election as United States senator, and the legislature was evenly divided politically. Senator Bogardus demonstrated his ability as a leader, and was rewarded with a return to the house in 1887. He was selected chairman of the republican caucus in 1887. In 1888 he was advanced to the senate, and in the sessions of 1889, 1893 and 1897 was chairman of the committee to make up the senate committees for the republicans. He was reëlected in 1892 to the senate, and in 1895 was chosen president pro tem by acclamation in the republican caucus—the highest place in the gift of the senate. In 1895, in absence of governor and lieutenant-governor, he was constitutional governor for some time.

SENATOR BOGARDUS.

JAMES H. FARRELL—House.

James H. Farrell (dem.), of Chicago, 21st district, in point of continuous service the oldest member of the house of representatives, was born in the Isle of Jersey, November 19, 1842. Capt. Farrell's father was born in the Isle of Guernsey, where Victor Hugo lived in exile, and his mother in Dublin. All the education he received from school books was obtained before he was ten years old, but he has been a close observer and received a good education in contact with the world. He arrived in New York in 1851 and began life as a clerk. When nineteen years old the war fever attacked him, and he enlisted in Co. H of the famous Fifth New York infantry, Col. Judson Kilpatrick, commanding, and beginning with the battle of Big Bethel, the first general engagement of the strife, he was in nearly every important battle and skirmish of the Army of the Potomac during the war. Honorably mustered out at the close of the struggle, he returned to peaceful pursuits, entering the largest wall paper manufacturing establishment in New York city, as clerk, and remained there until 1868, when he removed to Chicago, continuing in the same line for two years with G. L. Faxon & Co., on Lake street, before the big fire. He has been in the real estate business for the past twelve years, and it is his present occupation.

Capt. Farrell has always taken great interest in politics, and is a democrat. The will of the majority as honestly expressed in a democratic convention or caucus always met his approbation. His experience in the army peculiarly fitted him for the part he has played in politics during the past ten years. The Marching Club of the County Democracy of Cook County, of which he is marshal, and which he has commanded ever since its organization, has made a name for itself all over the United States, principally through the untiring efforts of its commanding officer. There is nearly a regiment of marchers in the club, and they create a sensation wherever they go. During the presidential campaigns of 1892 and 1896 Capt. Farrell had charge of the organization of marching clubs in Illinois for the Democratic National and State Committees. He was elected grand marshal of the democratic marching clubs of the state in 1884, and still retains the title.

In the house Capt. Farrell has been a member of all the important committees since his first session—1887—he is now serving his sixth—twelve years. A leader in his party on the floor, constantly in his seat, and ever ready to oblige a friend if consistent with his duty to the people, Capt. Farrell is one of the best-liked members of the General Assembly. He lost his first wife by death in 1883 and four years later married his present wife.

REPRESENTATIVE FARRELL.

CHARLES H. CRAWFORD—Senate.

Charles H. Crawford (rep.), of Chicago, 5th district, one of the most influential and aggressive members of the Illinois General Assembly, has been in the senate, excepting one term, since 1885, having been elected in 1884-1888-1894, and when his present term is completed will have been a member of the upper branch for twelve years. It is not too much to say that his influence has been felt in every General Assembly of which he was a member on every measure of importance. Many of the leading bills were presented to the senate by Mr. Crawford himself. He is the author of the Crawford Primary Election Law, which has worked a much-needed reform in the conduct of primary elections by the two great political parties in Illinois. Senator Crawford has been one of the organizers of the republican party in the senate of every session, excepting the present one. He is now chairman of the Committe on Elections and member of the most important committees in the senate. A parliamentarian without a peer in the state, he is quick to see a point in debate, and his opposition is feared as much as his friendly interest is desired by senators with measures to advance.

SENATOR CRAWFORD.

Senator Crawford was born in Bennington, Vermont, and was reared in Bureau and LaSalle counties, Illinois. He is a lawyer by profession, and has a large and lucrative practice. For twenty-two years he has lived in Chicago, and during that time has been prominent and active in republican party politics. He was elected to the state senate in 1894 by a majority of 10,000—6,000 more than the republicans had in the preceding election of 1892.

ORVILLE F. BERRY—Senate.

Orville F. Berry (rep.), of Carthage, 28th district, is one of the best parliamentarians in the country. He was born on a McDonough county farm, Feb. 16, 1852, and was early left an orphan. He obtained a fair common school education, however, and at the age of sixteen struck out for himself. At first he worked as a farm hand. Then he removed to Carthage, where he read law, and was admitted to the bar in 1877. Two years later he formed a partnership with Hon. Thomas C. Sharp, and in 1879 Senator Berry's brother, M. P., was added to the firm. They have had a very successful and lucrative practice, extending all over western Illinois.

SENATOR BERRY.

Senator Berry has filled many places of honor and trust. In 1883 he was elected mayor of Carthage, and was twice reëlected without opposition. He was secretary of the Hancock County Agricultural Board for four years. He is a Royal Arch Mason, a Knight of Pythias, a Modern Woodman, and member of the Ancient Order of United Workmen. He has been Grand Master Workman for Illinois, and several times has been supreme representative from the state to the Supreme Lodge. From the Supreme Lodge he has many times been chosen delegate to fraternal congresses.

In 1873 Senator Berry married Miss Anna M. Barr, of Hancock county.

In 1888 the democrats of Illinois made a herculean effort to carry the state and the Hancock district was regarded as doubtful. The republicans were importuned to name their strongest man, and Senator Berry was induced to make the race. He was elected. In 1892 the democrats swept the state, Senator Berry's district giving Harrison only 187 majority; while his own majority was 244. But the legislature of 1893 was democratic and a new gerrymander was made, throwing Senator Berry into what was thought to be a hopelessly democratic district. In '96 by a political trick and without warrant of law his opponent's name was placed on the ballot under the democratic and populist columns, and apparently defeated Mr. Berry by about 100 votes. The latter contested, however, and was awarded the seat, the senate holding that the secretary of state illegally certified his opponent's name as a candidate of the populists. Senator Berry was chairman of the judiciary committee during the session of 1895 and was also chairman of the republican state convention in 1896. He has been a leader in the legislature every session when he was a member. He has also been very prominent in state politics, and has been in demand at caucuses and conferences of party leaders. For many years he has been a close personal friend of Gov. Tanner.

ISAAC B. CRAIG—House.

Isaac B. Craig (dem.), of Mattoon, 40th district, is the descendant of a revolutionary soldier, his paternal grandfather, Robert Craig, having fought all through the war of the revolution. Mr. Craig's father, Isaac N., was a pioneer of Illinois, coming to this state in 1828, and settling in Coles county, where he was a man of prominence and standing. He died in January, 1893, at the ripe age of 83, leaving a large estate. He was a careful, prudent business man, whose opinion in commercial transactions was sought by many. He was a soldier in the Black Hawk war.

REPRESENTATIVE CRAIG.

Isaac B. Craig was born on his father's farm in Coles county, April 28, 1857, and received a good education in the public schools of his county and at Ann Arbor, Mich., and for fourteen years has been a very successful lawyar at Mattoon. His practice is not confined to Coles county, but extends to almost every county in eastern-central Illinois. He has always taken a deep interest in politics, and has been a prominent and influential figure in the democratic party since he attained his majority. Mr. Craig was elected to the house of representatives in 1888 and again in 1890. In 1892 he was advanced to the state senate, and served for one term of two sessions. In 1896, although reluctant to again become a candidate, he consented to the use of his name for the house. He was elected, and was complimented by the democratic house caucus with the highest honor within its gift—the nomination for speaker. He was named by acclamation. In one sense it is an empty honor, and in another it carries great responsibility with it. The minority nominee for speaker names the minority membership on all the committees, and is the leader of his party in the house.

He was chairman of the joint caucus in 1891 and appointed the steering committee of democrats who so successfully led the party to victory in the contest for United States senator that session. It was one of the closest contests a general assembly ever met, and the result was in doubt from the start to the finish.

In 1882 Mr. Craig was married to Miss Helen Hasbrouck, who is a member of an old New York Knickerbocker family, very prominent in Ulster county, New York. They have three children—Helen Louise, aged 6; Gertrude, aged 4, and Kathryn, aged 1½.

Mr. Craig is a member of Godfrey de Bouillon Commandery, No. 44, Knights Templar, of Mattoon.

JOHN HUMPHREY—Senate.

John Humphrey (rep.), of Orland, Cook county, 7th district, is a lawyer by profession and an Englishman by birth. He was born in the county of Norfolk, England, June 20, 1838, and was brought to this country by his parents when a lad of ten years. The family settled in Cook county, Illinois, where Senator Humphrey received a common school education. He read law in the office of Hon. James P. Root, and was admitted to the Illinois bar in 1872. He lives in Orland and practices his profession with an office in the Monadnock building, Chicago.

Senator Humphrey owns a large amount of farming land in Cook county. He has been treasurer of Orland for 24 years and supervisor of his township for 28 years. He has been president of the board of trustees of Orland for five years, and still holds the office, although he has not desired it. He was bailiff under Sheriff Bradley, of Cook county, for a time.

Senator Humphrey is one of the oldest members in point of consecutive service in the General Assembly. He was elected to the house in '70, '80 and '84, and was advanced to the senate in the next general election, 1886, and returned in 1890, in the face of determined opposition, and was again elected in 1894 by an enormous majority.

Senator Humphrey has attracted the attention of the entire state this session by the introduction of two bills of great importance. One of them provides for a commission to be appointed by the governor, which is given the power of granting franchises to all street railroads in Illinois, and the authority to pass on all regulations of street car lines, including the time card, heating apparatus, seating capacity, speed, motive power, etc. This commission is also empowered to decide whether there shall be any extensions of old lines or the establishment of new lines, and its powers are almost absolute. The municipalities are to be recompensed for the privileges granted the street car corporations, by receiving from one to seven per cent on the gross earnings of the lines, the per cent being determined by the population and time in which the franchise operates. The bill is only operative on corporations that accept its provisions. The franchises of such are extended for fifty years from September, 1897. The bills passed the senate April 16, 1897.

The startling provisions of the measures attracted the attention particularly of all the street railways in the state, and especially those in Chicago. If they become laws they will curtail the powers and perquisites of aldermen in Chicago and every other city in the state. Senator Humphrey is an able man, a clear and forcible talker in debate, well posted in parliamentary law, and thoroughly familiar with all the ways of a legislature.

SENATOR HUMPHREY.

HOMER F. ASPINWALL—Senate.

Homer F. Aspinwall (rep.), of Freeport, 12th district, was born in Stephenson county, Illinois, November 15, 1846. He was born on a farm and has lived on a farm all his life. His education was such as was furnished by the district schools of his boyhood, and was completed in the Freeport high school, from which he graduated. After his school days, he entered a wholesale notion store as clerk, remaining for two years. Later he returned to the farm and has been a practical agriculturist ever since. Senator Aspinwall owns 265 acres of Stephenson county soil, all well improved. For four years he was a member of the Stephenson county board of supervisors, and has held several minor offices. He was first elected to the state senate in 1892, and was reëlected in 1896, receiving 11,573 votes, to 7,567 for William A. Barber, democrat.

Northern Illinois has not been recognized by the republican party since Gen. Smith ran for state treasurer, away back early in the 80's, and the enormous republican vote and the heavy republican majorities in that section have more than once saved the party banner from being captured by the enemy at state elections. In 1896 Senator Aspinwall, whose record in the senate in the Thirty-eighth and Thirty-ninth General Assemblies, entitled him to consideration at the hands of the republican state convention, was importuned by many friends all over the state to permit the use of his name for a place on the state ticket. The neighboring county of Winnebago, to which Stephenson is attached by ties of the strongest kind politically, had a candidate for state auditor, and Senator Aspinwall did not feel that he ought to jeopardize the chances of any candidate from his own section by dividing the delegates. He gave a loyal and hearty support to the Winnebago candidate, who, however, was defeated in the state convention.

SENATOR ASPINWALL.

In some quarters, Senator Aspinwall's name is being discussed as a suitable candidate for higher honors and his record in the senate for three sessions—1893, 1895, 1897—will redound to his advantage. No member of the General Assembly has done more for the people of the state than Senator Aspinwall. He is regarded as one of the leaders in the senate, and a man of standing in the counsels of his party in the state.

Senator Aspinwall is a 32d degree Mason. He was married in 1874 to Miss Emma M. Sheetz, and they have two children.

FREEMAN P. MORRIS—House.

Freeman P. Morris (dem.), of Watseka, 16th district, chairman of the democratic house caucus, was born on a farm in Cook county, Illinois, March 19, 1854. He labored on the farm after the manner of all farmer boys and attended the district school when his work permitted. He completed his education in Chicago and graduated from the Union College of Law of that city. In 1874, when twenty years of age, he was admitted to practice at the bar in 1896. He has held various local offices, and has been a member of the General Assembly of Illinois five times—now serving his fifth term. He was a member of the house in 1885, 1889, 1893, 1895 and 1897.

At every session Mr. Morris has had a great deal to do with every important bill or measure that has been considered. He is one of the best lawyers in the legislature, and on the judiciary committee, as well as on the floor of the house, always commands attention from the members. Mr. Morris has been chairman

REPRESENTATIVE MORRIS.

Illinois, and immediately went to Watseka, which has been his home ever since. Mr. Morris has the best and most lucrative law practice of any attorney in the northeastern part of Illinois.

In 1882 Mr. Morris married Minnie D. Lott, of Denver, Colo., and they live in a handsome home in Watseka. They have one son, Eugene, aged eight.

April 21, 1893, Gov. Altgeld appointed Mr. Morris colonel and aide-de-camp on his personal staff, an appointment which Col. Morris resigned in

of the house caucus and of the steering committee every session. Always a democrat he has taken an active interest in furthering democratic policies and principles. During the presidential campaigns in 1892 and 1896 he made many speeches throughout the state for the democratic state and national ticket.

Mr. Morris is a member of Mary Commandery, Knights Templar, of Watseka. He was chancellor commander of the Watseka Knights of Pythias, and for six years was deputy chancellor of the same society.

ISAAC M. HAMILTON--Senate.

Isaac Miller Hamilton (rep.), of Cissna Park, 16th district, was born in Ash Grove, Iroquois county, Illinois, September 6, 1864, and received a common school education. His father died when he was eleven years of age and young Hamilton was compelled to leave school and begin life for himself. He worked for a stock buyer and later entered business for himself. He combined this with work in a general merchandise store, and valued clients in Chicago, and they have brought him much important litigation. He was never a candidate for office until last year. He was elected senator by the largest majority ever given a senator from his district. He is executive committeeman-at-large for Illinois of the National League of Republican Clubs, chairman of the Campaign Committee of the National Republican League, and member of the Executive Committee of the Illinois League of Republican Clubs. During the campaign of 1896

SENATOR HAMILTON.

in 1884 he formed a partnership, under the firm name of Young & Hamilton, which has existed ever since. In 1886 a banking business was added, and three years later the general merchandise store and stock buying were disposed of, and the firm is now exclusively in the banking and real estate business. In 1889 Senator Hamilton was admitted to the bar and since that time has devoted himself almost exclusively to his law practice, which has grown to be very large and remunerative. He has numerous he made many speeches in Michigan, Kentucky and Tennessee for the Republican National Committee, besides making a thorough canvass of his own district. He is a 32d degree Mason, a Knight Templar, a Shriner, and a Knight of Pythias. He is not married. He was appointed executor of the great Cissna estate some time ago, and in a day made a bond of half a million dollars, thirty-five of his friends and neighbors signing his bond, an evidence of the regard in which he is held in his home county.

ALMET POWELL—House.

Almet Powell (rep.), of Gilman, 16th district, was born in Albany county, New York, March 20, 1846, and came to Illinois in 1855, to Lawn Ridge, Marshall county, where his father engaged in the business of general merchandise. His son, Almet, acted as clerk in the store. Mr. Powell received a good common school education, such as was furnished in the district schools of Illinois of early days, but he learned more in the broad school of life, in contact with men. In 1871 Mr. Powell moved to Gilman, Iroquois county, and established himself in the same line of trade as was pursued by his father. He now owns one of the largest and most complete general merchandise stores in Iroquois county. It is really a department store, for about everything is handled except hardware, drugs and agricultural implements.

Mr. Powell owns many acres of fine farming lands near Gilman, and has always taken a practical interest in agriculture. This is his first political office of prominence, although he has served in various township offices. He always has been a stanch republican and cast his first vote for Gen. U. S. Grant for president. His father, Leander Powell, was an old-fashioned William Penn Quaker, and possessed of all the traditional virtues of that strict sect, including an aversion to quarrels and wars, and his standard of honesty and square dealing was measured in the Quaker balance. He reared his children in the same strict school, and the lessons learned in boyhood have not been thrown away in manhood, for no man stands higher in the community than the son of Quaker parents who followed the precepts of his fathers. Leander Powell was born in Albany county, New York, and came from a long line of Welsh ancestors.

REPRESENTATIVE POWELL.

Representative Powell is a member of Mt. Olive Commandery No. 38, Knights Templar, of Paxton. He is chairman of the committee on Live Stock and Dairying, and has taken great interest in state affairs all his life, but has never been an active office seeker. He is a member of the joint steering committee of the house and senate. He married Miss Cordella Borthwick, of Albany county, N. Y., and they have one son, Bruce B., now 22 years old.

C. M. NETTERSTROM—Senate.

Charles M. Netterstrom (rep.), of Chicago, 21st district, was born in Norway, September 24, 1847. Five years later he moved with his parents to Chicago, where he was educated in the public schools, and has lived ever since. Senator Netterstrom is a builder and street contractor with offices in the Portland building on Dearborn street. He was a Cook County Commissioner until elected to the state senate in 1894. trustee, from 1880 to 1887. The last time he was a candidate he received every vote that was cast—no opposition. He was nominated for the state senate by acclamation, and elected over his democratic opponent by a majority of 3,414.

In 1869 Senator Netterstrom married Miss Anna M. Anderson, and they have three sons, two daughters and two grandsons—Carl Netterstrom Allander is the eldest.

Mr. Netterstrom is not a politician—he is too good a business man to take kindly to politics as a profession.

SENATOR NETTERSTROM.

The new Criminal Court Building in Chicago, on the North Side, was erected and finished under his supervision. One remarkable circumstance in connection with this building, and one of which Senator Netterstrom is proud, is the fact that in all the thousands of dollars expended under his superintendency, there was not a dollar of expense for "extras" charged against Cook county.

Senator Netterstrom lives in Lake View, and he served that township for six years as commissioner and His position in the state senate is practically the only political office he ever filled. He is not an office seeker, and probably for this reason wields a great deal of influence in the politics of Cook county. In the session of 1895 as well as in the present session he has been favored with a list of good committees, and is disposed to apply business rules, rather than a strict partisan standard to legislative work. He has been a staunch republican since he became of age.

ROBERT B. FORT—*Senate.*

Robert B. Fort (rep.), of Lacon, 20th district, was born in Lacon, April 25, 1867, and received his education in the public schools of Washington, D. C., at Wyman Institute, and at Exeter, N. H., taking the classical course. Mr. Fort has been a farmer all his life, operating large farms in Illinois and Nebraska. He was elected mayor of Lacon in 1895, and he resigned to take his seat in the senate. He has always been a republican and has taken an active part in the politics of his section of the state, although this is the first office of state importance he ever held. Mr. Fort's father, Hon. Greenbury L. Fort, was a member of the Forty-third, Forty-fourth, Forty-fifth and Forty-sixth congresses, and was one of the eminent men of his day. Senator Fort is not married. He was elected from a district that gave a democratic majority of about 1,700 in 1892.

Senator Fort's father was born in Sciota county, O., and removed with his parents to Marshall county, Ill., where he was raised on a farm. He completed his education at Mt. Morris, Ill., where he was a schoolmate with Congressman Hitt. At the age of 24 he was elected sheriff of Marshall county after which he was elected circuit clerk, and subsequently probate judge, which position he held when in '61 he volunteered in the Union army. He served as a soldier until '65. In '66 he was elected state senator, and his congressional record is already indicated above. He retired voluntarily from congress, and died soon afterwards, leaving a widow and one son.

Senator Fort's maternal grandfather, Dr. Robert Boal, served several terms in the Illinois legislature with credit. He was born in Dauphin county, Pa., and graduated from the Medical College of Ohio in '28. He is now the oldest living alumnus of that institution. In '36 he removed to Lacon, Ill., where he practiced medicine for twenty-five years. He was elected to the state senate in '44 and was instrumental in establishing the hospital for the insane at Jacksonville, the first in the state. He was also active in advocating the Illinois and Michigan canal. In '54 he was elected to the house, and in the session of '55 voted for Lincoln for senator until the latter insisted on Trumbull being elected. Next year he was a delegate to the first republican state convention, which met at Bloomington. The same year he was again returned to the house. Gov. Bissell appointed Dr. Boal trustee for the deaf and dumb institution, and he served in that capacity for 17 years. In '65 he removed to Peoria, practicing his profession there 25 years. In '93 he retired from active work, and returned to his old home, Lacon.

SENATOR FORT.

CHARLES E. HULL—Senate.

Charles E. Hull (dem.), of Salem, 42d district, was born in Salem, Nov. 7, 1862, and graduated from the Salem High School in '77. He entered the Southern Illinois Normal, taking the classical course, and graduated with class honors in '80. He has followed the business of his father and grandfather—that of general merchants.

In '82 Senator Hull married Miss Lulu Hammond, daughter of Hon. J. E. W. Hammond, of Salem, who was a member of the house in '79, and was a prominent merchant and influential democrat before his death. They have one child—a daughter.

The present site of Salem was platted and named and the nucleus of the city made by a great-grandfather of Senator Hull, Mark Tully. His maternal grandfather, William Finley, was one of the pioneer preachers of southern Illinois and organized many of the early Cumberland Presbyterian churches. His paternal grandfather, Samuel Hull, was a veteran of the Black Hawk war and a prominent politician, being in office continuously from '33 until '61, holding successively the offices of recorder, sheriff, county judge and postmaster. He was sheriff six times, the last five having no opposition. He was a democrat up to 1861, when he became a republican. He lived with his wife for 57 years, and they died within a few hours of each other about seven years ago.

His father, Erasmus Hull, was a quiet, home-loving man, and never cared for business or office which took him away from his home. In addition to his regular line of business he was interested in and a director of the Salem National Bank from its organization and operated a large flouring and saw mill. He was a staunch democrat and was prominent in county politics, being chairman of the county board for years. In company with the Senator's grandfather, he established a general store in Salem in '53. In 1880 Senator Hull entered the business which has been extended and increased until there are now six general stores in Marion county in which the Senator is financially interested. The Senator owns large interests in three coal mines—Sandoval, Salem and Kinmundy—employing about 400 miners. He is also largely interested in farming and personally superintends the operation of the old country seat of Judge Hull, most of which is within the city limits of the old town of Salem. This farm has had but three owners—the United States, Judge Hull and the Senator.

SENATOR HULL.

Senator Hull was elected to the state senate after a fierce battle against the republican candidate, in 1896. He is an untiring worker, and made a close canvass of his district. He is editor and publisher of the Salem "Herald-Advocate," the oldest paper in the county, and an influential democratic organ.

EDWARD J. DWYER—Senate.

Edward J. Dwyer (rep.), of Chicago, 17th district, one of the leaders in the senate, was born in Chicago November 21, 1861, and educated in the public schools of that city. Leaving school, he was for six years superintendent of the mailing department of the Althrop Publishing House, and at the end of that time he entered politics. His first office was a clerical position in the city clerk's office in Chicago. In 1890 he was elected West Town Clerk, and after his term had expired was appointed assistant superintendent of the water department in the city government. In 1892 he was elected West Town Assessor, an office of great responsibility. He was the only republican who won at that election, and the same was true of his election as clerk in 1890. Senator Dwyer took an active part in the election of Mayor Hempstead Washburn, and was selected by the latter as Superintendent of Water Department.

Senator Dwyer's energy as well as his popularity among the people of his district, was demonstrated when he became a candidate for state senator in 1894. The district had been gerrymandered by the democrats in order to insure a democratic senator and two democrats as representatives. It was arranged for a democratic majority of 3,000. It was an enormous mountain to climb, but there were 382 more votes for Senator Dwyer than for his democratic opponent. Two democrats and one republican were chosen from the same district.

In 1894 Senator Dwyer was married to Miss Mollie Lawler, of Chicago.

Senator Dwyer was one of the controlling spirits in the organization of the senate for the present session. With four colleagues he arranged with a majority of the republican senators to control the republican senate caucus in January, 1897. Inasmuch as the republicans had a two-thirds majority in the senate, it was a virtual control of the organization.

SENATOR DWYER.

Mr. Dwyer is the chairman of the Committee on Municipalities this session, the most important committee in the senate for a Cook county member. He was appointed deputy city clerk of Chicago in 1895, and retained the office until the democrats took charge in April, 1897. He is in control of the republican party organization in the 17th ward of Chicago.

JAMES BRANEN—House.

James Branen (dem.), of Sycamore, 29th district, is serving his second term in the house—an unusual circumstance for a minority representative in northern Illinois. The twenty-ninth district is overwhelmingly republican. Mr. Branen was born in Ireland January 1, 1848, and when he was six months old his parents moved to Oneida county, New York, where he received a good common school education. He attended school and worked on a farm until twenty years old, when he entered an Oneida hotel as clerk, remaining for several years. In 1870 he moved to DeKalb county, Illinois, and has filled various positions since. He never was a candidate for office until 1894 when the democrats of DeKalb induced him to accept the nomination to the legislature. In the session of 1895 Mr. Branen was a member of the minority party, but so energetic was his work in committee and on the floor that the establishment of the Northern Normal College at DeKalb is due more to his efforts than that of any other man. There was great opposition manifested to it in house and senate. As a mark of appreciation of his efforts in behalf of the county, for securing the only state institution in the district, Mr. Branen was importuned in 1896 to become a candidate a second time for representative. He consented and was elected, sacrificing his own business interests.

REPRESENTATIVE BRANEN.

Mr. Branen is a member of all the important committees in the house. When the supreme court consolidation bill was under consideration he championed Ottawa, and so successfully did he labor that the bill passed the house with Ottawa substituted for Springfield, the state capital. The senate, however, amended the bill by again substituting Springfield, and the house finally concurred in the amendment.

Selby, Charles E. (rep.), of Springfield, 39th district, was born in Lancaster, O., October 7, 1855, and was educated at the Danville (Ind.) Normal. He moved to Sangamon county in '75, taught school for a time, read law and was admitted to the bar in '88. He is a Mason, a K. P., Odd Fellow and M. W. A. He is married and has one son and two daughters. As a boy he worked on a farm in summer to obtain money to attend school in winter. Since his admission to the bar he has enjoyed an excellent practice. Mr. Selby is now serving his second term in the house, having been elected in '94 and '96. He was a prominent candidate for speaker the present session, and was regarded as possessing all the qualifications for the place. Mr. Selby is one of the leaders of the house, is chairman of the republican steering committee,

REPRESENTATIVE SELBY.

and by virtue of that office, also chairman of the house caucus. He is also at the head of the important committee of revenue. He is a member of one of the strongest legal firms in Springfield, and for many years has been active in politics in central Illinois.

Anderson, James O. (rep.), of Decorra, 35th district, was born in Henderson county, August 1, 1845, was raised on a farm, received a common school education, and left Monmouth College when a student to enlist in the 28th Ill. Inf., in which he attained the rank of second lieutenant. Returning from the war he married and engaged in farming, which is his present occupation. He was sheriff of Henderson county for ten years. He was elected to the house in '88, '90, '92 and '96, and was on the steering committee the session of '93. He was chosen sergeant-at-arms of the senate by the republican caucus in Jan., '95, by acclamation. Mr. Anderson has been a prominent and in

REPRESENTATIVE ANDERSON.

fluential figure in western Illinois politics for years. He was a delegate to the republican national convention in '96, and in the present session is chairman of the committee on congressional apportionment and a member of other important committees.

Sullivan, William (rep.), of Chicago, 6th district, was born in Chicago December 17, 1862. He graduated from the Chicago public schools and also from the H. B. Bryant Business College. He was in the grocery business for several years after securing his education. During '90-'93 he was in

SENATOR SULLIVAN.

the revenue service for the national government. He was appointed deputy county clerk in '95, a position he resigned when elected state senator.

Kilcourse, Lawrence (rep.), of Chicago, 23d district, was born May 21, 1859, in Chicago, and was educated in the common schools, and took a course at a commercial college. For

REPRESENTATIVE KILCOURSE.

six years he was salesman for a big cigar manufacturer. He was revenue inspector in Chicago during President Harrison's administratioin. He is a single man. Mr. Kilcourse was nominated by acclamation in the convention. This is his second term in the house, having been elected in '94 and '96. He is chairman of the committee on license.

Busse, Fred A. (rep.), of Chicago, 21st district, was born in his present district March 3, 1866, and educated in the public schools of Chicago. He has been engaged in the hardware

REPRESENTATIVE FRED BUSSE.

business with his father for years. Mr. Busse was town clerk of North Chicago for a term, and was in the sheriff's office for four years. He was chief clerk in the North Town Collector's office for a year. Mr. Busse is not married. This is his second term, having been elected to the house in '94 and '96. This session he is chairman of the important committee on railroads, and is on several other committees of importance. Mr. Busse is a member of the firm of Schendorf & Busse, general contractors. He was nominated for the house both times by acclamation.

Funk, Duncan M. (rep.), of Bloomington, 22d district, was born in Funk's Grove township, McLean county, June 1, 1832, and received a limited education in the district schools. In '74 he was chosen president of the First National Bank of Bloomington, a position he now fills. The same year he was elected a member of the board of supervisors, an office he filled for twenty-one successive years, two years being chairman

REPRESENTATIVE FUNK.

of the board. He was trustee of the Soldiers' and Sailors' Orphans' Home at Normal for thirteen years, eight of which he was chairman of the board. Mr. Funk is also a director in the First National Bank of Normal and the State National at Lexington. He also owns and operates 2,400 acres of McLean county land. In 1857 he married Miss Elizabeth Richardson, who died in '96, being survived by one son and one daughter. It was Senator Isaac Funk, father of Mr. Funk, who, in the state senate in '63, when an effort was being made to kill an appropriation for Illinois soldiers in the field, hurled the fiercest invectives at the enemies of his country, and for his courage on that occasion no history of Illinois is complete without the incident. Mr. Funk is a Mason.

Bryan, Charles, P. (rep.), of Elmhurst, 14th district, was born in Chicago, October 2, 1855. He was educated at the University of Virginia and the Columbia Law School. He was admitted to practice in '78 and next year moved to Colorado. Col. Bryan was elected to the legislature of that state in '80, and was urged for higher preferment. He returned to Chicago in '83, and has since led a literary life. Col. Bryan was a member of Gov. Oglesby's and Gov. Fifer's military staffs with the rank of colonel, having previously served in the First regiment, I. N. G., and in the Guard of Colorado. Col. Bryan was elected to the house in '90, '92, '94 and '96 and during the session of '95 took an active part and succeeded in getting seven of his measures on the statute books. Col. Bryan takes a deep interest in legislation in regard to education and child labor. He was the first commissioner who went to Europe for the World's Fair, and afterwards returned to the continent as secretary of the Exposition Commission in '91-'92. Col. Bryan is not married. He was active in furthering the nomination and election of President McKinley and labored night and day in the national headquarters for the success of the ticket.

REPRESENTATIVE BRYAN.

Nicholls, Henry D. (rep.), of Chicago, 15th district, was born in Philadelphia, March 13, 1846, and received a high school education. After his school days he learned the carpenter's trade. In '65 he crossed the plains overland, returning to Philadelphia in '68, and entered the employ of Disston & Sons, the great saw manufacturers, as foreman. In '72 he moved to Chicago and there started a branch of the house and factory, and has filled the responsible position of manager ever since. This is his first political office, although he has always taken an active part in politics, always as a republican of the stalwart kind. He is a member of Apollo Commandery, K. T., and Medina Shrine. He is married.

REPRESENTATIVE NICHOLLS.

Sterchie, John C. (dem.), of Chicago, 1st district, was born in New York City, Dec. 24, 1856, and educated in the common schools. He moved to Chicago in '73 and it has been his home since. He was deputy assessor in the South Town office for two years, and for another two years was deputy clerk in the superior court. He is married and has two children. Mr. Sterchie has been active in democratic politics for the past fifteen years, and was elected to the 39th assembly by the largest vote any democrat ever received from the First senatorial district. He was returned to the house in '96.

REPRESENTATIVE STERCHIE.

McGee, William Q. (dem.), of Cairo, 51st district, was born in Stewart Co., Tenn., March 24, 1857, and his parents were driven from their home on account of their pronounced Uni n

REPRESENTATIVE McGEE.

sentiments. They moved to Cairo. He was educated at the Chicago University and Lafayette College, at Easton, Pa., then he read law with Judge Samuel P. Wheeler in Cairo; was admitted to the bar, and began practice immediately. His health failing, he spent two years on a famr, but in '93 resumed the practice of his profession. He was elected city attorney of Cairo, notwithstanding its tremendous republican majority.

Organ, Benjamin S. (dem.), of Carmi, 44th district, was born near Nash-

REPRESENTATIVE ORGAN.

ville, Tenn., April 2, 1847, and two years later his parents moved to Illinois. He was educated in the common schools and at Xenia Academy. He studied law and was admitted to practice in '68, when only 20 years of age. He practiced for five years in Missouri, and then returned to southern Illinois, served a term as county judge of White county, and one term as county treasurer of Wayne county. He is a Mason, a Workman and member of the G. A. R. He is married and has one son. At the age of 16 he joined the 136th Ill. Vols. and was discharged with his regiment at Springfield, Ill., in the fall of '64.

Nohe, Augustus W. (rep.), Chicago, 2d district, was born in Baden, Germany, Nov. 27, 1846, and came to this country in '51. He remained at Freeport until '75 when he moved to Chicago. He received a common school education. He is married. He was elected to the house in '90, returned in '92 by an increased majority, and again in '96. He has represented his

REPRESENTATIVE NOHE.

ward in the Chicago city council. During the war he was connected with the military telegraph and did valuable service for the Union armies. He was with Gen. Schofield for a time and joined Sherman at Goldsboro, N. C., finishing his field service at Raleigh. The government required his aid after the war, and he was sent to Nashville, Tenn., where he remained on duty until '67, when he was mustered out of the volunteer service, being probably the last war telegrapher to retire. Mr. Nohe is one of the most aggressive members, and has been a leader on the floor at every session. He was chairman of the republican house caucus last January when the officers of the house were nominated. He is chairman of the committee on insurance and on other important committees.

Shephard, John Adam (dem.), of Jerseyville, 47th district, was born in Jerseyville, March 21, 1847. His father, the late Hon. Wm. Shephard, was a native of England and came to America in '32, settling in Jersey county in '37. His wife was a daughter of Adam Gross, of Dauphin Co., Pa.; they were married in 1840, and the widow is still living in Jerseyville. J. A. Shephard was educated at the St. Louis University, a Catholic school. From '60-'67 he was a bookkeeper for his father in a store. From '67-'72 he aided his father in constructing railroads in Illinois and Texas, and from '72-'75 he was engaged in the banking business with his father in Jerseyville, which was closed up just before his father's death, August 12, '75. From '76-'82 with Judge A. A. Goodrich he was in

REPRESENTATIVE SHEPHARD.

the law and real estate business. In '79 he was elected county treasurer and reëlected in '82 and '90. In '83 he reëntered the banking business with his brother, H. A. Shephard, and in '90, on the organization of the State Bank of Jerseyville by S. H. Bowman and H. A. Shephard, he was made its vice president, a position he still holds. For the past twenty years he has been treasurer of the Jersey county fair. He was alderman for eighteen years. January 16, '78, he married Miss Hattie S. Ely, and they have three daughters.

LaMonte, William O. (rep.), of Chicago, 5th district, was born at Lyons, Iowa, April 20, 1862, and moved to Chicago in 1870. For ten years he was connected with the coal business in Chicago; for four years examiner of the money order division of the Chicago postoffice; two years deputy clerk of the Circuit Court, and two years Chief Clerk Water Department, Bureau of Public Works, of Chicago, which position he resigned when elected to the General Assembly. He

REPRESENTATIVE LA MONTE.

is a Blue Lodge and Chapter Mason and a Knight of Pythias. He is married, and has for many years taken an active part in Cook county politics.

Joy, John B. (rep.), of Concord, 34th district, was born in Morgan county, Ill., January 12, 1848. He is a farmer and has spent most of his life on the farm. He was educated in the common schools and at the Jacksonville high school. He is married and has two daughters and one son. This is his first political office. He received the nomination last year without solicitation on his part—in fact, a case

REPRESENTATIVE JOY.

of the office seeking the man. Mr. Joy was one of the stalwarts who were for Senator Wm. E. Mason from start to finish in the contest for United States senator in January, '97.

Gaines, Duane (dem.), of Newton, 45th district, was born on a Crawford county (Ill.) farm, November 2, 1862, and is a lawyer by profession and practice. He completed a thorough

REPRESENTATIVE GAINES.

education at the normal school at Danville, Ind., and taught school for a time. In '90 he was admitted to the bar, and three years later formed a partnership at Newton with Judge Kasserman, under the firm name of Gaines & Kasserman. He was appointed master in chancery in '95. He is married and has one daughter. This is his first political office. Mr. Gaines has taken an active interest this session in exposing the stuffed pay-rolls of the General Assembly.

Suttle, Henry C. (dem.), of Kenney, 30th district, was born in Franklin,

REPRESENTATIVE SUTTLE.

Kentucky, May 4, 1858. He moved to Lincoln, Ill., in 1866, and was educated in the Lincoln public schools, and in the office of the Lincoln Herald, where he learned the printer's trade from the ground up. In 1881 he went to Mt. Pulaski and purchased the "Citizen," which he ran until 1886. He was superintendent of a coal mine for two years. In 1888 he went into the real estate and loan business, dealing in western real estate. In 1890 he started a private bank at Kenney, DeWitt Co., which he is now running. He was mayor of Kenney in 1895 and has held minor offices. He is a Knight Templar, a Knight of Pythias and a Woodman. In 1878 he married Susan A. Scroggin, daughter of Leonard K. Scroggin, an old-time banker of Mt. Pulaski, and well-known all over Illinois.

Morrison, John J. (rep.), of Chicago, 15th district, was born in New Haven, Conn., Nov. 27, 1861, and graduated from the Chicago High School in '78. He was clerk in a railroad office for a time, and then was bill clerk in the

SENATOR MORRISON.

paint and oil store of John W. Masury & Son for seven years, leaving when he was credit man with full charge of the office. He resigned to become chief deputy assessor of the West Town of Chicago, and after this he was put in charge of all the Chicago police courts. At present he is a general contractor. He was elected to the senate by a majority of over 900 over his democratic opponent. The district gave Cleveland 3,500 and Mayor Hopkins 2,200 majority. He is married. Senator Morrison is chairman of the important committee of railroads this session. He was one of a limited number of republican senators to control the organization this session, defeating a coterie of the ablest politicians in Illinois. He has been prominent in Cook county politics for years.

Tisdel, Clark J. (rep.), of Evanston, 7th district, was born in Leroy, Boone county, Ill., March 10, 1867, and five years later moved with his parents to Wyoming. At the age of 9 he lived with his maternal grandfather in Manchester, Iowa, where he attended public school. In '82 he spent a term at Oberlin (O.) College, but was forced by ill health to quit. Later he entered Northwestern University, remaining four years. Then he became a partner with his father in the real estate business in Kearney, Wyo. On account of dullness of trade he returned to Chicago in '88. In the meantime he read law, and graduated from the Chicago College of Law in '89 and was admitted to practice the same year. He is married and has two children; Mrs. Tisdel is a niece of Senator W. E. Mason. In Dec., '91, Mr. Tisdel was elected secretary

REPRESENTATIVE TISDEL.

of the Northwestern University settlement, a society for the amelioration of the condition of the poor in Chicago. He is a member of Custer Camp, Sons of Veterans. In '95 he was appointed secretary of the Civil Service Commission of Evanston. During the recent warm contest in republican ranks for United States senator Mr. Tisdel was the executive head of Senator Mason's campaign committee, and not a little of the credit of the result is due to his untiring energy, foresight and ability. His entire time and attention were devoted to Senator Mason's cause from the day of election in '96 until the republican caucus decided the matter.

Hall, Ross C. (dem.), of Oak Park, 7th district, was born in Rushville, Ill., Oct. 29, 1866, and his education was completed at Georgetown (D. C.) College. He was admitted to the bar in Georgetown and also in Illinois in '88, and entered into partnership with Judge Montgomery in Rushville in '89. He was city attorney of Rushville for

REPRESENTATIVE ROSS HALL.

one term—his only office prior to the present one. In '92 he moved to Chicago and entered into partnership with Judge William Prentiss, which still continues. He is married and has two sons.

Murray, Hugh V. (dem.), of Carlyle, 42d district, was born in Carlyle September 21, 1870, and completed his education at St. Joseph's College, Teutopolis, graduating in '89. For two years he taught school in Clinton county, and then studied law with his father, M. P. Murray, of Carlyle, and was admitted to the bar in '94,

REPRESENTATIVE HUGH MURRAY.

and is now practicing his profession in Carlyle. He is not married. This is his first political office. Mr. Murray is taking a very active part in all general legislation and exerting more influence than is usually accorded a new member.

Bollinger, Albert C. (rep.), of Waterloo, 48th district, was born in Steelville, Ill., Nov. 22, 1870, and is the

SENATOR BOLLINGER.

youngest member of the senate. He read law in the office of Hartzell & Sprigg, famous southern Illinois democratic leaders, but retained his love for the principles of republicanism. Was admitted to the bar in '93; in '92 he declined the nomination for state's attorney of Randolph county. He was elected over a fusion of democrats and populists, the district giving the fusionists a majority on the presidential ticket. He is married and has a daughter.

Houghton, Edwin W. (rep.), of Galva, 33d district, was born in Hough-

REPRESENTATIVE HOUGHTON.

ton, N. Y., July 28, 1834. Houghton was named after his grandfather, who settled there. Mr. Houghton received a common school education and learned the carpenter's trade when quite young. He moved to Wyanet, Ill., in '62, and for about three years, followed the business of carpenter and builder. In '65 he established a lumber yard in Wyanet, maintaining it until '80, when he moved to Henry. In '83 he moved to Galva and has since lived there. He is now president of the E. W. Houghton Lumber Co., with five lumber yards in as many different towns—Galva, Altona, Bradford, Wyoming and Etherley. He was a member of the board of supervisors of Henry county for three years, was several times mayor, and has held various minor offices. Is married and has one son and two daughters. He is a stalwart republican.

Laub, William G. (rep.), of Chicago, 1st district, was born in Cincinnati, O., June 5, 1850, and when 15 years old was apprenticed to a stone cutter.

REPRESENTATIVE LAUB.

He finished his apprenticeship on the Chicago postoffice. Then he visited nearly every state in the Union, and crossed the ocean, spending three years in foreign countries. Eventually he returned to Chicago, but again becoming restless he went to Mexico. In '82 he again returned to Chicago, and worked twelve years at his trade, the last eight as foreman. In '94 he was appointed assistant chief deputy of the criminal court of Cook county, which he resigned to take his seat at Springfield. For nine consecutive terms he was president of the Stone cutters' union, and for years was chairman of the arbitration committee. He is also prominent in political, fraternal and benevolent societies, holding many offices of honor and trust. Is married and has three children.

Wathier, Charles A. (rep.), of Chicago, 1st district, was born in the Grand Duchy of Luxembourg, September 7, 1852; emigrated with his parents to the United States in 1860; came to Chicago the same year; was educated in the public schools and afterwards attended Dyrenfurth Business College. After leaving school he became a partner in the firm of Joseph P. Wathier & Bros., wholesale and retail jewelers. Retiring from business he was appointed a deputy collector of internal revenue by Collector Stone; was reappointed by Collectors Mamer and Mize, which position he resigned in 1893 to accept an appointment by Sheriff Gilbert as deputy sheriff, and was reappointed by Sheriff Pease, which position he resigned Dec. 31, 1896. He has been identified with his ward organization for twenty years, having been city central and senatorial committeeman, and is a member of the Hamilton club and other political and social clubs. He is married and has a wife and three children.

REPRESENTATIVE WATHIER.

McEniry, William (dem.), of Rock Island, 33d district, was born on a Rock Island farm, May 9, 1860, and completed his education at a commercial college at Prairie du Chien, Wis., and the University of Notre Dame, graduating from the latter in '83 in the scientific course. In October of the same year he entered the Ann Arbor law school, graduating in the class of '85, and immediately opened a law office in Rock Island, in partnership with his brother, who has an office in the city of Moline. The style of the firm is McEniry & McEniry. His brother is present postmaster of Moline. In '87 Mr. McEniry was elected city attorney of Rock Island. He has been identified with the democratic party all his life and has been prominent in party matters in northern Illinois. Is married and has two sons and one daughter. Two years ago he took an active part in locating the Western Hospital for the Insane at Rock Island.

REPRESENTATIVE McENIRY.

Wood, Charles Lee (rep.), of Hamburg, 47th district, was born in Alton, Aug. 24, 1849, and when nine years old his mother moved to Hamburg, and the same year died, leaving him an orphan. He attended the public schools, but learned considerably more by his own efforts. He has been a farmer all his life, and owns a fine farm in Calhoun county. He is a Mason, and has served as officer in all its branches, and is also a member of the Home Forum. He is married and has one daughter. Mr. Wood has always been a strong republican and very prominent in his section of

REPRESENTATIVE WOOD.

the state in republican conventions and party matters of every kind.

Hussman, Bernard L. (dem.), of Effingham, 43d district, was born August 2, 1855, in St. Clair county, Ill.,

REPRESENTATIVE HUSSMAN.

and when he was ten years old his parents moved to Shelby county. He received a good education in private and common schools, spending three years at St. Joseph's College, Teutopolis. He has taught school in Clinton, Effingham, Cumberland and Shelby counties, and was principal of the Aviston public schools. In '82 he moved to Effingham county and engaged in farming, his present occupation. He is married and has seven sons and five daughters.

McGinnis, Peter J. (dem.), of Chicago, 2d district, was born in New York City August 19, 1854, and was edu-

REPRESENTATIVE McGINNIS.

cated there in the public schools. He is from a family of Tammany democrats, and has never swerved from that line. When fourteen years old he moved to Chicago. In '89-'90 he was chief deputy assessor for the West Town of Chicago, and in connection with Senator E. J. Dwyer he was in the real estate business until '95. He is a Knight of Pythias, and a member of the A. O. U. W., Knights of Columbus, and C. O. F. He is married and has two sons. For twenty years he has been prominent in Twelfth ward politics, and is interested in a measure to compel mayors to choose chiefs of police and fire department from men in the ranks, and compel Pullman to lower rates for berths in Illinois to $1.50 and $1.

Alschuler, Samuel (dem.), of Aurora, 14th district, was born in Chicago, November 20, 1859. Two years later the family moved to Aurora, where Mr. Alschuler was educated in the public schools, and has ever since resided. He read law and was admit-

REPRESENTATIVE ALSCHULER.

ted to the bar in December, '80. He began the practice of his profession, and enjoys a large and remunerative clientage. He is now associated in partnership with Hon. J. C. Murphy, formerly United States attorney for the Territory of Dakota, under the firm name of Alschuler & Murphy. Mr. Alschuler has been prominent in politics in northern Illinois for years, and in '92 accepted the democratic nomination for congress in the Kane county district, which is the most intensely republican district in the state. In July, 1893, Gov. Altgeld appointed him a member of the State Commission of Claims. He was elected to the house in '96 and resigned his position on the Claims Commission. He is not married. In this legislature Mr. Alschuler is recognized as a democratic leader on the floor, although it is his first session.

Murray, Abner G. (rep.), of Springfield, 39th district, was born in Dayton, O., September 7, 1857, and received a good common school education followed by a special course at the Western Ohio Normal school at Lewisburg. He taught school for two years in Ohio, after which he studied law with Jordan & Linden at Dayton, and was admitted to practice at Columbus in '80. He began practice at Dayton. In October, '82, he moved to Springfield, where he has since practiced his profession, being very successful. He is a Modern Woodman and a member of Ben Hur. He is married and has two sons and one daughter. Mr. Murray is interested in all bills relating to educational work, being chairman of the committee on education. He has taken an active part in politics in central

REPRESENTATIVE A. G. MURRAY.

Illinois for many years, and his name was presented before the state convention in '92 as a candidate for lieutenant-governor.

White, David C. (rep.), of Forest City, 32d district, was born at Cameron, W. Va., August 26, 1842, and received a good common school education. He was attending Waynesburg College when the war broke out. Enlisted as a private in '61 in the 1st W. Va. Inf. Vol., and served for a short time, when he returned to college. In the fall of '62 he again enlisted, this time in the 15th Penn. Cav., was promoted to first lieutenant, and served until the close of the war. He moved to Mason county, Ill., in '65, near Forest City, where he now resides. He served two terms as supervisor, and has been school treasurer for twenty years. He is a member of the G. A. R., Grange, Patrons of Husbandry, Modern Woodmen, and is a Knight Templar Mason. Is married and has two sons and one daughter. Mr. White is interested in all measures relative to drainage and waterways.

REPRESENTATIVE WHITE.

He lives in a strong democratic county and district, and republicans have an up-hill job getting office.

Webb, Daniel R. (dem.), of Benton, 46th district, was born near Benton, October 11, 1861, and educated at Ewing College, graduating in '85, and at the Southern Illinois Normal. He taught school for a few years, then studied law, was admitted to practice in '88, and has since been practicing at Benton. He was chosen police magistrate in '95, and still retains the office. He is married and has two sons. He is an Odd Fellow. This is his first political office. Mr. Webb

REPRESENTATIVE WEBB.

while in college gained quite a reputation as an elocutionist, and won several contests in school societies. He is interested in legislation that will benefit the farming community.

Williams, Samuel A. (rep.), of Friendsville, 44th district, was born near Nashville, Tenn., Feb. 29, 1849; when he was two years old his parents moved to Illinois and settled in

REPRESENTATIVE WILLIAMS.

Wabash county near where he now lives. He received a good common school education; is a farmer, and owns one of the most fertile farms in the Wabash valley. This is the first political office he ever held, but he has been active as a political worker, and a life-long republican. He is married and has four sons and one daughter. Mr. Williams will champion anything in the interest of the farmer, fruit raiser or stockman.

Compton, William A. (dem.), of Macomb, 28th district, was born on a McDonough county farm March 5, 1864. He finished his education at

REPRESENTATIVE COMPTON.

the Macomb Normal College, graduating in '85. Then he taught school for several terms and entered the law office of Judge William Prentiss, then of Macomb, now of Chicago, and was admitted to practice in November, '88. In the spring of '89 he began practice in Macomb, and has had a lucrative business ever since. He was married in '90 and has one son, Wm. A. Compton, Jr. Mr. Compton was first assistant clerk of the house in '91, having been nominated in the democratic caucus by acclamation. This is the first elective office he has filled. He is chairman of the democratic county committee of McDonough county, and is a recognized leader in western Illinois. He is a K. P. and a Woodman.

Garver, Samuel B. (rep.), of Farmer City, 30th district, was born in Dauphin Co., Pa., August 2, 1839, and was educated in the common schools. In '55 he moved to Piatt county, Ill., and has lived there ever since. At first he engaged in farming, and left the

REPRESENTATIVE GARVER.

farm to enter the army during the war, being mustered in Co. D, 73d Ill. Inf. Vol., on July 25, '62. He took part in the battles of Stone River, Chickamauga, Kenesaw Mountain, Resaca, Peach Tree Creek, the Atlanta battles, Franklin and others. Mr. Garver was three times wounded, twice through the left shoulder and once through the right hand. May 29, '65, he was discharged on account of wounds, and returned home. He farmed for four years, and entered the drug business in March, '70, and it is his present occupation. He began voting for republicans in '60, when he voted for Lincoln, and is proud of his unbroken record as a republican voter and worker. He is married and has two sons and two daughters. He is a Mason, member of the G. A. R. and Woodmen. He never aspired for political preferment.

Lyon, George R. (rep.), of Waukegan, 8th district, was born at Little Fort, now Waukegan, July 19, 1846, and finished his education at the Northwestern University at Evanston. In July, '62, at the age of 15, he enlisted in the 69th Ill. Vol.—a 3-months' regiment. In February, '64, he reënlisted in the 64th Ill. Inf., and served with Sherman from Chattanooga to Atlanta, from Atlanta to the sea, and on the march through the Carolinas to Washington, participating in the grand review at the close of the war. He was mustered out at Louisville, Ky., and returned home on the last day of his eighteenth year. He engaged in merchandising with his father at Waukegan, later purchasing the stock, and has since been engaged in the business. For three terms he was supervisor, the last term as

REPRESENTATIVE LYON.

chairman. He is Past Commander of Waukegan Post, G. A. R.; also Past Eminent Commander of Waukegan Commandery, K. T.; member Oriental Consistory of Chicago, and Medinah Shrine, Chicago. He is married and has two sons. This is his first term in the legislature.

Lovett, O. E. (dem.), of St. Elmo, 26th district, was born October 20, 1834, at Frostburg, Md., and came to Illinois in '50, settling in Fayette county. At present he is engaged in farming and stock-raising. He was educated in the common schools, and has served as director and president of the Fayette County Fair for fourteen years. He is married and has one son and two daughters living. Mr. Lovett is a loyal and enthusiastic democrat of the Jacksonian type and makes it a point to be in his seat during all the sessions of the house. This is his first political office. He was a member of the advisory council of the World's Congress Auxiliary on farm culture and cereal industry

REPRESENTATIVE LOVETT.

and member of the World's Agricultural Congress at the World's Fair, '93.

Large, James M. (dem.), of Athens, 32d district, was born in Morgan county, Feb. 5, 1858. When quite young his father moved to Auburn, and here he received a good common school education. He taught school, and attended the Chicago College of Law. For the past fifteen years he has been engaged in the mining industry, having had charge of several large mines in central Illinois. He has served his county as surveyor and

REPRESENTATIVE LARGE.

his city as its attorney, and is a Mason and a Modern Woodman. Is married. He has for years been prominent in the councils of his party in his county.

Payne, Joseph T. (dem.), of Mt. Vernon, 46th district, was born on a farm in Jefferson county, February 16, 1847. Since '77 he has been engaged in the ministry, preaching the gospel

SENATOR PAYNE.

according to the creed of the Missionary Baptist denomination. He received a good common school education. He was supervisor for his township and chairman of the board; was twice married, in '66 and '80. Senator Payne is a democrat, but was elected by a fusion of populists and democrats. He is a practical farmer, has owned and operated a farm all his life, and lives on a farm now. He takes great pride in his agricultural life.

Landrigan, John (dem.), of Albion, 44th district, was born in County Tipperary, Ireland, in 1832 and came to America with his parents when less than a year old stopping in New Jersey. He spent his early life in Logansport, Indiana, and completed his

SENATOR LANDRIGAN.

education at Logansport Seminary. After leaving school he engaged in railroad and canal contracting. Senator Landrigan came to Illinois in '58, buying a farm in Edwards county, and has since remained there. This is his fourth term in the Illinois legislature, two terms in the house, 1869-1875, and twice in the senate, 1871-1897. He was president of the state board of agriculture from 1893-1896. He is married and has no children. Senator Landrigan is one of the most prominent men of the state, and has been a democratic leader in southern Illinois for many years.

Granger, Flavel K. (rep.), of West McHenry, 8th district, was born in Wayne county, New York, May 16, 1832, and was educated in the public schools of Sodus, New York. He settled in Illinois in '53 at Waukegan.

SENATOR GRANGER.

He studied law and was admitted to the bar in '55. The same year he moved to McHenry and began the practice of his profession and has since resided there. In '56 he engaged in the live stock, wool and farm produce business, and is still interested in it, incidentally with his law practice. He has always been prominent in politics, and has represented a democratic township for fifteen years on the county board. He was a member of the house in the 28th, 29th, 30th and 31st general assemblies and was temporary speaker in the 29th and 30th—the first two sessions held in the present capitol. He is married and has three sons and three daughters.

Horn, Joseph A. (dem.), of Mt. Pulaski, 32d district, was born in Graham, N. C., May 13, 1848, and educated in the common schools. He worked on a farm until he was 20 years of age. In '60 his father moved with his family to Mt. Pulaski and seven years later Mr. Horn carried a surveyor's chain across the country from the Missouri river to Denver and the west, surveying what is now the Kansas Pacific and several branches of the Union Pacific railroads. After the surveys he was timekeeper and bookkeeper in the construction department. He began the practice of law at Brookfield, Mo., in '77, and two years later was admitted to the bar. In '89 he returned to Mt. Pulaski, and has practiced his profession there ever since. He was city attorney of Mt. Pulaski for six years and has filled various minor offices. He is an Odd Fellow, a Knight of Pythias, and

REPRESENTATIVE HORN.

member of several fraternal orders. He is married. Mr. Horn always has been a democrat and prominent in central Illinois politics.

Pemberton, Stanton C. (rep.), of Oakland, 40th district, was born near Oakland, July 9, 1858, and lived on a farm until 20 years old. He completed his education by graduating in '79 from Lee's Academy. After this he embarked in the lumber and coal business in Oakland under the firm name of Green Bros. & Pemberton. This title was changed to Pemberton & Price, and it still exists. For eight years he was a member of the county board, four of which he was chairman of the board, and has filled various minor township and village offices. He is an Odd Fellow, a Knight of Pythias and a Woodman. He was married in '82 and has one son living. Senator Pemberton has been an active figure in republican politics in eastern Illinois for twenty years, and his popularity is attested by the fact that his district went democratic by over 500, while he was elected by over 100.

SENATOR PEMBERTON

He is a member of the most important committees in the senate.

Eldredge, Charles M. (rep.), of Chicago, 6th district, was born in Fairfield, O., August 26, 1867, and received his education in the common schools and at Beloit College, Wisconsin. He graduated from the Union College of Law, in Chicago, in '87, and when he came of age, in '88, was admitted to practice. He has practiced his profession in Chicago ever since. Mr. Eldredge's family moved to McHenry county, Ill., in '70, and it was there

REPRESENTATIVE ELDREDGE.

he lived until he went to Chicago to carve out a future for himself. This is his first political office, although he has always taken an active interest in politics. He is a Mason and a member of the Royal Arcanum. Is married.

Fuller, DuFay A. (rep.), of Belvidere, 8th district, was born in Boone county, Feb. 21, 1852, and received his education from the public schools of Belvidere. In 1892 he entered the

REPRESENTATIVE FULLER.

insurance business, and was appointed district manager of the New York Mutual Life, a position he yet holds. He is a Mason and an Odd Fellow. He is a brother of Hon. Charles E. Fuller, long prominent in state politics. The official returns show that there is only one vote between the totals for Mr. Fuller and his republican colleague—a singular circumstance.

Marquiss, Seymour (rep.), of DeLand, 30th district, was born near his present home, June 7, 1837, and has lived in Piatt county all his life. He was educated in the early district

REPRESENTATIVE MARQUISS.

schools of pioneer days. He has been a farmer all his life until within the last eight years, having rented his farm and moved to DeLand. He has filled various local offices, and was chairman of the republican county committee for two terms. His first ballot was cast for Lincoln in '60 and he has been a sturdy republican worker ever since. He is married. Mr. Marquiss is interested in all legislation that will benefit the farmer and the people in general, and is especially anxious to have the revenue laws revised.

Baxter, Delos W. (rep.), of Rochelle, 10th district, was born in Rochelle July 29, 1857, and was educated in the public schools. He graduated from the law department of the Iowa State University in June, '81. He was admitted to the bar in Illinois in December, '81, and has practiced his profession in Rochelle ever since. In '84 he was elected state's attorney of Ogle county and held the office for twelve years—until his election as

SENATOR BAXTER.

state senator in '96. He also has been mayor of Rochelle. Is a Knight Templar, Shriner, Odd Fellow and Knight of Pythias. He is married. Senator Baxter has been an influential member of the republican party all his life, and was elected by a majority of nearly 9,000.

Sparks, Capt. David R. (rep.), of Alton, 47th district, was born near Lanesville, Indiana, in 1823, and in the spring of '36 moved with his parents to Macoupin Co., Ill. In June, '47, he enlisted in the Mexican war in the infantry arm, and crossed the great plains to Santa Fé, returning in the fall of '48. He was married in February, '49, and in '50 he again crossed the plains and mountains in search of gold, driving an ox team to California. In the summer of '51 he returned via the Isthmus of Panama, Cuba, New Orleans and St. Louis. In company with Wesley Best he built a steam flouring mill at Staunton in '55, and in the spring of '60 he again crossed the plains with ox teams, taking a quartz mill, and erecting it near what is now Central City, Col., and started the second steam engine in those mines. He returned to Illinois in time to vote for Douglas, and two weeks later became a stalwart republican. He enlisted on the first call for 3-year volunteers, in '61, and as captain of the 3d Ill. Cav. he participated in several bloody battles, and was present at the fall of Vicksburg. After serving two years and a half he returned to his home, then at Litchfield. In '64 the same firm of Best & Sparks built a larger mill in Litchfield, and in '69 they bought the flour mill in Alton, built by S. & P. Wise. In '81 he bought the interest of Mr. Best and has materially enlarged and

SENATOR SPARKS.

improved the plant. Capt. Sparks has six children—one daughter, Mrs. Milnas, and five sons, four of whom have charge of the Alton mill. He was a member of the house in '89, and is the oldest member of the present state senate.

Berryman, James R. (rep.), of Scales Mound, 12th district, was born near Scales Mound October 17, 1850, where he has lived all his life. He received his education at the Galena Normal school, '71-'72. He has been a farmer all his life, added to which during the past ten years he has been in the grain and stock business at Scales Mound, living on his farm, which is about two miles from the town. He has filled various local offices, assessor, collector, etc., and has been supervisor for his township for the past eight years, for the past two years being chairman of the board, a position he now fills. For years he has taken a prominent part in the politics of northern Illinois. He is married and has two sons and two daughters.

REPRESENTATIVE BERRYMAN.

He is a Mason, a Woodman and a Knight of the Globe.

Harnsberger, George L. (dem.), of Springfield, 39th district, was born July 13, 1850, at Pleasant Plains, Sangamon Co., Ill. He went from the district school to Illinois College at Jacksonville. He graduated at Lincoln University and in '76 graduated from the law school at Ann Arbor, Mich., and was admitted to the bar the same year. His life was spent principally on the farm, until two years ago, when he moved to Springfield. He is still engaged in farming and in the mercantile business in this

REPRESENTATIVE HARNSBERGER.

city. He was married to Addie Houghton in '90. Mr. Harnsberger was a member of the board of supervisors for twelve terms, being twice its chairman.

Kain, Joseph (dem.), of Braidwood, 25th district, was born in Kilwinning, Scotland, December 4, 1854, and in '61 emigrated with his parents to Huntington Penn., and five years later

REPRESENTATIVE KAIN

they moved to Braidwood, which has been his home ever since. Here he attended the public schools. He is engaged in the business of undertaker, livery and sale stable, and owns a furniture store. Mr. Kain has been a member of the Will county board of supervisors for the past twelve years, is now a member, and has filled many minor official positions. He is married and has three sons and two daughters. Mr. Kain is a member of the Knights of Pythias and and Foresters. He has been an active democrat in his district for many years.

REPRESENTATIVE BOOTH.

Booth, Fenton W. (rep.), of Marshall, 43d district, was born in Marshall, May 12, 1869. His education was obtained in his native city, and at DuPauw University, Greencastle, Ind. He graduated from the Marshall High School, and spent three years at DuPauw, and he also graduated from the law department of the University of Michigan at Ann Arbor in '92, and immediately commenced practicing his profession of law in Marshall. This is his first political office, but he has been an active worker in republican ranks in eastern Illinois all his life. He is a Knight of Pythias. He was married in '93, but lost his wife by death in March, '95; he has one child, a daughter, Margaret.

Trousdale, Fletcher A. (dem.), of Metropolis, 51st district, was born on a White county, Ill., farm January 15, 1846, and received a good education in the public schools. He taught school for a short time, and after-

REPRESENTATIVE TROUSDALE.

wards went into the grain and pork business. Then he traveled for several years for wholesale dry goods houses in Cincinnati and Evansville, his territory being southern Illinois and Kentucky. In '75 he located in Metropolis and engaged in merchandise and grain buying. In '77 he established the Metropolis "Democrat," and became the proprietor and active editor—his present occupation. He extended his business in '90 by manufacturing cast iron water pipe. He is married and has two sons.

Allen, Robert H. (pop.-dem.), of Shiloh Hill, 48th district, was born in Randolph county, April 8, 1834, and spent his entire life on a farm. He received a good common school education, and in '62 enlisted in the 80th Ill. Inf., Co. F, and served until the close of the war. He participated in fourteen general battles, and was under fire for a total of fifty-two days. In April, '63, at Sand Mountain, he was wounded, captured and thrown into Libby prison. Received the pop-

REPRESENTATIVE ALLEN.

ulist nomination for member of the General Assembly in '92, again in '94 and in '96 he was the unanimous choice of democrats and populists. He is always in his seat and never dodges a roll call. He has one son by his first wife and two by his present wife.

McGoorty, John P. (dem.), of Chicago, 3d district, was born in Conneaut, O., August 25, 1866, and in '70 his parents moved to Berlin, Wis. Here he was educated in the public schools, completing the high school course. He moved to Chicago in '86, and finished a course in law at Lake

REPRESENTATIVE McGOORTY.

Forest University in '92; he was orator of his class in '91, and president of the class of '92. In June, '92, he began practicing his profession of law and was one of the counsel for Prendergast, who killed Mayor Carter H. Harrison, of Chicago, in '93. In '93 he married Miss Mary Wiggins, of Chicago. This is his first political office. In the election November, '96, he received 1,200 more votes than any of his colleagues on the democratic ticket—and there was no fusion in his district, either.

Rhodes, William V. (dem.), of Wrightsville, 36th district, was born in Bedford county, Pa., September 14, 1846, and was educated in the country schools. In '66 he moved to a Greene county (Illinois) farm, and has farmed ever since. He was county supervisor for four years and has held several minor offices. He is a Knight of Pythias. Mr. Rhodes is married and has four sons and two daughters. He is interested in everything that interests the farmer, and is anxious

REPRESENTATIVE RHODES.

for a revision of the revenue laws so the burden of taxes will be more equitably distributed. Mr. Rhodes is one of the best members of this General Assembly; is always in his seat. His work in committee room has been conspicuously good.

Butler, Michael J. (dem.), of Chicago, 4th district, was born at Carbondale, Pa., June 24, 1851. He attended the public schools and worked in the anthracite coal mines. In '81 he moved to Chicago and engaged in the packing business and later was employed in the Union Stock Yards blacksmith shops. For a time he was chief clerk of the Town of Lake Board of Health, and in '87 was appointed a United States gauger. In '90 he was a corporation inspector for the south division in Chicago, and in

'94 was appointed superintendent of sidewalks. He is a member of the National Union and other benevolent and fraternal societies. He lost his wife by death in '95. He has two

REPRESENTATIVE BUTLER.

sons and three daughters. Mr. Butler has been a prominent figure in Cook county politics for many years.

Murray, George (rep.), of Elmira, Stark Co., 31st district. Born in Roxburyshire, Scotland, May 1, 1840, and moved to America with his parents in '53, coming direct to Stark county, and has been there ever since. He received a common school education and is married. He began farm work when 14 years old and has been on a farm ever since. He has held several township and school offices, and was a member of the house in '93 and was

REPRESENTATIVE GEO. MURRAY

reëlected in '94 and '96. He is a typical farmer. Mr. Murray is always in his seat and informs himself as to the merits of all bills. This session he is chairman of the committee on contingent expenses, one of the most important and responsible committees in the house, to which all matters affecting expenses and pay-rolls are referred.

Case, Selon H. (rep.), of Chicago, 2d district, was born in Chicago, November 17, 1846, and finished his education by graduating in mathematics from Madison University in 1862. He served in the Union army until May 29, 1865. After the war he went to South America and the Sandwich Islands. Returning about 1871 he embarked in the iron manufacturing business, and later into the loan and discount business, his present occupation. He is married and has one son and two daughters. He is a Knight Templar, and until 1896 was a member of the republican state committee and on the executive com-

SENATOR CASE.

mittee a part of the time. During the recent contest for United States senator Mr. Case was a staunch friend of Senator Mason and was one of the leaders in Mason's campaign, representing Senator Mason's district in the state senate.

Walleck, Christian R. (dem.), of Chicago, 9th district, was born October 29, 1864, of Bohemian parents and has resided in Chicago since 1868. He received a common school education and since his thirteenth year has worked at various manual pursuits. Being fond of books he has devoted all his leisure moments to reading and storing his mind with useful knowledge, which he failed to obtain in his earlier days. For the last twelve years he has been engaged in the real estate and mortgage loan business in partnership with his brother. He is unmarried, a man of quiet habits and unassuming ways, very popular among his people and a

REPRESENTATIVE WALLECK.

member of several societies. This is his second term in the General Assembly, having been reëlected in '96 by an increased majority. He is mainly interested in labor and revenue legislation.

Harding, Fred E. (rep.), of Monmouth, 35th district, was born near Richfield Springs, N. Y., Sept. 20, 1847, and educated at Monmouth College and Union College, New York, graduating from the latter in '69 in the classical course. He has been connected with the Monmouth and Second National Banks, of Monmouth, for twenty-three years, beginning as a messenger, and he is now president. He

SENATOR HARDING.

has not been an office seeker. He has been on the Warren county republican committee for fifteen years, twelve of which he has been chairman. Is married, and was elected by a majority of 6,913 over his democratic opponent. Senator Harding is chairman of the committee on corporations this session, one of the most influential committees in the senate. Senator Harding has large financial interests in Warren county, and has been a prominent figure in western Illinois politics for many years. In the senate no man stands higher in the estimation of his colleagues. His record will bear the closest scrutiny.

Powell, Joseph (rep.), of Chicago, 5th district, was born in Calais, France, September 6, 1847. His parents came to America in '53, and located at Waterbury, Conn., where he attended the common schools. He removed to Bridgeport, where he identified himself with the Howe Sewing

REPRESENTATIVE JOSEPH POWELL.

Machine Company. When 23 years old he moved to Philadelphia, joining his brothers in the manufacture of hosiery. He now represents that establishment for the western territory with headquarters in Chicago. He was elected to the present house as an independent-anti-machine republican. This is his first political office. He is a Mason, is married and has one son, Burton. Mr. Powell was sent to the legislature to protest against gang methods, and is thoroughly in earnest in the reform movement.

Stewart, Eb (dem.), of Toledo, 43d district, was born on a Morgan county (Ind.) farm, September 14, 1860, and when very young his parents moved to a farm near Greenup, Ill. He completed his education at Lee's Academy, Loxa, Ill., taught a school for a short time, and then farmed and engaged in buying and selling live stock. In '86 with his partner. Mr. Jones, he erected one of the finest flouring mills in southern Illinois, operating it for nearly three years.

REPRESENTATIVE STEWART.

From '88 to '94 he was circuit clerk, running ahead of his ticket at the last election. He has lived in Cumberland county continuously since '65, and has been prominent in southern Illinois politics most of the time; was nominated by acclamation for his present office. Is unmarried.

Brignadello, Frank J. (dem.), of Chicago, 17th district, was born in Chicago February 22, 1865, of Italian parents. He was educated in the common schools of Chicago and clerked in a commission store for six years, when he went into the feed business with his brother under the

REPRESENTATIVE BRIGNADELLO.

firm name of Brignadello Bros. He is not married, and never held an office until '95, when he was elected to the house. He has been very active in democratic politics, and stands well with his constituents. Mr. Brignadello is a member of a number of societies. He is favored with a list of first class committees, among which is the steering committee, which controls democratic party management in the house. This is his second session, having been elected in '94 and '96.

Beer, Simon P. (dem.), of Fairview, 26th district, was born near his present home September 29, 1837, and finished a good education at Abingdon College, and also graduated at the Medical College of Ohio in '70. He began the practice of his profession at Ellisville, Fulton county, Ill., the same year, and moved in '86 to Fairview. For a period of twelve years he was a supervisor, four years of the time being chairman of the county board. In '62 he enlisted as first lieutenant

REPRESENTATIVE BEER.

in Co. B, 103d Ill. Inf., and participated in the great battles of Vicksburg, Chattanooga, Franklin and Nashville, and was mustered out at the close of the war, when he returned home and resumed practice as a physician. He is a member of the G. A. R., a Mason and Odd Fellow. Is married and has one daughter.

Montgomery, George W. (dem.), of Clayton, 37th district, was born near Wellsburg, W. Va., February 24, 1841; was educated in the common schools, and came to Illinois in '65. He began the practice of pharmacy in '67 and has been in the drug business most of the time since that date. He was the senior of the firm of Montgomery & Craig, bankers of Clayton, from '79 to '89, and since the latter date he has been in the real estate and insurance business. He has been supervisor, town clerk and member of the board of education, and is a Mason and Odd Fellow. He lost his wife by death

REPRESENTATIVE MONTGOMERY.

in November, '96. Mr. Montgomery's legislative record can be scanned closely without finding flaws. He stands well with his colleagues.

Barnes, John A. (dem.), of Louisville, 42d district, was born in Marion county, January 3, 1859, and educated in the common schools. He taught school for seven years meantime reading law. In August, '84, he was admitted to the bar, and two years later located in Louisville. Mr. Barnes is a Mason, an Odd Fellow, a Knight of Pythias and a Woodman. He is married to a daughter of Gov. John R.

REPRESENTATIVE BARNES.

Tanner and they have one son and one daughter. Mr. Barnes has been an active democrat in southern Illinois for several years. He has been master in chancery of Clay county for the past nine years. He is a member of the most important committees in the house and is on the democratic steering committee. This is his second term, having been elected '94 and '96.

Munroe, George H. (rep.), of Joliet, 25th district, was born in Jefferson Co., N. Y., Sept. 24, 1844, and came to Illinois in '49 with his parents; went to Joliet in '62 at the time his father was elected sheriff. He received a common school education, and when 19 years old was appointed by his father, George Munroe, deputy sheriff. In '65 he engaged in the merchandise business with his father under the firm name of George Munroe & Son. The firm was successful and at the end of fifteen years they sold out the retail trade and confined their efforts to the wholesale grocer trade

SENATOR MUNROE.

proper. In this they were also successful, but after a few years the firm sold part of their business to their employes, and opened up in the real estate and mortgage loan business. Senator Munroe's father died in '90, and the business was continued by Senator Munroe until '96, when his brother, Edwin S., became a partner. The firm is now doing one of the largest mortgage-loan businesses in Joliet, and they also own a large amount of business property. Senator Munroe has been connected with the stone business for the past twenty years and is a large stockholder and vice president of the Western Stone Co. He is also interested largely in farm lands, banking and other investments. He has been an earnest republican since he was of age, but never was an applicant for office until he received the nomination for senator in '94. Senator Munroe is a member of the Union League and Marquette clubs of Chicago. He is married, and lives just outside the limits of the city of Joliet.

Johnson, Caleb C. (dem.), of Sterling, 31st district, was born in Whiteside county, May 23, 1844, and educated in the common schools, and spent a term in the military academy at Fulton. He was admitted to the bar in '77, and two years later began practice. He enlisted in the army in Co. C, 69th Ill. Vol. Inf., and Co. D, 140th Ill. He has been a member of the board of supervisors and was deputy collector of internal revenue during Cleveland's first administration. He was a delegate to the democratic national convention in '88, and in '85 and '87 was a member of the house. He is married. Mr. Johnson has been

REPRESENTATIVE C. C. JOHNSON.

a leader in every general assembly of which he has been a member. By tacit consent he is the leader of the democratic side on the floor of the house at the present session. He is a good parliamentarian, and one of the ablest men in the legislature.

Allen, Charles A. (rep.), of Hoopeston, 18th district, was born in Danville, July 26, 1851, and received a good common school education. He graduated from the law department of Ann Arbor University in 1875, and was admitted to practice in Illinois the same year. During his school studies he taught school and worked on a farm to obtain the means to complete his education. He began practice at Rossville in '75, and in '81 moved to Hoopeston. He has earned and is receiving a lucrative practice, and is regarded as one of the ablest lawyers in eastern Illinois. He was a member of the house in '85, '87, '89, '91, retiring voluntarily until '97. He was a leader on his side of the house in every session, and during the great

REPRESENTATIVE CHARLES ALLEN.

Logan-Morrison fight for the United States senate in '85 Mr. Allen was one of the closest friends Gen. Logan had. Again in '91 when Palmer finally won the office of senator, Mr. Allen was a leader of his party in the legislature, and his counsel was always welcome. He was temporary speaker of the present house and is chairman of the committee on judiciary. He is married and has two sons.

Schubert, Ernest G. (rep.), of Chicago, 11th district, was born in Chicago June 9, 1863. He was educated in the public schools and at Bryant & Stratton's Business College. He has

REPRESENTATIVE SCHUBERT.

been in the printing and publishing business and owner of vessel property for seven years. He is a Mason and member of other fraternal and benevolent societies. He is married. This is Mr. Schubert's second session, having been elected in '94 and '96. In the session of '95 he was chairman of the committee on parks and boulevards, and this session is chairman of the committee on municipal corporations, and is on the most important committees in the house. Mr. Schubert was a leading candidate for speaker of the house this session, and only by his withdrawal the morning of the caucus was the selection of Speaker Curtis made possible. He is one of the republican leaders in Cook county and is influential in the General Assembly. He is on the steering committee.

O'Brien, William J. (dem.), of Chicago, 9th district, was born in Boston, Mass., March 20, 1851. During the thirty-four years he has lived in Chi-

SENATOR O'BRIEN.

cago he has risen step by step until today he is not only a political leader but a business man of wealth and influence. Senator O'Brien worked in the rolling mills for several years, then in the brick yards, and afterwards in the packing houses. In '66 he engaged in business for himself. Senator O'Brien is married. He took an active interest in politics and soon became one of the leaders of his party in the Sixth ward. In '89 and again in '91 he was elected alderman. He was elected to the senate in '94. In April, '97, he was again elected alderman. In '92 he aided in organizing the Citizens' Brewing Co., and the success of the institution financially is largely due to him. Senator O'Brien is also a large owner of real estate in Chicago.

Olson, Albert J. (rep.), of Chicago, 23d district, was born at Elgin June 24, 1865, and educated in Elgin's public schools. When he was 17 he moved to Chicago and began business in the wholesale dairy line, his present occupation, handling the products of

REPRESENTATIVE OLSON.

his own large dairy farm, as well as the best dairies in the vicinity of his McHenry county farm. He is married. He has been active in Chicago politics since attaining his majority, and is a popular member of the house. Is a Mason, a K. P., and A. O. U. W. Mr. Olson was a member of the house in '95 and was reëlected in '96 by an increased majority.

McConnel, Edward (dem.), of Jacksonville, 34th district, was born in Jacksonville, July 19, 1840, and received a collegiate education, graduating from Illinois College in '59 in the classical course. April 16, '61, he

SENATOR McCONNEL.

joined Co. B., 10th Ill. Inf., a three-months' regiment; afterwards he joined the 16th U. S. Inf., and resigned in March, '66, when he was captain and brevet-major. He returned to Jacksonville and resumed his studies. He studied law and was admitted to the bar in Jan., '79, and has practiced ever since, doing considerable newspaper work incidentally. Senator McConnel was a member of the house in '95 and was advanced to the senate in '96, running ahead of the democratic ticket. He is married and has one daughter. He has never been an office seeker.

Murdoch, Frank A. (rep.), of Oneida, 35th district. Born in Ayrshire, Scotland Sept. 2, 1843, and came to America in '52 with his parents, stopping first in Trumbull Co., O. Moved to Knox Co., Ill., in '57, and settled on a farm near Oneida. He was educated in the common schools and farmed until '73, when he went into the banking business and has been in it ever since.

REPRESENTATIVE MURDOCH.

The Exchange Bank of Oneida is owned by Anderson & Murdoch. He served ten years in the Illinois National Guard. He was elected alderman for eight years and mayor for four years, and he was a member of the school board for six years, resigning in '95; was chairman of the republican county committee for two years, and was a member of the house in '93 and was reëlected in '94 and '96. Is married. He is a 32d degree Mason; has been master of his lodge for eight or ten years; high priest of the Chapter; past commander of Galesburg Commandery No. 8, K. T., and a past grand in the Odd Fellows. Mr. Murdoch is also a member of Medinah Temple of the Mystic Shrine, Chicago. He was chairman of the important committee on corporations in the sessions of '95 and '97.

Novak, Edward J. (dem.), of Chicago, 13th district, was born in Chicago, Nov. 2, 1869, and with probably one exception is the youngest member of the General Assembly. He was edu-

REPRESENTATIVE NOVAK.

cated in the public schools of Chicago and at the Metropolitan Business College, graduating from the latter. In February, '95, he was admitted to the bar before the appellate court. Mr. Novak is now serving his third term, having been elected to the house in '92, '94 and '96. He is married and has one child, a boy. Mr. Novak is a member of the steering committee and one of the democratic leaders in the house. In Cook county he stands high as an influential democrat.

Miller, George W. (rep.), of Chicago, 3d district, was born on a farm near

REPRESENTATIVE MILLER.

Gilman, Ill., Jan. 12, 1869, and graduated from the Gilman high school in '87. He taught school for over a year, and went to Chicago in Sept.,

'89, entering the Union College of Law. In May, '90, he accepted a position in the interior department, and took a two years' course in the Columbian University at Washington, D. C., doing his office work at the same time, graduating in June, '91. He went back to Chicago and entered the law office of Congressman Mann; admitted to the bar in October, '91, and in January, '94, the style of the firm was changed to Mann, Hayes & Miller, and still exists. Mr. Miller is married. He is one of the clearest and most forcible speakers in the house, and as chairman of judicial department and practice this session, and member of other important committees, exerts considerable influence.

Sharrock, James E. (rep.), of Taylorville, 41st district, was born at Tower Hill, Ill., May 15, 1860, and received a good common school education. He studied law and was admitted to the bar in '86, commencing the practice of his profession immediately at Cowden. In May, '92, he removed to Taylorville, where he enjoys a large and lucrative practice. Mr. Sharrock has held several minor offices, and is married. He was a member of the last General Assembly, when he took prominent ground in favor of the curtailment of the expenses of the legislature. He was also active in exposing corruption in the General Assembly. This sesion he is chairman of the committe on drainage and waterways, and is one of the republican leaders. He made an eloquent speech naming Wm. E. Mason for United States senator in the joint assembly, and when he addresses the house commands close attention.

REPRESENTATIVE SHARROCK.

Quanstrum, John F. (rep.), of Chicago, 19th district, was born in Sweden, August 8, 1858. In 1862, his parents moved to Jordan, Minn., where Mr. Quanstrum attained a good education in the public schools. In May, '80, he moved to Chicago and entered the lathing business and subsequently established a bakery business. This is the first elective office he ever filled, although he has been active in politics in his ward, and always was a republican. Mr. Quanstrum is a Mason and a Shriner. He is married and has three daughters.

REPRESENTATIVE QUANSTRUM.

Perry, Elmer A. (dem.), of Mt. Sterling, 37th district, was born on a farm near Mt. Sterling, March 31, 1861, and graduated from the university at Valparaiso, Ind., in '84, with a degree of A. B. He taught school for seven years, reading law meantime, and was admitted to the bar in '88. He has practiced since February, '93. Mr. Perry was elected city attorney of Mt. Sterling in '93, '95 and again in '97. He

REPRESENTATIVE PERRY.

is a Mason, a Knight Pythias, and is not married. Mr. Perry is now serving his second term, having been elected to the house in '94 and again in '96. He is a forceful, eloquent speaker on the floor, but seldom exercises the privilege.

Anthony, George D. (rep.), of Chicago, 23d district, was born Feb. 18, 1863, in Chicago, and is the third son of Judge Elliott Anthony. He was educated at the Ogden school, followed by a course in the West Division High School, then four years at Amherst, where he graduated in '85 with degree of Bachelor of Arts; three years later was given degree of Master of Arts. He followed this up with a thorough course at the Union College of Law: admitted to the bar in '87. Then he spent a year visiting European countries. He is now a member of the law firm of C. E. & G. D. Anthony. He is married. He is a 32d degree Mason, an Odd Fellow, a Knight of Pythias, a Forester, and a member of the National Union. His majority over his democratic opponent in '94 was 1,153. Senator Anthony is chairman of judiciary, the most important committee in the senate. He was one of the organizers of the present senate, and is a republican leader.

SENATOR ANTHONY.

Salmans, George W. (dem.), of Danville, 18th district, was born in Vinton Co., O., January 9, 1849, and completed his education by graduating from the University of Michigan in the spring of '76. He was admitted to the bar the same year, but taught school and worked on a farm for ten years previous. He commenced the practice of his profession immediately in Vermilion county, and has been actively engaged in it ever since. He is married and has four sons and three daughters. This is the first political office he ever filled, there being little chance for democrats in Vermilion county, had he the desire for office-holding. He was born an abolitionist, "Greeleyized" in '72, and with many other republicans finally joined the democrats, and is a great admirer of Bryan and the last Chicago platform.

REPRESENTATIVE SALMANS.

Barricklow, Joseph P. (dem.), of Arcola, 40th district, was born near Rising Sun, Ind., Feb. 7, 1867, and came of a long line of Dutch ancestry, his forefathers being among the first settlers of New Amsterdam. In '71 he moved to Illinois with the family, settling on a farm near Arcola, where his mother still resides, his father having died in '75. He received a common school education, and began teaching in '85, studying law in the meantime; was admitted to the bar in '93, and immediately won his spurs

REPRESENTATIVE BARRICKLOW.

in a sensational murder trial, clearing his client. He has been identified with the Illinois National Guard since '85. Mr. Barricklow is now serving his second term, having been elected in '94 and again in '96 to the house. He is pushing a uniform text book bill, introduced by himself, and hopes to pass it. He is married and has one daughter.

Busell, David C. (rep.), of Milledgeville, 12th district, was born in Sandwich, N. H., June 20, 1837, and educated in the common schools. When seventeen years old he moved with his parents to Lee Co., Ill. After a year there he moved to Carroll county, and has since lived there, where he owns a valuable farm; he has been a farmer all his life. He was supervisor for fourteen years consecutively, the last three of which he was

REPRESENTATIVE BUSELL.

chairman of the board. He was also school treasurer for 25 years. He is president of the First National Bank of Lanark and is a Mason. He is married and has two daughters. He always has been a strong republican in politics, but this is his first political office. Mr. Busell is more of a business man than a politician. He has done all in his power to advance the interests of republican candidates and republican principles in his section of the state.

Thomas, John E. (rep.), of Belleville, 49th district, was born in Belleville, November 7, 1862. He was educated in the public schools of Belleville, in a private school in the east, and graduated in law at Ann Arbor in '83. After this he managed his father's extensive business, Col. John Thomas, one of Illinois' pioneers, being one of the largest land owners in St. Clair county. In '89 he purchased an interest in the Belleville "Advocate," and has had charge of the business department ever since. Is married.

REPRESENTATIVE THOMAS.

He is a 32d degree Mason, a Knight of Pythias, a Woodman and a member of several musical societies. He was a page in the house in '73. Mr. Thomas' father died December 15, '94, aged 95 years, and his mother is living at the age of 71.

Bryant, Nathan D. (peo.-dem.), of Omaha, 44th district, was born in Gallatin county, November 28, 1869, and spent his early life on a farm, but received a good district school education and taught school three years. He attended Hayward College at Fairfield, and returned to Gallatin county, where he taught school for four years

REPRESENTATIVE BRYANT.

more. When 21 years old he was elected town clerk, and later ran for county superintendent of schools of Gallatin county on the people's ticket, and was defeated. He was chosen to the present General Assembly by a fusion of people's and democrats. He is a Good Templar and a member of the Court of Honor and F. M. B. A. He is married. He is anxious to have the time for collection of taxes made in the fall after crops are marketed.

Blood, Fred G. (peo.-dem.), of Mt. Vernon, 46th district, was born on a dairy farm near Potsdam, N. Y., May 4. 1856, and completed the scientific and teacher's course at the State Normal school at Potsdam. He taught school to pay for his tuition and expenses. In '77 he came to Montgomery Co., Ill., and worked on a farm. In the fall he went to Franklin county, teaching school until '88. Then he moved to Marion and took charge of the F. M. B. A. "Binder," which he conducted until it was sold to the

REPRESENTATIVE BLOOD.

"Progressive Farmer." He moved to Mt. Vernon and entered the field as an organizer for the F. M. B. A. About '90 he was made state organizer for the F. A. & I. U. and elected state secretary. He was in the publishing business in Chicago for two years. In '95 he was admitted to the bar and has since practiced his profession at Mt. Vernon. He cast his last republican vote for Blaine and Logan and became an independent until the people's party was organized, and ever since has taken prominent part in all the conventions and movements of the new party. Is married and has two daughters. He is an Odd Fellow, a Knight Pythias, a Woodman, and member of the Court of Honor.

Edelstein, Jacob S. (dem.), of Belvidere, 8th district, was born in Courland, eastern province of Russia, October 16, 1857, and emigrated to Belvidere in '82. He engaged in the dry goods business and was very successful, retiring in '95. He is an Odd Fellow and a Woodman. He is married

REPRESENTATIVE EDELSTEIN.

and has three sons. Mr. Edelstein's education was obtained in the provincial schools of Russia. He is interested to a considerable extent in the real estate business in Boone county. He is an active worker in his party in northern Illinois, and the intense republicanism of his county and district is one reason why this is his first political office.

King, Joseph W. (rep.), of Eddyville, 51st district, was born in Pope county December 29, 1838. He attended the district school and spent his early life on a farm; has been a farmer all his life. He has served in minor

REPRESENTATIVE KING.

township political offices, but the present one is the only political office of consequence he ever filled. He enlisted in the army in '61, and was chosen captain of Co. E, 120th Ill. Vol. Inf., serving gallantly in many skirmishes. He was at the fall of Vicksburg, and mustered out at the close of the war. During President Harrison's administration Capt. King was superintendent of the great pension building in Washington. He is married and has five sons and five daughters.

Flannigan, Wallace B. (rep.), of McLeansboro, 46th district, was born in Union Co., Ky., May 8, 1859, although his parents were citizens of Hamilton Co. Ill., at the time. Soon after his birth they returned home, but moved to Franklin county the next year. In '64 his father, Samuel E., was appointed a federal judge at New Orleans, where the family resided for a year. His father was one of the board that selected the site of the Normal school at Carbondale. Returning to Franklin county from New Orleans, they remained there until '73, when they removed to McLeansboro, which has been Mr. Flannigan's home ever since. His education was completed at the Hamilton County College. He was admitted to the bar in '83 and has actively practiced his profession ever since, although for nine years he was interested in a general merchandise store. He is married and has two sons and two daughters. He is a Mason and a Woodman. He was instructed and voted for W. E. Mason for U. S. senator and is a very warm friend of the senator.

REPRESENTATIVE FLANNIGAN.

Andrus, Henry (rep.), of Cherry Valley, 10th district, was born in Harlem, Winnebago county, November 4, 1844. His early boyhood was spent assisting his father on the farm, attending the district school, and the high schools of Roscoe and Rockton, where he obtained his education. At the age of 24 he married and moved to Pecatonica, where he lived for six years. Then he bought a farm at Cherry Valley, on which he now lives. He was elected a county supervisor, a position which he has filled for nineteen years, and is now the oldest member in point of service on the board, and for the past six years has been chairman of that board. He is a Mason, an Odd Fellow, a Knight Pythias, a Red Man and a Woodman. Closely identified with farm work and farm life he is interested in any legislation pertaining to that industry. He is married and has one son and one daughter.

REPRESENTATIVE ANDRUS.

Price, Joseph P. (dem.), of Irving, 38th district, was born in Fayette county October 22, 1849, and has spent most of his life on a farm. When 15 years old he moved to Montgomery county, working on a farm and attend-

REPRESENTATIVE PRICE.

ing school in winter. He now owns a fertile farm of 400 acres, and is one of the most successful farmers and stock raisers in his section. He has served his township as supervisor for ten years. He is a Mason and Modern Woodman. He is married and has two sons and one daughter. Mr. Price is interested in bills regarding educational matters, and is always in his seat in the house.

Hunter, William F. (rep.), of Elgin, 14th district, was born in Goliad, Tex., near San Antonio, January 1, 1853, and was educated in Elgin and Ann Arbor graduating from the latter in the law class of '74, but never practiced his profession. In '63 Mr. Hunter's father and family were notified to leave Texas by the confederate authorities, Mr. Hunter, Sr., being strong in his Union sentiments. On the way north they stopped at St. Louis for a

REPRESENTATIVE HUNTER.

few months, but finally settled at Elgin. Mr. Hunter has been in the real estate business all his life. He has been a member of the board of supervisors for the past ten years. He has been prominent in politics all his life, and served two terms as postmaster of Elgin, under Garfield and Arthur and Harrison. He is married.

Hall, Frank L., A. M., M. D. (dem.), of Perry, 34th district, was born in Pike Co., Ill., September 10, 1861, and graduated in the classical course from Eureka College in '84. He obtained a medical degree in '87 from Rush Medical College, and commenced the practice of his profession immediately at Perry. He is now and has been for four years a member of the board of supervisors, was a member of the board of education for many years, and has filled many minor offices. He was one of the organizers and is a director in the State Bank of Perry. He is secretary of the St. L., P. & C. R. R., construction of which has been

REPRESENTATIVE FRANK HALL.

commenced. He is married, and is a member of the K. P., D. O. K. K., Odd Fellows and Woodmen. He has always been active in democratic politics in western Illinois.

Brown, Robert C. (rep.), of Sparta, 48th district, was born in Sparta, November 11, 1859, and received a good common school education. He learned the blacksmith's trade, working at it for ten years, and reading law in the meantime. He worked in a creamery for a time, and having perfected himself in the law by a course in the law department of Washington University in St. Louis, he was admitted to the

REPRESENTATIVE BROWN.

bar in '94. He promptly began the practice of his profession at Sparta. He was elected city attorney while attending school, and has filled other minor offices. He is a Knight of Pythias and a Woodman. Is married and has one daughter.

Nothnagel, Charles W. (rep.), of Chicago, 3d district, was born in Cleveland, O., February 7, 1863, and was educated in the Cleveland high school, after which he took up the study of architecture. In March, '84, he went to Chicago and identified himself with the firm of Adler & Sullivan, and later was connected with Edbrooke & Burnham, both firms leading architects of Chicago. In '88 he opened an office for himself, and still continues the practice of his profession. He holds a membership in the Illinois Chapter of the American Institute of Architects, and is vice president of the Chicago Architects' Business Association. This is his first political office. He is an Odd Fellow, and member of all its

REPRESENTATIVE NOTHNAGEL.

grand bodies. He drafted and is pushing a bill for licensing architects, and the appointment of a board of examiners to regulate the practice of architecture as a profession. In '86 he was married and has one son and two daughters.

English, Robert B. (dem.), of Hardin, 47th district, was born in Jersey county, December 30, 1853, and has lived in Illinois all his life. He was educated in the common schools, and studied law in the office of Judge Herdman. Subsequently he graduated at the Louisville (Ky.) Law school; admitted to the bar in '82, and began practice at Jerseyville; soon afterwards was elected city attorney. In '85 he removed to Hardin. He is a Modern Woodman, is married and has two sons and two daughters. The vote in the 47th district in '96 was very close, the returns electing two democrats and one republican. The second republican contested Mr. English's right to the seat, and on a recount of the ballots it was claimed

REPRESENTATIVE ENGLISH.

that Mr. English was defeated by Kirby, republican. As the house is republican Mr. English was unseated by a party vote.

Jarvis, Jule C. (dem.), of Centerville Station, 49th district, was born in St. Clair county, Illinois, October 9, 1849, and received a common school education. He has been a farmer all his life, and this is his first political office. He is married and has seven daughters and two sons. Mr. Jarvis never has been an office seeker, but has taken a deep interest in politics all his life. He has been favored with important committee assignments. Mr.

REPRESENTATIVE JARVIS.

Jarvis introduced bills affecting railroads—to compel them to block frogs and switches, and relating to their privileges crossing streets, alleys, etc.

Sullivan, Denis E. (dem.), of Chicago, 23d district, was born in Kewanee, Ill., November 16, 1869, and is one of the youngest members of the General Assembly. He finished his education in Lake Forest University, taking the classical course, also a course in law, graduating in the latter in '93, and was admitted to the bar the same year. He has been practicing ever since, principally in civil and corporation law. He is in partnership with Hon. D. P. Phelps, sub-treasurer at Chicago, and ex-Congressman John J. McDannold. This is his first political office. He is not married. Mr. Sullivan made a thorough canvass of Cook county for the democratic ticket last fall, and accompanied Hon. W. J. Bryan for three days during the latter's wonderful campaign in Chicago, just preceding the election.

REPRESENTATIVE SULLIVAN.

Guffin, Washington I. (rep.), of Paw Paw, 29th district, was born in Carlisle, N. Y., Jan. 17, 1840, and moved to Illinois in '69, settling on a farm near Mahigin's Grove, Lee county, where he went into the dairy and cheese industry. In '72 the Burlington railroad ran a branch through the county, and established the town of Compton, where Mr. Guffin built an elevator, also one at Paw Paw, and engaged in the grain business, with his home at Compton. Sixteen years later he moved to Paw Paw. He was educated in the common and select schools near his boyhood home. He owns real estate in Paw Paw and Evanston, and is married. He was on the county board in '72; but never was on a jury, was a witness in court only once, and never had a case in court as plaintiff or defendant. He is very independent in his utterance, and a good legislator. He was elected to the house in '92 and reëlected in '94 and '96, and has been a member of the committees on appropriations and revenue every session. He is chairman of the responsible committee on penal and reformatory institutions the present session.

REPRESENTATIVE GUFFIN.

Needles, Thomas B. (rep.), of Nashville, 42d district, was born in Monroe Co., Ill., April 26, 1837. He received an academic education. He served for four terms, sixteen years, as county clerk of Washington county, and for many years was a member of the republican state central committee. In '76 he was elected state auditor of public accounts, serving four years, and in '80 was elected a state senator, and in '94 and '96 was

REPRESENTATIVE NEEDLES.

elected to the house. He is a Mason and Odd Fellow; elected grand master of the latter in '70, and served four years as representative to the sovereign grand lodge; for many years he has been grand treasurer. He was United States marshal for Indian Territory — which included Oklahoma when that territory was opened to settlers—by appointment of President Harrison. He is married and has two daughters. Mr. Needles was chairman of appropriations committee last session, and also the present session, and is one of the republican leaders. He has been an active figure in republican state politics for the past twenty-two years.

Campbell, Daniel A. (rep.), of Chicago, 19th district, was born in Elgin, June 23, 1863, and was educated in the common schools and at the Chicago Union College of Law. Was admitted to the bar in '86, and has been in active practice ever since, principally in the real estate and commercial lines. Has met with very flattering success in his legal career. Was a member of the house in '93, being advanced to the senate from an overwhelming democratic district in '94 by a plurality of 2,400. He is held in high esteem by his colleagues, and is a hard worker in committees. Mr. Campbell is one of the youngest members, and one of the most diligent and best informed. He performs all his duties unostentatiously, but creditably to himself, his party and his constituents.

SENATOR CAMPBELL.

In Cook county politics he is an active and effective worker.

Stoskopf, Michael (dem.), of Freeport, 12th district, was born near Freeport June 7, 1845, and graduated from the Freeport High School about '63. He read law in the office of the late Justice Bailey, of the supreme court, and was admitted to the bar in '74.

REPRESENTATIVE STOSKOPF.

Mr. Stoskopf has had an extensive and lucrative law business ever since, extending all over northern Illinois. He has been master in chancery of Stephenson county for twelve years and was a member of the house in the 36th and 39th general assemblies—'89 and '95—and was reëlected in 1896. Mr. Stoskopf is not married. He is the only member of either house, or state officer, who is a 33d degree Mason. Mr. Stoskopf is a democratic leader in the house, and is on the steering committee. He is and has been for many years one of the most prominent democrats in northern Illinois, and one whose counsel is sought by the party managers.

Warder, Walter (rep.), of Cairo, 50th district, was born at Maysville, Ky., April 7, 1851, his father moving to Johnson Co. Ill., next year. He was raised on a farm, and completed a good education at Illinois University. After his school days he worked on the farm, taught school and studied law; was admitted to the bar in '74, and immediately began practice at Marion. In '76 he married Miss Dora Bain, of Vienna. In '80 he removed to Cairo, where he has since resided, and been very successful in the law. In '83 he was appointed state's attorney to fill a vacancy, and in '85 was appointed master in chancery, an office he has filled ever since. Senator Warder has always been a republican, and is one of the most influential republicans in southern Illinois. In '90 he was elected to the house, and earned the reputation of being an industrious member and a leader. He was on the steering committee, the judiciary and other important committees. He was returned in '92, and was nominated for temporary speaker and was identified with the most important legislation of the session. In '94 he was chairman of the Alexander county republican committee and assumed personal management of the campaign, which resulted in such a signal victory for his party. In '96 he was nominated unanimously for senator in a democratic district and was elected over the fusionist candidate by a majority of 264. As chairman of the judicial apportionment committee this session he had charge of the bill to reapportion the state judicially, and got it through the senate by practically a unanimous vote. He

SENATOR WARDER.

is thoroughly familiar with parliamentary law and legislative work, and there is no better off-hand debater in the senate. Senator Warder's name has been frequently mentioned as a candidate for congress, and his legislative record ought to commend him to the people.

Hunt, Daniel D. (rep.), of DeKalb, 29th district, was born in Wyoming Co., N. Y., September 19, 1835, and moved to DeKalb Co., Ill., in '57. He has been engaged in hotel and mercantile business and farming for 25 years, and is one of the oldest members of the General Assembly, having been elected to the house in '86 and '88 and to the senate in '90 and '94. Only four members have served longer consecutively. For sixteen years he was school trustee and for three years supervisor. Excepting one session he was on the appropriations committee every session, and has always been on important committees. The present

SENATOR HUNT.

session he led the fight for a bill to prevent the coloring of butter substitutes, and was so aggressive that the butterine people only had one majority in committee. At the last two sessions Senator Hunt endeavored to have a normal college established in his district. There was strong opposition from an element in the General Assembly that opposed new state schools. But mainly through the energy and influence of Senator Hunt the bill became a law in '95 and the school is now in process of construction at DeKalb.

REPRESENTATIVE SHANAHAN.

Shanahan, David E. (rep.), of Chicago, 9th district, was born in Lee county, Ill., September 7, 1862. Since he was six months old he has lived in Chicago, and was educated in the public schools of that city. Mr. Shanahan was elected South Town Supervisor in '85, and again in '86, running ahead of his ticket both times. Under the administration of President Harrison he was deputy United States marshal. He is not married. Mr. Shanahan is one of the best members of the General Assembly, a hard worker, and one whose record will bear the closest scrutiny. He is a member of the firm of M. W. & D. E. Shanahan, general agents for mining properties, and real estate interests. The firm represents a number of eastern capitalists. In this session Mr. Shanahan has had charge in the house of the best measures affecting Cook county.

Dunlap, Henry M. (rep.), of Savoy, 30th district, was born in Cook county Nov. 14, 1853, and four years later his parents moved to Savoy, where he has lived ever since. He was educated in the University of Illinois at Urbana, graduating in the class of '75 in the scientific course. Is married and owns 320 acres of land, 200 of which are in bearing apple orchard. Represented for six years Champaign township on the county board; has been president of the State Horticultural Society, and is now secretary of the society. Is a Knight of Pythias. He takes great interest in all matters pertaining to agriculture and horticulture, and was

SENATOR DUNLAP.

chairman of the committee on appropriations last session. Senator Dunlap was reëlected by an increased majority in '96, and is chairman of the important committee on revenue this session. He is also chairman of the republican steering committee. He represents the Illinois University district.

Bartling, Henry C. (dem.), of Chicago, 6th district, was born in Spring-

REPRESENTATIVE BARTLING.

field July 4, 1867, and moved with his parents to Chicago in '70. He was educated in the Lutheran parochial schools. Mr. Bartling was ledgerman at Marshall Field's for some time; has been in the commission business—grain and produce—for six years. He was elected supervisor for the North Town in '91, being second on the ticket, although the district was safely republican. He is very popular in his own district, and was elected state senator in '92 by a vote of 20,801 to 17,181 for his republican opponent—the district was overwhelmingly republican in '88. In '96 Mr. Bartling was elected to the house. He is one of the youngest men in the legislature, and is a member of some of the best and most important committees, including the democratic steering committee.

McLauchlan, John (dem.), of LaSalle, 27th district, was born Jan. 27, 1840, in Old Cumnock, Ayrshire, Scotland, and educated in the Free Church school. In '69 he emigrated to Luzerne Co., Pa., and in '71 he came to Illinois. Afterwards he returned to Pennsylvania, and in '76 he moved to LaSalle. He was raised a miner, which occupation he followed until '81, when he had a serious accident that nearly cost him his life. He has been supervisor and poormaster of his township for sixteen years; was chief of police of the house in the 38th General Assembly, and was a police officer in the session of '91. In '95 he was a member of the house and was reëlected in '96. Is married and has four sons and one daughter. To Mr.

REPRESENTATIVE McLAUCHLAN.

McLauchlan more than to any other man are the laboring men under obligations for the adoption of the resolution at the present session, submitting to the people the amendement to the constitution authorizing the legislature "to enact and provide for the enforcement of laws necessary to regulate and control contracts, conditions and relations, existing or arising from time to time between corporations and their employés."

Perrottet, Louis (rep.), of Mascoutah, 40th district, was born in the pro-

REPRESENTATIVE PERROTTET.

vince of Fribourg, Switzerland, March 29, 1843, and was educated in the common schools of Switzerland and the United States. In '55 he emigrated with his parents to St. Clair county, Ill., settling on a farm, and has farmed all his life. In '63 he enlisted in Co. E, 43d Ill. Inf., and served until the close of the war. He was on the St. Clair county board of supervisors for six years; was township collector for two years, and on the school board for sixteen years. He was also a member of the house in '91, was reëlected to the session of '95 and again elected to the present house. Mr. Perrottet is married and has one son and six daughters. He is interested in any measure that will reform the revenue system of the state, and in measures to protect the dairy interests.

McGuire, John L. (dem.), of Metamora, 20th district, was born in County Tipperary, Ireland, Aug. 27, 1844. In April, '53, with his father, his

REPRESENTATIVE McGUIRE.

mother having died, he emigrated to Ohio, and in '58 he moved to Woodford Co., Ill. He received a common school education, and was supervisor for nine successive years, resigning to take a seat in the house in '95. He was reëlected in '96. Jan. 30, '62, he enlisted in Co. D, 51st Ill. Inf., and served until March 1, '65. He was at Stone River and Chickamauga; at the latter place he was wounded and captured, spending seven months in the Richmond prison. At Kenesaw Mountain he rejoined his regiment and was with Thomas at the battles of Franklin and Nashville. Is married and has one son and one daughter. Is a Mason and M. W. A. He is anxious for uniform text book legislation, and any legislation in the interest of the masses.

McCloud, Sidney (rep.), of Chicago, 3d district, was born in Staffordshire, England, March 3, 1848, and received a good common school education in England and America. In '62 he came

SENATOR McCLOUD.

to America, to Pennsylvania, and to Illinois in '85, moving to Chicago and accepting the position of manager of the Corning Steel Co. He has been a trustee of the town of Hyde Park, and was elected to the state senate by a majority of 9,335 over his democratic opponent. He is married and has a family of five.

Lundin, Frederick (rep.), of Chicago, 11th district, was born in Sweden, May 18, 1868, and ten years later moved with his family to Chicago, where he was educated in the com-

SENATOR LUNDIN.

mon schools. After school hours he stationed himself at the corner of Washington and Clark streets with a bootblack's outfit and bundles of daily papers. Afterwards he accepted a position as messenger in the clothing firm of Gross & Co., and was soon promoted to be salesman. He was industrious and honest and was offered the place of manager, but declined, engaging with his brother in the manufacture of a well known proprietary article, and they have established a large and profitable business. Senator Lundin's ability as a political worker rapidly brought him prominently before the public. In '97 he received by acclamation in the Cook county republican convention the nomination for city clerk, and in the April election he ran 20,000 ahead of his ticket.

Curley, Daniel F. (dem.), of Chicago, 4th district, was born in Boston, Mass., January 1, 1861, and removed with his parents to Chicago in '68,

SENATOR CURLEY.

which has been his home ever since. He received a good common school education, and entered the employ of Armour & Co., in Chicago, obtaining a thorough knowledge of the packing business in all departments. He was assistant car accountant for this firm for four years. Mr. Curley is married and has four children. In '94 he received an appointment in the office of internal revenue collector for the Chicago district and resigned to accept a place in the house in '95, to which he was elected in '94. He was advanced to the senate in '96. Senator Curley is one of the most pleasing orators in the General Assembly. He made a canvass all over Cook county in '96, and also in the spring campaign in '97. He is a leader in his party at home and in Springfield. He ran ahead of his ticket in '96, receiving a plurality of 1,369 over his principal opponent.

Weidmaier, Charles F. (rep.), of Chicago, 4th district, was born in Reading, Pa., November 20, 1859, and moved to Chicago with his parents when five years old. Seven years later his father died, leaving him the only support of his mother. He attended the Chicago public schools, and learned the trade of machinist and engineer. For nearly fifteen years he was an engineer in the lumber district of Chicago. Then he went west and spent a number of years in the silver states, working at his trade. Subsequently he visited nearly every country of the old world. Returning to Chicago he accepted a place as superintendent with Coleman & Rhoads, steamfitters. He has always been active in party

REPRESENTATIVE WEIDMAIER.

politics, always as a staunch republican. This is his first political office. He is married and has one daughter. Mr. Weidmaier is a member of the National Association of Stationary Engineers, and United Order of American Mechanics.

Mounts, William L. (dem.), of Carlinville, 36th district, was born in Carlinville August 31, 1862, and educated at Blackburn University, graduating in the scientific course. Is married and owns and controls 2,000 acres of farm and coal land. He has held the offices of city treasurer, city attorney and was mayor of Carlinville from '91 to '93. He was secretary of the democratic committee of Macoupin county for eight years, and stands high in the estimation of his constituents. He believes that pledges are not made by politicians and parties to be broken. Mr. Mounts was a member of the democratic steering committee of the last house and also of the present senate, and is an influential worker. He is

SENATOR MOUNTS.

strong in debate and a good parliamentarian. This is his third session, having been elected in '92 and '94 to the house, and to the senate in '96.

Payne, William (rep.), of Osborn, 33d district. Born in Scott Co., Iowa, March 4, 1841, and lived on a farm for the first ten years of his life and then moved with his parents to Hampton, Ill. Was educated in the public schools, and at 18 taught school, leaving that occupation to enlist in the 13th Ill. Inf., the first 3-year regiment in the service. After

REPRESENTATIVE PAYNE.

four years' service he returned to Illinois, spending a year in a commercial college, and then entered the county treasurer's office, Rock Island. From

'66 to '70 he was deputy sheriff, and was sheriff from '70 to '74, and in '74 he moved on a farm in Zuma township and has been there ever since, as farmer, breeder and shipper of stock. Is married, and owns 540 acres. Elected to the house in '91 to fill vacancy caused by the ineligibility of W. F. Collins, he was re-elected in '92, '94 and '96. Mr. Payne has taken a deep interest in the establishment of an insane hospital northwest of the Illinois river, and introduced a bill which passed the house in '93. Again in '95 he presented his measure, and it became a law, and the institution was located in Rock Island county. He also introduced and secured the enactment of a bill giving state aid of $50 to each county farmers' institute.

Fitzpatrick, P. V. (rep.), of Chicago, 1st district, was born in Ireland, July

SENATOR FITZPATRICK.

17, 1840, and was educated in the schools of Toledo, O. In '58 he went to Chicago as a train boy, and attended a commercial college until '61, when he enlisted in the 9th Ill. Cav., and was made regimental sergeant-major in '62. He received a severe wound at Moscow, Tenn., in '63. Honorably discharged in April, '64, account of wounds. In '68 he started a book and stationery business and has continued it ever since. He is a G. A. R. and member Union Veteran League. He is married and has a daughter.

Merrill, Alva (rep.), of Northampton, 24th district, was born in Peoria county Oct. 9, 1854, and educated in the district schools. He was brought up on a farm and has held various township offices, and has been for four years and is now a member of the board of supervisors of Peoria county. Mr. Merrill's wife died in '92, leaving a son and daughter. He is an Odd Fellow and a Woodman. Mr. Merrill is always in his seat, and is

REPRESENTATIVE MERRILL.

above the average in this respect. This is his second term in the house, having been elected in '94 and '96. He is chairman of the committee on public charities, one of the important committees in the house.

Ely, John K. (rep.), of Mazon, 29th district, was born in Oneida Co., N. Y., Dec. 2, 1837, and moved to Kendall Co., Ill., in '44, and to Grundy county in '47. He was educated at the Rock River Seminary, graduating in '58. Then he taught school for seven years and since that time has been engaged

REPRESENTATIVE ELY.

in the farming and stock raising business. He has held several township offices. He enlisted in Chicago Aug. 12, '62, in Co. H, 88th Ill. Inf., and was discharged on account of disability at Nashville, Tenn., May 13, '65. He participated with his regiment in the battles of Stone River, Chickamauga, Missionary Ridge and in the battles of the Fourth Corps from Chattanooga to Atlanta. He was wounded at Peach Tree Creek, July 20, '64. He is a Knight Templar. Is married and has three sons and four daughters. He was a member in '95 and was reëlected in '96 by a majority of 23,700. Mr. Ely is very much interested in the enactment of a uniform school text book bill, the butterine and revenue bills, and an early adjournment. In the establishment of the normal school at DeKalb in '95 Mr. Ely was prominent and influential.

Willoughby, James A. (rep.), of Belleville, 49th district, was born on a St. Clair county farm May 2, 1855, and received his education at McKendree College, and in law at Ann Arbor, graduating from the latter in '76. He was admitted to the Michigan bar in '76, before he was 21. He was in the drug business in Lebanon for four years, and in '80 was elected recorder of St. Clair county, one of three republicans elected. In June, 85, he bought the "Belleville Advocate" and has conducted it since. He was chairman of the congressionel committee when Jehn Baker defeated Col. Morrison, and has been on the county committee almost constantly for the past twenty years, serving as chairman or secretary most of the time. He is married.

SENATOR WILLOUGHBY.

Senator Willoughby was elected by a majority of 1,211. He was on the committee to fix the membership of the republican end of the committees for this session.

Templeton, James W. (rep.), of Princeton, 31st district, was born in St. Clairsville, O., and received a common school education in his native town. In '63 he moved to Princeton

SENATOR TEMPLETON.

and the following year was appointed deputy county clerk. In '75 he was appointed postmaster, and served for a period of twelve years under republican administrations, and in all the elective and appointive offices with which he was honored, he was attentive, courteous and gave good satisfaction. Mr. Templeton was a delegate to the National Republican Convention in '72, and a member of the state republican committee from '84 to '86. He is married and has a son and a daughter. Since leaving the postoffice Senator Templeton has devoted his time to looking after his Bureau county farms, and prides himself on being a pretty good granger. At the present session Senator Templeton was honored with the chairmanship of the important committee on appropriations, one of the greatest responsibility in the senate.

McKinlay, Robert L. (dem.), of Paris, 43d district, was born in Cincinnati July 14, 1839, and moved to Paris in '68. He was edrcated in the common schools of Cincinnati, graduating in the high school, and spent some time at the Annapolis naval academy. Obtained his legal education at the Cincinnati Law School, graduating in '61, being admitted to the bar the same year. He was captain of Co. A, 59th, and adjutant of the 22d O. Inf.; saw hard service in West Virginia and west Tennessee. Returning from the army he took up the practice of his profession, and is regarded as one of the most successful lawyers in eastern Illinois. Is married and owns considerable property in Paris. He was city attorney of Paris for many years, and was

SENATOR McKINLAY.

elected to the house in '76, '78, '86, '92 and to the senate in '94. He made a magnificent canvass of the state in '84 as democratic candidate for attorney general. He is one of the strongest men in the senate. Senator McKinlay's seat was contested by his republican opponent in '95, but the senate, republican though it was, declared Senator McKinlay entitled to the seat.

Bovey, Victor H. (rep.), of Pine Creek, Ogle county, 10th district, was born at Pine Creek March 6, 1856, and

REPRESENTATIVE BOVEY

at the age of nine was left an orphan and nearly penniless. However, he obtained a fair education by hard work and close application. He completed his educational studies at Rock River Seminary. For several years he farmed in summer and taught school in winter. Mr. Bovey was township assessor for four years, and represented his township on the county board for eight years, the last four years being chairman. He always has taken an active interest in politics. He is married and has two sons and two daughters. This is his second term, having been elected in '94 and '96—his district broke the record in '96 by electing three republicans to the house. Mr. Bovey is chairman of manufactures and on the revenue and agricultural committees. His bill repealing the worst features of the flag statute is likely to become a law.

Noling, Lars M. (rep.), of Rockford, 10th district, was born May 4, 1843, in Westergotland, Sweden, and re-

REPRESENTATIVE NOLING.

ceived a common school education. In '64 he emigrated to Rockford, and for the past twenty-one years he has done much to build up the city. At first he took contracts for the manufacture of agricultural implements and is now president of eight manufactories, and holds stock in twelve; he is also financially interested in two banks, and is president of the Poston newspaper. He has been on the republican county committee for fourteen years, and was elected to the house in '92, '94 and '96, being nominated every time by acclamation. He is married and has one daughter. Mr. Noling was elected in '96 by a larger majority than ever before. He is chairman of the committee on building, loan and homestead associations. He is regarded as a leader in his party in northern Illinois, and is one of the most public-spirited citizens of Rockford. He was an influential member of every General Assembly of which he has been a member.

Sawyer, Lewis M. (rep.), of Streator, 27th district, was born in Waverly, N. Y., August 1, 1837, and five years later his parents moved with him to the great west, locating in LaSalle Co., Ill., where he received the ordinary education afforded by the schools of that day. Mr. Sawyer has been a farmer all his life, and a successful one, too. He has represented his township on the county board of supervisors several times and was a member of the house in '87. In '94 he was elected to the senate, and received one of the largest majorities ever given a candidate in LaSalle county—2,200. Senator Sawyer is married and has four sons and four daughters. He has been an active and influential figure in all the important legislation of the last and present session, and is regarded as one of the strongest men in the General Assembly. During the contest for U. S. senator before the republican caucus last January Senator Sawyer was one of the "inner circle" of Senator Mason's friends, and exhibited an energy and astuteness that made him a close friend of the senator's. If he is not U. S. marshal for the northern district it will not be the fault of Senator Mason or the LaSalle county republicans who are anxious for his appointment.

SENATOR SAWYER.

Kincheloe, Charles F. (rep.), of Loraine, 37th district, was born in Loraine March 13, 1865, and received a common school education. When 19 he began teaching and when nominated for the legislature was principal of the Loraine graded schools. He is married, and is a Mason, an Odd Fellow, a M. W. A. and a K. P. Mr. Kincheloe has been identified with every move against corporation lobbyists, and is particularly interested in legislation for uniform text books. He was a member of the house in '95. Mr. Kincheloe was a "Mason stalwart" from start to finish in the contest for the republican nomination for U. S. senator last January. He was prominent in all the moves and no man worked harder or accomplished more towards the election of Senator Mason. The strain was tremendous, and soon after the election of Senator Mason, Mr. Kincheloe was taken with an illness that almost cost him his life.

REPRESENTATIVE KINCHELOE.

Rowe, Peter A. (rep.), of Chicago, 2d district, was born in London, Ontario, March 24, 1855. While very young he became interested in the telegraph business, and at the age of 14 was so proficient that he entered an office in Detroit. Two years later he was assistant superintendent of the American Company, with headquarters at Jackson, Mich. Later he accepted a position with the Western Union in Chicago, where he was one of the most expert telegraphers of the early 70's. In '82 he connected himself with the old "Chicago Evening Journal" remaining until the sale of the paper two years ago to a syndicate. In '95 he was sent to Springfield by his paper to look after the interests of Hon. Geo. E. Adams, then a candidate for

United States senator. Last year he was urged for the legislature, and received a unanimous nomination. Always a warm personal friend of W. E. Mason, Mr. Rowe was active and

REPRESENTATIVE ROWE.

untiring in advancing Mr. Mason's candidacy. His joint resolution to amend the constitution, for abolishing justice courts, substituting therefor district courts in large cities, has won him great fame. He is married and has one son and two daughters.

Stubblefield, George W. (rep.), of Bloomington, 22d district, was born in

SENATOR STUBBLEFIELD.

McLean county, January 2, 1849. His father came to Illinois with the pioneers, in '24. Senator Stubblefield was educated in the district schools and at Wesleyan University. He has been a farmer and importer and breeder of draft and coach horses all his life, and has made eighteen trips across the ocean, and also traveled extensively in the United States. This is his first political office, although he has been active in the politics of Central Illinois; never asked for an office until '96. He is married. Is a member of the Odd Fellows, Red Men and Modern Woodmen, and has been representative to the grand encampment for many years. He is also a member of the Sons of the American Revolution, his ancestor on his father's side, Wm. Green Munford, having been colonel in the revolutionary army.

Busse, Robert C. (rep.), of Chicago, 19th district, was born in Chicago, January 2, 1859, and educated in the common schools and at the North-

REPRESENTATIVE ROBT. BUSSE.

western University at Watertown, Wis. In June, '90, he graduated from the Union College of Law, Chicago. He was admitted to practice law in March of the same year—previous to his graduation—and has practiced his profession since. He was assistant prosecuting attorney under Mayor Swift from May, '95, resigning to accept his seat in the legislature. He is married. He is a Mason, member of the Royal Arcanum and other fraternal and benevolent societies. Mr. Busse has taken an active part in Cook county politics since he was of age, and is one of the charter members of the German-American Republican Club of Cook county, and was chosen its first financial secretary.

Mahoney, Joseph P. (dem.), of Chicago, 13th district, was born in Oswego, N. Y., Nov. 1, 1863, and moved with his parents to Chicago in '66. He was educated in the public schools and graduated from the West Side high school. Then he read law in the office of Hon. John N. Jewett and was

SENATOR MAHONEY.

admitted to the bar in '84, and elected the same year to the house, being 21 years of age the Saturday preceding election day. He was reëlected to the house in '86 and '88, and advanced to the senate in '90 and reëlected in '94. He is one of the oldest members in the legislature in continuous service. Is not married. Senator Mahoney is one of the readiest debaters and best parliamentarians in the state; quick in retort and apt in repartee. He was appointed to the board of education in Chicago by Mayor Washburn, but resigned. He has an extensive law practice and is very successful in his profession and has been master in chancery of Cook county circuit court for eight years.

Avery, Oscar F. (rep.), of Pontiac, 20th district, was born in Hillsdale Co., Mich., November 19, 1841, and entered Hillsdale College in '60. In '61 he left school and enlisted in the 11th Mich. Inf., Co. B, and served until Nov., '65, when he was mustered out. He participated in the battles of Stone River and Chickamauga, where he was wounded in the right foot. He was detailed by Gen. Thomas to the Michigan military agency at Nashville. He served for six months in the quartermasters' department of the 40th U. S. C. T. Mr. Avery went to the West Virginia oil fields in the spring of '66. He soon tired of this, and came back to Illinois and began teaching school, which was his principal occupation from '66 until '76, except for a short time in '72 when he lived in Kansas. He was admitted to the bar in Kansas in '72, and in Illinois in '75. He was master in chancery of Livingston county two terms and public administrator for twelve years. He was deputy county clerk and afterwards deputy county treasurer until 1896, when he resigned to take his seat in the house. He is married and has two daughters. He is past grand president of the I. O. M. A., and state deputy head consul for Indiana of the M. W. A.; is a member of the G. A. R., F. M. C. and Uniform Degree I. O. O. F. Mr. Avery

REPRESENTATIVE AVERY.

has been on the council of administration of the G. A. R. for the past ten years.

Wylie, John (rep.), of Utica, 27th district, was born on a LaSalle county farm, December 6, 1855, and was educated in the public schools and at Knox College. He has farmed all his life. He was supervisor for his township for nine years. Mr. Wylie is married and has five daughters. He is a Knight Templar. This is his second session, having been elected in '94

REPRESENTATIVE WYLIE.

and '96. Mr. Wylie exerted his utmost to have the supreme court consolidated at Ottawa in his county, and was influential in getting the bill through the house.

The asterisk (*) preceding a legislative sketch indicates that no portrait accompanies the biography.

***Sherman, Lawrence Y.** (rep.), of Macomb, 28th district, is thirty-seven years old. He was born and raised on a farm. He received a common school education and was successively hired hand, farmer, school teacher, law student at McKendree College, lawyer, and is now serving his first term in the house.

***Bailey, Martin B.** (rep.), of Danville, 18th district, was born in Vermilion county, Jan. 22, 1858, and was educated at Earlham College and the Illinois State Normal. He farmed and taught school, and for three years worked in Colorado mines, and for a time was clerk in the treasury department at Washington. He was chief of the law department in the pension bureau during Harrison's administration. Is not married. He was a member of the house in '95.

SECRETARY PADDOCK.

James H. Paddock (rep.), of Springfield, secretary of the senate, and chairman of the Live Stock Commission, for thirty-two years past has been in Springfield during the sessions of the General Assembly. He was born in Lockport, Ill., May 29, 1850, and received a good education. He was page in the senate in '65. In '67 he was assistant postmaster of the senate, and in '69, '71, '73 and '75 he was assistant secretary of the senate. In '77, '79 and '81 he was secretary of the senate. From '81 to '89 he was assistant secretary of state, and early in '89 he was appointed secretary of the railroad and warehouse commission, which position he filled until March 1, '93, when the democrats took charge. He was selected by acclamation by the republican caucuses for secretary of the senate in '95 and '97. In '77 Mr. Paddock received the entire vote of the senate for secretary, when the farmers held the balance of power, and in '75 the democrats had the organization and they made him assistant secretary. Gov. Altgeld appointed him member of the live stock commission in '95 and Gov. Tanner reappointed him in '97. Undoubtedly he has a wider acquaintance among the public men of Illinois than any

SECRETARY PADDOCK.

other man, and in every position he has occupied he has discharged his duties with energy and faithfulness. In '73 he married Miss Mary L. Crawford of Kankakee, and they have two children—a son and a daughter.

ASST. SECRETARY CONWELL.

James Conwell, first assistant secretary of the senate, is a well known Chicago newspaper man, having worked principally as political reporter on all the morning and afternoon papers of that city during the last thirteen years. He was born in 1861, in the town of Leighlin Bridge, Carlow county, Ireland, and went to Chicago in '85, and has been almost continually engaged in newspaper work ever since. He was selected by Melville E. Stone as the representative of the Chicago Morning News to accompany the famous Irish member of parliament, William O'Brien, during the latter's campaign in Canada against the governor-general, Marquis of Lansdowne, and his letters attracted much attention. In '91 he was selected by

ASST. SECRETARY CONWELL.

Mayor Washburn, of Chicago, as his private secretary. Mr. Conwell has always been a prominent republican. His father was John Conwell, a well-known teacher under the national system of education in Ireland. Mr. Conwell's mother is still living at the old home at Leighlin.

THE PRESS GALLERY.

Hiram D. Fargo, in charge of the legislative bureau of the Chicago Evening Post, was born in Ionia, Mich., Nov. 6, 1868. Mr. Fargo has the personal friendship and confidence of every party leader, both republican and democratic, and has never violated that confidence in the least particular. He has represented his paper as its legislative correspondent during the regular sessions of '93, '95 and '97, and the special session of '95, and his newspaper work has been exclusively political for the last three years, although he has been connected with the Evening Post in various responsi-

MR. FARGO.

ble positions for over five years. Born of hardy Michigan stock, the great California boom of 1886 attracted the wideawake young man, and a printer's case on the leading republican daily of Santa Ana gave him his first opportunity to embark in the field of journalism. But such talents as his could not but gain recognition, and he soon worked up from the case to the position of editor-in-chief, resigning in '89 to go to Chicago, where his efforts have already won for him a high position in his chosen profession. He is married and lives in Buena Park.

MR. DAVIS.

John McCan Davis, in charge of the Associated Press and St. Louis Globe-Democrat, did his first newspaper work at Canton, Ill., as local editor of the Canton Republican. Afterward he became its editor. While in this position he was also official reporter for the circuit court. During the campaign of '88 he was managing editor of the Council Bluffs (Ia.) Daily Herald. In November of that year he removed to Springfield, where he has since resided. First employed on the Illinois State Journal, he subsequently devoted his attention chiefly to correspondence for metropolitan papers. He has represented the Globe-Democrat at the Illinois capital for more than six years. Upon the death of William M. Glenn, March 20, '97, Mr. Davis became manager of the legislative bureau of the Associated Press. In January, '95, he was admitted to the bar by the supreme court, and opened a law office at Springfield after the legislative extra session of that year. By recent appointment he is secretary of the state board of arbitration. He is an authority on the early life of Abraham Lincoln, and his extensive contributions to the "Life of Lincoln," which appeared in McClure's Magazine in 1895-6 attracted wide attention. He is married.

Harry Gilson Gardner, in charge of the Chicago Evening Journal bureau, was born in Chicago, March 16, 1869, and educated in the common schools, and graduated from the North Division High School in '88. Then Mr. Gardner went to Williams College at Williamstown, Mass., graduating with honors in '92. The next year he entered Northwestern University Law School at Chicago, graduating two years later, and admitted to practice

MR. GARDNER.

at the Illinois bar. Preferring the occupation of journalist he deserted the law to accept a position with the Chicago Daily News. A year later he accepted a place with the Chicago Evening Mail, which had been purchased by Mr. George Booth, of Detroit, and which after a somewhat brief but brilliant existence as the

MR. JOHN GLENN.

Evening Press, absorbed the Evening Journal. The title, "Evening Press" was dropped, and the old Evening Journal received all the push and brains and dash that characterized the Press. Mr. Gardner's work for the Journal the present session has been characterized by the sharp, spicy paragraphs that are a characteristic of the new management of the Journal. Unhampered by "the office," his matter is always interesting.

John M. Glenn, of Chicago, in charge of the legislative bureau of the Chicago Times-Herald since the resignation of Mr. Lahiff, who lately became private secretary to Mayor Harrison, of Chicago, is the local political editor of the Times-Herald, and has been on that paper since Dec., '95. He was born in Ft. Wayne, Ind., Nov. 14, 1859, and his parents moved to Monmouth, Ill., soon afterwards. He graduated from Monmouth College in the class of '83, and immediately entered a local newspaper office. In '86 he entered the Inter Ocean office as a reporter, and next year with his brother, William M., bought an interest in the Springfield State Journal, which they conducted until the spring of '88, when he returned to the Inter Ocean, and was local political editor for some time. In Aug., '90, he went to the Tribune, and for about a year was the New York correspondent of that paper, returning again to the local political field in Chicago, he remained until Dec., '95, when he accepted the city hall assignment with the Times-Herald. In '88 he married Miss Jeannie Chapin, and they have three children. Mr. Glenn has had a wide experience, is a breezy writer, and a great hustler for exclusive news. He is a son of Judge J. J. Glenn, of Monmouth, who has been on the bench for 20 years.

William M. Glenn, who died in Springfield March 20, 1897, for two sessions had charge of the legislative bureau of the Associated Press, and was in charge when he died. Mr. Glenn was born in Monmouth Jan. 6, 1862, and was educated at Monmouth College, where his first newspaper work was done on a college paper. After his school days he became a reporter on a Monmouth paper, and in '87 in partnership with his brother, John M., bought an interest in the Springfield Journal. After the national republican convention in '88 he went to Chicago, on the Inter Ocean. Two years later he joined the Tribune staff, and remained until '93, when the Associated Press secured his services. He covered many of the most important events for this great newsgathering concern, including the World's Fair, a special session of congress, the St. Louis cyclone, political national conventions, the Homestead strikes, the Cronin case and the Ohio mining troubles. He was in charge of the St. Louis agency of the Associated Press when he was ordered to Springfield to report the general assembly.

MR. WILL GLENN

His thoroughness and care in handling great assignments made him an invaluable man for great occasions. He was not only a journalist by close application, but by instinct, and was very popular with his colleagues and members of the legislature.

Edward M. Lahiff, in charge of the bureau of the Chicago Times-Herald,

MR. LAHIFF.

is one of the brightest young newspaper men that ever burned the wires from Springfield during a legislative session. He lives in Chicago and has been a member of the Herald staff for the past seven years. He is known and popular with every politician of any note, in all parties, in Chicago. Mr. Lahiff has had charge of the Herald bureau at many notable conventions and assemblies, and always acquitted himself creditably. The correspondent who scored a "beat" on him earned the privilege of boasting about it. He is an Irishman by birth, and although a gentleman of education and culture, spent his first year in America shoveling coal on a coal dock in Detroit owned by W. P. Rend. Mr. Lahiff is 34 years old and went to Chicago in 1886. He was appointed a Cook county civil service commissioner early in 1897, and in his career as a newspaper man has been very successful. In April, 1897, Mayor Carter H. Harrison appointed Mr. Lahiff his private secretary and he resigned his newspaper connection. In 1895 Mr. Lahiff married Eileen Malone of Cork, Ireland, and they have one son.

George Cushing Sikes has acted as legislative correspondent for the Chicago Record for the 39th and 40th general assemblies. Mr. Sikes learned the printer's trade in a country office at Dodge Center, Minn., the place of his birth. While acquiring his education he made his living by working at his trade on the Minneapolis Tribune. He graduated from the University of Minnesota in '92. After that he served on the Minneapolis Tribune as proofreader, reporter and telegraph editor. The last named position he left in the fall of '93 to put in a year of graduate study in political economy and political science at the University of Chicago, from which institution he holds a master's degree. For the last six months of '94 Mr. Sikes worked as copy editor on the Chicago Tribune. Since then he has been with the Record and for eighteen months previous to coming to Springfield he was editorial writer on that paper. Mr. Sikes takes special interest in social and municipal problems and in questions relating to labor. While an active printer he took deep interest in the affairs of the Typographical Union

MR. SIKES.

and was once president of the organization at Minneapolis. In order better to study social problems and conditions he spent some two years in residence at Hull House, the social settlement at 335 South Halsted street, Chicago. Mr. Sikes is 29 years old. He was married Feb. 6, 1897, to Miss Madeleine Wallin, daughter of Judge Wallin, of the North Dakota supreme court.

Dwight Wilcox, in charge of the Morning Monitor and Post-Dispatch bureaus, although young, has had quite an experience in the newspaper line. He was born in Sangamon county, June 2, 1867, and graduated from the Springfield High School. His first active work was on the Monitor in '88, and his first legislative session was in '93, when he was with the Associated Press bureau. He was also with the same concern in '95, and has had a long experience with Chicago and northwestern dailies. At the World's Fair he was attached to

MR. WILCOX.

the Associated Press bureau on the fair grounds, and his work there was so thorough and readable that he commended himself to his chief. He is not married.

Edward J. Hamilton, of the St. Louis Chronicle, was born in Salem, Ill., August 13, 1856. His father, Rev. Presley P. Hamilton, was a prominent minister of the Methodist Episcopal church. His mother was the daughter of Judge H. B. Jones, the first settler of Perry county. Mr. Hamilton was educated at McKendree College. Four terms he was justice of the peace of DuQuoin; city treasurer for one

MR. HAMILTON.

term and held other offices. He became a railway postal clerk early in the 80's, resigning to become assistant postmaster of DuQuoin, which position he held for six years. He was local correspondent at DuQuoin for the St. Louis Chronicle, Globe-Democrat, Inter Ocean and Associated Press, positions he held for ten or more years. He established the DuQuoin Evening News in '88. In '90 he relinquished the pen for a position as clerk in the secretary of state's office, which he held until the democrats released him from further service. Mr. Hamilton then accepted a position with the St. Louis Chronicle, which paper he still represents. He also represented the Chicago Times and does special work for New York, Cincinnati, Louisville, and Peoria papers, and for the past four years has furnished copy for the Journal, Register and Associated Press in Springfield, principally political and state capitol work. He has represented the St. Louis Chronicle for the last three general assemblies. Mr. Hamilton is married and has two sons and two daughters. He is an ardent republican.

MR. PICKERING.

John L. Pickering, of Springfield, in charge of the legislative bureau of the St. Louis Republic, and compiler of this Directory, has been in the newspaper business all his life. He learned the printer's trade in a country office in Arcola, Ill., beginning when he was ten years old. He completed a common school education at the Peoria High School and was a compositor on the old Peoria National Democrat at the same time. He was trainboy and afterwards brakeman on a freight train for several years when a youth. He solicited subscribers for Peoria and Chicago newspapers all over the northwest '80-'82. In '83-'85 he reported the Illinois legislature for the State Register at Springfield, and at every succeeding session has represented some first-class newspaper. With one exception he is the oldest legislative correspondent in Springfield. He was telegraph editor of the State Register for several years. From '84 to '90 inclusive he represented the Chicago Herald and St. Louis Republic as political correspondent. In '91 and early in '92 he was on the Washington staff of the Chicago Times. During the campaign of '92 he was with the Chicago Tribune, and in '96 he represented the Chicago Chronicle. In '93 he established the Evening Telegram in Springfield, using a leased wire telegraph service, the first in that city. It was a creditable newspaper, and he sold it at a profit in '95. Mr. Pickering was born seven miles east of Neoga, Sept, 12, 1860. His father died in '65, leaving no property and three small children to the care of his mother. In '67 the family moved to Neoga, and in '69 to Arcola, which was his home until '78, when he went to Peoria. In '83 he fixed his residence at Springfield. The same year he married Miss Etta Rountree, of Nashville, Ill., and they have two sons and two daughters.

SENATORS.

***Wells, Albert W.**(dem.), of Quincy, 37th district, who died March 5, 1897, was born in South Woodstock, Conn., May 9, 1841. Received an academic education, and spent his early days on a farm. Taught school in New Jersey for several years, resigning to enlist in the Union army. Senator Wells took a full law course at Columbia College and was admitted to the bar in New York City. He moved to Quincy in '70, and was a successful lawyer. He held various offices of trust and was a member and president of the board of education for several years. He was a director in the Ricker National Bank and in the Quincy Gas Company. He was a member of the house in '87 and '89, and advanced to the senate in '90 and '94. He was chairman of the democratic house caucus in '89 and of the senate caucus in '91 and '95, and served on important committees in both branches.

***Kanan, Michael F.** (rep.), of Decatur, 41st district, was born in Essex Co., N. Y., in November, 1837, and was educated in the public schools. In '57 he moved to Decatur and went on a farm. He enlisted in Co. A, 41st Ill. Inf., and served nearly four years. He was mayor of Decatur for six years, being chosen on an independent ticket. He was elected senator in '94.

***Kingsbury, Hiram H.** (rep.), of Olney, 45th district, was born in Meigs Co., O., April 3, 1840. In '46 his father emigrated to Illinois, locating at Mt. Carmel. He worked in the store of his father and on a farm until he was of age, when he enlisted in Co. B, 8th Ill. Inf. He was elected city clerk, and three times city treasurer, has been alderman and a supervisor and was police magistrate until elected senator. Is married and has three sons and three daughters.

***Chapman, Pleasant T.** (rep.), of Vienna, 51st district, was born in Johnson county Oct. 8, 1854. He graduated from McKendree College in '76, and was admitted to the bar at Mt. Vernon in '78. In '77 he was elected superintendent of the Johnson county schools, and reappointed for a short term in '81; next year was chosen county judge, and again in '86. In '90 and '94 he was elected to the senate. He is married.

***Leeper, Arthur A.** (dem.), of Virginia, 32d district, was born near Chandlerville, Cass Co., Ill., Aug. 21, 1855. He was educated in the common schools and at Eureka College, and graduated from the law department of the State University at Iowa City, in '75. He is married. Senator Leeper was state's attorney of Cass county from '76 to '80, and was elected state senator in '88, '92 and '96.

***Dresser, Nathaniel S.** (peo.-dem.), of Greenville, 38th district, was born in Temple, Me., June 24, 1825, came to Illinois in 1837, settling in Bond county, and has lived there ever since. He married in '43 and has one son and two daughters living.

***Putnam, James D.** (rep.), of Elmwood, 24th district, was born in St. Paul, Minn., March 13, 1859. He graduated from the Elmwood High School and from the law department of the Michigan University. For nine years he ran a hotel, four years of which he was a cigar manufactuer in Elmwood. He was police magistrate of Elmwood for eight years. He is not married and is a K. P.

***Edwards, W. Scott** (rep.), of Lewistown, 26th district, was born in Sciota Co., O., August 10, 1851, and completed his education at Hedding College, Abingdon, Ill., graduating in '76. He is married and this is his first office of consequence.

***Littler, David T.** (rep.), of Springfield, 39th district, was born at Clifton, O., Feb. 7, 1836. At the age of 21 he moved to Lincoln, Ill., and worked at the carpenter's trade for two years, meantime studying law; was admitted to the bar in '60, and soon afterwards elected justice of the peace, and later was appointed master in chancery. In '68 he moved to Springfield and formed a law partnership with H. S. Greene and M. Hay. It continued until '81. In '66 President Johnson appointed Mr. Littler collector of internal revenue at Springfield; he resigned in '68. He is a Knight Templar. He was elected to the house in '82 and '86 and to the senate in '94.

REPRESENTATIVES.

***Galligan, Peter F.** (dem.), of Chicago, 15th district, was born in Chicago January 20, 1860. He finished his education at St. Ignatius College. He was 15, and the eldest of six, when his father died, and he was compelled to quit school and go to work. He went into the office of the Adams & Westlake Co., remaining until '82. The next four years he was a clerk in the office of the Clerk of the Probate Court. He played professional ball with the Washingtons, the Minneapolis team and the famous Whitings, until '91. He was a U. S. gauger, resigning in '92. Is not married. He is a Knight Pythias.

***Dinneen, Jerry W.** (rep.), of Albany, 31st district, was born Sept. 17, 1843, in Franklin Co., N. Y.; was educated in the common schools near his early home, and moved to Albany in '68. He embarked in the manufacture of carriages, wagons and buggies, and at present is in the agricultural implement business. He is married and has two sons.

***Staudacher, John** (dem.-pop.), of Chicago, 4th district, was born in Austria, December 27, 1857, and educated in the public schools of Lincoln, Ill., to which city his parents emigrated in '69. He is a mechanic in tin and sheet iron work. For nine years he traveled for the Arlington-Curtis Mfg. Co., Saginaw, Mich., and in '86 moved to Chicago, embarking in the grocery business, which he continued for about a year, and then went to work at his trade, which he continued up to the fall of '96. He was nominated by populists and democrats. He is married and has one daughter.

***Morey, Thomas P.** (rep.), of Greenville, 38th district, was born in Mulberry Grove, September 27, 1847, and is a real estate dealer. He was educated at McKendree College. He taught school for six years, and was circuit clerk of Bond county from '76-'84; was chosen to fill vacancy in the county superintendency of schools and elected for a full term, serving five years. He is married and has one son and daughter.

***Schwab, Joseph S.** (dem.), of Chicago, 11th district, was born in New Orleans, Aug. 17, 1856, and graduated in '80 from the University of Louisiana and was admitted to the bar the same year. He was a Cleveland elector from that state in '84, and in '89 on account of ill health moved north to Chicago. He promoted the National White Lead and Oil Co., of which he is a large stockholder. Under Mayor Carter Harrison I he was superintendent of pipe extensions. Is married, has two children and is a K. P. and a Mason. He was a member of the house in '95 and was re-elected in '96.

***O'Donnell, James F.** (dem.), of Bloomington, 22d district, was born in Dubuque, Iowa, Feb. 1, 1864, and has resided since childhood in Bloomington. He received a common school education, and went into the newspaper business in '83 under Hon. John H. Oberly. Afterwards he purchased a half interest in the Bloomington "Bulletin," and is now associate editor of it. He made a campaign of Illinois in behalf of the democratic ticket in '94 and '96. He is not married.

***Meaney, Patrick J.** (rep.), of Chicago, 15th district, was born in Ireland March 8, 1849, and when he was three months old his parents emigrated to Buffalo, N. Y. In '58 they moved Chicago, where he completed his education. He learned the plumbing trade and in '76 engaged in the business for himself. He served as deputy sheriff, and bailiff of appellate court. He is married and has four daughters.

***Sayler, Walter** (rep.), of Chicago, 11th district, was born in Eaton, O., October 3, 1857, and graduated from the National Normal College, Lebanon, O. Mr. Sayler was admitted to practice in Ohio in '81. He opened an office at Eaton, but moved to Chicago in '87. He has been collector and afterwards was attorney for the Town of Jefferson. He is a member of the Cook county republican committee, and is a Knight Templar. Is married and has five children.

***Ward, Harry B.** (rep.), of DuQuoin, 48th district, was born in DuQuoin July 30, 1871, and was educated at Illinois College and at a business college in St. Louis. Is now in the boot and shoe business in DuQuoin. He is married and has one daughter.

***Kohlstedt, John** (rep.), of Monee, 25th district, was born in Hesse Cassel, Prussia, May 22, 1836, educated in Germany and came to Illinois when 17 years of age. He began life on a farm and in '69 moved to Monee. In '74 he embarked in the coal and lumber business, his present occupation. He was a supervisor for twelve years, and is a Mason and Odd Fellow. He is married and has ten children.

***Dickson, Elbert H.** (rep.), of Oakville, 50th district, was born near Oakville, January 28, 1867. When a year old his parents moved to Union county. Taught school fifteen years, and owns a farm which he works in summer. He is an Odd Fellow. Is married and has three children.

***Daugherty, Aquilla J.** (rep.), of Peoria, 24th district, was born in Butler Co., O., Dec. 6, 1842; was educated at Miami University. Was correspondent of the Louisville Journal and Cincinnati Gazette during the civil war. After the war he went on the Indianapolis Journal. In '67 he moved to Hancock Co., Ill., taught school and served three terms on the board of supervisors. From '75 to '90 he filled several responsible railroad positions. From '90 until '93 he was consul to Callao, Peru. He is married and has one son. He was a member of the house in '95.

***Scrogin, Arthur J.** (rep.), of Lexington, 22d district, was born in Lexington August 25, 1853, and educated at Shurtleff College. He has been a farmer all his life. He was a member of the board of supervisors for seven years. He is married and has one son and two daughters. He is a K. P.

***O'Shea, John** (dem.), of Chicago, 9th district, was born in Chicago, February 17, 1859, and educated in the public schools. He was a member of the house in '83 and '85. From '82 until '86 he was deputy county clerk under M. W. Ryan, and was division clerk in the water office under Mayor Cregier. Appointed deputy clerk in the office of the clerk of the superior court, he held the office until the legislature opened in January, '97, when he resigned. He is married and has two sons and three daughters. He has been prominently identified with the politics of Chicago for years.

***Thiemann, William** (rep.), of Itasca, 7th district, was born in Hanover, Germany, Feb. 11, 1849, and in '57 emigrated with his parents to DuPage county. He was elected to the house in '90, '92, '94 and '96; common school education. Is married.

***Huffman, John D.** (dem.), of Bluffs, 34th district, was born in Decatur Co., Ind., Jan. 1, 1850, and in '59 moved to Illinois. He received a limited education. Mr. Huffman has been a farm laborer all his life. He has worked at anything he could get, mainly on farms. He is married and has one daughter. He was a member of the house in '95.

***Carmody, William** (dem.), of Chicago, 13th district, was born in Simcoe, Can., Oct. 25, 1859, and two years later moved with his parents to Chicago, where he was educated in the common schools. He has held many minor offices and for four years was deputy coroner of Cook county. Is married and has one son and one daughter.

***Revell, David** (rep.), of Chicago, 21st district, was born in Chicago in October, 1866, and was educated in the common schools and the Union College of Law, graduating in '87, was admitted to the bar the same year. He is not married. He was a member of the house in '95.

***Trowbridge, Irving H.** (rep.), of Marseilles, 27th district, was born in Delta, Ohio., March 16, 1849, and was educated at Adrian College. He moved to Illinois in '76 and engaged in the drug business. He was a supervisor for three terms, and is a Mason, a Modern Woodman and a United Workman. He is married and has three sons and one daughter.

***Wilson, Ulysses A.** (rep.), of Rushville, 28th district, was born in Huntsville tp., Schuyler county, July 5, 1854, and was educated at Hedding College and Lincoln University. He was elected to the house in '94 and '96. He is married and has two sons and two daughters.

***Johnson, John W.** (rep.), of Canton, 26th district, was born in Marshall Co., W. Va., Nov. 24, 1837, and received a common school education. He moved to Fulton Co., Ill., in '57, and has farmed all his life. He served for twelve years on the county board of supervisors. Is married and has one son and one daughter. He was a member of the house in '95.

***Lathrop, William H.** (rep.), of Newton, 45th district, was born in Greensburg, Ind., Nov. 21, 1853, and later his parents moved to Olney, Ill.; public school education; learned marble cutting; engaged in that business for himself in '76 at Lawrenceville, and shortly afterwards moved to Newton. He is a Mason, a K. P. and M. W. A.; is married and has four children.

***Glade, Albert** (rep.), of Chicago, 17th district, was born in Chicago, February 22, 1859, and educated in the public schools. After school he entered a printing office, and then went into the teaming business, taking contracts for work from contractors. This is his present occupation. He is married and is a K. P. He was a member of the house in '95.

***Hammers, Isaac B.** (rep.), Panola, 20th district, was born in Green township, Woodford county, Oct. 20, 1861, and graduated from the State Normal in '83. He taught school in Woodford county for two years, and then went on a farm, where he has been ever since. Is married. He was a member of the house in '95.

***McDonough, Daniel V.** (dem.), of Chicago, 17th district, was born in Quebec, Canada, January 19, 1866, and moved to Chicago in '71. He graduated from St. Patrick's parochial college about '86. He was record writer in the office of the superior court clerk, was in the election commissioner's office and for nearly two years was in the postoffice. He is a K. P. and is not married.

*** Metcalf, George B.** (rep.), of Greenfield, 30th district, was born in Macoupin county, October 7, 1848, and was educated at Blackburn University. In '71 he engaged in the mercantile business at Greenfield. For 14 years he was on the city board of Greenfield; he is now and has been for the last two terms mayor. He is married and has two children.

***Torrence, Caleb R.** (rep.), of Cowden, 40th district, was born in Pickaway Co., O., Nov. 29, 1854, and came to Illinois in '59. He was educated at Ohio Wesleyan University. He taught school and studied law; was admitted to the bar in '79. Is a Mason, K. P., and a M. W. A.; is married and has seven children.

***Atchison, Oliver T.** (dem.), of Lovington, 41st district, was born in Bath Co., Ky., April 5, 1843, and was educated in the common schools. He has been a farmer all his life. In '62 he moved to Moultrie Co., Ill., and bought a farm. He is married and has one son and one daughter. He is a Mason and a Woodman.

***Cochran, William G.** (rep.), of Sullivan, 41st district, was born in Ross Co., O., Nov. 13, 1844, and moved to Moultrie Co., Ill., in '49. Was raised on a farm, enlisted in Co. A, 126th Ill. Inf., was mustered out Aug. 5, '65. Was admitted to practice in '79. Is married and has five children. He was elected to the house in '88, '94 and '96, and was speaker of the special sessions of '90 and '95. He is a Mason and Odd Fellow, and department commander of the G. A. R.

***Parish, William H., Jr.** (rep.), of Harrisburg, 51st district, was born December 1, 1849, in Saline county. Taught school four years and was admitted to the bar in '84. He was county judge '86-'90. He is married and has five children.

***Buckner, John C.** (rep.), of Chicago, 5th district, was born on a Kendall Co., Ill., farm, March 14, 1859, and received a collegiate education. He worked on a farm until he was 22, when he went to Chicago and became a caterer, his present occupation. In '91 he organized a colored company for the I. N. G., and afterwards was elected major of the colored battalion. He was a member of the house in '95 and is a member of the republican state committee.

***Merriam, Jonathan** (rep.), of Atlanta, 26th district, was born Nov. 1, 1834, in Vermont, and when two years old moved to Springfield, Ill., with his parents. In '39 the parents moved to Alton, Ill., and in '41 they moved to Tazewell county. He was educated at Wesleyan University and McKendree. Is largely interested in farm lands. Entered the army in '62, as lieutenant-colonel of the 117th Ill. Inf., and served three years. He was member of the last constitutional convention (1870). In '73 he was collector of internal revenue for the 8th district (Springfield) and held it until '83. He is married and has seven children. He was a member of the house in '95.

***Bristol, Almon H.** (dem.), of Chillicothe, 24th district, was born in Peoria county, March 25, 1853, and spent his early life on his father's farm, attending the common schools. He is an Odd Fellow; is married and has one son and one daughter.

***Conlee, William T.** (dem.), of Carlinville, 36th district, was born in Morgan county, September 24, 1849, and worked in his father's mills until he was 16. He learned the carpenter's trade, but gave it up and went to farming; was supervisor for nine years. He is a Modern Woodman; is married and has two sons and three daughters.

***Mitchell, B. M.** (dem.), of Chicago. Born in Quincy Jan. 30, 1869. When young his parents moved to Chicago: was bundle wrapper in Coutant & Co.'s and the Bee-Hive. Was a member of the house in '93. Is not married.

***Barnett, James R.** (dem.), of Coldbrooke, 35th district, was born near Athens, Ill., September 22, 1832. When two years old his parents moved to a farm near Nauvoo. He was educated at Knox Academy, and then taught school. He has held several minor offices. He is an Odd Fellow, and for 22 years has been a director of the local Farmers' Mutual Insurance company and president for several years. He is married and has four sons and two daughters.

***Boyd, George M.** (rep.), of Chicago, 6th district, was born in Allegheny Co., Pa., Oct. 7, 1849, and in '59 moved west. He was educated in Monmouth College and admitted to the bar and practiced law in Iowa for seven years. In '87 he moved to Chicago; is married and has four children. He was elected to the house in '94 and '96. He is a K. P. and M. W. A.

***Hart, William** (dem.), of Annapolis, 45th district, was born in Crawford county, February 24, 1840, and educated in the common schools. He is a farmer. He was supervisor for two terms. He is married and has two sons and four daughters.

***Steen, William H.** (rep.), of Braidwood, 25th district, was born in Johnstone, Renfrewshire, Scotland, July 29, 1849. He entered the coal mines at nine years of age, and in '65 he emigrated to this country and entered the Schulykill county mines, Pa., with his father. In '70 moved to Illinois, locating at Braidwood. He is married and has five children. He has been alderman, mayor and held minor township offices in Braidwood. He was a member of the house in '95.

***Cavanaugh, James P.** (rep.), of Chicago, 13th district, was born in Buffalo, N. Y., Feb. 27, 1858, and removed with his parents to Chicago a few months afterwards; was educated in the parochial schools. He learned the plumber's trade, and it is his present occupation. He is married and has three children. Mayor Washburn appointed him assistant superintendent of water main extension, and he was in the county clerk's office for a time. He was a member of the house in '95.

***Dewoody, William D.** (rep.), of Corinth, 50th district, was born in Lincoln county, Tenn., Oct. 22, 1844, and settled in Jefferson Co., Ill., in '60; common school education. In March, '62, he enlisted in the 60th Ill. Inf., and was in the battles of Chickamauga, Kenesaw Mountain, Atlanta, Peach Tree Creek, and with Sherman to the sea. He entered the drug business, which he sold in 1879 and returned to farming, his present occupation. Is married and has four children. Is an Odd Fellow and Methodist minister.

SENATE COMMITTEES.

Fortieth General Assembly.

JUDICIARY.—Anthony, Chairman. Berry, Putnam, Humphrey, Edwards, Crawford, Aspinwall, Netterstrom, Hamilton, Baxter, Dunlap, Campbell, Fisher, Lundin, Chapman, Littler, Kingsbury, Dwyer, Bollinger, Fitzpatrick, Warder, Wells, McConnel, McKinlay, Mounts, Leeper, Mahoney, Hull.

EDUCATION.—Bogardus, Chairman. Lundin, Fitzpatrick, Granger, Sullivan, Dunlap, Morrison, Sparks, Dwyer, Pemberton, Kingsbury, Bollinger, Hull, Mahoney, O'Brien, Wells.

RULES.—Fisher, Chairman. Putnam, Crawford, Harding, Bogardus, Mahoney, Leeper.

JUDICIAL DEPARTMENT.—Hamilton, Chairman. Berry, Putnam, Crawford, Littler, Anthony, Bollinger, Fitzpatrick, Baxter, Sawyer, Campbell, Edwards, Humphrey, Willoughby, Granger, Evans, Mounts, Hull, Leeper, Wells, McConnel.

REVENUE.—Dunlap, Chairman. Berry, Littler, Crawford, Bogardus, McCloud, Baxter, Templeton, Lundin, Granger, Harding, Kanan, Munroe, Evans, Putnam, Kingsbury, Hunt, Pemberton, Hamilton, Edwards, Leeper, Wells, Hull, Mahoney, O'Brien.

EXPENSES OF GENERAL ASSEMBLY.—Granger, Chairman. Campbell, Warder, Sparks, Kanan, Hunt, Dresser, McKinlay.

APPROPRIATIONS.—Templeton, Chairman. Berry, Fitzpatrick, Harding, Aspinwall, McCloud, Humphrey, Bogardus, Granger, Kanan, Sawyer, Kingsbury, Sparks, Willoughby, Hull, Landrigan, Mahoney, O'Brien.

LIVE STOCK AND DAIRYING.—Willoughby, Chairman. Dwyer, Evans, Anthony, Fitzpatrick, Hunt, Lundin, Granger, Stubblefield, Morrison, Edwards, Bollinger, Hull, Mahoney, O'Brien, Curley, Leeper.

COMMERCE.—Chapman, Chairman. Sullivan, Stubblefield, Littler, Morrison, Willoughby, Warder, Templeton, Wells, Mounts, O'Brien, Leeper.

RAILROADS.—Morrison, Chairman. Munroe, Kanan, Evans, Lundin, Stubblefield, Fitzpatrick, Willoughby, Humphrey, Dwyer, Edwards, Chapman, Sullivan, Kingsbury, Netterstrom, Mahoney, O'Brien, Landrigan, Hull, Curley.

MUNICIPALITIES.—Dwyer, Chairman. Pemberton, Warder, Fisher, Anthony, Evans, McCloud, Kanan, Humphrey, Netterstrom, Morrison, Hamilton, Lundin, Case, Leeper, Mahoney, Mounts, O'Brien.

CORPORATIONS.—Harding, Chairman. Berry, McCloud, Baxter, Willoughby, Dwyer, Hunt, Putnam, Evans, Anthony, Crawford, Fisher, O'Brien, Hull, Mahoney, Wells.

BUILDING AND LOAN ASSOCIATIONS.—Baxter, Chairman. Berry, Kanan, Case, Bogardus, Sawyer, Dunlap, Hunt, Morrison, Humphrey, Netterstrom, Aspinwall, Fort, Littler, Evans, Hull, Leeper, Wells, Mahoney, McKinlay.

COUNTY AND TOWNSHIP ORGANIZATION.—Warder, Chairman. Hamilton, McCloud, Baxter, Anthony, Hunt, Munroe, Humphrey, Stubblefield, Crawford, Case, Mounts, McKinlay, Curley.

MILITARY.—Sparks, Chairman. Fitzpatrick, Case, Fort, Warder, Bogardus, Templeton, Granger, Kingsbury, Evans, Curley, McKinlay, Mounts.

SENATORIAL APPORTIONMENT.—Pemberton, Chairman. Berry, Dwyer, Sparks, Kanan, Lundin, Stubblefield, Morrison, Bogardus, Anthony, Dunlap, Aspinwall, Campbell, Hamilton, Crawford, Templeton, Chapman, Humphrey, Harding, Hull, Landrigan, McConnel, Curley, Payne.

WAREHOUSES.—Lundin, Chairman. Sparks, Case, Fisher, Harding, Netterstrom, Baxter, McCloud, Pemberton, Sullivan, O'Brien, McKinlay, Curley.

LICENSE.—Netterstrom, Chairman Evans, Dwyer, Stubblefield, Morrison, Bollinger, Lundin, Willoughby, Sullivan, Campbell, Mahoney, Wells, O'Brien.

FISH AND GAME.—Campbell, Chairman. Berry, Edwards, Sullivan, Putnam, Fitzpatrick, Granger, Harding, Fort, Anthony, Fisher, Willoughby, Leeper, Mahoney, O'Brien, Wells.

AGRICULTURE AND HORTICULTURE.—Sawyer, Chairman. Berry, Bogardus, Humphrey, Sullivan, Hamilton, Munroe, Aspinwall, Dunlap, Pemberton, Kingsbury, Bollinger, Netterstrom, Landrigan, Curley, Wells, Mounts.

PRINTING.—Bollinger, Chairman. Kanan, Case, Willoughby, Campbell, Warder, Templeton, Hull, Mounts.

WATERWAYS AND DRAINAGE.—Munroe, Chairman. Dwyer, Bogardus, Bollinger, Fort, Humphrey, Putnam. Crawford, Edwards, Sparks, Sawyer, Anthony, Mahoney, O'Brien, Leeper.

CONGRESSIONAL APPORTIONMENT.—Aspinwall, Chairman. Harding, Sullivan, Willoughby, Fort, Anthony, Littler, Pemberton, Lundin, Bogardus, Dunlap, Dwyer, Fisher, Humphrey, Chapman, Putnam, Hamilton, Landrigan, Hull, Payne, McKinlay, Wells.

INSURANCE.—Fitzpatrick, Chairman. Sparks, Granger, Lundin, Morrison, Aspinwall, Dwyer, Hunt, Munroe, Fisher, Pemberton, Hull, McKinlay, Wells, O'Brien.

FEES AND SALARIES.—Kingsbury, Chairman. Campbell, Granger, Crawford, Warder, Sullivan, Baxter, Dresser, Payne.

ROADS, HIGHWAYS AND BRIDGES.—Humphrey, Chairman. Putnam, Aspinwall, Kingsbury, Dunlap, Baxter, Bollinger, Templeton, Chapman, Hunt, Hamilton, Dresser, Hull, Payne, Landrigan.

FARM DRAINAGE.—Hunt, Chairman. Dunlap, Bollinger, Chapman, Fort, Hamilton, Templeton, Sawyer, Edwards, Aspinwall, Littler, Curley, Landrigan, Payne, Dresser.

FEDERAL RELATIONS.—Dresser, Chairman. Hamilton, Pemberton, Fisher, Netterstrom, Chapman, McConnel.

STATE LIBRARY, ARTS AND SCIENCES.—Mahoney, Chairman. Munroe, Fort, Case, Stubblefield, Kanan, Crawford, Dunlap, Warder, Edwards, Leeper, McConnel.

ENROLLED AND ENGROSSED BILLS.—Sullivan, Chairman. Netterstrom, Hamilton, Pemberton, Stubblefield, Mounts, Payne.

FINANCE.—Case, Chairman. Bogardus, Sawyer, Harding, Munroe, Edwards, Granger, Dresser, McConnel.

PENAL AND REFORMATORY INSTITUTIONS.—Stubblefield, Chairman. Berry, Dunlap, Fitzpatrick, Morrison, Chapman, Fort, McCloud, Aspinwall, Kanan, Netterstrom, Monroe, Kingsbury, Sparks, Pemberton, McKinlay, Hull, Mahoney, O'Brien, Payne.

STATE CHARITABLE INSTITUTIONS.—Putnam, Chairman. Kingsbury, Sullivan, Granger, Templeton, Aspinwall, Stubblefield, Campbell, Fisher, Harding, Sparks, Dresser, McConnel, Payne, Mounts.

MINES AND MINING.—Edwards, Chairman. Bollinger, Littler, Willoughby, Sawyer, Harding, Templeton, Putnam, Fort, Baxter, Bogardus, Payne, Mounts, McConnel, McKinlay.

LABOR AND MANUFACTURES.—McCloud, Chairman. Munroe, Campbell, Pemberton, Stubblefield, Chapman, Crawford, Hunt, Fitzpatrick, Littler, Sawyer, Wells, Curley, Payne.

PUBLIC BUILDINGS AND GROUNDS.—Littler, Chairman. Evans, Netterstrom, Templeton, Chapman, Fort, Sawyer, Hunt, Stubblefield, McConnel, Landrigan, Payne, Dresser.

CANALS AND RIVERS.—Fort, Chairman. Lundin, Aspinwall, Munroe, Templeton, Case, Warder, Edwards, Campbell, Sawyer, Sparks, McConnel, Dresser, Payne, Curley.

ELECTIONS.—Crawford, Chairman. Anthony, Warder, Putnam, Baxter, McCloud, Dunlap, Fisher, McKinlay, Leeper, Mahoney, Mounts.

BANKS AND BANKING.—Kanan, Chairman. Fitzpatrick, Chapman, Harding, Fisher, Case, Bogardus, Dwyer, Hamilton, Morrison, Sullivan, Hull, Leeper, Wells.

LINCOLN MONUMENT.—Evans, Chairman. Kingsbury, Crawford, Sparks, Littler, McConnel, Landrigan.

JUDICIAL APPORTIONMENT.—Warder, Chairman. Harding, Sparks, Baxter, Templeton, Hamilton, Edwards, Pemberton, Dunlap, Aspinwall, Putnam, Kingsbury, Bollinger, Munroe, Fisher, Leeper, Mounts, Landrigan, Hull.

TO VISIT STATE CHARITABLE INSTITUTIONS.—McCloud, Chairman. Bollinger, McConnel.

TO VISIT PENAL AND REFORMATORY INSTITUTIONS.—Willoughby, Chairman. Anthony, Dresser.

TO VISIT EDUCATIONAL INSTITUTIONS.—Fort, Chairman. Munroe, Payne.

TO INVESTIGATE EMBEZZLEMENT OF ILLINOIS UNIVERSITY FUNDS.—Berry, Chairman. Aspinwall, Dunlap, Fisher, McKinlay.

HOUSE COMMITTEES.

Fortieth General Assembly.

JUDICIARY.—Allen of Vermilion, Chairman. Cochran, Selby, Sharrock, Boyd, Revell, Bailey, Kincheloe, Booth, Sherman, Sayler, Parish, Tisdel, Torrence, Brown, R. C. Busse, Murray of Sangamon, Eldredge, Flannigan, Avery, Craig, Morris, Barnes, Schwab, Stoskopf, Johnson of Whiteside, Barricklow, Novak, Perry, Organ, McGoorty, Hall of Cook, Sullivan, Salmans, McEniry, McGee, Alschuler.

ELECTIONS.—Sherman, Chairman. Miller Busse, F. A., Booth, Guffin, Anderson, Selby, Thomas, Kincheloe, Eldredge, Hammers, Walleck, Salmans, Alschuler, Compton, McGee, Shephard, Webb, Sullivan.

ENGROSSED BILLS.—Cavanaugh, Chairman, Booth, Hammers, Weidmaier, Lathrop, Perry, Murray of Clinton.

CONTINGENT EXPENSES.—Murray of Stark, Chairman. Kincheloe, Murdoch, Daugherty, Boyd, Kolstedt, Quanstrum, O'Donnell, Walleck, Montgomery, McLauchlan.

RULES.—Mr. Speaker, Allen of Vermilion, Craig, Morris, Schubert, Cochran, Sherman, Powell of Iroquois, Johnson of Whiteside.

APPROPRIATIONS.—Needles, Chairman. Guffin, Cochran, Shanahan, Merriam, Anderson, Wylie, Funk, Buckner, Booth, Sherman, Powell of Iroquois, Nicholls, Johnson of Fulton, Steen, Garver, Thomas, Ward, Busell, O'Donnell, Stoskopf, Branen, Harnsberger, Suttle, Price, McGoorty, McEniry, Conlee, Blood, Craig.

JUDICIAL DEPARTMENT.—Miller, Chairman. Selby, Cochran, Boyd, Sharrock, Kincheloe, Bailey, Booth, R. C. Busse, Parish, Sayler,

Tisdel, Avery, Flannigan, Eldredge, Alschuler, Blood, Horn, Murray of Clinton, English, Webb, Gaines, Compton, Bryant.

CIVIL SERVICE REFORM.—Bryan, Chairman. Tisdel, Hammers, Miller, Thiemann, Powell of Iroquois, Avery, Powell of Cook, Daugherty, Lathrop, Trowbridge, Rowe, McGuire, Bryant, Large, Perry, Huffman, Bristol, Suttle, Hussman, Alschuler.

CORPORATIONS.—Murdoch, Chairman. Selby, Revell, Fuller, Schubert, Andrus, Glade, Ely, F. A. Busse, Ward, Kilcourse, Brown, Buckner, Shanahan, Nohe, Meaney, Farrell, Novak, Branen, Johnson of Whiteside, Barnes, Walleck, McGuire, O'Shea, Carmody, Kain.

RAILROADS.—F. A. Busse, Chairman. Eldredge, Bryan, Powell of Iroquois, Kilcourse, Sherman, Weidmaier, Booth, Cavanaugh, Noling, Revell, Nohe, Thomas, Murray of Stark, Houghton, Glade, Morris, Stoskopf, Farrell, Barricklow, Stewart, Blood, Hall of Pike, Sterchie, Novak, Mitchell, Galligan.

WAREHOUSES.—Revell, Chairman. Thiemann, Daugherty, Eldredge, F. A. Busse, LaMonte, Wathier, Rowe, Quanstrum, Buckner, Brignadello, Bartling, English, Kain, Horn, Atchison, Sullivan.

CANAL AND RIVER IMPROVEMENT.—Wylie, Chairman. Payne, Merrill, Kolstedt, Merriam, Murray of Stark, Dinneen, White, Wood, Andrus, King, Dickson, Flannigan, McLauchlan, Jarvis, Suttle, McGoorty, McGinnis, Hall of Cook, McDonough, Kain.

FINANCE.—Thomas, Chairman. Houghton, Shanahan, Lyon, Miller, Andrus, Thiemann, Noling, Powell of Cook, Shephard, Bryant, O'Shea, Alschuler, Edelstein, Murray of Clinton.

MINES AND MINING.—Trowbridge, Chairman. Steen, Murray of Sangamon, Bailey, DeWoody, Sharrock, Thomas, Johnson of Fulton, Morey, Wood, Wylie, McLauchlan, Large, Webb, Kain, Bristol, Salmans, Jarvis, Staudacher.

FEES AND SALARIES.—Glade, Chairman. Booth, Boyd, Fuller, Perrottet, Nohe, Ward, Meaney, Stewart, O'Shea, Lovett, Allen of Randolph, Trousdale.

PENAL AND REFORMATORY INSTITUTIONS.—Guffin, Chairman. Needles, Anderson, Noling, Steen, Brown, Scrogin, Lyon, Avery, Houghton, Lathrop, Murray of Stark, Powell of Cook, Laub, Large, Montgomery, Rhodes, Huffman, Atchison, Murray of Clinton, Hussman, McEniry, Bristol.

MUNICIPAL CORPORATIONS.—Schubert, Chairman. Sherman, Revell, Cavanaugh, Perrottet, Nohe, Noling, Kilcourse, Houghton, R. C. Busse, Quanstrum, Sayler, Wathier, Weidmaier, Farrell, Johnson of Whiteside, Barricklow, Schwab, Morris, Brignadello, Bartling, Craig, McGinnis, Sterchie.

EDUCATION.—Murray of Sangamon, Chairman. Bryan, Merriam, Schubert, Hammer, Tisdel, Scrogin, Nohe, Wathier, Parish, Trowbridge, Joy, Dickson, Barricklow, Johnson of Whiteside, O'Donnell, Gaines, Alschuler, Trousdale, Hall of Cook, Suttle, Farrell.

STATE INSTITUTIONS.—Brown, Chairman. Daugherty, Payne, Wylie, Anderson, Kolstedt, Nothnagel, Marquiss, Joy, King, Large, Lovett, Hall of Pike, Edelstein, Allen of Randolph, English, Beer.

PUBLIC CHARITIES.—Merrill, Chairman. Funk, F. A. Busse, Dinneen, Lathrop, Kilcourse, Dickson, Williams, Joy, King, Morey, Horn, McGuire, Hussman, McLauchlan, Perry, Hart.

PUBLIC BUILDINGS AND GROUNDS.—Daugherty, Chairman. Cavanaugh, Buckner, Houghton, Glade, Laub, Torrence, Marquiss, Sayler, Metcalf, Atchison, Harnsberger, Conlee, McEniry, Montgomery.

REVENUE.—Selby, Chairman. Cochran, Shanahan, Guffin, Merriam, Needles, Schubert, Bovey, Glade, Daugherty, Hunter, Scrogin, Nicholls, Berryman, Sayler, Novak, Craig, Brignadello, Stoskopf, Walleck, Edelstein, Blood, Mitchell, Suttle, Stewart.

BANKS AND BANKING.—Boyd, Chairman. Funk, Lyon, Merriam, Needles, Glade, Murdoch, Busell, Powell of Iroquois, Wilson, Metcalf, Laub, Lathrop, Schwab, Barnes, Suttle, Shephard, Horn, Montgomery, Trousdale, Edelstein.

COUNTY AND TOWNSHIP ORGANIZATION.—Perrottet, Chairman. Andrus, Sharrock, Kolstedt, Kincheloe, Powell of Cook, Berryman, DeWoody, Laub, White, Williams, Huffman, Bryant, Lovett, Jarvis, Mitchell, Atchison, Salmans, Hussman.

AGRICULTURE.—Fuller, Chairman. Thiemann, Wilson, Bovey, Murray of Stark, Perrottet, Anderson, Scrogin, White, Williams, Marquiss, Berryman, Busell, DeWoody, Dickson, Branen, Huffman, Hart, Hussman, McGuire, Bristol, Atchison, Rhodes, Allen of Randolph, Price.

LIVE STOCK AND DAIRYING.—Powell of Iroquois, Chairman. Olson, Thiemann, Schubert, Miller, F. A. Busse, Perrottet, Andrus, Shanahan, Noling, Cavanaugh, Kolstedt, Brown, Hunter, Johnson of Whiteside, Branen, Morris, Farrell, Bartling, Butler, McGinnis, Galligan.

LABOR.—Steen, Chairman. Glade, Bailey, Murray of Sangamon, Ward, Bovey, Olson, Torrence, Eldredge, DeWoody, McLauchlan, Rhodes, Allen of Randolph, Huffman, Large, Salmans, Staudacher.

MANUFACTURES.—Bovey, Chairman. Cavanaugh, Guffin, Ely, Thiemann, Meaney, LaMont, Quanstrum, Sayler, Kolstedt, Novak, Hall of Cook, Carmody, Blood, Kain.

BUILDING LOAN AND HOMESTEAD.—Noling, Chairman. Lyon, Nothnagel, Needles, Murdoch, Murray of Sangamon, Rowe, Nicholls, Trowbridge, Avery, Laub, LaMonte, Garver, Barricklow, Shephard, Murray of Clinton, O'Donnell, Montgomery, Bryant, Atchison, Stewart.

STATUTORY REVISION.—Tisdel, Chairman. Miller, Williams, Murray of Sangamon, Boyd, Bailey, Torrence, Eldredge, Flannigan, Alschuler, Organ, Murray of Clinton, McGee, Horn, Compton.

SANITARY AFFAIRS.—Meaney, Chairman. Olson, Merrill, Quanstrum, Nothnagel, Steen, Dinneen, Powell of Cook, Morey, Mitchell, Beer, Sterchie, McDonough, Carmody, Bristol.

INSURANCE.—Nohe, Chairman. Fuller, LaMonte, Hunter, Schubert, Bovey, Kilcourse, Johnson of Fulton, Parish, Weidmaier, Glade, Laub, O'Donnell, Barnes, Novak, Stoskopf, Bartling, Craig, Schwab, McDonough, Barnett.

FEDERAL RELATIONS.—Flannigan, Chairman. Sharrock, Wilson, Hunter, Parish, Nothnagel, Williams, Houghton, Eldredge, Stoskopf, Salmans, Webb, O'Donnell, English, Hall of Cook.

CLAIMS.—Kincheloe, Chairman. Funk, Merrill, Ely, Berryman, Brown, Wathier, Murray of Sangamon, Dinneen, Schwab, Blood, Galligan, Atchison, Brignadello, Mitchell.

MILITARY AFFAIRS.—Buckner, Chairman. Bryan, Cochran, Nicholls, Payne, King, Rowe, Perrottet, Tisdel, White, Farrell, McLauchlan, Sullivan, McGuire, Horn, Price, Compton.

RETRENCHMENT.—Lyon, Chairman. Daugherty, Gufiin, Bailey, Ely, Ward, Marquiss, White, Torrence, Edelstein, Staudacher, Montgomery, Jarvis, Lovett, Beer.

PRINTING.—Rowe, Chairman. Wilson, Hunter, Morey, R. C. Busse, Andrus, Busell, Metcalf, Thomas, Kolstedt, Galligan, Storchle, Carmody, Bryant, Hart.

ROADS AND BRIDGES.—Thiemann, Chairman. Ely, Bovey, Perrottet, Guflin, Murray of Stark, Johnson of Fulton, Wilson, Berryman, Avery, Thomas, DeWoody, Garver, Marquiss, Morey, Price, McLauchlan, Stewart, Beer, Salmans, Bristol, Hart, Allen of Randolph, Conlee, Jarvis.

DRAINAGE AND WATER WAYS.—Sharrock, Chairman. Olson, Merriam, Buckner, Allen of Vermilion, Nohe, Houghton, Murray of Stark, Ely, Steen, Payne, Trowbridge, White, Nothnagel, Merrill, McGoorty, Hall of Cook, Atchison, Barricklow, Webb, Stewart, Kain, Barnes, Craig, McGinnis.

FISH AND GAME.—Nicholls, Chairman. Lyon, Allen of Vermilion, LaMonte, Wylie, Merrill, Perrottet, Hunter, Olson, Brown, Quanstrum, Wood, DeWoody, Bartling, Large, Price, Allen of Randolph, Hart, Montgomery, Jarvis, Barnett.

LICENSE.—Kilcourse, Chairman. Glade, Metcalf, Nothnagel, Joy, Tisdel, Schubert, Allen of Vermilion, Needles, Wathier, Trowbridge, Powell of Cook, Marquiss, Branen, Schwab, Barnes, Galligan, Morris, Craig, Novak, McDonough.

VISIT PENAL INSTITUTIONS.—Booth, Chairman. Parish, Lyon, Wood, Garver, King, Harnsberger, McGee, Blood.

VISIT EDUCATIONAL INSTITUTIONS.—Ward, Chairman. Allen of Vermilion, Powell of Cook, Torrence, Morey, Scrogin, Alschuler, Montgomery, Salmans.

VISIT CHARITABLE INSTITUTIONS.—Berryman, Chairman. Merriam, Funk, Powell of Iroquois, Metcalf, Dinneen, McGuire, Compton, O'Shea.

SOLDIERS' HOME.—Merriam, Chairman. Funk, Payne, Nicholls, Anderson, King, Joy, Wood, Garver, McGuire, Price, O'Donnell, Beer.

FARM DRAINAGE.—Payne, Chairman. Ely, Andrus, Johnson of Fulton, Rowe, Wylie, Thomas, Dickson, White, Scrogin, Trousdale, Hart, Conlee, Harnsberger, Barnett, Staudacher, Galligan.

PARKS AND BOULEVARDS.—Sayler, Chairman. Schubert, Bryan, Daugherty, Tisdel, Rowe, Olson, R. C. Busse, Revel, Cavanaugh, Wiedmaier, Kilcourse, Quanstrum, Meaney, Wathier, Laub, Glade, Storchle, Sullivan, Galligan, Walleck, McDonough, Butler, Mitchell, McGinnis, Carmody.

STATE AND COUNTY FAIRS.—Wilson, Chairman. Hammers, Sherman, Thiemann, Murdoch, Murray of Sangamon, Williams, Wood, Garver, Harnsberger, Large, McGuire, Barnett, Rhodes, Price.

HORTICULTURE—Garver, Chairman. Morey, Joy, Fuller, Nolling, Kolstedt, Dinneen, Dickson, Metcalf, Meaney, Johnson of Fulton, Flannigan, King, Jarvis, Hart, Horn, Allen of Randolph, Huffman, Hall of Pike, Rhodes, Hussman.

JUDICIAL APPORTIONMENT.—Cochran, Chairman. Bailey, Boyd, Merrill, Murdoch, R. C. Busse, Berryman, Lathrop, LaMonte, Torrence, Williams, Busell, Flannigan, Stoskopf, Atchison, Alschuler, Craig, Conlee, Gaines, Organ, Barnes.

CONGRESSIONAL APPORTIONMENT.—Anderson, Chairman. Needles, Sharrock, Miller, Cavanaugh, Ward, Nohe, Quanstrum, Powell of Iroquois, Wilson, Scrogin, Laub, Steen, Novak, O'Donnell, Large, Schwab, Blood, Shephard, Sullivan, Jarvis.

SENATORIAL APPORTIONMENT.—Busse, R. C., Chairman. Allen of Vermilion, Cochran, Selby, Shanahan, Sherman, Glade, Payne, Wathier, Fuller, Weidmaier, Parish, Williams, McGee, Stewart, Bryant, Hall of Cook, Price, Horn, McGoorty, Barricklow.

JOINT RULES.—Cochran, Chairman. F. A Busse, Wylie, Murray of Clinton.

INVESTIGATE STATE INSTITUTIONS.—Anderson, Chairman. Allen of Vermilion, Sherman, Booth, Cochran, Compton, Barricklow, Blood.

REPUBLICAN STEERING COMMITTEE.—Selby, Chairman. Allen, Miller, Bryan, Murdoch, Schubert, Sherman, Shanahan, Booth, Cochran, Needles, F. A. Busse.

DEMOCRATIC STEERING COMMITTEE.—Morris, Chairman. Craig, Sullivan, Johnson, Stoskopf, Bartling, Barricklow, Perry, Compton, O'Donnell, Barnes, Blood, Brignadello.

SPECIAL COMMITTEE ON CONSTITUTIONAL AMENDMENTS.—Allen of Vermilion, Chairman. Miller, Rowe, Cochran, Craig, Morris, Johnson of Whiteside.

Nativity of Members.

An even one hundred of the members of the present General Assembly were born in Illinois. Ohio and New York are neck and neck with a score of 17 each, and other states follow in this order: Pennsylvania, 7; Indiana, 5; Tennessee and Kentucky, 4 each; Connecticut, West Virginia and Iowa, 3 each; Vermont and Massachusetts, 2 each. In each of these states one member was born: Minnesota, Louisiana, Maryland, North Carolina, New Hampshire, Michigan and Texas. Only 30 members were born under a foreign potentate. Canada furnished 4; Scotland and Ireland, 5 each; Germany, 4; Sweden, 3; England, 2; Russia, Norway, Austria, France, Bohemia, Switzerland and the Isle of Jersey, 1 each. Senator Sparks with his 74 honorable years of life is the eldest member and Mr. Ward is the youngest. There are 28 old soldiers in the senate and house.

There are no Smiths nor Robinsons and only one Brown in the legislature. There are two Allens, two Johnsons, two Halls, three Murrays and two Powells. Twenty members answer to "John." "William" is a close second with 19, and there are 13 "Charles" and 12 "James." Three are bound to acknowledge "Isaac," 6 "David," 5 "Daniel," 3 "Samuel," and 8 "Joseph." Two begin with "Caleb," 1 "Obed," 1 "Ebenezer," 1 "Abner," 1 "Jacob," 2 "Michael," 2 "Patrick," 2 "Peter," 1 "Jeremiah," 1 "Jonathan," and 1 "Hiram." Of odd names there are these: Pleasant, Lars, Alva, Almet, Aquilla and Almon.

APPENDIX "A"

TO

LEGISLATIVE DIRECTORY

OF 1897

A Complete

STATISTICAL HISTORY

Of Illinois from 1800 to 1897

Followed by

PORTRAITS AND BIOGRAPHIES

Of all Illinois Governors, Present State Officers, etc.

A. Lincoln

ILLINOIS TERRITORY.

The Illinois Territory was established by act of Congress, approved Feb. 3, 1809, which provided as follows:

"That from and after the first day of March next, all that part of the Indiana Territory which lies west of the Wabash river and a direct line drawn from the said Wabash river and Post Vincennes due north, to the territorial line between the United States and Canada, shall, for the purpose of temporary government, constitute a separate territory, and be called 'Illinois.'"

The seat of government was fixed at Kaskaskia. The territorial government was continued under the first grade from 1809 until 1812, when by a vote of the people the second grade was adopted. Under the first grade, the Governor and Judges, who received their appointment from the President, constituted the Legislative Council, and enacted laws for the government of the people. The Governor possessed almost unlimited power in the appointment of officers; the Secretary of the Territory being the only officer not appointed by the Governor. Under the second grade, the people elected the Legislature, which was composed of a Legislative Council and a House of Representatives. The Legislative Council was composed of five members, and the House of Representatives of seven members.

The Legislature enacted the laws for the government of the people, but the Governor was possessed of the absolute veto power, and was therefore in a position to dictate the laws, if he chose to exercise the power.

The people also elected the Delegate to Congress by popular vote.

TERRITORIAL OFFICERS.

The following is a complete roster of territorial officers from 1809 until the organization of the State government in 1818. The term of the Governor's appointment was two years. Governor Edwards was reappointed from time to time, as his term expired, and served through the entire territorial government

GOVERNORS.

John Boyle, March 7, 1809. Declined.
Ninian Edwards, April 24, 1809 to Dec. 6, 1818.

SECRETARIES.

Nathaniel Pope, March 7, 1809 to Dec. 17, 1816.
Joseph Phillips, Dec. 17, 1816 to Oct. 6, 1818.

AUDITORS OF PUBLIC ACCOUNTS.

H. H. Maxwell, 1812 to 1816.
Daniel P. Cook, Jan. 13, 1816, to April, 1817.
Robert Blackwell, April 5, 1817, to Aug., 1817.
Elijah C. Berry, Aug. 28, 1817, to Oct. 9, 1818.

ATTORNEYS-GENERAL.

Benjamin H. Doyle, July 24, 1809, to Dec., 1809.
John J. Crittenden, Dec. 30, 1809, to April, 1810.
Thomas T. Crittenden, April 7, 1810, to Oct., 1810.
Benjamin M. Platt, Oct. 29, 1810, to June, 1813.
William Mears, June 23, 1813, to Feb. 17, 1818.

TREASURER.

John Thomas, 1812 to 1818.

DELEGATES TO CONGRESS.

Shadrach Bond, Dec. 1812, to 1814.
Benjamin Stephenson, Sept. 29, 1814, to 1817.
Nathaniel Pope, 1817 to 1818.

JUDGES.

Obadiah Jones, March 7, 1809.
Alexander Stuart, March 7, 1809. Resigned.
Jesse B. Thomas, March 7, 1809.
Stanley Griswold, March 16, 1810. Vice Stuart.
William Sprigg, July 29, 1813.
Thomas Towles, Oct. 28, 1815.
Thomas Towles, Jan. 16, 1816.
Daniel P. Cook (Western circuit), Jan. 13, 1818.
John Warnock (Western circuit), June 8, 1818.
John McLean (Eastern circuit), Jan. 13, 1818. Declined.
Elias Kent Kane (Eastern circuit), Feb. 17, 1818.
William Mears (Eastern circuit), Feb. 17, 1818.
Jeptha Hardin (Eastern circuit), March 3, 1818.

ADJUTANTS GENERAL.

Elias Rector, May 8, 1809, to July 18, 1809.
Robert Morrison, July 18, 1809, to May 28, 1810.
Elias Rector, May 28, 1810, to Oct. 25, 1813.
Benjamin Stephenson, Dec. 13, 1813, to Oct. 27, 1814.
Wm. Alexander, Oct. 27, 1814, to Dec., 1818.

FIRST TERRITORIAL LEGISLATURE—1812-14.

Convened at Kaskaskia the 25th day of November, 1812. Adjourned the 26th day of December, 1812. Second session convened and adjourned Nov. 8, 1813

LEGISLATIVE COUNCIL.

President—Pierre Menard.
Secretary—John Thomas.
Doorkeeper—Thomas Van Swearingen.

Pierre Menard, Randolph.
Benjamin Talbott, Gallatin.
William Biggs, St. Clair.
Samuel Judy, Madison.
Thomas Ferguson, Johnson.

HOUSE OF REPRESENTATIVES.

Speaker—George Fisher.
Doorkeeper—Thomas Van Swearingen.
Clerk—William C. Greenup.

George Fisher, Randolph.
Alexander Wilson, Gallatin.
Philip Trammel, Gallatin.
John Grammar, Johnson.
Joshua Oglesby, St. Clair.
Jacob Short, St. Clair.
William Jones, Madison.

SECOND TERRITORIAL LEGISLATURE—1814-16.

First session convened at Kaskaskia the 14th day of November, 1814. Adjourned Dec. 24, 1814. Second session convened Dec. 4, 1815. Adjourned Jan. 11, 1816.

LEGISLATIVE COUNCIL.

President—Pierre Menard,
Doorkeeper—Thomas Stuart.
Secretary—John Thomas.
Enrolling and Eng. Cl'k—Wm. C. Greenup.

Pierre Menard, Randolph.
William Biggs, St. Clair.
Benjamin Talbott, Gallatin
Samuel Judy, Madison.
Thomas Ferguson, Johnson.

HOUSE OF REPRESENTATIVES.

Speaker—Risdon Moore.
Doorkeeper—Thomas Stuart.
Clerk—William Mears.

Risdon Moore, St. Clair.
William Rabb, Madison.
James Lemen, Jr., St. Clair.
James Gilbreath, Randolph (expelled).
Jarvis Hazelton, Randolph (vice Gilbreath).
Philip Trammel, Gallatin.
Thomas C. Browne, Gallatin.
Owen Evans, Johnson (first session only).
John G. Lofton, Madison (sec'd session only).

THIRD TERRITORIAL LEGISLATURE—1816-18.

First session convened at Kaskaskia the 2d day of December, 1816. Adjourned Jan. 14, 1817. Second session convened Dec. 1, 1817. Adjourned Jan. 12, 1818.

LEGISLATIVE COUNCIL.

President—Pierre Menard.
Enrolling and Eng. Clerk—R. K. McLaughlin.
Secretary—Joseph Conway.
Doorkeeper—Ezra Owen.

Pierre Menard, Randolph.
John G. Lofton, Madison.
Abraham Amos, St. Clair.
John Grammar, Johnson.
Thomas C. Browne, Gallatin.

HOUSE OF REPRESENTATIVES.

Speaker—George Fisher.
Enrolling and Eng. Clerk—R. K. McLaughlin.
Clerk—Daniel P. Cook.
Doorkeeper—Ezra Owen.

George Fisher, Randolph.
C. R. Matheny, St. Clair.
Wm. H. Bradsby, St. Clair.
*Nathan Davis, Jackson.
†M. S. Davenport, Gallatin.
Joseph Palmer, Johnson.
*Seth Gard, Edwards.
*Samuel Omelveny, Pope.
†Willis Hargrave, White.

*First session only.
†Second session only.

ILLINOIS STATE.

CONSTITUTIONAL CONVENTIONS.

CONVENTION OF 1818.

Assembled at Kaskaskia July —, 1818. Adjourned Aug. 26, 1818. Thirty-three delegates. One member from Washington county died during the sitting of the convention; name unknown. Constitution adopted in convention without being submitted to a vote of the people. Approved by Congress Dec. 3, 1818.

President—Jesse B. Thomas.
Secretary—William C. Greenup.

St. Clair—Jesse B. Thomas, John Messinger, James Lemen, Jr.
Randolph—George Fisher, Elias Kent Kane.
Madison—Benjamin Stephenson, Joseph Borough, Abraham Prickett.
Gallatin—Michael Jones, Leonard White, Adolphus F. Hubbard.
Johnson—Hezekiah West, Wm. McFatridge.
Edwards—Seth Gard, Levi Compton.
White—Willis Hargrave, Wm. McHenry.
Monroe—Caldwell Carns, Enoch Moore.
Pope—Samuel Omelveny, Hamlet Ferguson.
Jackson—Conrad Will, James Hall, Jr.
Crawford—Joseph Kitchell, Edward N. Cullom.
Bond—Thomas Kirkpatrick, Samuel G. Morse.
Union—William Echols, John Whittaker.
Washington—Andrew Bankson.
Franklin—Isham Harrison, Thomas Roberts.

CONVENTION OF 1847.

Convened at Springfield, June 7, 1847. Adjourned Aug. 31, 1847. One hundred and sixty-two delegates. Constitution ratified by the people March 6, 1848; in force April 1, 1848.

President, pro tem.—Zadok Casey.
Secretary—Henry W. Moore.
President—Newton Cloud.
Sergeant-at-Arms—John A. Wilson.

Adams—Wm. Laughlin, W. B. Powers, Jacob M. Nichols.
Adams and Highland—Archibald Williams.
Alexander and Pulaski—Martin Atherton.
Bond—Michael G. Dale.
Boone—Daniel H. Whitney.
Brown—James W. Singleton.
Brown and Schuyler—James Brockman, Alexander McHatton.
Bureau—Simon Kinney.
Calhoun and Jersey—Wm. Bosbyshell.
Carroll and Ogle—Garner Moffett.
Cass—Henry E. Dummer.
Champaign and Vermilion — Thompson R. Webber.
Christian and Shelby—D. D. Shumway.
Clark—Wm. Tutt, Justin Harlan.
Clark, Edgar and Coles—Uri Manly.
Clay—Peter Green.
Clinton—Benjamin Bond.
Coles—Thomas A. Marshall, Thos. B. Trower.
Cook—Patrick Ballingall, Francis C. Sherman, Reuben B. Heacock, E. F. Colby, David L. Gregg.
Crawford—Nelson Hawley.
Cumberland and Effingham—Wm. H. Blakely.
DeKalb—George H. Hill.
DeWitt—George B. Lemen.
DuPage—Jeduthun Hatch.
DuPage and Will—Samuel Anderson.
Edgar—Wm. Shields, George W. Rives.
Edwards and Wayne—Alvin R. Kenner.
Fayette—John W. F. Edmonson, J. T. Eccles.
Franklin—George W. Akin.
Fulton—David Markley, Hezekiah M. Wead, Isaac Linley, George Kreider.
Gallatin—Albert G. Caldwell, Jacob Smith.
Greene—Franklin Witt, L. E. Worcester, D. M. Woodson.
Grundy and LaSalle—George W. Armstrong.
Hamilton—James M. Lasater.
Hancock—Thomas C. Sharpe, Wm. S. Moore, Charles Choate, Robert Miller, Thomas Geddes.
Hardin and Gallatin—Andrew McCallen.
Henderson—Gilbert Turnbull.
Henry and Knox—Joshua Harper.
Highland—Lewis J. Simpson.
Iroquois and Will—Jesse O. Norton.
Jackson—Alexander M. Jenkins.
Jasper and Crawford—Richard G. Morris.
Jefferson—Franklin S. Casey.
Jefferson, Marion and Hamilton—Zadok Casey, Walter B. Scates.
Jersey—A. R. Knapp.
JoDaviess—Thompson Campbell, W. B. Green, O. C. Pratt.
Johnson—John Oliver.
Kane—Alfred Churchill, Augustus Adams, Thomas Judd.
Kendall—John West Mason.
Knox—Curtis K. Harvey, James Knox.
Lake—Horace Butler, Hurlbut Swan.
LaSalle—Wm. Stadden, Abraham Hoes.
Lawrence—John Mieure.
Lee—John Dement.
Livingston and McLean—Samuel Lander.
Logan—James Tuttle.
McLean—David Davis.
Mason—F. S. D. Marshall.
Macoupin—James Graham, John M. Palmer.
McDonough—James M. Campbell.
McDonough and Warren—John Huston.
McHenry—John Sibley, Peter W. Deitz.
McHenry and Boone—Stephen A. Hurlbut.
Madison—Cyrus Edwards, E. M. West, Benaiah Robinson, George T. Brown.
Marshall and Stark—Henry D. Palmer.
Marion—George W. Pace.
Macon and Piatt—Edward O. Smith.
Massac—Thomas G. C. Davis.
Menard—Benjamin F. Northcott.
Mercer—Frederick Frick.
Montgomery—Hiram Rountree.
Montgomery and Bond—James M. Davis.
Moultrie and Shelby—Anthony Thornton.
Morgan—Newton Cloud, James Dunlap, Samuel D. Lockwood, William Thomas.
Monroe—James A. James, John D. Whiteside.
Ogle—Daniel J. Pinckney.
Perry—H. B. Jones.
Perry, Washington and Clinton—John Crain.
Peoria—Wm. W. Thompson, Lincoln B. Knowlton.
Peoria and Fulton—Onslow Peters.
Pike—Wm. R. Archer, Harvey Dunn, Wm. A. Grimshaw, Montgomery Blair.
Pope—William Sim.
Putnam—Oaks Turner.
Randolph—Ezekiel W. Robbins, Richard B. Servant.
Richland—Alfred Kitchell.
Rock Island—John W. Spencer.
Sangamon—John Dawson, James H. Matheny, Ninian W. Edwards, Stephen T. Logan.
Scott—N. M. Knapp, Daniel Dunsmore.
Schuyler—William A. Minshall.
Shelby—Edward Evey.
St. Clair—Wm. W. Roman, Wm. C. Kinney, John McCulley, George Bunsen.
Stephenson—Seth B. Farwell, Thomas B. Carter.
Tazewell—William H. Holmes, Henry R. Green.
Union—Samuel Hunsaker.
Vermilion—John Canady, John W. Vance.
Wabash—Charles H. Constable.
Warren—Abner C. Harding.
Washington—Zenas H. Vernor.
Wayne—James M. Hogue.
Whiteside—Aaron C. Jackson.
White—S. Snowden Hayes, Daniel Hay.
Woodford—Samuel J. Cross.
Winnebago—Selden M. Church, Robert J. Cross.
Williamson—John T. Loudon.
Williamson, Franklin and Jackson—Willis Allen
Will—Hugh Henderson, Wm. McClure.

CONVENTION OF 1862.

Convened at Springfield Jan. 7, 1862. Adjourned March 24, 1862. Seventy-five delegates Constitution rejected by the people at an election June 17, 1862.

President, pro tem.—John Dement.
Secretary—William M. Springer.
Assistant—John W. Merritt.
Postmaster—Robert H. Burton.
President—William A. Hacker.
Sergeant-at-Arms—John Schell.
Assistant—William Sands.

Adams—James W. Singleton, Austin Brooks.
Alexander, Pulaski and Union—Wm. A. Hacker.
Pope, Hardin and Massac—George W. Waters.
Williamson and Johnson—Wm. J. Allen.
Gallatin and Saline—Milton Bartley.
Franklin and Jackson—Andrew D. Duff.
Randolph Daniel Reilly.
Washington and Perry—George W. Wall.
Jefferson, Marion and Hamilton—H. K. S Omelveny, T. B. Tanner.
Wabash and White—Thomas W. Stone.
Wayne and Edwards—R. P. Hanna.
Monroe—Thomas W. Morgan.

St. Clair—Augustus C. French, James B. Underwood.
Clinton and Bond—Samuel Stevenson.
Madison—Solomon Kœpflie, Samuel A. Buckmaster.
Fayette and Effingham—Isaac L. Leith.
Richland, Clay and Jasper—James H. Parker.
Lawrence and Crawford—Harmon Alexander.
Cumberland and Shelby—Anthony Thornton.
Montgomery and Christian—Horatio M. Vandeveer.
Macoupin—Lewis Solomon.
Greene—John M. Woodson.
Edgar—James A. Eades.
Coles, Moultrie and Douglas—Orlando B. Ficklin.
Sangamon—Benj. S. Edwards, Jas. D. Smith.
Morgan and Scott—Joseph Morton, Albert G. Burr.
Pike and Brown—Alexander Starne, Archibald A. Glenn.
Schuyler—John P. Richmond.
Hancock—Milton M. Merrill.
McDonough—Joseph C. Thompson.
Fulton—Lewis W. Ross, John G. Graham.
Cass and Menard—Thompson W. McNeely.
Logan and Mason—E. L. Austin.
Macon, Platt, De Witt and Champaign—T. R. Webber.
Vermilion and Ford—Elias S. Terry.
McLean—Wm. W. Orme.
Tazewell—Robert B. M. Wilson.
Henderson and Warren—Jonathan Simpson.
Peoria and Stark—Julius Manning, Norman H. Purple.
Marshall, Woodford and Putnam—John Burns.
LaSalle, Livingston and Grundy—Alexander Campbell, Perry A. Armstrong.
Kendall—Thomas Finnie.
Will, DuPage, Kankakee and Iroquois—Francis Goodspeed, J. W. Paddock, Henry C. Childs.
Kane and DeKalb—Stephen B. Stinson, Adoniram J. Joslyn.
Knox—W. Selden Gale.
Jersey—Wm. H. Allen.
Clark—Timothy R. Young.
Bureau—Robert T. Templeton.
Mercer, Henry and Rock Island—George W. Pleasants.
Lee and Whiteside—John Dement.
Ogle—Charles Newcomer.
JoDaviess and Carroll—Wellington Weigley, Henry Smith.
Stephenson—Willard P. Naramore.
Winnebago—Porter Sheldon.
Boone and McHenry—Wm. M. Jackson, Luther W. Lawrence.
Lake—Elisha P. Ferry.
Cook—John Wentworth, Melville W. Fuller, Elliott Anthony, John H. Muhlke.

CONVENTION OF 1870.

Convened at Springfield, Dec. 13, 1869. Adjourned May 13, 1870. Eighty-five delegates. Constitution ratified by the people, July 2, 1870; in force August 8, 1870.

President, pro tem—John Dement.
President—Charles Hitchcock.
Secretary—John Q. Harmon.
First Assistant—Daniel Shepard.
Second Assistant—A. H. Swain.
Doorkeeper—J. S. Lothrop.
First Assistant—Cloyd Crouch.
Second Assistant—R. S. Moore.
Postmaster—James Whiteman.
Assistant—Wilson C. Garrard.

DELEGATES BY DISTRICTS.

1. William J. Allen.
2. George W. Brown.
3. W. G. Bowman.
4. James M. Sharp.
5. Wm. B. Anderson.
6. James M. Washburn.
7. Harvey P. Buxton.
8. J. H. Wilson, Geo. W. Wall.
9. Silas L. Bryan.
10. Robert P. Hanna.
11. James C. Allen.
12. James P. Robinson.
13. **Beverly W. Henry, †† Ferris Forman.
14. Charles E. McDowell.
15. Wm. H. Snyder, Wm. H. Underwood.
16. Charles F. Springer, ‡‡Henry W. Billings.
17. John Scholfield.
18. George R. Wendling.
19. Edward Y. Rice.
20. Milton Hay, Samuel C. Parks.
21. John W. Hankins.
22. Robert A. King.
23. James W. English.
24. Wm. R. Archer, John Abbott.
25. Wm. L. Vandeventer.
26. O. H. Wright.
27. Henry J. Atkins.
28. Orville H. Browning, Onias C Skinner.
29. W H. Neece.
30. Jesse C. Fox.
31. David Ellis.
32. James S. Poage.
33. *A. G. Kirkpatrick, †Henry Tubbs.
34. Alfred M. Craig.
35. Lewis W. Ross, Samuel P. Cummings.
36. Henry W. Wells, Miles A. Fuller.
37. Jonathan Merriam.
38. Reuben M. Benjamin, Clifton H. Moore.
39. John L. Tincher, Henry P. H. Bromwell, Richard B. Sutherland.
40. ‡Charles Emmerson, Abel Harwood.
41. §Wm. H. Patterson, ¶John P. Gamble.
42. Addison Goodell.
43. Wm. C. Goodhue, W. P. Peirce.
44. Geo. S. Eldridge, Joseph Hart, Nathaniel J. Pillsbury.
45. L. D. Whiting, J. G. Bayne, Peleg S. Perley.
46. George E. Wait.
47. Calvin Truesdale.
48. James McCoy.
49. John Dement.
50. Joseph Parker.
51. Westel W. Sedgwick, Jesse S. Hildrup.
52. Chas. Wheaton, Henry Sherrill.
53. Elijah M. Haines.
54. Lawrence S. Church.
55. Robert J. Cross.
56. Thomas J. Turner.
57. Wm. Cary, David C. Wagner.
58. Hiram H. Cody.
59. Joseph Medill, John C. Haines, S. Snowden Hayes.
60. Wm. F. Coolbaugh, Charles Hitchcock.
61. Elliott Anthony, Daniel Cameron.

*Died March 15.
†Vice A. G. Kirkpatrick.
‡Died April 16.
§Died Jan. 16.
¶Vice W. H. Patterson.
** Resigned March 8.
†† Vice B. W. Henry.
‡‡ Died April 19.

EXECUTIVE DEPARTMENT.

Under the constitution of 1818 the elective officers were the Governor and Lieutenant-Governor, who held office for four years. The election returns were transmitted by the returning officers, directed to the Speaker of the House of Representatives, whose duty it was to open and publish them in the presence of a majority of each house of the General Assembly. In case of a tie the choice was made by a joint ballot of both houses. The first election for Governor and Lieutenant-Governor was held on the third Thursday of September, 1818. Thereafter the elections were held every four years on the first Monday of August.

The Secretary of State was appointed by the Governor, with the advice and consent of the Senate.

The Auditor of Public Accounts, Treasurer and Attorney-General were elected by the General Assembly, and held office for two years respectively.

By the constitution of 1848 all these officers were made elective by the people, except the Attorney General, which office was abolished. The term of office for each was four years, except the Treasurer, which was two years.

The office of Attorney-General was again created by law in 1867, and the term fixed at two years. The office was first filled by appointment by the Governor, and at the expiration of the term by election by the people.

The constitution of 1870 provides that the Executive Department shall consist of a Governor, Lieutenant-Governor, Secretary of State, Auditor of Public Accounts, Treasurer, Superintendent of Public Instruction, and Attorney-General, who shall each, with the exception of the Treasurer, hold office for four years from the second Monday in January next after election. The Treasurer holds office for two years, and is ineligible for re-election until the expiration of two years next after the end of his term. The first election under the constitution of 1870 was held Nov. 5, 1872.

By a law passed in 1849 the Secretary of State was made *ex-officio* State Superintendent of Public Schools. In 1854 the law establishing a system of free schools created the office of State Superintendent, and provided for the appointment by the Governor, upon the taking effect of the law, of some person to hold office until the election in 1855, when a State Superintendent should be elected, and every two years thereafter.

The offices of Adjutant-General, State Geologist, and Entomologist, etc., are created by law, and filled by appointment.

[NOTE.—The early records on all State offices are very unsatisfactory.]

GOVERNORS.

Name.	When Inaugurated.	From what county.	Remarks.
Shadrach Bond	Oct. 6, 1818	St. Clair	
Edward Coles	Dec. 5, 1822	Madison	
Ninian Edwards, Dem	Dec. 6, 1826	Madison	
John Reynolds, Dem	Dec. 9, 1830	St. Clair	Resigned Nov. 17, 1834. Elected Representative to Congress.
Wm. L. D. Ewing, Dem	Nov. 17, 1834	Fayette	Vice Reynolds.
Joseph Duncan, Dem	Dec. 3, 1834	Morgan	
Thomas Carlin, Dem	Dec. 7, 1838	Green	
Thomas Ford, Dem	Dec. 8, 1842	Ogle	
Augustus C. French, Dem	Dec. 9, 1846	Crawford	
Augustus C. French, Dem	Jan. 8, 1849	Crawford	Re-elected under Constitut'n of 1847
Joel A. Matteson, Dem	Jan. 10, 1853	Will	
Wm. H. Bissell, Rep	Jan. 12, 1857	Monroe	Died March 15, 1860.
John Wood, Rep	Mar. 21, 1860	Adams	Succeeded to office vice Bissell.
Richard Yates, Rep	Jan. 14, 1861	Morgan	
Richard J. Oglesby, Rep	Jan. 16, 1865	Macon	
John M. Palmer, Rep	Jan. 11, 1869	Macoupin	
Richard J. Oglesby, Rep	Jan. 13, 1873	Macon	Resigned Jan. 23, 1873. Elected U. S. Senator.
John L. Beveridge, Rep	Jan. 23, 1873	Cook	Succeeded to office, vice Oglesby.
Shelby M. Cullom, Rep	Jan. 8, 1877	Sangamon	
Shelby M. Cullom, Rep	Jan. 10, 1881	Sangamon	Resigned Feb. 6, 1883. Elected U.S. Senator.
John M. Hamilton, Rep	Feb. 6, 1883	McLean	Vice Cullom, resigned.
Richard J. Oglesby, Rep	Jan. 30, 1885	Macon	
Joseph W. Fifer, Rep	Jan. 14, 1889	McLean	
John P. Altgeld, Dem	Jan. 9, 1893	Cook	
John R. Tanner, Rep	Jan. 11, 1897	Clay	

LIEUTENANT-GOVERNORS.

Name.	Date of Com'n. or Qualified.	From what county.	Remarks.
Pierre Menard, Dem...	Oct. 6, 1818..	Randolph	....
Adolphus F. Hubbard, Dem	Dec. 5, 1822..	Gallatin	....
William Kinney, Dem.......	Dec. 6, 1826..	St. Clair......	....
Zadok Casey, Dem....... ..	Dec. 9, 1830..	Jefferson	Resigned March 1, 1833.
Wm. L. D. Ewing, Dem ...	Mar. 1, 1833..	Fayette.......	Speaker of Senate and Acting Lieutenant-Governor.
Alex. M. Jenkins, Dem.....	Dec. 5, 1834..	Jackson	Resigned.
Wm. H. Davidson, Dem....	Dec. 9, 1836..	White	Speaker of Senate and Acting Lieutenant-Governor.
Stinson H. Anderson, Dem.	Dec. 7, 1838..	Jefferson	....
John Moore, Dem..........	Dec. 8, 1842..	McLean	....
Joseph B. Wells, Dem......	Dec. 9, 1846..	Rock Island..	....
Wm. McMurtry, Dem.......	Jan. 8, 1849..	Knox	....
Gustavus Koerner, Dem....	Jan. 10, 1853..	St. Clair......	....
John Wood, Rep...........	Jan. 12, 1857..	Adams........	Succeeded to office of Governor, vice Bissell, deceased.
Thomas A. Marshall, Dem.	Jan. 7, 1861..	Coles	President of Senate and Acting Lieutenant-Governor.
Francis A. Hoffman, Rep..	Jan. 14, 1861..	Cook	....
William Bross, Rep	Jan. 16, 1865..	Cook..........	....
John Dougherty, Rep......	Jan. 11, 1869..	Union	....
John L. Beveridge, Rep....	Jan. 13, 1873..	Cook..........	Succeeded to office of Gov., vice Oglesby elected U. S. Senator.
John Early, Rep	Jan. 23, 1873..	Winnebago ..	President of Senate and Acting Lieutenant-Governor.
Archibald A. Glenn, Dem..	Jan. 8, 1875..	Brown........	President of Senate and Acting Lieutenant-Governor.
Andrew Shuman, Rep......	Jan. 8, 1877..	Cook	....
John M. Hamilton, Rep ..	Jan. 10, 1881..	McLean.......	Succeeded to office of Gov., vice Cullom elected U. S. Senator.
Wm. J. Campbell, Rep.....	Feb. 6, 1883 .	Cook....	President of the Senate and Acting Lieut. Gov., vice Hamilton.
John C. Smith, Rep.........	Jan. 30, 1885..	Cook	....
Lyman B. Ray, Rep.........	Jan. 14, 1889..	Grundy.......	....
Joseph B. Gill, Dem........	Jan. 9, 1893..	Jackson	....
William A. Northcott, Rep.	Jan. 11, 1897..	Bond	....

SECRETARIES OF STATE.

Name.	Date of Com'n. or Qualified.	From what county.	Remarks.
Elias Kent Kane, Dem......	Oct. 6,1818..	Kaskaskia ...	Resigned Dec. 16,1822.
Samuel D. Lockwood, Dem.	Dec. 18,1822..	Madison......	Resigned April 2, 1823.
David Blackwell, Dem......	April 2,1823..	St. Clair......	Resigned Oct. 15, 1824.
Morris Birkbeck, Dem......	Oct. 15,1824..	Edwards	Resigned Jan. 15, 1825.
George Forquer, Dem.......	Jan. 15 1825..	Sangamon....	Resigned Dec. 31, 1828.
Alexander P. Field, Dem .	Jan. 23,1829..	Union	Removed Nov. 30, 1840.
Stephen A. Douglas, Dem..	Nov. 30,1840..	Morgan.......	Resigned Feb. 27, 1841.
Lyman Trumbull, Dem......	Mch. 1,1841..	St. Clair......	Removed March 4, 1843.
Thompson Campbell, Dem.	Mch. 6,1843..	JoDaviess....	Resigned Dec. 23, 1846.
Horace S. Cooley, Dem.....	Dec. 23,1846..	Adams..	Appointed by Gov. French.
Horace S. Cooley, Dem.....	Jan. 8,1849..	Adams........	Elected under Constitution of 1848 Died April 2, 1850.
David L. Gregg, Dem	April 2,1850..	Cook..........	....
Alexander Starne, Dem.....	Jan. 10,1853..	Pike	....
Ozias M. Hatch, Rep........	Jan. 12,1857..	Pike	....
Ozias M. Hatch, Rep........	Jan. 14,1861..	Pike	....
Sharon Tyndale, Rep.......	Jan. 16,1865.	St. Clair	....
Edward Rummel, Rep......	Jan. 11,1869.	Peoria........	....
Geo. H. Harlow, Rep.......	Jan. 13,1873	Tazewell	....
Geo. H. Harlow, Rep.......	Jan. 8,1877..	Tazewell	....
Henry D. Dement, Rep.....	Jan. 10,1881..	Lee	....
Henry D. Dement, Rep.....	Jan. 30,1885..	Lee	....
Isaac N. Pearson, Rep......	Jan. 14,1889..	McDonough..	....
Wm. H. Hinrichsen, Dem..	Jan. 9,1893..	Morgan.......	....
James A. Rose, Rep.........	Jan. 11, 1897..	Pope.....	....

AUDITORS OF PUBLIC ACCOUNTS.

Name.	Date of Com'n. or Qualified.	From what county.	Remarks.
Elijah C. Berry, Dem......	Oct. 9, 1818..	Fayette.......	....
Elijah C. Berry, Dem	April 6, 1819..	"	Continued in office until 1831.
James T. B. Stapp, Dem...	Aug. 27, 1831..	"	....
Levi Davis, Dem..........	Nov. 16, 1835..	"	....
James Shields, Dem........	Mch. 4, 1841..	Randolph	....
Wm. L. D. Ewing, Dem...	Mch. 26, 1843..	Fayette.......	Died March 26, 1846.
Thomas H. Campbell, Dem.	Mch. 26, 1846..	Randolph ...	Appointed, vice Ewing, deceased.
Thomas H. Campbell, Dem.	Jan. 7, 1847..	"	Elected by General Assembly.
Jesse K. Dubois, Rep	Jan. 12, 1857..	Lawrence	....
Jesse K. Dubois, Rep.... ...	Jan. 14, 1861..	"	....
Orlin H. Miner, Rep..... ...	Dec. 12, 1864..	Sangamon....	Died May 27, 1880.
Charles E. Lippincott, Rep	Jan. 11, 1869..	Cass	....
Charles E. Lippincott, Rep.	Jan. 13, 1873..	"	....
Thos. B. Needles, Rep.......	Jan. 8, 1877..	Washington..	....
Chas. P. Swigert, Rep.......	Jan. 10, 1881..	Kankakee....	....
Chas. P. Swigert, Rep	Jan. 30, 1885..	Kankakee....	....
Charles W. Pavey, Rep,.....	Jan. 14, 1889..	Jefferson......	....
David Gore, Dem...........	Jan. 9, 1893..	Macoupin	....
James S. McCullough, Rep.	Jan. 11, 1897..	Champaign...	....

STATE TREASURERS.

Name.	Date of Com'n. or Qualified.	From what county.	Remarks.
John Thomas, Dem.........	1818..	St. Clair......	....
R. K. McLaughlin, Dem...	Aug. 2, 1819..	Fayette.......	....
Abner Field, Dem...........	Jan. 14, 1823..	Union........	....
James Hall, Dem	Feb. 12, 1827..	Jackson	....
John Dement, Dem.........	Feb. 1, 1831..	Franklin . ..	Resigned Dec. 3, 1836.................
Charles Gregory, Dem	Dec. 5, 1836..	Greene	....
John D. Whiteside, Dem ...	Mch. 4, 1837..	Monroe	....
Milton Carpenter, Dem	Mch. 6, 1841..	Hamilton.....	Died.
John Moore, Dem	Aug. 14, 1848..	McLean.......	Appointed, vice Carpenter
John Moore, Dem	Dec. 16, 1850..	McLean.......	Elected.
James Miller, Rep..........	Jan. 12, 1857..	McLean.......	Resigned Sept. 3, 1859.
William Butler, Rep........	Sept. 3, 1859..	Sangamon....	Appointed, vice Miller.
William Butler, Rep	Jan. 14, 1861..	Sangamon....	....
Alexander Starne, Dem....	Jan. 12, 1863..	Sangamon....	....
James H. Beveridge, Rep..	Jan. 9, 1865..	DeKalb	....
George W. Smith, Rep	Jan. 10, 1867..	Cook..........	....
Erastus N. Bates, Rep......	Jan. 11, 1869..	Marion	....
Erastus N. Bates, Rep......	Nov. 8, 1870..	Marion	....
Edward Rutz, Rep..........	Jan. 13, 1873..	St. Clair......	....
Thos. S. Ridgway, Rep. ..	Jan. 11, 1875..	Gallatin	....
Edward Rutz, Rep..........	Jan. 8, 1877..	St. Clair......	....
John C. Smith, Rep...... ...	Jan. 13, 1879..	Jo Daviess....	....
Edward Rutz, Rep..........	Jan. 10, 1881..	Cook..	....
John C. Smith, Rep.........	Jan. 5, 1883..	Jo Daviess ...	....
Jacob Gross, Rep	Jan. 30, 1885..	Cook..........	....
John R. Tanner, Rep.......	Jan. 6, 1887..	Clay..........	....
Charles Becker, Rep........	Jan. 14, 1889..	St. Clair......	....
Edward S. Wilson, Dem ...	Jan. 12, 1891..	Richland	....
Rufus N. Ramsay, Dem	Jan. 9, 1893..	Clinton	Died Nov. 11, 1894.
Elijah P. Ramsay, Dem	Nov. 14, 1894..	Clinton	By app. of Gov., vice Ramsay, dec.
Henry Wulff, Rep.....	Jan. 14, 1895..	Cook	....
Henry L. Hertz, Rep.......	Jan. 11, 1897..	Cook..........	....

SUPERINTENDENTS OF PUBLIC INSTRUCTION.

Name.	Date Com'n. or Qualified.	County.	Remarks.
Ninian W. Edwards, Dem..	Mch. 24, 1854..	Sangamon....	Appointed by the Governor.
Wm. H. Powell, Rep	Jan. 12, 1857..	Peoria	....
Newton Bateman, Rep.....	Aug. 1, 1859..	Morgan........	....
Newton Bateman, Rep.....	Jan. 4, 1861..	Morgan......	....
John P. Brooks, Dem	Jan. 12, 1863 .	Sangamon....	....
Newton Bateman, Rep. ...	Jan. 10, 1865..	Sangamon....	....
Newton Bateman, Rep.....	Jan. 10, 1867..	Sangamon....	....
Newton Bateman, Rep.....	Nov. 8, 1870..	Sangamon....	Term extended to 4 years.
Sam'l M. Etter, Dem	Jan. 11, 1875	McLean.......	....
James P. Slade, Rep........	Jan. 13, 1879..	St. Clair......	....
Henry Raab, Dem..........	Jan. 5, 1883..	St. Clair......	....
Richard Edwards, Rep.....	Jan. 6, 1887..	Bureau	....
Henry Raab, Dem..........	Jan. 12, 1891..	St. Clair	....
Samuel M. Inglis, Rep......	Jan. 14, 1895..	Jackson	....

ATTORNEYS GENERAL.

Name.	Qualified.	County.	Remarks.
Daniel Pope Cook, Dem....	Mch. 5,1819..	Randolph	Resigned March 5,1819.
William Mears, Dem..	Dec. 14,1819..	St. Clair......	....
Samuel D. Lockwood, Dem.	Feb. 26,1821..	Madison......	Resigned Dec. 28,1822.
James Turney,Dem.........	Jan. 14,1823..	Washington..	Resigned Jan. 7, 1825.
James Turney,Dem.........	Jan. 15,1825..	"	....
George Forquer, Dem	Jan. 23,1829..	Monroe.	Resigned Dec. 3,1832.
James Semple, Dem.........	Jan. 30,1833..	Madison......	....
Ninian W. Edwards, Dem.	Sept. 1,1834..	Sangamon ...	....
Ninian W. Edwards, Dem	Jan. 19,1835..	"	Resigned Feb. 7,1835.
Jesse B. Thomas,Jr, Dem.	Feb. 12,1835..	Madison......	Resigned Jan. 8,1836.
Walter B. Scates,Dem.....	Jan. 16,1836..	Jefferson.....	Resigned Dec. 26,1836.
Usher F. Linder,Dem......	Feb. 4,1837..	Coles	Resigned June 11,1838.
George W. Olney,Dem.....	June 26,1838..	Madison	Resigned Feb. 1,1839.
Wickliffe Kitchell,Dem...	Mch. 5,1839..	Crawford.....	Resigned Nov. 19,1840.
Josiah Lamborn,Dem.......	Dec. 23,1840..	Morgan	....
James A. McDougall, Dem.	Jan. 12,1843..	"	....
David B. Campbell, Dem...	Dec. 21,1846..	Sangamon ...	....
Robert G. Ingersoll,Rep ..	Feb. 28,1867..	Peoria........	Appointed by Gov. Oglesby.
Washington Bushnell, Rep.	Jan. 11,1869..	LaSalle	....
James K. Edsall, Rep......	Jan. 13,1873..	Lee..........	....
James K. Edsall, Rep.......	Jan. 8,1877..	"	....
James McCartney,Rep	Jan. 10,1881..	Wayne........	....
George Hunt, Rep..	Jan. 30,1885..	Edgar.........	....
George Hunt, Rep....	Jan. 14,1889..	Edgar.........	....
Maurice T. Moloney, Dem..	Jan. 9,1893..	LaSalle	....
Edward C. Akin, Rep......	Jan. 11, 1897..	Will....... . .	....

STATE GEOLOGISTS.

Name.	Appointed.	County.	Remarks.
Joseph G. Norwood.........	July 21,1851..	Sangamon ...	Act of Feb. 17,1851.
Amos H. Worthen	Mch. 22,1858..	Hancock	Died May 6,1888.
Josua Lindahl...............	June 9,1888..	Rock Island..	....
Wm. F. E. Gurley...........	July 14,1893..	Vermilion....	Vice Lindahl.
C. H. Crantz.................	Feb. 10, 1897..	Cook..........	Vice Gurley.......... ....

STATE ENTOMOLOGISTS.

Name.	Appointed	County.	Remarks.
D. B. Walsh	June 11,1867..	Rock Island..	Died.
Wm. LeBarron	April 2,1870 .	Kane..........	Died.
Cyrus Thomas......	April 13,1875..	Jackson	....
S. A. Forbes	July 3,1882..	McLean......	....

ADJUTANTS GENERAL.

Term, two years.

Name.	Appointed.	County.	Remarks.
Wm. Alexander, Dem	April 24, 1819	Randolph	
Elijah C. Berry, Dem	June 11, 1821	Fayette	
James W. Berry, Dem	Dec. 19, 1828	"	Resigned Nov. 11, 1839.
Moses K. Anderson, Dem	Dec. 16, 1839	Sangamon	
Simon B. Buckner, Dem	April 3, 1857	Cook	Resigned Nov. 7, 1857.
William C. Kinney, Rep	Dec. 9, 1857	St. Clair	Died.
Thomas S. Mather, Rep	Oct. 28, 1858	Sangamon	Vice Kinney, deceased.
Allen C. Fuller, Rep	Nov. 11, 1861	Boone	
Isham N. Haynie, Rep	Jan. 16, 1865	Alexander	Died.
Edward P. Niles, Rep		Cook	Acting *ad interim*.
Hubert Dilger, Rep	Mch. 24, 1869	Sangamon	
Edwin L. Higgins, Rep	Jan. 24, 1873	"	
Edwin L. Higgins, Rep	July 1, 1874	"	Removed July 2, 1875.
Hiram Hilliard, Rep	July 2, 1875	Cook	
Hiram Hilliard, Rep	July 2, 1877	"	
Isaac H. Elliott, Rep	Aug. 1, 1881	Bureau	
Joseph W. Vance, Rep	May 15, 1884	Edgar	
Jasper N. Reece, Rep	June 28, 1891	Sangamon	
Alfred Orendorff, Dem	Jan. 20, 1893	Sangamon	
Charles C. Hilton, Dem	Jan. 4, 1896	Cook	Vice Orendorff, resigned Jan. 4, '96.
Jasper N. Reece, Rep	Feb. 2, 1897	Sangamon	Vice Hilton, resigned

BOARD OF R. R. AND WAREHOUSE COMMISSIONERS.

Term, two years.

Name.	Appointed.	County.	Remarks.
Gustavus Koerner, Rep	July 1, 1871	St. Clair	
Daniel S. Hammond, Rep	July 1, 1871	Cook	
Richard P. Morgan, Dem	July 1, 1871	McLean	
H. D. Cook, Rep	Mch. 13, 1873	McLean	Died.
David A. Brown, Dem	Mch. 13, 1873	Sangamon	
John M. Pearson, Rep	Mch. 13, 1873	Madison	
James Steele, Rep	Dec. 15, 1873	Edgar	Vice Cook.
John M. Pearson, Rep	Jan. 1, 1875	Madison	
David A. Brown, Dem	Jan. 1, 1875	Sangamon	
James Steele, Rep	Jan. 1, 1875	Edgar	
*William M. Smith, Rep	Feb. 21, 1877	McLean	
*George M. Bogue, Rep	Feb. 21, 1877	Cook	
*John H. Oberly, Dem	Feb. 21, 1877	Alexander	
Wm. H. Robinson, Rep	Feb. 10, 1881	Wayne	Vice Oberly.
William H. Smith, Rep	Mch. 26, 1881	McLean	
George M. Bogue, Rep	Mch. 26, 1881	Cook	
William N. Brainard, Rep	Mch. 8, 1883	Cook	
Edward C. Lewis, Rep	Mch. 8, 1883	LaSalle	
Chas. T. Strattan, Rep	Mch. 8, 1883	Jefferson	
John I. Rinaker, Rep	April 8, 1885	Macoupin	
Benj. F. Marsh, Rep	April 8, 1885	Hancock	
Wm. T. Johnson, Rep	April 8, 1885	Cook	
John I. Rinaker, Rep	April 8, 1887	Macoupin	
Benj. F. Marsh, Rep	April 8, 1887	Hancock	
Jason Rogers, Rep	April 8, 1887	Macon	Vice Johnson.
John R. Wheeler, Rep	Feb. 27, 1889	Cook	
Isaac N. Phillips, Rep	Feb. 27, 1889	McLean	
W. L. Crim, Rep	Feb. 27, 1889	Franklin	
John R. Wheeler, Rep	Mch. 18, 1891	Cook	
Isaac N. Phillips, Rep	Mch. 18, 1891	McLean	
John R. Tanner, Rep	Mch. 18, 1891	Clay	Resigned.
J. C. Willis, Rep	Oct. 3, 1891	Massac	Vice Tanner.
Thomas Gahan, Dem	Jan. 18, 1893	Cook	
Chas. F. Lape, Dem	Jan. 18, 1893	Sangamon	
William S. Cantrell, Dem	Jan. 18, 1893	Franklin	
George W. Fithian, Dem	Aug. 8, 1895	Jasper	Vice Lape, resigned Aug., '95
Cicero J. Lindly, Rep	Feb. 3, 1897	Bond	
Charles S. Rannells, Rep	Feb. 3, 1897	Morgan	
Joseph E. Bidwell, Rep	Feb. 3, 1897	Cook	

*All three were re-appointed Jan. 20, 1879.

CHIEF GRAIN INSPECTORS.

Term, two years.

Name.	Appointed.	County.	Remarks.
Wm. F. Tompkins, Rep...	July 3, 1871..	Cook..........	Removed April 1, 1873.
Wm. H. Harper, Rep........	April 1, 1873..	Cook..........	Vice Tompkins.
John C. Smith, Rep.........	April 24, 1875..	Jo Daviess ...	....
William H. Swett, Rep.....	Aug. 7, 1877..	Cook	Removed April 24, 1878.
John P. Reynolds, Rep	April 24, 1878..	Cook..........	Resigned.
P. Bird Price, Rep...........	Aug. 31, 1882..	Cook	Vice Reynolds.
Frank Drake, Rep...........	July 25, 1883..	Cook	....
P. Bird Price, Rep....... ...	July 22, 1885..	Cook..........	....
P. Bird Price, Rep...........	July 25, 1887..	Cook	....
P. Bird Price, Rep...........	July 1, 1889..	Cook..........	....
P. Bird Price, Rep...........	Aug. 4, 1891..	Cook	....
George P. Bunker, Dem.....	Mch. 2, 1893..	Cook..........	Resigned Dec. 16, 1895.
Dwight W. Andrews, Dem..	Dec. 17, 1895..	Cook...... ...	Vice Bunker.
Edwin J. Noble, Rep.........	Feb. 3, 1897..	Cook...... .	Vice Andrews.

BOARD OF FISH COMMISSIONERS.

Term, three years.

Name..	Appointed.	Post Office.	Remarks
W. A. Pratt, Rep............	May 24, 1875..	Elgin..........	....
N. K. Fairbank, Rep........	July 20, 1878..	Chicago.......	....
N. K. Fairbank, Rep........	July 2, 1879..	Chicago.......	....
S. P. Bartlett, Rep..........	July 2, 1879..	Quincy.........	....
J. Smith Briggs, Rep........	July 2, 1879..	Kankakee	....
S. P. McDole, Rep	Mch. 26, 1881..	Sugar Grove..	Vice Briggs..........................
S. P. Bartlett, Rep..........	July 11, 1881..	Quincy	Own successor,........ ....
N. K. Fairbank, Rep........	July 10, 1882..	Chicago.	Own successor...... ....
George Breuning, Rep	Oct. 30, 1883..	Centralia.....	Vice McDole.........................
George Breuning, Rep	July 2, 1886..	Centralia.....	Own successor.......................
S. P. Bartlett, Rep..........	Aug. 2, 1884..	Quincy	Own successor. ....
N. K. Fairbank, Rep........	July 10, 1885..	Chicago.	Own successor..... ....
S. P. Bartlett, Rep	Aug. 12, 1887..	Quincy..... ..	Own successor.......................
N. K. Fairbank, Rep........	Sept. 12, 1888..	Chicago.......	Own successor.......................
George Breuning, Rep......	July 3, 1889..	Centralia......	Own successor.......................
S. P. Bartlett, Rep..........	Sept. 9, 1890..	Quincy	Resigned July 14, 1893..........
N. K. Fairbank, Rep..	Sept. 19, 1891..	Chicago........	Rejected by Senate Feb 2, 1893 ....
George Breuning, Rep	July 16, 1892..	Centralia.. ...	Rejected by Senate Feb. 2, 1893.....
George W. Langford, Dem	July 14, 1893..	Havana.......	Vice Bartlett Langford Died Oct., '96
Richard Roe, Dem...........	July 14, 1893..	East St. Louis	Vice Breuning.........................
D. J. Sickler, Dem...........	July 29, 1893..	Geneva........	Vice Fairbank........................
Henry Schmidt, Dem........	Jan. 16, 1894..	Elgin	Vice Sickler, died..... ....
S. P. Bartlett, Rep...........	April 13, 1897..	Quincy........	....
Nathan H. Cohen, Rep.....	April 13, 1897..	Urbana........	....
August Lenke, Rep..........	April 13, 1897..	Chicago......	....

COMMISSION OF CLAIMS.

Term, four years. Auditor Public Accounts, Clerk of Commission ex-officio.

Name.	Appointed.	Post Office.	Remarks.
E. D. Blinn, Rep............	July 2, 1889..	Lincoln........	....
R. D. Adams, Rep............	July 2, 1889..	Fairfield.......	....
W. S. Kay, Dem..............	July 2, 1889..	Watseka.......	....
W. H. Dawdy, Dem..........	July 15, 1893..	Greenville....	To succeed Blinn....................
Samuel Alschuler, Dem.....	July 15, 1893..	Aurora	To succeed Kay.......................
H. G. Reeves, Rep...........	July 29, 1894..	Bloomington	To succeed Adams..................
Walter S. Louden, Rep......	April 7, 1897..	Carlyle.........	To succeed Dawdy...... ....
John C. McKenzie, Rep.....	April 7, 1897..	Elizabeth.....	To succeed Reeves..................
William C. Jones, Dem......	April 7, 1897..	Robinson.....	To succeed Alschuler........ ....

LEGISLATIVE DEPARTMENT.

APPORTIONMENT.

The following are the apportionments for members of the General Assembly from 1818 to 1893, inclusive:

APPORTIONMENT UNDER THE CONSTITUTION OF 1818.

Section 5, Article II. of the constitution of 1818 provided that—

"The number of Senators and Representatives shall, at the first session of the General Assembly holden after the returns herein provided for are made, be fixed by the General Assembly, and apportioned among the several counties or districts to be established by law, according to the number of white inhabitants. The number of Representatives shall not be less than twenty-seven nor more than thirty-six, until the number of inhabitants within this State shall amount to 100,000; and the number of Senators shall never be less than one-third or more than one-half of the number of Representatives."

Section 8 of the Schedule provided that the representation of the first General Assembly should be as follows:

"Section 8. Until the first census shall be taken as directed by this constitution, the county of Madison shall be entitled to one Senator and three Representatives; the county of St. Clair, to one Senator and three Representatives; the county of Bond, to one Senator and one Representative; the county of Washington, to one Senator and one Representative; the county of Monroe, to one Senator and one Representative; the county of Randolph, to one Senator and two Representatives; the county of Jackson, to one Senator and one Representative; the counties of Johnson and Franklin, to form one Senatorial district, and to be entitled to one Senator, and each county one Representative; the county of Union, to one Senator and two Representatives; the county of Pope, to one Senator and two Representatives; the county of Gallatin, to one Senator and three Representatives; the county of White, to one Senator and three Representatives; the county of Edwards, to one Senator and three Representatives; and the county of Crawford, to one Senator and two Representatives."

Apportionments were made by law as follows:

Feb. 14, 1821: Senate, 18; House, 36. Jan. 12, 1826: Senate, 19; House, 36. Feb. 7, 1831: Senate, 26; House, 55. Jan. 14, 1836, the ratio for a Senator was fixed at 7,000 white inhabitants, and for a Representative, 3,000. By this law the State was entitled to 40 Senators and 91 Representatives. Feb. 26, 1841, the ratio for a Senator was fixed at 12,000, and for a Representative, 4,000. The Senate consisted of 41 members, and the House of Representatives of 121 members.

Under the last two apportionments made, the membership of the General Assembly varies one or two from the number designated by the acts—probably owing to a variation of population.

Feb. 25, 1847, another apportionment was made, by which the ratio was fixed at 19,000 for a Senator, and 6,500 for a Representative. The Senate was made to consist of 34 and the House 100 members; but before an election was held under this law the constitution of 1848 was adopted, and the apportionment made thereby took effect.

APPORTIONMENT UNDER THE CONSTITUTION OF 1848.

Section 6, Article III., of the constitution of 1848 provided:

"Section 6. The Senate shall consist of 25 members, and the House of Representatives shall consist of 75 members, until the population of the State shall amount to one million of souls, when five members may be added to the House and five additional members for every 500,000 inhabitants thereafter, until the whole number of Representatives shall amount to 100; after which, the number shall neither be increased nor diminished; to be apportioned among the several counties according to the number of white inhabitants. In all future apportionments, where more than one county shall be thrown into a representative district, all the Representatives to which said counties may be entitled shall be elected by the entire district." By section 8 of the same article, an apportionment was required to be made in the year 1855, and every tenth year thereafter. Section 40, same article, apportioned the representation in the General Assembly at 25 Senators and 75 Representatives, and divided the State into districts, as follows:

SENATORIAL.

1—Alexander, Union, Pulaski, Johnson, Massac, Pope, Hardin.
2—Gallatin, Saline, Williamson, Franklin, White.
3—Jefferson, Wayne, Marion, Hamilton.
4—Washington, Perry, Randolph, Jackson.
5—St. Clair, Monroe.
6—Madison, Clinton.
7—Christian, Shelby, Montgomery, Bond, Fayette.
8—Effingham, Jasper, Clay, Richland, Lawrence, Edwards, Wabash.
9—Edgar, Clark, Crawford.
10—Vermilion, Champaign, Piatt, Moultrie, Coles, Cumberland.
11—Tazewell, McLean, Logan, DeWitt, Macon.
12—Sangamon, Menard, Mason.
13—Macoupin, Jersey, Greene, Calhoun.
14—Morgan, Scott, Cass.
15—Adams, Pike.
16—McDonough, Schuyler, Brown, Highland.
17—Hancock, Henderson.
18—Fulton, Peoria.
19—Rock Island, Henry, Mercer, Warren, Knox, Stark.
20—LaSalle, Bureau, Putnam, Marshall, Woodford, Livingston, Grundy.
21—DuPage, Kendall, Will, Iroquois.
22—Ogle, Lee, DeKalb, Kane.
23—JoDaviess, Stephenson, Carroll, Whiteside.
24—McHenry, Boone, Winnebago.
25—Cook, Lake.

REPRESENTATIVE.

1—Union, Alexander, Pulaski; one.
2—Massac, Pope, Hardin; one.
3—Gallatin, Saline; one.
4—Johnson, Williamson; one.
5—Jackson, Franklin, one.
6—Marion, Jefferson, Wayne, Hamilton, 3.
7—White; one.
8—Wabash, Edwards; one.
9—Lawrence, Richland; one.
10—Crawford, Jasper; one.
11—Coles; one.
12—Clark; one.
13—Cumberland, Effingham, Clay; one.
14—Fayette; one.
15—Montgomery, Bond, Clinton; two.
16—Washington, Perry; one.
17—Randolph; one.
18—Monroe; one.
19—St. Clair; two.
20—Madison; two.
21—Macoupin; one.
22—Jersey, Greene; two.
23—Scott; one.
24—Morgan; two.
25—Cass, Menard; one.
26—Sangamon; two.
27—Mason, Logan; one.
28—Tazewell; one.
29—McLean, DeWitt; one.
30—Vermilion; one.
31—Edgar; one.
32—Champaign, Piatt, Moultrie, Macon; one.
33—Shelby, Christian; one.
34—Pike, Calhoun; two.
35—Adams, Highland, Brown; three.
36—Schuyler; one.
37—Hancock, two.
38—McDonough; one.
39—Fulton; two.
40—Peoria; one.
41—Knox; one.
42—Warren, Mercer, Henderson; two.
43—Rock Island, Henry, Stark; one.
44—Whiteside, Lee; one.
45—Carroll, Ogle; one.
46—JoDaviess, Stephenson; two.
47—Winnebago; one.
48—Putnam, Marshall, Woodford; one.
49—LaSalle, Grundy, Livingston, Bureau; two.
50—DuPage, Kendall, Will, Iroquois; three.
51—Kane, DeKalb; two.
52—Boone, McHenry; two.
53—Lake; one.
54—Cook; two.

APPORTIONMENT OF 1854.

The Act of Feb. 27, 1854, apportioned the representation in the General Assembly at 25 Senators, and 75 Representatives, and divided the State into districts as follows:

SENATORIAL.

1—Cook.
2—Lake, McHenry.
3—Boone, Winnebago, Ogle, Carroll.
4—JoDaviess, Stephenson.
5—Kane, DeKalb, Lee, Whiteside.
6—Will, DuPage, Kendall, Iroquois, Kankakee.
7—LaSalle, Grundy, Livingston, Bureau.
8—Peoria, Marshall, Putnam, Woodford.
9—Knox, Warren, Mercer, Rock Island, Henry, Stark.
10—Fulton, McDonough.
11—Schuyler, Henderson, Hancock.
12—Adams, Brown.
13—Pike, Calhoun, Scott.
14—Greene, Macoupin, Jersey.
15—Sangamon, Morgan.
16—Champaign, DeWitt, Piatt, Macon, Moultrie, Christian, Shelby, McLean.
17—Cass, Menard, Logan, Mason, Tazewell.
18—Vermilion, Coles, Cumberland, Edgar.
19—Clark, Fayette, Effingham, Jasper, Lawrence, Crawford.
20—Jefferson, Wayne, Edwards, Wabash, Marion, Clay, Richland.
21—Madison, Bond, Montgomery.
22—Monroe, St. Clair.
23—Williamson, Saline, White, Hamilton, Franklin.
24—Randolph, Washington, Clinton, Perry, Jackson.
25—Alexander, Union, Johnson, Pulaski, Massac, Pope, Hardin, Gallatin.

REPRESENTATIVES.

1—Alexander, Pulaski, Union; one.
2—Pope, Hardin, Massac; one.
3—Williamson, Johnson; one.
4—Gallatin, Saline; one.
5—Franklin, Jackson; one.
6—Randolph; one.
7—Washington, Perry; one.
8—Jefferson, Marion, Hamilton; two.
9—Wabash, White; one.
10—Wayne, Edwards; one.
11—Monroe; one.
12—St. Clair; two.
13—Clinton, Bond; one.
14—Madison; two.
15—Fayette, Effingham; one.
16—Clay, Richland, Jasper; one.
17—Lawrence, Crawford; one.
18—Clark; one.
19—Cumberland, Shelby; one.
20—Montgomery, Christian; one.
21—Macoupin; one.
22—Jersey, Calhoun; one.

23—Greene; one.
24—Edgar; one.
25—Coles, Moultrie; one.
26—Sangamon; two.
27—Morgan, Scott; two.
28—Pike, Brown; two.
29—Adams; two.
30—Schuyler; one
31—Hancock; one.
32—McDonough; one.
33—Fulton; two.
34—Cass, Menard; one.
35—Mason, Logan; one.
36—Macon, DeWitt, Platt, Champaign; one.
37—Vermilion; one.
38—McLean; two.
39—Tazewell; one.
40—Henderson, Warren; one.
41—Peoria, Stark; two.
42—Marshall, Woodford, Putnam; one.
43—LaSalle, Livingston, Grundy; two.
44—Kendall; one.
45—Iroquois, Will, DuPage, Kankakee; three.
46—Kane, DeKalb; two.
47—Bureau; one.
48—Mercer, Henry, Rock Island; one.
49—Lee, Whiteside. one.
50—Ogle; one.
51—Carroll, JoDaviess; two.
52—Stephenson; one.
53—Winnebago; one.
54—Boone, McHenry; two.
55—Lake; one.
56—South Chicago, Lyons, Lake, Lemont, Palos, Worth, Orland, Breinen, Thornton, Rich, and Bloom, in Cook county; 2.
57—West Chicago, North Chicago, Jefferson, Leyden, Ridgeville, Niles, Maine, Elk Grove, Schaumburg, Hanover, Northfield, Wheeling, Palatine, Barrington, Proviso, and New Trier, in Cook Co.; 2.
58—Knox; one.

APPORTIONMENT OF 1861.

By act of Jan. 31, 1861, the representation was fixed at 25 Senators and 85 Representatives, and the State divided into 25 Senatorial and 61 Representative districts, as follows:

SENATORIAL.

1—Alexander, Pulaski, Massac, Union, Johnson, Pope, Hardin, Gallatin, Saline.
2—Hamilton, Wabash, Edwards, Wayne, Clay, Richland, White, Lawrence.
3—Williamson, Franklin, Jackson, Jefferson, Randolph, Monroe.
4—Perry, Washington, Clinton, Marion, Fayette, Bond.
5—St. Clair, Madison.
6—Jersey, Calhoun, Greene, Scott, Pike.
7—Macoupin, Montgomery, Christian, Shelby.
8—Effingham, Jasper, Crawford, Cumberland, Clark, Edgar.
9—Coles, Douglas, Champaign, Vermilion, Iroquois, Ford.
10—McLean, DeWitt, Platt, Moultrie, Macon.
11—Tazewell, Logan, Sangamon.
12—Menard, Cass, Schuyler, Brown, Morgan.
13—Adams, Hancock.
14—McDonough, Henderson, Mercer, Warren.
15—Mason, Fulton, Knox.
16—Peoria, Stark, Marshall, Putnam.
17—Woodford, Livingston, LaSalle.
18—Kankakee, Grundy, Will, Kendall.
19—DuPage, Kane, DeKalb.
20—Ogle, Lee, Whiteside.
21—Bureau, Henry, Rock Island.
22—Carroll, Jo Daviess, Stephenson.
23—Winnebago, Boone. McHenry, Lake.
24—North Chicago, South Chicago, Lake, Worth, Thornton, Bloom, of Cook Co.
25—Lakeview, Evanston, New Trier, Northfield, Wheeling, Palatine, Barrington, Hanover, Schaumburg, Elk Grove, Maine, Niles, West Chicago, Cicero, Jefferson, Leyden, Proviso, Lyons, Palos, Lemont, Orland, Rich, Bremen, in Cook county.

REPRESENTATIVE.

1—Union, Pulaski, Alexander; one.
2—Massac, Pope, Johnson; one.
3—Hardin, Saline, Gallatin; one.
4—Lawrence, Wabash; one.
5—Franklin, Jefferson; one.
6—Jackson, Williamson; one.
7—Clinton, Washington; one.
8—Monroe, Randolph, Perry; two.
9—Marion; one.
10—Wayne, Hamilton; one.
11—Jasper, Crawford; one.
12—Clay, Richland; one.
13—Fayette, Effingham; one.
14—Edwards, White; one.
15—St. Clair; two.
16—Madison, Bond; two.
17—Clark, Cumberland; one.
18—Shelby; one.
19—Christian, Montgomery; one.
20—Sangamon, Logan; two.
21—Macoupin; one.
22—Jersey, Calhoun; one.
23—Greene; one.
24—Pike, Scott; two.
25—Cass, Brown, one.
26—Mason, Menard; one.
27—Morgan; one.
28—Adams; two.
29—McDonough, one.
30—Schuyler; one.
31—Hancock; one.
32—Henderson, Mercer; one
33—Warren; one.
34—Knox; one.
35—Fulton; two.
36—Peoria, Stark; two.
37—Tazewell; one.
38—McLean, DeWitt; two.
39—Coles, Douglas, Vermilion, Edgar; three.
40—Champaign, Platt, Macon, Moultrie; two.
41—Kankakee; one.
42—Iroquois, Ford; one.
43—Will, Grundy; two.
44—LaSalle, Livingston; three.
45—Bureau, Putnam, Marshall, Woodford; three.
46—Henry; one.
47—Rock Island; one.
48—Whiteside; one.
49—Lee; one.
50—Ogle; one.
51—DeKalb, Boone; two.
52—Kane, Kendall; two.
53—Lake; one.
54—McHenry; one.
55—Winnebago; one.
56—Stephenson; one.
57—JoDaviess, Carroll; two.
58—DuPage; one.
59—West Chicago, Cicero, Jefferson, Leyden, Proviso, Lyons, Palos, Lemont, Orland, Bremen and Rich, in Cook county; three.
60—South Chicago, Lake, Worth, Thornton, and Bloom, in Cook county; two
61—North Chicago, Lakeview, Evanston, New Trier, Northfield, Wheeling, Palatine, Barrington, Hanover, Schaumburg. Elk Grove, Maine and Niles, in Cook county; two.

APPORTIONMENT UNDER THE CONSTITUTION OF 1870.

Section 13 of the Schedule, constitution of 1870, provided that, upon the adoption of the new constitution, the Governor and Secretary of State should immediately thereafter proceed to fix the apportionment for members of the House of Representatives; the apportionment to be based upon the United States Census of 1870, if the same should be ascertained in time therefor; if not, then to be based upon the State Census of 1865. The ratio of representation in the House was to be ascertained by dividing the population of the State by 153—the quotient to be the ratio; every county or district, when its population amounted to three-fifths of the ratio, to be entitled to one representative; each county or district having a population equal to a ratio and three-fifths, to be entitled to two representatives, and for each additional number of inhabitants equal to the ratio, one representative.

Section 14 of the Schedule directed that the districts should be regularly numbered, commencing with Alexander county, proceeding northwardly, and terminating with Cook.

Section 15 of the Schedule provided that the Senate, at its first session under the constitution of 1870, should consist of 50 members, being two for each district under the constitution of 1848.

The Minority-Representation section having been adopted, the legislative article of the constitution provides as follows:

The General Assembly shall apportion the State every ten years, beginning with the year 1871, by dividing the population of the State by 51, and the quotient shall be the ratio for representation in the Senate. The State shall be divided into 51 senatorial districts, each of which shall elect one senator, whose term of office shall be four years. The senators are elected every two years, in odd and even-numbered districts alternately, beginning with the even-numbered districts in 1872.

The House of Representatives consists of three times the number of members of the Senate, and the term of office is two years. Three representatives are elected in each senatorial district, at each general election for members of the General Assembly; the election occurring in each even-numbered year, on the first Tuesday after the first Monday in the month of November. Each qualified voter may cast as many votes for one candidate as there are representatives to be elected, or may distribute the same, or equal parts thereof, among the candidates, as he shall see fit; and the candidates highest in votes shall be declared elected.

APPORTIONMENT OF 1870.

The representation in the Twenty-seventh General Assembly, which convened Jan. 4, 1871, being the first under the constitution of 1870, as apportioned by the Governor and Secretary of State, consisted of 50 Senators and 177 Representatives, and the State was divided into districts as follows:

SENATORIAL.

1—Alexander, Pulaski, Massac, Hardin, Union, Pope, Johnson, Gallatin, Saline.
2—Hamilton, Wabash, Edwards, Wayne, Clay, Richland, White, Lawrence.
3—Williamson, Franklin, Jackson, Jefferson, Randolph, Monroe.
4—Perry, Washington, Clinton, Marion, Fayette, Bond.
5—St. Clair, Madison.
6—Jersey, Calhoun, Greene, Scott, Pike.
7—Macoupin, Montgomery, Shelby, Christian.
8—Effingham, Jasper, Cumberland, Crawford, Clark, Edgar.
9—Coles, Douglas, Champaign, Vermilion, Iroquois, Ford.
10—McLean, DeWitt, Platt, Moultrie, Macon.
11—Tazewell, Logan, Sangamon.
12—Menard, Cass, Schuyler, Brown, Morgan.
13—Adams, Hancock.
14—McDonough, Henderson, Mercer, Warren
15—Mason, Fulton, Knox.
16—Peoria, Stark, Marshall, Putnam.
17—Woodford, Livingston, LaSalle.
18—Kankakee, Grundy, Kendall, Will.
19—DuPage, Kane, DeKalb.
20—Ogle, Lee, Whiteside.
21—Bureau, Henry, Rock Island.
22—Carroll, JoDaviess, Stephenson.
23—Winnebago, Boone, McHenry, Lake.
24—North Chicago, South Chicago, Lake, Worth, Thornton, Bloom, in Cook county.
25—Lakeview, Evanston, New Trier, Northfield, Wheeling, Palatine, Barrington, Hanover, Schaumburg, Elk Grove, Maine, Niles, West Chicago, Cicero, Jefferson, Leyden, Proviso, Lyons, Palos, Lemont, Orland, Rich, Bremen, in Cook county.

REPRESENTATIVES.

1—Alexander, one.
2—Pulaski, Massac; one.
3—Pope; one.
4—Johnson; one.
5—Union; one.
6—Jackson; one.
7—Williamson; one.
8—Saline; one.
9—Gallatin, Hardin; one.
10—White; one.
11—Hamilton; one.
12—Franklin; one.
13—Perry; one.
14—Randolph; two.
15—Monroe; one.
16—St. Clair; three.
17—Washington; one.
18—Jefferson; one.
19—Wayne; one.
20—Edwards, Wabash; one.
21—Lawrence; one.
22—Richland; one.

23—Clay; one.
24—Marion; two.
25—Clinton; one.
26—Madison; three.
27—Bond; one.
28—Fayette; one.
29—Effingham; one.
30—Jasper; one.
31—Crawford; one.
32—Clark; one.
33—Cumberland; one.
34—Shelby; two.
35—Christian; two.
36—Montgomery; two.
37—Macoupin; two.
38—Jersey; two
39—Greene; one.
40—Pike; two.
41—Scott; one.
42—Morgan; two.
43—Sangamon; three.
44—Macon; two.
45—Moultrie; one.
46—Coles; two.
47—Edgar; two.
48—Douglas; one.
49—Vermilion; two.
50—Champaign; two.
51—Platt; one.
52—De Witt; one.
53—Logan; two.
54—Cass, Menard; two.
55—Brown; one.
56—Schuyler; one.
57—Adams; four.
58—Hancock; two.
59—McDonough; two.
60—Fulton; three.
61—Mason; one.
62—Tazewell; two.
63—McLean; four.
64—Iroquois; two.
65—Livingston; two.
66—Woodford; one.
67—Peoria; three.
68—Knox; three.
69—Warren; two.
70—Henderson; one.
71—Mercer; one.
72—Rock Island; two.
73—Henry; two.
74—Stark; one.
75—Marshall, Putnam; two.
76—Bureau; two.
77—LaSalle; four.
78—Grundy; one.
79—Kankakee, Ford; two.
80—Will; three.
81—Kendall; one.
82—DuPage; one.
83—Kane; three.
84—DeKalb; two.
85—Lee; two.
86—Ogle; two.
87—Whiteside; two.
88—Carroll; one.
89—JoDaviess; two.
90—Stephenson; two.
91—Winnebago; two.
92—Boone; one.
93—McHenry; two.
94—Lake; two.
95—West Chicago, and other towns in Cook; ten.
96—South Chicago, and other towns in Cook; six.
97—North Chicago, and other towns in Cook; six.

APPORTIONMENT OF 1872.

By the act of March 1, 1872, the State was divided into Senatorial districts as provided by the constitution, each district being entitled to one Senator and three Representatives, as follows:

SENATORIAL DISTRICTS.

1—First, Second, Tenth, Eleventh Wards of Chicago.
2—Third, Fourth, Fifth Wards of Chicago, and the towns of Hyde Park and Lake, in Cook county.
3—Sixth, Seventh and Eighth Wards of Chicago.
4—Ninth, Twelfth and Thirteenth Wards of Chicago.
5—Fourteenth, Fifteenth and Eighteenth Wards of Chicago.
6—Sixteenth, Seventeenth, Nineteenth and Twentieth Wards of Chicago.
7—The towns of New Trier, Northfield, Wheeling, Palatine, Barrington, Hanover, Schaumburg, Elk Grove, Maine, Niles, Evanston, Lakeview, Jefferson, Leyden, Proviso, Riverside, Cicero, Lyons, Lemont, Palos, Worth, Calumet, Thornton, Bremen, Orland, Rich and Bloom, in Cook county.
8—McHenry, Lake.
9—Winnebago, Boone.
10—JoDaviess, Stephenson.
11—Carroll, Whiteside.
12—Ogle, Lee.
13—DeKalb, Kendall, Grundy.
14—Kane, DuPage.
15—Will.
16—Kankakee, Iroquois.
17—LaSalle.
18—Livingston, Ford.
19—Bureau, Stark.
20—Putnam, Marshall, Woodford.
21—Rock Island, Henry.
22—Mercer, Knox.
23—Warren, McDonough.
24—Henderson, Hancock.
25—Fulton, Schuyler.
26—Peoria.
27—Tazewell, Logan.
28—McLean.
29—DeWitt, Macon.
30—Platt, Champaign.
31—Vermilion, Edgar.
32—Douglas, Coles, Moultrie.
33—Shelby, Cumberland, Effingham.
34—Christian, Montgomery.
35—Sangamon.
36—Mason, Brown, Cass, Menard.
37—Adams.
38—Scott, Pike, Calhoun.
39—Greene, Morgan.
40—Macoupin, Jersey.
41—Madison.
42—Bond, Clinton, Washington.
43—Fayette, Marion.
44—Clay, Wayne, Richland, Edwards, Wabash.
45—Clark, Crawford, Lawrence, Jasper.
46—Jefferson, Hamilton, White.
47—Franklin, Williamson, Saline, Gallatin.
48—Monroe, Randolph, Perry.
49—St. Clair.
50—Jackson, Union, Alexander.
51—Pulaski, Massac, Johnson, Pope, Hardin.

APPORTIONMENT OF 1882.

By act of May 6, 1882, the State was divided into Senatorial Districts as follows, each district being entitled to one senator and three representatives:

1. Ninth and Tenth wards, and all that part of the Eleventh ward north of the center line of Van Buren street, in Chicago.
2. That part of the Fourth ward south of the center line of Twenty-ninth street, in Chicago, and the towns of Hyde Park and Lake.
3. The First, Second and Third wards, and that part of the Fourth ward north of the center line of Twenty-ninth street, in Chicago.
4. That part of the Eighth ward north of the center line of Taylor street, that part of the Eleventh ward south of the center line of Van Buren street, and the Twelfth ward, in Chicago.
5. That part of the Sixth ward west of the center line of Throop street, the Seventh ward, and that part of the Eighth ward south of the center line of Taylor street, in Chicago.
6. The Eighteenth ward, that part of the Sixteenth ward east of the center line of Sedgwick street, and the Fifteenth ward, in Chicago, and the towns of Lake View and Evanston.
7. The towns of New Trier, Northfield, Wheeling, Palatine, Barrington, Hanover, Schaumburg, Elk Grove, Maine, Niles, Jefferson, Norwood Park, Leyden, Proviso, Cicero, Riverside, Lyons, Lemont, Palos, Worth, Calumet, Thornton, Bremen, Orland, Rich and Bloom, in Cook county.
8. Lake, McHenry and Boone.
9. The Thirteenth ward, and all of the Fourteenth ward except that portion thereof lying east of a line drawn from a point where the center line of Milwaukee avenue intersects the center line of Ohio street, northwest along said center line of Milwaukee avenue to the center line of Ashland avenue, thence north along the center line of Ashland avenue to the center line of Clybourne place, thence northeasterly along the center line of Clybourne place to the north branch of the Chicago river in Chicago.
10. Winnebago and Ogle.
11. The Fifth ward, and that part of the Sixth ward east of the center line of Throop street, in Chicago.
12. JoDaviess, Stephenson and Carroll.
13. That part of the Fourteenth ward lying east of a line drawn from the intersection of the center line of Milwaukee avenue with the center line of Ohio street northwest along the center line of said Milwaukee avenue, to the center line of Ashland avenue, thence north along the center line of Ashland avenue to the center line of Clybourne place, thence northeasterly along the center line of Clybourne place to the north branch of the Chicago river; that part of the Sixteenth ward west of the center line of Sedgwick street, and the Seventeenth ward, in Chicago.
14. Kane and DuPage.
15. Will.
16. Kankakee and Iroquois.
17. DeKalb, Kendall and Grundy.
18. Livingston and Ford.
19. Whiteside and Lee.
20. Marshall, Woodford and Tazewell.
21. Rock Island and Henry.
22. Knox and Fulton.
23. La Salle.
24. Hancock, Henderson and Mercer.
25. Bureau, Stark and Putnam.
26. Peoria.
27. Warren and McDonough.
28. McLean.
29. Logan and Macon.
30. Champaign, Piatt and DeWitt.
31. Vermilion and Edgar.
32. Douglas, Coles and Cumberland.
33. Moultrie, Shelby and Effingham.
34. Mason, Menard, Cass and Schuyler.
35. Adams.
36. Brown, Pike and Calhoun.
37. Scott, Greene and Jersey.
38. Macoupin and Morgan.
39. Sangamon.
40. Christian and Montgomery.
41. Madison.
42. Bond, Clinton and Washington.
43. Fayette, Marion and Jefferson.
44. Clay, Richland, Wayne and Edwards.
45. Clark, Jasper and Crawford.
46. Hamilton, White, Wabash and Lawrence.
47. St. Clair.
48. Monroe, Randolph and Perry.
49. Saline, Gallatin, Hardin, Pope and Massac.
50. Jackson, Union and Alexander.
51. Franklin, Williamson, Johnson and Pulaski.

APPORTIONMENT OF 1893.

By act of June 15, 1893, the State was divided into Senatorial Districts as follows, each district being entitled to one senator and three representatives:

1. The First and Fifth wards and the Second ward, except that part lying south of the center line of Twenty-second street, and west of the center line of State street, in Chicago.
2. The Twelfth ward, and Tenth ward, except that part lying south of the center line of West Twenty-first street, and east of the center line of Campbell avenue, in Chicago.
3. That part of the town of Calumet lying outside Chicago, and all of the Thirty-first, Thirty-third and Thirty-fourth wards, in Chicago.
4. The Twenty-ninth and Thirtieth wards, in Chicago.
5. The Third, Fourth and Thirty-second wards, and that part of the Second ward lying south of the center line of Twenty-second street, and west of the center line of State street, in Chicago.

6. The Twentieth ward and Twenty-sixth ward, lying south of the town of Evanston, that part of the Twenty-fifth ward lying north of the center line of Montrose boulevard and south of the town of Evanston, and that part of the Fifteenth ward lying east of the center line of Western avenue, in Chicago.
7. The towns of Thornton, Bloom, Rich, Bremen, Orland, Lemont, Palos, Worth, Lyons, Riverside, Cicero, Proviso, Leyden, Norwood Park, Maine, Elk Grove, Schaumburg, Hanover, Barrington, Palatine, Wheeling, Northfield, New Trier, Evanston and Niles, in Cook county.
8. Lake, McHenry and Boone.
9. The Sixth ward, that part of the Twenty-eighth ward lying between the center line of the Illinois and Michigan canal and the center line of Thirty-ninth street, that part of the Ninth ward lying south of the center line of West Sixteenth street, that part of the Tenth ward lying south of the center line of West Twenty-first street, and east of the center line of Campbell avenue, in Chicago.
10. Winnebago and Ogle.
11. The Fourteenth ward, that part of the Fifteenth ward lying west of the center line of Western avenue, the Twenty-eighth ward, except that part lying between the center line of the Illinois and Michigan canal and the center line of Thirty-ninth street, and the Twenty-seventh ward of Chicago.
12. Stephenson, JoDaviess and Carroll.
13. The Seventh ward, the Eighth ward, and that part of the Nineteenth ward bounded on the north by the center line of West Taylor street, on the east by the center line of Des-Plaines street, on the south by the center line of West Twelfth street, and on the west by the center line of Newberry avenue, in Chicago.
14. Kane and DuPage.
15. The Nineteenth ward, except that part bounded on the north by the center line of West Taylor street, on the east by the center line of DesPlaines street, on the south by the center line of West Twelfth street, on the west by the center line of Newberry avenue, that part of the Eleventh ward lying south of the center line of Lake street, and that part of the Ninth ward lying north of the center line of West Sixteenth street, in Chicago.
16. Kankakee and Iroquois.
17. That part of the Eleventh ward lying north of the center line of West Lake street, and the Seventeenth and Eighteenth wards, in Chicago.
18. Ford and Vermilion.
19. The Thirteenth ward and all of the Sixteenth, except that part lying northeasterly of the center line of Milwaukee avenue and east of the center line of Noble street and south of the center line of West Division street, and the north branch of the Chicago river, in Chicago.
20. Marshall, Woodford and Livingston.
21. The Twenty-first ward, the Twenty-second ward and that part of the Twenty-fifth ward lying south of the center line of Montrose boulevard, in Chicago.
22. McLean.
23. The Twenty-third ward, Twenty-fourth ward, and that part of the Sixteenth ward lying northeasterly of the center line of Milwaukee avenue and east of the center line of Noble street and south of the center line of West Division street and the north branch of the Chicago river, in Chicago.
24. Peoria.
25. Will.
26. Fulton and Tazewell.
27. LaSalle.
28. Hancock, McDonough and Schuyler.
29. Lee, DeKalb, Kendall and Grundy.
30. Champaign, DeWitt and Piatt.
31. Whiteside, Bureau, Putnam and Stark.
32. Cass, Menard, Mason and Logan.
33. Rock Island and Henry.
34. Pike, Scott and Morgan.
35. Knox, Warren, Henderson and Mercer.
36. Greene and Macoupin.
37. Adams and Brown.
38. Montgomery, Bond and Fayette.
39. Sangamon.
40. Douglas, Coles and Shelby.
41. Macon, Christian and Moultrie.
42. Clay, Marion, Clinton and Washington.
43. Edgar, Clark, Cumberland and Effingham.
44. Wabash, Edwards, White, Gallatin and Hardin.
45. Jasper, Crawford, Richland and Lawrence.
46. Franklin, Jefferson, Wayne and Hamilton.
47. Madison, Jersey and Calhoun.
48. Monroe, Randolph, Perry and Jackson.
49. St. Clair.
50. Williamson, Union and Alexander.
51. Pulaski, Massac, Johnson, Pope and Saline.

MEMBERS OF THE GENERAL ASSEMBLY.

FROM 1818 TO 1897 INCLUSIVE.

FIRST GENERAL ASSEMBLY, 1818–1820.

First session convened at Kaskaskia, Oct. 5, 1818; adjourned Oct. 13, 1818. Second session convened Jan. 4, 1819; adjourned March 31, 1819.

SENATE.

President—Pierre Menard.
Secretary—William C. Greenup.
Doorkeeper—Ezra Owen.

Barker, Lewis, Pope county.
Cadwell, George, Madison county.
Cox, Thomas, Union county.
Hargrave, Willis, White county.
Jamison, Alexander, Monroe county.
Jones, Martin, Bond county.
Jones, Michael, Gallatin county.
Kinney, William, St. Clair county.
Kitchell, Joseph, Crawford county.
Maddux, Zariah, Washington county.
McFerron, John, Randolph county.
Roberts, Thomas, Johnson and Franklin counties.
Smith, Guy W., Edwards county.
Will, Conrad, Jackson county.

HOUSE OF REPRESENTATIVES.

Speaker, pro tem.—Risdon Moore.
Speaker—John Messenger.
Clerk—Thomas Reynolds.
Enrolling and Eng. Clerk—Tim'y Davis.
Assistant—Milton Ladd.
Doorkeeper—Charles McNabb.

Alexander, William, Monroe county.
Compton, Levi, Edwards county.
Dalmwood, John G., Gallatin county.
Echols, Jesse, Union county.
Ewing, Elijah, Franklin county.
Field, Green B., Pope county.
Greggs, Jesse, Jackson county.
Hamilton, Robert, Pope county.
Howard, John, Madison county.
Hubbard, Adolphus F., Gallatin county.
Humphreys, Edward, Randolph county.
Kirkpatrick, Francis, Bond county.
*Marshall, John, Gallatin county.
McClintock, Samuel, Gallatin county.
McHenry, William, White county.
Messenger, John, St. Clair county.
Moore, Risdon, St. Clair county.
Nash, William, White county.
Phillips, Alexander, White county.
Porter, David, Crawford county.
Prickett, Abraham, Madison county.
Riggs, Scott, Crawford county.
Swearingen, Daniel S., Washington county.
Thomas, James D., St. Clair county.
Utter, Henry, Edwards county.
Walker, Samuel, Randolph county.
Whiteaker, John, Union county.
Whiteside, Samuel, Madison county.
Wilcox, Isaac D., Johnson county.

*Resigned.

SECOND GENERAL ASSEMBLY, 1820–1822.

Convened at Vandalia, Dec. 4, 1820; adjourned Feb. 15, 1821.

SENATE.

President—Pierre Menard.
Secretary—James Turner.
Enrolling and Eng. Clerk—Robt. Lemen.
Doorkeeper—Ezra Owen.

Barker, Lewis, Pope county.
Boon, William, Jackson county.
Cadwell, George, Madison county.
Crozier, Samuel, Randolph county.
Frazier, Robert, Edwards county.
Jamison, Alexander, Monroe county.
Jones, Edmund B. W., Union county.
Jones, Martin, Bond county.
Jones, Michael, Gallatin county.
Kitchell, Joseph, Crawford county.
Ladd, Milt., Johnson and Franklin counties.
Lemen, James, Jr., St. Clair.
Maddux, Zariah, Washington county.
White, Leonard, White county.

HOUSE OF REPRESENTATIVES.

Speaker—John McLean.
Clerk—Thomas Reynolds.
Enrolling and Eng. Clerk—Chas. Dunn.
Doorkeeper—Henry I. Mills.

*Alexander, Samuel, Union county.
Alexander, William M., Pope county.
Blackwell, David, St. Clair county.
Borough, Joseph, Madison county.
Buckmaster, Nathaniel, Madison county.
Cairns, Abraham, Crawford county.
Campbell, Alexander, Edwards county.
Crisp, William M., Bond county.
Dorris, Thomas M., Franklin county.
Eddy, Henry, Gallatin county.
Kitchell, Wickliffe, Crawford county.
Logan, John R., White county.
Matheny, Charles R., St. Clair county.
Mather, Thomas, Randolph county.
McClintock, Samuel, Gallatin county.
McFatridge, William, Johnson county.
McLean, John, Gallatin county.
McLean, William B., White county.
Michaels, Moses, Edwards county.
Moore, Enoch, Monroe county.
Moore, Risdon, St. Clair county.
†Omelveney, Samuel, Union county.
Otwell, William, Madison county.
Phillips, Alexander, White county.
Robinson, Edward, Pope county.
Slade, Charles, Washington county.
Widen, Raphael, Randolph county.
Will, Conrad, Jackson county.
Young, Richard M., Union county.

* Seat contested. † Vice Samuel Alexander, ousted.

THIRD GENERAL ASSEMBLY, 1822-1824.

Convened at Vandalia, Dec. 2, 1822; adjourned Feb. 18, 1823.

SENATE.

President—Adolphus F. Hubbard.
Secretary—Thomas Lippincott.
Enrolling and Eng. Clerk—H. S. Dodge
Doorkeeper—John O. Prentice.

Bankson, Andrew, Washington county.
Barker, Lewis, Pope county.
Beard, Joseph A., Monroe county.
Boon, William, Jackson county.
Cadwell, George, Green, Pike counties.
Crozier, Samuel, Randolph county.
Frazier, Robert, Edwards county.
Grammar, John, Union county.
Jones, Martin, Bond, Fayette, Montgomery counties.
Jones, Michael, Gallatin county.
Kinkead, William, Wayne, Lawrence counties.
Kinney, William, St. Clair county.
Ladd, Milton, Johnson, Franklin counties.
Parker, Daniel, Crawford, Clark counties.
Sloo, Thomas, Jr., Hamilton and Jefferson counties.
Smith, Theophilus W., Madison county.
Stillman, Stephen, Sangamon county.
White, Leonard, White county,

HOUSE OF REPRESENTATIVES.

Speaker—William M. Alexander.
Clerk—Charles Dunn.
Enrolling and Eng. Clerk—Winsted Davis
Doorkeeper—John Lee.

Alexander, Samuel, Pope county.
Alexander, William, Monroe county.
Alexander, William M., Alexander county.
Berry, William, Fayette, Montgomery counties.
Blakeman, C., Madison county.
Campbell, Alexander, Wayne county.
Cain, Abraham, Lawrence county.
Casey, Zadok, Hamilton, Jefferson counties.
Churchill, G., Madison county.
Dalmwood, J. G., Gallatin county.
Davenport, James S., Gallatin county.
Dorris, Thomas M., Franklin county.
Emmett, John, White county.
Field, Alexander P., Union county,
Ford, R. C., Crawford conuty.
*Hansen, Nicholas, Pike county.
Logan, George R., White county.
Lowery, William, Clark county.
Mather, Thomas, Randolph county.
McFatridge, William, Johnson county.
McFerron, John, Randolph county.
McGahey, David, Crawford county.
McIntosh, John, Union county.
Moore, Risdon, St. Clair county.
Ogle, Jacob, St. Clair county.
Pell, G. T., Edwards county.
Phillips, Alexander, White county.
Pugh, Jonathan C., Bond county.
Rattan, Thomas, Greene county.
†Shaw, John, Pike county.
Sims, James, Sangamon county.
Trotter, James, St. Clair county.
‡Turney, James, Washington county.
West, E. J., Madison county.
Whiteside, James A., Pope county.
Widen, Raphael, Randolph county.
Will, Conrad, Jackson county.

* Seat contested. † Vice Hansen, ousted. ‡ Resigned Feb. 18, 1823.

FOURTH GENERAL ASSEMBLY, 1824-1826.

First session convened at Vandalia, Nov. 15, 1824; adjourned Jan. 18, 1825. Second session convened Jan. 2, 1826; adjourned Jan. 28, 1826.

SENATE.

President—Adolphus F. Hubbard.
Second session—Raphael Widen.
Secretary—Emanuel J. West.
Enrolling and Eng. Clerk—Albert G. Sloo.
Sergeant-at-Arms—Benjamin Ogle.
Second session—Thomas Higgins.

Bankson, Andrew, Washington county.
Barker, Lewis, Pope county.
Beaird, Joseph A., Monroe county.
Bird, James, Wayne, Lawrence counties.
Bliss, Stephen, Edwards county.
Carlin, Thomas, Green, Morgan, Pike, Fulton counties.
†Conway, Joseph, Madison county.
Duncan, Joseph, Jackson county.
Ewing, John, Johnson, Franklin counties.
Grammar, John, Union, Alexander counties.
Hay, Daniel, White county.
Jones, Michael, Gallatin county.
Kirkpatrick, Francis, Bond, Fayette, Montgomery counties.
Lemen, James, St. Clair county.
Parker, Daniel, Crawford, Clark, Edgar counties.
Sloo, Thomas, Jr., Hamilton, Jefferson, Marion counties.
*Smith, Theophilus W., Madison county.
Stillman, Stephen, Sangamon county.
Widen, Raphael, Randolph county.

* Resigned. † Second session; vice Smith.

HOUSE OF REPRESENTATIVES.

Speaker—Thomas Mather.
Second session—David Blackwell.
Clerk—Charles Dunn.
Enrolling and Eng. Clerk—R. P. Allen.
Doorkeeper—James S. Smith; resigned.
Second session—Thos. Redman.

Acher, Wm. B., Clark, Edgar counties.
Brakeman, Curtis, Madison county.
Blackwell, David, St. Clair county.
Beers, Philo, Washington county.
Bridges, John, Johnson county.
Casey, Zadok, Hamilton, Jefferson, Marion counties.
Churchill, George, Madison county.
Dorris, Thomas M., Franklin county.
Eyman, Abraham, St. Clair county.
*Forquer, George, Monroe county.
Gard, Timothy, Gallatin county.
Hacker, John, Union county.
Hamilton, Wm. S., Sangamon county.
*Hansen, Nicholas, Pike, Fulton counties.
†James, Thomas, Monroe county.
Job, Archibald, Greene, Morgan counties.
‡Jones, Gabriel, Randolph county.
Jones, Richard T., Gallatin county.
*Kane, Elias K., Randolph county.
Logan, George R., White county.
*Mather, Thomas, Randolph county.
McGahey, David, Crawford county.
McHenry, Wm., White county.
Moore Risdon, Jr., St. Clair county.
Norton, Asa, Lawrence county.
Otwell, Wm., Madison county.
Phillips, Alexander, White county.
¶Roberts Levi, Pike, Fulton counties.
Russell, John, Bond county.
Sim, Wm., Pope county.
Slocum, Rigdon B., Wayne county.
§Smith, Samuel, Randolph county.
Stewart, David, Crawford county.
Utter, Henry, Edwards county.
Wakefield, John A., Fayette, Montgomery counties.
Walker, Samuel, Randolph county.
Webb, Henry L., Alexander county.
Whiteaker, John, Union county.
Whiteside, James A., Pope county.
Will, Conrad, Jackson county.

*Resigned. †Vice Forquer. ‡Second session, vice Kane. ¶Vice Hansen. §Vice Mather.

FIFTH GENERAL ASSEMBLY, 1826–1828.

Convened at Vandalia, Dec. 4, 1826; adjourned Feb. 19, 1827.

SENATE.

President—William Kinney.
Secretary—Emanuel J. West.
Enrolling and Eng. Clerk—A. F. Grant.
Sergeant-at-Arms—Joseph Chance.

Alexander, Samuel, Pope county.
Archer, Wm. B., Clark, Crawford, Edgar, Vermillion counties.
Beaird, Joseph A., Monroe, Clinton, Washington counties.
Bird, James, Wayne, Lawrence counties.
Bliss, Stephen, Wabash, Edwards counties.
Carlin, Thomas, Greene county.
Casey, Zadok, Jefferson, Hamilton, Marion, Clay counties.
Conway, Joseph, Madison county.
*Duncan, Joseph, Jackson county.
Ewing, John, Franklin, Jackson counties.
Gard, Timothy, Gallatin county.
Hay, Daniel, White county.
Hunsacker, George, Union, Johnson, Alexander counties.
Iles, Elijah, Sangamon county.
Job, Archibald, Pike, Fulton, Adams, Morgan, Peoria, Schuyler.
Kirkpatrick, Francis, Bond, Fayette, Montgomery counties.
Lemen, James, St. Clair county.
Widen, Raphael, Randolph county.

* Resigned, Feb. 19, 1827.

HOUSE OF REPRESENTATIVES.

Speaker—John McLean.
Clerk—William Lee D. Ewing.
Enrolling and Eng. Clerk—H. Rountree.
Doorkeeper—Bowling Greene.

Alexander, John, Clark, Edgar, Vermilion counties.
Alexander, John C., Crawford county.
Allen, John, Green, Calhoun counties.
Berry, Wm., Bond, Montgomery, Fayette counties.
Blackwell, David, St. Clair county.
Brooks, Benjamin W., Union, Johnson, Alexander counties.
Cavalry, Alfred W., Green, Calhoun counties.
Churchill, George, Madison county.
Clubb, Samuel H., Lawrence county.
Davis, Wm. B., Wayne county.
Dorris, Thomas M., Franklin county.
Field, Alexander P., Union, Johnson, Alexander counties.
Fletcher, Job, Sangamon county.
Hall, James, Hamilton county.

Ives, Charles, Clark, Edgar, Vermilion counties.
James, Thomas, Monroe county.
Lacy, John, Randolph county.
Leeper, John, Morgan county.
Lieb, Daniel, Morgan county.
McHenry, Wm., White county.
McLaughlin, Robert K., Bond, Montgomery, Fayette counties.
McLean, John, Gallatin county.
Mills, Henry I., Edwards county.
Mobley, Mordecai, Sangamon county.
Prickett, David, Madison county.
Prince, Francis, Gallatin county.
Pugh, Jonathan H., Sangamon county.
Reynolds, John, St. Clair county.
Reynolds, Thomas, Randolph county.
Ridgway, John, White county.
Ross, Henry J., Pike, Adams, Schuyler, Fulton, Peoria counties.
Sim, Wm., Pope county.
Slade, Charles, Clinton, Washington counties.
Utter, Henry, Wabash county.
Will, Conrad, Jackson county.
Wren, Nicholas, Jefferson, Marion and Clay.

SIXTH GENERAL ASSEMBLY, 1828–1830.

Convened at Vandalia, Dec. 1, 1828; adjourned Jan. 23, 1829.

SENATE.

President—William Kinney.
Secretary—Emanuel J. West.
Enrolling and Eng. Clerk—Jas. Whitlock.
Sergeant-at-Arms—John Grammar.

Alexander, Samuel, Pope county.
Archer, Wm. B., Clark, Edgar, Vermilion counties.
Beach, Enoch, Edwards, Wayne, Wabash counties.
Carlin, Thomas, Greene, Calhoun counties.
Casey, Zadok, Jefferson, Hamilton, Clay, Marion counties.
Conway, Joseph, Madison county.
Crawford, Samuel, Randolph, Perry counties.
Gard, Timothy, Gallatin county.
Hunsacker, George, Union, Johnson, Alexander counties.
Iles, Elijah, Sangamon county.
Job, Archibald, Morgan county.
Kitchell, Wickliffe, Crawford, Lawrence counties.
McHenry, Wm., White county.
McLaughlin, Robt. K., Fayette, Bond, Tazewell, Montgomery, Shelby counties.
*McRoberts, Samuel, Monroe, Clinton, Washington counties.
†Moore, Risdon, Jr., St. Clair county.
Ross, Henry J., Pike, Adams, Fulton, Schuyler, Peoria, JoDaviess counties.
Will, Conrad, Franklin, Jackson, Perry counties.

* Second session, vice Beaird deceased.
† Died.

HOUSE OF REPRESENTATIVES.

Speaker—John McLean.
Clerk—Wm. L. D. Ewing.
Enrolling and Eng. Clerk—H. Rountree.
Doorkeeper—Asa Haynes.

Allen, John, Greene, Calhoun counties.
Alexander, John C., Crawford county.
Black, James, Fayette, Bond, Shelby, Montgomery, Tazewell counties.
Brown, Wm. G., St. Clair county.
Carrigan, John S., Clinton and Washington counties.
Cartwright, Peter, Sangamon county.
Churchill, George, Madison county.
Dement, John, Franklin county.
Elkin, Wm. F., Sangamon county.
Eubanks, Wm., White county.
Field, Alexander P., Union, Alexander, Johnson counties.
Gillham, Henry M., Lawrence county.
Green, W. B., Morgan county.
Hall, James, Hamilton county.
Ives, Chas., Clark, Edgar, Vermilion counties.
Jennings, Israel, Jefferson, Marion and Clay.
Jones, Wm., Madison county.
Kimmel, Singleton H., Jackson county.
Lemen, Moses, Monroe county.
Mather, Thos., Randolph county.
May, Wm. L., Morgan county.
McLean, John, Gallatin county.
Menard, Hypolite, Randolph county.
Munday, Samuel, Wabash county.
Pell, Gilbert T., Edwards county.
Prentice, Charles, Fayette, Bond, Tazewell, Montgomery, Shelby counties.
Prince, Francis, Gallatin county.
Pugh, Jonathan H., Sangamon county.
Rattan, Thomas, Greene, Calhoun counties.
Reynolds, John, St. Clair county.
Shellody, Stephen B., Clark, Edgar, Vermilion counties.
Slocum, Rigdon B., Wayne county.
Stewart, Josiah, White county.
Turney, John, Pike, Adams, Fulton, Schuyler, Peoria, JoDaviess counties.
Whiteaker, John, Union, Alexander, Johnson counties.
Whiteside, James A., Pope county.

SEVENTH GENERAL ASSEMBLY, 1830–1832.

Convened at Vandalia, Dec. 6, 1830; adjourned Feb. 16, 1831.

SENATE.

President—Zadok Casey.
Secretary—Jesse B. Thomas.
Enrolling and Eng. Clerk—James Whitlock.
Sergeant-at-Arms—Champen Anderson.

Alexander, Samuel, Pope county.
Archer, Wm. B., Clark, Edgar, Vermilion counties.
Beach, Enoch, Wayne, Edwards, Wabash counties.
Carlin, Thomas, Greene, Calhoun, Macoupin counties.
Conway, Joseph, Madison county.
Crawford, Samuel, Randolph, Perry counties.

Evans, James, Morgan county.
Gard, Timothy, Gallatin county.
Grammar, John, Union, Johnson, Alexander.
Iles, Elijah, Sangamon county.
Kitchell, Wickliffe, Crawford county.
Lynch, Jonathan, Monroe, Clinton, Washington counties.
McHenry, Wm., White county.
Maulding, Ennis, Hamilton, Jefferson, Marion, Clay counties.
McLaughlin, Robt. K., Fayette, Bond, Tazewell, Montgomery, Shelby counties.
Ross, Henry J., Pike, Adams, Fulton, Peoria, Schuyler, JoDaviess counties.
*Snyder, Adam W., St. Clair county.
Will, Conrad, Jackson, Franklin counties.

*Vice Risdon Moore, Jr., deceased.

HOUSE OF REPRESENTATIVES.

Speaker—Wm. Lee D. Ewing.
Clerk—David Prickett.
Enrolling and Eng. Clerk—Hiram Rountree.
Doorkeeper—Bowling Greene.

Alexander, John C., Crawford county.
Atkins, John, Randolph, Perry counties.
Beckwith, W. D., Clark, Edgar, Vermilion counties.
Brown, Wm. G., St. Clair county.
Canal, John B. E., Madison and Macoupin counties.
Carrigan, John S., Clinton and Washington counties.
Churchill, George, Madison and Macoupin counties.
Clark, Alexander, Wayne county.
Cloud, Newton, Morgan county.
Davenport, John, Hamilton county.
Dawson, John, Sangamon county.
Dement, John, Franklin county.
Eubanks, Wm., White county.
Ewing, Wm. L. D., Fayette, Bond, Tazewell, Montgomery, Shelby counties.
Fairfield, Joseph M., Morgan county.
Gatewood, Wm. J., Gallatin county.
Gregory, Charles, Greene, Calhoun, Macoupin counties.
Jenkins, Alexander M., Jackson county.
Jordan, James, Edwards county.
Marshall, Wm., Jefferson, Marion, Clay counties.
McLean, James M., Lawrence county.
Munday, Samuel, Wabash county.
Ogle, Jacob, St. Clair county.
Owen, Thomas J. V., Randolph and Perry counties.
Pierce, Samuel C., Greene, Calhoun, Macoupin counties.
Priestly, Joseph L., Johnson, Union, Alexander counties.
Posey, John F., Fayette, Bond, Tazewell, Montgomery, Shelby counties.
Pugh, Jonathan H., Sangamon county.
Shellody, Stephen B., Clark, Edgar, Vermilion counties.
Stewart, Josiah, White county.
Taylor, Edmund D., Sangamon county.
Watkins, Joseph E., Gallatin county.
Whiteaker, John, Johnson, Union, Alexander counties.
Whiteside, John D., Monroe county.
Whiteside, James A., Pope county.
Wright, Joel, Pike, Adams, Fulton, Schuyler, Peoria, JoDaviess counties.

EIGHTH GENERAL ASSEMBLY, 1832–1834.

Convened at Vandalia, Dec. 3, 1832; adjourned March 2, 1833.

SENATE.

President—Zadok Casey, resigned.
President pro tem.—Wm. Lee D. Ewing.
Secretary—Jesse B. Thomas, Jr.
Enrolling and Eng. Clerk—James Whitlock.
Sergeant-at-Arms—Wm. Weatherford.

Archer, Wm. B., Edgar, Clark, Coles counties.
Bird, James, Tazewell, McLean counties.
Conway, Joseph, Madison county.
Craig, Larkin, Bond, Macoupin, Montgomery counties.
Davidson, Wm. H., White county.
Evans, James, Morgan county.
Ewing, Wm. Lee D., Fayette, Marion, Clay counties.
Forquer, George, Sangamon county.
Grammar, John, Alexander, Union counties.
Iles, Elijah, Sangamon county.
Jones, Waller, Morgan county.
Lynch, Jonathan, Monroe, Clinton counties.
Mather, Thos., Randolph, Perry counties.
Maulding, Ennis, Hamilton, Jefferson counties.
McCreery, Wm., Schuyler, Fulton, Knox, Henry, Calhoun, Mercer, McDonough, Warren counties.
McGahey, David, Lawrence, Crawford counties.
Mills, Henry I., Edwards, Wayne, Wabash counties.
Rattan, Thomas, Greene county.
*Raum, John, Pope, Johnson counties.
Snyder, Adam W., St. Clair county.
Strode, James M., Peoria, Putnam, Cook, LaSalle, JoDaviess counties.
Vance, John W., Vermilion county.
Watkins, Joseph B., Gallatin county.
Will, Conrad, Jackson, Franklin, Washington counties.
Williams, Archibald, Pike, Hancock, Adams counties.
Williamson, William, Macon, Shelby counties.

* Vice Samuel Alexander, resigned.

HOUSE OF REPRESENTATIVES.

Speaker—Alexander M. Jenkins.
Clerk—David Prickett.
Enrolling and Eng. Clerk—Thomas C. Kirkman.
Doorkeeper—Wm. C. Murphy.

Able, Wilson, Alexander county.
Anderson, Stinson H., Jefferson county.
Anderson, Wm. G., Wabash county.
Baldridge, David, Randolph, Perry counties.
Barnett, George, Vermilion county.
Beeler, George H., Shelby, Macon counties.
Blackwell, Robert, Fayette county.
Blockberger, Christian B., Montgomery county.

Borough, Joseph, Macoupin county.
Bowyer, George P., Franklin, Washington.
Briggs, Benjamin, McLean, Tazewell counties.
Carrico, John, Coles county.
Carrigan, John S., Clinton county.
Cartwright, Peter, Sangamon county.
Clark, Alexander, Wayne county.
Dougherty, John, Union county.
Edmondston, Wm., Calhoun, McDonough, Warren, Mercer counties.
Edwards, Cyrus, Madison county.
Enloe, Benj. S., Johnson county.
Essery, Jesse, Clark county.
Flood, Wm. G., Hancock, Pike, Adams counties.
Goode, Wm., Greene county.
Goudy, John C., White county.
Greer, Abner, Lawrence county.
Hackelton, Samuel, Fulton, Knox, Henry counties.
Hall, James, Hamilton county.
Hubbard, Gordon S., Vermilion county.
Hunt, Thomas, Edwards county.
Hunter, Wm., Bond county.
Highsmith, Wm., Crawford county.
Henry, John, Morgan county.
Jenkins, Alexander M., Jackson county.
Jones, Michael, Gallatin county.
Link, Lewis W., Greene county.
Marshall, Wm., Marion, Clay counties.
Martin, Philip W., Hancock, Pike, Adams counties.
Matthews, Samuel T., Morgan county.
McClintock, Samuel, Gallatin county.
McConnel, Murray, Morgan county.
McCown, John, White county.
Middlecoff, John, St. Clair county.
Mills, Benjamin, Peoria, JoDaviess, Putnam, LaSalle, Cook counties.
Minshall, Wm. A , Schuyler county.
Morris, Achilles, Sangamon county.
Murphy, Richard G., Randolph, Perry counties.
Noel, Lundsford R., Edgar county.
Pierce, Samuel C., Greene county.
Semple, James, Madison county.
Stuart, John T., Sangamon county.
Stuntz, John, St. Clair county.
Taylor, Edmund D., Sangamon county.
Whiteside, James A., Pope county.
Whiteside, John D., Monroe county.
Wren, Johnson, Franklin and Washington.
Wyatt, John, Morgan county.

NINTH GENERAL ASSEMBLY, 1834-1836.

First session convened at Vandalia, Dec. 1, 1834; adjourned Feb. 13, 1835; Second session Dec. 7, 1835; adjourned Jan. 18, 1836.

SENATE.

President—Alexander M. Jenkins.
Secretary—Leonard White.
Enrolling and Eng. Clerk—Wm. G. Flood.
Sergeant-at-Arms—Robert M. Gordon.

Bond, Benjamin, Monroe, Clinton counties.
Craig, Larkin, Bond, Montgomery, Macoupin counties.
Davidson, Wm. H., White county.
Edwards, Cyrus, Madison county.
Ewing, Wm. L. D., Fayette, Marion, Clay counties.
†Fletcher, Job, Sangamon county.
*Forquer, George, Sangamon county.
Gatewood, Wm. J., Gallatin county.
Hacker, John S., Union, Alexander counties.
‡Herndon, Archer G., Sangamon county.
¶Jones, Waller, Morgan county.
Lane, Levin, Hamilton, Jefferson counties.
*Mather, Thomas, Randolph, Perry counties.
Maxwell, George W. P., Schuyler, Fulton, Knox, Calhoun, McDonough and Warren counties.
McGahey, David, Lawrence, Crawford counties.
Mills, Henry I., Edwards, Wayne, Wabash counties.
Mitchell, Benjamin, McLean, Tazewell counties.
Noel, Lunsford R., Clark, Edgar and Coles.
§Parish, Braxton, Jackson, Franklin, Washington counties.
Rattan, Thomas, Greene county.
**Servant, Richard B., Randolph, Perry counties.
Snyder, Adam W., St. Clair county.
*Stephenson, James W., JoDaviess, Cook, LaSalle, Putnam, Peoria and Rock Island counties.
††Strode, James M., JoDaviess, Cook, LaSalle, Putnam, Peoria, Rock Island counties.
*Taylor, Edmund D., Sangamon county.
Thomas, Wm., Morgan county.
Vance, John W., Vermilion, Champaign and Iroquois counties.
‡‡Weatherford, Wm., Morgan county.
Whiteside, James A., Pope, Johnson counties.
¶Will, Conrad, Jackson, Franklin, Washington counties.
Williams, Archibald, Pike, Hancock, Adams counties.
Williamson, Wm., Shelby, Macon counties.

* Resigned. † Vice Taylor. ‡ Vice Forquer. ¶ Died. § Vice Will.
** Vice Mather. †† Vice Stephenson. ‡‡ Vice Jones.

HOUSE OF REPRESENTATIVES.

Speaker—James Semple.
Clerk—David Prickett.
Assistant—Walter B. Scates.
Enrolling and Eng. Clerk—Eb'z'r B. Ryan.
Doorkeeper—Wm. C. Murphy.

Able, Wilson, Alexander county.
*Anderson, Stinson H., Jefferson county.
*a*Blackford, Nathaniel, White county.
Blackwell, Robert, Fayette and Effingham counties.
Blockberger, Christian B., Montgomery county.
Bowyer, George P., Franklin, Washington counties.
Brown, Wm., McLean, Tazewell counties.
*b*Buckmaster, Nathaniel, Madison county.
Butler, Peter, Calhoun, McDonough, Warren, Mercer counties.
Carpenter, Milton, Hamilton county.
Carpenter, Wm., Sangamon county.
Clark, Benj. A., Wayne county.
Cloud, Newton, Morgan county.
*c*Craig, Bazel B., Union county.
Cunningham, James T., Coles county.
Dawson, John, Sangamon county.

*Dougherty, John, Union county.
Dubois, Jesse K., Lawrence county.
Dunn, Charles, Pope county.
Elliott, Asa, Vermillion, Champaign, Iroquois counties.
*Ficklin, Orlando B., Wabash county.
Fithian, Wm., Vermillion, Champaign, Iroquois counties.
Frazier, Elijah S., Marion, Clay counties.
Gordon, Wm., Morgan county.
Gregory, Charles, Greene county.
Hackelton, Samuel, Fulton, Knox, Henry counties.
Hamlin, John, Peoria, JoDaviess, Putnam, LaSalle, Cook, Rock Island counties.
Hampton, James, Gallatin county.
Harreld, James, Jackson county.
Harris, John, Macoupin county.
Henry, John, Morgan county.
Hughes, John D., St. Clair county.
Hunt, Thomas, Edwards county.
Hunter, Wm., Bond county.
Lincoln, Abraham, Sangamon county.
*aLink, Lewis W., Greene county.
Manly, Uri, Clark county.
dMcGahey, James D., Crawford county.
*aMcHenry, Wm., White county.
Moore, Wm., St. Clair county.
Murphy, Richard G., Randolph, Perry counties.
Nunnally, Nelson W., Edgar county.
Oliver, John, Johnson county.
Outhouse, James, Clinton county.
Owens, Thomas H., Hancock, Pike, Adams counties.
ePace, Harvey T., Jefferson county.
fPorter, David, Crawford county.
Ross, Wm., Hancock, Pike, Adams counties.
a*Rowan, Stephen R., Gallatin county.
Semple, James, Madison county.
gSmith, Edward, Wabash county.
Stuart, John T., Sangamon county.
*Thomas, Jesse B., Jr., Madison county.
Thompson, John, Randolph, Perry counties.
Trower, Thomas B., Shelby, Macon counties.
Tunnel, Calvin, Greene county.
hTurney, James, Greene county.
Vandeventer, Jacob, Schuyler county.
Webb, Edwin B., White county.
Whiteside, John D., Monroe county.
iWood, Daniel, Gallatin county.
Wren, Johnson, Franklin and Washington.
Wyatt, John, Morgan county.

*Resigned Feb. 13, 1835. *aResigned. aVice McHenry. bVice Thomas, Jr. cVice Dougherty. dDied. eVice Anderson. fVice McGahey. gVice Ficklin. hVice Link. iVice Rowan.

TENTH GENERAL ASSEMBLY, 1836–1838.

First session convened at Vandalia, Dec. 5, 1836; adjourned March 6, 1837; Second session July 10, 1837; adjourned July 22, 1837.

SENATE.

President—Wm. H. Davidson, vice Jenkins, resigned.
Secretary—Jesse B. Thomas, Jr.
Enrolling and Engrossing Clerk—William G. Flood.
Sergeant-at-Arms—David Campbell.

Allen, James, McLean, Macon counties.
Allen, John, Greene, Calhoun counties.
Bond, Benjamin, Clinton, Marion counties.
Borough, Joseph, Macoupin county.
Browning, Orville H., Adams county.
Butler, Peter, Warren, Knox, Henry counties.
Craig, Larkin, Montgomery, Bond counties.
Davidson, Wm. H., White county.
Edwards, Cyrus, Madison county.
Fletcher, Job, Sangamon county.
Gatewood, Wm. J., Gallatin county.
Hacker, John S., Union, Alexander counties.
Hackelton, Samuel, Fulton county.
Hamlin, John, Peoria, Putnam counties.
Herndon, Archer G., Sangamon county.
Lane, Levin, Hamilton, Jefferson counties.
Maxwell, Geo. W. P., Schuyler county.
McLaughlin, Robt. K., Fayette, Effingham, Clay counties.
Mills, Henry I., Edwards, Wayne, Wabash counties.
Mitchell, Benjamin, Tazewell county.
†Moore, James B., Madison, St. Clair, Monroe counties.
Murray, John, St. Clair county.
Noel, Lundsford R., Edgar county.
O'Rear, William, Morgan county.
Owens, Thomas H., McDonough, Hancock counties
Parish, Braxton, Franklin, Jackson counties.
Parker, Nathaniel, Clark, Coles counties.
Pruyne, Peter, Cook, Will counties.
Reilly, John C., Lawrence, Crawford, Jasper counties.
Ross, William, Pike county.
Servant, Richard B., Randolph county.
Stadden, William, LaSalle, Kane, Iroquois counties.
Thomas, William, Morgan county.
Turney, James, Greene county.
Vance, John W., Vermilion, Champaign counties.
Warren, Peter, Shelby county.
Weatherford, William, Morgan county.
Whiteside, James A., Pope and Johnson counties.
*Whiteside, John D., Madison, St. Clair, Monroe counties.
Wright, A. G. S., JoDaviess, Rock Island, Mercer counties.
Wood, John D., Washington, Perry counties.

*Resigned March 6, 1837. †Vice Whiteside, resigned.

HOUSE OF REPRESENTATIVES.

Speaker—James Semple.
Clerk—David Prickett.
Enrolling and Engrossing Clerk—Nelson W. Nunnally.
Doorkeeper—Jefferson Weatherford.

Abel, Wilson, Alexander county.
Aldrich, Mark, Hancock county.
Atwater, Thomas, Putnam county.
aBaker, Edward D., Sangamon county.
Ball, Asel F., Fulton county
Barnett, George, Vermilion county.
bBartlett, S. M., JoDaviess, Rock Island, Mercer counties.
Bentley, Richard, Bond county.
Carpenter, Milton, Hamilton county.

*Charles, Elijah, JoDaviess, Mercer, Rock Island counties.
Cloud, Newton, Morgan county.
cConnelly, Samuel, Edgar county.
dCopeland, James, Johnson county.
Courtright, Isaac, Iroquois county.
Craig, James, JoDaviess, Mercer, Rock Island counties.
Crain, John, Washington county.
Cullom, Richard N., Tazewell county.
eCunningham, J. T., Coles county.
Davis, Cyrus A., Greene county.
Davidson, Wm., Marion county.
Dawson, John, Sangamon county.
*Dement, John, Fayette, Effingham counties.
Dairman, Jonathan, Pope county.
Dollins, Archilles D., Franklin county.
Dougherty, John, Union county.
*Douglas, Stephen A., Morgan county.
Dubois, Jesse K., Lawrence c unty.
Dunbar, Alexander P., Coles county.
fDunn, Tarlton, Gallatin county.
Edmonston, Wm., McDonough county.
Edwards, Ninian W., Sangamon county.
English, Revill W., Greene county.
Elkin, Wm. F., Sangamon county.
*Enloe, Benjamin S., Johnson county.
gEwing, Wm. L. D., Fayette, Effingham counties.
*French, Augustus C., Edgar county.
†Galbraith, George, Adams county.
‡Graham, Resolve, Gallatin county.
Green, Joseph, St. Clair county.
hGreen, John, Greene, Calhoun counties.
Green, Peter, Clay county.
Hankins, Wm. J., Fayette, Effingham counties.
Happy, W. W., Morgan county.
Hardin, John J., Morgan county.
Harris, John, Macoupin county.
Henshaw, George, McLean county.
Hogan, John, Madison county.
Huey, Joseph, Clinton county.
Hunt, Thomas, Edwards county.
Lagow, Wilson, Crawford, Jasper counties.
*Lane, Wm., Calhoun, Greene counties.
Leary, Albert G., Cook county.
Lincoln, Abraham, Sangamon county.
*Linder, Usher F., Coles county.
Logan, John, Jackson county.
Lyons, James H., Champaign county.
Madden, Henry, LaSalle county.
Marrs, Wm. B., Clark county.
*McClernand, Jno. A., Gallatin county.
McCormick, Andrew, Sangamon county.
McCown, John, White county.
McMurtry, Wm., Warren, Knox, Henry counties.
Minor, Gideon, Edgar county.
Minshall, Wm. A., Schuyler county.
Moore, John, McLean county.
Morton, Joseph, Morgan county.
Moore, Wm., St. Clair county.
Murphy, John H., Vermilion county.
Murphy, Richard G., Perry county
Naper, John, Cook county.
*Nowlan, David, Monroe county.
Odam, Dempsey, Franklin county.
O'Neille, Edward J., Lawrence county.
Pace, Harvey T., Jefferson county.
Paullen, Parven, Pike county.
Ralston, James H., Adams county.
Rawalt, James, Fulton county.
Reddick, Wm. G., Macon county.
Richardson, Wm. A., Schuyler county.
Scarborough, George, Vermilion county.
Semple, James, Madison county.
Shields, James, Randolph county.
Smith, Edward, Wabash county.
Smith, Robert, Madison county.
*Stone, Daniel, Sangamon county.
Stuart, Robert, Tazewell county.
Stuntz, John, St. Clair county.
iSummerville, John A., Monroe county.
Thompson, Samuel G., Randolph county.
Turley, John S., Shelby county.
Turney, Daniel, Wayne county.
Voris, Francis, Peoria county.
Walker, James, Cook county.
Walker, Richard S., Morgan county.
jWatkins, Joseph E., Gallatin county.
Webb, Edwin B., White county.
Wheeler, Alpheus, Pike county.
Whitten, Easton, Montgomery county.
kWilliams, Archibald, Adams county.
Wilson, Robert L., Sangamon county.
Witt, Franklin, Greene county.
Wood, Daniel, Gallatin county.
lWyatt, John, Morgan county.

* Resigned. † Died. ‡ Died Dec. 27, 1836. *a* Vice Stone. *b* Vice Charles. *c* Vice French. *d* Vice Enloe. *e* Vice Linder. *f* Vice McClernand. *g* Vice Dement. *h* Vice Lane. *i* Vice Nowlan. *j* Vice Graham. *k* Vice Galbraith. *l* Vice Douglas.

ELEVENTH GENERAL ASSEMBLY, 1838-1840.

First session convened at Vandalia Dec. 3, 1838; adjourned March 4, 1839. Second session convened at Springfield Dec. 9, 1839; adjourned Feb. 3, 1840.

SENATE.

President—Stinson H. Anderson.
Enrolling and Eng. Clerk—William Moore.
Secretary—Benjamin Bond.
Sergeant-at-Arms—Levin Lane.

Allen, James, McLean, Macon counties.
Blackwell, R., Effingham, Clay counties.
Borough, Joseph, Macoupin county.
aBostwick, Monoah, Greene, Jersey counties.
Browning, Orville H., Adams county.
Butler, Peter, Warren, Knox, Henry counties.
Churchill, George, Madison county.
Davidson, Wm. H., White county.
Fithian, William, Vermilion, Champaign counties.
Fletcher, Job, Sangamon county.
Gaston, William, Clinton, Marion counties.
Gatewood, Wm. J., Gallatin county.
Gibbs, Worthington J., Pope, Johnson counties.
Greer, Abner, Lawrence, Crawford, Jasper counties.
Hacker, John S., Union, Alexander counties.
*Hackelton, Samuel, Fulton county.
Hamlin, John, Peoria, Putnam counties.
Harrison, Geo. W., JoDaviess, Rock Island, Stephenson, Winnebago, Ogle, Mercer, Boone counties.
Herndon, Archer G., Sangamon county.
Hunter, William, Montgomery, Bond counties.
Johnson, Noah, Hamilton, Jefferson counties.
Little, Sidney H., McDonough, Hancock counties.
bMarkley, David, Fulton county
Mills, Henry I., Edwards, Wabash, Wayne counties.
Mitchell, Benjamin, Tazewell county.
Monroe, Byrd, Clark, Coles counties.

Moore, James B., Madison, St. Clair, Monroe counties.
Murray, John, St. Clair county.
Nunnally, Nelson W., Edgar county.
O'Rear, William, Morgan county.
Parish, Braxton, Franklin, Jackson counties.
*Peck, Ebenezer, Cook, Will, McHenry counties.
Richardson, Wm. A., Schuyler county.
Ross, William, Pike county.
cSergeant, Wm. L., Morgan, Cass and Scott.
Stadden, Wm., LaSalle, Iroquois, Kane, De Kalb counties.
Servant, Richard B., Randolph county.
†Thomas, Wm., Morgan county.
*Turney, James, Greene county.
Warren, Peter, Shelby county.
Weatherford, Wm. B., Morgan county.
Witt, Franklin, Greene, Calhoun counties.
Wood, John D., Washington, Perry counties.
dWoodworth, James H., Cook, Will, Du Page, McHenry counties.

* Resigned. † Resigned March 4, 1839. a Vice Turney. b Vice Hackelton.
c Vice Thomas. d Vice Peck.

HOUSE OF REPRESENTATIVES.

Speaker—Wm. Lee D. Ewing.
Clerk—David Prickett.
Assistant—Ebenezer Z. Ryan; resigned.
Assistant—Isaac S. Berry (vice Ryan).
Enrolling and Engrossing Clerk—Joseph R. Loveless.
Doorkeeper—Wm. C. Murphy.

aAble, Wilson, Alexander county.
Aldrich, Mark, Hancock county.
Alexander, Harmon, Crawford and Jasper counties.
Allen, John, Greene county.
Allen, Willis, Franklin county.
Archer, Wm. B., Clark county.
Bainbridge, Allen, Franklin county.
Baker, Edward D., Sangamon county.
bBowman, Joseph G., Wabash county.
Brown, John, Schuyler county.
Calhoun, John, Sangamon county.
Carpenter, Milton, Hamilton county.
Churchill, Joseph W., LaSalle, Kane, De Kalb counties.
Cloud, Newton, Morgan county.
Compher, Wm., Peoria county.
Copeland, James, Johnson county.
Craig, James, JoDaviess, Mercer, Rock Island, Stephenson, Ogle, Winnebago counties.
Crain, John, Washington county.
Cunningham, James T., Coles county.
Daley, Edward M., Greene county.
Dawson, John, Sangamon county.
Dubois, Jesse K., Lawrence county.
Dunn, Tarlton, Gallatin county.
Edmonston, Wm., McDonough county.
Edwards, Ninian W. Sangamon county.
Elkin, William F., Sangamon county.
Elliott, Asa, Vermilion county.
Emmerson, Allan, Edwards county.
English, Revill W., Greene county.
Ewing, Wm. L. D., Fayette, Effingham.
Ficklin, Orlando B., Coles county.
Fisk, Josiah, Montgomery county.
*Flood, Wm. G., Adams county.
Foster, Hardy, Marion county.
French, Augustus C., Edgar county.
Gilham, William, Morgan county.
Gouge, Jesse Wilson, Macon county.
Green, John, Calhoun, Greene counties.
Green, Peter, Clay county.
Hankins, Wm. J., Fayette Effingham counties.
Happy, Wm. W., Morgan county.
Hardin, John J., Morgan county.
Harlan, Moses, Peoria county.
Harris, John, Macoupin county.
Henderson, Wm. H., Putnam, Bureau counties.
Henry, John, Morgan county.
Holmes, Wm., Cass county.
Houston, John, Crawford, Jasper counties.
Huey, Joseph, Clinton county.
Hull, Alden, Tazewell county.
Jarrot, Vital, St. Clair county.
Johnson, Benjamin, Bond.
Jones, Gabriel, Randolph county.
Kent, Germanicus, JoDaviess, Mercer, Rock Island, Stephenson, Ogle, Winnebago counties.
Kercheval, Gholson, Cook, Will, McHenry counties.
Kerr, Richard, Pike county.
Lincoln, Abraham, Sangamon county.
Logan, John, Jackson county.
Lyon, James H., Champaign county.
Marshall, Samuel D., Gallatin county.
Maus, Wm. S., Tazewell county.
McCormick, Andrew, Sangamon county.
McCutchen, Jesse M., Schuyler county.
McMillan, Robert, Edgar county.
McWilliams, James, Pike county.
Menard, Edward, Randolph county.
Moore, John, McLean county.
Morgan, Edward T., Monroe county.
Murphy, John H., Vermilion county.
Murphy, Richard, Cook, Will, McHenry counties.
Murphy, Richard G., Perry county.
Nance, Thomas J., Sangamon county.
Naper, Joseph, Cook, Will, McHenry counties.
Otwell, Wm., Madison county.
Pace, Harvey T., Jefferson county.
Phillips, Alexander, White county.
Rawalt, Jonas, Fulton county.
Read, John W., Pope county.
Roberts, Louis, Iroquois county.
Robinson, Jeffry, Wayne county.
Roman, Wm. W., St. Clair county.
Stapp, Wyatt B., Warren, Knox, Henry counties.
cStarr, Richard W., Adams counties.
dSimms, Hall, Edgar county.
†Smith, Edward, Wabash county.
Smith, George, Madison county.
Smith, Robert, Madison county.
Thomas, Cheney, McLean county.
Thomas, John, St. Clair county.
Thornton, Wm. F., Shelby county.
Walker, Isaac P., Vermilion county.
Walker, Newton, Fulton county.
Webb, Edwin B., White county.
Webb, Henry L., Alexander county.
Williams, Archibald, Adams county.
Williamson, William, Shelby county.
Wood, Daniel, Gallatin county.
Zimmerman, Jacob, Union county.

* Resigned Feb. 27, 1839. † Died. a Vice H. L. Webb. b Vice Smith.
c Vice Flood. d Vice French.

TWELFTH GENERAL ASSEMBLY, 1840-1842.

First session convened at Springfield, Nov. 23, 1840; adjourned Dec. 5, 1840. Second session Dec. 7, 1840; adjourned March 1, 1841.

SENATE.

President—Stinson H. Anderson.
Secretary—Merritt L. Covell.
Sergeant-at-Arms—Andrew J. Witt.
Enrolling and Eng. Clerk—Downing Baugh.

*Allen, John, Greene, Jersey counties.
Baker, Edward D., Sangamon, Menard, Logan, Christian counties.
Churchill, George, Madison county.
Cullom, Richard N., Tazewell county.
Davidson, Wm. H., White county
Evans, Aiken, Fayette, Clay, Effingham counties.
Feaman, Jacob, Randolph county.
Fithian, Wm., Vermilion, Champaign counties.
Gaston, Wm., Clinton, Marion counties.
Gatewood, Wm. J., Gallatin county.
Gibbs, Worthington J., Pope, Johnson counties.
Hacker, John S., Union, Alexander counties.
Hamlin, John, Peoria, Putnam, Marshall, Bureau, Stark counties.
Harris, John, Macoupin county.
Harrison, George W., JoDaviess, Rock Island, Stephenson, Ogle, Mercer, Whiteside, Winnebago, Boone, Carroll, Lee counties.
Henry, John, Morgan county.
Herndon, Archer G., Sangamon, Menard, Logan, Christian counties.
Houston, John, Crawford, Lawrence, Jasper counties.
Hunter, Wm., Montgomery, Bond counties.
James, James A., Monroe, Madison St. Clair counties.
Johnson, Noah, Hamilton and Jefferson.
Kilpatrick, T. M., Morgan, Scott, Cass counties.
Little, Sidney H., McDonough, Hancock counties.
Markley, David, Fulton county.
Moore, John, McLean, Macon, DeWitt, Livingston counties.
Monroe, Byrd, Clark, Coles counties.
Nunnally, Nelson W., Edgar county.
Parish, Braxton, Franklin, Williamson, Jackson counties.
Pearson, John, Cook, Will, DuPage, Lake, McHenry counties.
Ralston, James H., Adams county.
Richardson, Wm. A., Schuyler, Brown counties.
Ross, Wm., Pike county.
Sergeant, Wm. L., Morgan, Cass, Scott counties.
Slocum, Rigdon B., Wayne, Edwards, Wabash counties.
Snyder, Adam W., St. Clair county.
Stadden, Wm., LaSalle, Iroquois, Kane, DeKalb counties.
Stapp, Wyatt B., Warren, Knox, Henry counties.
Warren, Peter, Shelby county.
Witt, Franklin, Greene, Jersey, Calhoun counties.
Wood, John D., Washington, Perry counties.

*Died.

HOUSE OF REPRESENTATIVES.

Speaker—Wm. L. D. Ewing.
Clerk—John Calhoun.
Assistant—George Davis.
Enrolling and Eng. Clerk—Robert Smith.
Doorkeeper—Wm. C. Murphy.
Assistant—Benjamin Roberts.

Abel, Wilson, Alexander county.
Archer, Wm. B., Clark county.
Bailey, Wm. W., McDonough county.
Baldwin, Daniel, St. Clair county.
Barnett, Rob't F., Macon, DeWitt counties.
Beall, James, Wabash county.
Bennett, John, Menard county.
Bentley, Richard, Bond county.
Bissell, Wm. H., Monroe county.
Blackman, David J., Gallatin county.
Bradford, James M., Sangamon county.
Brown, James N., Sangamon county.
Brown, John J., Vermilion county.
Busey, Matthew W., Champaign county.
Canady, John, Vermilion county.
Carpenter, Milton, Hamilton county.
Cavalry, Alfred W., Greene, Jersey counties.
Charles, John F., Hancock county.
Courtright, Isaac, Iroquois county.
Cox, Jeremiah, Morgan county.
Crain, John, Washington county.
Cunningham, James T., Coles county.
Darnielle, John, Sangamon county.
Denny, John, Warren, Knox, Henry counties.
Dodge, Abram R., LaSalle county.
Dollins, Achilles D., Franklin, Williamson counties.
Dougherty, John, Union county.
Drummond, Thomas, JoDaviess, Rock Island, Stephenson, Ogle, Mercer, Whiteside, Winnebago, Boone, Carroll, Lee counties.
Dunlap, Samuel, Lawrence county.
Edwards, Cyrus, Madison county.
Emmerson, Allan, Edwards county.
English, Revill W., Greene, Jersey counties.
Ewing, Wm. L. D., Fayette, Effingham counties.
Francis, Josiah, Sangamon county.
Froman, Isaac, Vermilion county.
Funk, Isaac, McLean county.
Gillespie, Joseph, Madison county.
Green, Peter, Clay county.
Gridley, Asahel, McLean county.
Hankins, Wm. J., Fayette, Effingham counties.
Hardin, John J., Morgan county.
Henderson, Wm. H., Putnam, Bureau, Stark, Marshall counties.
Hicks, Stephen G., Jefferson county.
Hull, Alden, Tazewell county.
Humphrey, John G., Adams county.
Kelly, John M., Edgar county.
Kitchell, Wickliffe, Montgomery county.
Laughlin, Wm., Adams county.
Leary, Albert G., Cook, Will, McHenry counties.
Lester, Harvey, Brown county.
Lincoln, Abraham, Sangamon county.

Logan, John, Jackson county.
Marshall, James, Marion county.
McClernand, John A., Gallatin county.
McClurken, James, Randolph county.
McDonald, John, Greene, Jersey, Calhoun counties.
McGinnis, John P., Randolph county.
McLean, James, Lawrence county.
Menard, Pierre, Tazewell county.
Minshall, Wm. A., Schuyler county.
Moore, Daniel T., St. Clair county.
Munsell, Leander, Edgar county.
Murphy, Richard, Cook, Will, McHenry counties.
Murphy, Richard G., Perry county.
Odam, Dempsey, Franklin, Williamson counties.
Olds, Francis A., Macoupin county.
Oliver, John, Johnson county.
Ormsbee, Joseph W., Scott county.
Parkinson, James, Morgan county.
Parsons, Solomon, Pike county.
Peck, Ebenezer, Cook, Will and McHenry.
Phelps, Wm. J., Peoria county.
Phillips, Alexander, White county.
Prentice, Owen, Shelby county.
Reynolds, James, Madison county.
Ross, Lewis W., Fulton county.
Scott, John, Clinton county.
Shepley, Oliver, Fulton county.
Thornton, Hiram W., JoDaviess, Rock Island, Stephenson, Ogle, Mercer, Whiteside, Winnebago, Boone, Carroll and Lee.
Threlkeld, Thomas, Coles county.
Trumbull, Lyman, St. Clair county.
Troy, Daniel, Morgan county.
Turney, Daniel, Wayne county.
Waters, George T., Pope county.
Webb, Edwin B., White county.
West, Amos S., Cass county.
Wheeler, Alpheus, Pike county.
White, Martin, Logan, Christian counties.
Wilson, Wm., Crawford, Jasper counties.
Wood, Daniel, Gallatin county.
Woodson, David M., Greene, Jersey counties.

THIRTEENTH GENERAL ASSEMBLY, 1842-1844.

Convened at Springfield, Dec. 5, 1842; adjourned March 6, 1843.

SENATE.

President—John Moore.
Secretary—Isaac S. Berry.
Sergeant-at-Arms—Iram Nye.
Enrolling and Engrossing Clerk—William D. Latshaw.

Baker, Edward D., Christian, Menard, Logan, Sangamon counties.
Barnett, Robert F., McLean, DeWitt, Macon counties.
Buford, John, Rock Island, Henry, Lee, Whiteside counties.
Catlin, Seth, St. Clair county.
Cavalry Alfred W., Greene, Jersey counties.
Crain, John, Perry, Clinton, Washington counties.
Cullom, Richard N., Tazewell county.
Davis, Jacob C., Hancock county.
Dougherty, John, Union, Alexander counties.
*English, Revill W., Greene, Calhoun counties.
Evans, Aikens, Fayette, Clay, Effingham counties.
Feaman, Jacob, Randolph county.
Fithian, Wm., Vermilion and Champaign.
Gillham, James, Cass, Scott counties.
Harris, John, Macoupin county.
Harrison, George W., JoDaviess, Carroll, Stephenson counties.
Harrison, Reuben, Sangamon county.
Henry, John, Morgan county.
Hoard, Samuel, Cook, Lake counties.
Houston, John, Lawrence, Jasper, Crawford counties.
James, James A., Madison, St. Clair and Monroe counties.
Johnson, Benjamin, Bond, Christian and Montgomery counties.
Kilpatrick, T. M., Morgan, Scott counties.
Leviston, George, Gallatin county.
Markley, David, Fulton county.
Matteson, Joel A., Will, DuPage, Iroquois counties.
McMurtry, Wm., Knox, Mercer counties.
Minard, Ira, Kane, McHenry, Boone, DeKalb counties.
Nunnally, Nelson W., Edgar county.
Parker, Nathaniel, Coles, Clark counties.
Parish, Braxton, Franklin, Williamson, Jackson counties.
Pearson, John, Cook, Will, DuPage, Lake, McHenry counties.
†Ralston, James H., Adams county.
Ryan, Michael, LaSalle county.
Slocum, Rigdon B., Wayne, Edwards and Wabash counties.
Smith, George, Madison county.
Stapp, Wyatt B., Warren, Knox and Henry counties.
Thompson, W. W., Peoria, Stark, Bureau.
Vandeventer, Jacob, Schuyler and Brown counties.
Warren, Peter, Shelby county.
Waters, Geo. W., Pope, Hardin, Johnson counties.
Wilbanks, Robert A. D., Hamilton, Jefferson, Marion counties.
Worthington, Thomas, Pike county.
Wynne, Lewis B., Menard, Logan, Mason counties.

* Resigned Dec. 22, 1842. † Resigned Jan. 1, 1843.

HOUSE OF REPRESENTATIVES.

Speaker—Samuel Hackelton.
Clerk—Wm. L. D. Ewing.
Assistant—Washington J. Taylor.
Enrolling and Eng. Clerk—Robert Smith.
Doorkeeper—Wm. C. Murphy.
Assistant—Thomas Evans.

Adams, Darius, Winnebago county.
Aldrich, Robert, Madison county.
Ames, Alfred E., Boone county.
Anderson, Wm. G., Lawrence county.
Andrus, Leonard, Ogle county.
Arnold, Isaac, N., Cook county.
Ballhache, John, Madison county.
Bell, Robert F., Marshall, Putnam counties.
Bibbens, Elisha, LaSalle county.
Bishop, Mahlon, McLean county.
Blair, Wm., Pike county.
Blakeman, Curtis, Madison county.

Bone, Elisha, Menard county.
Bradley, Richard A., Jackson county.
Brinkley, Wm., Hamilton, Jefferson and Marion counties.
Brown, Benjamin D., Pike county.
Brown, James N., Sangamon county.
Browning, Orville H., Adams county.
Bryant, John H., Peoria, Stark and Bureau counties.
Burklow, John D., Perry county.
Busey, Matthew W., Champaign county.
Caldwell, Wm., Sangamon county.
Canady, John, Vermilion county.
Cloud, Newton, Morgan county.
Cochran, John, Alexander, Union counties.
Collins, Addison, DuPage, Will, Iroquois counties.
Compton, John, Wabash county.
Courtwright, Isaac, DuPage, Will, Iroquois counties.
Cushman, Wm. H., LaSalle county.
Danner, Jacob J., Monroe, Randolph counties.
Davis, James M., Bond county.
Davis, John T., Williamson county.
Dennis, Elias S., Clinton and Washington counties.
Dickinson, Andrew J., Monroe, Randolph counties.
Dollins, Achilles D., Franklin county.
Dougherty, Willis, Clark county.
Douglas, John, Hamilton county.
Dubois, Jesse K., Lawrence county.
Edwards, Lorenzo, Scott county.
Epler, David, Morgan county.
Ervin, Hugh, McDonough county.
Ewing, Charles F., Logan, Mason counties.
Ficklin, Orlando B., Coles county.
Flanders, Abner, Gallatin county.
Fowler, Joseph, Coles county.
Garrett, Peter B., Adams county.
Glass, Robert W., Macoupin county.
Gobble, Sergeant, Macoupin county.
Graves, Hubbard, Carroll and Stephenson counties.
*Green, John, Greene county.
Green, Peter, Clay county.
Gregg, David L., DuPage, Will and Iroquois counties.
Hackleton, Samuel, Peoria, Fulton counties.
Haley, Maxmillian, Warren and Henderson counties.
Hambaugh, Stephen D., Brown county.
Hannaford, Levi A., Peoria county.
Hanson, George M., Coles county.
Harper, Joshua, Rock Island, Henry counties.
Hatch, Jeduthan, DuPage, Will, Iroquois counties.
Hick, Thomas S., Gallatin county.
Hickman, Wm., Sangamon county.
Hicks, Stephen G., Jefferson county.
Hinton, Alfred, Greene county.
Horner, Samuel, Schuyler county.

* Died Feb. 3, 1843.

Howard, Jonathan B., Shelby county.
Hunsacker, James J., Union, Alexander counties.
Jackson, Aaron C., Whiteside, Lee counties.
Jackson, Wm. M., Kane, McHenry, Boone, DeKalb counties.
Jonas, Abraham, Adams county.
Kendall, Samuel T., Jersey county.
Kœrner, Gustavus, St. Clair county.
Kuykendall, Andrew J., Johnson county.
Langworthy, Cyrus, Stark, Bureau counties.
Lawler, John S., White county.
Lockard, James, Clark county.
Logan, Stephen T., Sangamon county.
Loy, Thomas M., Fayette, Effingham counties.
Madden, Henry, Boone, DeKalb, Kane, McHenry, Kendall counties.
Manning, Julius, Knox county.
Marshall, James, Marion county.
McBride, Wm., Monroe, Randolph counties.
McClernand, John A., Gallatin county.
McDonald, John, Greene, Calhoun counties.
McDonald, John, JoDaviess county.
McMillan, Andrew, McLean and Livingston counties.
Menard, Pierre, Tazewell county.
Miller, Harry L., Fulton county.
Mitchell, Edward, Scott county.
Murphy, Richard, Lake county.
Nesbitt, Samuel G., Macon, Platt counties.
Norris, James, Vermilion county.
Owen, Thomas H., Hancock county.
Penn, Philip, St. Clair county.
Pickering, Wm., Edwards county.
Pratt, John M., Cass county.
Scott, James K., DeWitt county.
Sharp, Joseph L., Fulton county.
Shirley, John, Fayette, Effingham counties.
Simms, Hall, Edgar county.
Smith, Guy W., Crawford, Jasper counties.
Smith, Wm., Hancock county.
Spicer, Reuben H., Knox, Mercer counties.
Starne, Alexander, Pike county.
Starr, Richard W., Adams county.
Stewart, Hart L., Cook county.
Stockton, Wm. S., Warren and Henderson counties.
Tackerberry, Middleton, Tazewell county.
Thompson, Amos, St. Clair county.
Turner, Horace, Fulton county.
Vandeveer, H. M., Christian county.
Vance, P. C., Schuyler, Brown counties.
Vineyard, Philip, Pope, Hardin counties.
Weatherford, Wm., Morgan county.
Wist, Edward, Wayne county.
Wheat, Almeron, Adams county.
Whitcomb, Lot, Cook county.
White, John, Clinton, Washington counties.
Whitten, Easton, Montgomery county.
Wilson, Wm., Crawford, Jasper counties.
Woodworth, James H., LaSalle county.
Yates, Richard, Morgan county.

FOURTEENTH GENERAL ASSEMBLY, 1844-1846.

Convened at Springfield, Dec. 2, 1844; adjourned March 3, 1845.

SENATE.

President—John Moore.
Secretary—Merit L. Covell.
Assistant—Henry W. Moore.
Enrolling and Eng. Clerk—Noah Johnson.
Sergeant-at-Arms—Wm. C. Murphy.

Allen, Willis, Williamson, Franklin, Jackson counties.
Boal, Robert, Tazewell, Marshall, Putnam, Woodford counties.
Buford, John, Rock Island, Henry, Whiteside, Lee counties.
Catlin, Seth, St. Clair county.
Cavarly, Alfred W., Greene, Calhoun counties.
Constable, Charles H., Wayne, Edwards, Wabash counties.
Crain, John, Perry, Clinton, Washington counties.
Davis, Jacob C., Hancock county.

Dougherty, John, Union, Alexander counties.
Dunlap, Samuel, Crawford, Lawrence, Jasper, Richland counties.
Edwards, Ninian W., Sangamon county.
Fithian, William, Vermilion, Champaign counties.
Forman, Ferris, Fayette, Effingham, Clay, Richland counties.
Harris, John, Macoupin, Jersey counties.
Harrison, George W., JoDaviess, Stephenson, Carroll counties.
Henry, John, Morgan county.
Johnson, Benjamin, Bond, Christian, Montgomery counties.
Judd, Norman B., Cook, Lake counties.
Kilpatrick, Thos. M., Scott, Cass counties.
Leviston, George, Gallatin county.
Markley, David, Fulton county.
Matteson, Joel A., Will, DuPage, Iroquois counties.
McMillan, Wm., Warren, McDonough, Henderson counties.
Minard, Ira, Kane, McHenry, Boone, DeKalb counties.
McMurtry, William, Knox, Mercer counties.
Morrison, Joseph, Randolph, Monroe counties.
Nunnally, Nelson W., Edgar county..
Parker, Nathaniel, Coles, Clark counties.
Powers, Geo. W., McLean, Macon, Livingston, Platt, DeWitt counties.
Ruggles, Spooner, Winnebago, Ogle counties.
Ryan, Michael, LaSalle county.
Smith, George, Madison county.
Smith, Jacob, Adams county.
Thompson, W. W., Peoria, Stark, Bureau counties.
Vandeventer, Jacob, Schuyler, Brown counties.
Warren, Peter, Shelby, Moultrie counties.
Webb, Edwin B., White county.
Waters, George W., Pope, Johnson, Hardin counties.
Wilbanks, Robert A. D., Hamilton, Jefferson, Marion counties.
Worthington, Thomas, Pike county.
Wynne, Lewis B., Menard, Logan, Mason counties.

HOUSE OF REPRESENTATIVES.

Speaker—William A. Richardson.
Clerk—Newton Cloud.
Assistant—John McDonald.
Enrolling and Eng. Clerk—F. D. Preston.
Doorkeeper—Jarvis Pierce.
Assistant—Jefferson Weatherford.

Adams, E., Monroe, Randolph counties.
Aldrich, Cyrus, JoDaviess county.
Alexander, W., Edgar county.
Anderson, Samuel, St. Clair county.
Anderson, Wm. G., Lawrence county.
Arenz, Francis, Morgan county.
Armstrong, Geo. W., LaSalle, Kendall and Grundy counties.
Arnold, Isaac N., Cook county.
Babbitt, A. W., Hancock county.
Backenstos, J. B., Hancock county.
Barnsback, George, Madison county.
Benedict, Kirby, Macon, Platt counties.
Berry, Isaac S., Fayette, Effingham counties.
Blair, William, Pike county.
Boyakin, H. P., Marion county.
Bradley, Richard A., Jackson county.
Brinkley, Wm., Hamilton county.
Brown, John, Schuyler county.
Burnett, John M., Gallatin county.
Butler, H., Lake county.
Campbell, Joseph, Wayne county.
Churchill, George, Madison county.
Cochran, John, Union, Alexander counties.
Collins, A., DuPage, Will, Iroquois counties.
Cox, David, Champaign county.
Cushman, W. H. W., LaSalle, Kendall and Grundy counties.
Davis, David, McLean county.
Davis, John T., Williamson county.
Denning, Wm. A., Alexander, Pulaski counties.
Deskines, John, Logan, Mason counties.
Dunbar, A. P., Coles county.
Emerson, R., White county.
Fletcher, Job, Sangamon county.
Funkhouser, P., Fayette, Effingham counties.
Gregg, D. L., DuPage, Will, Iroquois counties.
Haley, Maximillian, Warren and Henderson counties.
Hannaford, Levi A., Peoria county.
Hanson, Geo. M., Coles county.
Hardie, H., Knox, Mercer counties.
Harper, Joshua, Rock Island, Henry counties.
Harriott, James, Jersey county.
Henderson, Wm. H., Warren, Henderson counties.
Hendry, William, Adams county.
Herndon, Wm. D., Sangamon county.
Hick, Thomas S., Gallatin county.
Hicks, Stephen G., Jefferson county.
Hitt, Samuel M., Ogle county.
Huffman, Samuel, Vermillion county.
Jackson, B. M., Peoria, Stark, Bureau counties.
Jackson, Wm. M., Kane, McHenry, Boone, De Kalb counties.
Janney, E. S., Crawford, Jasper counties.
Jewell, E. G., Kane, McHenry, Boone, De Kalb counties.
Kirkpatrick, John, Montgomery county.
Kuykendall, Andrew J., Johnson, Massac counties.
Leighton, James, Scott county.
Lockard, James, Clark county.
Logan, Stephen T., Sangamon county.
Loop, James L., Kane, McHenry, Boone, De Kalb counties.
Lott, Peter, Adams county.
Manning, Julius, Knox county.
Matthews, Samuel T., Morgan county.
McDonald, John, Greene, Calhoun counties.
Metz, B. B., Pike county.
Miller, Anson S., Winnebago county.
Miller, Harry L., Fulton county.
Miller, William, Adams county.
Moore, Wm J., Vermillion county.
Morrill, Jacob C., Marshall, Putnam counties.
Morris, R. G., Crawford, Jasper counties.
Morrison, J. L. D., St. Clair county.
Myers, Elias B., McLean, Livingston counties.
Nye, Iram, Brown county.
O'Conner, A., LaSalle, Kendall and Grundy counties.
Oglesby, John M., Hamilton, Jefferson and Marion county.
Parish, Braxton, Franklin county.
Pickering, William, Edwards county.
Pitner, Franklin R., Clay county.
Pratt, John W., Cass county.
Prevo, Samuel, Clark county.
Randolph, Wm. H., McDonough county.
Rawlings, Isaac D., Morgan county.
Reed, J. H., Richland, Lawrence counties.
Richardson, Wm. A., Schuyler and Brown counties.
Ricks, William S., Christian county.
Robbins, E. W., Monroe, Randolph counties.
Ross, Lewis W., Fulton county.
Scott, James K., DeWitt county.
Scott, John, Macoupin county.
Sexton, Orvall, Gallatin county.
Sharp, Joseph L., Fulton county.
Sherman, Francis C., Cook county.
Smith, Benjamin L., Stark, Bureau counties.
Smith, Henry, Carroll, Stephenson counties.
Smith, Joseph, Sangamon county.

Starkweather, Elisha H., Cumberland county.
Starne, Alexander, Pike county.
Steele, John, Perry county.
Stewart, Hart L., Cook county.
Strong, N. D., Madison county.
Thompson, Amos, St. Clair county.
Tunnel, Calvin, Greene county.
Turley, John S., Shelby county.
Vedder, F. P., Greene county.
Vineyard, Philip, Pope, Hardin counties.
Wagner, Jacob, DuPage, Will and Iroquois counties.
Warren, J. M., DuPage, Will and Iroquois counties.
White, James, Menard county.
White, John, Clinton, Washington counties.
White, John, Scott county.
Whiteside, John D., Monroe and Randolph counties.
Wilcox, Charles C., Tazewell and Woodford counties.
Wilkinson, W. S., Whiteside, Lee counties.
Williams, Isaac, Tazewell and Woodford counties.
Wood, John T., Macoupin county.
Woodburn, Wm., Clinton and Washington counties.
Woolard, James B., Bond county.
Yates, Richard, Morgan county.
Youngkin, John F., Wabash county.
Zeiber, John S., Peoria, Fulton counties.

FIFTEENTH GENERAL ASSEMBLY, 1846-1848.

Convened at Springfield Dec. 7, 1846; adjourned March 1, 1847.

SENATE.

President—Joseph B. Wells.
Secretary—Henry W. Moore.
Assistant—Nelson D. Elwood.
Enrolling and Eng. Clerk—F. D. Preston.
Sergeant-at-Arms—William J. Cline.
Assistant—Alfred Hinton.

Allen, Willis, Franklin, Williamson, Jackson counties.
Allison, John Y., Edgar county.
Boal, Robert, Tazewell, Putnam, Marshall and Woodford counties.
Brown, John, Schuyler, Brown counties.
Catlin, Seth, St. Clair county.
Cavarly, Alfred W., Greene and Calhoun counties.
Constable, Charles H., Wayne, Edwards and Wabash counties.
Davis, Jacob C., Hancock county.
Davis, Thomas G. C., Pope, Johnson, Hardin counties.
Dennis, Elias S., Clinton, Washington, Perry counties.
Denny, John, Knox, Mercer.
Dougherty, John, Union, Pulaski, Alexander counties.
Dunlap, Samuel, Crawford, Lawrence, Jasper counties.
Edwards, Ninian W., Sangamon county.
Gillespie, Joseph, Madison county.
Goudy, Oliver, Bond, Christian, Montgomery counties.
Hanson, George M., Cumberland, Coles, Clark counties.
Harris, John, Macoupin, Jersey counties.
Henry, John, Morgan county.
Houston, Samuel, Fayette, Effingham, Clay counties.
Judd, Norman B., Cook, Lake county.
Kilpatrick, Thos. M., Scott, Cass counties.
Leviston, George, Gallatin county.
Markley, David, Fulton county.
Matteson, Joel A., Will, DuPage and Iroquois counties.
McMillan, Wm., McDonough, Warren and Henderson counties.
McRoberts, Josiah, Vermilion, Champaign counties.
Miller, Anson S., Ogle, Winnebago counties.
Morrison, Joseph, Randolph and Monroe counties.
Noble, Silas, Lee, Whiteside, Rock Island and Henry counties.
Powers, George W., McLean, Livingston, Piatt, Macon and DeWitt counties.
Reddick, William, LaSalle, Grundy, Kendall counties.
Sanger, Lorenzo P., JoDaviess, Stephenson, Carroll county.
Smith, Jacob, Adams, Marquette counties.
Stephenson, Wm. J., Hamilton, Jefferson, Marion counties.
Sutphin, Hugh L., Pike county.
Sweat, Peter, Peoria, Stark, Bureau counties.
Warren, Peter, Shelby, Moultrie counties.
Webb, Edwin B., White county.
Wilcox, Elijah, Kane, McHenry, Boone and DeKalb counties.

HOUSE OF REPRESENTATIVES.

Speaker—Newton Cloud.
Clerk—John McDonald.
Assistant—William W. Pace.
Enrolling and Eng. Clerk—A. J. Galloway.
Doorkeeper—John A. Wilson.
Assistant—Isham G. Davidson.

aAiken, Walter S., Franklin county.
Archer, Wm. B., Clark county.
Austin, Henry S., Fulton, Peoria counties.
Bailey, Evon, Fulton county.
Bailey, John S., Brown, Schuyler counties.
Bailey, William, Rock Island and Henry counties.
Barber, William, LaSalle, Kendall, Grundy counties.
Blakeman, Curtis, Madison county.
Boyakin, Henderson P., Marion county.
Boyle, Marmontel, Crawford and Jasper counties.
Bragg, Henry, Greene county.
Brown, James N., Sangamon county.
Buckley, Edward H., Marquette county.
Campbell, John B., Scott county.
Cantrill, William, Macon, Piatt counties.
Casey, Lewis F., Jefferson county.
Caswell, Josiah, Greene county.
Chapman, Wyllys H., Marquette county.
Cloud, Newton, Morgan county.
Cockle, Washington, Peoria county.
Constant, Resin H., Sangamon county
Creel, Berryman, Clinton county.
Cross, Robert J., Winnebago county.
Cummings, Thomas, Jersey county.
Cunningham, John W., Williamson county.
Curts, John, Warren, Henderson counties.
Dana, Wm. G., Ogle county.
Davis, Wm. P., Vermilion county.
Dawson, John, Brown county.
*Denning, Wm. A., Franklin county.
DeWolf, Wm. F., Madison county.
bDiarman, Joseph, Pope, Hardin counties.
Eads, Abner, JoDaviess county.

Eddy, Henry, Gallatin county.
Ela, George, Lake county.
Enloe, Enoch, Johnson, Massac counties.
Epperson, Thomas, Stark, Peoria, Bureau counties.
Erwin, Lewis D., Schuyler county.
Everett, J. J., Cook county.
Fry, John D., Greene, Calhoun counties.
Funkhouser, P., Fayette, Effingham counties.
Gilmore, Ephraim, Knox, Mercer counties.
Glenn, Samuel P., DeWitt county.
Glover, James O., LaSalle, Kendall, Grundy counties.
Griffith, John M., Clay county.
Grubb, Alfred, Pike county.
Hansford, Charles, Knox county.
Harpole, Wm. P., Pike county.
Herrington, James, Kane, McHenry, Boone, De Kalb counties.
Hart, Thomas, Macoupin county.
Hayes, Samuel S., White county.
Hendry, William, Adams county.
Hick, Thomas, Gallatin county.
Higgins, James M., Pike county.
Hodges, John, Alexander, Pulaski counties.
Huffman, Samuel, Vermilion county.
Janney, Eldridge S., Crawford, Jasper counties.
Johnson, Noah, Marion, Hamilton, Jefferson counties.
Kretsinger, George W., Kane, McHenry, Boone, De Kalb counties.
Kinney, Captain E., Will, DuPage, Iroquois.
Linder, Usher F., Coles county.
Little, Thomas A., Fulton county.
Little, Wm. E., Will, DuPage and Iroquois.
Logan, John, Jackson county.
Logan Stephen T., Sangamon county.
Long, Wm. H., Morgan county.
Lukins, Samuel S., Wabash county.
Munn, Robert, Randolph, Monroe counties.
†Marshall, Samuel S., Hamilton county.
Martin, Wm., Madison county.
McConnel, Robert, Stephenson and Carroll.
McDowell, Reuben R., Fulton county.
McLean, Michael C., Lawrence, Richland.
Miller, John, Will, DuPage, Iroquois counties.
Miner, Edward G., Scott county.
Morris, Isaac N., Adams county.
Morrison, John, Randolph, Monroe counties.
Morrison, Thomas, Hancock county.
Morton, Joseph, Morgan county.
O'Conner, Ambrose, LaSalle, Kendall and Grundy counties.
Omelveny, Edward, Randolph and Monroe.
Osburn, Hawkins S., Perry county.
Pickering, Wm., Edwards county.
Pierson, James T., Kane, McHenry, Boone, De Kalb counties.
Prevo, Samuel, Clark county.
Randolph, Wm. H., McDonough county.
Remann, Frederick, Fayette and Effingham.
Reynolds, John, St Clair county.
‡Rhodes, William, Pope, Hardin counties.
Robb, Matthew, McLean county.
Robeson, James, McLean, Livingston, Woodford counties.
Robinson, James M., Menard county.
Ruddle, John M., Adams county.
Rutledge, James M., Montgomery county.
Seehorn, James M., Adams county.
Sherman, Francis C., Cook county.
Shumway, Dorice D., Christian county.
Sims, Hall, Edgar county.
Skinner, Mark, Cook county.
Slocumb, Rigdon B., Wayne county.
Smith, Wm. S., Bond county.
Stanley, Micagah J., Will, DuPage, Iroquois counties.
Stark, James, Hancock county.
Starkweather, Elisha H., Cumberland county
Stickney Wm. H., Gallatin county.
Stokes, Matthew, Union county.
Stookey, Samuel, St. Clair county.
Swing, Michael W., Logan, Mason counties.
Tappan, Harman, V. A., Macoupin county.
Thomas, Samuel, Bureau, Stark counties.
Thomas, William, Morgan county.
Tucker, James, Warren, Henderson counties.
Turner, Edward W., Cass county.
Underwood, Wm. H., St. Clair county.
Wallace, Hugh, Whiteside, Lee counties.
Wardlaw, Andrew, Marshall, Putnam counties.
Watson, Wm. D., Coles county.
West, Benjamin, Sangamon county.
White, John, Washington county.
Wilcox, Charles C., Tazewell, Woodford.
Williams, Isaac, Tazewell, Woodford counties.
Williamson, Wm., Shelby county.
Wright, James S. Champaign county.
Wynne, Josiah R., Lawrence and Richland.

* Resigned. † Resigned March 12, 1847. ‡ Died Jan. 4, 1847. *a* Vice Denning. *b* Vice Rhodes.

SIXTEENTH GENERAL ASSEMBLY, 1848-1850.

First Session convened at Springfield Jan. 1, 1849; adjourned Feb. 12, 1849. Second session Oct. 22, 1849; adjourned Nov. 7, 1849.

SENATE.

President—Wm. McMurtry.
Secretary—William Smith.
Assistant—Dorice D. Shumway.
Enrolling and Eng. Clerk—A. C. Dickson.
Sergeant-at-Arms—I. G. Davidson.
Assistant—John Oliver.

Dist.	Name.	County.	Dist.	Name.	County.
1	William Y. Davis	Johnson	13	Franklin Witt	Greene
2	Dempsey Odam	Williamson	14	Newton Cloud	Morgan
3	Jeduthan P. Hardy	Hamilton	15	Hugh L. Sutphin	Pike
4	Hawkins S. Osburn	Perry	16	John P. Richmond	Schuyler
5	J. L. D. Morrison	St. Clair	17	Azro Patterson	Henderson
6	Joseph Gillespie	Madison	18	David Markley	Fulton
7	Hiram Rountree	Montgomery	19	John Denny	Knox
8	Alfred H. Grass	Lawrence	20	William Reddick	LaSalle
9	William Tichenor	Edgar	21	Joel A. Matteson	Will
	*Url Manly	Clark	22	Wm. B. Plato	Kane
10	Josiah McRoberts	Vermilion	23	Hezekiah H. Gear	JoDaviess
11	Edward O. Smith	Macon	24	Alfred E. Ames	Winnebago
12	John T. Stuart	Sangamon	25	Norman B. Judd	Cook

* Vice Tichenor, absent from State.

HOUSE OF REPRESENTATIVES.

Speaker—Zadok Casey.
Clerk—Nathaniel Niles.
Assistant—Harmon G. Reynolds.

Enrolling and Eng. Clerk—A. J. Galloway
Doorkeeper—Samuel Ewing.
Assistant—Samuel B. Smith.

Dist.	Name.	County.	Dist.	Name.	County.
1	John Cochran	Union	30	John H. Seonce	Vermilion
2	Wesley Sloan	Pope	31	George W. Rives	Edgar
3	David J. Blackman	Saline	32	Reuben B. Ewing	Moultrie
4	David Y. Bridges	Johnson	33	Edward Evey	Shelby
5	Richard A. Bradley	Jackson	34	Tyree Jennings	Pike
6	James J. Richardson	Marion		George Pattison	Calhoun
	John A. Campbell	Wayne	35	Onias C. Skinner	Adams
	Zadok Casey	Jefferson		Jonathan Dearborn	Brown
7	Samuel S. Hayes	White		John Marrett	Adams
8	William Pickering	Edwards	36	Jesse Darnell	Schuyler
9	Ebenezer Z. Ryan	Lawrence	37	George Walker	Hancock
10	Richard G. Morris	Crawford		S. H. Tyler	Hancock
11	Usher F. Linder	Coles	38	Josiah Harrison	McDonough
12	Joshua P. Cooper	Clark	39	William Kellogg	Fulton
13	Elisha H. Starkweather	Cumberland		Edward Sayre	Fulton
14	John McDonald	Fayette	40	Ezra G. Sanger	Peoria
15	Edward Y. Rice	Montgomery	41	Henry J. Runkel	Knox
	Richard S. Bond	Clirton	42	Gilbert Turnbull	Henderson
16	Zenas H. Vernor	Washington		Abner C. Harding	Warren
17	Samuel H. Guthrie	Randolph	43	John W. Henderson	Stark
18	Xerxes F. Trail	Monroe	44	Joseph Crawford	Lee
19	Simon Stookey	St. Clair	45	Dauphin Brown	Ogle
	*Samuel B. Chandler	St. Clair	46	Abner Eads	JoDaviess
	Edward Abend	St. Clair		Cyrenius B. Denio	JoDaviess
20	Edward Keating	Madison	47	Wilson H. Crandell	Winnebago
	Curtis Blakeman	Madison	48	John Page	Woodford
21	F. A. Olds	Macoupin	49	George W. Gilson	LaSalle
22	Isaac Darneille	Jersey		Melancthon E. Lasher	Bureau
	†Joel Corey	Jersey	50	William E. Little	Will
	John D. Fry	Greene		Warren L. Wheaton	DuPage
	‡Thomas Carlin	Greene		Lorenzo D. Brady	Kendall
23	Charles F. Keener	Scott		§Orlando H. Haven	Kendall
24	George B. Waller	Morgan	51	H. W. Fay	DeKalb
	Richard Yates	Morgan		E. W. Austin	Kane
25	Richard S. Thomas	Cass	52	John F. Gray	McHenry
26	Ninian W. Edwards	Sangamon		Selby Leach	Boone
	John W. Smith	Sangamon	53	Life Wilson	Lake
27	John Lucas	Logan	54	Philip Maxwell	Cook
28	Middleton Tackerberry	Tazewell		Francis C. Sherman	Cook
29	James B. Price	McLean			

* Vice Stookey, deceased † Vice Darneille, deceased. ‡ Vice Fry, resigned. § Vice Brady, resigned.

SEVENTEENTH GENERAL ASSEMBLY, 1850-1852.

First session convened at Springfield, Jan. 6, 1851; adjourned Feb. 17, 1851. Second session June 7, 1852; adjourned June 23, 1852.

SENATE.

President—William McMurtry.
Secretary—William Smith.
Assistant—William D. Latshaw.

Enrolling and Eng. Clerk—A. C. Dickson.
Sergeant-at-Arms—Edward A. Bedell.
Assistant—Benjamin N. Wyatt.

Dist.	Name.	County.	Dist.	Name.	County.
1	Andrew J. Kuykendall	Johnson	13	‡John M. Palmer	Macoupin
2	Dempsey Odam	Williamson	14	Newton Cloud	Morgan
3	Jeduthan P. Hardy	Hamilton	15	John Wood	Adams
	*Hugh Gregg	Hamilton	16	John P. Richmond	Schuyler
4	Hawkins S. Osborn	Perry	17	Jacob C. Davis	Hancock
5	J. L. D. Morrison	St. Clair	18	Peter Sweat	Peoria
6	Joseph Gillespie	Madison	19	John Denny	Knox
7	Hiram Rountree	Montgomery		§Samuel Webster	Rock Island
	†Jacob D. Lansing		20	William Reddick	LaSalle
8	Alfred H. Grass	Lawrence	21	Joel A. Matteson	Will
9	Josiah R. Wynn	Crawford	22	William B. Plato	Kane
10	Nathaniel Parker	Coles	23	Hugh Wallace	Whiteside
11	Ashel Gridley	McLean	24	Thomas B. Talcott	Winnebago
12	John T. Stuart	Sangamon	25	Norman B. Judd	Cook
13	Franklin Witt	Greene			

* Vice Hardy, resigned. † Vice Rountree, resigned. ‡ Vice Witt, deceased.
§ Vice Denny, resigned.

HOUSE OF REPRESENTATIVES.

Speaker—Sidney Breese.
Clerk—Isaac R. Diller.
Assistant—William A. J. Sparks.

Enrolling and Eng. Clerk—Wm. J. Allen.
Assistant—William M. Osman.
Doorkeeper—Samuel B. Smith.
Assistant—Chester Carpenter.

Dist.	Name.	County.	Dist.	Name.	County.
			29	Robt. F. Barnett	DeWitt
1	Cyrus G. Simonds	Union	30	Oliver L. Davis	Vermilion
2	Wesley Sloan	Pope	31	Ozias Bailey	Edgar
3	A. G. Caldwell	Gallatin	32	Charles Emerson	Macon
	*Orville Sexton	Gallatin	33	Anthony Thornton	Shelby
4	Wilfred Ferrell	Williamson	34	Wm. D. Hamilton	Calhoun
5	Thomas M. Sams	Franklin		Ozias M. Hatch	Pike
6	Zadok Casey	Jefferson	35	James W. Singleton	Brown
	Isham N. Haynie	Marion		J. R. Hobbs	Adams
	Wm. L. Gash	Wayne		J. M. Pitman	Adams
7	Samuel H. Martin	White	36	Allen Persinger	Schuyler
8	Wm. Pickering	Edwards	37	Joseph Sibley	Hancock
9	Aaron Shaw	Lawrence		John Carlin	Hancock
10	James C. Allen	Crawford	38	John Huston	McDonough
11	Usher F. Linder	Coles	39	Thomas J. Little	Fulton
12	T. C. Moore	Clark		Isaac Linley	Fulton
13	Wm. H. Blakely	Effingham	40	David Sanborn	Peoria
14	Akins Evans	Fayette	41	Henry Arms	Knox
15	Sidney Breese	Clinton	42	Azro Patterson	Henderson
	Wm. Brewer	Montgomery		Thomas Willits	Mercer
16	Richard G. Murphy	Perry	43	James M. Allen	Henry
17	John E. Detrich	Randolph	44	Van J. Adams	Whiteside
18	Thomas Quick	Monroe	45	Wm. T. Miller	Carroll
19	Wm. H. Snyder	St. Clair	46	D. Wilson	Stephenson
	Harbert Patterson	St. Clair		B. B. Howard	JoDaviess
	Philip B. Fouke†	St. Clair	47	Horace Miller	Winnebago
20	Andrew Miller	Madison	48	E. B. Ames	Putnam
	N. G. Edwards	Madison	49	Abraham L. Phillips	Bureau
	Samuel A. Buckmaster‡	Madison		John Hise	LaSalle
21	B. T. Burke	Macoupin	50	S. H. Randall	Kendall
22	Charles D. Hodges	Greene		Jesse O. Norton	Will
	J. C. Winters	Jersey		W. F. Jones	DuPage
23	Nathan N. Knapp	Scott		¶Julius M. Warren	DuPage
24	William Thomas	Morgan	51	Augustus Adams	Kane
	B. F. Bristow	Morgan		Benj. F. Hall	DeKalb
25	Wm. T. Beckman	Menard	52	A. H. Nixon	McHenry
26	Ninian W. Edwards	Sangamon		George Gage	McHenry
	Preston Breckenridge	Sangamon	53	Hurlbut Swan	Lake
	§James C. Conkling	Sangamon	54	Philip Maxwell	Cook
27	John Pemberton	Mason		Thomas Dyer	Cook
28	Robt. W. Briggs	Tazewell			

* Vice A. G. Caldwell, deceased. † Vice Harbert Patterson, resigned.
‡ Vice Nelson G. Edwards, resigned. § Vice Ninian W. Edwards, resigned.
¶ Vice W. F. Jones, resigned.

EIGHTEENTH GENERAL ASSEMBLY, 1852-1854.

First session convened at Springfield, Jan. 3, 1853; adjourned Feb. 14, 1853. Second session Feb. 9, 1854; adjourned March 4, 1854.

SENATE.

President—Gustavus Kœrner.
Secretary—R. Eaton Goodell.
Assistant—Wm. D. Latshaw.
Enrolling and Eng. Clerk—A. C. Dickson.

Assistant—John Crain.
Sergeant-at-Arms—Edward A. Bedell.
Assistant—John Oliver.

Dist.	Name.	County.	Dist.	Name.	County.
1	Andrew J. Kuykendall	Johnson	14	Joseph Morton	Morgan
2	Anderson P. Corder	Williamson	15	John Wood	Adams
3	Silas L. Bryan	Marion	16	James M. Campbell	McDonough
4	John E. Detrich	Randolph	17	Jacob C. Davis	Hancock
5	Edward Omelveny	Monroe	18	Peter Sweat	Peoria
6	Joseph Gillespie	Madison	19	Benj. Graham	Henry
7	Gabriel R. Jernigan	Christian	20	Burton C. Cook	LaSalle
8	Mortimer O'Kean	Jasper	21	Uri Osgood	Will
9	Josiah R. Wynn	Crawford	22	Wm. B. Plato	Kane
10	Nathaniel Parker	Coles	23	Hugh Wallace	Whiteside
11	Ashel Gridley	McLean	24	Thomas B. Talcott	Winnebago
12	James M. Ruggles	Mason	25	Norman B. Judd	Cook
13	John M. Palmer	Macoupin			

HOUSE OF REPRESENTATIVES.

Speaker—John Reynolds.
Clerk—Isaac R. Diller (resigned).
John Calhoun (vice Diller).
Assistant—Finney D. Preston.

Enrolling and Eng. Clerk—Wm. M. Osman
Assistant—Robert Voceth.
Doorkeeper—M. R. Owen.
Assistant—J. J. Richey.

Dist.	Name.	County.	Dist.	Name.	County.
1	John Cochran	Union	31	William Shields	Edgar
2	Wesley Sloan	Pope	32	Henry Prather	Macon
3	David B. Russell	Saline	33	Samuel W. Moulton	Shelby
4	David Y. Bridges	Johnson	34	Henry B. Buchanan	Calhoun
5	John A. Logan	Jackson		Hugh L. Sutphin	Pike
6	John Wilbanks	Jefferson	35	James M. Pitman	Adams
	Alexander Campbell	Wayne		John C. Moses	Brown
	John A. Wilson	Hamilton		David Wolf	Adams
7	Daniel L. Jones	White		James W. Singleton*	Brown
8	Victor B. Bell	Wabash		Hiram Boyle†	Adams
9	William H. Christy	Lawrence	36	Francis E. Bryant	Schuyler
10	William H. Sterrett	Crawford	37	David Gochenour	Hancock
11	William D. Watson	Coles		Joseph Sibley	Hancock
12	Url Manly	Clark	38	James M. Randolph	McDonough
13	Presley Funkhouser	Effingham	39	W. K. Johnson	Fulton
14	A. J. Gallagher	Fayette		L. H. Bradbury	Fulton
	N. M. McCurdy‡	Fayette	40	Charles P. King	Peoria
15	William H. Maddux	Clinton	41	Thomas McKee	Knox
	William Young	Montgomery	42	Samuel Darnell	Henderson
16	William M. Phillips	Washington		E. A. Paine	Warren
17	Joseph Williamson	Randolph	43	William Marshall	Rock Island
18	Thos. Winstanley	Monroe	44	Joseph Crawford	Lee
19	John Reynolds	St. Clair	45	E. S. Potter	Ogle
	Wm. H. Snyder	St. Clair	46	Cyrenius B. Denio	JoDaviess
20	Samuel A. Buckmaster	Madison		W. P. Narramore	Stephenson
	Thomas Judy	Madison	47	A. J. Enoch	Winnebago
21	Lewis Solomon	Macoupin	48	Silas Ramsey	Marshall
22	Giles H. Turner	Jersey	49	C. R. Potter	LaSalle
	Charles D. Hodges	Greene		C. L. Starbuck	Grundy
23	Royal Mooers	Scott	50	Joseph Thomas	Iroquois
24	William Brown	Morgan		R. N. Matthews	Kendall
	Edward Lusk	Morgan		Joseph Naper	DuPage
25	Cyrus Wright	Cass	51	John Ransted	Kane
26	Pascal P. Enos	Sangamon		Wm. Shepherdson	DeKalb
	James N. Brown	Sangamon	52	H. C. Miller	Boone
27	Colby Knapp	Logan		A. H. Nixon	McHenry
28	Richard N. Cullom	Tazewell	53	Henry W. Blodgett	Lake
29	John E. McClun	McLean	54	W. B. Eagan	Cook
30	Thomas Haywood	Vermilion		Homer Wilmarth	Cook

* Vice John C. Moses, resigned. † Vice James M. Pitman.
‡ Vice A. J. Gallagher, resigned.

NINETEENTH GENERAL ASSEMBLY, 1854-1856.

Convened at Springfield, Jan. 1, 1855; adjourned Feb. 15, 1855.

SENATE.

President—Gustavus Kœrner.
Secretary—George T. Brown.
Assistant—Daniel Evans.

Enrolling and Eng. Clerk—Chas. H. Ray.
Assistant—Isaac R. Womath.
Sergeant-at-Arms—William J. Heath.
Assistant—Wesley Davidson.

Dist.	Name.	County.	Dist.	Name.	County.
1	Norman B. Judd	Cook	14	John M. Palmer	Macoupin
2	George Gage	McHenry	15	Joseph Morton	Morgan
3	Waite Talcott	Winnebago	16	Gabriel R. Jernigan	Christian
4	John H. Addams	Stephenson	17	James M. Ruggles	Mason
5	Augustus Adams	Kane	18	William D. Watson	Coles
6	Url Osgood	Will	19	Mortimer O'Kean	Jasper
7	Burton C. Cook	LaSalle	20	Silas L. Bryan	Marion
8	J. D. Arnold	Peoria	21	Joseph Gillespie	Madison
9	Benjamin Graham	Henry	22	J. L. D. Morrison	St. Clair
10	James M. Campbell	McDonough	23	Anderson P. Corder	Williamson
11	Jacob C. Davis	Hancock	24	John E. Detrich	Randolph
12	William H. Carlin	Adams	25	Andrew J. Kuykendall	Johnson
13	Hugh L. Sutphin	Pike			

HOUSE OF REPRESENTATIVES.

Speaker—Thomas J. Turner.
Clerk—Edwin T. Bridges.
Assistant—J. W. Kitchell.

Enrolling and Eng. Clerk—Alex. Simpson.
Assistant—B. J. F. Hanna.
Doorkeeper—H. S. Thomas.
Assistant—Gershom Martin.

Dist.	Name.	County.	Dist.	Name.	County.
1	F. M. Rawlings	Alexander	32	Louis H. Waters	McDonough
2	George W. Gray	Massac	33	William M. Cline	Fulton
3	William J. Allen	Williamson		Amos C. Babcock	Fulton
4	Benjamin P. Hinch	Gallatin	34	S. D. Masters	Cass
5	Thomas M. Sams	Franklin	35	Samuel C. Parks	Logan
6	James C. Holbrook	Randolph	36	Henry C. Johns	Macon
7	P. E. Hosmer	Perry	37	James Courtney	Vermilion
8	T. B. Tanner	Jefferson	38	John McClun	McLean
	Hugh Gregg	Marion	39	Henry Riblett	Tazewell
9	S. H. Martin	White	40	William C. Rice	Henderson
10	C. C. Hopkins	Edwards	41	Henry Grove	Peoria
11	William R. Morrison	Monroe		Thomas J. Henderson	Stark
12	Albert H. Trapp	St. Clair	42	Robert Boal	Marshall
	William C. Kinney	St. Clair	43	David Strawn	LaSalle
13	J. Bradford	Bond		Frederick S. Day	Grundy
14	G. T. Allen	Madison	44	Alanson K. Wheeler	Kendall
	Henry S. Baker	Madison	45	G. D. A. Parks	Will
15	Presley Funkhouser	Effingham		John Strunk	Kankakee
16	Finney D. Preston	Richland		Erastus O. Hills	DuPage
17	Randolph Heath	Crawford	46	Benjamin Hackney	Kane
18	Thomas R. McClure	Clark		William Patten	DeKalb
19	Samuel W. Moulton	Shelby	47	Owen Lovejoy	Bureau
20	Henry Richmond	Montgomery	48	William L. Lee	Rock Island
21	George H. Holliday	Macoupin	49	Miles S. Henry	Whiteside
22	Lafayette McCrillis	Jersey	50	Daniel J. Pinckney	Ogle
23	J. M. Pursley	Greene	51	Porter Sargent	Carroll
24	Dudley McLain	Edgar		Wallace A. Little	JoDaviess
25	Albert Jones	Coles	52	Thomas J. Turner	Stephenson
26	Stephen T. Logan	Sangamon	53	William Lyman	Winnebago
	Jonathan McDaniel	Sangamon	54	S. W. Lawrence	Boone
27	Isaac R. Bennet	Scott		W. Diggins	McHenry
	Horace A. Brown	Morgan	55	Hurlbut Swan	Lake
28	Chauncey L. Higbee	Pike	56	Robert H. Foss	Cook
	Jonathan Dearborn	Brown		Thomas Richmond	Cook
29	Eli Seehorn	Adams	57	M. L. Dunlap	Cook
	Henry Sullivan	Adams		George F. Foster	Cook
30	John P. Richmond	Schuyler	58	Samuel W. Brown	Knox
31	George Walker	Hancock			

TWENTIETH GENERAL ASSEMBLY, 1856-1858.

Convened at Springfield Jan. 5, 1857; adjourned Feb. 19, 1857.

SENATE.

President—John Wood.
Secretary—Benjamin Bond.
First Assistant—Wilford D. Wyatt.
Second Assistant—Wm. D. Latshaw.

Enrolling and Eng. Clerk—John S. Roberts.
First Assistant—Thos. H. Smith.
Second Assistant—Lewis Hite.
Sergeant-at-Arms—David J. Waggoner.
Assistant—Thomas W. Stone.

Dist.	Name.	County.	Dist.	Name.	County.
1	Norman B. Judd	Cook	14	Linus E. Worcester	Greene
2	George Gage	McHenry	15	Cyrus W. Vanderen	Sangamon
3	Waite Talcott	Winnebago	16	Joel S. Post	Macon
4	John H. Addams	Stephenson	17	Samuel W. Fuller	Tazewell
5	Augustus Adams	Kane	18	Wm. D. Watson	Coles
6	G. D. A. Parks	Will	19	Mortimer O'Kean	Jasper
7	Burton C. Cook	LaSalle	20	Silas L. Bryan	Marion
8	J. D. Arnold	Peoria	21	Joseph Gillespie	Madison
9	Thomas J. Henderson	Stark	22	William H. Underwood	St. Clair
10	William C. Goudy	Fulton	23	Samuel H. Martin	White
11	Hiram Rose	Henderson	24	E. C. Coffey	Washington
12	William H. Carlin	Adams	25	Andrew J. Kuykendall	Johnson
13	Hugh L. Sutphin	Pike			

HOUSE OF REPRESENTATIVES.

Speaker—Samuel Holmes.
Clerk—Charles Leib.
First Assistant—W. C. B. Gillespie.
Second Assistant—E. Z. Ryan.

Enrolling and Eng. Clerk—Tevis Greathouse.
First Assistant—Cloyd Crouch.
Second Assistant—John A. Apperson.
Doorkeeper—William T. Gibbons.
Assistant—James M. Blades.

Dist.	Name.	County.	Dist.	Name.	County.
1	John Dougherty	Union	32	George Hire	McDonough
2	Wesley Sloan	Pope	33	Joseph Dyckes	Fulton
3	Thomas Jones	Johnson		James H. Stipp	Fulton
4	Ebon C. Ingersoll	Gallatin	34	Samuel Christy	Cass
5	John A. Logan	Jackson	35	Alexander W. Morgan	Logan
6	James H. Watt	Randolph	36	Jerome R. Gorin	Macon
7	H. S. Osburn	Washington	37	Oliver L. Davis	Vermilion
8	John A. Wilson	Hamilton	38	John H. Wickizer	McLean
	W. B. Anderson	Jefferson	39	Daniel Trail	Tazewell
9	John E. Whiting	White	40	A. V. T. Gilbert	Warren
10	Charles P. Burns	Wayne	41	M. Shallenberger	Stark
11	Wm. R. Morrison	Monroe		John T. Lindsey	Peoria
12	Vital Jarrot	St. Clair	42	Robert Boal	Marshall
	Wm. W. Roman	St. Clair	43	Elmer Baldwin	LaSalle
13	Wm. A. J. Sparks	Clinton		James M. Reading	Grundy
14	Lewis Ricks	Madison	44	John M. Crothers	Kendall
	Aaron P. Mason	Madison	45	Truman W. Smith	Will
15	Daniel Gregory	Fayette		Franklin Blades	Iroquois
16	Finney D. Preston	Richland		Wm. A. Chatfield	Kankakee
17	Isaac Wilkins	Crawford	46	David M. Kelsey	DeKalb
18	Nathan Willard	Clark		Wm. R. Parker	Kane
19	Samuel W. Moulton	Shelby	47	George W. Radcliffe	Bureau
20	Calvin Goudy	Christian	48	H. G. Little	Henry
21	B. T. Burke	Macoupin	49	John V. Eustace	Lee
22	Wright Casey	Jersey	50	Daniel J. Pinckney	Ogle
23	John W. Huitt	Greene	51	C. B. Denio	JoDaviess
24	Samuel Connelly	Edgar		Rollin Wheeler	Carroll
25	James E. Wyche	Coles	52	John A. Davis	Stephenson
26	James S. Megredy	Sangamon	53	Wm. Lathrop	Winnebago
	Shelby M. Cullom	Sangamon	54	L. S. Church	McHenry
27	Cyrus Epler	Morgan		L. W. Lawrence	Boone
	E. B. Hitt	Scott	55	W. M. Burbank	Lake
28	John L. Grimes	Pike	56	John H. Dunham	Cook
	King Kerley	Brown		George W. Morris	Cook
29	Samuel Holmes	Adams	57	Isaac N. Arnold	Cook
	M. M. Bane	Adams		A. F. C. Mueller	Cook
30	Lewis D. Erwin	Schuyler	58	David H. Frisbie	Knox
31	Wm Tyner	Hancock			

TWENTY-FIRST GENERAL ASSEMBLY, 1858–1860.

Convened at Springfield Jan. 3, 1859; adjourned Feb. 24, 1859.

SENATE.

President—John Wood.
Secretary—Finney D. Preston.
First Assistant—Timothy S. Fitch.
Second Assistant—Thomas H. Smith.

Enrolling and Eng. Clerk—John S. Roberts.
First Assistant—Lewis Hite.
Second Assistant—L. Wilson Sheppard.
Sergeant-at-Arms—David J. Waggoner.
Assistant—John Williams.
Postmaster—Rigdon S. Barnhill.

Dist.	Name.	County.	Dist.	Name.	County.
1	Norman B. Judd	Cook	14	Anthony L. Knapp	Jersey
2	Henry W. Blodgett	Lake	15	Cyrus W. Vanderen	Sangamon
3	Zenas Applington	Ogle	16	Joel S. Post	Macon
4	John H. Addams	Stephenson	17	Samuel W. Fuller	Tazewell
5	Richard F. Adams	Lee	18	Thomas A. Marshall	Coles
6	G. D. A. Parks	Will	19	Mortimer O'Kean	Jasper
7	Burton C. Cook	LaSalle	20	Silas L. Bryan	Marion
8	George C. Bestor	Peoria	21	Samuel A. Buckmaster	Madison
9	Thomas J. Henderson	Stark	22	Wm. H. Underwood	St. Clair
10	Wm. C. Goudy	Fulton	23	Samuel H. Martin	White
11	John P. Richmond	Schuyler	24	E. C. Coffey	Washington
12	Austin Brooks	Adams	25	Andrew J. Kuykendall	Johnson
13	Chauncey L. Higbee	Pike			

HOUSE OF REPRESENTATIVES.

Speaker—William R. Morrison.
Clerk—David E. Head.
First Assistant—Green B. Raum.
Second Assistant—Ebenezer Z. Ryan
Third Assistant—H. L. Clay.
Enrolling and Eng. Clerk—John Connelly, Jr.
First Assistant—John A. Apperson.
Second Assistant—Joseph Chapman.
Third Assistant—E. C. Weatherbee.
Doorkeeper—J. W. Connett.
First Assistant—James M. Blades.
Second Assistant—D. B. Cox.
Postmaster—Charles E. Foote.

Dist.	Name.	County.	Dist.	Name.	County.
1	Wm. A. Hacker	Union	32	Wm. Berry	McDonough
2	Wm. H. Green	Massac	33	John G. Graham	Fulton
3	J. D. Pulley	Johnson		Samuel P. Cummings	Fulton
4	Thos. S. Hick	Gallatin	34	Wm. Engle	Menard
5	James Hampton	Franklin	35	George H. Campbell	Logan
6	John E. Detrich	Randolph	36	Daniel Stickel	DeWitt
7	John D. Wood	Washington	37	Oscar F. Harmon	Vermilion
8	J. McIlvaine	Hamilton	38	Leonard Swett	McLean
	Wm. B. Anderson	Jefferson	39	R. B. M. Wilson	Tazewell
9	John G. Powell	White	40	William C. Rice	Henderson
10	R. T. Forth	Wayne	41	Thomas C. Moore	Peoria
11	Wm R. Morrison	Monroe		Myrtle G. Bruce	Stark
12	John Scheel	St. Clair	42	J. S. McCall	Marshall
	Vital Jarrot	St. Clair	43	Alexander Campbell	LaSalle
13	Charles Hoyles	Bond		Richardson S Hick	Livingston
14	Z. B. Job	Madison	44	Valentine Vermilyea	Kendall
	Joseph H. Sloss	Madison	45	Hiram Norton	Will
15	Stephen Hardin	Effingham		Alonzo W. Mack	Kankakee
16	W. G. Stephenson	Clay		J. M. Hood	DuPage
17	H. C. McCleave	Crawford	46	Wm. Patton	DeKalb
18	J Updegraff	Clark		Wm. B. Plato	Kane
19	Thomas Brewer	Cumberland	47	John H. Bryant	Bureau
20	James M. Davis	Montgomery	48	Ephraim Gilmore, Jr	Rock Island
21	Wm. C. Shirley	Macoupin	49	Wm. Prothrow	Whiteside
22	F. P. Rush	Calhoun	50	Joshua White	Ogle
23	Alexander King	Greene	51	James DeWolf	Carroll
24	Robert Mosely	Edgar		Halsted S. Townsend	JoDaviess
25	Wm. W. Craddock	Coles	52	John A. Davis	Stephenson
26	James W. Barrett	Sangamon	53	Elijah W. Blaisdell, Jr	Winnebago
	Daniel Short	Sangamon	54	L. H. Church	McHenry
27	Cyrus Epler	Morgan		Stephen A. Hurlbut	Boone
	Elisha B. Hitt	Scott	55	Elijah M. Haines	Lake
28	Gilbert J. Shaw	Pike	56	Van H. Higgins	Cook
·	King Kerley	Brown		Samuel L. Baker	Cook
29	Moses M. Bane	Adams	57	Ebenezer Peck	Cook
	Western Metcalf	Adams		Casper Butz	Cook
30	Lewis D. Erwin	Schuyler	58	Rufus W. Miles	Knox
31	Wm. H. Rosevelt	Hancock			

TWENTY-SECOND GENERAL ASSEMBLY, 1860-1862.

First Session convened at Springfield Jan. 7, 1861; adjourned Feb. 22, 1861. Second session April 23, 1861; adjourned May 3, 1861.

SENATE.

President pro tem.—Thomas A. Marshall.
President—Francis A. Hoffman.
Secretary—Campbell W. Waite.
First Assistant—John F. Nash.
Second Assistant—Sharon Tyndale (resigned).
Second Assistant—John Belser (vice Tyndale).
Enrolling and Eng. Clerk—David L. Phillips (resigned).
Enrolling and Eng. Clerk—Robert P. Tansey (vice Phillips).
First Assistant—James W. Fishback (resigned).
First Assistant—Henry L. Warren (vice Fishback).
Second Assistant—Julian Kune.
Sergeant-at-Arms—Richard T. Gill.
Assistant—Charles A. Thompson.
Postmaster—C. B. Denio (resigned).
Postmaster—Benj. Pyatt (vice Denio).

Dist.	Name.	County.	Dist.	Name.	County.
1	Wm. B. Ogden	Cook	14	Anthony L. Knapp	Jersey
2	Henry W. Blodgett	Lake	15	William Jayne	Sangamon
3	Zenas Applington	Ogle	16	Richard J. Oglesby	Macon
4	John H. Addams	Stephenson	17	Henry E. Dummer	Cass
5	Richard F. Adams	Lee	18	Thomas A. Marshall	Coles
6	Alonzo W. Mack	Kankakee	19	Presley Funkhonser	Effingham
7	Washington Bushnell	LaSalle	20	Zadok Casey	Jefferson
8	George C. Bestor	Peoria	21	Samuel A. Buckmaster	Madison
9	Thomas J. Pickett	Rock Island	22	Wm. H. Underwood	St. Clair
10	Wm. Berry	McDonough	23	Hugh Gregg	Williamson
11	John P. Richmond	Schuyler	24	James M. Rodgers	Clinton
12	Austin Brooks	Adams	25	Andrew J. Kuykendall	Johnson
13	Chauncey L. Higbee	Pike			

HOUSE OF REPRESENTATIVES.

Speaker—Shelby M. Cullom.
Clerk—Harley Wayne.
First Assistant—John W. Kitchell (resigned).
First Assistant—Harmon G. Reynolds (vice Kitchell).
Second Assistant—Wm. H. Robinson.
Third Assistant—David T. Linegar.

Enrolling and Eng. Clerk—J. F. Alexander.
First Assistant—Henry C. Latham.
Second Assistant—J. H. Yeager.
Doorkeeper—Caswell P. Ford.
First Assistant—E. Denman.
Second Assistant—Gershom Martin.
Postmaster—B. C Lundy.
Assistant—W. A. Schmitt.
Assistant—Marshal L. Stephenson.

Dist.	Name.	County.	Dist.	Name.	County.
1	Wm. A. Hacker	Union	32	S. H. McCandless	McDonough
2	Wm. H. Green	Massac	33	John G. Graham	Fulton
3	James D. Pulley	Johnson		Samuel P. Cummings	Fulton
4	William Elder	Saline	34	Frederick Rearick	Menard
5	Peter Keifer	Jackson	35	Robert B. Latham	Logan
6	Edmund Faherty	Randolph	36	Lawrence Weldon	DeWitt
7	Orson Kellogg	Perry	37	Samuel G. Craig	Vermilion
8	Cloyd Crouch	Hamilton	38	Harvey Hogg	McLean
	Cyrus W. Webster	Marion	39	David Kyes	Tazewell
9	James M. Sharp	White	40	Wm. C. Maley	Warren
10	Nathan Crews	Wayne	41	Elbridge G. Johnson	Peoria
11	H. C. Talbott	Monroe		Theodore F. Hurd	Stark
12	Vital Jarrot	St. Clair	42	Henry D. Cook	Woodford
	Samuel Stookey	St. Clair	43	Andrew J. Cropsey	LaSalle
13	Joshua P. Knapp	Clinton		John W. Newport	Grundy
14	Cyrus Edwards	Madison	44	Valentine Vermilyea	Kendall
	Garrett Crownover	Madison	45	Franklin Blades	Iroquois
15	F. H. Stoddard	Fayette		Samuel Storer	Will
16	Isaac H. Walker	Clay		Frederick H. Mather	DuPage
17	Aaron Shaw	Crawford	46	Edward R. Allen	DeKalb
18	John Scholfield	Clark		Thos. S. Terry	Kane
19	Thomas W. Harris	Shelby	47	Joseph W. Harris	Bureau
20	Horatio M. Vandeveer	Christian	48	Robert W. Smith	Rock Island
21	James T. Pennington	Macoupin	49	George Ryan	Lee
22	John N. English	Jersey	50	Francis A. McNeil	Ogle
23	Benjamin Baldwin	Greene	51	Benj. L. Patch	Carroll
24	Napoleon B. Stage	Edgar		J. Russell Jones	JoDaviess
25	Smith Nichols	Coles		*Robert H. McClellan	JoDaviess
26	Shelby M. Cullom	Sangamon	52	John F. Ankeny	Stephenson
	Norman M. Broadwell	Sangamon	53	Alfred A. Hale	Winnebago
27	Isaiah Turney	Morgan	54	Stephen A. Hurlbut	Boone
	Albert G. Burr	Scott		L. S. Church	McHenry
28	Wm. R Archer	Pike	55	Elijah M. Haines	Lake
	Benj. F. DeWitt	Brown	56	J. Young Scammon	Cook
29	James W. Singleton	Adams		Wm. H. Brown	Cook
	Wm. C. Harrington	Adams	57	Solomon M. Wilson	Cook
30	Lewis D. Erwin	Schuyler		Homer Wilmarth	Cook
31	Wm. H. Rollason	Hancock	58	Arthur A. Smith	Knox

* Vice J. Russell Jones, resigned.

TWENTY-THIRD GENERAL ASSEMBLY, 1862-1864.

Convened at Springfield Jan. 5, 1863; adjourned Feb. 14, 1863, till June 2, 1863; prorogued by the Governor June 10, 1863, until Dec. 31, 1864; convened and adjourned Dec. 31, 1864.

SENATE.

President—Francis A. Hoffman.
Secretary—Manning Mayfield.
First Assistant—Nelson Abbott.
Second Assistant—William Ronseville.
Postmaster—James Ward.

Enrolling and Eng. Clerk—Louis Houck.
First Assistant—Mathias J. Murray.
Second Assistant—James Lowe.
Sergeant-at-Arms—David J. Waggoner.
Assistant—James M. Blades.

Dist.	Name.	County.	Dist.	Name.	County.
1	Wm. H. Green	Massac	13	Bryant T. Scofield	Hancock
2	Hugh Gregg	Williamson	14	Wm. Berry	McDonough
3	Israel Blanchard	Jackson	15	Albert C. Mason	Knox
4	James M. Rodgers	Clinton	16	John T. Lindsay	Peoria
	*W. A. J. Sparks	Clinton	17	Washington Bushnell	LaSalle
5	Wm. H. Underwood	St. Clair	18	Alonzo W. Mack	Kankakee
6	Linus E. Worcester	Greene	19	Edward R. Allen	Kane
7	Horatio M. Vandeveer	Christian	20	Daniel Richards	Whiteside
8	Samuel Moffatt	Effingham	21	Thomas J. Pickett	Rock Island
9	Joseph Peters	Vermilion	22	John H. Addams	Stephenson
10	Isaac Funk	McLean	23	Cornelius Lansing	McHenry
11	Colby Knapp	Logan	24	Wm. B. Ogden	Cook
12	Henry E. Dummer	Cass	25	Jasper D. Ward	Cook

* Vice James M. Rodgers, deceased.

HOUSE OF REPRESENTATIVES.

Speaker—Samuel A. Buckmaster.
Clerk—John Q. Harmon.
First Assistant—Zimri S. Mastin.
Second Assistant—Claiborne Winston.
Second Assistant—Wm. M. Springer.
Third Assistant—Wm. A. Turney.

Enrolling and Eng. Clerk—John Hise.
First Assistant—Hubert Kelley.
Second Assistant—Joseph Merritt.
Doorkeeper—Charles Walsh.
First Assistant—John Husted.
Second Assistant—W. C. Davis.
Postmaster—Reuben Wood.

Dist.	Name.	County.	Dist.	Name.	County.
1	James H. Smith	Union	27	John T. Springer	Morgan
2	Thomas B. Hicks	Massac	28	Alexander E. Wheat	Adams
3	James B. Turner	Gallatin		Wm. J. Brown	Adams
4	James W. Sharp	Wabash	29	Lewis G. Reid	McDonough
5	Henry M. Williams	Jefferson	30	Joseph Sharon	Schuyler
6	James M. Washburn	Williamson	31	Milton M. Morrill	Hancock
7	Jesse R. Ford	Clinton	32	Thomas B. Cabeen	Mercer
8	Stephen W. Miles	Monroe	33	Henry K. Peffer	Warren
	Edward Menard	Randolph	34	Joseph M. Holyoke	Knox
9	John W. Merritt	Marion	35	John G. Graham	Fulton
10	James M. Heard	Wayne		Simeon P. Shope	Fulton
11	David W. Odell	Crawford	36	James Holgate	Stark
12	John W. Wescott	Clay		Wm. W. O'Brien	Peoria
13	Robert H. McCann	Fayette	37	Elias Wenger	Tazewell
14	Chauncy L. Conger	White	38	Harrison Noble	McLean
15	Joseph B. Underwood	St. Clair		Boynton Tenny	DeWitt
	John Thomas	St. Clair	39	John Tenbrook	Coles
16	Samuel A. Buckmaster	Madison		John Gerrard	Edgar
	Wm. Watkins	Bond		John Monroe	Vermilion
17	Philander Daughterty	Clark	40	James Elder	Macon
18	Reuben Roessler	Shelby		*William N. Coler	Champaign
19	Gustavus F. Coffeen	Montgomery		†John S. Busey	Champaign
20	Ambrose M. Miller	Logan	41	Chauncey A. Lake	Kankakee
	Charles A. Keyes	Sangamon	42	Addison Goodell	Iroquois
21	Charles A. Walker	Macoupin	43	John W. Newport	Grundy
22	John N. English	Jersey		Charles E. Boyer	Will
23	Wm. B. Witt	Greene		‡Perry A. Armstrong	Grundy
24	Scott Wike	Pike	44	Theodore C. Gibson	LaSalle
	Albert G. Burr	Scott		Mercy B. Patty	Livingston
25	James M. Epler	Cass		John O. Dent	LaSalle
26	Lyman Lacy	Menard	45	George Dent	Putnam

* Seat contested. † Admitted to seat of Wm. N. Coler. ‡ Vice John W. Newport, dec.

House of Representatives—*Continued.*

Dist.	Name.	County.	Dist.	Name.	County.
45	Jefferson A. Davis	Woodford	55	Selden M. Church	Winnebago
	Daniel R. Howe	Bureau	56	Horatio C. Burchard	Stephenson
46	Nelsen Lay	Henry	57	Henry Green	JoDavless
47	John Kistler	Rock Island		Joseph F. Chapman	Carroll
48	Leander Smith	Whiteside	58	Algernon S. Barnard	DuPage
49	Demas L. Harris	Lee	59	Ansell B. Cook	Cook
50	James V. Gale	Ogle		Amos G. Throop	Cook
51	Westel W. Sedgwick	DeKalb		Wm. E. Ginther	Cook
	Luther W. Lawrence	Boone	60	Melville W. Fuller	Cook
52	Sylvester S. Mann	Kane		*George W. Gage	Cook
	Jacob P. Black	Kendall		†Michael Brandt	Cook
53	Elijah M. Haines	Lake	61	Francis A. Eastman	Cook
54	Thaddeus B. Wakeman	McHenry		Lorenzo Brentano	Cook

* Seat contested. † Admitted to seat of Geo. W. Gage.

TWENTY-FOURTH GENERAL ASSEMBLY, 1864–1866.

Convened at Springfield, Jan. 2, 1865; adjourned Feb. 16, 1865.

SENATE.

President—William Bross.
Secretary—John F. Nash.
First Assistant—George H. Harlow.
Second Assistant—Thomas C. Moore.
Third Assistant—James Dowling.
Enrolling and Eng. Clerk—John R. Howlett
First Assistant—John H. Cacy.
Second Assistant—David H. Porter.
Sergeant-at-Arms—Caswell P. Ford.
Assistant—John I. Mussy.
Postmaster—Daniel C. Lockwood.

Dist.	Name.	Postoffice.	Dist.	Name.	Postoffice.
1	Wm. H. Green	Cairo	14	James Strain	Monmouth
2	John W. Wescott	Xenia	15	Albert C. Mason	Galesburg
3	Daniel Reilly	Kaskaskia	16	John T. Lindsay	Peoria
4	David K. Green	Salem	17	Washington Bushnell	Ottawa
5	Andrew W. Metcalf	Edwardsville	18	Alonzo W. Mack	Kankakee
6	Linus E. Worcester	Whitehall	19	Ew'd R. Allen	Aurora
7	Horatio M. Vandeveer	Taylorville	20	Daniel Richards	Sterling
8	Andrew J. Hunter	Paris	21	Alfred Webster	Rock Island
9	Joseph Peters	Danville	22	John H. Addams	Cedarville
10	Isaac Funk	Bloomington	23	Cornelius Lansing	Marengo
11	John B. Cohrs	Pekin	24	Francis A. Eastman	Chicago
12	Murray McConnell	Jacksonville	25	Jasper D. Ward	Chicago
13	Bryant T. Scofield	Carthage			

HOUSE OF REPRESENTATIVES.

Speaker—Allen C. Fuller.
Clerk—Walter S. Frazier.
First Assistant—Charles Turner.
Second Assistant—Alex. S. Thomson
Doorkeeper—Gershom Martin.
First Assistant—J. Y. Antrim.
Second Assistant—Alexander Pender.
Enrolling and Eng. Clerk—Aaron K. Stiles.
First Assistant—C. C. Mason.
Second Assistant—Robt. K. Dewey.
Third Assistant—Henry Clay.
Postmaster—Andrew T. Sherman.

Dist.	Name.	Postoffice.	Dist.	Name.	Postoffice.
1	Henry W. Webb	Cairo	11	Thomas Cooper	Willow Hill
2	Wm. A. Looney	Vienna	12	Lewis W. Miller	Olney
3	Charles Burnett	Elizabetht'n	13	George H. Deickman	Vandalia
4	D. H. Morgan	Russellville	14	Jonathan Shelby	Maple Grove
5	John Ward	Benton	15	Nathaniel Niles	Belleville
6	Wm. H. Logan	Murphysboro		John Thomas	Belleville
7	Isaac Miller	Nashville	16	Julius J. Barnsback	Troy
8	Wm. K. Murphy	Pinckn'yville		Hiram Dresser	Cottonw'd Gr.
	Austin James	Mitchie	17	Hiram B. Decius	Majority P'nt.
9	Samuel E. Stephenson	Salem	18	Wm. Middlesworth	Windsor
10	Valentine S. Benson	Mc Leansboro	19	Elisha E. Barrett	Butler

House of Representatives—*Continued.*

Dist.	Name.	Postoffice.	Dist.	Name.	Postoffice.
20	Ambrose M. Miller	Lincoln	43	Archibald J. McIntyre	Wilmington
	James W. Patton	Berlin		Wm. T. Hopkins	Morris
21	Sergeant Gobble	Scottville	44	Franklin Corwin	LaSalle
22	John McDonald	Hardin		John Miller	Freedom
23	Nathaniel M. Perry	Kane		Jason W. Strevell	Pontiac.
24	James F. Curtis	Manchester	45	Henry D. Cook	Kappa
	Scott Wike	Pittsfield		George D. Henderson	Granville
25	King Kerley	Mt. Sterling		Wm. C. Stacy	Princeton
26	John Hill	Petersburg	46	Milton M. Ford	Galva
27	John T. Springer	Jacksonville	47	Joseph W. Lloyd	Edington,
28	Thomas Redmon	Quincy	48	Leander Smith	Fulton
	Wm T. Yeargain	Columbus	49	Obed W. Bryant	Paw Paw Gr.
29	Wm. H. Neece	Macomb	50	Daniel J. Pinckney	Mt. Morris
30	Joseph Sharon	Augusta	51	Allen C. Fuller	Belvidere
31	Milton M. Morrill	Nauvoo		Ira V. Randall	DeKalb
32	Jonathan Simpson	Oquawka	52	Oliver C. Johnson	Kendall
33	James H. Martin	Monmouth		Sylvester S. Mann	Burlington
34	Joseph M. Holyoke	Wataga.	53	Eugene B. Payne	Waukegan
35	Lawrence W. James	Lewiston	54	Merritt L. Joslyn	Woodstock
	Timothy M. Morse	Fairview	55	Wm. Brown	Rockford
36	Richard C. Dunn	Toulon	56	Horatio C. Burchard	Freeport
36	Alexander McCoy	Peoria	57	John D. Platt	Warren.
37	Samuel R. Saltonstall	Tremont		Daniel W. Dame	Lanark
38	Harrison Noble	Heyworth	58	Henry C. Childs	Wheaton
	John Warner	Clinton	59	Nathan W. Huntley	Chicago
39	Malden Jones	Tuscola		Ansel B. Cook	Chicago
	John L. Tincher	Danville		Wm. Jackson	Orland
	Solomon L. Spink	Paris	60	Edward S. Isham	Chicago
40	Isaac C. Pugh	Decatur		Andrew H. Dalton	Hope
	Lewis J. Bond	Monticello	61	Alex. F. Stevenson	Chicago
41	Chauncey A. Lake	Kankakee		George Strong	Wheeling
42	Charles H. Wood	Onarga			

TWENTY-FIFTH GENERAL ASSEMBLY, 1866-1868.

First session convened at Springfield, Jan. 7, 1867; adjourned Feb. 28, 1867. Second session June 11, 1867; adjourned June 13, 1867. Third session June 14, 1867; adjourned June 28, 1867.

SENATE.

President—William Bross.
Secretary—Chas. E. Lippincott, resigned.
Chauncey Elwood, vice Lippincott.
First Assistant—John M. Adair.
Second Assistant—Isaac L. Mitchell.
Third Assistant—John Maxton.
Enrolling and Eng. Clerk—John M. Barber.
First Assistant—Bailey D. Dawson.
Second Assistant—Charles D. Rice.
Third Assistant—Isaac L. Mitchell.
Sergeant-at-Arms—William Mitchell.
First Assistant—J. S. Lothrop.
Postmaster—Lawson A. Parks.
Assistant—James H. Paddock.

Dist.	Name.	Postoffice.	Dist.	Name.	Postoffice.
1	Daniel W. Munn	Cairo	14	James Strain	Monmouth
2	John W. Wescott	Xenia	15	Thomas A. Boyd	Lewiston
3	Daniel Reilly	Kaskaskia	16	Greenbury L. Fort	Lacon
4	Daniel K. Green	Salem	17	Washington Bushnell	Ottawa
5	Andrew W. Metcalf	Edwardsville	18	Alonzo W. Mack	Kankakee
6	William Shephard	Jerseyville	19	William Patton	Sandwich
7	John M. Woodson	Carlinville	20	Daniel J. Pinckney	Mt. Morris
8	Andrew J. Hunter	Paris	21	Alfred Webster	Rock Island
9	John L. Tincher	Danville	22	John H. Addams	Cedarville
10	William H. Cheney	Cheney's Gr.	23	Allen C. Fuller	Belvidere
11	John B. Cohrs	Pekin	24	Francis A. Eastman	Chicago
12	Murray McConnell	Jacksonville	25	Jasper D. Ward	Chicago
13	Samuel R. Chittenden	Mendon			

HOUSE OF REPRESENTATIVES.

Speaker—Franklin Corwin.
Clerk—Stephen G. Paddock.
First Assistant—Charles H. Wood.
Second Assistant—Alex. S. Thomson.
Third Assistant—James K. Magie.
Fourth Assistant—C. C. Mason.
Postmaster—Andrew J. Alden.
Assistant—Modesto J. Green.
Enrolling and Eng. Clerk—Sam'l P. Moore.
First Assistant—Henry C. Latham.
Second Assistant—Maurice J. McGrath.
Third Assistant—William E. Clark.
Doorkeeper—Francis Sequin.
First Assistant—Alexander Pender.
Second Assistant—John A. Wall.

Dist.	Name.	Postoffice.	Dist.	Name.	Postoffice.
1	Newton R. Casey	Mound City	36	Sylvester F. Ottman	Wyoming
2	Phil. G. Clemens	New Liberty	37	William W. Sellers	Pekin
3	James Macklin	Harrisburg	38	William M. Smith	Lexington
4	James M. Sharp	Mt. Carmel		Henry S. Green	Clinton
5	Noah Johnson	Mt. Vernon	39	James M. True	Mattoon
6	Hugh Gregg	Marion		Malden Jones	Tuscola
7	Daniel Hay	Nashville		Napoleon B. Stage	Bloomfield
8	William K. Murphy	Pinckneyville	40	Clark R. Griggs	Urbana
	John Campbell	Steel's Mills		Abraham B. Bunn	Decatur
9	Erastus N. Bates	Centralia	41	Daniel S. Parker	Kankakee
10	Robert P. Hanna	Fairfield	42	George E. King	Watseka
11	David W. Odell	Oblong	43	Phil. Collins	Morris
12	Eli Bower	Olney		Robert Clow	E. Wheatland
13	George W. Cornwell	Mason	44	William Strawn	Odell
14	Patrick Dolan	Enfield		Elmer Baldwin	Farm Ridge
15	Abraham B. Pope	East St. Louis		Franklin Corwin	LaSalle
	Amos Thompson	Belleville	45	William C. Stacy	Princeton
16	John H. Yaeger	Alton		Robert T. Cassell	Metamora
	Jediah F. Alexander	Greenville		Alanson P. Webber	Henry
17	Edward Harlan	Marshall	46	Augustus Allen	Geneseo
18	Charles Voris	Windsor	47	Albert S. Coe	Port Byron
19	John B. Ricks	Taylorville	48	James Dinsmore	Sterling
20	James C. Conkling	Springfield	49	George Ryan	Paw Paw Gr.
	William McGalliard	Lincoln	50	Thomas J. Hewett	Foreston
21	William C. Shirley	Staunton	51	Stephen A. Hurlbut	Belvidere
22	Robert M. Knapp	Jerseyville		Robert Hampton	E. Paw Paw
23	Henry C. Withers	Carrollton	52	James W. Eddy	Batavia
24	James H. Dennis	Chambersb'g.		William P. Pierce	Lisbon
	Thomas Hollowbush	Naples	53	Eugene B. Payne	Waukegan
25	James M. Epler	Virginia	54	Thaddeus B. Wakeman	Harvard
26	John M. Beesley	Bath	55	Abram I. Enoch	Rockford
27	Felix G. Farrell	Jacksonville	56	Joseph M. Bailey	Freeport
28	Henry L. Warren	Quincy	57	Elijah Funk	Mt. Carroll
	Philip J. Corkins	Fairweather		Henry Green	Elizabeth
29	Amaziah Hanson	Bushnell	58	Henry C. Childs	Wheaton
30	George W. Metz	Rushville	59	Lester L. Bond	Chicago
31	John G. Fonda	Fount'nGreen		Joseph S. Reynolds	Chicago
32	Daniel W. Sedgwick	Suez		Horace M. Singer	Chicago
33	Francis M. Bruner	Monmouth	60	Moses W. Leavitt	Chicago
34	John Gray	Wataga		Henry M. Shepard	Chicago
35	Caleb B. Cox	Vermont	61	Alexander F. Stevenson	Chicago
	George W. Fox	Ellisville		Edward S. Taylor	Evanston
36	Thomas C. Moore	Peoria			

TWENTY-SIXTH GENERAL ASSEMBLY, 1868–1870.

Convened at Springfield Jan. 4, 1869; Adjourned April 20, 1869.

SENATE.

President—John Dougherty.
Secretary—Chauncey Elwood.
First Assistant—James B. Beggs.
Second Assistant—R. W. Coon.
Third Assistant—James H. Paddock.
Postmaster—Thos. J. Larrison.
Assistant—Geo. M. Dougherty.

Enrolling and Eng. Clerk—John M. Adair.
First Assistant—John H. Barton.
Second Assistant—John W. Dales.
Third Assistant—Robert D. Addis.
Sergeant-at-Arms—John A. Wall.
Assistant—Wm. Mitchell.

Dist.	Name.	Postoffice.	Dist.	Name.	Postoffice.
1	Daniel W. Munn	Cairo	14	Isaac McManus	Keithsburg
2	J. J. R. Turney	Fairfield	15	Thomas A. Boyd	Lewiston
3	Samuel K. Casey	Mt. Vernon	16	Greenbury L. Fort	Lacon
4	John P. VanDorston	Vandalia	17	Jason W. Strevell	Pontiac
5	Willard C. Flagg	Moro	18	Henry Snapp	Joliet
6	Wm. Shephard	Jerseyville	19	Wm. Patton	Sandwich
7	John M. Woodson	Carlinville	20	Daniel J. Pinckney	Mt. Morris
8	Edwin Harlan	Marshall	21	Andrew Crawford	Geneseo
9	John L. Tincher	Danville	22	John H. Addams	Cedarville
10	John McNulta	Bloomington	23	Allen C. Fuller	Belvidere
11	Aaron B. Nicholson	Lincoln	24	John C. Dore	Chicago
12	James M. Epler	Virginia	25	Jasper D. Ward	Chicago
13	Samuel R. Chittenden	Mendon			

HOUSE OF REPRESENTATIVES.

Speaker—Franklin Corwin.
Clerk—James P. Root.
First Assistant—James K. Magie.
Second Assistant—Albert Bliss, Jr.
Third Assistant—Ira J. Halstead.
Postmaster—Andrew J. Alden.
Assistant—E. F. Chittenden.

Doorkeeper—Francis Sequin.
First Assistant—L. O. Gillman.
Second Assistant—Gustave Wetzlau.
Enrolling and Eng. Clerk—Jas. V. Mahoney.
First Assistant—C. M. Whitney.
Second Assistant—Maurice Savage.
Third Assistant—Chas. H. Mitchell.

Dist.	Name.	Postoffice.	Dist.	Name.	Postoffice.
1	Newton R. Casey	Mound City	36	Wm. E. Phelps	Elmwood
2	Jonathan C. Willis	Metropolis	37	*Jonathan Merriam	Hittle
3	Charles Burnett	Shawneet'wn		†Samuel R. Saltonstall	Tremont
4	D. H. Morgan	Russellville	38	Wm. M. Smith	Lexington
5	C. C. M. V. B. Payne	Benton		Jacob Swigart	DeWitt
6	Edward L. Denison	Marion	39	George W. Parker	Charleston
7	George Gundlach	Carlyle		James E. Callaway	Tuscola
8	John M. McCutcheon	Sparta		Silas H. Elliott	Paris
	Thos. H. Burgess	DuQuoin	40	Wilson M. Stanley	Sullivan
9	Thos. E. Merritt	Salem		John W. Scroggs	Champaign
10	John Halley	Lovilla	41	James M. Perry	Kankakee
11	Joseph Cooper	Willow Hill	42	Calvin H. Frew	Paxton
12	Alex. W. Bothwell	Clay City	43	George Gaylord	Lockport
13	Leonard Rush	Vandalia		Phillip Collins	Morris
14	John Landrigan	Albion	44	Wm. Strawn	Odell
15	James R. Miller	Caseyville		Franklin Corwin	Peru
	Alexander Ross	Mascoutah		Samuel Wiley	Earlville
16	Daniel Kerr	Edwardsville	45	Lorenzo D. Whiting	Tiskilwa
	Samuel H. Challis	Pocahontas		Charles G. Reed	Malden
17	Lewis Brookhart	Majority P'nt		Joel W. Hopkins	Granville
18	Charles Voris	Windsor	46	Philip K. Hanna	Green River
19	Ephriam M. Gilmore	Litchfield	47	Hiram F. Sickles	Moline
20	John Cook	Springfield	48	James Dinsmoor	Sterling
	Silas Beason	Lincoln	49	Alonzo Kinyon	Amboy
21	Beatty T. Burke	Carlinville	50	Ogden B. Youngs	Hale
22	Thos. B. Fuller	Hardin	51	Charles W. Marsh	DeKalb
23	David M. Woodson	Carrollton		Elisha H. Talbott	Belvidere
24	Abraham Mittower	Milton	52	Irus Coy	Bristol
	Henry Dresser	Naples		Needham N. Ravlin	Kaneville
25	James G. Phillips	Mound Stat'n.	53	Ansel B. Cook	Libertyville
26	Edward Laning	Petersburg	54	Peter W. Deitz	Marengo
27	Smith M. Palmer	Jacksonville	55	Ephriam Sumner	Pecatonica
28	Thomas Jasper	Quincy	56	Joseph M. Bailey	Freeport
	James E. Downing	Camp Point	57	Adam Nase	Mt. Carroll
29	Humphrey Horrabin	Blandinsville		Henry Green	Elizabeth
30	John Ewing	Littleton	58	Henry C. Childs	Wheaton
31	Andrew J. Bradshaw	LaHarpe	59	Henry B. Miller	Chicago
32	David M. Findley	Oquawka		Lester L. Bond	Chicago
33	John Porter	Monmouth		Joseph S. Reynolds	Chicago
34	W. Selden Gale	Galesburg	60	Francis Munson	Chicago
35	Timothy M. Morse	Middle Grove		Joshua C. Knickerbocker	Chicago
	John W. Ross	Lewiston	61	Iver Lawson	Chicago
36	Bradford F. Thompson	Bradford		Edward S. Taylor	Evanston

* Seat contested. † Admitted to seat of Merriam.

TWENTY-SEVENTH GENERAL ASSEMBLY, 1870–1872.

First session convened at Springfield, Jan. 4, 1871; adjourned April 17, 1871, until Nov. 15, 1871. First special session May 24, 1871; adjourned June 22, 1871. Second special session Oct. 13, 1871; adjourned Oct. 24, 1871. Convened in regular adjourned session Nov. 15, 1871; adjourned, *sine die*, April 9, 1872.

SENATE.

President—John Dougherty.
Secretary—E. H. Griggs.
First Assistant—Z. S. Swan.
Second Assistant—James H. Paddock.
Third Assistant—Henry L. Boris.
Enrolling and Eng. Clerk—R. H. Gettamy.

Assistant—Gershom Martin.
Sergeant-at-Arms—Lewis Zeigler.
First Assistant—John F. Moore.
Second Assistant—B. B. Harlan.
Postmaster—John B. Turchin.
Assistant—R. C. Staples.

Dist.	Name.	Postoffice.	Dist.	Name.	Postoffice.
1	*Simeon K. Gibson	Equality	13	Jesse C. Williams	Carthage
	T. A. E. Holcomb.	South Pass	14	Benj. R. Hampton	Macomb
	‡Wm. G. Bowman			Harvey S. Senter	Aledo
2	John Jackson	Lawrencev'le	15	Thomas A. Boyd	Lewiston
	John Landrigan	Albion		Henry J. Vaughn	Victoria
3	*Samuel K. Casey	Mt. Vernon	16	Mark Bangs	Lacon
	James M. Washburn	Fredonia		Lucien H. Kerr	Peoria
	§Wm. B. Anderson	Mt. Vernon	17	Jason W. Strevell	Pontiac
4	John P. VanDorston	Vandalia		Wm. Reddick	Ottawa
	Jediah F. Alexander	Greenville	18	†Henry Snapp	Joliet
5	Williard C. Flagg	Moro		Wm. P. Pierce	Minooka
	Wm. H. Underwood	Belleville		‖John F. Daggatt	
6	†Wm. Sheppard	Jerseyville	19	Chas. W. Marsh	Sycamore
	J. M. Bush	Pittsfield		James W. Eddy	Batavia
*	¶Wm. H. Allen		20	James K. Edsall	Dixon
7	Lewis Solomon	Vancil's Point		Winfield S. Wilkinson	Morrison
	Charles Voris	Windsor	21	Andrew Crawford	Geneseo
8	Edwin Harlan	Marshall		Lorenzo D. Whiting	Tiskilwa
	Robert N. Bishop	Paris	22	*Wallace A. Little	Elizabeth
9	John N. Tincher	Danville		James M. Hunter	Mt. Carroll
	James W. Langley	Champaign	23	Allen C. Fuller	Belvidere
1	John McNulta	Bloomington.		John Early	Rockford
	Michael Donahue	Clinton	24	John C. Dore	Chicago
11	Aaron B. Nicholson	Lincoln		John N. Jewett	Chicago
	Alex. Starne	Springfield	25	Willard Woodard	Chicago
12	James M. Epler	Jacksonville		†John L. Beveridge	Evanston
	Edward Laning	Petersburg		**Artemus Carter	Chicago
13	James H. Richardson	Quincy			

* Died. † Resigned. ‡ Vice Simeon K. Gibson, deceased.
§ Vice Samuel K. Casey, deceased. ¶ Vice Wm. Shephard, resigned.
‖ Vice Henry Snapp, resigned. ** Vice John L. Beveridge, resigned.

HOUSE OF REPRESENTATIVES.

Speaker—Wm. M. Smith.
Clerk—Daniel Shepard.
First Assistant—Jasper N. Reece.
Second Assistant—Eric Johnson.
Third Assistant—Samuel R. Hay.
Doorkeeper—W. A. Moore.
First Assistant—Gustave Wetzlau.
Second Assistant—Henry Plasnick.

Enrolling and Eng. Clerk—W. W. Lowdermilk.
First Assistant—C. C. Kohlsaat.
Second Assistant—Wm. P. Squires.
Third Assistant—C. T. Heydecker.
Postmaster—J. W. Ayres.
Assistant—Wm. F. Wilton.

Dist.	Name.	Postoffice.	Dist.	Name.	Postoffice.
1	H. Watson Webb	Cairo	20	Walter L. Mayo	Albion
2	Wm. R. Brown	Metropolis	21	John D. Sage	Lawrenc'ville
3	George W. Waters	Glendale	22	Israel A. Powell	Olney
4	James B. Morray	Reynoldsb'rg	23	Osman Pixley	Ingraham
5	Wm. C. Rich	South Pass	24	Thomas E. Merritt	Salem
6	*Wm. Schwartz	Elkville		Samuel L. Dwight	Centralia
	‡Wm. A. Lemma	Carbondale	25	Samuel Burnside	Carlyle
7	Addison Reese, Jr	Marion	26	Daniel B. Gillham	Alton
8	Wm. Elder	Eldorado		A. F. Rodgers	Upper Alton
9	Wm. N. Ayres	Elizabethtwn		Theodore Miller.	St. Jacob
10	Frank E. Hay	Carmi	27	William Brown	Old Ripley
11	Calvin Allen	McLeansboro	28	Jacob Fouke	Vandalia
12	W. W. Barr	Benton	29	*David Leith	Mason
13	Wm. R. Gass	DuQuoin		B. F. Kagay	Effingham
14	James M. Ralls	Chester	30	William McElwee	Greenup
	Daniel R. McMasters	Sparta	31	William C. Jones	Robinson
15	Wm. R. Morrison	Waterloo	32	William T. Briscoe	Westfield
16	James R. Miller	Caseyville	33	Edward Barrett	Neoga
	Gustavus Kœrner	Belleville	34	John Casey	Moweaqua
	John Hinchcliffe	Belleville		Edward Roessler	Shelbyville
17	A. S. Rowley	Richview	35	William B. Hundley	Taylorville
18	Thos. S. Casey	Mt. Vernon		*Thomas Finley	Pana
19	Ashley T. Galbraith	Johnsonville.		Benj. Dornblaser	Assumption

House of Representatives—*Continued.*

Dist.	Name.	Postoffice.	Dist.	Name.	Postoffice.
36	James M. Berry	Irving	71	Stephen F. Flaharty	Swedonia
	James N. McElvain	Litchfield	72	John Morris	Rock Island
37	John N. McMillan	Carlinville		Edwin H. Johnson	Port Byron
	George A. W. Cloud	Girard	73	Levi North	Kewanee
38	George W. Herdman	Jerseyville		Jonas W. Olson	Galva
	Robert A. King	Jerseyville	74	Miles A. Fuller	Toulon
39	Thomas H. Boyd	Carrollton	75	Joseph H. Jones	Henry
40	Charles Kenny	Griggsville		Joseph Reinhardt	Granville
	Albert Landrum	El Dara	76	Robert Hunter	Tiskilwa
41	James M. Riggs	Winchester		Perry F. Remsberg	Limerick
42	Newton Cloud	Waverly	77	George W. Armstrong	Seneca
	William H. Barnes	Jacksonville		Benjamin Edgecomb	Utica
43	Charles H. Rice	Springfield		James Clark	Utica
	Wm. M. Springer	Springfield		H. M. Gallagher	Peru
	Ninian R. Taylor	Williamsville	78	Phillip Collins	Morris
44	William E. Nelson	Decatur	79	Warren R. Hickox	Kankakee
	William T. Moffitt	Decatur		Calvin H. Frew	Paxton
45	Jonathan Meeker	Sullivan	80	John H. Daniels	Wilmington
46	James R. Cunningham	Charleston		W. S. Brooks	Joliet
	Azariah Jeffries	Mattoon		Robert Clow	E. Wheatland
47	James Gaines	Ridge Farm	81	Henry Sherrill	Lisbon
	George W. Rives	Paris	82	William M. Whitney	Hinsdale
48	John Cofer	Arcola	83	Anson S. Clark	Elgin
49	John C. Short	Danville		Julius A. Carpenter	Carpenterv'le
	Wm. P. Chandler	Danville		Wm. H. Miller	Aurora
50	Randolph C. Wright	Homer	84	Reuben M. Prichard	Shabbona
	Jarius C. Sheldon	Urbana		Lewis M. McEwen	DeKalb
51	Andrew L. Rodgers	Cerro Gordo	85	Norman H. Ryan	Amboy
52	William R. Carle	Wapella		Miles J. Braiden	Rochelle
53	Peter J. Hawse	Atlanta	86	Mortimer W. Smith	Oregon
	Augustus Reise	Atlanta		Jeremiah Davis	Beacon
54	Wm. W. Easley	Virginia	87	Nathan Williams	Sterling
	Samuel C. Knoles	Petersburg		Dean S. Efner	Albany
55	James G. Phillips	Mt. Sterling	88	James Shaw	Mount Carroll
56	Samuel S. Benson	Huntsville	89	William Cary	Galena
57	A. H. Trimble	Marcelline		Halstead S. Townsend	Warren
	Maurice Kelly	Liberty	90	Thomas J. Turner	Freeport
	Joseph H. Stewart	Quincy		Wm. Massenberg	Freeport
	George J. Richardson	Quincy	91	James M. Wight	Rockford
58	Lemuel Mussetter	Warsaw		D. Emmons Adams	Laona
	Milton M. Morrill	Nauvoo	92	Jesse S. Hildrup	Belvidere
59	William H. Neece	Macomb	93	William A. McConnell	Richmond
	James Manley	Macomb		Ira R. Curtis	Marengo
60	John W. Ross	Lewiston	94	William B. Dodge	Waukegan
	Samuel P. Cummings	Astoria		Elijah M. Haines	Waukegan
	Timothy M. Morse	Middle Grove	95	Henry W. Austin	Chicago
61	Matthew Langston	Manito		Robert H. Foss	Chicago
62	Cæsar A. Roberts	Pekin		James L. Campbell	Chicago
	Ira B, Hall	Delavan		Carlisle Mason	Chicago
63	William M. Smith	Lexington		Wiley M. Egan	Chicago
	†Edward R. Roe	Bloomington		Richard P. Derrickson	Chicago
	Warren C. Watkins	Bloomington		John D. Easter	Chicago
	George W. Funk	McLean		John Humphrey	Orland
	§Leonidas H. Kerrick	Bloomington		Alexander L. Morrison	Chicago
64	Addison Goodell	Loda		John W. Heafield	Chicago
	Thomas Vennum	Watseka	96	A. J. Galloway	Chicago
65	John Stillwell	Chatsworth		Hardin B. Brayton	Chicago
	James G. Strong	Dwight		Simon D. Phelps	Chicago
66	Allison M. Cavan	El Paso		James P. Root	Chicago
67	James M. Rice	Peoria		William H. King	Chicago
	Samuel Caldwell	Peoria		Arthur Dixon	Chicago
	John S. Lee	Peoria	97	Horace F. Waite	Chicago
68	Oscar F. Price	Galesburg		Rollin S. Williamson	Chicago
	Joseph F. Latimer	Abingdon		Augustus H. Burley	Chicago
	Patrick H. Sanford	Knoxville		William Vocke	Chicago
69	Samuel T. Shelton	Monmouth		W. K. Sullivan	Chicago
	John T. Morgan	Monmouth		Henry C. Senne	DesPlaines
70	Wm. A. M. Crouch	Rozetta			

* Died. † Resigned. ‡ Vice Schwartz, resigned. § Vice E. R. Roe, resigned.

TWENTY-EIGHTH GENERAL ASSEMBLY, 1872–1874.

First session convened at Springfield Jan. 8, 1873; adjourned May 6, 1873, until Jan 8, 1874. Convened Jan. 8, 1874; adjourned *sine die* March 31, 1874.

SENATE.

President—J. L. Beveridge (became Gov.)
President—John Early, vice Beveridge.
Secretary—Daniel A. Ray.
First Assistant—James H. Paddock.
Second Assistant—Cyrus D. Kendall.
Third Assistant—Samuel Parker.
Enrolling and Eng. Clerk—Andrew J. Alden
Assistant—Henry C. Bolland.
Sergeant-at-Arms—Wm. A. Moore.
Assistant—Francis M. Malone.
Postmaster—Roswell C. Staples.
Assistant—A. W. Kellogg.

Dist.	Name.	Postoffice.	Dist.	Name.	Postoffice.
1	Joseph S. Reynolds	Chicago	27	Aaron B. Nicholson	Lincoln
2	Richard S. Thompson	Chicago	28	John Cusey	Downs
3	Miles Kehoe	Chicago	29	Michael Donohue	Clinton
4	Samuel K. Dow	Chicago	30	J. C. Sheldon	Urbana
5	J. McGrath	Chicago	31	John C. Short	Danville
6	Horace F. Waite	Chicago	32	Charles B. Steele	Mattoon
7	Rollin S. Williamson	Chicago	33	Charles Voris	Windsor
8	Clark W. Upton	Waukegan	34	Wm. B. Hundley	Taylorville
9	John Early	Rockford	35	Alexander Starne	Springfield
10	Henry Green	Elizabeth	36	Archibald A. Glenn	Mt. Sterling
11	Joseph M. Patterson	Sterling	37	*George W. Burns	Quincy
12	George P. Jacobs	Oregon		†Maurice Kelly	Liberty
13	Miles B. Castle	Sandwich	38	Wm. R. Archer	Pittsfield
14	Eugene Canfield	Aurora	39	Wm. Brown	Jacksonville
15	Wm. S. Brooks	Joliet	40	Beatty T. Burke	Carlinville
16	Almon S. Palmer	Onarga	41	John H. Yeager	Alton
17	Elmer Baldwin	Farm Ridge	42	Geo. Gundlach	Carlyle
18	James G. Strong	Dwight	43	John Cunningham	Salem
19	Lorenzo D. Whiting	Tiskilwa	44	Geo. W. Henry	Louisville
20	Edward A. Wilcox	Minonk	45	Wm. J. Crews	Lawrencev'le
21	Wm H. Shepard	Cambridge	46	Thos. S. Casey	Mt. Vernon
22	Patrick H. Sanford	Knoxville	47	Francis M. Youngblood	Benton
23	Benj. R. Hampton	Macomb	48	Wm. K. Murphy	Pinckneyville
24	Benj. Warren	LaHarpe	49	John Hinchcliffe	Belleville
25	Samuel P. Cummings	Astoria	50	Jesse Ware	Jonesboro
26	John S. Lee	Peoria	51	Chas. M. Ferrell	Elizabetht'n

* Resigned, Sept. 20, 1873. † Vice Geo. W. Burns.

HOUSE OF REPRESENTATIVES.

Speaker—Shelby M. Cullom.
Clerk—Daniel Shepard.
First Assistant—J. F. Allison (resigned).
First Assistant—John D. Hamilton (vice Allison).
Second Assistant—John D. Hamilton (elected First).
Second Assistant—G. W. Johns (vice Hamilton).
Third Assistant—G. W. Johns (elected Second).
Third Assistant—Miss Mary O. Charlton.
Reading Clerk—James K. Magie.
Enrolling and Eng. Clerk—Wm. I. Allen.
First Assistant—V. W. Dashiel.
Second Assistant—Edmund Roche.
Doorkeeper—Andrew B. Kirkbride.
First Assistant—Thomas Rountree.
Second Assistant—Joseph P. Roberts.
Postmaster—W. F. Wilton.
Assistant—Thomas E. Woods.

Dist.	Name.	Postoffice.	Dist.	Name.	Postoffice.
1	James B. Bradwell	Chicago	6	Otto Peltzer	Chicago
	John A. Lomax	Chicago		John M. Rountree	Chicago
	Wm. Wayman	Chicago		Geo. E. Washburn	Chicago
2	Solomon P. Hopkins	Chicago	7	Daniel Booth	Chicago
	Frank T. Sherman	Chicago		Chas. H. Dolton	Dolton Stat'n
	Charles G. Wicker	Chicago		Henry C. Senne	DesPlaines
3	E. F. Cullerton	Chicago	8	Richard Bishop	McHenry
	Constantine Kann	Chicago		Flavel K. Granger	McHenry
	Thos. M. Halpin	Chicago		Elisha Gridley	Half Day
4	John F. Scanlon	Chicago	9	*a*Robert J. Cross	Roscoe
	Thos. E. Ferrier	Chicago		Jesse S. Hildrup	Belvidere
	Wm. H. Condon	Chicago		Duncan J. Stewart	Durand
5	Wm. A. Herting	Chicago		*b*Richard F. Crawford	....
	Ingwell Oleson	Chicago	10	Edw. L. Cronkrite	Freeport
	Hugh McLaughlin	Chicago		Alfred M. Jones	Warren

House of Representatives—*Continued.*

Dist.	Name	Postoffice.	Dist.	Name.	Postoffice.
10	James S. Taggart	Ridott	32	John A. Freeland	Sullivan
11	James Shaw	Mt. Carroll		James A. Connolly	Charleston
	James E. McPherran	Sterling		*d*Joseph H. Ewing	Arcola
	Dean S. Efner	Albany	33	Wm. H. McDonald	Majority P'nt.
12	Isaac Rice	Mt. Morris		Wm. H. Blakely	Effingham
	Henry D. Dement	Dixon		Benson Wood	Effingham
	Frederick H. Marsh	Oregon	34	James M. Truitt	Hillsboro
13	Lyman B. Ray	Morris		Hiram P. Shumway	Taylorville
	Geo. M. Hollenback	Milbrook		Elias J. C. Alexander	Hillsboro
	Perry A. Armstrong	Morris	35	Alfred Orendorff	Springfield
14	Sylvester S. Mann	Elgin		Milton Hay	Springfield
	Julius A. Carpenter	Carp'nt'rsv'le		Shelby M. Cullom	Springfield
	James Herrington	Geneva	36	Henry H. Moose	Havana
15	Amos Savage	Lockport		Wm. W. Easley	Virginia
	John S. Jessup	Wilmington		Nathaniel W. Branson	Petersburg
	Jabez Harvey	Joliet	37	Charles Ballou	Clayton
16	Millard J. Sheridan	Momence		*a*Nehemia Bushnell	Quincy
	Erasmus B. Collins	Momence		Ira M. Moore	Quincy
	Thos. S. Sawyer	Chebanse		*e*John Tillson*f*	Quincy
17	Lewis Soule	Ottawa		*g*Albert J. Griffith	
	Joseph Hart	Earlville	38	Melville D. Massie	Pleasant Vale
	Geo. W. Armstrong	Seneca		Stephen G. Lewis	Hardin
18	John P. Middlecoff	Paxton		Henry Dresser	Naples
	Lucian Bullard	Forrest	39	Jerome B. Nulton	Carrollton
	John Pollock	Paxton		John W. Meacham	Waverly
19	Joab R. Mulvane	Princeton		John Gordon	Lynnville
	Cyrus Bocock	Castleton	40	Wm. McAdams	Jerseyville
	Mark R. Dewey	Ohio		Jonathan Plowman	Virden
20	Dwight J. Webber	Minonk		Archibald L. Virden	Virden
	Nathaniel Moore	Wenona	41	Henry Weinheimer	Highland
	John G. Freeman	Snachwine		Benj. R. Hite	Collinsville
21	Wilder W. Warner	Orion		Thomas T. Ramey	Collinsville
	Edwin H. Johnson	Port Byron	42	Fred. A. Lietze	Carlyle
	Charles Dunham	Geneseo		Charles D. Hoiles	Greenville
22	Alson J. Streeter	New Windsor		Andrew G. Henry	Greenville
	Geo. P. Graham	Aledo	43	Napoleon B. Morrison	Odin
	Jacob S. Chambers	Altona		Charles G. Smith	Vandalia
23	Wm. A. Grant	Monmouth		*f*Ziba S. Swan	Vandalia
	John E. Jackson	Colchester		*h*Alfred P. Crosly	
	E. K. Westfall	Bushnell	44	Isaac N. Jaquess	Mt. Carmel
24	Wm. Scott	Dallas City		Robert T. Forth	Keenville
	David Rankin	Biggsville		David W. Barkley	Fairfield
	Edward E. Lane	Warsaw	45	J. L. Flanders	Olive
25	Stephen Y. Thornton	Canton		Thos. J. Golden	Marshall
	John A. Gray	Lewiston		Harmon Alexander	Robinson
	John M. Darnell	Pleasantview	46	Leonidas Walker	McLeansboro
26	Julius S. Starr	Peoria		Robert S. Anderson	McLeansboro
	Michael C. Quinn	Peoria		Patrick Dolan	Enfield
	Ezra G. Webster	Elmore	47	John G. Newton	Marion
27	Laban M. Stroud	Atlanta		James R. Loomis	Shawneet'wn.
	Peter J. Hawes	Atlanta		Samuel M. Mitchell	Corinth
	Herman W. Snow	Washington	48	John W. Platt	Cutler
28	Archibald E. Stewart	Heyworth		William Neville	Chester
	Thomas P. Rogers	Bloomington		Austin James	Mitchie
	John Cassedy	Lexington	49	*f*Bernhard Wiek	Belleville
29	Job A. Race	Decatur		Luke H. Hite	East St. Louis
	Tillman Lane	Clinton		John Thomas	Belleville
	Wm. T. Moffett	Decatur		*i*Spencer M. Kase	Belleville
30	John Penfield	Rantoul	50	Wm. A. Lemma	Carbondale
	C. P. Davis	Monticello		Matthew J. Inscore	Anna
	Francis E. Bryant	Bement		John H. Oberly	Cairo
31	Willis O. Pinnell	Paris	51	James L. Wymore	Vienna
	Henri B. Bishop	Paris		Francis M. McGee	Reynoldsb'rg
	Jacob H. Oakwood	Catlin		Newton R. Casey	Mound City
32	*c*Wm. T. Sylvester	Arcola			

a Died. *f* Resigned. *g* Vice John Tillson, resigned. *h* Vice Ziba S. Swan, resigned. *i* Vice Bernhard Wiek, resigned. *e* Vice Nehemia Bushnell, deceased. *c* Removed. *b* Vice Robt. J. Cross, deceased. *d* Vice Wm T. Sylvester, removed.

TWENTY-NINTH GENERAL ASSEMBLY, 1874-1876.

Convened at Springfield, Jan. 6, 1875; adjourned April 15, 1875.

SENATE.

President—Archibald A. Glenn.
Secretary—R. R. Townes.
First Assistant—James M. Washburn.
Second Assistant—W. C. Garrard.
Third Assistant—James H. Paddock.
Enrolling and Eng. Clerk—H. F. Potter.
First Assistant—R. Emmet Morris.
Second Assistant—H. C. Bolland.
Sergeant-at-Arms—Patrick O'Conner.
Assistant—Samuel McCrary.
Postmaster—Henry J. Stierling.
Assistant—J. B. Roper.

Dist.	Name.	Postoffice.	Dist.	Name.	Postoffice.
1	John C. Haines	Chicago	27	James W. Robison	Tremont
2	Richard S. Thompson	Chicago	28	John Cusey	Heyworth
3	Miles Kehoe	Chicago	29	Jesse F. Harrold	Clinton
4	Samuel K. Dow	Chicago	30	Jairus C. Sheldon	Urbana
5	John Buehler	Chicago	31	George Hunt	Paris
6	Horace F. Waite	Chicago	32	Charles B. Steele	Mattoon
7	Michael W. Robinson	Chicago	33	Thomas Brewer	Majority P'nt.
8	Clark W. Upton	Waukegan	34	Wm. H. Hundley	Taylorville
9	John Early	Rockford	35	Wm. E. Shutt	Springfield
10	Henry Green	Elizabeth	36	Archibald A. Glenn	Mt. Sterling
11	Henry A. Mills	Mt. Carroll	37	Bernard Arntzen	Quincy
12	George P. Jacobs	Oregon	38	Wm. R. Archer	Pittsfield
13	Miles B. Castle	Sandwich	39	Charles D. Hodges	Carrollton
14	Eugene B. Canfield	Aurora	40	Beatty T. Burke	Carlinville
15	Albert O. Marshall	Joliet	41	Wm. H. Krome	Edwardsville
16	Almon S. Palmer	Onarga	42	George Gundlach	Carlyle
17	Fawcett Plumb	Streator	43	John Thompson	Vandalia
18	James G. Strong	Dwight	44	George W. Henry	Louisville
19	Lorenzo D. Whiting	Tiskilwa	45	O. V. Smith	Lawr'nceville
20	Edward A. Wilcox	Minonk	46	Thos. S. Casey	Mt. Vernon
21	E. O. Moderwell	Geneseo	47	Wm. H. Parish	Eldorado
22	Patrick H. Sanford	Knoxville	48	Wm. K. Murphy	Pinckn'yville
23	John T. Morgan	Monmouth	49	Jefferson Rainey	Belleville
24	Benj. Warren	LaHarpe	50	Jesse Ware	Jonesboro
25	Robert Brown	Rushville	51	Samuel Glassford	Vienna
26	John S. Lee	Peoria			

HOUSE OF REPRESENTATIVES.

Speaker—Elijah M. Haines.
Clerk—Jeremiah J. Crowley.
First Assistant—John M. Darnell.
Second Assistant—Robert W. Ross.
Third Assistant—L. M. Babcock.
Postmaster—Annie F. Owsley.
Assistant—James M. Sharp.
Doorkeeper—Peter W. Taylor.
First Assistant—N. L. Wickwire.
Second Assistant—John Cockrell.
Reading Clerk—John H. Merritt.
Enrolling and Eng. Clerk—Thomas Wolfe.
First Assistant—B. Cremer.
Second Assistant—Callie D. M. Springer.

Dist.	Name.	Postoffice.	Dist.	Name.	Postoffice.
1	James B. Bradwell	Chicago	9	Andrew Ashton	Durand
	Lincoln Dubois	Chicago		Richard F. Crawford	Rockford
	Moses J. Wentworth	Chicago		Myron K. Avery	Belvidere
2	John Hise	Chicago	10	Forest Turner	Nora
	George M. Bogue	Chicago		E. L. Cronkrite	Freeport
	Solomon P. Hopkins	Chicago		Alfred M. Jones	Warren
3	William Honan	Chicago	11	Albert R. McCoy	Fulton City
	Conrad L. Niehoff	Chicago		Norman D. French	Thompson
	Thomas M. Halpin	Chicago		Tyler McWhorter	Sterling
4	Orrin L. Mann	Chicago	12	Henry D. Dement	Dixon
	Wm. H. Condon	Chicago		Isaac Rice	Mt. Morris
	Michael M. Miller	Chicago		Fred'k H. Marsh	Oregon
5	Michael J. Dunne	Chicago	13	Philip Collins	Morris
	John S. Arwedson	Chicago		Joshua McGrath	Lisbon
	Carl L. Linderberg	Chicago		D. B. Bailey	Gardner
6	Robert Thiem	Chicago	14	Victor Fredenhagen	Downer's Gr.
	John C. Barker	Chicago		James F. Claflin	Lombard
	Wm. H. Stickney	Chicago		James Herrington	Geneva
7	Wm. H. Skelly, Jr.	Lemont	15	Wm. Mooney	Braidwood
	George Dunlap	Norwood P'rk		Henry H. Stassen, Jr.	Monee
	Wm. Freise	Desplaines		Lake H. Goodrich	Braidwood
8	Wm. A. James	HighlandP'rk	16	George W. Parker	Watseka
	Elijah M. Haines	Waukegan		George C. Wilson	Onarga
	Flavel K. Granger	McHenry		Reuben Richardson	Yellowhead

House of Representatives—*Continued.*

Dist.	Name.	Postoffice.	Dist.	Name.	Postoffice.
17	Charles L. Hoffman.	Farm Ridge..	34	Wm. F. Mulkey	Nokomis
	George W. Armstrong	Seneca	35	Joseph L. Wilcox	Loami
	Elijah H. Spicer	Marseilles		Fred Gehring	Springfield
18	Albert M. Haling	Roberts		Shelby M. Cullom	Springfield
	Joseph I. Robinson	Elliott	36	Nathaniel W. Branson	Petersburg
	David McIntosh			A. G. Nance	Petersburg
19	A. G. Hammond	Toulon		John W. Pugh	Mason City
	J. H. Moore	Tiskilwa	37	Thomas J. Bates	Camp Point..
	J. J. Herron	Princeton		Ira M. Moore	Quincy
20	Henry Frantz	Roanoke		Rezin H. Downing	Keokuk Junc.
	James T. Thornton	Magnolia	38	James Callans	Winchester
	Nathaniel Moore	Wenona		John Moses	Winchester
21	Rufus M. Grinnell	Cordova		Joseph S. Harvey	Belleview
	John T. Browning	Moline	39	Andrew J. Thompson	Bethel
	John P. Fox	Windsor		Samuel Woods	Pisgah
22	John H. Lewis	Knoxville		John Gordon	Lynnville
	John T. McGinnes	Joy	40	Samuel S. Gilbert	Carlinville
	Curtis K. Harvey	Knoxville		Oliver P. Powell	Jerseyvill e
23	Isaac L. Christie	Monmouth		Henry F. Martin	Brighton
	C. W. Boydston	Cameron	41	Franklin S. Pike	St. Jacob
	A. W. King	Macomb		George A. Smith	Alton
24	David Rankin	Biggsville		George H. Weigler	Alton
	Wellington Jenney	Burnside	42	J. K. McMasters	Nashville
	Paul D. Salter	Biggsville		Andrew G. Henry	Greenville
25	James DeWitt	Littleton		William H. Moore	Nashville
	Sam'l P. Cummings	Astoria	43	Wm. R. Hubbard	Kinmundy
	Stephen Y. Thornton	Canton		Thomas E. Merritt	Salem
26	Wm. Rowcliffe	Robin's Nest.		John B. Johnson	Alma
	Julius S. Starr	Peoria	44	Samuel R. Hall	Albion
	Patrick W. Dunn	Peoria		Byron J. Rotan	Louisville
27	Richard Holmes	Delavan		John Landrigan	Albion
	R. A. Talbott	Burton View.	45	Ethelbert Callahan	Robinson
	Thomas Windle	Lincoln		John H. Halley	Newton
28	Thomas P. Rogers	Bloomington.		John W. Briscoe	Darwin
	John F. Winter	Bloomington.	46	Hiram W. Hall	Knight's Pr..
	Archibald E. Stewart	Bloomington.		Amos B. Barrett	Mt. Vernon
29	Shaw Pease	Niantic		Boon Kershaw	Grayville
	John H. Tyler	DeWitt	47	John N. Wasson	Shawneet'wn
	Sam'l S. Jack	Decatur		A. C. Nellson	Marion
30	Wm. M. Phillips	Rantoul		Isaac Smith	Ridgway
	Geo. H. Benson	Rantoul	48	Joseph W. Rickert	Waterloo
	Wm. C. Hubbart	Monticello		Samuel McKee	Blair
31	Wm. S. O'Hair	Paris		Jonathan Chestnutwood	Evansville
	John Sidell	Fairmount	49	William G. Kase	E. St. Louis..
	Andrew Gundy	Bismark		John Thomas	Belleville
32	James A. Connolly	Charleston		James Rankin	Lebanon
	E. M. Vance	Mattoon	50	Fountain E. Albright	Murphysboro
	Rich'd A. Wilson	Williamsburg		Matthew J. Inscore	Anna
33	Wm. Gillmore	Edgewood		Claiborne Winston	Cairo
	Wm. Middlesworth	Shelbyville	51	Benj. O. Jones	Metropolis
	William Chew	Shelbyville		James R. Steagall	Oak
34	Levi Scott	Pana		Lewis F. Plater	Elizabethto'n
	John C. Hagler	Pana			

THIRTIETH GENERAL ASSEMBLY, 1876–1878.

Convened at Springfield, Jan. 3, 1877; adjourned May 24, 1877.

SENATE.

President—Andrew Shuman.
Secretary—James H. Paddock.
First Assistant—J. J. Crowley.
Second Assistant—Thomas Wolfe.
Third Assistant—Wm. C. Garrard.
Postmaster—Fred Gehring.
Assistant—P. H. Redmond.

Sergeant-at-Arms—P. O'Connor.
First Assistant—Boone Kershaw.
Second Assistant—R. M. Springer.
Enrolling and Eng. Clerk—H. F. Potter.
First Assistant—H. L. Glessner.
Second Assistant—F. E. Frantz.

Dist.	Name.	Postoffice.	Dist.	Name.	Postoffice.
1	John C. Haines	Chicago	27	James W. Robison	Tremont
2	Daniel N. Bash	Chicago	28	John M. Hamilton	Bloomington.
3	Miles Kehoe	Chicago	29	Jesse F. Harrold	DeWitt
4	Francis H. Riddle	Chicago	30	Chester P. Davis	Monticello
5	John Buehler	Chicago	31	George Hunt	Paris
6	Martin A. DeLany	Chicago	32	Malden Jones	Tuscola
7	Michael W. Robinson	Chicago	33	Thomas Brewer	Majority Poi't
8	Merritt L. Joslyn	Woodstock	34	Elizur Southworth	Litchfield
9	*John Early	Rockford	35	Wm. E. Shutt	Springfield
10	Robt. H. McClellan	Galena	36	Luther Dearborn	Havana
11	Henry A. Mills	Mt. Carroll	37	Bernard Arntzen	Quincy
12	Henry D. Dement	Dixon	38	Wm. R. Archer	Pittsfield
13	Miles B. Castle	Sandwich	39	Charles D. Hodges	Carrollton
14	Joseph H. Mayborne	Geneva	40	Geo. W. Herdman	Jerseyville
15	Albert O. Marshall	Joliet	41	Wm. H. Krome	Edwardsville.
16	Thomas P. Bonfield	Kankakee	42	F. E. W. Brink	Hoyleton
17	Faucett Plumb	Streator	43	John Thompson	Vandalia
18	Sam'l T. Fosdick	Chatsworth	44	Robt. P. Hanna	Fairfield
19	Lorenzo D. Whiting	Tiskilwa	45	O. V. Smith	Lawrenc'ville
20	Henry J. Frantz	Roanoke	46	Charles E. McDowell	Carmi
21	Erastus C. Moderwell	Geneseo	47	Wm. H. Parish	Eldorado
22	Benj. C. Taliaferro	Keithsburg	48	Ambrose Hoener	Waterloo
23	John T. Morgan	Monmouth	49	Jefferson Rainey	Belleville
24	William Scott	Dallas City	50	Jesse Ware	Jonesboro
25	Robert Brown	Rushvile	51	Sam'l M. Glassford	Vienna
26	John S. Lee	Peoria			

* Died September, 1877.

HOUSE OF REPRESENTATIVES.

Speaker—James Shaw.
Clerk—E. F. Dutton.
First Assistant—James E. Jewett.
Second Assistant—F. W. Fletcher.
Third Assistant—W. B. Taylor.
Postmaster—Miss Fannie Wallace.
Assistant—Wm. F. Wilton.

Doorkeeper—Clark C. Morse.
First Assistant—Wm. Baker.
Second Assistant—A. J. Babcock.
Third Assistant—Wm. Duncan.
Enrolling and Eng. Clerk—Wm. I. Allen.
First Assistant—Israel A. Powell.
Second Assistant—Miss Susan Foulke.

Dist.	Name.	Postoffice.	Dist.	Name.	Postoffice.
1	W. H. Thompson	Chicago	13	Peter S. Lott	Newark
	Charles L. Easton	Chicago		Wm. M. Byers	Sycamore
	Moses J. Wentworth	Chicago		Amos D. Clover	Gardner
2	Solomon P. Hopkins	Chicago	14	Henry H. Evans	Aurora
	J. W. E. Thomas	Chicago		James G. Wright	Naperville
	Joseph E. Smith	Chicago		James Herrington	Geneva
3	James B. Taylor	Chicago	15	Fred Kouka	Eagle Lake
	Henry F. Sheridan	Chicago		Luke H. Goodrich	Braidwood
	P. J. Hickey	Chicago		D. H. Pinney	Joliet
4	Elijah B. Sherman	Chicago	16	Conrad Secrest	Watseka
	George W. Reed	Chicago		John A. Koplin	Buckley
	Joseph J. Kearney	Chicago		Daniel C. Taylor	Kankakee
5	John A. Roche	Chicago	17	Lucien B. Crooker	Mendota
	Peter Kiolbassa	Chicago		Sam'l M. Heslet	Meriden
	Michael J. Dunne	Chicago		Geo. W. Armstrong	Seneca
6	Eugene A. Sittig	Chicago	18	Geo. B. Gray	Pontiac
	Arno Voss	Chicago		John H. Collier	Gibson
	Austin O. Sexton	Chicago		Eben C. Allen	Long Point
7	J. S. Bielefeldt	Thornton	19	Charles Baldwin	Princeton
	John H. Kedzie	Evanston		Daniel J. Hurd	Lafayette
	George C. Klehm	NilesCenter		James J. Herron	Princeton
8	Flavel K. Granger	McHenry	20	Joel A. Ranney	Metamora
	Wm. A. James	Highl'ndPark		Chas. Fosbender	Sparland
	Edw'd M. Dennis	Waukegan		Eli V. Raley	Granville
9	Geo. H. Hollister	Rockton	21	John T. Browning	Moline
	John Budlong	Rockford		John P. Fox	Geneseo
	Andrew Ashton	Durand		Rufus M. Grennel	Cordova
10	James S. Taggert	Ridott	22	Alfred S. Curtis	Oneida
	Hiram Tyrrell	Plum River		Joseph F. Latimer	Abingdon
	Edw'd L. Cronkrite	Freeport		Abraham M. Brown	Galesburg
11	James Shaw	Mt. Carroll	23	C. W. Boydston	Cameron
	Edw'd H. Nevitt	Albany		E. K. Westfall	Bushnell
	John M. Stowell	Mt. Carroll		Charles H. Whitaker	Macomb
12	Abijah Powers	Sterling	24	Charles F. Gill	LaHarpe
	Frank N. Tice	Forreston		Geo. P. Walker	Warsaw
	Bernard H. Truesdell	Lee		John J. Reaburn	Denver

House of Representatives—*Continued.*

Dist.	Name.	County	Dist.	Name.	County.
25	John A. Leeper	Farmington	38	B. J. Hall	Hardin
	Charles F. Robison	Ellisville	39	Isaac L. Morrison	Jacksonville
	Wm. T. McCreery	Huntsville		Wm. P. Callon	Jacksonville
26	Latham A. Wood	Chillicothe		Lucien King	Kane
	Nelson D. Jay	Elmwood	40	Richard Rowett	Carlinville
	Robert S. Bibb	Peoria		Hampton W. Wall	Staunton
27	Joseph C. Ross	Lincoln		John N. English	Jerseyville
	Dietrich C. Smith	Pekin	41	John S. Dewey	Troy
	Wm. A. Moore	Morton		Sam'l A. Buckmaster	Alton
28	Thomas F. Mitchell	Bloomington		Francis M. Pearce	Alhambra
	‡John F. Winter	Bloomington	42	Rich'd Tierney	Okawville
	Thomas P. Rogers	Bloomington		William M. Evans	Greenville
29	Thomas J. Abel	Decatur		George F. Berry	Greenville
	Sam'l S. Jack	Decatur	43	Fred. Remann	Vandalia
	Wm. L. Chambers	Clinton		Andrew J. Hogge	Loudon
30	Robert A. Bower	Tolono		Thomas E. Merritt	Salem
	E. C. Bartholo	Mahomet	44	Hiram H. Chessley	Louisville
	Simeon H. Busey	Urbana		Wm. R. Wilkinson	Friendsville
31	Jacob H. Oakwood	Catlin		George D. Ramsey	Xenia
	Alvin Gilbert	Rossville	45	Wm. Lindsey	Martinsville
	Robert L. McKinlay	Paris		*John H. Halley	Newton
32	Henry A. Neal	Charleston		Andrew J. Reavill	Flat Rock
	R. Heffernan	Mattoon	46	Ross Graham	Carmi
	Stephen Cannon	Sullivan		Thomas Connelly	McLeansboro
33	Gershom Monohon	Greenup		Thomas J. Williams	Spring G'rden
	Nathaniel P. Robinson	Effingham	47	Peter Phillips	Webb's Hill
	Thomas J. Fritts	Cold Springs		James M. Washburn	Marion
34	David H. Zepp	Nokomis		Thomas M. Mooneyham	Benton
	Wm. E. Morrison	Morrisonville	48	Theophilus T. Fountain	DuQuoin
	Burrel Phillips	Hillsboro		John Boyd	Pinckneyville
35	John Foutch	New Berlin		Septimus M. Mace	Percy
	John Mayo Palmer	Springfield	49	John W. Wells	Marissa
	D. W. Smith	Bates		Alonzo S. Wilderman	Belleville
36	Jacob Wheeler	Havana		James M. Whitaker	Summerfield
	Wm. L. Vandeventer	Mt. Sterling	50	Wm. H. Woodward	Carbondale
	Cornelius Rourke	Petersburg		†Alex. H. Irvin	Cairo
37	Thomas G. Black	Clayton		Fountain E. Albright	Murphysboro
	Hope S. Davis	Quincy	51	Wm. S. Morris	Elizabethto'n
	James H. Hendrickson	Mendon		Alonzo D. Pierce	Golconda
38	Asa C. Mathews	Pittsfield		E. B. Watkins	Mound City
	Starkey R. Powell	Winchester			

* Resigned Aug. 2, 1877. † Resigned Feb. 12, 1878. ‡ Resignation accepted Aug. 8, 1877.

THIRTY-FIRST GENERAL ASSEMBLY, 1878-1880.

Convened at Springfield Jan. 8, 1879; adjourned May 31, 1879.

SENATE.

President—Andrew Shuman.
Secretary—James H. Paddock.
First Assistant—George Terwilliger.
Second Assistant—R. W. Gates.
Sergeant-at-Arms—J. L. Wheat.
First Assistant—Thomas Penlwell.
Second Assistant—A. A. Benjamin.

Enrolling and Eng. Clerk—Chas. H. Greenleaf.
First Assistant—Frank E. Stephens.
Second Assistant—W. H. Brown.
Postmaster—Kate C. Hayes.
Assistant—Lizzie M. Harris.
Bill Clerk—Charles R. Haws.

Dist.	Name.	Postoffice.	Dist.	Name.	Postoffice.
1	George E. White	Chicago	13	John R. Marshall	Yorkville
2	Daniel N. Bash	Chicago	14	Joseph H. Mayborne	Geneva
3	Sylvester Artley	Chicago	15	Sylvester W. Munn	Joliet
4	Francis A. Riddle	Chicago	16	Thomas P. Bonfield	Kankakee
5	Wm. T. Johnson	Chicago	17	Samuel R. Lewis	Ottawa
6	Martin A. DeLany	Chicago	18	Samuel T. Fosdick	Chatsworth
7	W. J. Campbell	Chicago	19	Lorenzo D. Whiting	Tiskilwa
8	Merritt L. Joslyn	Woodstock	20	Henry J. Frantz	Roanoke
9	Charles E. Fuller	Belvidere	21	Milton M. Ford	Galva
10	Rob't H. McClellan	Galena	22	Benj. C. Tallaferro	Keithsburg
11	Charles Bent	Morrison	23	Wm. H. Neece	Macomb
12	Henry D. Dement	Dixon	24	William Scott	Dallas City

Senate—*Continued.*

Dist.	Name.	Postoffice.	Dist.	Name.	Postoffice.
25	Meredith Walker	Canton	39	Wm. P. Callon	Jacksonville.
26	John S. Lee	Peoria	40	Geo. W. Herdman	Jerseyville
27	Abram Mayfield	Lincoln.	41	Alfred J. Parkinson	Highland
28	John M. Hamilton	Bloomington.	42	F. E. W. Brink	Hoyleton
29	Wm. T. Moffett	Decatur	43	Thos. E. Merritt	Salem
30	Chester P. Davis	Monticello	44	Robert P. Hanna	Fairfield
31	George Hunt	Paris	45	Wm. C. Wilson	Robinson
32	Malden Jones	Tuscola	46	Chas. E. McDowell	Carmi
33	Erastus N. Rinehart	Effingham	47	Samuel L. Cheaney	Harrisburg
34	Elizur Southworth	Litchfield	48	Ambrose Hœner	Waterloo
35	Wm. E. Shutt	Springfield	49	John Thomas	Belleville
36	Luther Dearborn	Havana	50	Jesse Ware	Jonesboro
37	Maurice Kelly	Liberty.	51	Andrew J. Kuykendall	Vienna
38	Wm. R. Archer	Pittsfield			

HOUSE OF REPRESENTATIVES.

Speaker—William A. James.
Clerk—W. B. Taylor.
First Assistant—T. J. Vernor.
Second Assistant—W. B. Hawkins.
Third Assistant—E. T. Whitcomb.
Postmaster—Miss Lilly Ray.
Assistant—W. F. Wilton.

Enrolling and Eng. Clerk—Sam'l P. Mooney.
First Assistant—Ross Mathews.
Second Assistant—Daniel B. Dyer.
Doorkeeper—Nathan Crews.
First Assistant—Isaac H. Kelly.
Second Assistant—M R. Cunningham.
Third Assistant—Benj. B. Longnecker.

Dist.	Name.	Postoffice.	Dist.	Name.	Postoffice.
1	W. H. Thompson	Chicago	16	Conrad Secrest	Watseka
	Moses J. Wentworth	Chicago		Matthew H. Peters	Watseka
	David W. Clark, Jr	Chicago		Azariah Buck	Pilot Center
2	Benjamin M. Wilson	Chicago	17	Lucien B. Crooker	Mendota
	Solomon P. Hopkins	Chicago		Francis Bowen	Sheridan
	Patrick T. Barry	Chicago		David Richey	Tonica
3	Leo Meilbeck	Chicago	18	George B. Gray	Pontiac
	T. J. Walsh	Chicago		Norman E. Stevens	Paxton
	John R. Taylor	Chicago		Calvin H. Frew	Paxton
4	Lewis H. Bisbee	Chicago	19	Alfred G. Scott	Sheffield
	Elijah B. Sherman	Chicago		Sylvester F. Otman	Wyoming
	James Emmet Murray	Chicago		Simon Elliott	Princeton
5	William E. Mason	Chicago	20	Joel A. Ranney	Cazenovia
	Charles Ehrhardt	Chicago		George F. Wightman	Lacon
	Thomas F. O'Malley	Chicago		Charles Fosbender	Sparland
6	Christian Meyer	Chicago	21	Anthony R. Mock	Cambridge
	Austin O. Sexton	Chicago		John W. Foy	Atkinson
	Horace H. Thomas	Chicago		James W. Simonson	Port Byron
7	Lorin C. Collins, Jr	Norwood P'rk	22	Rufus W. Miles	Gilson
	George G. Struckman	Hanover		Joseph F. Latimer	Abingdon
	Bernhart F. Weber	Havelock		John Sloan	Douglas
8	Flavel K. Granger	McHenry	23	Henry M. Lewis	Berwick
	William A. James	Highland P'rk		Henry Black	Doddsville
	William Price	Waukegan		Edwin W. Allen	Berwick
9	Omar H. Wright	Belvidere	24	Thomas B. Brumback	Plymouth
	Thomas Butterworth	Rockford		John J. Reaburn	Denver
	Horace W. Taylor	Rockford		Brooks R. Hamilton	Nauvoo
10	James I. Neff	Freeport	25	Hosea Davis	Littleton
	Andrew Hinds	Oneco		Charles F. Robison	Ellisville
	Charles S. Burt	Dunleith		William T. McCreery	Birmingham.
11	James Shaw	Mt. Carroll	26	Horace R. Chase	Robin's Nest.
	W. H. Allen	Erie		Bernard Cremer	Peoria
	J. M. Pratt	Pratt		*Washington Cockle	Peoria
12	Frank N. Tice	Forreston	27	David H. Harts	Lincoln
	Bernard H. Truesdell	Amboy		Green P. Orendorff	Hopedale
	Alexander P. Dysart	Nachusa		William R. Hall	Pekin
13	William M. Byers	Sycamore	28	Thomas F. Mitchell	Bloomington.
	Robert M. Brigham	Sandwich		Henry A. Ewing	Bloomington.
	Alonzo B. Smith	Oswego.		Thomas P. Rogers	Bloomington.
14	Edward C. Lovell	Elgin	29	John H. Tyler	DeWitt
	*James G. Wright	Naperville		George K. Ingham	Kenney
	James Herrington	Geneva		Bradford K. Durfee	Decatur
15	Jerry Kenniston	Wilton Center	30	*George Scroggs	Champaign
	Fred Kouka	Beecher		James Core	Homer
	William P. Thompson	Joliet		William A. Day	Champaign

* Resigned.

House of Representatives—*Continued.*

Dist.	Name.	Postoffice.	Dist.	Name.	Postoffice.
31	John G. Holden	Danville	41	John S. Dewey	Troy
	Lyford Marston	Hoopeston	42	T. Duane Hinckley	Hoyleton
	Robert L. McKinlay	Paris		Samuel W. Jones	Nashville
32	Orlando B. Ficklin	Charleston		John L. Nichols	Clement
	Arnold Thomason	Lovington	43	John E. W. Hammond	Omega
	Henry A. Neal	Charleston		Francis M. Bolt	Ramsey
33	William M. Abraham	Watson		James S. Jackson	Iuka
	James L. Ryan	Greenup	44	Jacob Zimmerman	Mt. Carmel
	Bartley Scarlett	Moweaqua		William Bower	Olney
34	John B. Jones	Taylorville		Charles Churchill	Albion
	William Y. Crosthwait	Grove City	45	Jesse R. Johnson	West Liberty
	George L. Zink	Litchfield		James W. Graham	Marshall
35	William L. Gross	Springfield		Andrew J. Reavill	Flat Rock
	John C. Snigg	Springfield	46	Alfred M. Green	Mt. Vernon
	Carter Tracy	Rochester		John R. Moss	Mt. Vernon
36	John F. Snyder	Virginia		Charles M. Lyon	McLeansboro
	John W. Savage	Virginia	47	James M. Gregg	Harrisburg
	*Jacob Wheeler	Havana		Samuel C. Hall	New Haven
37	Samuel Mitcham	Camp Point		Wesley Trammell	Stone Fort
	Absalom M. Samuel	Burton	48	John T. McBride	Chester
	Josiah N. Carter	Quincy		John R. McFie	Coulterville
38	Asa C. Mathews	Pittsfield		Philip C. O. Provart	Paradise Pr.
	Starkey R. Powell	Winchester	49	Thomas C. Jennings	East St. Louis
	James H. Pleasants	Hardin		Joseph Veile	Millstadt
39	Isaac L. Morrison	Jacksonville		Henry Seiter	Lebanon
	Richardson Vasey	Jacksonville	50	Charles H. Layman	Murphysboro
	Francis M. Bridges	Carrollton		Thomas T. Robinson	Pomona
40	Hampton W. Wall	Staunton		Thomas W. Halliday	Cairo
	John N. English	Jerseyville	51	James H. Carter	Vienna
	George E. Warren	Jerseyville		Henry H. Spencer	Mound City
41	William R. Prickett	Edwardsville		†Thomas G. Farris	Vienna
	John M. Pearson	Godfrey		‡William V. Eldredge	Golconda

* Resigned. † Died, Dec. 10, 1878. ‡ Vice Farris, deceased; elected Jan. 4, 1879.

THIRTY-SECOND GENERAL ASSEMBLY, 1880-1882.

Convened at Springfield Jan. 5, 1881; adjourned May 30, 1881. Second session convened March 23, 1882; adjourned May 6, 1882.

SENATE.

President ..... John M. Hamilton, Bloomington.
President pro tem ..... William J. Campbell, Chicago.
Secretary ..... James H. Paddock, Kankakee.
First Assistant ..... George Terwilliger, Fulton.
Second Assistant ..... J. B. Castle, Sandwich.
Bill Clerk ..... L. H. Craig, Greenville.
Sergeant-at-Arms ..... James L. Wheat, LaGrange.
First Assistant ..... J. B. Mordoff, Belvidere.
Second Assistant ..... Joseph W. Hartwell, Marion.
Enrolling and Engrossing Clerk ..... R. W. Gates, Aurora.
First Assistant ..... James R. B. VanCleave, Chicago.
Second Assistant ..... A. H. Reed, Flora.
Postmaster ..... J. S. Fredericks, Paxton.
Assistant ..... Charles W. Rhodes, Chicago.
Superintendent of Ventilation ..... C. N. Whitney, Kewanee.
President's Private Secretary ..... Lincoln H. Weldon, Bloomington.

Republicans 32; Democrats 18; Socialist 1.

Dist.	Name.	Postoffice.	Dist.	Name.	Postoffice.
1	George E. White, rep	Chicago	10	David H. Sunderland, rep	Freeport
2	Leander D. Condee, rep	Chicago	11	Charles Bent, rep	Morrison
3	Sylvester Artley, soc.	Chicago	12	Isaac Rice, rep	Mt. Morris
4	Christopher Mamer, rep	Chicago	13	John R. Marshall, rep	Yorkville
5	*Fred. C. DeLang, rep	Chicago	14	Henry H. Evans, rep	Aurora
6	George E. Adams, rep	Chicago	15	Sylvester W. Munn, rep	Joliet
7	W. J. Campbell, rep	Chicago	16	Conrad Secrest, rep	Watseka
8	George Kirk, rep	Waukegan	17	Samuel R. Lewis, rep	Ottawa
9	Charles E. Fuller, rep	Belvidere	18	George Torrance, rep	Chatsworth

* Admitted by Senate, vice Wm. T. Johnson—no record of election of DeLang.

Senate—*Continued*

Dist.	Name.	Postoffice.	Dist.	Name.	Postoffice.
19	Lorenzo D. Whiting, rep	Tiskilwa	36	Edward Laning, dem	Petersburg
20	Thomas M. Shaw, dem	Lacon	37	Maurice Kelly, dem	Liberty
21	Milton M. Ford, rep	Galva	38	Wm. R. Archer, dem	Pittsfield
22	August W. Berggren, rep	Galesburg	39	Wm. P. Callon, dem	Jacksonville
23	Wm. H. Neece, dem	Macomb	40	Charles A. Walker, dem	Carlinville
24	John Fletcher, rep	Carthage	41	Alfred J. Parkinson, rep	Highland
25	Meredith Walker, dem	Canton	42	Thomas B. Needles, rep	Nashville
26	Andrew J. Bell, dem	Peoria	43	Thomas E. Merritt, dem	Salem
27	Abram Mayfield, dem	Lincoln	44	John R. Tanner, rep	Louisville
28	Joseph W. Fifer, rep	Bloomington	45	William C. Wilson, dem	Robinson
29	Wm. T. Moffett, rep	Decatur	46	John C. Edwards, dem	McLeansboro
30	James S. Wright, rep	Champaign	47	Samuel L. Cheaney, dem	Harrisburg
31	George Hunt, rep	Paris	48	Louis Ihorn, rep	Harrisonville
32	Horace S. Clark, rep	Mattoon	49	John Thomas, rep	Belleville
33	Erastus N. Rinehart, dem	Effingham	50	William A. Lemma, dem	Carbondale
34	Wm. T. Vandeveer, dem	Taylorville	51	Andrew J. Kuykendall, rep	Vienna
35	Wm. E. Shutt, dem	Springfield			

HOUSE OF REPRESENTATIVES.

Speaker ..... Horace H. Thomas, Chicago.
Clerk ..... W. B. Taylor, Wenona.
First Assistant ..... John A. Reeve, Cairo.
Second Assistant ..... H. W. Rowell, Decatur.
Third Assistant ..... Frank W. Latimer, Abingdon.
Postmaster ..... J. H. Melven, Equality.
Assistant ..... Miss Mollie McCabe, Springfield.
Doorkeeper ..... P. W. Wilcox, Mendota.
First Assistant ..... Isaac H. Kelly, Alton.
Second Assistant ..... W. F. Wilton, Clement.
Third Assistant ..... James H. Robinson, Walnut.
Enrolling and Engrossing Clerk ..... Benj. F. Ives, Springfield.
First Assistant ..... Miss Clara E. Patton, Quincy.
Second Assistant ..... C. H. Noel, Cherry Valley.
Speaker's Secretary ..... G. S. Willits, Chicago.
Chaplain ..... Rev. Albert Hale, Springfield.

Republicans 82; Democrats 71.

Dist.	Name.	Postoffice.	Dist.	Name.	Postoffice.
1	David Sullivan, dem	Chicago	12	†John H. White, dem	StillmanVal'y
	Addis L. Rockwell, rep	Chicago		Alexander P. Dysart, rep	Nachusa
	Madison R. Harris, rep	Chicago		Albert F. Brown, rep	StillmanVal'y
2	John R. Cook, dem	Chicago	13	Henry Wood, rep	Sycamore
	Randall H. White, rep	Chicago		Hiram Loucks, rep	Somonauk
	Orrin S. Cook, rep	Chicago		John Clark, dem	Somonauk
3	Thomas Cloonan, dem	Chicago	14	Oliver P. Chisholm, rep	Elgin
	George W. Kroll, rep	Chicago		James Herrington, dem	Geneva
	Joseph R. Gorman, dem	Chicago		James G. Wright, rep	Naperville
4	Patrick J. McMahon, dem	Chicago	15	F. B. Shumway, dem	Peotone
	John L. Parish, rep	Chicago		Michael Collins, rep	Peotone
	Robert N. Pierson, rep	Chicago		Harvey Stratton, rep	Plainfield
5	William A. Phelps, rep	Chicago	16	George B. Winter, dem	Onarga
	Thomas H. McKone, dem	Chicago		James Chatfield, rep	Momence
	S. D. Microslawski, dem	Chicago		Edward Rumley, rep	Gilman
6	Austin O. Sexton, dem	Chicago	17	Alexander Vaughey, dem	Seneca
	Horace H. Thomas, rep	Chicago		Isaac Ames, rep	Streator
	Nathan Plotke, rep	Chicago		Francis M. Robinson, rep	Seneca
7	George G. Struckman, rep	Elgin	18	John H. Collier, rep	Gibson City
	Lorin C. Collins, Jr., rep	Chicago		Albert G. Goodspeed, rep	Odell
	Bernard F. Weber, dem	Chicago		Leander L. Green, dem	Odell
8	Orson C. Diggins, rep	Harvard	19	John H. Welsh, dem	Tiskilwa
	James Thompson, dem	Harvard		Sylvester F. Otman, rep	Wyoming
	James Pollock, rep	Millburn		Charles Baldwin, rep	Princeton
9	Edward B. Sumner, rep	Rockford	20	Euclid Martin, dem	Minonk
	Omar H. Wright, rep	Belvidere		Calvin Stowell, rep	LaPrairie Ctr.
	Laurence McDonald, dem	Pecatonica		James T. Thornton, rep	Magnolia
10	William Cox, rep	Winslow	21	Anthony R. Mock, rep	Cambridge
	Edward L. Cronkrite, dem	Freeport		James W. Simonson, rep	Port Byron
	*Joseph H. Moore, rep	Plum River		Patrick O'Mara, dem	Rock Island
11	William H. Allen, rep	Erie	22	Martin A. Boyd, dem	Aledo
	Emanuel Stover, rep	Lanark		Alexander P. Petrie, rep	New Windsor
	Henry Bitner, dem	Mt. Carroll		Hannibal P. Wood, rep	Wataga

House of Representatives—*Continued.*

Dist.	Name.	Postoffice.	Dist.	Name.	Postoffice.
23	William C. McLeod, dem	Macomb	37	William A. Richardson, dem.	Quincy
	Simeon B. Davis, rep	Blandinsville	38	John L. Underwood, rep	Barry
	Daniel D. Parry, rep	Monmouth		William Mortland, dem	Hardin
24	Robert A. McKinley, dem.	Biggsville		Starkey R. Powell, dem	Winchester
	Henry M. Whiteman, rep	Biggsville	39	Ornan Pierson, rep	Carrollton
	James Peterson, rep	Oquawka.		Oliver Coultas, dem	Lynnville
25	Joseph L. McCune, rep	Ipava		Joseph S. Carr, dem	Kane
	William C. Reno, dem	Browning	40	Balfour Cowen, rep	Virden
	Inmon Blackaby, dem	Civer		John N. English, Sr., dem	Jerseyville
26	Joseph Gallup, dem	Lawn Ridge.		Archelaus N. Yancey, dem	Bunker Hill.
	David Heryer, rep	Brimfield	41	Henry O. Billings, dem	Alton
	J. M. Niehaus, dem	Peoria		John M. Pearson, rep	Godfrey
27	John H. Crandall, dem	Morton		Jones Tontz, rep	Grant Fork
	Wesley B. Harvey, rep	Washington	42	Frederick Becker, dem	Germantown
	Allen Lucas, dem	Mt. Pulaski		John L. Nichols, rep	Clement
28	William Hill, dem	Bloomington		Ervin H. Simmons, rep	Greenville
	George B. Okeson, rep	Lexington	43	Iverson M. Little, rep	Vera
	Thomas F. Mitchell, rep	Bloomington		‡Tilman Raser, dem	Kinmundy
29	Lewis Ludington, rep	Farmer City		Manell A. Harris, dem	Ramsey
	Jason Rogers, rep	Decatur	44	Nathan Crews, rep	Fairfield
	Bradford K. Durfee, dem	Decatur		James Keen, dem	Six Mile
30	Charles F. Tenney, dem	Bement		Ezra B. Keen, rep	Keensburg
	Ashbel H. Bailey, rep	Rantoul	45	Jacob C. Olwin, rep	Robinson
	Herbert D. Peters, rep	Monticello		James C. Bryan, dem	Marshall
31	Joseph B. Mann, dem	Danville		William H. H. Mieure, dem.	Lawr'nceville
	Bradley Butterfield, rep	Rankin	46	Charles T. Strattan, rep	Mt. Vernon
	John G. Holden, rep	Danville		Samuel H. Martin, dem	Carmi
32	Thomas E. Bundy, rep	Tuscola		Robert A. D. Wilbanks, dem.	Mt. Vernon
	John W. R. Morgan, dem	Sullivan	47	Milo Erwin, rep	Crab Orchard
	Eugene B. Buck, dem	Charleston		Francis M. Youngblood, dem.	Benton
33	George D. Chaffee, rep	Shelbyville		James M. Gregg, dem	Harrisburg
	Alfred C. Campbell, dem	Moweaqua	48	Isaac M. Kelly, rep	DuQuoin
	Francis M. Richardson, dem.	Neoga		William K. Murphy, dem.	Pinckn'yville
34	Robert McWilliams, rep	Litchfield		Austin James, dem	Mitchie
	George R. Sharp, dem	Sharpsburg	49	John N. Perrin, dem	Belleville
	George W. Paisley, dem	Hillsboro		Philip H. Postel, rep	Mascoutah
35	A. N. J. Crook, dem	Springfield		Joseph Veile, rep	Millstadt
	DeWitt Smith, dem	Bates	50	Harmon H. Black, rep	Cairo
	James M. Garland, rep	Springfield		David T. Linegar, dem	Cairo
36	Linus C. Chandler, rep	Chandlerville		Holly R. Buckingham, dem.	Alto Pass
	William M. Duffy, dem	San Jose	51	William A. Spann, dem	Vienna
	J. Henry Shaw, dem	Beardstown		William S. Morris, rep	Elizab'tht'wn
37	Joseph N. Carter, rep	Quincy		John D. Young, rep	Pellonia
	John McAdams, dem	Ursa			

* Died; James Bayne, Rep., of JoDaviess, elected his successor for second session March 21, 1882. † Died; Frank N. Tice, Rep., of Ogle, elected March 21, 1882. ‡ Died; Dwight W. Andrews, Dem., of Marion, elected March 21, 1882.

THIRTY-THIRD GENERAL ASSEMBLY, 1882–1884.

Convened at Springfield Jan. 3, 1883; adjourned June 18, 1883.

SENATE.

President........John M. Hamilton, Bloomington, (became Governor).
President pro tem........Wm. J. Campbell, Chicago, (became President).
Secretary........Lorenzo F. Watson, Watseka.
First Assistant........Fred K. Root, Chicago.
Second Assistant........Ed. E. Mitchell, Marion.
Bill Clerk........Edward I. Boles, Sycamore.
Enrolling and Engrossing Clerk........R. W. Gates, Aurora.
First Assistant........R. W. Wright, Boone county.
Second Assistant........F. D. Hitchcock, Clay county.
Postmaster........J. S. Fredericks, Paxton.
Assistant........Henry Glinnett, Clinton county.
Sergeant-at-Arms........P. W. Wilcox, Mendota.
First Assistant........W. M. Robbins, Charleston.
Second Assistant........Simon S. Barger, Eddyville.
President's Private Secretary........John F. Dewey, Aurora.

Republicans, 31; Democrats, 20.

Dist.	Name.	Postoffice.	Dist.	Name.	Postoffice.
1	George E. White, rep	Chicago	27	Henry Tubbs, rep	Kirkwood
2	Leander D. Condee, rep	Chicago	28	Joseph W. Fifer, rep	Bloomington.
3	John H. Clough, rep	Chicago	29	Jason Rogers, rep	Decatur
4	Christopher Mamer, rep	Chicago	30	James S. Wright, rep	Champaign
5	Wm. H. Ruger, rep	Chicago	31	*George Hunt, rep	Paris
6	Geo. E. Adams, rep	Chicago		†Henry Van Sellar, rep	Paris
7	Wm. J. Campbell, rep	Chicago	32	Horace S. Clark, rep	Mattoon
8	George Kirk, rep	Waukegan	33	Erastus N. Rinehart, dem	Effingham
9	Wm. E. Mason, rep	Chicago	34	Wm. T. Vandeveer, dem	Taylorville
10	David H. Sunderland, rep	Freeport	35	Maurice Kelly, dem	Liberty
11	Thomas Cloonan, dem	Chicago	36	Edward Laning, dem	Petersburg
12	Isaac Rice, rep	Mt. Morris	37	Francis M. Bridges, dem	Carrollton
13	Millard B Hereley, dem	Chicago	38	Wm. R. Archer, dem	Pittsfield
14	Henry H. Evans, rep	Aurora	39	Lloyd F. Hamilton, dem	Springfield
15	E. B. Shumway, dem	Peotone	40	Chas. A. Walker, dem	Carlinville
16	Conrad Secrest, rep	Watseka	41	Daniel B. Gillham, dem	Upper Alton.
17	Lyman B. Ray, rep	Morris	42	Thomas B. Needles, rep	Nashville
18	George Torrance, rep	Pontiac	43	Thomas E. Merritt, dem	Salem
19	Wm. C. Snyder, rep	Fulton	44	John R. Tanner, rep	Louisville
20	Thos. M. Shaw, dem	Lacon	45	Wm. H. McNary, dem	Martinsville
21	H. A. Ainsworth, rep	Moline	46	John C. Edwards, dem	McLeansboro
22	August W. Berggren, rep	Galesburg	47	Henry Seiter, dem	Lebanon
23	James W. Duncan, dem	Ottawa	48	Louis Ihorn, rep	Harrisonville
24	John Fletcher, rep	Carthage	49	Wm. S. Morris, rep	Golconda
25	L. D. Whiting, rep	Tiskilwa	50	Wm. A. Lemma, dem	Carbondale
26	Andrew J. Bell, dem	Peoria	51	Daniel Hogan, rep	Mound City

* Resigned; elected Attorney General in 1884. † Elected Nov., '84, vice Hunt, resigned.

HOUSE OF REPRESENTATIVES.

Speaker .... Lorin C. Collins Jr., Chicago.
Clerk .... John A. Reeve, Cairo.
First Assistant .... Joseph F. Allison, Mt. Carroll.
Second Assistant .... Bailey D. Dawson, Chicago.
Third Assistant .... Rector C. Hitt, Ottawa.
Enrolling and Engrossing Clerk .... Miss Clara E. Patton, Quincy.
First Assistant .... W. I. Allen, Springfield.
Second Assistant .... A. R. Dow, Belvidere.
Doorkeeper .... Lindsay Steele, Chester.
First Assistant .... Edward Smith, Bloomington.
Second Assistant .... Archie Ward, Peoria.
Third Assistant .... John W. Heiderman, Metropolis.
Postmaster .... John W. January, Minonk.
Assistant .... Miss Lizzie Gilmer, Pittsfield.
Chaplain .... Rev. Albert Hale, Springfield.

Republicans, 77; Democrats, 75; Independent, 1.

Dist.	Name.	Postoffice.	Dist.	Name.	Postoffice.
1	John Fairbanks, rep	Chicago	9	Julius Pederson, rep	Chicago
	R. B. Kennedy, rep	Chicago		August Wendell, rep	Chicago
	David Sullivan, dem	Chicago		Mark J. Clinton, dem	Chicago
2	Wm. H. Harper, rep	Chicago	10	Albert F. Brown, rep	Stillman V'l'y
	Hilon A. Parker, rep	Chicago		John C. Seyster, dem	Oregon
	Eugene J. Fellows, dem	Chicago		Ed. B. Sumner, rep	Rockford
3	J. W. E. Thomas, rep	Chicago	11	Jesse J. Rook, rep	Chicago
	Thos. J. McNally, dem	Chicago		John O'Shea, dem	Chicago
	Isaac Abrahams, dem	Chicago		August Motte, dem	Chicago
4	John L. Parish, rep	Chicago	12	Geo. L. Hoffman, rep	Mt. Carroll
	J. F. Lawrence, rep	Chicago		J. A. Hammond, rep	Hanover
	R. F. Sheridan, dem	Chicago		E. L. Cronkrite, dem	Freeport
5	David W. Walsh, dem	Chicago	13	Peter Sundelius, rep	Chicago
	James A. Taylor, dem	Chicago		Geo. A. Klupp, dem	Chicago
	Edwin E. Wood, rep	Chicago		John F. Dugan, dem	Chicago
6	Edward D. Cooke, rep	Chicago	14	Luther L. Hiatt, rep	Wheaton
	Theo. Stimming, rep	Chicago		James Herrington, dem	Geneva
	Austin O. Sexton, dem	Chicago		Henry F. Walker, rep	Hinsdale
7	Lorin C. Collins, Jr., rep	Chicago	15	George Bez, dem	Wilmington
	Geo. G. Struckman, rep	Chicago		John O'Connell, dem	Joliet
	Clayton E. Crafts, dem	Chicago		James L. Owen, rep	Frankfort
8	Chas. E. Fuller, rep	Belvidere	16	John H. Jones, rep	Milford
	Chas. H. Tryon, rep	Richmond		Wm. S. Hawker, rep	Salina
	Elijah M. Haines, ind	Waukegan		Daniel C. Taylor, dem	Kankakee

House of Representatives—*Continued.*

Dist.	Name.	Postoffice.	Dist.	Name.	Postoffice.
17	Henry Wood, rep	Sycamore	34	T. L. Mathews, rep	Virginia
	H. M. Boardman, rep	Shabbona	35	James E. Purnell, dem	Quincy
	Andrew Welch, dem	Yorkville		J. E. Downing, dem	Camp Point
18	John H. Collier, rep	Gibson		T. G. Black, rep	Clayton
	A. G. Goodspeed, rep	Odell	36	Thos. Worthington, Jr., rep	Pittsfield
	Michael Cleary, dem	Odell		John W. Moore, dem	Mound Stat'n
19	Sol. H. Bethea, rep	Dixon		Francis M. Greathouse, dem	Hardin
	J. G. Manahan, rep	Sterling	37	Walter E. Carlin, dem	Jerseyville
	John B. Felker, dem	Amboy		Geo. W. Murray, dem	Winchester
20	Revilo Newton, dem	Minonk		John H. Coats, rep	Winchester
	John H. Crandall, dem	Morton	38	A. N. Yancey, dem	Bunker Hill
	Robert S. Hester, rep	Belle Plain		E. M. Kinman, dem	Jacksonville
21	Thos. Nowers, Jr., rep	Atkinson		Isaac L. Morrison, rep	Jacksonville
	Henry C. Cleaveland, rep	Rock Island	39	Ben F. Caldwell, dem	Chatham
	Patrick O'Mara, dem	Rock Island		Geo. W. Murray, dem	Springfield
22	F. A. Willoughby, dem	Galesburg		David T. Littler, rep	Springfield
	W. H. Emerson, rep	Astoria	40	E. E. Cowperthwait, rep	Moawequa
	A. S. Curtis, rep	Oneida		John B. Ricks, dem	Taylorville
23	Wright Adams, rep	Sheridan		G. M. Stevens, dem	Nokomis
	Alex. Vaughey, dem	Seneca	41	John M. Pearson, rep	Godfrey
	Sam'l C. Wiley dem	Earlville		Henry O. Billings, dem	Alton
24	David Rankin, rep	Biggsville		R. D. Utiger, dem	Alhambra
	Josiah M. Ansley, rep	Swedonia	42	J. L. Nichols, rep	Clement
	John D. Stephens, dem	Carthage		F. E. W. Brink, dem	Hoyleton
25	James T. Thornton, rep	Magnolia		James M. Rountree, dem	Nashville
	John Lackey, rep	Osceola	43	Geo. H. Varnell, dem	Mt. Vernon
	John H. Welsh, dem	Tiskilwa		J. D. Jennings, dem	Beecher City
26	Sam'l H. Thompson, rep	Peoria		Seth F. Crews, rep	Mt. Vernon
	M. C. Quinn, dem	Peoria	44	Elbert Rowland, dem	Olney
	Joseph Gallup, dem	Lawn Ridge		J. S. Symonds, dem	Flora
27	Isaac N. Pearson, rep	Macomb		Henry Studer, rep	Olney
	C. M. Rogers, rep	Monmouth	45	Grandison Clark, dem	Newton
	Isaac L. Pratt, dem	Roseville		Wm. Updyke, dem	Robinson
28	Lafayette Funk, rep	Shirley		J. M. Honey, rep	Newton
	Thos. F. Mitchell, rep	Bloomington	46	W. H. Johnson, rep	Carmi
	Simeon H. West, dem	Arrowsmith		Lowery Hay, dem	Carmi
29	John W. Crocker, rep	Maroa		F. W. Cox, dem	Bridgeport
	John T. Foster, rep	Elkhart	47	M. A. Sullivan, dem	East St. Louis
	R. H. Templeman, dem	Mt. Pulaski		Louis C. Starkel, dem	Belleville
30	Wm. A. Day, dem	Champaign		Joseph B. Messick, rep	East St. Louis
	Wm. F. Calhoun, rep	Clinton	48	James F. Canniff, dem	Waterloo
	James A. Hawks, rep	Atwood		John J. Higgins, dem	DuQuoin
31	E. R. E. Kimbrough, dem	Danville		John R. McFie, rep	Coulterville
	W. J. Calhoun, rep	Danville	49	James M. Gregg, dem	Harrisburg
	Robert B. Ray, rep	Fairmount		Wm. H. Boyer, rep	Harrisburg
32	Jos. H. Ewing, rep	Arcola		R. W. McCartney, rep	Metropolis
	W. H. DeBord, rep	Greenup	50	Sidney Grear, dem	Jonesboro
	F. M. Richardson, dem	Neoga		David T. Linegar, dem	Cairo
33	Thos. N. Henry, dem	Windsor		James M. Scurlock, rep	Carbondale
	John H. Baker, dem	Sullivan	51	*A. N. Lodge, dem	Marion
	Chas. L. Roane, rep	Sullivan		W. W. Hoskinson, rep	Benton
34	Wm. M. Duffy, dem	San Jose		Milo Erwin, rep	Marion
	Henry C. Thompson, dem	Virginia			

* Seat contested by Wm. A. Spann, Dem.; latter was declared elected.

THIRTY-FOURTH GENERAL ASSEMBLY, 1884-1886.

Convened at Springfield Jan. 7, 1885; adjourned June 26, 1885.

SENATE.

President.......John C. Smith, Chicago.
President pro tem.......Wm. J. Campbell, Chicago.
Secretary.......L. F. Watson, Watseka.
First Assistant.......Edward I. Boles, Sycamore.
Second Assistant.......John D. Gerlach, Randolph County.
Enrolling and Engrossing Clerk.......R. W. Gates, Aurora.
First Assistant.......A. H. Reed, Flora.
Second Assistant.......John H. Barton, Carbondale.
Postmaster.......J. A. Hunter, Livingston County.
Assistant.......Miss Hattie B. Thompson, Urbana.
Sergeant-at-Arms.......F. A. Freer, Galesburg.
First Assistant.......George Morris, Golconda.
Second Assistant.......Frederick W. Scharlau, Chicago.
President's Private Secretary.......E. A. Routh, Springfield.

Republicans, 26; Democrats, 24; Greenback-Democrat, 1.

Dist.	Name.	Postoffice	Dist.	Name.	Postoffice.
1	George E. White, rep	Chicago	27	Henry Tubbs, rep	Kirkwood
2	Charles H. Crawford, rep	Hyde Park	28	LaFayette Funk, rep	Shirley
3	John H. Clough, rep	Chicago	29	Jason Rogers, rep	Decatur
4	Thomas A. Cantwell, dem.	Chicago	30	Martin B. Thompson, rep	Urbana
5	W. H. Ruger, rep	Chicago	31	Henry Van Sellar, rep	Paris
6	Henry W. Leman, rep	Chicago	32	Wm. B. Galbreath, dem	Charleston
7	Wm. J. Campbell, rep	Chicago	33	Erastus N. Rinehart, dem	Effingham
8	Ira R. Curtiss, rep	Marengo	34	John M. Darnell, dem	Rushville
9	Wm E. Mason, rep	Chicago	35	Maurice Kelly, dem	Liberty
10	Edward B. Sumner, rep	Rockford	36	James W. Johnson, dem	Pittsfield
11	Thomas Cloonan, dem	Chicago	37	*Francis M. Bridges, dem	Carrollton
12	James S. Cochran, rep	Freeport		†Robt. H. Davis, dem.	Carrollton
13	Millard B. Hereley, dem	Chicago	38	David Gore, dem	Carlinville
14	Henry H. Evans, rep	Aurora	39	Lloyd F. Hamilton, dem	Springfield
15	E. B. Shumway, dem	Peotone	40	Elizur Southworth, dem	Litchfield
16	Hamilton K. Wheeler, rep	Kankakee	41	Daniel B. Gillham, dem	Upper Alton
17	Lyman B. Ray, rep	Morris	42	William S. Forman, dem	Nashville
18	George Torrance, rep	Pontiac	43	Thomas E. Merritt, dem	Salem
19	William C. Snyder, rep	Fulton	44	Robley D. Adams, rep	Fairfield
20	Green P. Orendorff, dem	Hopedale	45	William H. McNary, dem	Martinsville
21	Henry A. Ainsworth, rep	Moline	46	Richard L. Organ, dem	Carmi
22	August W. Berggren, rep	Galesburg	47	Henry Seiter, dem	Lebanon
23	James W. Duncan, dem	Ottawa	48	John J. Higgins, dem	DuQuoin
24	Alson J. Streeter, gr dem	New Windsor	49	Wm. S. Morris, rep	Golconda
25	L. D. Whiting, rep	Tiskilwa	50	Geo. W. Hill, dem	Murphysboro
26	Andrew J. Bell, dem	Peoria	51	Daniel Hogan, rep	Mound City

* Died March 20, 1885. † Vice Bridges, elected April 11, 1885.

HOUSE OF REPRESENTATIVES.

Speaker .... Elijah M. Haines, Waukegan.
Clerk .... R. A. D. Wilbanks, Mt. Vernon.
First Assistant .... Chas. F. Strubbe, Chicago.
Second Assistant .... C. V. Jaquith, Paris.
Third Assistant .... G. C. Sanderson, Plano.
Enrolling and Engrossing Clerk .... Thos. H. Stokes, Lincoln.
First Assistant .... W. H. Matlack, Belleville.
Second Assistant .... Miss Helen LaBonte, Springfield.
Postmistress .... Mrs. Mary O'Connor, Springfield.
Assistant .... Miss Mollie McCabe, Springfield.
Doorkeeper .... Thos. B. Carson, Urbana.
First Assistant .... Daniel Delaney, Girard.
Second Assistant .... George Howard, Chicago.
Third Assistant .... A. Longworth, McLeansboro.

Republicans, 76; Democrats, 76; Independent, 1.

Dist.	Name.	Postoffice.	Dist.	Name.	Postoffice.
1	Robert B. Kennedy, rep	Chicago	8	James Pollock, rep	Milburn
	Francis W. Parker, rep	Chicago		Chas. E. Fuller, rep	Belvidere
	James McHale, dem	Chicago		Elijah M. Haines, ind	Waukegan
2	Wm. H. Harper, rep	Chicago	9	Fred S. Baird, rep	Chicago
	Hilon A. Parker, rep	Normal Park		Chas. E. Scharlau rep	Chicago
	Ernst Hummel, dem	Hyde Park		Dennis Considine, dem	Chicago
3	Abner Taylor, rep	Chicago	10	Albert F. Brown, rep	StillmanVal'y
	John W. E. Thomas, rep	Chicago		David Hunter, rep	Rockford
	Thos. J. McNally, dem	Chicago		Edwin M. Winslow, dem	Winnebago
4	Thos. C. MacMillan, rep	Chicago	11	Adam C Oldenburg, rep	Chicago
	Matthew Murphy, dem	Chicago		John O'Shea, dem	Chicago
	James F. Quinn, dem	Chicago		J. J. Schlesinger, dem	Chicago
5	Wm. S. Powell, rep	Chicago	12	Daniel A. Sheffield, rep	Apple River
	Jos. P. Mahoney, dem	Chicago		Simon Greenleaf, rep	Savanna
	Wm. A. Dorman dem	Chicago		E. L. Cronkrite, dem	Freeport
6	Henry S. Boutelle, rep	Chicago	13	Peter A. Sundelius, rep	Chicago
	Eugene A. Sittig, rep	Chicago		Barney Bruchteudorf, dem	Chicago
	Stephen F. Sullivan, dem	Chicago		Thomas F. Mulheran, dem	Chicago
7	John Humphrey, rep	Orland	14	Luther L. Hiatt, rep	Wheaton
	George G. Stuckman, rep	Elgin		John Stewart, rep	Campton
	Clayton E. Crafts, dem	Austin		Thomas O'Donnell, dem	Aurora

House of Representatives—*Continued.*

Dist.	Name.	Postoffice.	Dist.	Name.	Postoffice.
15	Henry H. Stassen, rep	Monee	33	Walter C. Headen, rep	Shelbyville
	James C. Morgan, dem	Joliet	34	Perry Logsdon, rep	Rushville
	George Bez, dem	Wilmington		†J. Henry Shaw, dem	Beardstown
16	Matthew F. Campbell, rep	Kankakee		George W. Langford, dem	Havana
	John L. Hamilton, rep	Watseka	35	Fred. P. Taylor, dem	Quincy
	Free P. Morris, dem	Watseka		Samuel Mileham, dem	Camp Point
17	Henry C. Whittemore, rep	Sycamore		Wm. H. Collins, rep	Quincy
	Wm. M. Hanna, rep	Lisbon	36	Wm. H. Brackenridge, rep	Versailles
	Andrew Welch, dem	Yorkville		John W. Moore, dem	Mound Stat'n
18	Albert G. Goodspeed, rep	Odell		Peter C. Barry, dem	Hardin
	Charles Bogardus, rep	Paxton	37	Henry C. Massey, dem	Jerseyville
	Michael Cleary, dem	Odell		Byron McEvers, dem	Glasgow
19	Charles H. Ingalls, rep	Sublette		Theodore S. Chapman, rep	Jerseyville
	*Dwight S. Spafford, rep	Morrison	38	Edward L. McDonald, dem	Jacksonville
	Caleb C. Johnson, dem	Sterling		Frank R. McAlinney, dem	Staunton
20	Julius Watercott, dem	Henry		George J. Castle, rep	Carlinville
	Samuel Patrick, dem	Washburn	39	Ben F. Caldwell, dem	Chatham
	Ernest F. Unland, rep	Pekin		Charles A. Keyes, dem	Springfield
21	Henry C. Cleaveland, rep	Rock Island		Charles Kerr, rep	Pawnee
	Thomas Nowers, Jr., rep	Atkinson	40	Robert A. Gray, dem	Blue Mound
	James H. Paddelford, dem	Cleveland		George M. Stevens, dem	Nokomis
22	Orrin P. Cooley, rep	Oneida		H. H. Hood, rep	Litchfield
	Wm. J. Orendorff, rep	Canton	41	Wm. R. Prickett, dem	Edwardsville
	Samuel P. Marshall, dem	Ipava		Wm. W. Pearce, dem	Alhambra
23	Samuel C. Wiley, dem	Earlville		Jones Tontz, rep	Grant Fork
	Charles L. Hoffman, dem	Farm Ridge	42	M. A. Morgan, rep	Okawville
	Frank P. Snyder, rep	Mendota		Milton M. Sharp, dem	Greenville
24	Abner W. Graham, rep	Biggsville		Charles C. Moore, dem	Carlyle
	Clarence R. Gittings, rep	Terre Haute	43	George H. Varnell, dem	Mt. Vernon
	Alfred N. Cherry, dem	Tioga		Geo. H. Dieckmann, dem	Vandalia
25	Albert W. Boyden, rep	Sheffield		Henry C. Goodnow, rep	Salem
	James H. Miller, rep	Toulon	44	William T. Prunty, rep	Olney
	Eli V. Raley, dem	Granville		Alfred Brown, rep	Albion
26	Mark M. Bassett, rep	Peoria		Edward McClung, dem	Fairfield
	John Downs, dem	Peoria	45	John M. Highsmith, dem	Robinson
	William McLean, dem	Chillicothe		Isaac M. Shup, dem	Newton
27	Calvin M. Rodgers, rep	Monmouth		David Trexler, rep	Newton
	W. H. McCord, rep	Blandinsville	46	James R. Campbell, dem	McLeansboro
	Wm. H. Weir, dem	Colchester		James M. Sharp, dem	MountCarmel
28	Samuel B. Kinsey, rep	McLean		Wm. T. Buchanan, rep	Lawrenc'ville
	Ivory H. Pike, rep	Bloomington	47	James M. Dill, dem	Belleville
	Simeon H. West, dem	Arrowsmith		Ferdinand Heim, dem	East St. Louis
29	Charles S. Lawrence, rep	Elkhart		Joseph B. Messick, rep	East St. Louis
	R. H. Templeman, dem	Mt. Pulaski	48	Thomas James, dem	Chester
	James M. Graham, dem	Niantic		Peter Bickelhaupt, dem	Waterloo
30	Wm. F. Calhoun, rep	Clinton		Henry Clay, rep	Tamaroa
	Virgil S. Ruby, rep	Bement	49	John Yost, rep	Elba
	Wm. B. Webber, dem	Urbana		Simon S. Barger, rep	Eddyville
31	Elliott E. Boudinot, rep	Danville		W. V. Choisser, dem	Harrisburg
	Charles A. Allen, rep	Hoopeston	50	David T. Linegar, dem	Cairo
	E. R. E. Kimbrough, dem	Danville		Philip V. N. Davis, dem	Anna
32	S. M. Long, rep	Newman		Wm. S. Rogers, rep	Murphysboro
	Henry Shepler, dem	Greenup	51	James M. Fowler, rep	Marion
	J. P. McGee, dem	Brushy Fork		William C. Allen, rep	Vienna
33	Thomas N. Henry, dem	Windsor		Quincy E. Browning, dem	Benton
	John H. Baker, dem	Sullivan			

* Vice R. E. Logan, rep., deceased; election March 21, 1885.

† Deceased; Wm. H. Weaver, rep., Petersburg, elected to succeed him May 6, 1885, giving Republicans a majority in the House and on joint ballot, and electing Gen. Logan to the United States Senate.

THIRTY-FIFTH GENERAL ASSEMBLY, 1886-1888.

Convened at Springfield Jan. 5, 1887; adjourned June 15, 1887.

SENATE.

President ..... John C. Smith, Chicago.
President pro tem ..... August W. Berggren, Galesburg.
Secretary ..... Lorenzo F. Watson, Watseka.
First Assistant ..... John W. Bailey, Princeton.
Second Assistant ..... J. M. Marks, Marengo.
Third Assistant ..... H. H. Peck, Chicago.
Bill Clerk ..... H. E. Torrance, Pontiac.

Enrolling and Engrossing Clerk....John F. Dewey, Aurora.
First Assistant....H. H. Reed, Flora.
Second Assistant....Chas. D. Patch, Sycamore.
Sergeant-at-Arms....Wm. B. Lynn, Carrollton.
First Assistant....Fred. Newland, Macomb.
Second Assistant....Robert F. Shipley, Mendota.
Postmistress....Miss Hattie B. Thompson, Urbana.
Assistant....Theodore Tromley, Enfield.
Chaplain....Rev. R. O. Post, Springfield.
Private Secretary to President....Robt. W. Smith, Chicago.

Republicans, 32; Democrats, 17; Labor, 1; Greenback-Democrat, 1.

Dist.	Name.	Postoffice.	Dist.	Name.	Postoffice.
1	Bernard A. Eckhart, rep	Chicago	27	Isaac N. Pearson, rep	Macomb
2	Chas. H. Crawford, rep	Chicago	28	Lafayette Funk, rep	Shirley
3	George A. Gibbs, rep	Chicago	29	Wm. C. Johns, rep	Decatur
4	Thomas A. Cantwell, dem	Chicago	30	Martin B. Thompson, rep	Urbana
5	James Monahan, rep	Chicago	31	George E. Bacon, rep	Paris
6	Henry W. Leman, rep	Chicago	32	*Thos. L. McGrath, rep	Mattoon
7	John Humphrey, rep	Orland	33	Lloyd B. Stephenson, dem	Shelbyville
8	Ira R. Curtiss, rep	Marengo	34	John M. Darnell, dem	Rushville
9	Philip Knopf, rep	Chicago	35	Geo. W. Dean, dem	Adams P. O.
10	Edward B. Sumner, rep	Rockford	36	James W. Johnson, dem	Pittsfield
11	Richard M. Burke, lab	Chicago	37	Theodore S. Chapman, rep	Jerseyville
12	James S. Cochran, rep	Freeport	38	David Gore, dem	Carlinville
13	Michael F. Garrity, rep	Chicago	39	Wm. E. Shutt, dem	Springfield
14	Henry H. Evans, rep	Aurora	40	Elizur Southworth, dem	Litchfield
15	Chas. H. Bacon, rep	Lockport	41	Wm. F. L. Hadley, rep	Edwardsville
16	Hamilton K. Wheeler, rep	Kankakee	42	Wm. S. Forman, dem	Nashville
17	Chas. F. Greenwood, rep	Waterman	43	Augustus M. Strattan, dem	Mt. Vernon
18	George Torrance, rep	Pontiac	44	Robley D. Adams, rep	Fairfield
19	John D. Crabtree, rep	Dixon	45	Andrew J. Reavill, dem	Flat Rock
20	Green P. Orendorff, dem	Hopedale	46	Richard L. Organ, dem	Carmi
21	John H. Pierce, rep	Kewanee	47	Henry Seiter, dem	Lebanon
22	August W. Berggren, rep	Galesburg	48	John J. Higgins, dem	DuQuoin
23	Joseph Reinhardt, rep	Peru	49	John Yost, rep	Elba
24	A. J. Streeter, gr-dem	New Windsor	50	Geo. W. Hill, dem	Murphysboro
25	Edward A. Washburn, rep	Princeton	51	Daniel Hogan, rep	Mound City
26	Andrew J. Bell, dem	Peoria			

* Elected Nov. 2, 1886, to succeed Galbreath, dem., deceased.

HOUSE OF REPRESENTATIVES.

Speaker....Wm. F. Calhoun, Clinton.
Clerk....John A. Reeve, Cairo.
First Assistant....Edward D. Northam, Aurora.
Second Assistant....S. D. Hall, Galesburg.
Third Assistant....John E. Melick, Springfield.
Fourth Assistant....John E. Blakemore, Moline.
Bill Clerk....Bailey D. Dawson, Chicago.
Reading Clerk....Wm. A. Rogers, Carbondale.
Enrolling and Engrossing Clerk....Harrison Black, Marshall.
First Assistant....J. B. Matlack, Chester.
Second Assistant....J. H. Lott, Paxton.
Postmaster....John W. January, Minonk.
Assistant....Mabel Allen, Springfield.
Doorkeeper....Chas. P. Loop, Belvidere.
First Assistant....J. O. Burton, Flora.
Second Assistant....J. O. P. Vandevost, Effingham.
Third Assistant....J. H. Robinson, Princeton.
Chaplain....Rev. Francis Springer, Springfield.
Private Secretary to Speaker....James M. North, Clinton.

Republicans, 78; Democrats, 66; Labor, 8; Prohibitionist, 1.

Dist.	Name.	County.	Dist.	Name.	County.
1	David W. Clark, rep	Chicago	3	Francis A. Brokoski, rep	Chicago
	John S. Ford, rep	Chicago		Geo. F. Ecton, rep	Chicago
	James O'Connor, lab	Chicago		Thos. J. Moran, dem	Chicago
2	Durfee C. Chase, rep	Englewood	4	James F. Gleason, dem	Chicago
	John W. Farley, dem	Chicago		Thos. C. MacMillan, rep	Chicago
	Wm. P. Wright, lab	Chicago		John Meyer, rep	Chicago

House of Representatives—*Continued*.

Dist.	Name.	Postoffice.
5	Kirk N. Eastman, rep	Chicago
	Joseph P. Mahoney, dem	Chicago
	Leo. P. Dwyer, lab	Chicago
6	James H. Farrell, dem	Chicago
	Michael J. Dwyer, lab	Chicago
	Chas. G. Neeley, rep	Chicago
7	Clayton E. Crafts, dem	Austin
	O. W. Herrick, rep	Chicago
	S. A. Reynolds, rep	Chicago
8	Charles E. Fuller, rep	Belvidere
	Charles A. Partridge, rep	Waukegan
	George Waite, dem	Volo
9	Charles E. Scharlau, rep	Chicago
	Henry Decker, rep	Chicago
	Chas. G. Dixon, lab	Chicago
10	David Hunter, rep	Rockford
	James P. Wilson, dem	Woosung
	James Lamont, pro	Rockford
11	Geo. F. Rohrbach, lab	Chicago
	Thomas G. McElligott, dem	Chicago
	Bryan Conway, dem	Chicago
12	Emanuel Stover, rep	Lanark
	George W. Pepoon, rep	Warren
	James Carr, dem	Scales Mound
13	Frank E. Schoenewald, rep	Chicago
	Victor Karlowski, lab	Chicago
	J. J. Furlong, dem	Chicago
14	Charles Curtiss, rep	Downers Gr'e
	James Herrington, dem	Geneva
	John Stewart rep	Elburn
15	Dwight Haven, rep	New Lenox
	Daniel McLaughlin, rep	Braidwood
	Thos. H. Reilly, dem	Joliet
16	Hiram M. Keyser, rep	Momence
	John L. Hamilton, rep	Watseka
	Truman Hulling, dem	Kankakee
17	Daniel D. Hunt, rep	DeKalb
	E. W. Faxon, rep	Fox
	Hiram Holcomb, dem	Sycamore
18	O. W. Pollard, rep	Dwight
	Charles Bogardus, rep	Paxton
	Michael Cleary, dem	Odell
19	Benjamin H. Bradshaw, rep.	Compton
	John W. White, rep	Tampico
	Caleb C. Johnson, dem	Sterling
20	Aaron H. Brubaker, rep	Benson
	Wm. H. Kister, dem	Henry
	*Samuel Patrick, dem	Washburn
21	Hendrick V. Fisher, rep	Geneseo
	Wm. F. Crawford, rep	Taylor Ridge.
	John T. Platt, dem	Cambridge
22	Orrin P. Cooley, rep	Oneida
	Thomas Hamer, rep.	Vermont
	Samuel P. Marshall, dem	Ipava
23	James P. Trench, dem	LaSalle
	Edgar S. Browne, dem	Mendota
	Lewis M. Sawyer, rep	Streator
24	Wesley C. Williams, dem	Carthage
	Clarence R. Gittings, rep	Terre Haute
	Wm. C. Galloway, rep	Aledo
25	James H. Miller, rep	Toulon
	Sterling Pomeroy, rep	Ohio
	Anthony Morrasy, dem.	Sheffield
26	N. D. Jay, dem	Elmwood
	James Kenney, dem	Peoria
	John M. Hart, rep	Eden
27	James P. Firoved, dem	Monmouth
	Henry W. Allen, rep	Kirkwood
	Richard G. Breeden, rep	Tennessee
28	Frank Y. Hamilton, rep	Bloomington
	Samuel B. Kinsey, rep	McLean
28	John Eddy, dem	Bloomington.
29	Hiram L. Pierce, dem	Lincoln
	Wm. H. Kretzinger, rep	Latham.
	Wm. Grason, rep	Cerro Gordo.
30	Francis M. Peel, dem	White Heath.
	Wm. F. Calhoun, rep	Clinton
	Virgil S. Ruby, rep	Bement
31	Hiram P. Blackburn, rep	Danville
	Charles A. Allen, rep	Hoopeston
	Robert L. McKinlay, dem	Paris
32	Samuel F. Wilson, rep	Neoga
	Eugene Rice, rep	Camargo
	F. M. Richardson, dem	Neoga
33	John H. Baker, dem	Sullivan
	John J. Schneider, dem	Effingham
	Joseph P. Condo, rep	Moccasin
34	Michael D. Halpin, dem	Beardstown
	Fred Wilkinson, dem	Petersburg
	James M. Ruggles, rep	Havana
35	Albert W. Wells, dem	Quincy.
	Ira Tyler, dem	Richfield
	Wm. H. Collins, rep	Quincy
36	Wm. R. Archer, dem	Pittsfield
	John McNabb, dem	Hardin
	Alex K. Lowry, rep	Mt. Sterling
37	Wm. M. Ward, rep	Greenfield
	Robert H. Davis, dem	Carrollton
	J. D. Sawyers, dem	Oxville
38	Geo. W. Smith, dem	Jacksonville.
	James B. Wilson, dem	Carlinville
	John E. Wright, rep.	Murrayville
39	Albert L. Converse, dem	Springfield
	Wiley E. Jones, dem	Springfield
	¶David T. Littler, rep	Springfield
40	Robert A. Gray, dem	Blue Mound
	Colman C. George, rep	Blackburn
	Burrell Phillips, dem	Hillsboro
41	John W. Coppinger, dem	Alton
	Isaac Cox, rep	Marine
	John Wedig, rep	Nameoki
42	M. A. Morgan, rep	Okawville
	**H. H. Helman, dem	Aviston.
	C. W. Seawell, dem	Greenville
43	Thomas E. Merritt, dem	Salem
	Granville V. E. Fletcher, dem	St. Elmo
	John J. Brown, rep	Vandalia
44	John S. Symonds, dem	Flora
	Thos. A. Wilson, rep	Flora
	†Alfred Brown, rep	Albion
45	Chas. A. Purdunn, dem	Marshall
	James Larrabee, dem	Latona
	Alfred H. Jones, rep	Robinson
46	James R. Campbell, dem	McLeansboro
	Geo. F. French, dem	Sumner
	Edward B. Green, rep	Mt. Carmel
47	Joseph B. Messick, rep	East St. Louis
	Joseph Velle, rep	Millstadt
	Geo. S. Bailey, lab	East St. Louis
48	Everett J. Murphy, rep	Chester
	Chas. B. Cole, dem	Chester
	Peter Bickelhaupt, dem	Waterloo
49	Wm. G. Sloan, rep	Harrisburg
	Simon S. Barger, rep	Eddyville
	Jonathan F. Taylor, dem	Elizabethto'n
50	Reuben S. Yocum, dem	Cairo
	Wm. S. Day, dem	Jonesboro
	Chas. F. Nellis, rep	Cairo
51	Wm. H. Bundy, dem	Marion
	‡W. W. Hoskinson, rep	Benton
	Alonzo K. Vickers, rep	Vienna

¶ Resigned April 30, 1887; no successor. † Died Feb. 21, 1887; Albert Rude, rep., Bone Gap, elected March 22, 1887. ‡ Died Feb. 25, 1887; W. L. Crim, rep., Frankfort, elected, April 5, 1887. * Died; Samuel A. Miller, dem., Minonk, elected, Jan. 18, 1887. ** Died; Wm. G. Kaune, Breese, elected Feb. 15 1887.

THIRTY-SIXTH GENERAL ASSEMBLY, 1888-1890.

Convened at Springfield Jan. 9, 1889; adjourned May 28, 1889. Second session convened July 23, 1890; adjourned Aug. 1, 1890.

SENATE.

President........ Lyman B. Ray, Morris.
President pro tem........ Theodore S. Chapman, Jerseyville.
Secretary........ Lorenzo F. Watson, Watseka.
First Assistant........ John W. Bailey, Princeton.
Second Assistant........ A. W. Sawyer, Rockford.
Bill Clerk........ Frank H. Guflin, Morrison.
Enrolling and Engrossing Clerk........ John F. Dewey, Aurora.
First Assistant........ Chas. D. Patch, Sycamore.
Second Assistant........ S. C. Jordan, Menard.
Sergeant-at-Arms........ Stephen Maddock, Paris.
First Assistant........ Fred. Newland, Macomb.
Second Assistant........ Ben Cleary, Chicago.
Postmistress........ Hattie B. Thompson, Urbana.
Assistant........ Alice Vaughn, Chicago.
Chaplain........ Rev. A. A. Burleigh, Springfield.
Private Secretary to President........ E. B. Fletcher, Morris.

Republicans 35; Democrats 15; Labor 1.

Dist.	Name.	Postoffice.	Dist.	Name.	Postoffice.
1	Bernard A. Eckhart, rep.....	Chicago	27	‡William J. Frisbee, rep......	Bushnell .....
2	Charles H. Crawford, rep ...	Chicago	28	Thomas C. Kerrick, rep	Bloomington.
3	George A. Gibbs, rep.........	Chicago	29	William C. Johns, rep.......	Decatur ......
4	Thomas C. MacMillan, rep...	Chicago	30	Milton W. Mathews, rep	Urbana. ......
5	James Monahan, rep	Chicago	31	George E. Bacon, rep	Paris..........
6	Horace H. Thomas, rep......	Chicago	32	*Lewis L. Lehman, rep......	Mattoon......
7	John Humphrey, rep.	Orland........	33	Lloyd B. Stephenson, dem.....	Shelbyville...
8	Charles E. Fuller, rep	Belvidere	34	Arthur A. Leeper, dem......	Virginia ......
9	Philip Knopf, rep............	Chicago	35	George W. Dean, dem........	Adams... ....
10	Benjamin F. Sheets, rep	Oregon	36	Harry Higbee, dem...........	Pittsfield.....
11	Richard M. Burke, lab....	Chicago	37	Theodore S. Chapman, rep ..	Jerseyville...
12	Robert H. Wiles, rep	Freeport	38	Edward L. McDonald, dem ..	Jacksonville.
13	Michael F. Garrity, rep	Chicago	39	William E. Shutt, dem	Springfield...
14	Henry H. Evans, rep..........	Aurora	40	Hiram P. Shumway, dem	Taylorville...
15	Charles H. Bacon, rep........	Lockport.....	41	Wm. F. L. Hadley, rep ...	Edwardsville
16	Conrad Secrest, rep	Watseka......	42	F. E. W. Brink, dem	Hoyleton.....
17	Charles F. Greenwood, rep..	Waterman ...	43	Augustus M. Strattan, dem ..	Mt. Vernon ..
18	Charles Bogardus, rep.	Paxton	44	Dios C. Hagle, rep	Flora ....
19	†Charles A. Griswold, rep ...	Fulton........	45	Andrew J. Reavill, dem	Flat Rock ....
20	Martin L. Newell, dem	Minonk.......	46	James R. Campbell, dem.....	McLeansboro
21	John H. Pierce, rep.........	Kewanee......	47	Henry Seiter, dem	Lebanon .....
22	Thomas Hamer, rep..........	Vermont	48	Joseph W. Rickert, dem	Waterloo ...
23	Joseph Reinhardt, rep......	Peru..........	49	John Yost, rep	Elba.... .....
24	Orville F. Berry, rep	Carthage	50	David W. Karraker, dem.....	Jonesboro....
25	Edward A. Washburn, rep...	Princeton	51	Daniel Hogan, rep	Mound City ..
26	Mark M. Bassett, rep.........	Peoria........			

* Elected Jan. 3, 1889, successor of T. L. McGrath, Rep., deceased, who was elected in Nov., 1888. † Successor to John D. Crabtree, Rep., resigned—elected circuit judge. ‡ Successor to I. N. Pearson, Rep., resigned—elected Secretary of State.

HOUSE OF REPRESENTATIVES.

Speaker........ *Asa C. Mathews, Pittsfield.
Speaker........ †James H. Miller, Toulon.
Speaker........ Wm. G. Cochran, Sullivan (second session.)
Clerk........ John A. Reeve, Cairo.
First Assistant........ Geo. T. Buckingham, Danville.
Second Assistant........ O. W. Walls, Vandalia.
Third Assistant........ Ed. E. McCoy, Auburn.
Bill Clerk........ Lincoln Ryan, Lawrenceville.
Enrolling and Engrossing Clerk........ J. B. Matlack, Chester.
First Assistant........ A. H. Bridgeman, Paxton.
Second Assistant........ J. E. Blakemore, Moline.
Postmaster........ Mrs. Lorraine J. Pitkin, Chicago.
Assistant........ Miss Mabel Allen, Springfield.
Doorkeeper........ James H. Robinson, Walnut.
First Assistant........ John A. Barr, Chicago.
Second Assistant........ Henry C. Henry, Mason.
Third Assistant........ William Watson, Bloomington.
Chaplain........ Rev. Francis Springer, Springfield.
Private Secretary to Speaker........ Delos Grigsby, Pittsfield.

* Resigned to be First Comptroller of the Treasury, May 10. † Succeeded Mathews; died before second session.

Republicans 80; Democrats 72; Independent 1.

Dist.	Name.	Postoffice.	Dist.	Name.	Postoffice.
1	John S. Ford, rep	Chicago	26	David B. Stookey, dem	Cramer
	Jethro M. Getman, rep	Chicago	27	Henry W. Allen, rep	Kirkwood
	James Walsh, dem	Chicago		Richard G. Breeden, rep	Tennessee
2	Bushrod E. Hoppin, rep	Englewood		Horatio R. Bartleson, dem	Macomb
	James N. Buchanan, rep.	Chicago	28	Ivory H. Pike, rep	Bloomington
	James J. O'Toole, dem	Chicago		Henry L. Terpening, rep	Cropsey
3	Francis A. Brokoski, rep	Chicago		John Eddy, dem	Bloomington
	George F. Ecton, rep	Chicago	29	Wm. H. Kretzinger, rep	Latham
	William Buckley, dem	Chicago		David P. Keller, rep	Macon
4	John Meyer, rep	Chicago		Robert H. Hill, dem	Boody
	Quida J. Chott, rep	Chicago	30	Julius A. Brown, rep	Monticello
	James F. Quinn, dem	Chicago		William H. Oglevee, rep	Clinton
5	James L. Monaghan, rep	Chicago		Joseph C. Myers, dem	Clinton
	Joseph P. Mahoney, dem	Chicago	31	Charles A. Allen, rep	Hoopeston
	Frank J. Wisner, dem	Chicago		Milton Lee, rep	Rossville
6	Jacob Miller, rep	Chicago		George R. Tilton, dem	Danville,
	George S. Baker, rep.	Chicago	32	Eugene Rice, rep	Camargo
	James H. Farrell, dem	Chicago		James Park McGee, dem	Tuscola
7	Stephen A. Reynolds rep.	Chicago		Isaac B. Craig, dem	Mattoon
	Edward J. Whitehead, rep	Austin	33	William G. Cochran, rep	Lovington
	Clayton E. Crafts, dem.	Austin		John J. Schneider, dem	Effingham
8	Charles A. Partridge, rep	Waukegan		Frank Spitler, dem	Sullivan
	Gardner S. Southworth, rep	Woodstock	34	Perry Logsdon, rep	Rushville
	*Elijah M. Haines, Ind	Waukegan		John W. Pugh, dem	Mason City
9	Samuel C. Hayes, rep	Chicago		William T. McCreery, dem	Huntsville
	William F. Wilk, rep	Chicago	35	‖Andrew S. McDowell, rep	Clayton
	Joseph A. O'Donnell, dem	Chicago		Albert W. Wells, dem	Quincy
10	David Hunter, rep	Rockford		Ira Tyler, dem	Richfield
	William H. Cox, rep	Grand Detour	36	‡Asa C. Mathews, rep	Pittsfield
	Robert Simpson, dem	Rockford		§John J. Teefey, dem	Mt. Sterling
11	William E. Kent, rep	Chicago		John McDonald, dem	Hardin
	Thomas G. McElligott, dem	Chicago	37	Edwin A. Doolittle, rep	Carrollton
	Henry P. Carmody, dem.	Chicago		Robert H. Davis, dem	Carrollton
12	George W. Pepoon, rep	Warren		Sylvester Allen, dem	Oxville
	Levi T. Bray, rep	Lanark	38	Watson A. Towse, rep	Carlinville
	Michael Stoskopf, dem	Freeport		David C. Enslow, dem	McVey
13	Peter A. Sundelius, rep	Chicago		Eugene K. Blair, dem	Waverly
	Stanley H. Kunz, dem	Chicago	39	Andrew J. Lester, rep	Springfield
	Wm. H. Lyman, dem	Chicago		Wiley E. Jones, dem	Springfield
14	Edgar C. Hawley, rep	Dundee		Albert L. Converse, dem	Springfield
	Robert M. Ireland, rep	Elgin	40	John Carstens, rep	Nokomis
	Nicholas R. Graham, dem	Wheaton		Pierson B. Updike, dem	Litchfield
15	Daniel McLaughlin, rep	Braidwood		Josiah A. Hill, dem	Sharpsburg
	Fred. Wilke, rep	Beecher	41	David R. Sparks, rep	Alton
	William Mooney, dem	Braidwood		Thomas T. Ramey, rep	Brooks
16	Wm. L. R. Johnson, rep	Buckley		Henry H. Padon, dem	Troy
	Daniel H. Paddock, rep	Kankakee	42	Joseph A. Combs, rep	Mulberry Grv.
	Free P. Morris, dem	Watseka		Rufus N. Ramsay, dem	Carlyle
17	Daniel D. Hunt, rep	DeKalb		Edward L. Willeford, dem	Old Ripley
	Reuben W. Willett, rep	Yorkville	43	Matthew Telford, rep	Dix
	Dwight Crossett, dem	Courtland		Thomas E. Merritt, dem	Salem
18	O. W. Pollard, rep	Dwight		William M. Farmer, dem	Vandalia
	N. J. Myer, rep	Ocoya	44	Edson Gould, rep	Bone Gap
	James A. Smith, dem	Chatsworth		Joseph B. Scudamore, rep	Wayne City
19	Benjamin H. Bradshaw, rep.	Compton		John S. Cochennour, dem	Olney
	John W. White, rep	Tampico	45	Walter Cole, rep	Marshall
	Sherwood Dixon, dem	Dixon		William G. Williams, dem	Newton.
20	Peter A. Coen, rep	Washburn		William G. Delashmutt, dem.	Martinsville .
	Jonas T. Ball, dem	Toluca	46	¶Charles M. Lyon, rep	McLeansboro
	John W. White, dem	Allentown		Wm. H. H. Mieure, dem	Lawr'nceville
21	William F. Crawford, rep	Taylor Ridge.		Samuel H. Martin, dem	Carmi
	Hendrick V. Fisher, rep	Geneseo	47	Samuel C. Smiley, rep	O'Fallon
	Elmore W. Hurst, dem	Rock Island		Frederick B. Phillips, dem	Belleville
22	Orrin P. Cooley, rep	Oneida		William H. Bowler, dem	O'Fallon
	George W. Prince, rep	Galesburg	48	James R. Walker, rep	Columbia
	James W. Hunter, dem	Hermon		William M. Schuwerk, dem	Evansville
23	David Ross, rep	Oglesby		Thomas J. Rice, dem	Tamaroa
	Edgar S. Browne, dem	Mendota	49	William G. Sloan, rep	Harrisburg
	James P. Trench, dem	LaSalle		Royal R. Lacey, rep	Elizab'tht'wn
24	James O. Anderson, rep	Oquawka		Hugh C. Gregg, dem	Elba
	John P. McClanahan, rep	Alexis	50	Robert B. Stinson, rep	Anna
	Thomas A. Marshall, dem	Keithsburg		Reed Green, dem	Cairo
25	†James H. Miller, rep	Toulon		Joseph B. Gill, dem	Murphysboro
	Peter McCall, rep	Spring Valley	51	Thomas Sullivan, Jr., rep	Akin
	Anthony Morrasy, dem.	Sheffield		James M. Fowler, rep	Marion
26	John M. Hart, rep	Eden		Isaac A. J. Parker, dem	Vienna
	James Kenny, dem	Peoria			

* Died April 25, 1889; R. J. Beck., Rep., elected July 15, 1890. † Died; Samuel White, Rep., elected July 21, 1890. ‡ Resigned May 10, 1889; Geo. B. Childs, Rep., elected July 15, 1890. § Died Feb. 26, 1889; G. M. Black, Dem., elected July 15, 1890. ¶ Resigned; J. E. Black, Dem., elected July 15, 1890. ‖ Resigned; Mitchell Dazey, Dem., Lima, elected July 15, 1890.

THIRTY-SEVENTH GENERAL ASSEMBLY, 1890–1892.

Convened at Springfield Jan. 7, 1891; adjourned June 12, 1891.

SENATE.

President .... Lyman B. Ray, Morris.
President pro tem .... Milton W. Mathews, Urbana.
Secretary .... L. F. Watson, Watseka.
First Assistant .... Henry C. Ebel, Jr., Chicago.
Second Assistant .... F. M. Moore, Golconda.
Bill Clerk .... Alvin Walt, Pontiac.
President's Private Secretary .... Geo. W. Huston, Morris.
Enrolling and Engrossing Clerk .... Frank E. Hills, Sycamore.
First Assistant .... John McFadden, Marengo.
Second Assistant .... S. C. Jordan, Menard.
Sergeant-at-Arms .... W. H. Kretzinger, Latham.
First Assistant .... H. K. Sikes, Peoria.
Second Assistant .... John Bell, Chicago.
Chaplain .... Rev. Preston Wood, Springfield.
Postmaster .... Mrs. Lorraine J. Pitkin, Chicago.
Assistant .... Mrs. Mary S. Munn, Aurora.

Republicans, 27; Democrats, 24.

Dist.	Name.	Postoffice.	Dist.	Name.	Postoffice.
1	Edward T. Noonan, dem.	Chicago	27	Perry Anderson, rep.	Alexis
2	Charles H. Crawford, rep.	Chicago	28	Thomas C. Kerrick, rep.	Bloomington.
3	George Bass, rep.	Chicago	29	Harmon Manecke, dem	Oakley
4	Thomas C. MacMillan, rep.	Chicago	30	Milton W. Mathews, rep.	Urbana
5	Joseph P. Mahoney, dem	Chicago	31	George E. Bacon, rep.	Paris
6	Horace H. Thomas, rep.	Chicago	32	Lewis L. Lehman, rep.	Mattoon
7	John Humphrey, rep.	Orland	33	Samuel W. Wright, Jr., dem.	Sullivan
8	Charles E. Fuller, rep.	Belvidere	34	Arthur A. Leeper, dem.	Virginia
9	Philip Knopf, rep.	Chicago	35	Albert W. Wells, dem.	Quincy
10	Benjamin F. Sheets, rep.	Oregon	36	Harry Higbee, dem.	Pittsfield
11	Emil Thiele, dem.	Chicago	37	Sylvester Allen, dem.	Oxville
12	Robert H. Wiles, rep	Freeport	38	Edward L. McDonald, dem.	Jacksonville.
13	John F. O'Malley, dem.	Chicago	39	Ben F. Caldwell, dem.	Chatham
14	Henry H. Evans, rep.	Aurora	40	Hiram P. Shumway, dem.	Taylorville.
15	John W. Arnold, dem.	Lockport	41	John W. Coppinger, dem.	Alton
16	Conrad Secrest rep.	Watseka.	42	F. E. W. Brink, dem.	Hoyleton
17	Daniel D. Hunt, rep	DeKalb	43	Wm. M. Farmer, dem	Vandalia
18	Charles Bogardus, rep.	Paxton	44	Dios C. Hagle, rep.	Flora
19	Virgil S. Ferguson, rep.	Sterling	45	Andrew J. Reavill, dem.	Flat Rock
20	Martin L. Newell, dem.	Minonk	46	James R. Campbell, dem.	McLeansboro
21	William F. Crawford, rep.	Taylor Ridge.	47	Peter Seibert, dem.	Fayetteville.
22	Thomas Hamer, rep.	Vermont	48	Joseph W. Rickert, dem.	Waterloo
23	Andrew J. O'Conor, dem.	LaSalle	49	Thomas H. Sheridan, rep.	Golconda
24	Orville F. Berry, rep.	Carthage	50	David W. Karraker, dem	Jonesboro
25	Louis Zearing, rep.	Ladd	51	P. T. Chapman, rep.	Vienna
26	Mark M. Bassett, rep.	Peoria.			

HOUSE OF REPRESENTATIVES.

Speaker .... Clayton E. Crafts, Austin.
Clerk .... W. H. Hinrichsen, Quincy.
First Assistant .... W. A. Compton, Macomb.
Second Assistant .... W. B. Morris, Golconda.
Third Assistant .... E. P. Kimball, Virden.
Fourth Assistant .... G. S. Clendenin, Springfield.
Fifth Assistant .... T. B. Castleman, Danville.
Doorkeeper .... E. S. Browne, Mendota.
First Assistant .... B. W. Rives, Kankakee.
Second Assistant .... James W. Coleman, Jonesboro.
Third Assistant .... John Cockrell, Marion county.
Enrolling and Engrossing Clerk .... A. H. Wagoner, Oregon.
First Assistant .... A. L. Hereford, El Paso.
Second Assistant .... G. E. Quinby, Clay county.
Postmaster .... Mrs. M. O'Conner, Springfield.
Assistant .... Miss Emma T. Hoehn, Springfield.
Chaplain .... William Steens, Sangamon county.
Speaker's Private Secretary .... Fred'k Merritt, Springfield.

Republicans, 73; Democrats, 77; Farmers' Alliance, 3.

Dist.	Name.	Postoffice.	Dist.	Name.	Postoffice.
1	William Burke, dem	Chicago	26	John L. Geher, dem	Edwards
	James J. Townsend, dem	Chicago		Thomas J. Edwards, rep	Edwards
	W. A. Hutchings, rep	Chicago	27	Eli Dixon, dem	Roseville
2	Michael McInerny, dem	Chicago		Charles V. Chandler, rep	Macomb
	William J. Kenney, dem	Chicago		Dominick C. Graham, rep	Cameron
	H. Dorsey Patton, rep	Chicago	28	John Eddy, dem	Bloomington.
3	Solomon Van Praag, dem	Chicago		Henry L. Terpening, rep	Cropsey
	Stephen D. May, dem	Chicago		Edmund O'Connell, rep	Bloomington.
	Edward H. Morris, rep	Chicago	29	Lawrence B. Stringer, dem	Lincoln
4	James F. Quinn, dem	Chicago		W. S. Smith, dem	Mt. Zion
	Quida J. Chott, rep	Chicago		David P. Keller, rep	Macon
	Wilson Brooks, rep	Chicago	30	Thomas B. Carson, dem	Urbana
5	Jacob J. Kern, dem	Chicago		Julius A. Brown, rep	Monticello
	William E. Burns, dem	Chicago		Jacob Zeigler, rep	Clinton
	Augustus W. Nohe, rep	Chicago	31	John F. Rowand, dem	Sidell
6	James H. Farrell, dem	Chicago		Charles A. Allen, rep	Hoopeston
	Edward H. Griggs, rep	Chicago		Thomas L. Spellman, rep	Danville
	Jacob Miller, rep	Chicago	32	Isaac B. Craig, dem	Mattoon
7	Clayton E. Crafts, dem	Austin		Henry J. Jansen, dem	Teutopolis
	Edward J. Whitehead, rep	Austin		George A. Neal, rep	Janesville
	William Thiemann, rep	Itasca	33	James Laughlin, dem	Prairie Home
8	John C. Donnelly, dem	Woodstock		Philip Wiwi, dem	Montrose
	Charles A. Partridge, rep	Waukegan		Walter C. Headen, rep	Shelbyville
	George Reed, rep	Belvidere	34	Fred Wilkinson, dem	Petersburg
9	Joseph A. O'Donnell, dem	Chicago		Bernard P. Preston, dem	Littleton
	Samuel C. Hayes, rep	Chicago		Homer J. Tice, rep	Greenview
	William F. Wilk, rep	Chicago	35	Ira Tyler, dem	Richfield
10	James P. Wilson, dem	Woosung		Jonathan Parkhurst, dem	Quincy
	David Hunter, rep	Rockford		George C. McCrone, rep	Quincy
	Prescott H. Talbot, rep	Lindenwood	36	Ernst Meyer, dem	Deer Plain
11	Henry P. Carmody, dem	Chicago		Joseph M. Hambaugh, dem	Versailles
	Bryan Conway, dem	Chicago		H. D. L. Grigsby, rep	Pittsfield
	Julius A. Lense, rep	Chicago	37	Thomas F. Ferns, dem	Jerseyville
12	George W. Curtiss, dem	Stockton		Frederick M. Fishback, dem	Carrollton
	Daniel S. Berry, rep	Savanna		Henry Miner, rep	Winchester
	Henry N. Frentress, rep	East Dubuque	38	David C. Enslow, dem	McVey
13	William H. Lyman, dem	Chicago		John W. Springer, dem	Jacksonville.
	John A. Kwasigroch, dem	Chicago		Edward P. Kirby, rep	Jacksonville.
	Samuel E. Erickson, rep	Chicago	39	Edward L. Merritt, dem	Springfield
14	Luther M. Dearborn, dem	Aurora		Frank H. Jones, dem	Springfield
	Edgar C. Hawley, rep	Dundee		John S. Lyman, rep	Farmingdale.
	Charles P. Bryan, rep	Elmhurst	40	Elijah H. Donaldson, dem	Nokomis
15	David Forsythe, dem	Elwood		Joseph Adams, dem	Moweaqua
	Fred Wilke, rep	Beecher		William W. Weedon, rep	Taylorville
	John Corlett, rep	Ritchie	41	Henry C. Picker, dem	Worden
16	J. W. Allison, dem	Essex		William H. Faires, dem	St. Jacobs
	Daniel H. Paddock, rep	Kankakee		William McKittrick, rep	Staunton
	John L. Hamilton, rep	Watseka	42	Rufus N. Ramsay, dem	Carlyle
17	William G. Dawkins, dem	Braceville		William H. Dawdy, dem	Greenville
	William Scaife, rep	Coal City		William D. Jacobs, rep	Venedy
	Charles T. Cherry, rep	Oswego	43	James H. Watson, dem	Wood Lawn
18	James A. Smith, dem	Chatsworth		Eugene L. Stoker, rep	Centralia
	Nelson J. Myer, rep	Ocoya		James Cockrell, F. A	Kinmundy
	Rufus C. Straight, rep	Fairbury	44	Elijah S. Shirley, dem	Xenia
19	Sherwood Dixon, dem	Dixon		Gideon D. Slanker, rep	Olney
	John W. White, rep	Tampico		Hosea H. Moore, F. A	Mount Erie
	Luther W. Mitchell, rep	Woosung	45	Lawrence Kelly, dem	Martinsville
20	John W. White, dem	Allentown		Ethelbert Callahan, rep	Robinson
	James O. Garrett, dem	Sparland		Herman E. Taubeneck, F. A	Ernst
	John H. Anthony, rep	Washington	46	John T. Norsworthy, dem	Carmi
21	George W. Vinton, dem	Moline		Albert B. Denham, dem	Cowling
	Reuben F. Beals, rep	Oneida		Thomas G. Parker, rep	Grayville
	*William C. Collins, rep	Rock Island	47	Daniel G. Ramsay, dem	East St. Louis
	†William Payne, rep	Osborn		Nicholas Boul, dem	FrenchVill'ge
22	James W. Hunter, dem	Hermon		Louis Perrottet, rep	Mascoutah
	George W. Prince, rep	Galesburg	48	John T. Pollock, dem	Chester
	Oscar J. Boyer, rep	Canton		John A. Bowlin, dem	DuQuoin
23	Louis Rohrer, dem	Somonauk		Albert H. Evans, rep	Tamaroa
	Michael O'Loughlin, dem	Seneca	49	George B. Parsons, dem	Shawneeto'n.
	Urbin S. Ellsworth, rep	Deer Park		Fowler A. Armstrong, rep	Massac Creek
24	Amos Edmunds, dem	Disco		Thomas R. Reid, rep	Shawneeto'n.
	William H. Myers, dem	Terre Haute	50	Reed Green, dem	Cairo
	James O. Anderson, rep	Oquawka		Joseph B. Gill, dem	Murphysboro
25	Michael Barton, dem	Spring Valley		Walter Warder, rep	Cairo
	Samuel White, rep	Lafayette	51	M. N. Webb, dem	Taylor Hill
	Archibald W. Hopkins, rep	Granville		W. J. N. Moyers, rep	Benton
26	John Johnston, dem	Peoria		John H. Duncan, rep	Marion

* Resigned Nov. 29, 1890. † Vice William C. Collins, resigned.

THIRTY-EIGHTH GENERAL ASSEMBLY, 1892-1894.

Convened at Springfield, Jan. 4, 1893; adjourned June 16, 1893.

SENATE.

President .... Joseph B. Gill, Murphysboro.
President pro tem .... John W. Coppinger, Alton.
Secretary .... Finis E. Downing, Virginia.
First Assistant .... Edward P. Kimball, Virden.
Second Assistant .... R. S. Bane, Varna.
Reading Clerk .... Phocion Howard, Danville.
Enrolling and Engrossing Clerk .... Fred J. Kern, Belleville.
First Assistant .... Harry J. Jones, Carlyle.
Second Assistant .... Gerhart Weber, Hillsboro.
Sergeant-at-Arms .... Robert H. Davis, Carrollton.
First Assistant .... Edward Bowen, Decatur.
Second Assistant .... Robert Welch, Chicago.
Postmaster .... Mrs. Michael O'Connor, Springfield.
Assistant .... Miss Mary Turner, Mattoon.
Chaplain .... Rev. Dr. F. W. Taylor, Springfield.
Private Secretary to President .... C. D. Tufts, Centralia.

Republicans, 22; Democrats, 29.

Dist.	Name.	Postoffice.	Dist.	Name.	Postoffice.
1	Edward T. Noonan, dem	Chicago	27	Perry Anderson, rep..........	Alexis .. ..
2	C. Porter Johnson, dem......	Chicago	28	Vinton E. Howell, rep.........	Bloomington.
3	George Bass, rep	Chicago	29	Harmon Manecke, dem.......	Oakley........
4	Moses Salomon, dem..........	Chicago	30	Henry M. Dunlap, rep.........	Savoy.........
5	Joseph P. Mahoney, dem	Chicago	31	George E. Bacon, rep.........	Paris.........
6	Henry C. Bartling, dem	Chicago	32	Isaac B. Craig, dem...........	Mattoon......
7	John Humphrey, rep.	Orland........	33	Samuel W. Wright, Jr., dem	Sullivan ......
8	Reuben W. Coon, rep.........	Waukegan ...	34	Arthur A. Leeper, dem.	Virginia ......
9	Philip Knopf, rep....	Chicago	35	Albert W. Wells, dem	Quincy.........
10	David Hunter, rep	Rockford.....	36	Harry Higbee, dem	Pittsfield .....
11	Emil Thiele, dem.	Chicago	37	Sylvester Allen, dem..........	Oxville ....
12	Homer F. Aspinwall, rep. ...	Freeport	38	Hampton W. Wall, dem......	Staunton......
13	John F. O'Malley, dem	Chicago	39	Ben F. Caldwell, dem.........	Chatham .. ..
14	Henry H. Evans, rep	Aurora..	40	George W. Paisley, dem......	Hillsboro ....
15	John W. Arnold, dem..... ...	Lockport.....	41	John W. Coppinger, dem.....	Alton ....
16	George R. Letourneau, rep ..	Kankakee...	42	Thomas E. Ford, dem	Carlyle ....
17	Daniel D. Hunt, rep...........	DeKalb	43	William M. Farmer, dem.....	Vandalia .....
18	Charles Bogardus, rep........	Paxton........	44	William A. Mussett, rep......	Grayville.....
19	Virgil S. Ferguson, rep.......	Sterling	45	Andrew J. Reavill, dem.......	Flat Rock ....
20	Charles N. Barnes, dem.....	Lacon	46	James R. Campbell, dem.....	McLeansboro
21	William F. Crawford, rep....	Taylor Ridge.	47	Peter Seibert, dem............	Fayetteville..
22	Thomas Hamer, rep	Vermont	48	Albert L. Brands, dem........	Pr'e du Roch'r
23	Andrew J. O'Conor, dem.....	LaSalle..	49	Thomas H. Sheridan, rep ...	Golconda.....
24	Orville F. Berry, rep.........	Carthage	50	Reed Green, dem..............	Cairo ... .
25	Louis Zearing, rep........ ..	Ladd....	51	Pleasant T. Chapman, rep...	Vienna........
26	John M. Niehaus, dem........	Peoria			

HOUSE OF REPRESENTATIVES.

Speaker .... Clayton E. Crafts, Austin.
Clerk .... Robert W. Ross, Vandalia.
First Assistant .... W. E. Handy, Tolono.
Second Assistant .... Wm. B. Morris, Golconda.
Third Assistant .... James E. Vail, McDonough County.
Fourth Assistant .... H. B. Lichtenberger, Freeport.
Doorkeeper .... Edgar S. Browne, Mendota.
First Assistant .... John N. Summers, Chicago.
Second Assistant .... John McDarrah, Rock Island.
Third Assistant .... Ben W. Rives, Kankakee.
Enrolling and Engrossing Clerk .... A. E. Simonson, Dixon.
First Assistant .... Adam Gard, Marshall.
Second Assistant .... Louis I. Hutchins, Aledo.
Postmaster .... Miss Mollie McCabe, Springfield.
Assistant .... Miss Kathryn Gallagher, Springfield.
Private Secretary to Speaker .... Will E. McGurren, Chicago.
Chaplain .... Rev. Joseph Hawkins, Lincoln.

Democrats, 78; Republicans, 75.

Dist.	Name.	Postoffice.
1	James O'Connor, dem	Chicago
	William Burke, dem	Chicago
	William W. Wheelock, rep.	Chicago
2	Michael McInerny, dem	Chicago
	Charles S. Deneen, rep	Chicago
	Robert McMurdy, rep	Chicago
3	Stephen D. May, dem	Chicago
	James E. Bish, rep	Chicago
	William H. King, rep	Chicago
4	James E. McGinley, dem	Chicago
	James F. Gleeson, dem	Chicago
	John Meyer, rep	Chicago
5	Edward J. Novak, dem	Chicago
	Edward J. Hayes, dem	Chicago
	Augustus W. Nohe, rep	Chicago
6	James H. Farrell, dem	Chicago
	Edward H. Griggs, rep	Chicago
	Godfred Langhenry, rep	Chicago
7	Clayton E. Crafts, dem	Austin
	Robert H. Muir, rep	Clyde
	William Thiemann, rep	Itasca
8	John C. Donnelly, dem	Woodstock
	Robert J. Beck, rep	Chemung
	George Reed, rep	Belvidere
9	Benjamin M. Mitchell, dem	Chicago
	Joseph A. O'Donnell, dem	Chicago
	Daniel A. Campbell, rep	Chicago
10	James P. Wilson, dem	Woosung
	Prescott H. Talbot, rep.	Lindenwood
	Lars M. Noling, rep	Rockford
11	Bryan Conway, dem	Chicago
	Henry P. Carmody, dem	Chicago
	William E. Kent, rep	Chicago
12	John N. Brandt, dem	Polo
	John C. McKenzie, rep	Elizabeth
	Daniel S. Berry, rep	Savanna
13	William H. Lyman, dem	Chicago
	John A. Kwasigroch, dem	Chicago
	Samuel E. Erickson, rep	Chicago
14	Luther M. Dearborn, dem.	Aurora
	Edgar C. Hawley, rep	Dundee
	Charles P. Bryan, rep	Elmhurst
15	Conrad Wilkening, dem	Crete
	David Forsythe, dem	Elwood
	Fred Wilke, rep	Beecher
16	Freeman P. Morris, dem	Watseka
	Daniel H. Paddock, rep	Kankakee
	Alba M. Jones, rep	Milford
17	Edgar L. Henning, dem	Plano
	Charles F. Meyer, rep	Kirkland
	Charles T. Cherry, rep	Oswego
18	James A. Smith, dem	Chatsworth
	Rufus C. Straight, rep	Fairbury
	Bailey A. Gower, rep	Odell
19	Caleb C. Johnson, dem.	Sterling
	Washington I. Guffin, rep	Paw Paw
	John Dyer, rep	Fulton
20	William A. Moore, dem	Morton
	Samuel H. McClure, dem	Eureka
	Oscar Painter, rep	Metamora
21	Joseph H. Mulligan, dem	Kewanee
	William Payne, rep	Osborn
	Reuben F. Beals, rep	Galva
22	Stephen E. Carlin, dem	Canton
	Jay L. Hastings, rep	Galesburg
	Frank Murdoch, rep	Oneida
23	Michael O'Loughlin, dem	Seneca
	Louis Rohrer, dem	Somonauk
	Urbin S. Ellsworth, rep	Deer Park
24	William H. Myers, dem	Terre Haute
	Noah H. Guthrie rep	Aledo
	James O Anderson, rep	Decorra
25	Michael Barton, dem	Spring Valley
	Archibald W. Hopkins, rep	Granville
	George Murray, rep.	Elmira
26	Peter Cahill, dem	Brimfield
	John Holmes, dem	Alta
26	William O. Clark, rep	Peoria
27	Thomas J. Sparks, dem	Bushnell
	Louis Kaiser, rep	Bushnell
	D. Caswell Hanna, rep	Monmouth
28	Bernard J. Claggett, dem	Lexington
	Edmund O'Connell, rep	Bloomington
	Edward Stubblefield, rep	McLean
29	Lawrence B. Stringer, dem.	Lincoln
	Washington S. Smith, dem	Mt. Zion
	Thomas N. Leavitt, rep	Maroa
30	Thomas B. Carson, dem	Urbana
	John Casey rep	Farmer City
	James A. Hawks, rep.	Atwood
31	Robert L. McKinlay, dem	Paris
	Thomas L. Spellman, rep.	Danville
	James P. Fletcher, rep	Ridge Farm
32	J. Park McGee, dem	Tuscola
	Charles Hanker, rep	Toledo
	William H. Wallace, rep	Humboldt
33	Philip Wiwi, dem	Montrose
	Leverett S. Baldwin, dem	Windsor
	Albert Campbell, rep	Effingham
34	Bernard P. Preston, dem	Littleton
	Robert S. Carter, dem	Petersburg
	Homer J. Tice, rep.	Greenview
35	Mitchell Dazey, dem	Lima
	Joel W. Bonney, dem	Quincy
	Geo. C. McCrone, rep	Quincy
36	*Ernst Meyer, dem	Deer Plain
	Frederick W. Rottger, dem	Mt. Sterling
	Augustus Dow, rep	Pittsfield
37	Thomas F. Ferns, dem	Jerseyville
	Norman L. Jones, dem	Carrollton
	Orville A. Snedeker, rep	Jerseyville
38	William L. Mounts, dem	Carlinville
	James T. McMillan, dem	Jacksonville
	Sargeant McKnight, rep	Girard
39	Edward L. Merritt, dem	Springfield
	Langley St. A. Whitley, dem.	Springfield
	H. Clay Wilson, rep	Springfield
40	Walter S. Parrott, dem	Litchfield
	Alex. B. Herdman, dem	Morrisonville
	Charles A. Ramsey, rep	Hillsboro
41	Michael J. Gill, dem	Alton
	Conrad A. Ambrosius, dem	Collinsville
	Thomas T. Ramey, rep	Brooks
42	James J. Anderson, dem	Nashville
	Charles W. Seawell, dem	Greenville
	George S. Caughlan, rep	Trenton
43	James H. Watson, dem	Woodlawn
	Daniel W. Holstlaw, dem	Iuka
	Richard T. Higgins, rep	Vandalia
44	Captain T. Taggart, dem	Cisne
	Thomas H. Creighton, rep	Fairfield
	John D. Edmiston, rep	Olney
45	Lawrence Kelly, dem	Martinsville
	James P. Warren, dem	Rose Hill
	Ethelbert Callahan, rep	Robinson
46	J. Edwin Black, dem	Bridgeport
	Jacob Zimmerman, dem	Mt. Carmel
	John S. Martin, rep	Bridgeport
47	William H. Snyder, Jr., dem	Belleville
	Joseph E. Miller, dem	Belleville
	Frederick S. Weckler, rep	Darmstadt
48	Joseph W. Drury, dem	Waterloo
	Joseph L. Murphy, dem	Pinckneyville
	John J. Douglas, rep	Chester
49	H. Robert Fowler, dem	Elizabetht'n.
	Fowler A. Armstrong, rep	Massac Creek
	Albert W. Lewis, rep	Harrisburg
50	Philip H. Kroh, dem	Anna
	William O. Dean, dem	Ava
	Walter Warder, rep	Cairo
51	Samuel H. Goodall, dem	Marion
	John H. Duncan, rep	Marion
	Richard M. Johnson, rep	Levings

* Died May 11, 1893; Wm. Mortland, dem., Calhoun county, elected June 19, 1893.

THIRTY-NINTH GENERAL ASSEMBLY, 1894–1896.

Convened at Springfield, Jan. 9, 1895; adjourned June 14, 1895. Special session, June 25 to August 2, 1895

SENATE.

President..........Joseph B. Gill, Murphysboro
President pro tem..........Charles Bogardus, Paxton
Secretary..........James H. Paddock, Springfield
First Assistant..........Penn V. Trovillion, Golconda
Second Assistant..........Samuel H. Cochran, Chicago
Third Assistant..........J. E. Cooke, Ottawa
Reading Clerk..........Bailey D. Dawson, Chicago
Bill Clerk..........Clarence J. Root, Chicago
Enrolling and Engrossing Clerk..........Frank E. Hills, Sycamore
First Assistant..........Julius Johnson, Rock Island
Second Assistant..........Wm. A. Schwarze, Freeport
Third Assistant..........W. P. Craig, Champaign
Sergeant-at-Arms..........J. O. Anderson, Decorra
First Assistant..........Frank E. Stanley, Chicago
Second Assistant..........Wm. F. Riley, Springfield
Chaplain..........Rev. M. F. Troxell, Springfield
Postmaster..........Fannie M. Worthington, Sterling
Assistant..........Winnie Cressey, Chicago
President's Private Secretary..........C. D. Tufts, Centralia
Superintendent of Ventilation..........E. A. Flood, Waukegan
Assistant..........Fayette Adams, Rockford

Republicans, 33; Democrats, 18. State was re-districted in 1893.

Dist.	Name.	Postoffice.	Dist.	Name.	Postoffice.
1	P. V. Fitzpatrick, rep	Chicago	27	Lewis M. Sawyer, rep	Streator
2	Moses Salomon, dem	Chicago	28	Orville F. Berry, rep	Carthage
3	Sidney McCloud, rep	Chicago	29	Daniel D. Hunt, rep	DeKalb
4	C. Porter Johnson, dem	Chicago	30	Henry M. Dunlap, rep	Savoy
5	Charles H. Crawford, rep	Chicago	31	James W. Templeton, rep	Princeton
6	Henry C. Bartling, dem	Chicago	32	Arthur Allen Leeper, dem	Virginia
7	John Humphrey, rep	Orland	33	Hendrick V. Fisher, rep	Geneseo
8	Reuben W. Coon, rep	Waukegan	34	Harry Higbee, dem	Pittsfield
9	William J. O'Brien, dem	Chicago	35	Fred E. Harding, rep	Monmouth
10	David Hunter, rep	Rockford	36	H. W. Wall, dem	Staunton
11	Frederick Lundin, rep	Chicago	37	Albert W. Wells, dem	Quincy
12	Homer F. Aspinwall, rep	Freeport	38	George W. Paisley, dem	Hillsboro
13	Joseph P. Mahoney, dem	Chicago	39	David T. Littler, rep	Springfield
14	Henry H. Evans, rep	Aurora	40	Isaac B. Craig, dem	Mattoon
15	John J. Morrison, rep	Chicago	41	M. F. Kanan, rep	Decatur
16	George R. Letourneau, rep	Kankakee	42	Thomas E. Ford, dem	Carlyle
17	Edward J. Dwyer, rep	Chicago	43	*Robert L. McKinlay, dem	Paris
18	Charles Bogardus, rep	Paxton	44	William A. Mussett, rep	Grayville
19	Daniel A. Campbell, rep	Chicago	45	Hiram H. Kingsbury, rep	Olney
20	Charles N. Barnes, dem	Lacon	46	James R. Campbell, dem	McLeansboro
21	Charles M. Netterstrom, rep	Chicago	47	Charles A. Herb, rep†	Alton
22	Vinton E. Howell, rep	Bloomington	48	Albert L. Brands, dem	Pr. du Rocher
23	George D. Anthony, rep	Chicago	49	James A. Willoughby, rep	Belleville
24	John M. Niehaus, dem	Peoria	50	Reed Green, dem	Cairo
25	George H. Munroe, rep	Joliet	51	Pleasant T. Chapman, rep	Vienna
26	Thomas Hamer, rep	Vermont			

* Seat contested, but decided in his favor. † Died Oct. 16, 1895.

HOUSE OF REPRESENTATIVES.

Speaker..........John Meyer, Chicago, died July 3, 1895. W. G. Cochran elected
Clerk..........John A. Reeve, Decatur.
First Assistant..........Alfred Bayliss, Sterling.
Second Assistant..........Carey E. Barnes, Springfield.
Third Assistant..........G. L. Peterson, Rock Island.
Fourth Assistant and Typewriter..........Wm. A. Ramplin, Chicago.
Bill Clerk..........W. H. Kretzinger, Latham.
Enrolling and Engrossing Clerk..........Charles E. Dole, Mattoon.
First Assistant..........Theo. Schultze, Nashville.
Second Assistant..........Moses W. Porter, Aledo.
Doorkeeper..........Ed. Harlan, Marshall.
First Assistant..........S. G. Sparks, Greenville.
Second Assistant..........George Sanderson, Galesburg.
Third Assistant..........T. T. Allain, Chicago.
Postmaster..........Mary Rowett, Carlinville.
Assistant..........Carrie Stephenson, Petersburg.
Chaplain..........A. G. Goodspeed, Minonk.
Speaker's Private Secretary..........James Morris, Chicago.

Republicans 92; Democrats 61.

Dist.	Name.	Postoffice.
1	John C. Sterchie, dem.	Chicago
	Stephen D. May, dem.	Chicago
	William E. Kent, rep.	Chicago
2	Rudolph Mulac, rep.	Chicago
	Oscar L. Dudley, rep.	Chicago
	Sherman P. Cody, dem.	Chicago
3	Alexander J. Jones, dem.	Chicago
	George W. Miller, rep.	Chicago
	S. L. Lowenthal, rep.	Chicago
4	William C. Eakins, rep.	Chicago
	Timothy Hogan, rep.	Chicago
	Daniel F. Curley, dem.	Chicago
5	Milroy H. Gibson, rep.	Chicago
	John C. Buckner, rep.	Chicago
	Angelo S. Cella, dem.	Chicago
6	George M. Boyd, rep.	Chicago
	Bernard J. Mahony, dem.	Chicago
	Isadore Plotke, rep.	Chicago
7	Robert H. Muir, rep.	Clyde.
	Clayton E. Crafts, dem.	Austin
	William Thiemann, rep.	Itasca.
8	George Reed, rep.	Belvidere
	Robert J. Beck, rep.	Harvard
	P. H. DeLany, dem.	Wadsworth
9	Christian R. Walleck, dem.	Chicago
	Philip Steiner, dem.	Chicago
	David E. Shanahan, rep.	Chicago
10	Lars M. Nolling, rep.	Rockford
	C. Harry Woolsey, dem.	Rockford
	Victor H. Bovey, rep.	Pine Creek
11	Joseph S. Schwab, dem.	Chicago
	Ernest G. Schubert, rep.	Chicago
	M. G. Mauritzon, rep.	Chicago
12	Daniel S. Berry, rep.	Savanna
	Michael Stoskopf, dem.	Freeport
	John C. McKinzie, rep.	Elizabeth
13	James P. Cavanagh, rep.	Chicago
	Simon Shaffer, dem.	Chicago
	Edward J. Novak, dem.	Chicago
14	Charles P. Bryan, rep.	Elmhurst
	Edgar C. Hawley, rep.	Dundee
	Luther M. Dearborn, dem.	Aurora
15	John Meyer, rep.*	Chicago
	John T. Fleming, dem.	Chicago
	Wm. F. McCarthy, rep.	Chicago
16	Ed C. Curtis, rep.	Grant Park
	Free P. Morris, dem.	Watseka
	A. M. Jones, rep.	Milford
17	William Burke, dem.	Chicago
	Frank J. Brignadello, dem.	Chicago
	Albert Glade, rep.	Chicago
18	James P. Fletcher, rep.	Ridge Farm
	M. A. Bailey, rep.	Danville
	William M. Bines, dem.	Ridge Farm
19	James W. FitzSimons, dem.	Chicago
	Sewell B. Weston, rep.	Chicago
	Charles G. Johnson, rep.	Chicago
20	Isaac B. Hammers, rep.	Panola
	John L. McGuire, dem.	Metamora
	Bailey A. Gower, rep.	Odell
21	James H. Farrell, dem.	Chicago
	David Revell, rep.	Chicago
	Fred A. Busse, rep.	Chicago
22	Edward Stubblefield, rep.	McLean
	James F. O'Donnell, dem.	Bloomington
	John L. White, rep.	Bloomington
23	William H. Lyman, dem.	Chicago
	Albert J. Olson, rep.	Chicago
	Lawrence Kilcourse, rep.	Chicago
24	Aquilla J. Daugherty, rep.	Peoria
	Alva Merrill, rep.	Northampton
	Peter Cahill, dem.	Brimfield
25	John M. Thompson, dem.	Joliet
	Addison B. Hallock, rep.	Peotone
	W. H. Steen, rep.	Braidwood
26	Lute C. Breeden, dem.	Lewistown
	Jonathan Merriam, rep.	Atlanta
26	John W. Johnson, rep.	Canton
27	John Wylie, rep.	Utica
	Urbin S. Ellsworth, rep.	Deer Park
	John McLauchlan, dem.	LaSalle
28	U. A. Wilson, rep.	Huntsville
	Louis Kaiser, rep.	Bushnell
	James A. Teel, dem.	Rushville
29	Washington I. Gullin, rep.	Paw Paw
	John K. Ely, rep.	Mazon
	James Brazen, dem.	Sycamore
30	W. H. Taylor, rep†	Weldon
	William C. Hubbart, rep.	Monticello
	James P. Ownby, dem.	Milmine
31	J. W. White, rep.	Rock Falls
	William M. Pilgrim, dem.	Bradford
	George Murray, rep.	Elmira
32	William S. Dunham, rep.	Atlanta
	Emeziah J. Mell, dem.	San Jose
	George Wendell, dem.	New Holland.
33	Joseph H. Mulligan, dem.	Kewanee
	William C. Stickney, rep.	Woodhull
	William Payne, rep.	Osborn
34	John D. Huffman, dem.	Bluffs
	Wilfred I. Klein, rep.	Barry
	Edward McConnel, dem.	Jacksonville.
35	Frank Murdoch, rep.	Oneida
	Noah H. Guthrie, rep.	Aledo
	LaVergne B. DeForest, dem.	N. Henders'n
36	William L. Mounts, dem.	Carlinville
	James W. Kitzmiller, rep.	Medora
	Norman L. Jones, dem.	Carrollton
37	Elmer A. Perry, dem.	Mt. Sterling
	George W. Dean, dem.	Adams
	Charles F. Kincheloe, rep.	Loraine
38	John R. Challacombe, rep.	Hillsboro.
	Emmet P. Poindexter, dem.	Greenville
	James G. Miller, rep.	Avena
39	Charles E. Selby, rep.	Springfield
	Edward L. Merritt, dem.	Springfield
	William J. Butler, rep.	Springfield
40	Alex. H. McTaggart, rep.	Pana
	Joseph P. Barricklow, dem.	Arcola
	W. H. Wallace, rep.	Humboldt
41	Murray McDonald, dem.	Sullivan
	James E. Sharrock, rep.	Taylorville
	W. G. Cochran, rep.	Sullivan
42	Thomas B. Needles, rep.	Nashville
	Morrison J. O'Harnett, rep.	Carlyle
	John A. Barnes, dem.	Louisville
43	Joseph P. Condo, rep.	Moccasin
	Polk B. Briscoe, dem.	Westfield
	Geo. M. LeCrone, dem.	Effingham
44	Samuel M. Smyth, rep.	Shawneetown
	M. W. Spencer, dem.	Carmi
	Ross Graham, rep.	Carmi
45	Ethelbert Callahan, rep.	Robinson
	J. Edwin Black, dem.	Bridgeport
	Thomas Tippit, dem.	Olney
46	William H. Green, dem.	Mt. Vernon
	Samuel H. Watson, rep.	Mt. Vernon
	Charles A. Aiken, rep.	Benton
47	Thomas F. Ferns, dem.	Jerseyville
	Orville A. Snedeker, rep.	Jerseyville
	Thomas P. McFee, rep.	Venice
48	Ezekiel J. Ingersoll, rep.	Carbondale
	John J. Douglas, rep.	Chester
	Harmon P. Burroughs, dem.	Elkville
49	William H. Snyder, dem.	Belleville
	Michael Kelly, rep.	Belleville
	Louis Perrottet, rep.	Mascoutah
50	Martin M. McDonald, rep.	Crab Orchard
	Andrew J. Pickrell, rep.	Anna
	William T. Davis, dem.	Marion
51	Fowler A. Armstrong, rep.	Massac Creek
	Richard M. Johnson, rep.	Levings
	C. A. F. Rondeau, dem.	Golconda

* Died July 3, 1895. † Murdered, fall of 1895.

FORTIETH GENERAL ASSEMBLY, 1896–1898.

Convened at Springfield, Jan. 6, 1897; adjourned, ———, 1897.

SENATE.

President ($1,000) .... William A. Northcott, Greenville.
President pro tempore (salary of Senator) .... Hendrick V. Fisher, Geneseo.
Secretary ($6.00) .... James H. Paddock, Springfield.
First Assistant ($4.00) .... James Conwell, Chicago.
Second Assistant ($4.00) .... C. J. McManis, Princeton.
Third Assistant ($4.00) .... Charles Wanger, Chicago.
Reading Clerk ($4.00) .... W. E. Lewis, Watseka.
Bill Clerk ($4.00) .... Clarence J. Root, Chicago.
President's Private Secretary ($3.00) .... W. W. Lowis, Greenville.
Enrolling and Engrossing Clerk ($5.00) .... Charles W. Baldwin, Chicago.
First Assistant ($4.00) .... P. M. Warner, Rossville.
Second Assistant ($4.00) .... Charles F. Herb, Alton.
Third Assistant ($4.00) .... W. B. Merrill, Bloomington.
Sergeant-at-Arms ($5.00) .... J. C. Ware, Champaign.
First Assistant ($3.00) .... H. C. Dempsey, Decatur.
Second Assistant ($3.00) .... William F. McCarthy, Chicago.
Chaplain ($3.00) .... Rev. A. G. Goodspeed, Minonk.
Postmaster ($4.00) .... Mrs. Fannie M. Worthington, Sterling.
Assistant ($3.00) .... Mrs. Ida M. Bacon, Aurora.
Superintendent of Ventilation .... N. N Coons, Monmouth.

Republicans, 39; Democrats, 11; Populist, 1.

Dist.	Name.	Postoffice.	Dist.	Name.	Postoffice.
1	Patrick V. Fitzpatrick, rep.	Chicago	27	Lewis M. Sawyer, rep.	Streator
2	Solon H. Case, rep.	Chicago	28	†Orville F. Berry, rep.	Carthage
3	Sidney McCloud, rep.	Chicago	29	Daniel D. Hunt, rep.	DeKalb
4	Daniel F. Curley, dem.	Chicago	30	Henry M. Dunlap, rep	Savoy
5	Charles H. Crawford, rep.	Chicago	31	James W. Templeton, rep	Princeton
6	William Sullivan, rep.	Chicago	32	Arthur A. Leeper, dem.	Virginia
7	John Humphrey, rep.	Orland	33	Hendrick V. Fisher, rep.	Geneseo
8	Flavel K. Granger, rep.	McHenry	34	Edward McConnel, dem.	Jacksonville
9	William J. O'Brien, dem.	Chicago	35	Fred. E. Harding, rep.	Monmouth
10	Delos W. Baxter, rep.	Rochelle	36	William L. Mounts, dem.	Carlinville
11	Frederick Lundin, rep.	Chicago	37	‡Albert W. Wells, dem.	Quincy
12	Homer F. Aspinwall, rep.	Freeport	38	Nathaniel S. Dresser, pop.	Greenville
13	Joseph P. Mahoney, dem.	Chicago	39	David T. Littler, rep	Springfield
14	Henry H. Evans, rep.	Aurora	40	Stanton C. Pemberton, rep.	Oakland
15	John J. Morrison, rep.	Chicago	41	M. F. Kanan, rep.	Decatur
16	Isaac M. Hamilton, rep.	Cissna Park	42	Charles E. Hull, dem.	Salem
17	Edward J. Dwyer, rep.	Chicago	43	Robert L. McKinlay, dem	Paris
18	Charles Bogardus, rep	Paxton	44	John Landrigan, dem.	Albion
19	Daniel A. Campbell, rep	Chicago	45	Hiram H. Kingsbury, rep.	Olney
20	Robert B. Fort, rep.	Lacon	46	Joseph T. Payne, dem.	Mt. Vernon
21	Charles M. Netterstrom, rep.	Chicago	47	*David R. Sparks, rep.	Alton
22	George W. Stubblefield, rep.	Bloomington	48	Albert C. Bollinger, rep.	Waterloo
23	George D. Anthony, rep	Chicago	49	James A. Willoughby, rep.	Belleville
24	James D. Putnam, rep	Elmwood	50	Walter Warder, rep.	Cairo
25	George H. Munroe, rep.	Joliet	51	Pleasant T. Chapman, rep.	Vienna
26	W. Scott Edwards, rep.	Lewistown			

*To succeed Charles A. Herb, deceased, rep., Alton. †Vice Wm. E. Manifold, dem., of LaHarpe, unseated March 18, 1897. ‡Died March 5, 1897.

HOUSE OF REPRESENTATIVES.

Speaker (salary of Member) .... Ed C. Curtis, Grant Park.
Clerk ($6.00) .... John A. Reeve, Decatur.
First Assistant ($4.00) .... B. H. McCann, Bloomington.
Second Assistant ($4.00) .... Geo. K. Adams, Waukegan.
Third Assistant ($4.00) .... G. L. Peterson, Chicago.
Bill Clerk ($4.00) .... W. H. Kretzinger, Latham.
Enrolling and Engrossing Clerk ($5.00) .... Charles E. Dole, Mattoon.
First Assistant ($4.00) .... S. M. Smyth, Shawneetown.
Second Assistant ($4.00) .... Moses W. Porter, Aledo.
Doorkeeper ($5.00) .... Ed. Harlan, Marshall.
First Assistant ($3.00) .... A. B. Hallock, Peotone.
Second Assistant ($3.00) .... J. F. Spalding, Bourne.
Third Assistant ($3.00) .... Geo. S. Caughlan, East St. Louis.
Postmaster ($4.00) .... Mrs. Millie Jackson, Salem.
Assistant ($3.00) .... Miss Mamie Cowan, Pana.
Chaplain ($3.00) .... Rev. David G. Bradford, Peotone.
Speaker's Private Secretary ($3.00) .... Ernest A. Curtis, Grant Park.
Superintendent of Ventilation ($3.00) .... J. H. Wasple, Springfield.

Republicans, 87; Democrats, 62; Populists, 4.

Dist.	Name.	Postoffice.	Dist.	Name.	Postoffice.
1	William Laub, rep.	Chicago	26	Simon B. Heer, dem.	London Mills.
	Charles A. Wuthler, rep.	Chicago	27	John Wylie, rep.	Utica
	John C. Sterchle, dem.	Chicago		Irving H. Trowbridge, rep.	Marseilles
2	Peter A. Rowe, rep.	Chicago		John McLauchlan, dem.	LaSalle
	Augustus W. Nohe, rep.	Chicago	28	Lawrence Y. Sherman, rep.	Macomb
	Peter J. McGinnis, dem.	Chicago		Ulysses A. Wilson, rep.	Rushville
3	George W. Miller, rep.	Chicago		William A. Compton, dem.	Macomb
	Charles W. Nothnagel, rep.	Chicago	29	Washington I. Guffin, rep.	Paw Paw
	John P. McGoorty, dem.	Chicago		John K. Ely, rep.	Mazon
4	Charles F. Weldmaler, rep.	Chicago		James Brunen, dem.	Sycamore
	Michael J. Butler, dem.	Chicago	30	Samuel B. Garver, rep.	Farmer City.
	John Staudacher, dem.	Chicago		Seymour Marquiss, rep.	DeLand
5	John C. Buckner, rep.	Chicago		Henry C. Suttle, dem.	Kenney
	William O. LaMonte, rep.	Chicago	31	George Murray, rep.	Elmira
	Joseph Powell, rep.	Chicago		Jerry W. Dinneen, rep.	Albany
6	George M. Boyd, rep.	Chicago		Caleb C. Johnson, dem.	Sterling
	Charles M. Eldredge, rep.	Chicago	32	David C. White, rep.	Forest City
	Henry C. Bartling, dem.	Chicago		Joseph A. Horn, dem.	Mt. Pulaski
7	William Thiemann, rep.	Elk Grove		James M. Large, dem.	Athens
	Clark J. Tisdel, rep.	Evanston	33	William Payne, rep.	Osborn
	Ross C. Hall, dem.	Oak Park		Edwin W. Houghton, rep.	Galva
8	DuFay A. Fuller, rep.	Belvidere		William McEniry, dem.	Rock Island
	George R. Lyon, rep.	Waukegan	34	John B. Joy, rep.	Concord
	Jacob S. Edelstein, dem.	Belvidere		John D. Huffman, dem.	Bluffs
9	David E. Shanahan, rep.	Chicago		Frank L. Hall, dem.	Perry
	John O'Shea, dem.	Chicago	35	Frank A. Murdoch, rep.	Oneida
	Christian R. Walleck, dem.	Chicago		James O. Anderson, rep.	Decora
10	Lars M. Noling, rep.	Rockford		James R. Barnett, dem.	Coldbrook
	*Victor H. Bovey, rep.	Pond Creek	36	George B. Metcalf, rep.	Greenfield
	*Henry Andrus, rep.	Cher'y Valley		William T. Conlee, dem.	Carlinville
11	Ernest G. Schubert, rep.	Chicago		William V. Rhodes, dem.	Wrightsville
	Walter Sayler, rep.	Chicago	37	Charles F. Kincheloe, rep.	Loraine
	Joseph S. Schwab, dem.	Chicago		Elmer A. Perry, dem.	Mt. Sterling
12	James R. Berryman, rep.	Scales Mound		George W. Montgomery, dem.	Clayton
	David C. Busell, rep.	Milledgeville	38	Thomas P. Morey, rep.	Greenville
	Michael Stoskopf, dem.	Freeport		Obed E. Lovett, dem.	St. Elmo
13	James P. Cavanaugh, rep.	Chicago		Joseph P. Price, dem.	Irving
	William Carmody, dem.	Chicago	39	Charles E. Selby, rep.	Springfield
	Edward J. Novak, dem.	Chicago		Abner G. Murray, rep.	Springfield
14	Charles P. Bryan, rep.	Elmhurst		George L. Harnsberger, dem.	Springfield
	William F. Hunter, rep.	Elgin	40	Caleb R. Torrence, rep.	Cowden
	Samuel Alschuler, dem.	Aurora		Isaac B. Craig, dem.	Mattoon
15	Patrick J. Meaney, rep.	Chicago		Joseph P. Barricklow, dem.	Arcola
	Henry D. Nicholls, rep.	Chicago	41	James E. Sharrock, rep.	Taylorville
	Peter F. Galligan, dem.	Chicago		William G. Cochran, rep.	Sullivan
16	Ed. C. Curtis, rep.	Grant Park		Oliver T. Atchison, dem.	Lovington
	Almet Powell, rep.	Gilman	42	Thomas B. Needles, rep.	Nashville
	Freeman P. Morris, dem.	Watseka		John A. Barnes, dem.	Louisville
17	Albert Glade, rep.	Chicago		Hugh V. Murray, dem.	Carlyle
	Daniel V. McDonough, dem.	Chicago	43	Fenton W. Booth, rep.	Marshall
	Frank J. Brignadello, dem.	Chicago		Bernard L. Hussman, dem.	Effingham
18	Charles A. Allen, rep.	Hoopeston		Eb. Stewart, dem.	Toledo
	Martin B. Bailey, rep.	Danville	44	Samuel A. Williams, rep.	Friendsville
	G. W. Salmans, dem.	Danville		Benjamin S Organ, dem.	Mt. Carmel
19	Robert C. Busse, rep.	Chicago		Nathan D. Bryant, pop.	Omaha
	John F. Quanstrum, rep.	Chicago	45	William H. Lathrop, rep.	Newton
	Benjamin M. Mitchell, dem.	Chicago		Duane Gaines, dem.	Newton
20	Oscar F. Avery, rep.	Pontiac		William Hart, dem.	Annapolis
	Isaac B. Hammers, rep.	Panola	46	Wallace B. Flannigan, rep.	Mc Leansboro
	John L. McGuire, dem.	Metamora		Daniel R. Webb, dem.	Benton
21	Fred A. Busse, rep.	Chicago		Fred G. Blood, pop.	Mt. Vernon
	David Revell, rep.	Chicago	47	Charles L. Wood, rep.	Hamburg
	James H. Farrell, dem.	Chicago		John A. Shephard, dem.	Jerseyville
22	Duncan M. Funk, rep.	Bloomington	†	Robert B. English, dem.	Hardin
	Arthur J. Scrogin, rep.	Lexington	48	Harry B. Ward, rep.	DuQuoin
	James F. O'Donnell, dem.	Bloomington		Robert C. Brown, rep.	Sparta
23	Lawrence Kilcourse, rep.	Chicago		Robert H. Allen, dem.	Shiloh Hill
	Albert J. Olson, rep.	Chicago	49	John E. Thomas, rep.	Belleville
	Denis E. Sullivan, dem.	Chicago		Louis Perrottet, rep.	Mascoutah
24	Aquilla J. Daugherty, rep.	Peoria		Jule C. Jarvis, dem.	Centrev'e Sta
	Alva Merrill, rep.	Hallock	50	Elbert H. Dickson, rep.	Oakville
	Alvon H. Bristol, dem.	Chillicothe		William D. DeWoody, rep.	Corinth
25	John Kohlstedt, rep.	Monee		William Q. McGee, dem.	Cairo
	William H. Steen, rep.	Braidwood	51	Joseph W. King, rep.	Eddyville
	Joseph Kain, dem.	Braidwood		William H. Parish, rep.	Harrisburg
26	Jonathan Merriam, rep.	Atlanta		Fletcher A. Trousdale, dem.	Metropolis
	John W. Johnson, rep.	Canton			

*Seat contested by Joseph W. Bacharach, dem., Rockford; Andrus and Bovey retain their seats. †Seat contested by Jett A. Kirby, rep., Jerseyville; Kirby was seated.

JUDICIAL DEPARTMENT.

We are indebted to the late Norman L. Freeman, Esq., Reporter of the Supreme Court, for the following interesting sketch of the early history of the Supreme and Circuit Courts under the constitutions of 1818, 1848 and 1870.

The first constitution of the State declared that the judicial power of the State of Illinois should be vested in one Supreme Court and such inferior courts as the General Assembly should, from time to time, ordain and establish.

The Supreme Court was vested with appellate jurisdiction only, except in cases relating to the revenue, in cases of *mandamus*, and such cases of impeachment as might be required to be tried before it. It consisted of a chief justice and three associates, though the number of justices might be increased by the General Assembly, after 1824.

The justices of the Supreme Court and the judges of the inferior courts were appointed by joint ballot of both branches of the General Assembly, and commissioned by the Governor, and held their offices during good behavior, until the end of the first session of the General Assembly which was begun and held after the first day of January, in the year 1824, at which time their commissions expired; and until that time the justices of the Supreme Court were required to hold the circuit courts in the several counties, in such manner and at such times, and were to have and exercise such jurisdiction, as the General Assembly should, by law, prescribe.

But after the period mentioned, the justices of the Supreme Court and the judges of the inferior courts held their offices during good behavior; and the justices of the Supreme Court were no longer compelled to hold the circuit courts unless required by law. The State was accordingly divided into four judicial circuits, within which the chief justice and associate justices of the Supreme Court were assigned to perform circuit duties, which they continued to do until the year 1824.

On the 29th of December, 1824, an act was passed declaring that, in addition to the justices of the Supreme Court, there should be appointed by that General Assembly five circuit judges, who should continue in office during good behavior, and by the same act the State was divided into five judicial circuits. Thus, for the first time, the justices of the Supreme Court were relieved from the performance of circuit duties, which now devolved upon the five circuit judges.

The circuit judges, however, were permitted to remain in office only about two years, as, by the act of 12th January, 1827, those sections of the act of 1824, which provided for the appointment of five circuit judges, and dividing the State into five judicial circuits, were repealed; and the State was again divided into four judicial circuits, in which the chief justice and three associate justices were again required to perform circuit duties.

The justices of the Supreme Court then continued to hold all the circuit courts until a circuit judge was elected by the General Assembly, in pursuance of the act of Jan. 8, 1829, which declared that there should be elected, by joint ballot of both branches of the General Assembly, at that session, one circuit judge, who should preside in the circuit to which he might be appointed, north of the Illinois river. A circuit judge was elected in pursuance of that act, and at the same time the Fifth judicial circuit was created, in which the circuit judge was required to preside, the justices of the Supreme Court continuing to perform their duties in the other four circuits.

The circuit courts continued to be thus held until the passage of the act of Jan. 7, 1835, by which all laws requiring the justices of the Supreme Court to hold the circuit courts were repealed, and it was provided that there should be elected by the General Assembly, at that session, five judges, in addition to the one then authorized by law, who should preside in the several circuit courts then or thereafter required to be held in the several counties in the State. The five additional circuit judges were accordingly elected, and at the same session the Sixth judicial circuit was created. The justices of the Supreme Court were thus again relieved from the performance of circuit duties, which, for the second time in the judicial history of the State, devolved upon the circuit judges exclusively.

The judiciary remained unchanged until 1841, the number of judicial circuits and of circuit judges being increased from time to time, as the business of the courts required. The

Seventh judicial circuit was created by the act of Feb. 4, 1837, and an additional circuit judge was elected; and by the act of Feb. 23, 1839, the Eighth and Ninth circuits were created, and provision made for the election of two additional judges, which was done.

The judiciary of the State was reorganized by the act of Feb. 10, 1841, which repealed all former laws authorizing the election of circuit judges, or establishing the circuit courts, thus again legislating out of office all the circuit judges in the State. The act then provided that there should be appointed, by joint ballot of both branches of the General Assembly, at that session, five additional associate justices of the Supreme Court, who, in connection with the chief justice and the three associates then in office, should constitute the Supreme Court of the State. The State was at the same time divided into nine judicial circuits, and the chief justice and eight associate justices were required to perform circuit duties in those circuits; the circuit courts being again created at the same session. The judiciary as thus organized continued until the entire system was changed by the constitution of 1848.

CONSTITUTION OF 1848.

It has been seen that under the constitution of 1818, the Supreme Court was the only court created by that instrument, and the circuit courts had no existence except by legislative enactment; but upon organizing the judiciary as it existed under the constitution of 1848, the circuit courts constituted a part of the judicial system as created by the new constitution—it being declared in that instrument that the judicial power of the State shall be vested in one Supreme Court, in circuit courts, in county courts and in justices of the peace, and the General Assembly is authorized to establish inferior local courts of civil and criminal jurisdiction, in the cities of the State, but such courts must have uniform organization and jurisdiction in such cities.

The Supreme Court consisted of three judges. The State was divided into three grand divisions, the people in each division electing one of said judges, for the term of nine years; though after the first election of judges under the constitution, the General Assembly could provide by law for their election by the whole State, or by divisions, as they might deem most expedient; but no change in that respect was made, and the judges of the Supreme Court continue to be elected by divisions, as provided in the constitution.

These three grand divisions were established by the new constitution, but after the taking of each census by the State they might be altered, if necessary, to equalize them in population, the alteration being required to be made by adding to either of the districts such adjacent counties as would make them nearest equal in population. Appeals and writs of error could be taken from the circuit court of any county to the Supreme Court, held in the division which included such county; or with the consent of all parties in the cause, to the Supreme Court in the next adjoining division.

It is provided in the constitution, that the State should be divided into nine judicial circuits, but the General Assembly might increase the number to meet the future exigencies of the State. The number of circuits was afterwards increased from time to time, as the business of the courts required, so that there were thirty judicial circuits in the State, in all, created under the constitution of 1848. In each of the nine circuits the constitution required that one circuit judge should be elected by the people thereof, who should hold his office for the term of six years, and until his successor should be commissioned and qualified.

The first election for justices of the Supreme Court and judges of the circuit courts under the constitution, was required to be held on the first Monday of September, 1848, and it was further provided, that on the first Monday of June, 1855, and every sixth year thereafter, an election should be held for judges of the circuit courts; and whenever an additional circuit was created, such provision should be made as to hold the second election of such additional judge at the regular elections provided in the constitution. All vacancies, either in the Supreme or circuit courts, must be filled by an election by the people, though if the unexpired term did not exceed one year, such vacancy might be filled by executive appointment.

It was required that there should be two or more terms of the circuit court held annually in each county in the State, at such times as might be provided by law, and the circuit courts to have jurisdiction in all cases at law and in equity, and in all cases of appeal from all inferior courts.

Those were the constitutional provisions as to the organization and jurisdiction of the circuit courts as they existed under the constitution of 1848—the schedule to the constitution of 1848 further declaring, that the judges of the circuit courts should have and exercise the powers and jurisdiction conferred upon the former judges of those courts, subject to the provisions of this constitution.

CONSTITUTION OF 1870.

The constitution of 1870 vested the judicial powers in one Supreme Court, circuit courts, county courts, justices of the peace, police magistrates, and such courts as may be created by law, in and for cities and incorporated towns.

The Supreme Court consists of seven judges, and has original jurisdiction, similar to that granted by the constitution of 1848. There is one chief justice, selected by the court; four judges constitute a quorum, and the concurrence of four judges is necessary to a decision. The three grand divisions established by the constitution of 1848 for holding the Supreme Court are retained in the present constitution. The terms of the court, the judicial divisions and places of holding court are regulated by law.

The State, for the election of supreme judges, is divided, by the constitution, into seven districts, one judge being elected from each district. The election occurs on the first Monday in June, in each year, in such districts, as the terms of any of the judges may expire. The term of office is nine years.

Appeals and writs of error may be taken to the Supreme Court held in the grand division in which the case is decided, or, by consent of parties, to any other grand division. The officers of the Supreme Court, as fixed by the constitution, are: one reporter of its decisions, who is appointed by the court, holds office six years, and is subject to removal by the court; one clerk in each of the three grand divisions, to be elected by the voters in their respective divisions, and hold office six years.

APPELLATE COURTS.

The constitution also provided for the creation of Appellate Courts, after the year 1874, of uniform organization and jurisdiction, in districts created for that purpose, to which such appeals and writs of error, as the General Assembly may provide, may be prosecuted from circuit and other courts, and from which appeals and writs of error may lie to the Supreme Court, in all criminal cases, and cases in which a franchise, or freehold, or the validity of a statute is involved, and in such other cases as may be provided by law. Such Appellate Courts to be held by such number of judges of the circuit courts, and in such times and places, and in such manner, as might be provided by law; but no judge shall sit in review upon cases decided by him, nor shall said judges receive any additional compensation for such services.

Under the above provisions of the constitution, the legislature, in 1877, created four Appellate Courts, and provided districts as follows: the first to consist of the county of Cook; the second to include all of the Northern grand division of the Supreme Court except the county of Cook; the third to consist of the Central grand division of the Supreme Court, and the fourth the Southern grand division of the Supreme Court. Each court to be held by three of the judges of the circuit court, to be assigned by the Supreme Court, three to each district, for the term of three years, at each assignment.

Two terms of the Appellate Court are held in each district, in every year. One presiding justice is chosen in each district by the judges thereof, for such time and in such manner as they may determine. Two judges constitute a quorum, and the concurrence of two is necessary to a decision. Clerks of the Appellate Court are elected, one for each district, and hold office six years.

The Appellate Courts have appellate jurisdiction only, and have jurisdiction of all matters of appeal or writs of error from the final judgments, orders or decrees of any of the circuit courts, or the Superior Court of Cook county, or from the city courts, in any suit or proceeding at law, or in chancery, other than criminal cases, and cases involving a franchise or freehold, or the validity of a statute. Appeals and writs of error lie from the final orders, judgments or decrees of the circuit or city courts, and from the Superior Court of Cook county, directly to the Supreme Court, in all criminal cases, and in cases involving a franchise or freehold, or the validity of a statute. In all cases determined in the Appellate Courts, in actions, *ex-contractu* (except those involving a penalty), wherein the amount involved is less than $1,000, exclusive of costs, and in all cases *sounding* in damages, wherein the judgment of the court below is less than $1,000 exclusive of costs, and the judgment is affirmed or otherwise finally disposed of in the Appellate Court, the judgment, order or decree of the Appellate Court shall be final, and no appeal shall lie or writ of error be prosecuted therefrom. In all other cases, appeals shall lie and writs of error may be prosecuted from the final judgments, orders or decrees of the Appellate Courts to the Supreme Court. A majority of the judges of the Appellate Court may, however, if they be of the opinion that any case decided by them, involving a less sum than $1,000, also involves questions of law of such importance, either on account of principal or collateral interests, as that it should be passed upon by the Supreme Court, in such cases, grant appeals and writs of error to the Supreme Court, on petition of parties to the cause, in which case they shall certify to the Supreme Court the grounds upon which the appeal is granted.

The law establishing the Appellate Courts went into effect July 1, 1877, the election of circuit judges took place in August, and the first assignment of Appellate judges was made by the Supreme Court at the September term, in the same year. These are substantially the constitutional and statutory provisions as to the organization and jurisdiction of the Appellate Courts.

CIRCUIT COURTS.

The constitution provides that the circuit courts shall have original jurisdiction of all causes in law and equity, and such appellate jurisdiction as is or may be provided by law, and shall hold two or more terms each year in every county. The judges are elected by districts, and hold office six years.

Section 13 of the judiciary article of the constitution provides that the State, exclusive of Cook and other counties having a population of 100,000, shall be divided into judicial circuits, to be formed of contiguous counties, and not over one circuit for each 100,000 population; one judge to be elected for each circuit. The first election for circuit judges was required to be held on the first Monday in June, 1873, and every six years thereafter.

The legislature, in 1873, in accordance with above section, divided the State, exclusive of Cook county, into twenty-six judicial circuits, and at the election in June, 1873, one judge was elected for each circuit, for the term of six years.

Section 15 provides that the General Assembly may divide the State into judicial circuits of greater population and territory, in lieu of the circuits provided for in section 13, and provide for the election therein, severally, by the electors thereof, by general ticket, of not exceeding four judges, who shall hold the circuit courts in the circuit for which they shall be elected, in such manner as may be provided by law.

The legislature, in 1877, in order to increase the number of circuit judges, and to provide for the organization of the appellate courts, divided the State into thirteen districts, and provided for the election of one additional judge in each district, in August, 1877, for two years, making three judges in each district and thirty-nine in the State. The election took place in August accordingly, and in September following the Supreme Court assigned twelve of the circuit judges to appellate duty, and the remaining judges held the circuit courts in their respective districts.

In June, 1879, three judges were elected in each of the thirteen judicial circuits, as created by the act of 1877. A second assignment was made by the Supreme Court, of circuit judges for appellate duty, at the June term, 1879, and the remaining judges perform circuit duty in the districts for which they were respectively elected.

COURTS OF COOK COUNTY.

The constitution of 1870 recognizes Cook county as a unit in the judiciary system of the State, by providing that the Supreme Court may hold one or more sessions each year in the city of Chicago, whenever suitable rooms are provided, without expense to the State; and also constitutes the county of Cook one judicial circuit, and excepts the county in the districting of the State by the legislature into circuits.

The circuit court of Cook county is made to consist of five judges, until their number shall be increased as provided by the constitution. The constitution provides that the General Assembly may increase the number of judges by adding one for every additional 50,000 inhabitants in the county over and above a population of 400,000. The term of office of the judges of the Cook county circuit court is also six years.

The Superior Court of Chicago, established by law, 1849, formerly the Cook County Court of Common Pleas, was continued by the constitution, and called the Superior Court of Cook Cou ty. The constitution provides for an increase of judges of the Superior Court the same as the circuit court of Cook county.

By an act of 1875, it is provided that for every 50,000 inhabitants over and above 400,000 in Cook county, there shall be added one judge, until the court shall be composed of nine judges. It is also made the duty of the Governor, whenever he shall ascertain from the census that the county of Cook is entitled to one or more additional judges, to issue a writ of election therefor, for the number to which the county is entitled.

Accordingly, it appearing by the United States census of 1880 that the population of the county of Cook exceeded 400,000, an election was ordered to be held for four additional judges of the Superior Court of Cook county, at the November election, 1880, and the court was increased by that number in accordance with the statute of 1875.

The above comprises a concise history of the State courts; and a comprehensive though brief outline of the judicial system of the State from its organization to the present time.

JUDGES OF THE SUPREME COURT.

Name.	When appointed or elected.	Expiration of term.	Remarks.
Joseph Phillips, C. J.	Oct. 9, 1818	July 4, 1822	Resigned
Thomas C. Browne	Oct. 9, 1818	Jan. 18, 1825	
William P. Foster	Oct. 9, 1818	July 7, 1819	Resigned
John Reynolds	Oct. 9, 1818	Aug. 31, 1822	
John Reynolds, C. J	Aug. 31, 1822	Jan. 19, 1825	
William Wilson	July 7, 1819	Jan. 19, 1825	
William Wilson, C. J	Jan. 19, 1825	Dec. 4, 1848	
Samuel D. Lockwood	Jan. 19, 1825	Dec. 4, 1848	
Theophilus W. Smith	Jan. 19, 1825	Dec. 26, 1842	Resigned.
Thomas C Browne	Jan. 19, 1825	Dec. 4, 1848	
Thomas Ford	Feb. 15, 1841	Aug. 4, 1842	Resigned
Sidney Breese	Feb. 15, 1841	Dec. 19, 1842	Resigned
Walter B. Scates	Feb. 15, 1841	Jan. 11, 1847	Resigned
Samuel H. Treat	Feb. 15, 1841	Dec. 4, 1848	
Stephen A. Douglas.	Feb. 15, 1841	June 28, 1843	Resigned.
John D. Caton	Aug. 20, 1842	March 6, 1843	Vice Ford
James Semple	Jan. 16, 1843	Aug. 16, 1843	Vice Breese, resigned
Richard M. Young	Feb. 4, 1843	Jan. 25, 1847	Resigned
John M. Robinson	March 6, 1843	April 27, 1843	Died
John D. Caton	May 2, 1843	Dec. 4, 1848	Vice Robinson
Jesse B. Thomas	Aug. 6, 1843	Aug. 8, 1845	Vice Douglas, resigned
James Shields	Aug. 16, 1843	April 2, 1845	Vice Semple, resigned
Gustavus Kœrner	April 2, 1845	Dec. 4, 1848	Vice Shields
William A. Denning	Jan. 19, 1847	Dec. 4, 1848	Vice Scates.
Jesse B. Thomas	Jan. 27, 1847	Dec. 4, 1848	Vice Young
Samuel H. Treat, C. J	Dec. 4, 1848	1855	Resigned
John D. Caton, C. J	Dec. 4, 1848	Jan. 9, 1864	Resigned
Lyman Trumbull	Dec. 4, 1848	July 4, 1853	Resigned.
Walter B. Scates, C. J	1854	May 1857	Resigned
Onias C. Skinner	June 4, 1855	April 19, 1858	Resigned.
Sidney Breese, C. J	Nov. 23, 1857	June 28, 1878	Vice Scates, resigned
Pinkney H. Walker, C. J.	April 19, 1858	June 3, 1867	Vice Skinner, resigned
Sidney Breese	July 6, 1861	June 6, 1870	Re-elected
Corydon Beckwith	Jan. 7, 1864	June 6, 1864	Vice Caton, resigned
Charles B. Lawrence	June 6, 1864	June 2, 1873	To succeed Beckwith
Pinkney H. Walker	June 3, 1867	June 1876	Re-elected
Sidney Breese	June 6, 1870	June 28, 1878	Died, June 28, 1878
Anthony Thornton	July 2, 1870	May 31, 1873	Resigned
John M. Scott	July 2, 1870	June 2, 1879	
Benjamin R. Sheldon	July 2, 1870	June 2, 1879	
Wm. K. McAllister	July 2, 1870	Nov. 26, 1875	Resigned
John Scholfield	June 2, 1873	June 2, 1879	Vice Thornton
Alfred M. Craig	June 2, 1873	June 1882	To succeed Lawrence
T. Lyle Dickey	Dec. 21, 1875	June 2, 1879	To succeed McAllister
Pinkney H. Walker	June 5, 1876	June 1885	Re-elected. Died
David J. Baker	July 9, 1878	June 2, 1879	Appointed vice Breese
John M. Scott	June 2, 1879	June 1888	Re-elected
Benjamin R. Sheldon	June 2, 1879	June 1888	Re-elected
John Scholfield	June 2, 1879	June 1888	Re-elected.
T. Lyle Dickey	June 2, 1879	June 1888	Re-elected. Died
John H. Mulkey	June 2, 1879	June 1888	To succeed Baker
Alfred M. Craig	June 5, 1882	June 1891	Re-elected
Damon G. Tunnicliffe	Feb. 16, 1885	June 1885	Appointed vice Walker
Simeon P. Shope	June 1, 1885	June 1894	To succeed Tunnicliff
Benj. D. Magruder	Nov. 3, 1885	June 1888	Vice Dickey
David J. Baker	June 4, 1888	June 1897	Vice Mulkey.
John Scholfield	June 4, 1888	June 1897	Re-elected. Died
Jacob W. Wilkin	June 4, 1888	June 1897	To succeed Scott
Joseph M. Bailey*	June 4, 1888	June 1897	To succeed Sheldon.
Benj. D. Magruder	June 4, 1888	June 1897	Re-elected
Alfred M. Craig	June 1, 1891	June 1900	Re-elected.
Jesse J. Phillips	June 5, 1893	June 1897	To succeed Scholfield
Joseph N. Carter	June 4, 1894	June 1903	To succeed Shope
James H. Cartwright	Dec. 17, 1895	June 1897	Vice Bailey, deceased

* Died Oct. 16, 1895.

JUDGES OF THE CIRCUIT COURT

APPOINTED OR ELECTED UNDER THE CONSTITUTION OF 1818.

Under the act of 1824 the State was divided into five circuits, and the following judges were elected by the General Assembly, all of whom were commissioned Jan. 19, 1825, and legislated out of office by the act of Jan. 12, 1827:

1st Circuit.......John Y. Sawyer.
2d Circuit.......Samuel McRoberts.
3d Circuit.......Richard M. Young.
4th Circuit.......James Hall.
5th Circuit.......James O. Wattles.

In pursuance of an act of the General Assembly, Jan. 8, 1829, the Fifth Judicial Circuit, comprising all the territory in the State, was created. Richard M. Young was elected by the General Assembly Judge of this circuit, and commissioned Jan. 23, 1829. By the act of Jan. 7, 1835, five additional circuit judges were provided for, and the Sixth Judicial Circuit created.

FIRST CIRCUIT.

Stephen T. Logan.......Elected 1835; resigned 1837.
William Brown.......Commissioned March 20, 1837; resigned July 20, 1837.
Jesse B. Thomas, Jr.......Commissioned July 20, 1837; resigned, 1839.
William Thomas.......Commissioned Feb. 25, 1839.

SECOND CIRCUIT.

Sidney Breese.......Elected 1835.

THIRD CIRCUIT.

Henry Eddy.......Elected Jan., 1835; resigned Feb. 10, 1835.
Alexander F. Grant.......Commissioned Feb., 1835.
Jeptha Hardin.......Commissioned Jan. 18, 1836.
Walter B. Scates.......Commissioned Dec. 26, 1836.

FOURTH CIRCUIT.

Justin Harlan.......Commissioned Jan. 4, 1835.

FIFTH CIRCUIT.

Richard M. Young.......Commissioned Jan. 23, 1829; resigned Jan. 2, 1837.
James H. Ralston.......Commissioned Feb. 4, 1837; resigned Aug. 31, 1839.
Peter Lot.......Commissioned Sept. 9, 1839; elected and re-commissioned Dec. 20, 1839.

SIXTH CIRCUIT.

Thomas Ford.......Commissioned Jan. 19, 1835; resigned March, 1837.
Daniel Stone.......Commissioned March 4, 1837.

SEVENTH CIRCUIT.

John Pearson.......Commissioned Feb. 4, 1837; resigned Nov. 20, 1840.

EIGHTH CIRCUIT.

Stephen T. Logan.......Commissioned Feb. 29, 1839; resigned.
Samuel H. Treat.......Commissioned May 27, 1839; elected and recommissioned Jan. 30, 1840.

NINTH CIRCUIT.

Thomas Ford.......Commissioned Feb. 25, 1839.

JUDGES OF THE CIRCUIT COURT

ELECTED OR APPOINTED UNDER THE CONSTITUTION OF 1848.

By the constitution of 1848, the State was divided into nine judicial circuits, in each of which a judge was elected Sept., 1848. The legislature was authorized to increase the number of circuits as might be required

FIRST CIRCUIT.

David M. Woodson.......Commissioned Dec. 4, 1848, June 25, 1855, and July 1, 1861.
Charles D. Hodges.......Commissioned June 27, 1867.

SECOND CIRCUIT.

William H Underwood.......Commissioned Dec. 4, 1848.
Sidney Breese.......Commissioned June 25, 1855; resigned.
Harvey K. Omelveny.......Commissioned March 1, 1858, vice Breese.
Silas L. Bryan.......Commissioned July 1, 1861; and July 11, 1867.

THIRD CIRCUIT.

William A. Denning.......Commissioned Dec. 4, 1848.
W. K. Parrish.......Commissioned Jan. 4, 1854, and June 25, 1855; resigned June 15, 1859.
Alex. M. Jenkins, Commissioned Aug. 27, 1859, vice Parrish, and July 1, 1861; died Feb. 13, 1864.
John H. Mulkey.......Commissioned April 22, 1864, vice Jenkins; resigned.
William H. Green.......Commissioned Dec. 28, 1865, vice Mulkey, resigned.
Monroe C. Crawford.......Commissioned June 27, 1867.

FOURTH CIRCUIT.

Justin Harlan.......................................Commissioned Dec. 4, 1848, and June 25, 1855.
Charles H. Constable...Commissioned July 1, 1861; died.
Hiram B. Decius.................Commissioned Dec. 1, 1865, vice Constable, and June 27, 1867.

FIFTH CIRCUIT.

William A. Minshall...Commissioned Dec. 4, 1848.
Pinkney H. Walker....Commissioned March 17, 1853, and June 25, 1855; resigned April 19, 1858.
John S. Bailey.................................Commissioned June 24, 1858; vice Walker, resigned.
Chauncey L. Higbee..............................Commissioned July 1, 1861, and June 27, 1867.

SIXTH CIRCUIT.

Benjamin R. Sheldon...Commissioned Dec. 4, 1848.
Ira O. Wilkinson...Commissioned May 14, 1851.
J. Wilson Drury.......................................Commissioned June 25, 1855; resigned March, 1860.
John H. Howe..Commissioned March 16, 1860, vice Drury.
Ira O. Wilkinson...Commissioned June 13, 1861.
George W. Pleasants..Commissioned June 27, 1867.

SEVENTH CIRCUIT.

Hugh T. Dickey..Commissioned Dec. 4, 1848.
Buckner S. Morris...Commissioned May 24, 1853.
George Maniere..............Commissioned June 25, 1855, and July 1, 1861; died July 9, 1863.
Erastus S. Williams..............Commissioned July 9, 1863, vice Maniere; and June 27, 1867.

EIGHTH CIRCUIT.

David Davis....Commissioned Dec. 4, 1848, June 25, 1855, and July 1, 1861; resigned Nov. 1, 1862.
John M. Scott..............Commissioned Dec. 2, 1862, vice Davis; and June 27, 1867; resigned.
Thomas F. Tipton...Commissioned Aug. 18, 1870, vice Scott.

NINTH CIRCUIT.

T. Lyle Dickey...Commissioned Dec. 4, 1848.
Edwin S. Leland...Commissioned Aug. 11, 1852.
Madison E. Hollister.....Commissioned June 25, 1855, and July 1, 1861; resigned Dec. 4, 1866.
Edwin S. Leland..................Commissioned Dec. 4, 1866, vice Hollister, and June 27, 1867.

TENTH CIRCUIT.

William Kellogg..Commissioned Feb. 12, 1850.
Hezekiah M. Wead...Commissioned Nov. 19, 1852.
John S. Thompson..........................Commissioned June 25, 1855; resigned Aug. 20, 1860.
Aaron Tyler...Commissioned Aug. 20, 1860, vice Thompson.
Charles B. Lawrence.............................Commissioned July 1, 1861; resigned July 21, 1864.
John S. Thompson.....Commissioned Sept. 5, 1864, vice Lawrence; resigned February, 1867.
Arthur A. Smith................Commissioned Feb. 19, 1867, vice Thompson, and June 27, 1867.

ELEVENTH CIRCUIT.

Hugh Henderson...Commissioned April 4, 1849; died.
S. H. Randall........Commissioned Oct. 31, 1854, vice Henderson, and June 25, 1855; resigned.
Jesse O. Norton...Commissioned March 14, 1857, vice Randall.
Sidney W. Harris...Commissioned July 1, 1861.
Josiah McRoberts............Commissioned Oct. 1, 1866, vice S. W. Harris; and June 27, 1867.

TWELFTH CIRCUIT.

Samuel S. Marshall......................Commissioned March 26, 1851; resigned Aug. 10, 1854.
Downing Baugh...Commissioned Aug. 11, 1854, vice Marshall.
Edwin Beecher..Commissioned June 25, 1855.
Samuel S. Marshall..................................Commissioned July 1, 1861; resigned Feb. 24, 1865.
James M. Pollock...............Commissioned April 6, 1865, vice Marshall; and June 27, 1867.

THIRTEENTH CIRCUIT.

Isaac J. Wilson..Commissioned June 18, 1851, and June 25, 1855.
Allen C. Fuller..Commissioned July 1, 1861; resigned July 18, 1862.
Theodore D. Murphy.................Commissioned Sept. 1, 1862, vice Fuller; and June 27, 1867.

FOURTEENTH CIRCUIT.

Benjamin R. Sheldon........Commissioned June 18, 1851; June 25, 1855; July 1, 1861; and June 27, 1867, resigned.
William Brown..Commissioned Aug. 18, 1870, vice Sheldon.

FIFTEENTH CIRCUIT.

Onias C. Skinner...Commissioned May 22, 1851.
Joseph Sibley.......................Commissioned June 21, 1855; July 1, 1861; and June 27, 1867.

SIXTEENTH CIRCUIT.

Onslaw Peters....................................Commissioned March 28, 1853; and June 25, 1855; died.
Jacob Gale...Commissioned April 10, 1856, vice Peters.
Elihu N. Powell...Commissioned Nov. 11, 1856, vice Gale.
Amos L. Merriman.....................................Commissioned July 1, 1861; resigned Nov. 28, 1863;
Marion Williamson...Commissioned Nov. 28, 1863, vice Merriman.
Sabin D. Puterbaugh.............................Commissioned June 20, 1867; resigned March 14, 1873.
Henry B. Hopkins..Commissioned March 17, 1873, vice Puterbaugh

SEVENTEENTH CIRCUIT.

Charles Emerson ....Commissioned April 2,1853; June 25, 1855; and July 1, 1861.
Arthur J. Gallagher............ .... Commissioned June 25, 1867.

EIGHTEENTH CIRCUIT.

Edward Y. Rice......Commissioned April 13, 1857; July 1,1861; and July 27, 1867; resigned Aug. 20, 1870.
Horatio M. Vandeveer....................................Commissioned Nov. 14, 1870; vice Rice.

NINETEENTH CIRCUIT.

Wesley Sloan ....Commissioned March 19, 1857; and July 1, 1861.
John Olney...Commissioned June 27, 1867.
David J. Baker, Jr. ....Commissioned March 22, 1869.

TWENTIETH CIRCUIT.

Charles R. Starr......... Commissioned March 19,1857; and July 1,1861; resigned March 8,1867.
Charles H. Wood ....Commissioned March 8, 1867, vice Starr; and June 7, 1867.

TWENTY-FIRST CIRCUIT.

James Harriott....................................Commissioned March 25, 1857; and July 1, 1861.
Charles Turner...Commissioned June 27, 1867.

TWENTY-SECOND CIRCUIT.

John V. Eustace ....Commissioned March 16, 1857.
William W. Heaton......................... ....Commissioned July 1, 1861; and June 7, 1867.

TWENTY-THIRD CIRCUIT.

Martin Ballou...... ....Commissioned March 31, 1857.
Mark Bangs...... ....Commissioned April 22, 1859.
Samuel L. Richmond...........Commissioned July 1, 1861, and June 27, 1867; died Feb. 19, 1873.
Mark Bangs...Commissioned March 5, 1873, vice Richmond.

TWENTY FOURTH CIRCUIT.

William H. Snyder .... Commissioned April 11, 1857.
Joseph Gillespie......................... .... Commissioned July 1, 1861, and June 27, 1867.

TWENTY-FIFTH CIRCUIT.

Alfred Kitchell.................................... ....Commissioned April 21, 1859.
James C. Allen.................. ....Commissioned July 1, 1861; resigned Dec 31, 1862.
Aaron Shaw...... ....Commissioned March 2, 1863, vice Allen.
Richard S. Canby.. ....Commissioned July 2, 1867.

TWENTY-SIXTH CIRCUIT.

Willis Allen............. ... .Commissioned March 2, 1859; died June 2, 1859.
William J. Allen.... ....Commissioned June 24, 1859, vice Willis Allen.
Andrew D. Duff... ....Commissioned July 1, 1861, and June 27, 1867.

TWENTY-SEVENTH CIRCUIT.

Oliver L. Davis..........Commissioned March 22, 1861, and July 1, 1861; resigned Aug —, 1866.
James Steele..........................Commissioned Aug. 6, 1866, vice Davis; and June 27, 1867.

TWENTY-EIGHTH CIRCUIT.

Isaac G. Wilson...................................... ....Commissioned July 1, 1861.
Sylvanus Wilcox ....Commissioned June 14, 1867.

[No record of the establishment of the Twenty-ninth Circuit, or the commission of judges can be found.]

THIRTIETH CIRCUIT.

Benjamin S. Edwards...........................Commissioned April 9, 1869; resigned June 1, 1870.
John A. McClernand...Commissioned July 12, 1870.

JUDGES OF THE CIRCUIT COURTS

ELECTED OR APPOINTED UNDER THE CONSTITUTION OF 1870.

The General Assembly, by act of March 28, 1873, divided the State into twenty-six judicial circuits, in each of which one judge of the circuit court was elected on the 2d day of June, 1873, for the term of six years, as follows:

1. William Brown .... Rockford
2. Theodore D. Murphy.........Woodstock
3. William W. Heaton.............. ..Dixon
4. *Sylvanus Wilcox.................. ..Elgin
   †Hiram H. Cody ....Naperville
5. George W. Pleasants... .....Rock Island
6. Edwin S. Leland ....Ottawa
7. Josiah McRoberts ....Joliet
8. Arthur A. Smith ....Galesburg
9. Joseph W. Cochran ....Peoria
10. Joseph Sibley.........................Quincy
11. Chauncey L. Higbee... ....Pittsfield
12. John Burns ....Lacon
13. Nathaniel J. Pillsbury............Pontiac
14. *Thomas F. Tipton.........Bloomington
    ‡Owen T. Reeves............Bloomington
15. Oliver L. Davis............... ....Danville
16. Charles B. Smith............ .Champaign
17. Lyman Lacy..........................Havana
18. Cyrus Epler..................Jacksonville
19. Charles S. Zane ....Springfield
20. Horatio M. Vandeveer.... ...Taylorville
21. James C. Allen...................Palestine
22. Wm. H. Snyder .. .. Belleville
23. Amos Watts..........................Nashville
24. Tazewell B. Tanner ....Mt. Vernon
25. Monroe C. Crawford...........Jonesboro
26. David J. Baker....... ....Cairo

* Resigned. † Vice Wilcox. ‡ Vice Tipton.

JUDGES OF THE CIRCUIT COURTS

In the thirteen judicial circuits created by the act of 1877; with dates of commission and residence. Dates beginning with 1885 and all following, indicate date of election.

FIRST CIRCUIT.

David J. Baker..June 16, '73; Cairo; resigned Aug. 13, '78.
Monroe C. Crawford..June 16, '73; Jonesboro
John Dougherty..... Aug. 20, '77; Jonesboro
Oliver A. Harker....Aug. 26, '78; Vienna; vice Baker.
David J. Baker ....June 16, '79; Cairo
D. M. Browning..........June 16, '79; Benton
Oliver A. Harker. ....June 16, '79; Vienna
David J. Baker...June 1, '85; Cairo; resigned
Oliver A. Harker..........June 1, '85; Vienna
Robt. W. McCartney ..June 1, '85; Metropolis
Geo. W. Young ......Nov. 6, '88; Marion; vice Baker.
Oliver A. Harker..... ... June 1, '91; Vienna
Joseph P. Robarts ...June 1, '91; Mound City
Alonzo K. Vickers ....June 1, '91; Vienna

SECOND CIRCUIT.

Tazewell B. Tanner..June 16, '73; Mt. Vernon
James C. Allen...... ...June 16, '73; Palestine
John H. Halley..........Aug. 20, '77; Newton
Chauncey S. Conger ......June 16, '79; Carmi
Thomas S. Casey....June 16, '79; Mt. Vernon
William C. Jones ......June 16, '79; Robinson
Chauncy S. Conger ....June 1, '85; Carmi
William C. Jones ...... June 1, '85; Robinson
Carroll C. Boggs.... ....June 1, '85; Fairfield
Carroll C. Boggs.........June 1, '91; Fairfield
Silas Z. Landes ....June 1, '91; Mt. Carmel
Edmund D. Youngblood ...June 1, '91; Shawneetown.

THIRD CIRCUIT.

Amos Watts............June 16, '73; Nashville
William H. Snyder... June 16, '73; Belleville
George W. Wall........Aug. 20, '77; DuQuoin
William H. Snyder...June 16, '79; Belleville
Amos Watts..... .....June 16, '79; Nashville
George W. Wall....... June 16, '79; DuQuoin
William H. Snyder.....June 1, '85; Belleville
Amos Watts......June 1, '85; Nashville; died
George W. Wall..........June 1, '85; DuQuoin
B. R. Burroughs....Jan. 26, '89; Edwardsville; vice Watts.
George W. Wall.........June 1, '91; DuQuoin
B. R. Burroughs.. June 1, '91; Edwardsville
Alonzo S. Wilderman..June 1, '91; Belleville

FOURTH CIRCUIT.

C. B. Smith.... .....June 16, '73; Champaign
Oliver L. Davis..........June 16, '73; Danville
William E. Nelson......Aug. 20, '77; Decatur
Oliver L. Davis..........June 16, '79; Danville
C. B. Smith..........June 16, '79, Champaign
Jacob W. Wilkin.......June 16, '79; Marshall
J. W. Wilkin..June 1, '85; Danville; resigned
Charles B. Smith.....June 1, '85; Champaign
James F. Hughes .... June 1, '85; Mattoon
Edward P. Vail. .. June 4, '88; Decatur; vice Wilkins.
Ferdinand Bookwalter...June 1, '91; Danville
Edward P. Vail...........June 1, '91; Decatur
Francis M. Wright ...... June 1, '91; Urbana

FIFTH CIRCUIT.

H. M. Vandeveer. ...June 16, '73; Taylorville
Charles S. Zane .....June 16, '73; Springfield
Wm. R. Welch ....Aug. 20, '77; Carlinville
C. S. Zane..June 16, '79; Springfield; resigned
Wm. R. Welch ....June 16, '79; Carlinville
Jesse J. Phillips ....June 16, '79; Hillsboro
Wm. R. Welch ..June 1, '85; Carlinville; died
Jesse J. Phillips........June 1, '85; Hillsboro
James A. Creighton ..June 1, '85; Springfield
W. L. Gross...Appointed Sept. 1, '84; Springfield; vice Zane.
J. Fouke...Nov. 6, '88; Vandalia; vice Welch
Jacob Fouke.. ....June 1, '91; Vandalia
Jesse J. Phillips...June 1, '91; Hillsboro; resigned.
James A. Creighton..June 1, '91; Springfield
R. B. Shirley....July 31, '93; Carlinville; vice Phillips.

SIXTH CIRCUIT.

Chauncey L. Higbee...June 16, '73; Pittsfield
Joseph Sibley.............June 16, '73; Quincy
Simeon P. Shope.....Aug. 20, '77; Lewistown
Simeon P. Shope.....June 16, '79; Lewistown
Chauncey L. Higbee...June 16, '79; Pittsfield
John H. Williams........June 16, '79; Quincy
William Marsh............ June 1, '85; Quincy
Charles J. Scofield......June 1, '85; Carthage
John C. Bagby...........June 1, '85; Rushville
Oscar P. Bonney...........June 1, '91; Quincy
Charles J. Scofield......June 1, '91; Carthage
Jefferson Orr............June 1, '91; Pittsfield

SEVENTH CIRCUIT.

Cyrus Epler.........June 16, '73; Jacksonville
Lyman Lacy............ June 16, '73; Havana
Albert G. Burr.........Aug. 20, '77; Carrollton
Albert G. Burr........June 16, '79; Carrollton
Cyrus Epler.........June 16, '79; Jacksonville
Lyman Lacy..............June 16, '79; Havana
Cyrus Epler..........June 1, '85; Jacksonville
Lyman Lacy...............June 1, '85; Havana
George W. Herdman..June 1, '85; Jerseyville
Cyrus Epler..........June 1, '91; Jacksonville
Lyman Lacy...............June 1, '91; Havana
George W. Herdman..June 1, '91; Jerseyville

EIGHTH CIRCUIT.

John Burns ....June 16, '73; Lacon
Joseph W. Cochran ... ..June 16, '73; Peoria
David McCulloch..........Aug. 20, '77; Peoria
David McCulloch..........June 16, '79; Peoria
John Burns...... ....June 16, '79; Lacon
Milton M. Laws............June 16, '79; Lacon
Thomas M. Shaw...........June 1, '85; Lacon
Samuel S. Page..June 1, '85; Peoria; resigned
Nathaniel W. Green........June 1, '85; Pekin
L. W. James..April 1, '90; Peoria; vice Page
Nathaniel W. Green........June 1, '91; Pekin
Thomas M. Shaw...........June 1, '91; Lacon
Nicholas E. Worthington..June 1, '91; Peoria

NINTH CIRCUIT.

Josiah McRoberts..........June 16, '73; Joliet
Edwin S. Leland..........June 16, '73; Ottawa
Francis Goodspeed.. .....Aug. 20, '77; Joliet
George W. Stipp......June 16, '79; Princeton
Josiah McRoberts........ .June 16, '79; Joliet
Francis Goodspeed.........June 16, '79; Joliet
Josiah McRoberts....June 1, '85; Joliet, died
Charles Blanchard........June 1, '85; Ottawa
George W. Stipp.......June 1, '85; Princeton
Dorrance Dibell. .....Nov. 3, '85; Joliet, vice McRoberts.
George W. Stipp.......June 1, '91; Princeton
Charles Blanchard........June 1, '91; Ottawa
Dorrance Dibell....... ......June 1, 91; Joliet

TENTH CIRCUIT.

Arthur A. Smith.......June 16, '73; Galesburg
Geo. W. Pleasants..June 16, '73; Rock Island
John J. Glenn.........Aug. 20, '77; Monmouth
Geo. W. Pleasants .June 16, '79; Rock Island
Arthur A. Smith.......June 16, '79; Galesburg
Geo. W. Pleasants...June 1, '85; Rock Island
John J Glenn..........June 1, '85, Monmouth
Arthur A. Smith........June 1. '85; Galesburg
Arthur A. Smith..June 1, '91; res. Nov. 15, '94
John J. Glenn.......... June 1, '91; Monmouth
Geo. W. Pleasants....June 1, '91, Rock Island
Hiram Bigelow..Jan. 7, '95; Galva; vice Smith

ELEVENTH CIRCUIT.

Owen T. Reeves ..March 6, '77; Bloomington
Nathaniel J. Pillsbury...June 16, '73; Pontiac
Franklin Blades ....Aug. 20, '77; Watseka
Franklin Blades ....June 16, '79; Watseka
Nathaniel J. Pillsbury..June 16, '79; Pontiac
Owen T. Reeves....June 16, '79; Bloomington
Owen T. Reeves....June 1, '85; Bloomington
Alfred Sample.. ....June 1, '85; Paxton
Nathaniel J. Pillsbury....June 1, '85; Pontiac
Thos. F. Tipton....June 1, '91; Bloomington
Alfred Sample.... ....June 1, '91; Paxton
Charles R. Starr.........June 1, '91; K'kakee

TWELFTH CIRCUIT.

Theo. D. Murphy....June 16, '73; Woodstock
Hiram H. Cody ......Sept. 15, '74; Naperville
Clark W. Upton .... Aug. 20, '77; Waukegan
Clark W. Upton .....June 16, '79; Waukegan
Isaac G. Wilson...........June 16, '79; Geneva
Charles Kellum ....June 16, '79; Sycamore
Isaac G. Wilson..... . ...June 1, '85; Geneva
Clark W. Upton...... June 1, '85; Waukegan
Charles Kellum ....June 1, '85; Sycamore
Charles Kellum ....June 1, '91; Sycamore
Clark W. Upton.......June 1, '91; Waukegan
Henry B. Willis..............June 1, '91; Elgin

THIRTEENTH CIRCUIT.

Wm. W. Heaton ....June 16, '73; Dixon; died
Wm. Brown............June 16, '73; Rockford
Joseph M. Bailey.......Aug. 20, '77; Freeport
J. V. Eustace........March 1, '78; Dixon; vice Heaton.
John V. Eustace...........June 16, '79; Dixon
William Brown ....June 16, '79; Rockford
Joseph M. Bailey.......June 16, '79; Freeport
J. M. Bailey...June 1, '85; Freeport; resigned
William Brown......... June 1, '85; Rockford
J. V. Eustace..........June 1, '85; Dixon; died
J. D. Crabtree..June 4, '88. Dixon; vice Bailey
J. H. Cartwright......June 4, '88; Oregon, vice Eustace.
James H. Cartwright.....June 1, '91; resigned
John D. Crabtree............June 1, '91; Dixon
James Shaw............June 1, '91; Mt. Carroll
J. C. Garver....April 7, '96; Rockford; vice Cartwright.

JUDGES OF COOK COUNTY CIRCUIT COURT.

William W. Farwell................Aug. 11, '71.
Henry Booth........ ....Aug. 11, '71
John G. Rogers ....Aug. 11, '71
Lambert Tree........................Dec. 1, '71
Erastus S. Williams...... ....Jan. 16, '73
Henry Booth.......... ....Jan. 16, '73
John G. Rogers.... ....Jan. 16, '73
William W. Farwell. ....Jan. 16, '73
*Lambert Tree..........................Jan. 16, '73
†William K. McAllister............Nov. 26, '75
William K. McAllister............June 16, '79
John G. Rogers.............. .....June 16, '79
Thomas A. Moran...... ....June 16, '79
Murray F. Tuley....................June 16, '79
‡William H. Barnum.... ....June 16, '79
§Lorin C. Collins, Jr. ..... Elected Dec. 2, '84
John G. Rogers...June 1, '85; died Jan. 10 '87
Thomas A. Moran...................June 1, '85
Murray F. Tuley.................. June 1, '85
Lorin C. Collins, Jr.................June 1, '85
Wm. K. McAllister.June 1, '85; died Oct. 29, '88
R. S. Tuthill.. ....April '87; Vice Rogers
¶R. W. Clifford.........................June 6, '87
¶Frank Baker. ....June 6, '87
**¶Rollin S. Williamson. ....June 6, '87
¶A. N. Waterman................. .June 6, '87
¶Oliver H. Horton....................June 6, '87
††¶Julius S. Grinnell...............June 6, '87
‖George Driggs.................... Nov. 23, '89
S. P. McConnell..April 2, '89; Vice McAllister
Murray F. Tuley......................June 1, '91
Richard W. Clifford.................June 1, '91
Oliver H. Horton....... ....June 1, '91
Richard S. Tuthill....................June 1, '91
Francis Adams....... ....June 1, '91
Frank Baker.................. ......June 1, '91
S. P. McConnell....June 1, '91; res. Oct. 8, '94
Lorin C. Collins, Jr.....June 1, '91; resigned
Arba N. Waterman. ....June 1, '91
George Driggs...............June 1, '91; died
Thomas A. Moran..June 1, '91; res. Apr. 13, '92
Thos. G. Windes..........Dec. 1, '92, (com.)
Edward F. Dunne.........Dec. 1, '92, (com.)
Edmund W. Burke..Nov. 7, '93; vice Collins
John Gibbons ....Nov. 7, '93
Elbridge Haneey ....Nov. 7, '93
Abner Smith....... ....Nov. 7, '93
C. G. Neeley......April 2, '95, vice McConnell

* Resigned Sept. 1, 1875. † Vice Tree. ‡ Resigned Dec. 1, 1884. § Vice Barnum.
** Died Oct. 9, 1889. †† Resigned May 11, 1891. ‖ Vice Williamson. ¶ Act. May 4, 1887.

JUDGES OF THE SUPERIOR COURT OF COOK COUNTY—COMMISSIONED.

Joseph E. Gary........ } Designated by the
John A. Jamieson...... } Constitution of 1870
Samuel H. Moore.. .. .. .Dec. 1, '73
Joseph E. Gary..... ... .Dec. 1, '75
John A. Jamieson...............Nov. 24, '77
Sidney Smith....... .... .Nov. 22, '79
Rollin S. Williamson..............Nov. 23, '80
Elliott Anthony.......... ....Nov. 30, '80
Kirk Hawes........................Dec. 1, '80
George Gardner....................Dec. 1, '80
Joseph E. Gary ....Dec. 1, '81
Henry M. Shepard........... .....Nov. 21, '83
Gwynne Garnett........Nov. 16, '85; resigned
Elliott Anthony ....Dec. 6, '86
Kirk Hawes...........................Dec. 6, '86
Egbert Jamieson...... Dec. 6, '86; resigned
John P. Altgeld..........Dec. 6, '86; resigned
Joseph E. Gary ....Nov. 28, '87
Henry M. Shepard....................Nov. 23, '89
Geo. H. Kettelle..Nov. 26, '90; vice Jamieson
Theodore Brentano.Nov. 26, '90; vice Garnett
Theodore Brentano......... ......Nov. 20, '91
Jonas Hutchinson..Nov. 20, '91; vice Altgeld
Philip Stein. . ...Dec. 1, '92
William G. Ewing.......... .. ..Dec. 1, '92
Jonas Hutchinson....................Dec. 1, '92
George F. Sugg......... .....Dec. 1, '92; died
James Goggin...................... . Dec 1, '92
George H. Kettelle. ....Dec 1, '92; died
Arthur H. Chetlain..Nov. 25, '93; vice Kettelle
Henry V. Freeman.....Nov. 25, '93; vice Sugg
John Barton Payne...............Nov. 25, '93
Nathaniel C. Sears. ....Nov. 29, '93
George E. Blanke..Nov. 29, '93; dec. July 28, '95
Joseph E. Gary............ ....Nov. 28, '93
Farlin Q. Ball........Nov. 16, '95; vice Blanke
Henry M. Shepard....................Nov. 16, '95

JUDGES OF APPELLATE COURTS.—DATE OF ASSIGNMENTS.

FIRST DISTRICT.

W. W. Heaton, Dixon..... ....Sept. '77
Geo. W. Pleasants, Rock Island ....Sept. '77
Theo. D. Murphy, Woodstock.......Sept. '77
Joseph M. Bailey, Freeport.... .... June '79
Isaac G. Wilson, Geneva............ June '79
William K. McAllister, Chicago......June '79
Joseph M. Bailey, Freeport ... .June '82
Isaac G. Wilson, Geneva..............June '82
William K. McAllister, Chicago......June '82
Joseph M. Bailey, Freeport ....June '85
Isaac G. Wilson, Geneva..............June '85
William K. McAllister, Chicago......June '85
William K. McAllister, Chicago......June '88
Thomas A. Moran, Chicago...........June '88
Gwynne Garnett, Chicago ....June '88
Joseph E. Gary, Chicago ....June '91
Thomas A. Moran, Chicago...........June '91
Arba N. Waterman, Chicago....... ..June '91
Joseph E. Gary, Chicago..............June '94
Arba N. Waterman, Chicago ....June '94
Henry M. Shepard, Chicago. . .....June '94

SECOND DISTRICT.

Edwin S. Leland, Ottawa....... .....Sept. '77
Nathaniel J. Pillsbury, Pontiac......Sept. '77
Joseph Sibley, Quincy............... Sept. '77
Nathaniel J. Pillsbury, Pontiac. ...June '79
Geo. W. Pleasants, Rock Island . ...June '79
Lyman Lacy, Havana .... .June '79
Nathaniel J. Pillsbury, Pontiac.......June '82
Geo. W. Pleasants, Rock Island .....June '82
Lyman Lacy, Havana ....June '82
David J. Baker, Cairo..................June '85
Lyman Lacy, Havana ....June '85
Wm. R. Welch, Carlinville...........June '85
Lyman Lacy, Havana .... .June '88
Murray F. Tuley, Chicago............June '88
Clark W. Upton, Waukegan ....June '88
*C. B. Smith, Champaign...... ......June '88
Lyman Lacy, Havana ....June '91
James H. Cartwright, Oregon.. .....June '91
Oliver A. Harker, Vienna.............June '91
Lyman Lacy, Havana ....June '94
†James H. Cartwright, Oregon........June '94
Oliver A. Harker, Vienna........ .....June '94

THIRD DISTRICT.

Chauncey L. Higbee, Pittsfield......Sept. '77
Oliver L. Davis, Danville.............Sept. '77
Lyman Lacy, Havana.................Sept. '77
Chauncey L. Higbee, Pittsfield.......June '79
Oliver L. Davis, Danville.............June '79
David McCulloch, Peoria ....June '79
Chauncey L. Higbee, Pittsfield.......June '82
Oliver L. Davis, Danville.............June '82
David McCulloch, Peoria. ....June '82
Geo. W. Pleasants, Rock Island.... .June '85
Chauncey S. Conger, Carmi ....June '85
George W. Wall, DuQuoin............June '85
Geo. W. Pleasants, Rock Island......June '88
Chauncey S. Conger, Carmi...........June '88
George W. Wall, DuQuoin........... June '88
George W. Wall, DuQuoin............June '91
Geo. W. Pleasants, Rock Island......June '91
Carroll C. Boggs, Fairfield............June '91
George W. Wall, DuQuoin.......... .June '94
Geo. W. Pleasants, Rock Island......June '94
Carroll C. Boggs, Fairfield............June '94

FOURTH DISTRICT.

James C. Allen, Palestine...... .... .Sept. '77
Tazewell B. Tanner, Mt. Vernon.....Sept. '77
George W. Wall, DuQuoin............Sept. '77
George W Wall, DuQuoin.............June '79
David J. Baker, Cairo..................June '79
Thomas S. Casey, Mt. Vernon........June '79
David J. Baker, Cairo............ .June '82
Thomas S. Casey, Mt. Vernon........June '82
George W Wall, DuQuoin............June '82
Nathaniel W. Green, Pekin............June '85
Jacob W. Wilkin, Marshall...........June '85
Nathaniel J. Pillsbury, Pontiac .. ...June '85
Nathaniel W. Green, Pekin ....June '88
Jesse J. Phillips, Hillsboro. ....June '88
Owen T. Reeves, Bloomington...... .June '88
Nathaniel W. Green, Pekin ....June '91
Jesse J. Phillips, Hillsboro ....June '91
Alfred Sample, Paxton...... .... .June '91
Nathaniel W. Green, Pekin...........June '94
Alfred Sample, Paxton.................June '94
Charles J. Scofield, Carthage....... .June '94

* Vice Tuley, relieved at his own request.
† Resigned; John D. Crabtree, Dixon, assigned.

CLERKS OF THE SUPREME COURT.

Prior to the adoption of the constitution of 1848 the Clerk of the Supreme Court was appointed by the court. Since 1848 one clerk has been elected in each of the three Grand Divisions. The records as to dates of appointments are somewhat obscure. James M. Duncan was appointed July 12, 1819. Ebenezer Peck appears as the successor of Mr. Duncan. Wm. B. Warren seems to have been the successor of Mr. Peck.

ELECTIONS UNDER THE CONSTITUTION OF 1848.

First Grand Division.

Finney D. Preston..........Sept. 4, 1848
Noah Johnson..........June 4, 1855
Noah Johnson..........June 3, 1861
Robert A. D. Wilbanks..........June 3, 1867

Second Grand Division.

Wm. B. Warren..........Sept. 4, 1848
Wm. A. Turner..........June 4, 1855
Wm. A. Turner..........June 3, 1861
Wm. A. Turner..........June 3, 1867

Third Grand Division.

Lorenzo Leland..........Sept. 4, 1848
Lorenzo Leland..........June 4, 1855
Lorenzo Leland..........June 3, 1861
Woodbury M. Taylor..........June 3, 1867

ELECTIONS UNDER THE CONSTITUTION OF 1870.

Under the constitution of 1870 the Grand Divisions were continued, and designated as the Southern, Central and Northern.

Southern Grand Division.

Robert A. D. Wilbanks, dem..........Nov. 5, 1872
Jacob O. Chance, dem..........Nov. 5, 1878
Jacob O. Chance, dem..........Nov. 4, 1884
Frank W. Havill, dem., Mt. Carmel, Nov. 4, 1890
Jacob O. Chance, dem., Mt. Vernon, Nov. 3, 1896

Central Grand Division.

Emanuel C. Hamburger, rep..........Nov. 5, 1872
Ethan A. Snively, dem..........Nov. 5, 1878
Ethan A. Snively, dem..........Nov. 4, 188
E. A. Snively, dem., Carlinville...Nov. 4, 1890
Albert D. Cadwallader, rep., Lincoln..........Nov. 3, 1896

Northern Grand Division.

Cairo D. Trimble, rep..........Nov. 5, 1872
Everell F. Dutton, rep..........Nov. 5, 1878
Alfred H. Taylor, rep..........Nov. 4, 1884
Alfred H. Taylor, rep..........Nov. 4, 1890
Christopher Mamer, rep., Chicago, Nov. 3, 1896

CLERKS OF THE APPELLATE COURTS.

By the act approved June 2, 1877, in force July 1, for the organization of the Appellate Courts of the State, it was provided that the Supreme Court clerks should also act as Appellate Court clerks until the expiration of the terms for which they were elected—1878—when clerks for both Supreme and Appellate courts were elected for six years, and every six years thereafter. First district, Cook county; second, all of the Northern Division of Supreme Court except Cook county; third, Central Grand Division of the Supreme Court; fourth, Southern Grand Division of the Supreme Court.

First District—Eli Smith, Chicago, Nov. 5, 1878. John J. Healy, Chicago, Nov 4, 1884. Thos. G. McElligott, dem., Chicago, Nov. 4, 1890. Thomas N. Jamieson, rep., Chicago, Nov. 3, 1896.

Second District—James R. Combs, Ottawa, Nov. 5, 1878; re-elected Nov. 4, 1884. Christopher C. Duffy, rep., Plano, Nov. 4, 1890; re-elected Nov. 3, 1896.

Third District—George W. Jones, dem., Pittsfield, Nov. 5, 1878; re-elected Nov. 4, 1884, and Nov. 4, 1800. William C. Hippard, rep., Marshall, Nov. 3, 1896.

Fourth District—John Q. Harmon, Cairo, Nov. 5, 1878; died. R. A. D. Wilbanks, Mt. Vernon, Nov. 7, 1882, succeeded Harmon, filling out the term. John W. Burton, dem., Marion, Nov. 4, 1884; re-elected Nov. 4, 1890. Frank W. Havill, dem., Mt. Carmel, Nov. 3, 1896.

REPORTERS OF THE SUPREME COURT.

The Reporter of the decisions of the Supreme Court is appointed by the court.

Sidney Breese was first authorized by the court to report and publish its decisions, and published the first volume of the Supreme Court Reports, which includes all the decisions of the court from its first organization, in 1819, to the close of the December term, 1831, and was the only volume published by him.

John Young Scammon, Esq., of Chicago, was appointed by the court, July, 1839, to succeed Judge Breese, and published four volumes, which are known as "Scammon's" Reports.

Charles Gilman, Esq., of Quincy, Illinois, succeeded Mr. Scammon, who had resigned, and was appointed Jan. 30, 1845. Mr. Gilman died July 24, 1849, when the fifth volume of his report was about four-fifths completed. Charles B. Lawrence, at the request of the administrators of the estate of Mr. Gilman, and the approbation of the court, completed the volume and superintended its publication. Mr. Gilman published five volumes, which are known as "Gilman's" Reports.

Ebenezer Peck, Esq., of Chicago, succeeded Mr. Gilman in 1849. Mr. Peck adopted the title of "Illinois Reports," which has continued since, and published his first number as "Illinois Reports—Volume XI." The last volume published by Mr. Peck was Volume XXX. Mr. Peck resigned in April, 1863.

Norman L. Freeman, Esq., was appointed in April, 1863, to succeed Mr. Peck, and was appointed from time to time by the court as his own successor, until his death, which occurred in Springfield, Aug. 23, 1894. Mr. Freeman issued Volume XXXI. of the Illinois Reports, and the last volume was the 151st.

On Oct. 24, 1894, the court appointed Isaac N. Phillips, of Bloomington, as Reporter, and he is the present incumbent.

STATE BOARDS OF EQUALIZATION.

The State Board of Equalization was organized by act of the General Assembly, approved March 8, 1867. As at first composed, the board consisted of twenty-five members, one elected from each Senatorial district. In 1872 the law was so amended as to reduce the number of members to nineteen, one being elected from each Congressional district. The first board, under the act of 1867, was appointed by the Governor and held office two years. Since the first board, the term has been four years. The Auditor of Public Accounts is, *ex-officio*, a member of the board.

The duties of the board are to equalize the assessment between counties, by adding or deducting the per cent. necessary to do so. The board is prohibited by law from reducing the aggregate assessment, but may increase it not to exceed one per cent. The board makes the assessment upon capital stock of incorporated companies and railroad property. The sessions of the board are held annually, in August.

STATE BOARD OF EQUALIZATION 1867-1868.

Chairman—Orlin H. Miner. *Secretary*—William Stadden.

Dist.	Name.	Postoffice.	Dist.	Name.	Postoffice.
1	William H. Parish	Raleigh	14	Harvey S. Senter	Aledo
2	Jasper Partridge	Carmi	15	Rufus W. Miles	Knoxville
3	Robert Kirkman	Carbondale	16	E. H. Clapp	Rome
4	Thomas H. Burgess	DuQuoin	17	Charles H. Gilman	Mendota
5	Frederick E. Scheil	Belleville	18	William P. Caton	Plainfield
6	James H. Vanarsdale	Carrollton	19	Needham N. Ravlin	Kanesville
7	Joseph C. Howell	Carlinville	20	Henry R. Sampson	Morrison
8	E. Callahan	Robinson	21	Holmes O. Sleight	Cambridge
9	William Hancock	Brushy Fork	22	John D. Platt	Warren
10	Henry B. Durfee	Decatur	23	James Y. Cory	Waukegan
11	Tels Smith	Pekin	24	Charles B. Farwell	Chicago
12	William H. Ray	Rushville	25	Henry Greenebaum	Chicago
13	John M. Ferris	Carthage		Orlin H. Miner, *ex-officio*	Springfield

STATE BOARD OF EQUALIZATION, 1868-1872.

Chairman—Charles E. Lippincott. *Secretary*—William Stadden.

Dist.	Name.	Postoffice.	Dist.	Name.	Postoffice.
1	Thomas Wilson	Cairo	15	Rufus W. Miles	Knoxville
2	William Friend	Mier	16	Ela H. Clapp	Rome
3	Henry C. Talbott	Waterloo	17	James Piper	Low Point
4	Zebedee P. Curlee	Tamaroa	18	Ira C. Mosier	Wilmington
5	Irwin B. Randle	Upper Alton	19	‡Wash. L. Simmons	Sandwich
6	William H. Reed	Vedder		§James H. Furman	Sandwich
7	Bushrod W. Henry	Shelbyville	20	Leander A. Devine	Dixon
8	Joseph J. Petri	Hutsonville	21	Holmes O. Sleight	Cambridge
9	William Hancock	Brushy Fork	22	‡John D. Platt	Warren
10	Henry B. Durfee	Decatur	23	‡W. A. McConnell	Richmond
11	*Tels Smith	Pekin		¶C. O. Parsons	McHenry
	†John T. Jenkins	Lincoln	24	Andrew H. Dolton	Dolton Stat'n
12	Archibald A. Glenn	Mt. Sterling	25	Homer Wilmarth	Barrington
13	Alpha Forsyth	Chili		Chas. E. Lippincott, *ex-officio*	Springfield
14	Benj. A. Griffith	Blandinsville			

* Died. † Vice Smith. ‡ Resigned. § Vice Simmons. ¶ Vice McConnell.

CONGRESS OF THE UNITED STATES.

APPORTIONMENT OF REPRESENTATIVES FROM ILLINOIS.

The State of Illinois, until the year 1832, constituted one congressional district.

APPORTIONMENT UNDER THE ACT OF 1831.

By the act approved Feb. 13, 1831, the State was divided into three districts. First election, first Monday in August, 1832.

1. Gallatin, Pope, Johnson, Alexander, Union, Jackson, Franklin, Perry, Randolph, Monroe, St. Clair, Washington, Clinton, Bond, Madison and Macoupin.
2. White, Hamilton, Jefferson, Wayne, Edwards, Wabash, Lawrence, Clay, Marion, Fayette, Montgomery, Shelby, Vermilion, Edgar, Coles, Clark and Crawford.
3. Greene, Morgan, Sangamon, Tazewell, Macon, McLean, LaSalle, Cook, Putnam, Peoria, Henry, Knox, JoDaviess, Mercer, Warren, Hancock, McDonough, Fulton, Schuyler, Adams, Pike and Calhoun.

APPORTIONMENT UNDER THE ACT OF 1843.

By the act of March 1, 1843, the State was divided into seven districts. First election, first Monday in August, 1843.

1. Alexander, Union, Jackson, Perry, Randolph, Monroe, Washington, St. Clair, Bond and Madison.
2. Johnson, Pope, Hardin, Williamson, Gallatin, Franklin, Hamilton, White, Wabash, Edwards, Wayne, Jefferson, Marion and Massac.
3. Lawrence, Richland, Crawford, Jasper, Effingham, Fayette, Montgomery, Christian, Shelby, Moultrie, Coles, Clark, Clay, Edgar, Macon, Piatt and DeWitt.
4. Lake, McHenry, Boone, Cook, Kane, DeKalb, DuPage, Kendall, Grundy, LaSalle, Will, Iroquois, Livingston, McLean, Champaign, Vermilion and Bureau.
5. Greene, Jersey, Calhoun, Pike, Adams, Marquette, Brown, Schuyler, Fulton, Peoria and Macoupin.
6. JoDaviess, Stephenson, Winnebago, Carroll, Ogle, Lee, Whiteside, Rock Island, Henry, Stark, Mercer, Henderson, Warren, Knox, McDonough and Hancock.
7. Putnam, Marshall, Woodford, Tazewell, Mason, Menard, Cass, Morgan, Scott, Logan and Sangamon.

APPORTIONMENT UNDER THE ACT OF 1852.

y the act of Aug. 22, 1852, the State was divided into nine districts. The first election, November, 1852.

1. Lake, McHenry, Boone, Winnebago, Stephenson, JoDaviess, Carroll and Ogle.
2. Cook, DuPage, Kane, DeKalb, Lee, Whiteside and Rock Island.
3. Will, Kendall, Grundy, LaSalle, Putnam, Bureau, Livingston, Iroquois, Vermilion, Champaign, McLean and DeWitt.
4. Fulton, Peoria, Knox, Henry, Stark, Warren, Mercer, Marshall, Woodford, Mason and Tazewell.
5. Adams, Pike, Calhoun, Brown, Schuyler, McDonough, Hancock and Henderson.
6. Morgan, Scott, Sangamon, Macoupin, Greene, Montgomery, Christian, Shelby, Cass, Menard and Jersey.
7. Logan, Macon, Piatt, Moultrie, Coles, Edgar, Clark, Cumberland, Effingham, Jasper, Clay, Crawford, Lawrence, Richland and Fayette.
8. Randolph, Monroe, St. Clair, Madison, Bond, Clinton, Washington, Jefferson and Marion.
9. Alexander, Pulaski, Massac, Union, Johnson, Pope, Hardin, Gallatin, Saline, Williamson, Jackson, Perry, Franklin, Hamilton, White, Wayne, Edwards and Wabash.

APPORTIONMENT UNDER THE ACT of 1861.

By the act of April 24, 1861, the State was divided into thirteen districts. The first election was held in November, 1862. By an error in the apportionment, the number of Representatives was fixed at thirteen, though the State was entitled to fourteen. The error was corrected by electing one member from the State at large.

1. Cook.
2. Lake, McHenry, Boone, Winnebago, DeKalb and Kane.
3. JoDaviess, Stephenson, Carroll, Ogle, Lee and Whiteside.
4. Adams, Hancock, Warren, Henderson, Mercer and Rock Island.
5. Peoria, Knox, Stark, Marshall, Putnam, Bureau and Henry.
6. LaSalle, Grundy, Kendall, DuPage, Will and Kankakee.
7. Macon, Piatt, Champaign, Douglas, Moultrie, Coles, Cumberland, Edgar, Vermilion, Iroquois and Ford.
8. Sangamon, Logan, DeWitt, McLean, Tazewell, Woodford and Livingston.
9. Fulton, Mason, Menard, Cass, McDonough, Schuyler, Brown and Pike.
10. Bond, Morgan, Scott, Calhoun, Jersey, Greene, Macoupin, Montgomery, Christian and Shelby.
11. Marion, Fayette, Clay, Richland, Jasper, Clark, Crawford, Lawrence, Wayne, Hamilton, Franklin, Jefferson and Effingham.
12. St. Clair, Madison, Clinton, Washington, Randolph and Monroe.
13. Alexander, Pulaski, Union, Johnson, Williamson, Jackson, Perry, Massac, Pope, Hardin, Saline, Gallatin, White, Edwards and Wabash.

APPORTIONMENT UNDER THE ACT OF 1872.

By the act of July 1, 1872, the State was divided into nineteen districts. The first election was held in November, 1872.

1. First, Second, Third, Fourth, Fifth, Sixth and Seventh Wards of Chicago, the towns of Hyde Park, Lake, Lyons, Riverside, Lemont, Palos, Worth, Calumet, Orland, Bremen, Thornton, Rich and Bloom, in Cook county, and the county of DuPage.
2. Eighth, Ninth, Tenth, Eleventh, Twelfth, Thirteenth, Fourteenth and Fifteenth Wards of Chicago.
3. Sixteenth, Seventeenth, Eighteenth, Nineteenth and Twentieth Wards of Chicago, the towns of Cicero, Proviso, Jefferson, Leyden, Lake View, Evanston, Niles, Maine, Elk Grove, Schaumburg, Hanover, Barrington, Palatine, Wheeling, Northfield and New Trier, in Cook county and the county of Lake.
4. Kane, DeKalb, McHenry, Boone and Winnebago.
5. Stephenson, JoDaviess, Carroll, Whiteside and Ogle.
6. Lee, Bureau, Putnam, Henry and Rock Island.
7. LaSalle, Kendall, Grundy and Will.
8. Kankakee, Iroquois, Ford, Livingston, Woodford and Marshall.
9. Stark, Peoria, Knox and Fulton.
10. Mercer, Henderson, Warren, Hancock, McDonough and Schuyler.
11. Adams, Brown, Pike, Calhoun, Greene and Jersey.
12. Scott, Morgan, Cass, Menard, Sangamon and Christian.
13. Mason, Tazewell, McLean, Logan and DeWitt.
14. Macon, Piatt, Champaign, Douglas, Coles and Vermilion.
15. Edgar, Clark, Cumberland, Moultrie, Shelby, Effingham, Jasper, Crawford and Lawrence.
16. Montgomery, Fayette, Bond, Clinton, Washington, Marion and Clay.
17. Macoupin, Madison, St. Clair and Monroe.
18. Randolph, Perry, Jackson, Union, Williamson, Johnson, Pope, Massac, Pulaski and Alexander.
19. Richland, Wayne, Edwards, Wabash, Jefferson, Franklin, Hamilton, White, Saline, Gallatin and Hardin.

APPORTIONMENT UNDER THE ACT OF 1882.

By the act of April 29, 1882, the State was divided into twenty districts. The first election was held in November, 1882.

1. First, Second, Third and Fourth Wards in Chicago, the towns of Riverside, Hyde Park, Lake, Lyons, Calumet, Worth, Palos, Lemont, Thornton, Bremen, Orland, Bloom and Rich in Cook county.
2. Fifth, Sixth and Seventh Wards in Chicago, and that part of the Eighth Ward which is south of the center of Polk street and the center of Macalester Place.
3. Ninth, Tenth, Eleventh, Twelfth, Thirteenth and Fourteenth Wards in Chicago, and that part of the Eighth Ward in Chicago which is north of the center of Polk street and the center of Macalester Place.
4. Fifteenth, Sixteenth, Seventeenth and Eighteenth Wards in Chicago, and the towns of Lakeview, Jefferson, Leyden, Norwood Park, Evanston, Niles, Maine, Elk Grove, Schaumburg, Hanover, New Trier, Northfield, Wheeling, Palatine, Barrington, Cicero and Proviso, in Cook county.
5. Lake, McHenry, Boone, DeKalb and Kane.
6. Winnebago, Stephenson, JoDaviess, Ogle and Carroll.
7. Lee, Whiteside, Henry, Bureau and Putnam.
8. LaSalle, Kendall, Grundy, Will and DuPage.
9. Kankakee, Iroquois, Ford, Livingston, Woodford and Marshall.
10. Peoria, Knox, Stark and Fulton.
11. Rock Island, Mercer, Henderson, Warren, Hancock, McDonough and Schuyler.
12. Cass, Brown, Adams, Pike, Scott, Greene, Jersey and Calhoun.
13. Tazewell, Mason, Menard, Sangamon, Morgan and Christian.
14. McLean, DeWitt, Platt, Macon and Logan.
15. Coles, Edgar, Douglas, Vermilion and Champaign.
16. Cumberland, Clark, Jasper, Crawford, Clay, Richland, Lawrence, Wayne, Edwards and Wabash.
17. Macoupin, Montgomery, Shelby, Moultrie, Effingham and Fayette.
18. Bond, Madison, St. Clair, Monroe and Washington.
19. Marion, Clinton, Jefferson, Franklin, Hamilton, White, Saline, Gallatin and Hardin.
20. Perry, Randolph, Jackson, Williamson, Union, Johnson, Pope, Alexander, Pulaski and Massac.

APPORTIONMENT UNDER THE ACT OF 1893.

By the act of June 9, 1893, the State was divided into twenty-two districts. The first election was held in November, 1894.

1. The towns of Rich, Bloom, Orland, Bremen, Thornton, Calumet and Worth, in Cook county, and the Fourth ward east of the center line of Wentworth avenue, the Third ward, the Thirty-first ward, the Thirty-second ward, the Thirty-third ward and the Thirty-fourth ward of Chicago.
2. The towns of Lemont, Palos, Lyons, Proviso, Riverside, Cicero, Leyden, Norwood Park, Maine, Elk Grove, Schaumburg and Hanover, in Cook county, and the Tenth, Twenty-eighth, Twenty-ninth and Thirtieth wards of Chicago.
3. First, Second, Fifth, Sixth and Seventh wards and that part of the Fourth ward west of the center line of Wentworth avenue, in Chicago.
4. Eighth, Ninth, Twelfth and Nineteenth wards of Chicago.
5. Eleventh, Thirteenth, Sixteenth, Eighteenth and Seventeenth wards of Chicago.
6. Twentieth, Twenty-first, Twenty-second, Twenty-third and Twenty-fourth wards, also that part of the Twenty-fifth ward south of the center line of Diversey street and west

of the center line of Halsted street, and that part of the Twenty-sixth ward south of the center line of Belmont avenue, in Chicago.

7. Fourteenth, Fifteenth and Twenty-seventh wards, the Twenty-fifth ward except that part south of the center line of Diversey street and west of the center line of Halsted street, that part of the Twenty-sixth ward north of the center line of Belmont avenue, in Chicago; also the towns of Evanston, Niles, New Trier, Northfield, Wheeling, Palatine and Barrington, in Cook county, and the county of Lake.

8. McHenry, DeKalb, Kane, DuPage, Kendall and Grundy.

9. Boone, Winnebago, Stephenson, JoDaviess, Carroll, Ogle and Lee.

10. Whiteside, Rock Island, Mercer, Henry, Knox and Stark.

11. Bureau, LaSalle, Livingston and Woodford.

12. Will, Kankakee, Iroquois and Vermilion.

13. Ford, McLean, DeWitt, Piatt, Champaign and Douglas.

14. Putnam, Marshall, Peoria, Fulton, Tazewell and Mason.

15. Henderson, Warren, Hancock, McDonough, Adams, Brown and Schuyler.

16. Cass, Morgan, Scott, Pike, Greene, Macoupin, Calhoun and Jersey.

17. Menard, Logan, Sangamon, Macon and Christian.

18. Madison, Montgomery, Bond, Fayette, Shelby and Moultrie.

19. Coles, Edgar, Clark, Cumberland, Effingham, Jasper, Crawford, Richland and Lawrence.

20. Clay, Jefferson, Wayne, Hamilton, Edwards, Wabash, Franklin, White, Gallatin and Hardin.

21. Marion, Clinton, Washington, St. Clair, Monroe, Randolph and Perry.

22. Jackson, Union, Alexander, Pulaski, Johnson, Williamson, Saline, Pope and Massac.

MEMBERS OF CONGRESS FROM ILLINOIS.

UNITED STATES SENATORS.

Name.	Term of Service	Residence.	Remarks.
Ninian Edwards, dem	1818-1819.........	Kaskaskia......	....
Jesse B. Thomas, dem.....	1818-1823........	Kaskaskia.....	....
Ninian Edwards, dem.......	1819-1824.........	Edwardsville...	His own successor. Resigned 1824.
Jesse B. Thomas, dem.....	1823-1829.	Edwardsville...	His own successor.
John McLean, dem.........	1824-1825.........	Shawneetown..	Vice Edwards, resigned.
Elias Kent Kane, dem	1825-1831.........	Kaskaskia.. ..	To succeed McLean.
John McLean, dem.........	1829-1830.........	Shawneetown..	Died ——, 1830.
David J. Baker, dem.......	Nov12-Dec.11,'30	Kaskaskia......	Ap'd by Gov. Edw'ds, suc'd McL'n
John M. Robinson, dem....	1830-1835.........	Carmi...........	Elected to succeed McLean.
Elias Kent Kane, dem......	1831-1835.........	Kaskaskia......	Suc'ded himself. Died Dec. 12, '35
John M. Robinson, dem....	1835-1841.........	Carmi...........	His own successor.
Wm. L. D. Ewing, dem....	1835-1837.........	Vandalia.	Vice Kane, deceased.
Richard M. Young, dem....	1837-1843.........	Jonesboro.....	To succeed Ewing.
Samuel McRoberts, dem...	1841-1843.........	Waterloo.......	Vice Robinson. Died Mar. 22, '43
Sidney Breese, dem.........	1843-1849.........	Carlyle.........	To succeed Young.
James Semple, dem.	1843-1847...	Alton............	App'ted vice McRoberts, dec'd.
Stephen A. Douglas, dem..	1847-1853.........	Quincy....	To succeed Semple.
James Shields, dem.........	1849-1855.........	Springfield	To succeed Breese.
Stephen A. Douglas, dem..	1853-1859.........	Chicago.........	His own successor.
L. Trumbull, anti-Neb. dem	1855-1861.........	Belleville.	To succeed Shields.
Stephen A. Douglas, dem..	1859-1861.........	Chicago.........	Suc'd himself. Died June 3, '61.
Lyman Trumbull, rep......	1861-1867.........	Chicago.........	His own successor.
Orville H. Browning, rep ..	1861-1863.........	Quincy..........	App'd vice Douglas June 26, '61.
Wm. A. Richardson, dem..	1863-1865..... ..	Quincy..........	Elected to succeed Browning.
Richard Yates, rep.........	1865-1871.........	Jacksonville...	To succeed Richardson.
Lyman Trumbull, rep......	1867-1873.........	Chicago.........	His own successor.
John A. Logan, rep.........	1871-1877........	Chicago.........	To succeed Yates.
Richard J. Oglesby, rep....	1873-1879.........	Decatur.........	To succeed Trumbull.
David Davis, ind...... ...	1877-1883.........	Bloomington .	To succeed Logan.
John A. Logan, rep..........	1879-1885.........	Chicago.........	To succeed Oglesby.
Shelby M. Cullom, rep......	1883-1889.........	Springfield......	Succeeded Davis.
John A. Logan, rep.........	1885-1886.........	Chicago.........	Died Dec. 26, 1886.
Charles B. Farwell, rep	1887-1891.........	Chicago.........	Elected vice Logan, deceased.
Shelby M. Cullom, rep	1889-1895.........	Springfield......	Succeeded himself.
John M. Palmer, dem	1891-1897.........	Springfield......	Succeeded Farwell.
Shelby M. Cullom, rep	1895-1901.........	Springfield......	Succeeded himself.
William E. Mason Rep.....	1897-1903...	Chicago.........	Succeeded Palmer ....

REPRESENTATIVES TO CONGRESS.

ILLINOIS TERRITORY.

Shadrach Bond was the first delegate to Congress from the territory, serving in the Twelfth and Thirteenth Congresses. He took his seat at the second session of the Twelfth Congress, Dec. 3, 1812, and served until Oct. 3, 1814, when he was appointed receiver of public moneys. Residence, Kaskaskia.

Benjamin Stephenson succeeded Bond, and took his seat at the third session of the Thirteenth Congress, Nov. 14, 1814, and served during the third session of the Thirteenth and first session of the Fourteenth Congresses, when he was also appointed receiver of public moneys April 29, 1816. Residence, Edwardsville.

Nathaniel Pope was elected the successor of Benjamin Stephenson, and entered Congress at the second session of the Fourteenth Congress, Dec. 2, 1816, and served during that session and the first session of the Fifteenth Congress—he being the delegate at the time of the admission of the territory as a State. Residence Kaskaskia.

ILLINOIS STATE.

Daniel P. Cook, dem., was the first Representative to Congress from the State, taking his seat at the second session of the Fifteenth Congress. He continued to represent the State during the Sixteenth, Seventeenth, Eighteenth and Nineteenth Congresses, a period of nearly nine years, being from Dec., 1818, to March, 1827. Residence, Kaskaskia.

Joseph Duncan, dem., succeeded Daniel P. Cook, and took his seat at the first session of the Twentieth Congress in 1827. He represented the State in the Twentieth, Twenty-first and Twenty-second Congresses, being from 1827 to 1833. Residence, Jackson and Morgan counties.

TWENTY-THIRD CONGRESS, 1833-1835.

Dist.	Name.	Residence.	Dist.	Name.	Residence.
1	*Charles Slade, dem...........	Belleville.....	3	‡Joseph Duncan, dem........	Jacksonville.
	†John Reynolds, dem.........	Belleville.....		§Wm. L. May, dem.....	Springfield...
2	Zadok Casey, dem............	Mt. Vernon...			

* Died. † Vice Slade, deceased. ‡ Resigned; elected Governor. § Vice Duncan.

TWENTY-FOURTH CONGRESS, 1835-1837.

Dist.	Name.	Residence.	Dist.	Name.	Residence.
1	John Reynolds, dem.....	Belleville.....	3	Wm. L. May, dem.......	Springfield...
2	Zadok Casey, dem......... ..	Mt. Vernon...			

TWENTY-FIFTH CONGRESS, 1837-1839.

Dist.	Name.	Residence.	Dist.	Name.	Residence.
1	Adam W. Snyder, dem..	Belleville.....	3	Wm. L. May, dem............	Springfield ...
2	Zadok Casey, dem....	Mt. Vernon...			

TWENTY-SIXTH CONGRESS, 1839-41.

Dist.	Name.	Residence.	Dist.	Name.	Residence.
1	John Reynolds, dem..........	Belleville.....	3	John T. Stuart, whig..... ..	Springfield ...
2	Zadok Casey, dem....	Mt. Vernon...			

TWENTY-SEVENTH CONGRESS, 1841-1843.

Dist.	Name.	Residence.	Dist.	Name.	Residence.
1	John Reynolds, dem..........	Belleville.....	3	John T. Stuart, whig..... ...	Springfield ...
2	Zadok Casey, dem....	Mt. Vernon...			

TWENTY-EIGHTH CONGRESS, 1843-1845.

Dist.	Name.	Residence.	Dist.	Name.	Residence.
1	Robert Smith, dem...........	Alton	5	Stephen A. Douglas, dem	Quincy........
2	John A. McClernand, dem...	Shawneet'wn	6	Joseph P. Hoge, dem.........	Galena.......
3	Orlando B. Ficklin, dem.....	Charleston...	7	John J. Hardin, whig....	Jacksonville.
4	John Wentworth, dem........	Chicago			

TWENTY-NINTH CONGRESS, 1845-1847.

Dist.	Name.	Residence.	Dist.	Name.	Residence.
1	Robert Smith, dem	Alton	5	†Wm. A. Richardson, dem	Rushville
2	John A. McClernand, dem	Shawneetown	6	Joseph P. Hoge, dem	Galena
3	Orlando B. Ficklin, dem	Charleston	7	‡Edward D. Baker, whig	Springfield
4	John Wentworth, dem	Chicago		§John Henry, whig	Jacksonville
5	*Stephen A. Douglas, dem	Quincy			

* Resigned April 7, 1847. † Vice Douglas. ‡ Resigned Dec. 30, 1846.
§ Vice Baker, Feb. 5, 1847.

THIRTIETH CONGRESS, 1847-1849.

Dist.	Name.	Residence.	Dist.	Name.	Residence.
1	Robert Smith, dem	Upper Alton	5	Wm. A. Richardson, dem	Rushville
2	John A. McClernand, dem	Shawneetown	6	Thomas J. Turner, dem	Freeport
3	Orlando B. Ficklin, dem	Charleston	7	Abraham Lincoln, whig	Springfield
4	John Wentworth, dem	Chicago			

THIRTY-FIRST CONGRESS, 1849-1851.

Dist.	Name.	Residence.	Dist.	Name.	Residence.
1	Wm. H. Bissell, dem	Belleville	5	Wm. A. Richardson, dem	Rushville
2	John A. McClernand, dem	Shawneetown	6	Edward D. Baker, whig	Galena
3	Timothy R. Young, dem	Marshall	7	Thos. L. Harris, dem	Petersburg
4	John Wentworth, dem	Chicago			

THIRTY-SECOND CONGRESS, 1851-1853.

Dist.	Name.	Residence.	Dist.	Name.	Residence.
1	Wm. H. Bissell, dem	Belleville	5	Wm. A. Richardson, dem	Quincy
2	Willis Allen, dem	Marion	6	Thompson Campbell, dem	Galena
3	Orlando B. Ficklin, dem	Charleston	7	Richard Yates, whig	Jacksonville
4	Richard S. Molony, dem	Belvidere			

THIRTY-THIRD CONGRESS, 1853-1855.

Dist.	Name.	Residence.	Dist.	Name.	Residence.
1	Elihu B. Washburne, whig	Galena	6	Richard Yates, whig	Jacksonville
2	John Wentworth, dem	Chicago	7	James C. Allen, dem	Palestine
3	Jesse O. Norton, rep	Joliet	8	Wm. H. Bissell, dem	Belleville
4	James Knox, rep	Knoxville	9	Willis Allen, dem	Marion
5	Wm. A. Richardson, dem	Quincy			

THIRTY-FOURTH CONGRESS, 1855-1857.

Dist.	Name.	Residence.	Dist.	Name.	Residence.
1	Elihu B. Washburne, rep	Galena	6	Thomas L. Harris, dem	Petersburg
2	James H. Woodworth, dem	Chicago	7	‡James C. Allen, dem	Palestine
3	Jesse O. Norton, rep	Joliet		§James C. Allen, dem	Palestine
4	James Knox, rep	Knoxville	8	¶Lyman Trumbull, dem	Belleville
5	*Wm. A. Richardson, dem	Quincy		‖J. L. D. Morrison, dem	Belleville
	†Jacob C. Davis, dem		9	Samuel S. Marshall, dem	McLeansboro

* Resigned Aug. 18, 1856.
† Vice Richardson, Aug. 25, 1856.
‡ Seat contested; declared vacant.
§ Elected to fill vacancy, Aug. 25, 1856.
¶ Resigned; elected U. S. Senator.
‖ Vice Trumbull.

THIRTY-FIFTH CONGRESS, 1857-1859.

Dist.	Name.	Residence.	Dist.	Name.	Residence.
1	Elihu B. Washburne, rep.	Galena	6	*Thomas L. Harris, dem	Petersburg
2	John F. Farnsworth, rep.	Chicago		†Charles D. Hodges, dem	Carrollton
3	Owen Lovejoy, rep	Princeton	7	Aaron Shaw, dem	Lawrenceville
4	William Kellogg, rep	Canton	8	Robert Smith, dem	Alton
5	Isaac N. Morris, dem	Quincy	9	Samuel S. Marshall, dem	McLeansboro

* Died Nov. 24, 1858. † Vice Harris, Jan. 20, 1859.

THIRTY-SIXTH CONGRESS, 1859-1861.

Dist.	Name.	Residence.	Dist.	Name.	Residence.
1	Elihu B. Washburne, rep.	Galena	6	John A. McClernand, dem	Springfield
2	John F. Farnsworth, rep.	Chicago	7	James C. Robinson, dem	Marshall
3	Owen Lovejoy, rep	Princeton	8	Philip B. Fouke, dem	Belleville
4	William Kellogg, rep	Canton	9	John A. Logan, dem.	Benton
5	Isaac N. Morris, dem	Quincy			

THIRTY-SEVENTH CONGRESS, 1861-1863.

Dist.	Name.	Residence.	Dist.	Name.	Residence.
1	Elihu B. Washburne, rep	Galena	6	†A. L. Knapp, dem	Jerseyville
2	Isaac N. Arnold, rep	Chicago	7	James C. Robinson, dem	Marshall
3	Owen Lovejoy, rep	Princeton	8	Philip B. Fouke, dem	Belleville
4	William Kellogg, rep	Canton	9	‡John A. Logan, dem	Benton
5	Wm. Richardson, dem	Quincy		§Wm. J. Allen, dem	Marion
6	*John A. McClernand, dem	Springfield			

* Resigned. † Vice McClernand, Dec. 12, 1861. ‡ Resigned April 4, 1862.
§ Vice Logan, June 2, 1862.

THIRTY-EIGHTH CONGRESS, 1863-1865.

Dist.	Name.	Residence.	Dist.	Name.	Residence.
	*James C. Allen, dem	Palestine	7	John R. Eden, dem	Sullivan
1	Isaac N. Arnold, rep	Chicago	8	John T. Stuart, rep	Springfield
2	John F. Farnsworth, rep	St. Charles	9	Lewis W. Ross, dem	Lewistown
3	Elihu B. Washburne, rep	Galena	10	Anthony L. Knapp, dem	Jerseyville
4	Charles M. Harris, dem	Oquawka	11	James C. Robinson, dem.	Marshall
5	†Owen Lovejoy, rep	Princeton	12	Wm. R. Morrison, dem	Waterloo
	‡Ebon C. Ingersoll, rep	Peoria	13	Wm. J. Allen, dem	Marion
6	Jesse O. Norton, rep	Joliet			

* For the State-at-large. † Died March, 1864. Vice Lovejoy, May 20, 1864.

THIRTY-NINTH CONGRESS, 1865-1867.

Dist.	Name.	Residence.	Dist.	Name.	Residence.
	*Samuel W Moulton, rep	Shelbyville	7	Henry P. H. Bromwell, rep.	Charleston
1	John Wentworth, dem	Chicago	8	Shelby M. Cullom, rep	Springfield
2	John F. Farnsworth, rep	St. Charles	9	Lewis W. Ross, dem	Lewistown
3	Elihu B. Washburne, rep	Galena	10	Anthony Thornton, dem	Shelbyville
4	Abner C. Harding, rep	Monmouth	11	Samuel S. Marshall, dem	McLeansboro
5	Ebon C. Ingersoll, rep	Peoria	12	Jehu Baker, rep	Belleville
6	Burton C. Cook, rep	Ottawa	13	Andrew J. Kuykendall, rep	Vienna

* For the State-at large.

FORTIETH CONGRESS, 1867-1869.

Dist.	Name.	Residence.	Dist.	Name.	Residence.
	*John A. Logan, rep	Carbondale	7	Henry P. H. Bromwell, rep	Charleston
1	Norman B. Judd, rep	Chicago	8	Shelby M. Cullom, rep	Springfield
2	John F. Farnsworth, rep	St. Charles	9	Lewis W. Ross, dem	Lewistown
3	Elihu B. Washburne, rep	Galena	10	Albert G. Burr, dem	Carrollton
4	Abner C. Harding, rep	Monmouth	11	Samuel S. Marshall, dem	Mc Leansboro
5	Ebon C. Ingersoll, rep	Peoria	12	Jehu Baker, rep	Belleville
6	Burton C. Cook, rep	Ottawa	13	Green B. Raum, rep	Metropolis

* For the State-at-large.

FORTY-FIRST CONGRESS, 1869-1871.

Dist.	Name.	Residence.	Dist.	Name.	Residence.
	*John A. Logan, rep	Carbondale	7	Jesse H. Moore, rep	Decatur
1	Norman B. Judd, rep	Chicago	8	Shelby M. Cullom, rep	Springfield
2	John F. Farnsworth, rep	St. Charles	9	Thompson W. McNeely, dem	Petersburg
3	†Elihu B. Washburne, rep	Galena	10	Albert G. Burr, dem	Carrollton
	‡Horatio C. Burchard, rep	Freeport	11	Samuel S. Marshall, dem	Mc Leansboro
4	Jno. B. Hawley, rep	Rock Island	12	John B. Hay, rep	Belleville
5	Ebon C. Ingersoll, rep	Peoria	13	John M. Crebs, dem	Carmi
6	Burton C. Cook, rep	Ottawa			

* For State-at-large. † Resigned March 9, 1869. ‡ Vice Washburn, Dec. 6, 1869.

FORTY-SECOND CONGRESS, 1871-1873.

Dist.	Name.	Residence.	Dist.	Name.	Residence.
	*John A. Logan, rep	Carbondale	6	§Henry Snapp, rep	Joliet
	†John L. Beveridge, rep	Evanston	7	Jesse H. Moore, rep	Decatur
1	Charles B. Farwell, rep	Chicago	8	James C. Robinson, dem	Springfield
2	Jno. F. Farnsworth, rep	St. Charles	9	Thompson W. McNeely, dem	Petersburg
3	Horatio C. Burchard, rep	Freeport	10	Edward Y. Rice, dem	Hillsboro
4	John B. Hawley, rep	Rock Island	11	Samuel S. Marshall, dem	Mc Leansboro
5	Bradford N. Stevens, rep.	Princeton	12	John B. Hay, rep	Belleville
6	‡Burton C. Cook, rep	Ottawa	13	John M. Crebs, dem	Carmi

* For State at large; resigned. † Vice Logan, Dec. 4, '71; resigned Jan. 4, '73. ‡ Resigned. § Vice Cook, Dec. 4, '71.

FORTY-THIRD CONGRESS, 1873-1875.

Dist.	Name.	Residence.	Dist.	Name.	Residence.
1	*John B. Rice, rep	Chicago	10	William H. Ray, rep	Rushville
	†Bernard G. Caulfield, dem	Chicago	11	Robert M. Knapp, dem	Jerseyville
2	Jasper D. Ward, rep	Chicago	12	James C. Robinson, dem	Springfield
3	Charles B. Farwell, rep	Chicago	13	John McNulta, rep	Bloomington
4	Stephen A. Hurlbut, rep	Belvidere	14	Joseph G. Cannon, rep	Tuscola
5	Horatio C. Burchard, rep	Freeport	15	John R. Eden, dem	Sullivan
6	John B. Hawley, rep	Rock Island	16	James S. Martin, rep	Salem
7	Franklin Corwin, rep	Peru	17	Wm. R. Morrison, dem	Waterloo
8	Greenbury L. Fort, rep	Lacon	18	Isaac Clements, rep	Carbondale
9	Granville Barriere, rep	Canton	19	Samuel S. Marshall, dem	Mc Leansboro

* Died Dec. '74. † Vice Rice; elected Jan. 23, '75, took seat Feb. 1, '75.

FORTY-FOURTH CONGRESS, 1875-1877.

Dist.	Name.	*Residence.	Dist.	Name.	Residence.
1	Bernard G. Caulfield, dem.	Chicago	10	John C. Bagby, dem.	Rushville
2	Carter H. Harrison, dem.	Chicago	11	Scott Wike, dem.	Pittsfield
3	*Charles B. Farwell, rep.	Chicago	12	Wm. M. Springer, dem.	Springfield
	†John V. LeMoyne, rep.	Chicago	13	Adlai E. Stevenson, greenb.	Bloomingtn.
4	Stephen A. Hurlbut, rep.	Belvidere	14	Joseph G. Cannon, rep.	Tuscola
5	Horatio C. Burchard, rep.	Freeport	15	John R. Eden, dem.	Sullivan
6	Thos. J. Henderson, rep.	Princeton	16	Wm. A. J. Sparks, dem.	Carlyle
7	Alex'r Campbell, greenb.	LaSalle	17	Wm. R. Morrison, dem.	Waterloo
8	Greenbury L. Fort, rep.	Lacon	18	Wm. Hartzell, dem.	Chester
9	Rich'd H. Whiting, rep.	Peoria	19	Wm. B. Anderson, greenb.	Mt. Vernon

* Seat contested; declared vacant. † Vice Farwell, May 6, '76.

FORTY-FIFTH CONGRESS, 1877-1879.

Dist.	Name.	Residence.	Dist.	Name.	Residence.
1	Wm. Aldrich, rep.	Chicago	11	Rob't M. Knapp, dem.	Jerseyville
2	Carter H. Harrison, dem.	Chicago	12	Wm. M. Springer, dem.	Springfield
3	Lorenzo Brentano, rep.	Chicago	13	Thos. F. Tipton, rep.	Bloomington.
4	William Lathrop, rep.	Rockford	14	Joseph G. Cannon, rep.	Danville
5	Horatio C. Burchard, rep.	Freeport	15	John R. Eden, dem.	Sullivan
6	Thomas J. Henderson, rep.	Princeton	16	Wm. A. J. Sparks, dem.	Carlyle
7	Philip C. Hayes, rep.	Morris	17	Wm. R. Morrison, dem.	Waterloo
8	Greenbury L. Fort, rep.	Lacon	18	Wm. Hartzell, dem.	Chester
9	Thos. A. Boyd, rep.	Lewistown	19	Rich'd W. Townshend, dem.	Shawneet'wn
10	Benj. F. Marsh, rep.	Warsaw			

FORTY-SIXTH CONGRESS, 1879-1881.

Dist.	Name.	Residence.	Dist.	Name.	Residence.
1	Wm. Aldrich, rep.	Chicago	11	Jas. W. Singleton, dem.	Quincy
2	Geo. R. Davis, rep.	Chicago	12	Wm. M. Springer, dem.	Springfield
3	Hiram Barber, Jr., rep.	Chicago	13	Adlai E. Stevenson, dem.	Bloomington.
4	John C. Sherwin, rep.	Geneva	14	Joseph G. Cannon, rep.	Danville
5	Rob't M. A. Hawk, rep.	Mt. Carroll	15	Albert P. Forsythe, greenb.	Isabel
6	Thos J. Henderson, rep.	Princeton	16	Wm. A. J. Sparks, dem.	Carlyle
7	Philip C. Hayes, rep.	Morris	17	Wm. R. Morrison, dem.	Waterloo
8	Greenbury L. Fort, rep.	Lacon	18	John R. Thomas, rep.	Metropolis
9	Thos. A. Boyd, rep.	Lewistown	19	Rich'd W. Townshend, dem.	Shawneet'wn
10	Benj. F. Marsh, rep.	Warsaw			

FORTY-SEVENTH CONGRESS, 1881-1883.

Dist.	Name.	Residence.	Dist.	Name.	Residence.
1	Wm. Aldrich, rep.	Chicago	10	Benj. F. Marsh, rep.	Warsaw
2	Geo. R. Davis, rep.	Chicago	11	Jas. W. Singleton, dem.	Quincy
3	Chas. B. Farwell, rep.	Chicago	12	Wm. M. Springer, dem.	Springfield
4	John C. Sherwin, rep.	Elgin	13	Dietrich C. Smith, rep.	Pekin
5	*Robt. M. A. Hawk, rep.	Mt. Carroll	14	Jos. G. Cannon, rep.	Danville
	†Robt. R. Hitt, rep.	Mt. Morris	15	Samuel W. Moulton, dem.	Shelbyville
6	Thos. J. Henderson, rep.	Princeton	16	Wm. A. J. Sparks, dem.	Carlyle
7	William Cullen, rep.	Ottawa	17	Wm. R. Morrison, dem.	Waterloo
8	Lewis E. Payson, rep.	Pontiac.	18	Jno. R. Thomas, rep.	Metropolis
9	John H. Lewis, rep.	Knoxville	19	Richard W. Townshend, dem.	Shawneetown

* Died. † Elected Nov. 7, 1882, vice Hawk.

FORTY-EIGHTH CONGRESS, 1883-1885.

Dist.	Name.	Residence.	Dist.	Name.	Residence.
1	Ransom W. Dunham, rep....	Chicago.......	11	Wm. H. Neece, dem	Macomb......
2	John F. Finerty, ind-dem....	Chicago.......	12	James M. Riggs, dem.........	Winchester...
3	Geo. R. Davis, rep..........	Chicago.......	13	Wm. M. Springer, dem.......	Springfield...
4	Geo. E. Adams, rep..........	Chicago.......	14	Jonathan H. Rowell, rep......	Bloomington.
5	Reuben Ellwood, rep	Sycamore ..	15	Jos. G. Cannon, rep	Danville......
6	Robert R. Hitt, rep	Mt. Morris...	16	Aaron Shaw, dem	Olney.........
7	Thos. J. Henderson, rep. ...	Princeton.....	17	Sam'l W. Moulton, dem......	Shelbyville...
8	Wm. Cullen, rep............	Ottawa........	18	Wm. R. Morrison, dem.......	Waterloo .....
9	Lewis E. Payson, rep...... ...	Pontiac.......	19	Richard W. Townshend, dem	Shawneetown
10	Nichol's E. Worthington, dem	Peoria	20	John R. Thomas, rep.........	Metropolis...

FORTY-NINTH CONGRESS, 1885-1887.

Dist.	Name.	Residence.	Dist.	Name.	Residence.
1	Ransom W. Dunham, rep....	Chicago	11	Wm. H. Neece, dem..........	Macomb.. ...
2	Frank Lawler, dem	Chicago	12	James M. Riggs, dem..........	Winchester...
3	James H. Ward, dem...	Chicago ..,...	13	Wm. M. Springer, dem.......	Springfield ...
4	Geo. E. Adams, rep...........	Chicago	14	Jonathan H. Rowell, rep.....	Bloomington.
5	*Reuben Ellwood, rep........	Sycamore	15	Joseph G. Cannon, rep.......	Danville .....
	†Albert J. Hopkins, rep	Aurora.........	16	Silas Z. Landes, dem..........	Mt. Carmel...
6	Robert R. Hitt, rep	Mt. Morris....	17	John R. Eden, dem	Sullivan ......
7	Thos. J. Henderson, rep.....	Princeton.....	18	Wm. R. Morrison, dem... ...	Waterloo .....
8	Ralph Plumb, rep.	Streator	19	Richard W. Townshend, dem	Shawneetown
9	Lewis E. Payson, rep..... ..	Pontiac.......	20	John R. Thomas, rep.........	Metropolis ...
10	Nichol's E. Worthington, dem	Peoria			

* Died. † Vice Ellwood, deceased.

FIFTIETH CONGRESS, 1887-1889.

Dist.	Name.	Residence.	Dist.	Name.	Residence.
1	Ransom W. Dunham, rep....	Chicago	11	Wm. H. Gest, rep...........	Rock Island..
2	Frank Lawler, dem.....	Chicago	12	Geo. A. Anderson, dem	Quincy........
3	Wm. E. Mason, rep,...	Chicago	13	Wm. M. Springer, dem........	Springfield ...
4	Geo. E. Adams, rep...........	Chicago	14	Jonathan H. Rowell, rep.....	Bloomington.
5	Albert J. Hopkins, rep.	Aurora.........	15	Jos. G. Cannon, rep	Danville .....
6	Robert R. Hitt, rep	Mt. Morris....	16	Silas Z. Landes, dem..........	Mt. Carmel...
7	Thos. J. Henderson, rep.....	Princeton ...	17	Edward Lane, dem......	Hillsboro.....
8	Ralph Plumb, rep..............	Streator	18	Jehu Baker, rep..............	Belleville. ...
9	Lewis E. Payson, rep.........	Pontiac.......	19	Richard W. Townshend, dem	Shawneetown
10	Philip S. Post, rep	Galesburg....	20	John R. Thomas, rep	Metropolis...

FIFTY-FIRST CONGRESS 1889-1891.

Dist.	Name.	Residence.	Dist.	Name.	Residence.
1	Abner Taylor, rep.	Chicago	12	Scott Wike, dem..............	Pittsfield .....
2	Frank Lawler, dem............	Chicago	13	Wm. M. Springer, dem.	Springfield ...
3	Wm. E. Mason, rep...........	Chicago	14	Jonathan H. Rowell, rep.....	Bloomington.
4	Geo. E. Adams, rep...........	Chicago	15	Jos. G. Cannon, rep	Danville......
5	Albert J. Hopkins, rep	Aurora	16	Geo. W. Fithian, dem	Newton........
6	Robt. R. Hitt, rep..	Mt. Morris....	17	Edward Lane, dem...........	Hillsboro.....
7	Thos. J. Henderson, rep	Princeton ...	18	Wm. S. Forman, dem.........	Nashville.....
8	Chas A. Hill, rep.............	Joliet.........	19	*Richard W. Townshend, dem	Shawneetown
				†James R. Williams, dem ...	Carmi. ....
9	Lewis E. Payson, rep........	Pontiac.......			
10	Philip S. Post, rep	Galesburg....	20	Geo. W. Smith, rep	Murphysboro
11	Wm. H. Gest, rep	Rock Island.			

* Died March 9, 1889. † Vice Townshend, deceased

FIFTY-SECOND CONGRESS, 1891-1893.

Dist.	Name.	Residence.	Dist.	Name.	Residence.
1	Abner Taylor, rep	Chicago	11	Ben T. Cable, dem	Rock Island
2	Lawrence E. McGann, dem	Chicago	12	Scott Wike, dem	Pittsfield
3	Allen C. Durborow, Jr., dem	Chicago	13	Wm. M. Springer, dem	Springfield
4	Walter C. Newberry, dem	Chicago	14	Owen Scott, dem	Bloomington.
5	Albert J. Hopkins, rep	Aurora	15	Samuel T. Busey, dem	Urbana
6	Robert R. Hitt, rep	Mt. Morris	16	Geo. W. Fithian, dem	Newton
7	Thos. J. Henderson, rep	Princeton	17	Edward Lane, dem	Hillsboro
8	Lewis Steward, dem	Plano	18	Wm. S. Forman, dem	Nashville
9	Herman W. Snow, dem	Sheldon	19	James R. Williams, dem	Carmi
10	Philip S. Post, rep	Galesburg	20	Geo. W. Smith, rep	Murphysboro

FIFTY-THIRD CONGRESS, 1893-1895.

Dist.	Name.	Residence.	Dist.	Name.	Residence.
1	J. Frank Aldrich, rep	Chicago	11	Benj. F. Marsh, rep	Warsaw
2	Lawrence E. McGann, dem	Chicago	12	John J. McDannold, dem	Mt. Sterling
3	Allen C. Durborow, Jr., dem	Chicago	13	Wm. M. Springer, dem	Springfield
4	Julius Goldzler, dem	Chicago	14	Benj. F. Funk, rep	Bloomington.
5	Albert J. Hopkins, rep	Aurora	15	Jos. G. Cannon, rep	Danville
6	Robert R. Hitt, rep	Mt. Morris	16	Geo. W. Fithian, dem	Newton
7	Thos. J. Henderson, rep	Princeton	17	Edward Lane, dem	Hillsboro
8	Robert A. Childs, rep	Hinsdale	18	Wm. S. Forman, dem	Nashville
9	Hamilton K. Wheeler, rep	Kankakee	19	James R. Williams, dem	Carmi
10	Philip S. Post, rep	Galesburg	20	Geo. W. Smith, rep	Murphysboro

At Large—Gen. John C. Black, dem., Chicago; Andrew J. Hunter, dem., Paris.

FIFTY-FOURTH CONGRESS, 1895-1897.

Dist.	Name.	Residence.	Dist.	Name.	Residence.
1	J. Frank Aldrich, rep	Chicago	12	Jos. G. Cannon, rep	Danville
2	Wm. Lorimer, rep	Chicago	13	Vespasian Warner, rep	Clinton
3	†Lawrence E. McGann, dem	Chicago	14	Joseph V. Graff, rep	Pekin
4	Chas. W. Woodman, rep	Chicago	15	Benj. F. Marsh, rep	Warsaw
5	Geo. E. White, rep	Chicago	16	†Finis E. Downing, dem	Virginia
6	Edward D. Cooke, rep	Chicago	17	James A. Connolly, rep	Springfield
7	Geo. Edmund Foss, rep	Chicago	18	Frederick Remann, rep	Vandalia
8	Albert J. Hopkins, rep	Aurora	19	Benson Wood, rep	Effingham
9	Robert R. Hitt, rep	Mt. Morris	20	Orlando Burrell, rep	Carmi
10	*Philip Sidney Post, rep	Galesburg	21	Everett J. Murphy, rep	East St. Louis
11	Walter Reeves, rep	Streator	22	Geo. W. Smith, rep	Murphysboro

* Died Jan. 6, 1895; Geo. W. Prince, rep., Galesburg, elected. † Seat contested.

W. F. L. Hadley, rep., Edwardsville, elected, vice Remann, who died July 14, 1895. John I. Rinaker, rep., Carlinville, seated, vice Downing. Hugh R. Belknap, rep., Chicago, seated, vice McGann.

FIFTY-FIFTH CONGRESS, 1897-1899.

Dist.	Name.	Residence.	Dist.	Name.	Residence.
1	James R. Mann, rep	Chicago	12	Joseph G. Cannon, rep	Danville
2	William Lorimer, rep	Chicago	13	Vespasian Warner, rep	Clinton
3	Hugh R. Belknap, rep	Chicago	14	Joseph V. Graff, rep	Pekin
4	Daniel W. Mills, rep	Chicago	15	Benjamin F. Marsh, rep	Warsaw
5	George E. White, rep	Chicago	16	William H. Hinrichsen, dem	Jacksonville
6	Edward D. Cooke, rep	Chicago	17	James A. Connolly, rep	Springfield
7	George E. Foss, rep	Chicago	18	Thomas M. Jett, dem	Hillsboro
8	Albert J. Hopkins, rep	Aurora	19	Andrew J. Hunter, dem	Paris
9	Robert R. Hitt, rep	Mt. Morris	20	James R. Campbell, dem	McLeansboro
10	George W. Prince, rep	Galesburg	21	Jehu Baker, pop	Belleville
11	Walter Reeves, rep	Streator	22	George W. Smith, rep	Murphysboro.

PRESIDENTIAL ELECTORS.

1820—DEMOCRATIC.

James B. Moore,
Adolphus F. Hubbard,
Michael Jones.

1824—DEMOCRATIC.

William Harrison,
Henry Eddy,
Alexander P. Field.

1828—DEMOCRATIC.

Richard M. Young,
A. M. Houston,
John Taylor.

1832—DEMOCRATIC.

John C. Alexander,
Adams Dunlap,
Abner Flack,
Daniel Stookey,
James Evans,
Thomas Ray.

1836—DEMOCRATIC.

Samuel Hackelton,
John Wyatt,
John Pearson,
Samuel Leach,
John D. Whiteside.

1840—DEMOCRATIC.

Adam W. Snyder,
J. P. Walker,
John A. McClernand,
John W. Eldridge,
James H. Ralston.

1844—DEMOCRATIC.

A. W. Cavarly,
John D. Wood,
Willis Allen,
Augustus C. French,
Wm. A. Richardson,
John Dement,
John Calhoun,
Isaac N. Arnold,
Norman H. Purple.

1848—DEMOCRATIC.

Ferris Forman,
Cornelius Lansing,
William Martin,
Samuel S. Hayes,
H. M. Vandeveer,
Madison E. Hollister,
Lewis W. Ross,
Julius Manning,
William I. Ferguson,
Montgomery Sweeny (vice Ross, absent).

1852—DEMOCRATIC.

David L. Gregg,
Calvin A. Warren,
John A. McClernand,
Richard I. Hamilton,
Edward Omelveny,
James Mahon,
Kirby Benedict,
E. P. Ferry,
Ezra G. Sanger,
Joseph Knox,
John Calhoun.

1856—DEMOCRATIC.

Augustus M. Herrington,
Charles H. Constable,
Merritt L. Joslyn,
Hugh Maher,
Milton T. Peters,
Robert Holloway,
John P. Richmond,
Samuel W. Moulton,
Orlando B. Ficklin,
Wm. A. J. Sparks,
John A. Logan.

1860—REPUBLICAN.

John M. Palmer,
Leonard Swett,
Allen C. Fuller,
William B. Plato.
Lawrence Weldon,
William P. Kellogg,
James Stark,
James C. Conkling,
Henry P. H. Bromwell,
Thomas G. Allen,
John Olney.

1864—REPUBLICAN.

John Dougherty,
Francis A. Hoffman,
Benjamin M. Prentiss,
John V. Farwell,
Anson S. Miller,
John V. Eustace,
James S. Poage,
John I. Bennett,
William T. Hopkins,
Franklin Blades,
James C. Conkling,
William Walker,
Thomas W. Harris,
N. M. McCurdy,
Henry S. Baker,
Z. S. Clifford.

1868—REPUBLICAN.

Gustavus Kœrner,
Stephen A. Hurlbut,
Thomas J. Henderson.
Lorenzo Brentano,
Jesse L. Hildrup,
James McCoy,
Henry W. Draper,
Thomas G. Frost,
Joseph O. Glover,
John W. Blackburn,
Samuel G. Parks,
Damon G. Tunnicliff,
John D. Strong,
Edward Kitchell,
Charles F. Springer,
Daniel W. Munn.

1872—REPUBLICAN.

Henry Greenbaum,
David T. Linegar,
Chauncey T. Bowen,
Lester L. Bond,
Mahlon D. Ogden,
Richard L. Devine,
James Shaw,
Norman H. Ryan,
Irus Coy,
Joseph J. Cassell,
William Selden Gale,

1872—*Continued*.

William D. Henderson,
Moses M. Bane,
George A. Sanders,
Hugh Fullerton,
Martin B. Thompson,
Jacob W. Wilkin,
John P. Van Dorston,
John I. Rinaker,
John Dougherty,
William H. Robinson.

1876—REPUBLICAN.

John I. Rinaker,
Peter Shuttler,
George Armour,
Bolivar G. Gill,
Louis Schaffner,
Allen C. Fuller,
Joseph M. Bailey,
John B. Hawley,
Franklin Corwin,
Jason W. Strevell,
Oscar F. Price,
Alexander McLean,
David E. Beaty,
Philip N. Minlere,
Michael Donahue,
Hugh Crea,
George D. Chafee,
James M. Truitt,
Cyrus Happy,
George C. Ross,
Joseph J. Castles.

1880—REPUBLICAN.

George Schneider,
Ethelbert Callahan,
Robert T. Lincoln,
John M. Smyth,
James A. Kirk,
Christopher M. Brazee,
Robert E. Logan,
Isaac H. Elliott,
James Goodspeed,
Alfred Sample,
Sabin D. Puterbaugh,
Emery C. Humphrey,
William A. Grimshaw,
James C. McQuigg,
Jonathan H. Rowell,
William R. Jewell,
Jackson M. Sheets,
James W. Peterson,
Wilbur T. Norton,
George W. Smith,
William H. Johnson.

1884—REPUBLICAN.

Andrew Shuman,
Isaac Lesem,
George Bass,
John Tegtmeyer,
John M. Smyth,
James A. Sexton,
Albert J. Hopkins,
Conrad J. Fry,
Wm. H. Shepard,
Robert A. Childs,
David McWilliams,
Rufus W. Miles,
John A. Harvey,
Francis M. Davis
J Otis Humphrey,
Edward D. Blinn,
Wm. O. Wilson,
Rufus Cope,
John H. Dunscomb,
Cicero J. Lindley,
Jasper Partridge,
Matthew J. Inscore.

1888—REPUBLICAN.

Chas. H. Deere,
James M. Truitt,
John Crerar,
Michael B. Kearney,
John R. Wheeler,
Orrin W. Potter,
Harvey A. Jones,
Duncan Mackay, Jr.,
James Dinsmoor,
Isaac C. Norton,
Richard J. Hanna,
Edgar A. Bancroft,
Robert Moir,
Thos. Worthington, Jr ,
Dietrich C. Smith,
Vespasian Warner,
Wm. R. Jewell,
Ethelbert Callahan,
Alex. H. McTaggart,
Emery P. Slate,
Allen Bleakley,
Henry C. Horner.

1892—DEMOCRATIC.

At large—Potter Palmer and Geo. P. Bunker, Chicago; Prince Albert Pearce, Carmi; Andrew J. O'Conor, LaSalle.
1—Rensselaer Stone, Chicago.
2—Frank Lawler, Chicago.
3—William G. Legner, Chicago.
4—Frederick H. Atwood, Chicago.
5—Frederick B. Townsend, Sycamore.
6—Elijah W. Blaisdell, Rockford.
7—Owen Lovejoy, Princeton.
8—Darius W. Cresey, Downer's Grove.
9—Michael Cleary, Odell.
10—Meredith Walker, Canton.
11—John H. Hanley, Monmouth.
12—Mark Meyerstein, Whitehall.
13—Thompson W. McNeely, Petersburg.
14—Thomas H. Stokes, Lincoln.
15—John Ervin, Tuscola.
16—Charles H. Martin, Lawrenceville.
17—David C. Enslow, McVey.
18—William R. Prickett, Edwardsville.
19—William V. Choisser, Harrisburg.
20—David W. Karraker, Jonesboro.

1896—REPUBLICAN.

At large—Emil G. Hirsch, Chicago; Horace S. Clark, Mattoon.
1—Noble B. Judah, Chicago.
2—Dayton C. Gray, Chicago.
3—Charles L. Sherlock, Chicago.
4—Frederick M. Blount, Chicago.
5—Ephraim Banning, Chicago.
6—Chester M. Dawes, Chicago.
7—Washington Van Horn, Chicago.
8—William L. Sackett, Morris.
9—Eugene W. Montgomery, Galena.
10—Augustus G. Hammond, Wyoming.
11—Marcellus W. Willson, Metamora.
12—William R. Jewell, Danville.
13—Allen T. Barnes, Bloomington.
14—Edward S. Easton, Peoria.
15—Warren E. Taylor, Monmouth.
16—John H. Coats, Winchester.
17—Henry N. Schuyler, Pana.
18—John R. Pogue, Sullivan.
19—Joseph Hall, Westfield.
20—Theodore G. Risley, Mt. Carmel.
21—Walter S. Louden, Trenton.
22—Warren W. Duncan, Marion.

List of Counties in Illinois, Dates of Organization and County Seats.

Counties.	When Organized.	County Seats.	Counties.	When Organized.	County Seats.
Adams	Jan. 13, 1825	Quincy	Lee	Feb. 27, 1839	Dixon
Alexander	March 4, 1819	Cairo	Livingston	Feb. 27, 1837	Pontiac
Bond	Jan. 4, 1817	Greenville	Logan	Feb. 15, 1839	Lincoln
Boone	March 4, 1837	Belvidere	Macon	Jan. 19, 1829	Decatur
Brown	Feb. 1, 1839	Mt. Sterling	Macoupin	Jan. 17, 1829	Carlinville
Bureau	Feb. 28, 1837	Princeton	Madison	Sept. 14, 1812	Edwardsville
Calhoun	Jan. 10, 1825	Hardin	Marion	Jan. 24, 1823	Salem
Carroll	Feb. 22, 1839	Mt. Carroll	Marshall	Jan. 19, 1839	Lacon
Cass	March 3, 1837	Virginia	Mason	Jan. 20, 1841	Havana
Champaign	Feb. 20, 1833	Urbana	Massac	Feb. 8, 1843	Metropolis
Christian	Feb. 15, 1839	Taylorville	McDonough	Jan. 25, 1826	Macomb
Clark	March 22, 1819	Marshall	McHenry	Jan. 16, 1836	Woodstock
Clay	Dec. 23, 1824	Louisville	McLean	Dec. 25, 1830	Bloomington
Clinton	Dec. 27, 1824	Carlyle	Menard	Feb. 15, 1839	Petersburg
Coles	Dec. 25, 1830	Charleston	Mercer	Jan. 13, 1825	Aledo
Cook	Jan. 15, 1831	Chicago	Monroe	June 1, 1816	Waterloo
Crawford	Dec. 31, 1816	Robinson	Montgomery	Feb. 12, 1821	Hillsboro
Cumberland	May 1, 1843	Toledo	Morgan	Jan 31, 1823	Jacksonville
DeKalb	March 4, 1837	Sycamore	Moultrie	Feb. 16, 1843	Sullivan
DeWitt	March 1, 1839	Clinton	Ogle	Jan. 16, 1836	Oregon
Douglas	Feb. 13, 1857	Tuscola	Peoria	Jan. 13, 1825	Peoria
DuPage	Feb. 9, 1839	Wheaton	Perry	Jan. 29, 1827	Pinckneyville
Edgar	Jan. 3, 1823	Paris	Platt	Jan. 27, 1841	Monticello
Edwards	Nov. 28, 1814	Albion	Pike	Jan. 31, 1821	Pittsfield
Effingham	Feb. 15, 1831	Effingham	Pope	April 1, 1816	Golconda
Fayette	Feb. 14, 1821	Vandalia	Pulaski	March 3, 1843	Mound City
Ford	Feb. 17, 1859	Paxton	Putnam	Jan. 13, 1825	Hennepin
Franklin	Jan. 2, 1818	Benton	Randolph	April 28, 1809	Chester
Fulton	Jan. 28, 1823	Lewistown	Richland	Feb. 24, 1841	Olney
Gallatin	Sept. 14, 1812	Shawneet'wn	Rock Island	Feb. 9, 1831	Rock Island
Greene	Jan. 20, 1821	Carrollton	Saline	Feb. 25, 1847	Harrisburg
Grundy	Feb. 17, 1841	Morris	Sangamon	Jan. 30, 1821	Springfield
Hamilton	Feb. 8, 1821	McLeansboro	Schuyler	Jan. 13, 1825	Rushville
Hancock	Jan. 13, 1825	Carthage	Scott	Feb. 16, 1839	Winchester
Hardin	March 2, 1839	Elizabetht'wn	Shelby	Jan. 23, 1827	Shelbyville
Henderson	Jan. 20, 1841	Oquawka	Stark	March 2, 1839	Toulon
Henry	Jan. 13, 1825	Cambridge	St. Clair	April 28, 1809	Belleville
Iroquois	Feb. 26, 1833	Watseka	Stephenson	March 4, 1837	Freeport
Jackson	Jan. 10, 1816	Murphysboro	Tazewell	Jan. 31, 1827	Pekin
Jasper	Feb. 15, 1831	Newton	Union	Jan. 2, 1818	Jonesboro
Jefferson	March 26, 1819	Mt. Vernon	Vermilion	Jan. 18, 1826	Danville
Jersey	Feb. 28, 1839	Jerseyville	Wabash	Dec. 27, 1824	Mt. Carmel
JoDaviess	Feb. 17, 1827	Galena	Warren	Jan. 13, 1825	Monmouth
Johnson	Sept. 14, 1812	Vienna	Washington	Jan. 2, 1818	Nashville
Kane	Jan. 16, 1836	Geneva	Wayne	March 26, 1819	Fairfield
Kankakee	Feb. 11, 1851	Kankakee	White	Dec. 9, 1815	Carmi
Kendall	Feb. 19, 1841	Yorkville	Whiteside	Jan. 16, 1836	Morrison
Knox	Jan. 13, 1825	Galesburg	Will	Jan. 12, 1836	Joliet
Lake	March 1, 1839	Waukegan	Williamson	Feb. 28, 1839	Marion
LaSalle	Jan. 15, 1831	Ottawa	Winnebago	Jan. 16, 1836	Rockford
Lawrence	Jan. 16, 1821	Lawrenceville	Woodford	Feb. 27, 1841	Metamora

Population by Counties, According to United States Census.

Counties	1800	1810	1820	1830	1840	1850	1860	1870	1880	1890
Adams	......	......	......	2,186	14,476	26,508	41,323	56,362	59,148	61,888
Alexander	......	......	626	1,390	3,313	2,484	4,707	10,564	14,809	16,563
Bond	......	......	2,931	3,124	5,060	6,144	9,815	13,152	14,873	14,550
Boone	......	......	......	......	1,705	7,624	11,678	12,942	11,527	12,203
Brown	......	......	......	......	4,183	7,198	9,938	12,205	13,044	11,951
Bureau	......	......	......	......	3,067	8,841	26,426	34,415	33,189	35,014
Calhoun	......	......	......	1,090	1,741	3,231	5,144	6,562	7,471	7,652
Carroll	......	......	......	......	1,023	4,586	11,733	16,705	16,985	18,320
Cass	......	......	......	......	2,981	7,253	11,325	11,580	14,494	15,963
Champaign	......	......	......	......	1,475	2,649	14,629	32,737	40,869	42,159
Christian	......	......	......	......	1,878	3,203	10,492	20,363	28,232	30,531
Clark	......	......	931	3,940	7,453	9,532	14,987	18,719	21,900	21,899
Clay	......	......	......	755	3,228	4,289	9,336	15,875	16,195	16,772
Clinton	......	......	......	2,330	3,718	5,139	10,941	16,285	18,718	17,411
Coles	......	......	......	......	9,616	9,335	14,203	25,235	27,055	30,093
Cook	......	......	......	......	10,201	43,385	144,354	349,966	607,719	1,191,922
Crawford	......	......	2,999	3,117	4,422	7,133	11,551	13,889	16,190	17,283
Cumberland	......	......	......	......	......	3,718	8,311	12,223	13,762	15,443
DeKalb	......	......	......	......	1,697	7,540	19,086	23,265	26,774	27,066
DeWitt	......	......	......	......	3,247	5,002	10,820	14,768	17,014	17,011
Douglas	......	......	......	......	......	......	7,140	13,484	15,857	17,669

Counties.	1800	1810	1820	1830	1840	1850	1860	1870	1880	1890
DuPage					3,535	9,290	14,701	16,685	19,187	22,551
Edgar				4,071	8,225	10,692	16,925	21,450	25,504	26,787
Edwards			3,444	1,649	3,070	3,524	5,454	7,565	8,600	9,444
Effingham					1,675	3,799	7,816	15,653	18,924	19,358
Fayette				2,704	6,328	8,075	11,189	19,638	23,243	23,367
Ford							1,979	9,103	15,105	17,035
Franklin			1,763	4,083	3,682	5,681	9,393	12,652	16,129	17,138
Fulton				1,841	13,142	22,508	33,338	38,291	41,249	43,110
Gallatin			3,155	7,405	10,760	5,448	8,055	11,134	12,862	14,935
Greene				7,674	11,951	12,429	16,093	20,277	23,014	23,791
Grundy						3,023	10,379	14,938	16,738	21,024
Hamilton				2,616	3,945	6,362	9,915	13,014	16,712	17,800
Hancock				483	9,946	14,652	29,061	35,935	35,352	31,907
Hardin					1,378	2,887	3,759	5,113	6,024	7,234
Henderson						4,612	9,501	12,582	10,755	0,876
Henry				41	1,260	3,809	20,660	35,506	36,600	33,338
Iroquois					1,695	4,149	12,325	25,782	35,457	35,167
Jackson			1,542	1,828	3,566	5,862	9,589	19,634	22,508	27,809
Jasper					1,472	3,220	8,364	11,238	14,515	18,188
Jefferson			691	2,555	5,762	8,109	12,965	17,864	20,686	22,590
Jersey					4,535	7,354	12,051	15,054	15,546	14,810
JoDaviess				2,111	6,180	18,604	27,325	27,820	27,534	25,101
Johnson			843	1,596	3,626	4,114	9,342	11,248	13,079	15,013
Kane					6,501	16,703	30,062	39,091	44,956	65,061
Kankakee							15,412	24,352	24,961	28,732
Kendall						7,730	13,074	12,399	13,084	12,106
Knox				274	7,060	13,278	28,663	39,522	38,360	38,752
Lake					7,654	14,226	18,257	21,014	21,299	24,235
LaSalle					9,348	17,815	48,332	60,792	70,420	80,798
Lawrence				3,668	7,092	6,121	9,214	12,533	13,663	14,693
Lee					2,035	5,292	17,6[illegible]1	27,171	27,494	26,187
Livingston					759	1,552	11,637	31,471	38,450	38,455
Logan					2,333	5,128	14,272	23,053	25,041	25,489
Macon				1,122	3,039	3,988	13,738	26,481	30,671	38,083
Macoupin				1,990	7,826	12,355	24,602	32,726	37,705	40,380
Madison			13,550	6,221	14,433	20,441	31,351	44,131	50,141	51,535
Marion				2,125	4,742	6,720	12,739	20,622	23,691	24,341
Marshall					1,849	5,180	13,437	16,956	15,036	13,653
Mason						5,021	10,931	16,184	16,244	16,067
Massac						4,092	6,213	9,581	10,443	11,313
McDonough					5,308	7,616	20,069	26,509	27,984	27,467
McHenry					2,578	14,978	22,089	23,762	24,914	26,114
McLean					6,565	10,163	28,772	53,988	60,115	63,036
Menard					4,431	6,349	9,584	11,735	13,028	13,120
Mercer				26	2,352	5,246	15,042	18,769	19,501	18,545
Monroe			1,516	2,000	4,481	7,679	12,832	12,982	13,682	12,948
Montgomery				2,953	4,490	6,277	13,979	25,314	28,086	30,003
Morgan				12,714	19,547	16,064	22,112	28,463	31,519	32,636
Moultrie						2,234	6,385	10,385	13,705	14,481
Ogle					3,479	10,020	22,888	27,492	29,946	28,710
Peoria					6,153	17,547	36,601	47,540	55,419	70,378
Perry				1,215	3,222	5,278	9,552	13,723	16,008	17,529
Platt						1,606	6,127	10,953	15,583	17,062
Pike				2,396	11,728	18,819	27,249	30,768	33,761	31,000
Pope			2,610	3,316	4,094	3,975	6,742	11,437	13,256	14,016
Pulaski						2,264	3,943	8,752	9,507	11,355
Putnam				1,310	2,131	3,924	5,587	6,280	5,555	4,730
Randolph	1,103	7,275	3,492	4,429	7,944	11,079	17,205	20,859	25,691	25,049
Richland						3,012	9,711	12,803	15,546	15,019
Rock Island					2,610	6,937	21,005	29,783	38,314	41 917
Saline						5,588	9,331	12,714	13,940	19,342
Sangamon				12,960	14,716	19,228	32,274	46 352	52,902	61,195
Schuyler				2,959	6,972	10,573	14,684	17,419	16,249	16,013
Scott					6,215	7,914	9,069	10,530	10,745	10,304
Shelby				2,972	6,659	7,807	14,613	25,476	30,282	31,191
Stark					1,573	3,710	9,004	10,751	11,209	9,982
St. Clair	1,255	5,007	5,248	7,078	13,631	20,180	37,694	51,068	61,850	66,571
Stephenson					2,800	11,667	25,112	30,608	31,970	31,338
Tazewell				4,716	7,221	12,052	21,470	27,903	29,679	29,556
Union			2,362	3,239	5,524	7,615	11,181	16,518	18,100	21,549
Vermilion				5,836	9,303	11,402	19,800	30,388	41,600	49,905
Wabash				2,710	4,240	4,690	7,313	8,841	9,945	11,866
Warren				308	6,739	8,176	18,336	23,174	22,940	21,281
Washington			1,517	1,675	4,810	6,953	13,731	17,599	21,117	19,262
Wayne			1,114	2,553	5,133	6,825	12,223	10,758	21,297	23,8[illegible]6
White			4,828	6,601	7,919	8,925	12,403	16,846	23,089	25,005
Whiteside					2,514	5,361	18,737	27,503	30,888	30,854
Will					10,167	16,703	29,321	43,013	53,424	62,007
Williamson					2,457	7,216	12,205	17,329	19,326	22,226
Winnebago					4,609	11,773	24,491	29,301	30,518	39,938
Woodford						4,415	13,282	18,956	21,630	21,429
Aggregate	2,358	12,282	55,162	157,445	476,183	851,470	1,711,951	2,539,891	3,078,636	3,826,351

SHADRACH BOND, of St. Clair, Democrat, first Governor of Illinois, from Oct. 6, 1818, to Dec. 5, 1822, was born at Fredericktown, Md., Nov. 24, 1778, and was raised a farmer, on his father's plantation, and agriculture was his pursuit in Illinois, whither he emigrated in 1794. He had received a plain English education. He was 6 feet high, and weighed 200 pounds. His features were strongly masculine, dark complexion, hair jet, and hazel eyes. He was a favorite with the ladies. His disposition was jovial, thoroughly honest and unostentatious, and he was the most popular man of the day. He was a member of the Legislature when Illinois was a part of Indiana territory, and was a Delegate in Congress in 1812, and in the latter capacity procured the right of pre-emption on the public domain. In 1814 he was appointed receiver of public moneys at Kaskaskia. After his gubernatorial term expired, in 1824, he ran for Congress against Daniel P. Cook, but was beaten. Afterwards he was appointed register of the land office at Kaskaskia, where he died April 12, 1832. The county of Bond was named after him. He was elected without opposition and party politics were unknown. The election was held on the third Thursday and two following days in September, 1818. Governor Bond was in favor of making Illinois a slave State, and is classed as a Democrat. His remains were removed from Kaskaskia and re-interred at Chester, several years ago, with a handsome monument above it, the Illinois Legislature having made an appropriation by a special act for that purpose.

Edward Coles

EDWARD COLES, second Governor, anti-slavery Democrat, of Madison, from Dec. 5, 1822, to Dec. 6, 1826, was born in Albemarle county, Virginia, Dec. 15, 1786, and was among the youngest of ten children. His father was a planter and owned many slaves. During college Gov. Coles' mind was impressed with the moral wrongfulness and political impolicy of slaveholding, and he resolved when he came into possession of his share of his father's slaves he would set them free. When his father died in 1808 he became entitled to twenty-five slaves and 1,000 acres of land. Mr. Coles became the private secretary of President Madison. In person he was tall and graceful. He was gifted with a wide fund of information, social tact and conversational powers. He is said to have brought about a reconciliation between Madison and Monroe and also Adams and Jefferson, who had become estranged. In 1816 he was sent on a special mission to Russia. He spent the summer of 1818 in Illinois and witnessed the efforts to form a constitution. In the spring of 1819 he moved with his slaves to Illinois One moonlight night, while floating down the Ohio to Illinois in flatboats, Gov. Coles called all his slaves around him and in a speech set them free. They tendered him a year's service free, but he declined the offer. He gave the head of each family 160 acres of land near Edwardsville, some money, and exercised a paternal care over them. When elected Governor he was register of the land office at Edwardsville. In 1833 he moved to Philadelphia, married Miss Sallie Logan Roberts, by whom he had one daughter and two sons. He died July 7, 1868. For Governor, Coles received 2,810 votes, and Gen. Moore, 522 (both anti-slavery); Joseph Phillips, 2,760, and Thomas C. Brown, 2,543, (both pro slavery) In 1825 Gov. Coles was temporarily absent in Virginia, and Lieut. Gov. Hubbard declined to yield the office when he returned. The Supreme Court decided against Hubbard, however.

Ninian Edwards

NINIAN EDWARDS, third Governor, Democrat, of Madison, from Dec. 6, 1826, to Dec. 9, 1830, was born in Montgomery county, Maryland, in March, 1775, and was Territorial Governor of Illinois. He was a life-long friend of William Wirt. He had a collegiate course at Carlyle, Pa., and studied law, but was sent into Kentucky to select lands for his brothers and sisters and open a farm. He located in Nelson county, and was early chosen a member of the Kentucky legislature. Before he was 32 years old he had filled the offices of presiding judge of the general court, circuit judge, fourth judge of the appeals and chief justice of the State, which last he held when his associate, Justice Boyle, was appointed Territorial Governor of Illinois. A change was made—Edwards, through the friendship of Henry Clay, being appointed Governor of Illinois, and Boyle chief justice in Kentucky. Gov. Edwards was a fine-looking man, large and with a distinguished air and courtly manners. He was fluent of speech and wielded a ready pen. He was elected Governor at the regular election in August, 1826. "Edwards," says Gov. Ford, "was a large, well-made man, with a noble, princely appearance, who never condescended to the common low arts of electioneering. Whenever he went out among the people he arrayed himself in the style of a gentleman of the olden time, dressed in fine broadcloth, with short breeches, long stockings and high, fair topped boots; was drawn in a fine carriage driven by a negro; and for success he relied on his speeches, which were delivered in great pomp and in a style of diffuse and florid eloquence. When he was inaugurated he appeared before the general assembly wearing a gold-laced cloak, and with great pomp he pronounced his first message to the legislature." He died July 20, 1833. He received 6,299 votes to 5,818 for Thos. Sloo, Jr.

John Reynolds

JOHN REYNOLDS, fourth Governor, Democrat, of St. Clair, Dec. 9, 1830, to Nov. 17, 1834, was born in Montgomery county, Pennsylvania, Feb. 26, 1789, of Irish parents, who removed to Tennessee while he was an infant, and to Illinois in 1800. He afterwards returned to Tennessee, where he received "a classical education," as he asserts in his "Life and Times," but for this information no one would have ever suspected it, either from his conversation, public addresses or writings. He disliked polish, condemned fashion, and was profane. These weregarnished by his varied learning, native shrewdness and wonderful faculty ofgarrulity. He wastall; his face long and bony and deeply furrowed, and under his high, narrow forehead rolled his eyes, large and liquid, expressive of volubility. His nose projected well downward to his ample mouth. His thoroughly democratic manners, social disposition and talkative habit caused him to mingle readily with the people and enjoy their confidence. He was a judge, served three terms in congress, was afterward commissioned one of the State financial agents to negotiate large sums to carry on internal improvements He was always a staunch Democrat. In 1858, however, he refused to follow Douglas, siding with Buchanan in his effort to fasten slavery on Kansas, and his hatred for Douglas was such that he preferred Lincoln for the senate to Douglas. In 1860, old and infirm, he attended the Charleston convention an anti-Douglas delegate, supporting Breckenridge. After the October elections, foreshadowing the election of Lincoln, he published an address urging Democrats to rally to the support of Douglas, hoping that the election would be thrown into the house, which would have elected Breckenridge. During the war he was clearly in sympathy with the South. He died in Belleville May 8, 1865 He served in the legislature in 1846-48 and 1852-54; he was speaker the last term. In 1858 he was the Buchanan-Democrat candidate for Superintendent of Public Instruction. He wrote several books. He was elected to congress in 1834, and on Nov 17 resigned the office of Governor. He received 12,835 votes to 8,946 for William Kinney, Whig.

WM. LEE D. EWING, Democrat, of Fayette, served but seventeen days—Nov. 17, 1834, to Dec. 3, 1834—having been elected a State Senator and president pro tem. of the senate. Lieut. Gov. Casey resigning, Mr. Ewing became Lieutenant Governor, and Gov. Reynolds resigning to become a member of congress, Mr. Ewing filled the interim until Gov. Duncan qualified. Mr. Ewing was a native of Kentucky, born Aug. 31, 1798. He was a man of fine education and polished manners. He was appointed receiver of public moneys at Vandalia soon after the organization of the State, and was a colonel in the Black Hawk war. He was clerk of the house in the Fifth and Sixth general assemblies. In the Seventh general assembly he was speaker of the house. In the Eighth he was president pro tem. of the Senate. He was a member of the Tenth general asssembly, member and speaker of the house in the Eleventh and Twelfth, and again clerk of the Thirteenth (1842). Dec. 29, 1835, he was elected United States Senator to succeed Senator Elias Kent Kane, deceased. In 1842 he was elected State Auditor on the ticket with Gov. Ford, but did not qualify until after his term as clerk of the house expired. He died March 26, 1846, while in office. He was a lawyer by profession, and one of the most popular men in the State in his time. Mr. Ewing was clerk, speaker, president pro tem., United States Senator, Governor, clerk of the house again, and finally auditor of public accounts. His remains are interred in Oak Ridge cemetery, Springfield.

JOSEPH DUNCAN, fifth Governor elected, Democrat, of Morgan, Dec. 3, 1834, to Dec. 7, 1838, was born at Paris, Ky., Feb. 23, 1790. He served gallantly in the war of 1812. In Illinois he was major general of militia. Subsequently he became a State senator, and introduced the first bill providing for a free school system. In 1826 he gained great eclat by defeating Daniel P. Cook for congress. He retained his seat in congress until elected Governor, when he resigned. For Governor he received 17 330 votes to 10,224 for William Kinney, Whig, and 4,320 for Robert McLaughlin and 887 for James Adams. He served the first year in the Black-hawk war as brigadier-general of volunteers. Gov Duncan was a man of limited education, but natural abilities. He was well adapted to gain the admiration of the people, and in his intercourse with them he was affable, courteous and dignified. He did not personally participate in the campaign, but remained in Washington. Illinois then was divided politically by Whigs and "Jackson Democrats," and Duncan was the candidate of the latter, who worshipped Old Hickory. However, unknown to the people of the State, Congressman Duncan had become estranged from Jackson, and now as cordially hated the President as before he had loved him. The Whigs and leading Jackson Democrats tried to make the people believe this, but they would not Jackson had vetoed bills for the improvement of the harbor of Chicago and the great Wabash river, and had crushed the United States bank, measures which Duncan had set his heart on. The means of communication in those days were limited, and the people did not know Duncan's sentiments until he presented his inaugural. He died Jan. 15, 1844. After his election he was classed as a Whig, and eight years after his election was nominated by the Whigs for Governor, but was defeated.

THOMAS CARLIN, sixth Governor elected, Democrat, of Greene, Dec. 7, 1838, to Dec 8, 1842, was born near Frankfort, Ky., July 18, 1789. His father was an Irishman. Gov. Carlin's education was meagre, and in early manhood he supplied the deficiency by becoming his own tutor. In 1803 his father removed to Missouri, then Spanish, where he died in 1810. In 1812 Gov. Carlin moved to Illinois, and proved himself a soldier of undaunted bravery in battles with the Indians. He was married to Rebecca Huitt in 1814, and lived on the banks of the Mississippi, opposite the mouth of the Missouri, for four years, when he moved to Greene county. He located near Carrollton and made a liberal donation of land for county buildings in 1825. He was the first sheriff of the county, and afterwards was twice elected to the State Senate. In the Blackhawk war he commanded a spy battalion, a position of great danger and hardship. In 1834 he was appointed receiver of public moneys by President Jackson and removed to Quincy. After his term as Governor he returned to Greene county and was elected to the legislature in 1849 vice J. D. Fry, resigned. He spent the remainder of his life in agricultural pursuits. He died Feb 14, 1852, leaving a wife and seven children, out of thirteen born to them. He was elected as a straight Democrat against a straight Whig, the vote standing: Carlin, 30,573; Cyrus Edwards (brother of Ninian Edwards), 29,629. Gov. Carlin has the reputation of being one of the best Governors Illinois ever had.

THOMAS FORD, seventh Governor elected, Democrat, of Ogle, the first Governor from Central or Northern Illinois, Dec. 8, 1842, to Dec. 9, 1846, was born at Uniontown, Pa., Dec. 5, 1800. His father was killed by Indians in the mountains of Pennsylvania. His mother was left in poor circumstances with a large family, mostly girls, and she concluded to move to Missouri in 1804. There was some sickness in the family, and the mother decided to move from Missouri to Illinois, which she did, settling three miles south of Waterloo. Gov. Ford received a limited common school education. In 1829 Gov. Edwards appointed him prosecuting attorney; two years later Gov Reynolds reappointed him, and after that the legislature four times elected him judge—twice as circuit judge, as judge of Chicago and as associate judge of the supreme court, when in 1841 that tribunal was reorganized and five Democrats elected. He resigned to become Governor. The Democrats, in Dec., 1841, met and nominated Adam W. Snyder, of St. Clair county, for Governor for the election of Aug. 1842, but he died in the spring of 1842, and Gov. Ford was named to succeed him. Ex-Gov. Duncan ran as the Whig candidate, but was badly beaten, receiving 38,584 votes to Ford's 46,901. He died Nov. 3, 1850, at Peoria, in very indigent circumstances. He wrote an excellent history of Illinois from 1818 to 1847. Gov. Ford is regarded as one of the great men of his time in Illinois. He retained the respect of everybody to the time of his death.

AUGUSTUS C. FRENCH, eighth and ninth Governor elected, Democrat, of Crawford, Dec. 9, 1846, to Jan. 10, 1853, was born in the town of Hill, N. H., Aug. 2, 1808. He received a common school education and spent a short time at Dartmouth. He was admitted to the bar in 1831 and shortly afterwards settled in Albion. After a year he moved to Paris. Here he entered public life by going to the legislature A strong attachment sprang up between him and Stephen A. Douglas. In 1839 Gov. French was appointed receiver of the United States land office at Palestine, Crawford county, then an important point, where he resided when named for Governor. Lyman Trumbull, John Calhoun and Walter B. Scates were among the candidates for the Democratic nomination for Governor that year, but after the fourth ballot all withdrew in favor of French. He received 58,700 votes to 36,775 for Thos. M. Kilpatrick, Whig. In 1844 Gov. French was a Polk elector. After the expiration of his term as Governor he occupied for some years the professor's chair in the law department at McKendree college, Lebanon, and did not appear in public life again except as a member of the constitutional convention of 1862. In 1858 the Democrats nominated Gov. French for State superintendent of public instruction, but he was defeated by Newton Bateman, Republican, who received 124,556 votes to 122,413 for French and 5,173 for Ex Gov John Reynolds, who ran as a Buchanan Democrat. Gov. French died at Lebanon Sept. 4, 1864. The constitution of 1848 was adopted in March, 1848, and provided a term of four years for all State officers, and ordered an election for Nov. 1848. At this election there was no organized opposition to Gov. French, and he received 67,453 votes to 5,639 for Pierre Menard, Jr., 4,748 for Chas. V. Dyer, 3,834 for W. L. D. Morrison and 1,361 for J. L. D. Morrison. Gov. French thus served six years.

JOEL A. MATTESON, tenth Governor elected, Democrat, of Will, Jan. 10, 1853, to Jan. 12, 1857, was born Aug. 8, 1808, in Jefferson county, New York. He received a common school education, taught school, improved a farm his father left him, built railroads in the South, and in 1833 he removed with his family to Illinois, taking a claim near the head of Au Sable river, in the present Kendall county. In 1835 he bought largely at government land sales, and next year during the speculative mania that pervaded Chicago and the State he sold his lands at inflated prices and moved to Joliet. In 1838 he took heavy contracts with the Illinois and Michigan canal. When he completed his job in 1841, when hard times prevailed, business at a stand, contracts paid in State scrip, he bought from the State 700 tons of railroad iron. He sold this in Detroit, paid his debts and had several thousands left. He started a woolen mill in Joliet, which assumed enormous proportions. In 1842 he was elected State senator, but by a bungling apportionment John Pearson held over from the same district. Mr. Pearson immediately resigned for the two years he had to serve, a bill was passed in a few hours, and in ten days Matteson took his seat. He was made chairman of the finance committee, which he held for ten years. Besides his woolen mill, when work was resumed on the canal under the new loan of $1,600,000, he again became a heavy contractor, and subsequently extensively engaged in railroad building. In his message he strongly urged the passage of a free school bill, and in 1855 it was passed. He died in Chicago Jan. 31, 1873. His Whig opponent for Governor was E. B. Webb, of White. Matteson received 80,789 votes, and Webb 64,408. Two years after Matteson had left the office it was discovered that $224,182.66 of 90-day canal scrip that had once been redeemed by the State, but not canceled, had been stolen from the State treasury and was in possession of ex-Gov. Matteson. He maintained that he came honestly by it, and courted the fullest investigation, meantime turning over all his property to the State until the truth was discovered. The thief was never found, and the State realized $255,500 from the sale of Matteson's property.

WILLIAM H. BISSELL, of St. Clair, eleventh Governor elected, the first Republican Governor, from Jan. 12, 1857, to March 15, 1860, was born April 25, 1811, near Painted Post, Yates county, N. Y. He received an academic education. Early in life he moved to Monroe county and took up the law. In 1840 he was elected to the Illinois house as a Democrat. When he returned he qualified for the law. He was twice married, his first wife being Miss James, of Monroe county, by whom he had two daughters, probably yet living in Belleville, where he lived when elected Governor; his wife died about 1840. His second wife was a daughter of Elias K. Kane, United States Senator from Illinois; she survived him but a short time and died without issue. In 1846 he enlisted in the Mexican war and was chosen colonel over Don Morrison by an almost unanimous vote—807 to 6. After the war he was elected to congress twice as a Democrat over P. B Fouke and Joseph Gillespie. His lower extremities became paralyzed before his term of office expired, caused by exposure in the war, and he died March 15, 1860, in Springfield, nine months before his term expired. He died in the faith of the Roman Catholic church, of which he had been a believer since 1854. While in congress he accepted a challenge from Jefferson Davis to fight a duel, and when he took the oath of office was obliged to swear he had never fought a duel or accepted a challenge. It was made the text for John A. Logan, then a Democratic member of the Illinois house, who delivered a speech of two days' length, extremely bitter and vituperative. Evidence from a number of Democrats, including Wm. R. Morrison, was given to show that Bissell had accepted the Davis challenge. Bissell, who was an anti-Nebraska Democrat when nominated, received 111,466 votes; William A. Richardson (Democrat), 106,769; Buckner S. Morris (Knownothing), 19,088.

JOHN WOOD, Republican, of Adams, who succeded on Bissell's death, March 21, 1860, to Jan. 14, 1861, was born in Moravia, N. Y., Dec. 20, 1798. His father was a surgeon in the Revolutionary war. He moved to Shawneetown in the summer of 1819, and in March, 1820, settled in Pike county, thirty miles southeast of Quincy. In 1821 he visited the present site of Quincy, bought a quarter section of land and in the fall of 1822 erected a cabin on it. It was the first building in Quincy. In 1824 he gave newspaper notice that he would apply to the legislature to form a new county. It was done in the winter of 1825, and in the summer Quincy was selected as the county seat, when there were four male adult and two female inhabitants. He made that his home thereafter. He was mayor and alderman many times, and in 1850 was elected to the State senate. In 1856 he was nominated for Lieutenant Governor by the Republicans, and on Gov. Bissell's death in 1860 became Governor. He was one of the five delegates sent by Illinois to the famous Peace Conference in 1861, and was quartermaster general in Illinois during the war. He was married two times, and died in Quincy June 4, 1880. Gov. Wood was a Whig and afterwards a Republican. It was his influence that named Adams county and the town of Quincy, after his famous hero, John Quincy Adams. He has many descendants left in Quincy and Adams county.

Richd. Yates.

RICHARD YATES, Republican, of Morgan, twelfth Governor elected, Jan. 14, 1861, to Jan. 16, 1865, was born Jan. 18, 1818, at Warsaw, Gallatin county, Ky. In 1831 his father moved to Illinois, stopping for a short time at Springfield, and then settling at Island Grove, Sangamon county. He graduated from Illinois college, Jacksonville, in 1837 with first honors. He chose the law as a profession and soon rose to the first rank. He was a passionate admirer of Henry Clay, and, of course, a Whig. He was elected to the legislature in 1842 from Morgan county. He served several terms, and in 1850 was unanimously chosen as the Whig candidate for congress in a district that extended from Sangamon on the south to LaSalle on the north, and was elected. He was re-elected, and took pronounced grounds against slavery in any form. In 1854 Gov. Yates was defeated for re-election. He was elected Governor in 1860, receiving 172,196 votes to 159,253 for James C. Allen, Democrat, and discharged his duties during the war in a manner to make him the idol of the people. In 1865 he was elected United States Senator to succeed Wm. A. Richardson, Democrat, and was in turn succeeded by Gen. Logan in 1871. He died in St. Louis, Nov. 27, 1873, on his way home from a trip over the Southwestern railroad lines, of which he was a government commissioner.

R. J. Oglesby

RICHARD J. OGLESBY, Republican, of Macon, thirteenth, fifteenth and eighteenth Governor elected, from Jan. 16, 1865, to Jan. 11, 1869; Jan. 13, 1873, to Jan. 23, 1873, and Jan. 30, 1885, to Jan. 14, 1889, was born July 25, 1824, in Oldham county, Kentucky. When 12 years of age he moved with an uncle to Decatur; was apprenticed to a carpenter, farmed and studied law, essaying to practice at Sullivan. He was first lieutenant, Co. C, Fourth Illinois infantry, in the Mexican war. On returning he took a course of law lectures at Louisville, but caught the gold fever and crossed the plains to California. Returning in 1852, he made his first bow in politics as a Scott elector. Later he visited Europe and the Holy Land, and in 1858 was a candidate for congress against James C. Robinson, but was defeated. Was elected State senator in 1860, but resigned, organized a regiment and was made colonel of the Eighth Illinois infantry in the rebellion. He lost 500 men in his corps at Fort Donelson. He has a magnificent war record, and in 1863 was given charge of the Sixteenth army corps, but on account of wounds resigned and returned home. He received 190,376 votes to 158,701 for James C. Robinson, Democrat. Gov. Oglesby was elected United States Senator in 1873 to succeed Lyman Trumbull, resigning the office of Governor, to which he had again been chosen in 1872, when he received 237,774 votes to 197,084 for Gustavus Kœrner, Democrat. Again in 1884 he was elected Governor over Carter H. Harrison, Democrat, receiving 334,234 votes to Harrison's 319,635. He is living on a magnificent farm at Elkhart, Ill.—"Oglehurst."

JOHN M. PALMER, Republican, of Macoupin, fourteenth Governor elected, Jan. 11, 1869, to Jan. 13, 1873, was born in Scott county, Kentucky, Sept. 13, 1817; removed with his father to Madison county, Illinois, in 1831; educated in common schools and spent one year at Shurtleff college, Alton; in 1838 taught school and studied law; admitted to the bar in Dec., 1839; in 1843 was elected probate judge of Macoupin county; was a member of the constitutional convention in 1847; was county judge from 1848 to 1852, when he was elected to the State senate to fill a vacancy; was re-elected in 1854 as an anti-Nebraska Democrat, and nominated and voted for Lyman Trumbull for United States Senator. In 1856 he resigned his seat, having decided to act with the Republicans. He was chairman of the first Republican State convention; delegate to the Philadelphia convention that nominated Fremont; was defeated for congress in 1859; in 1860 was an elector-at-large for Lincoln; member of the Peace Conference of 1861; colonel of the Fourteenth Illinois infantry, and in Nov., 1861, was promoted to brigadier general; has a gallant war record; was promoted to major general in 1863, and in October of that year was given command of the Fourteenth army corps; was relieved at his own request in Aug., 1864; commanded military department of Kentucky from Feb., 1865, to May, 1866. He removed to Springfield in 1867 and was elected Governor in 1868, receiving 249,912 votes to 199,813 for John R. Eden, Democrat. He became a Democrat again in 1872-74, disagreeing with the Republicans on tariff and State rights. He was nominated by the Democrats in 1888, but was defeated by Fifer. He was nominated in State convention by the Democrats for United States Senator in 1890 and elected by the legislature in April, 1891, two farmer Independents voting with the Democrats to elect him. He lives in Springfield.

Oglesby succeeded him in 1873 as Governor, but immediately resigned, having been elected United States Senator, after his inauguration as Governor.

John L. Beveridge

JOHN L. BEVERIDGE, Republican, of Cook, Jan. 23, 1873, to Jan. 8, 1877, who succeeded to office when Gov. Oglesby resigned, was born in Greenwich, Washington county, N. Y., July 6, 1824. He was reared upon a farm and received a common school education. He moved to DeKalb county, Illinois, in 1842, and attended Granville academy and Rock River seminary, located at Mt. Morris. In 1845 he began teaching school in Tennessee; then he read law and was admitted to practice. In 1849, through the mismanagement of his partner, he lost all he had accumulated. In 1851 he had paid his creditors, and then he moved back to DeKalb county. He entered a law office in Sycamore. In 1854 he moved to Evanston, and in the spring of 1855 he opened a law office in Chicago. In 1861 he enlisted (Aug. 27) in the Eighth Illinois cavalry, and was chosen captain of Co. F, which he had raised. Next day he was elected major. In October his regiment joined the Army of the Potomac in Washington. In Nov., 1863, he resigned to organize the Seventeenth cavalry, of which he was elected colonel in Jan., 1864, which he commanded until Oct., 1865; he was mustered out Feb. 6, 1866; in March, 1865, he was brevetted a brigadier general. After the war he resumed the practice of his profession, and in the summer of 1866 was elected sheriff of Cook county. In Nov., 1870, he was elected State senator, resigning in 1871; was elected congressman-at-large in Dec., 1871, vice Logan, resigned to run for United States Senator. In Nov., 1872, was elected lieutenant governor, and in Jan., 1873, resigned as congressman-at-large. When Governor Oglesby was elected United States Senator in 1873 Beveridge became Governor for nearly the full term. He is still living in Chicago and actively practicing his profession.

SHELBY M. CULLOM, Republican, of Sangamon, sixteenth and seventeenth Governor elected, Jan. 8, 1877, to Jan. 10, 1881, Jan. 10, 1881, to Feb. 6, 1883, was born in Wayne Co., Ky, Nov. 22, 1829. His father moved with him to Tazewell Co., Ill., in 1830; he received an academic and university education; went to Springfield in 1853 to study law, and has since lived there; was immediately elected city attorney; was an elector in 1856 on the Fillmore ticket; was elected to the Illinois House in 1856, 1860, 1872 and 1874, and was chosen speaker in 1861 and 1873; was elected to the 39th, 40th and 41st Congresses; delegate to the Philadelphia convention in 1872 and placed Grant in nomination; chairman of the Illinois delegation to the Republican national convention of 1884; was elected governor in 1876, receiving 215,414 votes to 208,580 for Lewis Steward, Democrat and Greenback; was re-elected in 1880, receiving 245,905 votes to 214,515 for Lyman Trumbull, Democrat; Feb. 6, 1883, he resigned, having been elected to the United States Senate to succeed David Davis. In 1889, and again in 1895 he was re-elected. He lives in Springfield. He has never been defeated for any office for which he has been a candidate, and is the only Governor of Illinois elected to succeed himself, excepting Gov. French. Gov. Cullom is married and has one daughter.

JOHN M. HAMILTON, Republican, of McLean, Feb. 6, 1883, to Jan. 30, 1885, who succeeded to the office of Governor, was born in Union county, Ohio, May 28, 1847. In 1854 he came with his parents to Illinois, where he worked upon his father's farm until 16 years of age, when he enlisted in the army. In 1865 he entered Wesleyan university at Delaware, O., graduating in 1868. In 1869 he located in Bloomington, Ill., read law and was admitted to the bar in 1870. He then formed a partnership with J. H. Rowell, which lasted until Gov. Hamilton was inaugurated Governor. He was elected State senator in 1876; was president pro tem. of the senate in the Thirty-first general assembly, and was elected Lieutenant Governor in 1880 with Gov. Cullom. He was, while a member of the senate, the author of the bill creating appellate courts. After retirement from the executive office Gov. Hamilton moved to Chicago, where he is practicing his profession.

He was succeeded on Jan. 30, 1885, by Richard J. Oglesby, eighteenth Governor elected, Republican, of Logan, Jan. 30, 1885, to Jan. 14, 1889. For portrait, biography and vote, see a preceding page. Gov. Oglesby's inauguration was delayed by the failure of the house to permanently organize, the session of 1885 being the one in which Elijah M. Haines, having been elected temporary speaker, declined to permit the election of a speaker, holding that he had been elected to that position; that the constitution did not contemplate a temporary speaker. He finally abdicated the chair, but, being an Independent and holding the balance of power, he then compelled the Democrats to elect him speaker.

JOSEPH W. FIFER, nineteenth governor elected, Republican, of McLean, Jan. 14, 1889, to Jan. 10, 1893, was born in Staunton, Va., Oct. 28, 1842. In 1857 his father moved to McLean Co., Ill. He practically educated himself. His father was a brick mason, and the son was taught that trade. When the war broke out Joseph W. Fifer and his brother, George, enlisted in the 33d Illinois Infantry. He participated in the battles of the Vicksburg campaign, and at Jackson, Miss., on July 13, 1863, in an assault on breastworks he was desperately wounded by a rifle ball, which passed through his right lung and also through the upper portion of his liver. After a time in the hospital he was discharged and returned to his regiment, serving out his time. Returning home in 1864 he entered the Illinois Wesleyan University at Bloomington, from which he graduated in 1868. Then he studied law and was admitted in 1869, beginning practice immediately in Bloomington. He was corporation counsel of Bloomington, states attorney two terms, was elected to the State Senate in 1880, and in 1888 was elected governor by the Republicans after a hot campaign against ex-Gov. Palmer, the Democratic nominee, Fifer receiving 367,860 votes to Palmer's 355,313. After his term as governor he returned to the practice of his profession at Bloomington. He is married and has one son and one daughter.

JOHN P. ALTGELD, twentieth governor elected, Democrat, of Cook, January 10, 1893, to January 11, 1897, was born in Prussia in 1848 and came to this country with his parents when a boy, his father settling on a farm near Mansfield, Ohio. He attended the district school when farm work was not pressing, but at the age of 16 enlisted in the 163d Ohio Infantry, and participated in the closing campaign of the great civil war. After the war he returned home and for the next few years taught school, worked as a farm hand and studied when opportunity offered. He went to St. Louis, working at odd jobs to support himself, and while there, and between the hours of labor, studied law. At Savannah, Mo., he entered a law office and continued his studies. His intense application and faculty for getting at the heart of a subject combined with his natural ability soon brought him to the front. In '74 he was elected prosecuting attorney of Andrew county, but in the fall of '75 he resigned and removed to a wider field—Chicago. He took little interest in politics for several years, but in '84 accepted the Democratic nomination to Congress, and largely reduced the overwhelming republican majority. In '86, without solicitation on his part, he was nominated for Superior Court judge of Cook county, and was elected. His power for organization and close attention to every detail became apparent in this canvass, and was a factor in determining the Democratic State convention in '92 to nominate him for Governor. He resigned from the bench in August, '91. The campaign of '92 was remarkable for the work done by Gov. Altgeld. He received 425,558 votes to 402,676 for Joseph W. Fifer, Republican. Gov. Altgeld is the author of several valuable literary works dealing with economic questions, the most important probably, being "Live Questions." His messages to the General Assembly are considered valuable additions to State papers. He was renominated for Governor by acclamation by the Democratic and Populist State conventions in 1896 and received 474,256 votes to 587,637 for John R. Tanner, Republican. In 1878 he married Miss Emma Ford, of Chicago. Gov. Altgeld resides in Chicago.

THE SENIOR U. S. SENATOR.

Shelby Moore Cullom, son of Richard Northcraft and Elizabeth Coffey Cullom, was born in Monticello, Wayne Co., Ky., Nov. 22, 1829. The following year his father moved to Tazewell Co., Ill. R. N. Cullom was a prominent and influential whig and frequently represented his district in the legislature. Senator Cullom spent two years at Rock River Seminary, Mt. Morris; though in order to maintain himself he found it necessary to devote some time to teaching. In '53 he began the study of law in Springfield. His health becoming impaired his progress was slow and he was admitted to practice in '55. Soon after this he was elected city attorney. In '56 he entered political life as a member of the legislature, and despite the variance of political creed between himself and his constituents, he was returned in '60, although Sangamon county gave the Douglas electors a small majority. Mr. Cullom was chosen speaker. In '62 he was appointed by President Lincoln, with ex-Gov. Boutwell and Charles A. Dana, a commissioner to examine and pass upon the accounts of the quartermasters and U. S. disbursing officers. In '64 he was elected to congress, transforming a democratic majority of 1,365 into a republican majority of 1,785. He introduced a bill on polygamy, for "an act to aid in the execution of the laws," and succeeded in securing its passage through the house. He also secured an appropriation of $320,000 for a federal building in Springfield. He was reëlected in '66 and '68, but in '70 a factious opposition had been aroused, he was defeated for the nomination, and the district was lost to the republicans. In '72 he was returned to the General Assembly, and unanimously chosen speaker by the republican caucus. In '74 he was again elected to the house.

In '76 he was elected governor, and in the administration he developed the highest qualities of statesmanship. In '80 he was again elected governor, the first and only time a governor has been elected to succeed himself for two full terms. In '83 he was advanced to the U. S. senate and was reëlected in '89 and '95. His senatorial career has been brought most prominently before the public through his Inter-State Commerce bill. Senator Cullom has been in the service of his state and country over a third of a century, and there are years of usefulness yet before him. Should the day come when the people shall call upon him to fill the chair occupied by those two other great sons of Illinois—Lincoln and Grant— the record of his past affords the surest guarantee that the destinies of the republic may safely be entrusted to him.

U. S. SENATOR CULLOM.

THE JUNIOR U. S. SENATOR.

William Ernest Mason, was born in Franklinville, N. Y., July 7, 1850. In '58 the family moved to Bentonsport, Iowa, where the father died in '65. The senator had received the rudiments of an education, and had studied two years at Birmingham College. He began teaching school and devoted himself alternately to teaching and studying until '68. During the next two years he taught in the public schools of Des Moines.

He then began the study of law and removed to Chicago. In '77 he formed a partnership with Judge M. R. M. Wallace and later with Mr. Ennis. He was known as a safe connselor and especially as an able and eloquent advocate. Mr. Mason has always been a staunch republican, and an enthusiastic worker in the interest of that party. Before he was 30 years old he was a member of the General Assembly of Illinois, and in '82 was sent to the senate. In the legislature he was conspicuous for his ability, devotion to the interests of his constituency, and close attention to business.

In '86 he was elected congressman from the Third district, was reëlected in '88, and won honor for himself, and reflected credit upon those who elected him. Possessing oratorical powers of high order, a ready wit and a broad knowledge of public affairs, he distinguished himself on the floor of the house on numerous occasions.

Senator Mason is a man of the people, and from experience knows their needs, their hopes and their ambitions, and enters heartily into any movement calculated to better their condition. He was one of the most popular men in congress, being under all circumstances a most genial and affable gentleman.

In the presidential campaign of '88 he became widely known as an effective political speaker, and during the hotly contested campaign of '90 in Ohio in which he participated, he won renown as a campaign orator.

U. S. SENATOR MASON.

In the campaign of '96 he stumped Illinois from one end to the other untiringly for five months, and after the election he went into his own campaign for the United States senate, which terminated successfully Jan. 20, '97. He has already distinguished himself as a parliamentarian in the senate, and is destined to become one of the leaders of that august body.

Senator Mason has recently formed a partnership, under the title of Mason, Holmes & Mason. Judge Holmes is a distinguished lawyer from Sioux City, and the junior member of the firm is Mr. Mason's eldest son, Lewis F., who is a promising young man.

In '73, Mr. Mason was married to Miss Edith Julia White, of Des Moines, Iowa, and they have seven children.

THE SECRETARY OF STATE.

James A. Rose, secretary of state of Illinois, was born October 13, 1850, and has spent his entire life in Illinois, having been raised in Golconda, the county seat of Pope county. Mr. Rose's opportunity for an education was confined to the public schools and to one term in the Northern Illinois Normal University. He commenced teaching before he was 17 years old, in a country school in his own county. Four years thereafter he was elected as principal of the graded schools of his home town, Golconda.

At the age of 22 he was elected county superintendent of schools of Pope county, as a republican, and was reëlected four years thereafter. Before the close of his second term he was admitted to the bar and a year later was petitioned by the citizens of his county to resign the office of county superintendent of schools to become state's attorney of the county, which he did, being elected without opposition. At the end of his first term as state's attorney he was renominated and reëlected. He refused to be a candidate for a third term.

In 1889 he was appointed by Governor Fifer one of the trustees of the Pontiac Reformatory, in which position he served not quite one year, when the governor appointed him one of the commissioners of the Southern Illinois Penitentiary at Chester, in which position he remained until the change in administrations in 1893. In the spring of 1896, Mr. Rose having been solicited by a number of friends throughout the state, became a candidate for the office of secretary of state. He received the nomination from the republican state convention in the spring and was elected by a majority of 137,611.

SECRETARY OF STATE ROSE.

Mr. Rose is a married man, having been wedded on July 14, 1874, to Miss Elizabeth Young, of Golconda. His acquaintance throughout the state is quite extensive. He was one of the leading campaign speakers during the last three campaigns. During the campaign of 1896 perhaps no speaker or candidate traveled more miles or made more speeches than he.

In his new office Mr. Rose has instituted several needed reforms, and bids fair to administer the affairs of his responsible office in a manner to merit the commendation of the people.

Harrington Clanahan, of Golconda, Chief Clerk in the Secretary of State's office, was born on a farm in Pope county, Ill., Oct. 21, 1850. He completed his education at the Illinois

MR. CLANAHAN.

State Normal in '71. In '72 he married Mary E. Hodge and they have two daughters, Myrtle and Lucy, and one son, Robert. Mr. Clanahan taught school for ten years and in '80 declined the principalship of the Golconda public schools, to accept the republican nomination for circuit clerk, to which office he was elected five times in succession, each time by an increased majority and in every case running ahead of his ticket, his last election being in '96. After the election he accepted the position he now holds and on February 15, '97, resigned the office of circuit clerk. For many years Mr. Clanahan has been an influential factor in southern Illinois politics and his counsel was usually sought in all party matters.

MR. SPEAR.

Stephen L. Spear, of Bloomington, Chief of the Index Department, was born at Alton, Ill., in 1848. He grew up on a farm near Carrollton, and taught school for a number of years in Greene, Pope and McLean counties, attending school at the Illinois State Normal in intervals of teaching. He was for a while editor of the Golconda Herald, and in '82 was elected county superintendent of schools for Pope county, which office he resigned in '84 to accept a position with a Chicago manufacturing concern. In '93 he went to Australia as the representative of an American manufacturing company, returning in time to take an active part in the campaign of '96. He proved himself a logical and forcible speaker and writer on the financial questions so largely discussed during the late campaign.

Theodore S. McCoy, of Golconda, Private Secretary to the Secretary of State, was born July 28, 1871, at Golconda, and completed his education at the Southern Illinois Normal. In '91 he was appointed official court reporter for the First Judicial circuit.

MR. McCOY.

and served until Dec., '94. In the spring of '94, Mr. McCoy received the republican nomination for county clerk, being but 22 years of age. He was elected by a large majority. During the last campaign he was secretary of the county committee, also a member of the senatorial committee of his district, and did good work for the success of his party. Jan. 18, '97, he resigned as county clerk to accept his present position.

Albert Brown, of Springfield, Chief Engineer, was born in Washington, D. C., October 6, 1846, and moved to Springfield with his parents in '50. Here he received a common school education, and at 15 started to learn the trade of machinist. Soon after he enlisted in Co. G, 114th Ill. Inf. (Aug. '62), serving nearly three years, and participating in the battles of Jackson, siege of Vicksburg, retaking of Jackson, Guntown, Tupelo, Nashville and

Spanish Fort; mustered out at Vicksburg, Sept., '65. Then he returned home and finished his trade at the Wabash shops. For six years he was with the C. & A. R. R., building loco-

MR. BROWN.

motives, and for three years was in the North Chicago Rolling Mills. Mr. Brown had charge of the hydraulic machinery in the Bessemer steel mill. From there he returned to Springfield, and entered the Watch Factory, where he remained for eighteen years, resigning to take his present place. He is married and has two children.

Oscar D. Spotts, of Springfield, Chief Carpenter, was born at DuQuoin February 12, 1860. He was educated in the high school and soon afterwards learned the carpenter's trade. He came to Springfield in '92, and was foreman for the Springfield Planing Mill. When James A. Rose became

MR. SPOTTS.

secretary of state he appointed Mr. Spotts as chief carpenter. Mr. Spotts was highly endorsed by the labor unions, trades assembly and other organizations. He has been president and vice president of the local Carpenters' Union. He was president of the Springfield Federated Trades Assembly for three successive terms, and holds that position now. Mr. Spotts is one of the leading republicans of his ward. He is married and has a son and a daughter.

George H. Switzer, of London Mills, Chief of Shipping Department, Secretary of State's office, was born in Chestnut township, Knox Co., Ill., May 22, 1862, and finished his education at Hedding College. In '85-'86 he taught school and in '87 he was general traveling agent for a law publishing house in Chicago. Subsequently he engaged in the insurance business in Knoxville. Early in '90 he leased the Times, published at London Mills, an independent newspaper, which he published for nearly a year. In '90 he married Miss M. Ella VanCleave, of Knoxville, and they have one daughter. In '92 he again became connected with the London Times as foreman and editor of a department, a position which he re-

MR. SWITZER.

tained until his appointment to his present position. Mr. Switzer is a republican, a Methodist in religion, and a Woodman. Mr. Switzer has inaugurated needed reforms in his department, and a better system prevails than ever before. He gives his personal attention to every detail of the office.

William Hamilton Miller, of Streator, Chief of Supply Department, was born at Woodside, Lanarkshire, Scotland, June 18, 1866, and was brought to this country when an infant. The family settled in Streator, Ill., in '77, where Mr. Miller worked in coal mines when a boy, and obtained a fair education. He learned the printer's trade and helped organize the local typographical union. He did reportorial and editorial work on Streator dailies for ten years, and was advertising manager for two years for Heenan's large department store. He served on the LaSalle county board from '93-'97. He is not married. Mr. Miller has been active in politics since he attained his majority, and there was no more

MR. MILLER.

active or energetic republican worker in Streator or LaSalle county during the hotly contested campaign of '96 than he.

Charles S. Whitney, of Springfield, Chief Electrician, Secretary of State's office, was born in Springfield, October 25, 1865, and obtained a common school education. Then he served his time in modern machine shop practice. In '84 he entered the Springfield Electric Light Co., and two years later was made superintendent and electrician. In '93 he was superintendent and manager of the electric light company of Pekin, and later was chief engineer of the Bloomington Electric Light Co., and for the past few years electrician and superintendent of electrical con-

MR. WHITNEY.

struction of the R. Haas Electric and Mfg. Co., of Springfield. He is married and has one son. He is a Mason and an Odd Fellow. Mr. Whitney has made a life study of electricity and its application to light and power purposes. In Springfield he is a recognized authority on the subject. Since he assumed control of the electric department of the capitol, one of the most responsible positions in the state, there has been a great improvement in the service.

THE PRINTER EXPERT.

John H. Barton, printer expert, was born in West Carlyle, O., Jan. 2, 1837. Completed his education at the West Bedford (O.) Academy. In '51 he apprenticed himself to the Coshocton (O.) Republican to learn the printers' trade. The Republican was then under the management of Hon. Joseph Medill, now of the Chicago Tribune. After completing his apprenticeship Mr. Barton worked as a journeyman in all the larger western cities, making a specialty of fine job printing. In the fall of '60 he established the Union Dem-

MR. BARTON.

ocrat, at Anna. In May, '61, he enlisted in the army and was commissioned first lieutenant of Co. I, 18th Ill. Vol. Inf. In '65 he returned to his trade as a journeyman, and the next year purchased the New Era at Carbondale, and except a term of five years as postmaster at Carbondale, has ever since been a publisher and editor in Carbondale. At present he is editor of the Southern Illinois Herald. He was appointed printer expert by Gov. Tanner March 17, '97. Mr. Barton is one of the best known newspaper men in Illinois, and for years has been one of the most prominent journalists of southern Illinois. He is the first member of the Typographical Union to fill the position. Mr. Barton's appointment was especially gratifying to labor organizations for this reason. In politics he has been a prominent and influential figure in Illinois for a great many years. Always active and earnest, he was never an office seeker.

AUDITOR OF PUBLIC ACCOUNTS.

James Skiles McCullough, Auditor of Public Accounts of Illinois, was born near Mercersburg, Franklin county, Pa., and moved to Urbana with his father in April, 1854. He attended the Urbana High School for one year, and the Illinois Soldiers' College at Fulton for two years after his discharge from the army. Mr. McCullough followed farming until the summer of 1862, when he enlisted in Company G, Seventy-sixth Illinois Volunteer Infantry, and participated in the battles of Vicksburg, Jackson, Benton, Jackson Cross Roads, Vaughan's Station, the Meridian campaign, Fort Blakely and others of importance. Mr. McCullough lost his left arm in the assault on Fort Blakely, April 9, 1865, from the effects of a grape shot. In 1868 he returned home from the Fulton College and entered the county clerk's office as a deputy, and served for five years. Then he was elected county clerk, and served continuously from 1873 until 1896, when he resigned to take his present office—a total of twenty-three years in the same office.

STATE AUDITOR McCULLOUGH.

In 1869 Mr. McCullough was married to Miss Celinda Harvey, of Urbana, and they have one son and one daughter. The family are Presbyterians.

Mr. McCullough has always been a stalwart republican, and is personally acquainted with probably 90 per cent of the people of Champaign county. He never sought an office outside his own county until 1896, when he was induced to permit the use of his name for state auditor before the republican state convention. Of course his old comrades were enthusiastically for him, and as the campaign before the state convention progressed, friends sprang up unexpectedly in all parts of the state. He was nominated and added strength to the ticket. Mr. McCullough received 601,574 votes to 463,561 for A. L. Maxwell, the candidate of the democrats and populists, running ahead of a majority of his colleagues on the republican state ticket. He is a member of Black Eagle Post 129, G. A. R., of Urbana.

George S. Thomas, of Chicago, Chief of Banking Department, Auditor's office, was born in Whitehall, Ill., July 6, 1846. His father organized the First National Bank in Champaign in

MR. THOMAS.

'66, and Mr. Thomas became paying teller and acting cashier. Three years later he was one of the organizers of the private bank of Thomas Bros. & Weedman at Farmer City. In '76 he sold his interest to his partners and went into the mining and railroad construction business in Colorado, which he continued for five years. In '84 he started a real estate and mortgage business in Chicago. Mr. Thomas always has been a republican and active in politics, yet this is his first political office. He is thoroughly acquainted with the banking business in all its details.

MR. EUBANKS.

William H. Eubanks, of Marion, Chief Clerk to the State Auditor, was born in Williamson county, Dec. 13, 1846, and finished his education at the State Normal. After his school days he entered the county offices in Williamson county and was deputy county clerk and deputy sheriff until '73, when he was elected county clerk, which he held for nine years. In Dec., '82, he was appointed chief clerk in the office of the internal revenue collector at Cairo, serving four years. After this he engaged in the mercantile business until Jan., '89, when State Auditor Pavey tendered him the position of chief clerk in the auditor's office. He filled this place until the advent of the democrats in '93. Mr. Eubanks was elected secretary of the State Board of Equalization in '89, and in Jan., '97, he accepted his old place in the auditor's office. In Jan., '64, when 17 years old, he enlisted in the Mississippi Marine Brigade, serving on the ram Monarch until the close of the war. Mr. Eubanks is married and has one daughter living. He is one of the republican leaders in southern Illinois and has always taken an active part in politics.

MR. WILLIAMS.

H. D. Williams, of Charleston, Chief Clerk Warrant Department, Auditor's office, was born in New York city in 1845 and came to Illinois with his father in '54, locating on a farm in Edgar county. He volunteered as a member of Co. I, 66th Ill., during the war, participating in the battles of Corinth, Iuka, Snake Creek Gap, Resaca, Dallas, Altoona, Atlanta, Kenesaw Mountain and Jonesboro; was with Sherman on his march to the sea, also through the Carolinas, taking part in the battle of Bentonville, N. C. He was in the grand review at Washington. Mr. Williams never had a furlough during the war. He has been engaged in business most of the time since the war, filling some minor political positions; was deputy county clerk and deputy treasurer six years in Coles county.

THE STATE TREASURER.

Henry L. Hertz, State Treasurer of Illinois, was born Nov. 19, 1847, in Copenhagen, Denmark, his grandparents having emigrated there from Hanover and Bavaria, Germany. He received a classic education in the Metropolitan Latin School and graduated from the University of Copenhagen with honors receiving the degree of arts in 1866, and the degree of philosophy in 1867. He studied medicine two years and in 1869 emigrated to the United States, and made his home in Chicago, on the northwest side, where he has resided ever since. His first years passed as those of any immigrant, trying to make a living by hard work. He was agent for Wheeler & Wilson's Sewing Machine Company for a while, was clerk in a bank for a couple of years, and immediately after the fire he worked as a farm hand on a farm near Dixon, in Lee county.

STATE TREASURER HERTZ.

In 1878 he was transferred from a clerkship in the recorder's office to the position of record writer in the office of the clerk of the Criminal Court, where he remained until he, in 1884, was elected coroner of Cook county by 10,000 majority. In 1888 he was reëlected coroner by an overwhelming majority, running about 5,000 ahead of his ticket. In 1892 he was nominated for state treasurer, but was beaten, together with the balance of the republican ticket, in the big landslide.

He is one of the active working republicans of this county, and has for many years been one of the best organizers within the ranks of the republican party. As an instance of his organization and his general work for the party, we call attention to the vote on the northwest side twelve years ago and now. Twelve years ago that part of the county gave about 3,000 democratic majority. In 1894 the same territory gave about 7,000 republican majority.

Mr. Hertz is a member of a great many societies. He is a life member of Oriental Consistory, Thirty-Second Degree Masons; belongs to the Odd Fellows, Royal Arcanum, Knights of Pythias, Royal League, I. O. M. A., Knights of Honor, Covenant Lodge No. 526, A. F. and A. M., and Medinah Temple, Nobles of the Mystic Shrine. Mr. Hertz married Miss Mary P. Power in 1880 and with his wife and five children lives a happy home life at No. 628 North Hoyne avenue.—Inter Ocean, April 29, 1896.

In '96 Mr. Hertz received 589,714 to 473,050 for Edward C. Pace, fusion candidate of the democrats and populists.

THE ATTORNEY GENERAL.

Edward C. Akin, Attorney General of Illinois, was born in Will county, July 19, 1852, and was educated in the public schools of Joliet, and at Ann Arbor, Mich. For four years he was paying and receiving teller in the First National Bank of Joliet, where he acquired an extensive acquaintance throughout Will county. He was admitted to the bar in the fall of 1878, and has continued in active practice ever since. He began his political career in 1887, when he was nominated as the republican candidate for city attorney of Joliet, and although the city was at the time democratic from 500 to 600 he defeated the democratic nominee by a majority of 716. In 1888 he was nominated for state's attorney of Will county, and at the election led the entire state and county ticket by 800 votes. In 1892 he was renominated and again led his ticket by hundreds of votes, and is credited by the leaders of both political parties with having saved the republican county ticket from defeat. His most brilliant political victory was achieved in the spring of 1895, when he ran as the republican candidate for mayor of Joliet. Although opposed by a citizens' ticket, led by a republican, he defeated the democratic nominee by a majority of 260 votes, receiving nearly as many votes as both his opponents combined.

As a lawyer he stands among the leaders at the Will county bar. As a public prosecutor he has no superior in the state, and his conduct of municipal affairs won for him the admiration of all good citizens, regardless of party. He is a man of high character and sterling integrity, and although he has been prominently before the people of his county for the past ten years, no breath of suspicion has ever been cast upon his private life or official acts. Mr. Akin is a man of fine appearance and pleasing address, and has won an enviable reputation throughout the state as a public speaker.

ATTORNEY GENERAL AKIN.

Attorney General Akin has rendered opinions on several very important questions thus early in his incumbency, and the Supreme Court has taken the same view as Mr. Akin on every question submitted to it, in which the attorney general has been interested.

Mr. Akin is married to Louise M. McRoberts, eldest daughter of Judge Josiah McRoberts, and they have one child, Gertrude McR., aged 18.

Mr. Akin received 598,965 votes for his present office to 466,306 for M. C. Crawford, fusionist.

THE ADJUTANT-GENERAL.

Gen. J. N. Reece is a prominent and well known citizen of Springfield. He has ably served the state in various important official capacities and is a conspicuous figure in military circles. He was born in Abingdon, Knox Co., April 30, 1841, and passed his boyhood days in obtaining an education, and was one of the first students to enter Hedding College at Abingdon. He was scarcely 20 when he enlisted as a private in the early part of the war. Later he enlisted in another regiment and in Oct., '64, was mustered out as a captain of his company. He saw much service in the southwest, his command being engaged in clearing that region from the terror of bushwhackers. The pursuit of the guerillas kept his command busily at work in the saddle for days.

After the war he gave his attention to farming and mercantile pursuits at and near Monmouth for seven years. In '71 he was elected first assistant clerk of the house, and in '73 he was assistant secretary of state under Col. Harlow. In '77 he became assistant adjutant general of the Second Brigade, I. N. G., Brigadier General E. N. Bates commanding. In the latter capacity, under the direction of his commanding officer, he was in charge of the military during the riots in July, 1877, at East St. Louis. In November following he was made brigadier-general, commanding the Second Brigade. In '81-'82 he was chief clerk in the United States marshal's office, and was private secretary to Gov. Hamilton, '83-'85. In '86 he was in command of the forces at East St. Louis during the railroad riots, which lasted six weeks, and it was owing to his firmness and courage that the rioters were held in check. Gen. Reece also in charge of the troops during other strikes.

Gen. Reece is recognized as one of the best military men and organizers in the citizen soldiery of the country.

Gen. Reece ranks high in the Masonic order. He is prominent in all benevolent societies, and is at present a director of the Modern Woodmen of America, one of the largest and most successfully managed fraternal societies in the world. He is a man of great social prominence in city, county and state.

Politically he is a republican—unswerving and uncompromising. July 1, '91, he was appointed adjutant-general by Gov. Fifer, retiring from command of the Second Brigade after a service of fourteen years as its commander. He held the position of adjutant-general until the change of administration in '93. For four years he devoted his time to the interests of the Modern Woodmen of America and to farming. Feb. 2, '97, he was appointed by Gov. Tanner as adjutant general, his present position.

ADJUTANT-GENERAL REECE.

APPELLATE COURT—1st District.

Thomas Nevin Jamieson, of Chicago, Clerk of the Appellate Court, First District, was born in Durham, County of Grey, Province of Ontario, Canada, February 29, 1848, of Scotch parents. He received a good education in the famous schools of Ontario, and at the age of 14 he was apprenticed to a druggist. At the age of 18 he went to Chicago, his ambition being for a larger field. In '70 he embarked in the drug business on his own account, and ever since has been identified with the drug business in Chicago. For three years he was president of the Retail Drug Association of Chicago, and for five years was president of the State Board of Pharmacy. Notwithstanding the prominence he has attained in politics he still retains his drug stores in Chicago. He was city sealer under Mayor Washburn, and later was superintendent of public service of Cook county for two years. Dr. Jamieson is happily married and has two sons and two daughters.

APPELLATE COURT CLERK JAMIESON.

Dr. Jamieson early identified himself with the republican party, and being endowed with a natural genius for political organization and management, he soon came to the front among the political leaders of that organization, and his skill, sagacity and good judgment soon became recognized. He was secretary of the republican state committee during the campaign of 1888 when "Private Joe" Fifer was elected governor of Illinois, and was the principal manager of the campaign which made James H. Gilbert sheriff of Cook county; also of the campaign which resulted in the election of Hempstead Washburn mayor of Chicago. During the Washburn administration Dr. Jamieson was entrusted with the distribution of the offices, and exerted an important influence on the general policy of the administration. In the election of 1894, which resulted in such a notable triumph of his party, Dr. Jamieson exerted a powerful influence. He was chairman of the state committee in 1896, which he resigned to accept the position of national committeeman for Illinois. In this capacity he was frequently called into counsel with Chairman Hanna of the national committee, and was one of the most prominent figures in the political world during the fierce battle between the republicans and democrats. For clerk of the appellate court he received 218,853 votes to 153,272 for Thomas G. McElligott, fusion.

APPELLATE COURT—2nd District.

Christopher C. Duffy is now serving his second term as clerk of the Appellate Court, Second district, having been elected in 1890 and again in 1896. He was born in Dublin, Ireland, April 15, 1843, and moved to Chicago with his parents in 1850. During the terrible cholera epidemic that swept Chicago in 1854, Mr. Duffy lost both his parents, and he was thrown on his own resources. He entered the newspaper business in the humble capacity of carrier for the Chicago Times, and after his route was delivered sold papers on the streets of Chicago. At that time twelve boys covered the streets of Chicago by selling papers. Every one of them attained more or less celebrity afterwards in the political and financial world. Young Duffy wanted an education, and leaving Chicago he worked on a DeKalb county farm in summer and did chores in winter to pay for his schooling. For several summers he sailed before the mast on Lake Michigan to vary the monotony of farm life.

In 1862 he enlisted from the harvest field in the 105th Illinois Infantry, and never was absent from his regiment from the time it left Chicago until it was honorably mustered out after the grand review in Washington at the close of the war. After the war he attended the Northern Illinois College at Fulton, graduating in 1871. After this he taught school in Kendall county, and remained in that county for nineteen years—until his election as clerk of the Appellate Court in 1890 seven years he was a teacher and principal of Plano's public schools, and twelve years he was county superintendent of schools. He was elected in 1890 by a majority of 28,000 and in 1896 received 164,443 votes to 90,459 for Wm. D. Stewart, democrat. His term expires in 1902. The consolidation of the supreme court at Springfield does not affect Mr. Duffy's office.

APPELLATE COURT CLERK DUFFY.

Mr. Duffy is married and has six children. He always has been an ardent republican, and served a term on the state committee in 1888. The Second Appellate district comprises the thirty-two northern counties of the state except Cook county.

APPELLATE COURT—4th District.

Frank W. Havill, Clerk of the Appellate Court, Fourth District, came to Illinois from Ohio at the age of 14. He was born at Roscoe, O., on the Muskingum, and now lives at Mt. Carmel, on the Wabash. He has worked at a little of everything from driving a dirt cart on a new railroad to playing politics in Egypt. He has been a success at everything. He was private, first lieutenant, captain and assistant inspector general in the civil war, serving four years in the 15th Army Corps. He was twice severely wounded, being shot through the right leg at Shiloh and the left shoulder at Kenesaw Mountain. He struck his gait in civil life when he entered the newspaper business, and as publisher of the Mt. Carmel Register (established 1839) he has achieved an unqualified success. When he bought the paper it was printed with "shoe pegs and apple butter on a cheese press." Now the Register office is one of the most complete country printing offices in the west, and the paper is more frequently quoted than any other in southern Illinois. Mr. Havill has held all the offices that Mt. Carmel could induce him to take. He was also postmaster under Cleveland's first administration. He hopes he will sometime be forgiven for accepting anything from Cleveland. He was twice master in chancery of Wabash county, and in 1890 was elected clerk of the supreme court, Southern grand division. He declined to be a candidate for reëlection, but was drafted into service for his present place. At the election in 1894 the counties comprising the present Fourth Appellate district gave a republican plurality of 12,324, and a clear republican majority of 3,000 over all. He was honored with the people's party nomination in 1896, as well as his own party. To the surprise of the opposition he succeeded in being elected by a majority of 1,416, running about 1,000 votes ahead of Mr. Bryan. Frank's democracy is stalwart, and he believes in lambasting the enemy upon every occasion, but his keen assaults are usually directed against parties, not individuals. His friends are not restricted by party lines. He is at home in all the lodges—Knights Templar, Shriners, Masons, Workmen, Red Men, Odd Fellows, Grangers, Knights of Labor, and Providence only knows what else. He is married and has a cozy home in Mt. Carmel, where he lives with his wife and two younger boys, and where the latchstring is always out. The eldest son, Orra, is publisher of the Lawrenceville News. The second son, a bright handsome youth, was killed by the cars in 1895. Frank is at present member-at-large of the democratic state committee.

APPELLATE COURT CLERK HAVILL.

SUPREME COURT CLERK CHANCE.

SUPREME COURT—So. Grand Div.

Jacob O. Chance, Clerk of the Supreme Court of the Southern Grand Division, is now a resident of Mt. Vernon. He was born in the country, about eight miles southeast of Salem, where his father, Reuben Chance, located at an early day. Upon the old home farm Jacob O. Chance was reared and in the public schools was educated. In '56 he was assistant circuit clerk and in '60 was elected circuit clerk for four years. On the expiration of his term he was appointed master in chancery by the Hon. Silas L. Bryan, circuit judge, and in 1869 he was elected county clerk, serving until 1873. During that time he read law and was admitted to the bar. He also made the first set of abstract books ever made in the county and continued in the abstract business in connection with real estate dealing until the fall of 1878, when he was elected clerk of the Supreme Court for the Southern grand division, and in 1884 he was reëlected, filling the office for two terms, or twelve years. In 1896 he was again elected to the same position.

Mr. Chance is a Royal Arch Mason and in politics has been a life-long democrat. Since attaining his majority he has almost continuously been connected with public office and in the discharge of his official duties he has ever been found faithful and true, and Jefferson county recognizes in him one of its best citizens. His residence is the old place settled by Gov. Zadok Casey, at a very early day, adjoining Mt. Vernon.

Mr. Chance received 87,463 votes to 86,093 for R. E. Mabery, republican, for his present office.

SUPREME COURT—Cent. Grand Div.

Albert D. Cadwallader, of Lincoln, was born in Ohio in 1846, and came to Illinois with his parents in '54. He received his education in the common schools and at the age of 16 enlisted in Co. B, 85th Ill. Vol. as a private, was promoted to orderly sergeant of his company and afterwards to first lieutenant, and upon the captain of his company being wounded, he took command. At the battle of Peach Tree Creek he lost his right arm. Prior to being wounded he participated in a number of battles, Perryville, Stone River, Chickamauga, Resaca, Kenesaw Mountain, Missionary Ridge, and others of minor importance. After the war he was a telegrapher for a number of years and in '69 was appointed postmaster at Lincoln, which office he held for about seventeen years; in '83 he was admitted to the bar and was in the active practice of his profession until December, '96, when he took

CLERK CADWALLADER.

charge of his present office. He was elected in '96, receiving 133,450 to 131,-164 for E. A. Snively, fusion. For many years he has been an enthusiastic member of the Grand Army of the Republic and has been a member of the council of administration of that order in this state for a number of years.

APPELLATE COURT—3rd Dist.

William C. Hippard, of Marshall, Clerk of the Appellate Court, Third district, was born December 6, 1863, at Marshall. His father was one of the early settlers of that section, having moved there from Virginia when quite a young man. Mr. Hippard was married to Mary Grace Littlefield, daughter of John Littlefield, editor of the democratic organ of Clark county, and a man of many notable characteristics, June 30, '86. They have two children, George, aged 10, and Lenore, aged 5. He is a republican in politics, and was elected city clerk of Marshall, April 17, '88, and has been reëlected without opposition ever since, resigning that office before en-

CLERK HIPPARD.

tering upon the duties of his present position. He received 133,346 votes to 131,318 for Geo. W. Jones, fusion candidate.

THE STATE GEOLOGIST.

C. Henry Crantz, of Chicago, State Geologist and Curator of the Illinois State Museum of Natural History, was born Oct. 3, 1849, in Wexio, Sweden, where he went through the schools and graduated at the University of Upsala. He moved to Chicago in '73, where he soon engaged in business, being for a number of years a member of the Board of Trade, in the meantime keeping up his studies of the natural sciences. In Feb., '97, he was appoint-

MR. CRANTZ.

ed state geologist by the governor, secretary of state and superintendent of public instruction. He is married and has two children. He is a Mason and Odd Fellow of many years' standing.

INSURANCE SUPERINTENDENT.

James R. B. VanCleave, of Chicago, Insurance Superintendent, was born at Knoxville, Ill., October 9 1853, and received his education at Knox College, Galesburg, working for the money necessary to pay his expenses at school. He was traveling correspondent for the Chicago Times in the south and also in the employ of the New York Herald, and established many branch news agencies for the Herald. In January, '80 he was elected secretary of the first Blaine club organized in Chicago. After the national ticket. In March, '95, he was again elected city clerk by a majority of 45,000. When he originally came into this office it was nearly impossible to find many of the papers and documents. Mr. VanCleave indexed and numbered all the papers from the time of the fire down, and otherwise placed the business under a complete and convenient system. Since '78 he has been at every republican state convention, and has attended all republican national conventions since '76, holding official positions in all of them. Since '76 he has held official position in the First Ward republican club and in all that time no candidate that he and his

SUPERINTENDENT VANCLEAVE.

republican convention Mr. VanCleave was called to Mentor to act as assistant secretary to the candidate until the arrival of Gen. Swain and Col. Rockwell—personal friends of Mr. Garfield. In Jan., '81 he was elected an enrolling and engrossing clerk of the Illinois senate and acted as private secretary to Wm. J. Campbell. In July, '81, he was appointed by William Henry Smith, collector of customs for Chicago, as his private secretary and chief clerk of the Chicago custom house. He was reappointed by Jesse Spaulding and Anthony F. Seeberger. In '87 he was made deputy city clerk of Chicago under D. W. Nickerson and also under City Clerk Amberg. In April, '91, he was elected city clerk, leading his ticket by 10,000. In '93 he was defeated for reëlection, but received 13,000 more votes than any other candidate on the friends selected as delegates, has been defeated. He has been secretary of the Cook county committee for years and since '81 has beeen secretary of every state and county convention. In '96 he was secretary of the state committee, and one of the executive officers in charge of the campaign.

He is connected with the Union League, Chicago Athletic, Marquette, LaSalle, Miltona, Cumberland and Eagle River Shooting and Fishing clubs, Apollo Commandery, K. T.; Medinah Temple, Mystic Shrine, Knights of Pythias, A. O. U. W., Royal Arcanum and National Union. Appointed inspector of rifle practice, I.N.G. by Gov. Tanner. He married Miss Josephine Helen Sweich, of Richmond, Mo., in '81, and they have two children, Helen Farwell (10), and Bruce (1).

R.R. and WAREHOUSE COMMISSION

Cicero J. Lindly, of Greenville, chairman of the Railroad and Warehouse Commission, was born on a farm near St. Jacobs, Madison Co., Ill., December 11, 1857. His ancestors were early settlers in Madison county, although his father and mother were native born Illinoisians. His mother, Amanda Agnes Palmer, was born where a portion of Joliet now stands, and his father was born in Madison county. Mr. Lindly's father moved his family to Lebanon in 1867 to take advantage of McKendree College for his children, and in this excellent school Cicero J. Lindly received his education. He graduated in the scientific course in 1877, and from the law department two years later. The same year he was examined by the supreme court at Mt. Vernon and passed, but the license to practice could not be issued, on account of Mr. Lindly being under twenty-one years old. He went to St. Louis with ex.-Gov. Fletcher, and at the Court of Appeals in that city was examined again, passing with credit and was admitted to practice before he was of age.

December 22, 1880, Mr. Lindly married Miss Alice J. McNeill, of Greenville, daughter of an extensive stockdealer and banker. They moved to the old homestead near St. Jacobs, where he farmed for two years. In 1882 Mr. Lindly purchased a section of land near Greenville, and it has since been his home.

Mr. Lindly has been in politics all his life, and has had an active and sometimes personal interest in every biennial election in Illinois since 1886. In 1880 he was secretary of the St. Clair county républican convention, and was prominently connected with the Grant and anti-Grant fight that year. In 1884 he was a delegate to the republican state convention at Peoria, and was presidential elector that year. In 1886 he was elected county judge of Bond county. In 1888 he was a delegate to the republican national convention, and represented Illinois on the committee on credentials. He was chairman of the special committee that drafted the report to the national convention on the Mahone-Wise contested case from Virginia.

In 1890 he was nominated for congress and largely reduced the democratic majority. In 1891 he was the "last-ditch" candidate of the republicans for United States senator, when three alleged farmer members held the balance of power between the two old parties. He has been a personal friend of Gov. Tanner for twenty years, and was active in his interest long before the state convention met in 1896. No man worked harder in that campaign than Mr. Lindly. He spoke night and day for three months preceding the election.

COMMISSIONER LINDLY.

COMMISSIONER RANNELLS.

R.R. and WAREHOUSE COMMISSION

Charles S. Rannells, of Jacksonville, member of the Railroad and Warehouse Commission, was born on a Morgan county (Illinois) farm, December 5, 1857. His early life was that of the farmers' boys of the '60's. He went to school and finished his education by graduating from that famous Jacksonville institution, Illinois College, class of '79, in the classical course. He has been trustee of Illinois College for the past ten years, and for the past eight years he has been a trustee of the Young Ladies' Presbyterian Seminary, at Jacksonville.

The first political office Mr. Rannells ever filled is his present one on the Railroad and Warehouse Commission. He was highly endorsed for the position by farmers and stockmen from every section of the state, and represents that element of Illinois' population on the board.

Mr. Rannells has been an active figure in state politics for several years. In 1894 he was chosen member of the republican state committee, and was placed on the executive committee by Chairman John R. Tanner of the state committee. He was also a member of the finance committee. He was reëlected to the state committee in 1896, chosen chairman of the executive committee and was actively engaged in directing the campaign from the committee headquarters in Chicago. Mr. Rannells' labors in the campaign of 1896 were appreciated by the republicans of the state, and he received complimentary mention when he made his report at the close of the campaign.

In 1880 Mr. Rannells married Miss Cornelia May Stevenson, daughter of S. C. Stevenson, of Orleans, Morgan county.

He has been a farmer and cattle feeder all his business life and has been very successful.

R.R. and WAREHOUSE COMMISSION

Joseph E. Bidwell, member of the Railroad and Warehouse Commission, was born in Chicago, February 21, 1857, and received his education in the Foster public school of Chicago. After his school days he entered a packing box manufactory. In '78 he went into the grain inspection department in Chicago in a very humble position, that of helper. The department at that time was under the supervision of the veteran John P. Reynolds, chief inspector. Mr. Bidwell did his work so thoroughly and was so apt and energetic in the performance of his duties that his promotion followed. He worked his way up the ladder to a position as first assistant inspector, passing through several grades. He resigned when the democrats came into power in 1893. Four times he was elected to represent the Ninth ward of Chicago in the city council, his term of service being for eight years consecutively. He was offered the nomination for congress twice, and declined it. He was a delegate to the republican national conventions of 1892 and 1896, and has been a member of the Cook county republican committee for twelve years, and of the city committee also. He is now a member of the republican state committee, representing the Fourth congressional district. He took an active and energetic interest in the election of 1896, and contributed of his means and time to the success of the republican ticket. The Ninth ward, which he represented in the council, was always good for a democratic majority of 1,800 to 2,500, but every time Mr. Bidwell ran he carried it. Mr. Bidwell was married in 1882 to Miss Mary A. Sullivan, and they have three children. He is a member of the Independent Order of Foresters and the Ancient Order of United Workmen.

COMMISSIONER BIDWELL.

Mr. Bidwell's thorough knowledge of the grain inspection department in Chicago, which is one of the most important and largest inspection departments in the world, was taken advantage of by Gov. Tanner, who wanted not only a thorough business man, but also one familiar with the office, to take charge of that section of the Railroad and Warehouse Commission, and the governor's desire that Mr. Bidwell oversee that department has been endorsed by the board.

Mr. Bidwell's father was a soldier in the Nineteenth Wisconsin Volunteer Infantry, and was killed in the battle of Gettysburg.

THE GRAIN REGISTRAR.

Daniel Hogan, Registrar, Grain Department, Railroad and Warehouse Commission, one of the most important and lucrative offices in the state, was born in County Kilkenny, Ireland, July 4, 1849. Three years later his father came to Pulaski county, Illinois. It has been Mr. Hogan's home ever since. The early days of his life were spent on a farm. He completed his education by taking the high school course at Cairo, learning telegraphy at night. This was of great benefit to him during the war. He was too young to enlist, but was smuggled by an elder brother into the camp of the 31st Infantry, Col. John A. Logan commanding, and a few months later was regularly enrolled in the army and attached to the telegraph corps of Gen. Grant's brigade as confidential cipher clerk, with the rank of lieutenant and afterwards captain. He was under fire at Fort Donelson, Corinth and Iuka. He was with Gens. Hatch and Grierson in their cavalry raids in Tennessee, Mississippi and Alabama. Mr. Hogan accompanied Gen. W. T. Sherman to Chattanooga, and was his confidential cipher clerk and telegrapher, but was soon sent to Memphis as chief of military lines. At the close of the war he was honorably mustered out "for faithful and important military services." He graduated from a business college and became one of the Western Union's most expert operators in various large cities. In 1867 Mr. Hogan returned to Mound City, in order to be near his aged parents. The ability and high standing of Mr. Hogan was recognized and although very young in 1873 he was elected county clerk of Pulaski county. He was reëlected twice and held the office until 1882, when he was elected to the state senate. He took an active part in legislation, and formed a close friendship with Senator Tanner, now the governor, which has existed ever since. During his legislative career Senator Hogan developed a political shrewdness that placed him in the front rank in southern Illinois, a position which he has maintained for fifteen years. He was reëlected to the senate in '86, and in '89 he was appointed collector of internal revenue for the Cairo district by President Harrison. This he resigned in '93 when Cleveland came into office as president. He was member-at-large of the republican state committee in '94, and contributed not a little to the sweeping republican successes of that year.

GRAIN REGISTRAR HOGAN.

In '76 Mr. Hogan married Dora W. Carter, the youngest daughter of the late Judge G. W. Carter, of Versailles, Ky., and they have three children.

THE PRIVATE SECRETARY.

J. Mack Tanner, private secretary to the governor, was born in Bates Co., Mo., Nov. 10, 1868, and came to Illinois with his parents the following spring. He completed his education by graduating from Knox College in '91 as salutatorian of his class. He was superintendent of the shipping department in Tanner Bros.' lumber mill for three years, and when his father was chosen assistant treasurer of the United States in Chicago, J. Mack Tanner was a coin and currency clerk and afterwards held the responsible position of paying teller. He resigned some time after the democrats took charge, in Dec., '94, to accept a position as assistant cashier to the county treasurer of Cook county, which he retained until called by Gov. Tanner to become his private secretary. Mr. Tanner took considerable interest in

MR. TANNER.

military matters while in college, was major of the college battalion, has since been adjutant of the 6th Inf., I. N. G., and is now judge advocate on Gen. Barkley's staff. In '94 he married Miss Flora E. Ingersoll, of Galesburg, and they have two sons—John R., Jr., and Bruce Ingersoll Tanner.

STATE LIVE STOCK COMMISSION.

James P. Lott, of Chicago, State Live Stock Commissioner, was born in Clark Co., O., October 12, 1839, and spent his early life in farming and stock raising. At the age of 17 he commenced handling stock, taking a drove of sheep from Ohio to the Philadelphia market by land. In 1860 he moved to Illinois, settling in Bloomington, where he engaged in the mercantile and stock business for several years. In 1870 he removed to Chicago and engaged in the live stock business, which he has followed continuously ever since. He has always been an active republican and cast his first vote for Abraham Lincoln in 1860. Has never held any elective or appointive office prior to his appointment to

COMMISSIONER LOTT.

his present position. Mr. Lott is a married man and has no children .

James R. Goddard, of Galesburg, State Live Stock Commissioner, was born at Palmyra, Wayne Co., N. Y., January 22, 1844, and moved to Adrian, Mich., in 1853. His parents settled on a farm in 1855 and lived on a farm farm continuously to within the past ten years. For eight years he was one of the traveling auditors of the Chicago, Burlington & Quincy Railroad Company, on the Galesburg division. Two years ago, in 1895, he was elected city treasurer of Galesburg. He is a married man with a family of four

COMMISSIONER GODDARD.

children. Mr. Goddard was prominent during the campaign of 1896 as a gold democrat, earnestly and enthusiastically supporting Senator Palmer for president.

C. P. Johnson, of Springfield, Secretary of the State Board of Live Stock

Commissioners, was born at Oskaloosa, Iowa, in 1857, and he has resided in Sangamon county since '63. Mr. Johnson was raised on a farm eight miles west of Springfield. At the age of 17 he commenced teaching school in Sangamon county, continuing for eight consecutive years, the last three years as principal of the school at Pleasant Plains. Subsequently was city editor of the Evening Post, now the Evening News. In '84 and '85 was city editor of the State Journal and correspondent for the Chicago Tribune and Chicago News. In Aug., '85, on the organization of the State Live Stock Board, he was elected secretary and continued in that position until July, '93. The first year of his connection with that board he was also extensively engaged as stenographer in court reporting in the courts of Sangamon county. In Jan., '94, he was elected State President of the American Protective Association, and for three years gave his entire time to that position. For the

SECRETARY JOHNSON.

past twelve years he has taken an active and influential part in political campaigns, county, state and national.

(Portrait and sketch of James H. Paddock, president of the Commission, appears on page 73 of the Legislative Directory.)

The Deaf and Dumb Institution.

Gates Strawn, President of the Board of Trustees, Institution for Education of the Deaf and Dumb, was born at Jacob Strawn's "Home Farm," four miles southwest of Jacksonville. He was a student at Ohio Wesleyan University for some years, and left school to enlist in the 84th Ohio Vol., under Col. Lawrence. This was in '62. He served for several years and was honorably mustered out. Then he entered Harvard University, graduating from the law school department in '65. Two years later he made a trip to California, and returned home via Mexico, Isthmus of Panama, Peru, Bolivia, Chile, Buenos Ayres, Rio Janiero and the Amazon to New York, and thence to his home in Jacksonville. Mr.

TRUSTEE STRAWN.

Strawn married Miss Almyra Trabue. Mr. Strawn is a son of the famous old pioneer Jacob Strawn, known all over Illinois as one of the best citizens and hardiest of Illinois' early settlers. Mr. Strawn has always been a republican and an influential member of his party.

George W. Harper, of Robinson, Secretary Board of Trustees, Institution for Education of the Deaf and Dumb, was born in Wayne Co., Ind.; learned the printing business at Richmond. He came to Illinois while in his teens, and established The Argus at Robinson, in '63, and has been its editor and publisher ever since. He has been

TRUSTEE HARPER.

quite successful in his business, having one of the best equipped country plants in southern and central Illinois. It is located in a home of its own, and Mr. Harper has other property to show for his frugality and industry. Mr. Harper has always been a republican and was postmaster under President Harrison, and added many needed improvements to the Robinson postoffice, which resulted in a largely increased business. He is a member of several secret orders, and also of the Christian church, of which he has been an elder for several years. The Argus is one of the best and most influential newspapers in eastern Illinois, no paper standing higher. Mr. Harper is married and has children and grandchildren.

James R. Smith, of Taylorville, Trustee, Institution for Education of the Deaf and Dumb, was born in Clinton Co., Ill., in 1851, and has lived principally in Shelby and Christian counties all his life. He was married to Mary A. Adams in '73, who died Aug., '96, leaving two sons to the care of their father. Mr. Smith moved to Taylorville in '81 and engaged in the harness

TRUSTEE SMITH.

and buggy business, his present occupation. He was mayor for two years, and elected member of the republican county committee in '88, and in '92 made chairman. In '96 he was elected member of the republican state committee, and served on the committee on speakers during that fierce campaign. Mr. Smith has been an active figure in the politics of central Illinois for many years, and always has been a stalwart republican.

Kankakee Hospital for the Insane.

Lennington Small, of Kankakee, President Board of Trustees, Kankakee Hospital for the Insane, was born on a Kankakee county farm, June 16, 1862. The main buildings of the hospital now stand on 40 acres of Mr. Small's father's farm. Mr. Small received a good education, and has been in the nursery business all his life, and has been identified with agricultural interests for years. He represented his congressional district on the State Board of Agriculture, and is now serving his second term; has served

TRUSTEE SMALL.

as chairman of the republican county committee, and at the fall election of '96 he was elected circuit clerk by the largest majority ever given a candidate for that office. He was elected on the board of supervisors in '95, and is still a member. He has been in active politics for four years, and has always been a republican. He is married and has three children. Mr. Small was not only the personal choice of Gov. Tanner and Speaker Curtis but was almost unanimously endorsed for trustee by the business men and farmers of Kankakee county.

John J. Magee, of Chicago, Trustee for Kankakee Hospital for Insane,

TRUSTEE MAGEE.

was born near Decatur, Ill., on a farm, August 23, 1867, and moved to Chicago in '87, where he has lived ever since. He graduated from the Decatur High School in the class of '84, and graduated from the pharmacy department in the class of '88. He established his present pharmacy at Fifty-seventh street and Lake avenue in '90. He is not married. He is a member of Chevalier Bayard Commandery, Knights Templar, and has been active in Thirty-fourth ward politics in Chicago for some time. In the spring campaign in '96, Mr. Magee was energetic in securing a first class candidate for alderman on the republican ticket, and was successful.

George T. Buckingham, of Danville, Trustee Kankakee Hospital for the Insane, was born at Delphi, Ind., April 21, 1864, and moved with his parents to Vermilion Co., Ill., in '70, where he has since resided. He was educated at Ladoga, Ind., and went to Danville in '84, where he engaged in mercantile pursuits. He began the study of law with Hon. W. J. Calhoun in '89, was subsequently admitted to the bar, and began practice in '91. In '89 Mr. Buckingham was first assistant clerk of the Illinois House of Representatives, and at the World's Fair session the next year was elected chief clerk of the same body. He was appointed the same year as special agent of the U. S. Treasury Department, by President Harrison, and served for four years, during which time he visited most of the principal points in this country, Mexico and Canada, and made one trip to Europe in the interest of that department. In '94 he returned to Danville, where he has since been engaged in the practice of his profession, in partnership with S. G. Wilson, state's attorney. He is married and has one son; belongs to a number of fraternal orders, and for the last eight

TRUSTEE BUCKINGHAM.

years has been an active factor in the politics of eastern Illinois.

Dr. William G. Stearns, Superintendent of the Kankakee Hospital for the Insane, was reared on a farm near Fond du Lac, Wis., and was educated in the state and normal schools of Wisconsin and New York. For several years he was operator, station agent and business agent of the C., M. & St. P. R. R. For a time he managed the Cornell Advertising Agency and was managing editor of the Methodist Home Journal. In '93 he grad-

SUPERINTENDENT STEARNS.

uated from the medical department of the Northwestern University. By competitive examination he won the position of first house physician of St. Luke's hospital, Chicago. He became a life member of the Chicago Medical Alumni association for the achievement. For three years he has been a member of the faculty of the Northwestern University as professor of general pathology, and pathological anatomy. He is a member of the American Medical Association. Dr. Stearns early decided to make a life study of mental and nervous diseases, and he promptly accepted the tender of a place as assistant physician in '94 at the Kankakee hospital. He has devoted his entire time to a study of the insane. From ward physician he was promoted until in '95 he was appointed pathologist. His promotion was made over those many years his senior at the hospital.

The Southern Illinois Penitentiary.

Joseph B. Messick, of East St. Louis, Chairman of the Board of Commissioners, Chester Penitentiary, was born on a farm in Macoupin county, Ill., Jan. 29, 1847. He lived on his father's farm until he was 21, except one year, spent in the army. In '72 he was admitted to the bar and immediately began practice of his profession at East St. Louis, and has been for years one of the most successful lawyers and most prominent men in southern Illinois. He was a member of the house in the 33d, 34th and 35th General Assemblies, and in each was regarded as a leader on the republican side. He was particularly active during the session of '85, when the famous contest between Col. W. R. Morrison and Gen. J. A. Logan for United States senator was the sensational feature. Judge

COMMISSIONER MESSICK.

Messick was one of Senator Logan's most trusted lieutenants. From '75-'79 he was judge of the East St. Louis city court. He was commissioner of the Chester prison under Gov. Fifer, and was reappointed by Gov. Tanner. No political or business events of importance have taken place in southwestern Illinois within the last fifteen years that Judge Messick has not been connected with. He always has been a stalwart republican. He is married and has one son, J. B., Jr.

James E. Jobe, of Harrisburg, Commissioner Chester Penitentiary, was born in Zionsville, Boone Co., Ind., Feb. 19, 1856, and received a good academic education in Zionsville. He varied his school work by learning the

COMMISSIONER JOBE.

carpenter's trade, and labored at it when not in school. In October, '73, he moved to Saline Co., Ill., and in September, '75, married Miss Mollie Bickers, daughter of Rev. Wm. C. Bickers, and they have four children. He commenced teaching school in the autumn of '76, and continued that occupation for ten years, when he was nominated by the republicans for county superintendent of schools of Saline county. He was elected in November, the first time Saline county was carried by the republicans for that office. He proved so good an official and was so popular with the people that he was reelected in '90 and again in '94, and resigned the office March 25, '97, to accept a place on the Chester Penitentiary Board. Mr. Jobe is credited with having the best endorsements, more of them, and in better shape, than any other candidate for an appointive office under Gov. Tanner. He was a delegate to the national republican convention in '96, and has taken a lively interest in republican success for many years.

Col. Thomas W. Scott, of Fairfield, Commissioner for the Chester Peniten-

COMMISSIONER SCOTT.

tiary, was born near Danville, Ill. He enlisted first in the 8th Ill. Vol. Inf., afterwards in the 98th Ill. Vol. Inf., and devoted nearly four years of his life in the service. He was four times promoted for gallant and meritorious conduct on the field of battle, and when mustered out at Nashville, Tenn., July, '65, was A. A. G. on the staff of Gen. Long, commanding 2d Div. Cav. Corps, military division of the Mississippi. It was Col. Scott who detailed a detachment to pursue Jefferson Davis and party, capturing him near Irwinsville, Ga., and the first official report of his capture was made to him. At the close of the war he returned to Olney, engaging in mercantile pursuits. He was commander of the first post G. A. R. organized in Olney. In '73 he moved to Fairfield, and has since lived there. From '84 to '92 he was A. Q. M. G., Department of Illinois, G. A. R., and is now a member of the executive committee, national council of administration. Always prominent and active in politics, and a staunch republican, he has held many places of trust, and none of profit, in his party. From '76 to '84 he was member of the executive committee of the state committee. He always was a close friend of Gov. Tanner and during the campaign of '96 was one of the governor's chief counsellors. He was a delegate to the national conventions in '88 and '96. For many years he was a director in the L., E. & St. L. R. R., and is president of the First National Bank of Fairfield. Col. Scott was an aide-de-camp on Gov. Fifer's staff '88-'92. He is married and has two daughters.

Lincoln Asylum for Feeble-Minded.

Clarence R. Gittings, of Terre Haute, President Board of Trustees, Asylum for Feeble-Minded Children, was born

TRUSTEE GITTINGS.

on a farm near La Harpe, Ill., June 28, 1848, and has lived continuously on the farm ever since, except one year at school at Denmark, Iowa, and two years in Adrian College, Adrian, Mich. He was married in '71 and has two children—Robert Frederick, who lives in Chicago, and Charles Sumner, who is a young farmer at home. For 16 years he has been justice of the peace. In '84 he was elected from the 24th district to the house and takes pride in the fact that he is one of the 103 that sent John A. Logan to the United States senate the last time. Mr. Gittings now lives in a cozy home near Terre Haute, Ill., a retired farmer and takes the world easy by living like a quiet conscientious citizen, enjoying the respect of all his neighbors.

Zeno K. Wood, of Mt. Pulaski, Trustee, Asylum for Feeble-Minded Children, was born in West Yarmouth, Mass., September 29, 1841. He finished his education in the New Bedford High School. In July, '62, he enlisted in Co. A, 41st Mass. Vol. Inf., and when in New Orleans assisted in raising a regiment of Union troops in that confederate city—the 1st New Orleans

TRUSTEE WOOD.

Vol. Inf. In April, '64, Mr. Wood was appointed adjutant of his regiment. Afterwards he was detached and appointed assistant adjutant general and A. D. C. on the staff of Gen. T. W. Sherman. June 1, '66, he received an honorable discharge at New Orleans. After the war he spent seven years on the plains in Kansas. For the past 22 years he has been in the grain business in Illinois, principally in Mt. Pulaski. Mr. Wood is married and has two children. He has held minor city offices, and is a member of Mt. Pulaski Commandery No. 39, Knights Templar.

Samuel C. Smiley, of O'Fallon, Trustee, Asylum for Feeble-Minded Children, was born on a St. Clair county

TRUSTEE SMILEY.

(Ill.) farm, near O'Fallon, October 12, 1841, and entered McKendree College to complete his education. After one term he left school to enlist in the army, joining Co. I, 117th Ill. Inf., August 12,

'62. When honorably discharged he returned to the farm, and operated it until '91, when he moved to town and became vice president in the Tiedmann Milling Co. He is president and superintendent of the O'Fallon Electric Light Co., and is a stockholder in the Wiggins Ferry Co. Mr. Smiley owns several valuable farms in St. Clair county. He was a member of the house in '89, and has been prominent in southern Illinois politics for many years. He is married and has four children. He is a Mason and member of the G. A. R.

Illinois and Michigan Canal Board.

Clarence E. Snively, of Canton, President Board of Canal Commissioners, was born in Ellisville, Fulton county, July 4, 1854, and when 10 years old entered the office of the Rushville Times to learn the trade of printer. He has been in the business all his life, and was educated principally in a country printing office. About '75 he bought one-half interest in the Carlinville Democrat, a republican newspaper, and in the summer of '78 he purchased the Canton Weekly Register, and in '90 he established a daily in connection with the weekly. No country paper in Illinois wields more influence, is handsomer typographically, or more ably edited than the Canton Register. In '85 he was appointed postmaster of Canton by President Arthur. He was an alternate to the republican national convention in '84, and in '88 and '96 he was a delegate, being secretary of the Illinois delegation both times. He was a member and secretary of the Canal Board under Gov. Fifer, and for 18

COMMISSIONER SNIVELY.

years has been secretary of the Fulton county republican committee. For 16 years he has practically had charge of the organization of the party in the county, and during that time the county has changed from democratic to republican. For 15 years he has been a prominent figure in state politics. He is married and has eight children. He is a K. P., I. O. O. F. and Red Man.

COMMISSIONER RYON.

Frank M. Ryon, of Streator, Canal Commissioner, was born in Kendall county, Ill., and was educated and raised to manhood in that county. In December, '67, he moved to Streator, and it has ever since been his home. He engaged in the mercantile business, which he continued until '74, when he was appointed by President Grant as postmaster of Streator. He held the position for twelve consecutive years, until the democrats came into power. Then he entered the glass business in Streator and still has interests and connections with that industry. For the last eight years he has been connected with the Streator National Bank, and for several years has been and now is a director and its vice president. Mr. Ryon has been active in party politics for many years. He is married and has two children.

Howard O. Hilton, of Rockford, Canal Commissioner, was born in Atchison Co., Kan., 33 years ago, and completed his education at Lincoln University, Lincoln, Ill. He worked on a farm, taught school and finally drifted into newspaper work, working on newspapers in various cities in Illinois. In '90 he founded the Rockford Republic and is now the political editor of that prosperous paper. In '94 he was chosen member of the republican state committee from the 9th district, and was reëlected by acclamation in '96, and was one of the most energetic and valuable members of the executive committee during the recent campaign. He is one of the youngest members of the state committee, and is also one of the youngest of Gov.

Tanner's appointees. He never held nor sought any other office. Mr. Hilton is married and has two daughters. He has worked early and late for the republican party as writer, worker and

COMMISSIONER HILTON.

campaign speaker. He stands high in business circles in northern Illinois.

William L. Sackett, of Morris, Chief Clerk, Canal Board, was born in Holyoke, Mass., May 21, 1862, and in early boyhood moved to Amboy, Ill. He was educated in the graded schools of Hartford, Conn. At the age of 12, he entered a printing office at Hartford. In '85 he became night editor of the Springfield (Ill.) Journal. In '87 he was appointed private secretary to Attorney General George Hunt. He also served in this capacity for Hon. (now Governor) John R. Tanner, state treasurer. In '91 he purchased the Morris Herald, and is now publishing that paper.

CHIEF CLERK SACKETT.

Mr. Sackett has been active in state politics the past twelve years, and was presidential elector for the 8th district in '96. He was appointed chief clerk and paymaster of the Canal Commission by Gov. Tanner, Feb. 15, '97.

Leon McDonald, of Lockport, General Superintendent Illinois and Michigan Canal, was born November 2, 1860, at New Lennox, Will Co., Ill., and finished a good education at the University of Wisconsin, at Madison, in '80. He has been engaged in the newspaper business all his life, having been connected with his father most of the time on the Lockport Phenix. He began as a "devil," on the bottom round, and is now proprietor and publisher of the Phenix, which he purchased from his father in '84. He always has been active in politics and has been continuously a member of the county committee since he was a voter. For two successive terms he was elected president of the village of Lockport. He was one of the organizers of the Sons of Veterans in Will county; is Past State Adviser of the M. W. A., and is

SUPERINTENDENT McDONALD.

Past Exalted Ruler of the B. P. O. E. Mr. McDonald is not married.

The Anna Hospital for the Insane.

Col. Louis Krughoff, of Nashville, Chairman of Board of Trustees, Anna Hospital for Insane, was born in Minden, Westphalia, November 25, 1836, and came to Washington Co., Ill., in '51. He worked on a farm, clerked in a store and attended school until the war. In June, '61, he enlisted in Co. H., 1st Ill. Cav. Three months later he was wounded in the arm, and returned home. He recruited a company which was assigned to the 49th Ill. Inf. as Co. C. He was wounded in the head at Fort Donelson, but participated in the siege of Corinth. The 49th was on the Red River expedition, chased Price in Missouri, traveling 750 miles in thirty-five days, and closed its active work in the battle of Nashville, and pursuit of Hood. Col. Krughoff was mustered out in '65 with the brevet of major "for gallant and meritorious services." In '74, when the Washington County Bank was organized, he was made cashier. It is now the private bank of Needles, Krughoff & Co., and is as sound an institution as there is in Illinois. Col. Krughoff is married and has two sons and two daughters. He always has been a republican, and was one of the "famous 306" delegates in the republican national convention who stood so long for Grant. In '77 he organized and was elected captain of a militia company at Nashville, and was chosen lieut.-colonel of the 11th regiment. He was elected colonel of the 9th Inf., I. N. G., May 17, '82; resigned Feb. 22, '85, and was colonel and aide-de-camp during Gov. Oglesby's administration. His record in the G. A. R. is long and honorable. Seven times he has been post commander, a place he now holds; many times delegate to national encampments; in '92 was de-

TRUSTEE KRUGHOFF.

partment inspector; on council of administration under Gen. Harlan; A. D. C. and chief of staff under Gen. Powell; is now department inspector.

Samuel Hastings, of Cairo, Trustee Anna Hospital for Insane, was born on a farm in Noble county, Ohio, in 1850, and moved to Illinois with his father when he was about 4 years old. Mr. Hastings, Sr., settled in Jasper county, purchased a farm, and educated his children in the district schools. Samuel Hastings finished a scientific course at McKendree College, Lebanon, graduating in '72. He taught school for several years, and in '84 moved to Cairo, which has been his home ever since. He embarked in the commission business, which is his present occupation, dealing in oats, corn and hay. Mr. Hastings has been a member of the county board of Alexander county, county commissioner for six years, and at present is chairman of the board. His appointment as a trustee for the Anna Hospital was without solicitation on his part, and for some time he hesitated to accept. He was married in '76, and has three

TRUSTEE HASTINGS.

daughters and one son. Mr. Hastings lived in Clay county about ten years, and is personally acquainted with Gov. Tanner, and has taken active part in several campaigns when the governor was a candidate for office.

James C. Mitchell, of Marion, Trustee Anna Hospital for Insane, was born in Williamson Co., Ill., Oct. 31, 1852, and attended school when he could, at the old log school house near the farm. The father and older brothers entered the army, and Mr. Mitchell, then 10 years old, with his younger brother, Edward, and his mother, ran the farm, successfully, until the close of the war. At 18 he attended McKendree College, and in '71 entered a Marion drugstore as clerk. In '76 he bought a drug store, which he ran for

TRUSTEE MITCHELL.

ten years, when he was elected county clerk, and was reëlected in '90. When first elected the county finances were in a deplorable condition, warrants being sold for 40 to 45 cents on the dollar. There was a floating debt of $30,000 and a railroad bond debt of $100,000. Mr. Mitchell's ability as a financier was exercised and within two years after his election county warrants were at par, and before his eight yearsof service had expired $20,000 of the floating debt had been paid, and the levy was not increased. The railroad debt was funded at 4½ per cent and $5,000 laid aside every year to pay the principal. The county had paid 8 per cent interest on this debt for 22 years. He was elected cashier of the First National Bank in '91 and still retains it. Mr. Mitchell resides with his wife and four sons and three daughters in a beautiful home in Marion.

W. A. Stoker, of Centralia, Superintendent Anna Hospital for Insane, was born at Centralia, Ill., August 18, 1864. and graduated at McKendree College. Lebanon, Ill., in '83, and at the Medical College of Ohio, Cincinnati, March 5, '85. He was appointed assistant physician at the Southern Illinois Penitentiary, Jan., 7, '86, and resigned Jan. 1, '88. Dr. Stoker then returned to Centralia and practiced his profession with great success. Feb. 19, '97, he was appointed superintendent of the Asylum for the Criminal Insane, and on March 2, was selected for superintendent of the Anna hospital, resigning from the Criminal Insane, March 4. Dr. Stoker has been very active in politics of southern Illinois for years,and was electeda member of the republican state committee in '94 and again in '96. He was elected city treasurer of Centralia in April, '95,

SUPERINTENDENT STOKER.

without opposition. Was married to Miss Lillian B. Tucker in Denver, Colo., Dec. 3, 1890, and they have two children—Annie E., aged 5, and Eugene T., aged 3.

Jacksonville Hospital for the Insane.

F. L. Sharpe, of Jacksonville, President of the Board of Trustees, Central Hospital for the Insane, was born

TRUSTEE SHARPE.

in Pike Co., Ill., his parents having moved there from Connecticut in 1834. Mr. Sharpe's early life was spent on the farm where he was born. He received a common school education, and at the age of 20 began teaching school, farming in the summer. In '77 he moved to Jacksonville and engaged in the manufacture of hardwood lumber. He abandoned this in '93 and embarked in the retail lumber business. Mr. Sharpe now owns branch lumber yards at Virginia and Franklin, as well as a large one at Jacksonville. He also owns a small farm near Jacksonville. In '79 he was married to Nettie M., daughter of Duncan Mackay, of Mt. Carroll, and they have four children. He always has been an ardent republican and an active party worker, but not a seeker for office.

Morris Emmerson, of Mt. Vernon, Trustee Jacksonville Hospital for the Insane, was born June 7, 1853, at Wanboro, Ill., and was educated in the Albion public schools and Bryant & Stratton's Business College, St. Louis. At the age of 16 he engaged to Churchill & Dalby, at Albion, general merchants and pork packers, as bookkeeper, and remained with them until '75. He spent a year at Red Oak, Ia., as clerk in a store. Returning to Illinois in '76 he clerked in the store of Hon. Thos. W. Scott, of Fairfield, and then in partnership with E. Balentine purchased the Albion Journal. At the end of one year Mr. Emmerson became sole proprietor, and he published the paper until the spring of '84 when he sold it and removed to Mt. Vernon, where he established the Register. A daily edition of the Register was started in '92, and is one of the brightest and most influential republican newspapers in Southern Illinois. Mr. Emmerson is director in the Mt. Vernon Car Works, and secretary of

TRUSTEE EMMERSON.

the Mt. Vernon Loan and Building association. He was the republican candidate for clerk of the Appellate Court in the campaign of '96, but was defeated by the demo-populistic combine. He is a Royal Arch Mason.

J. A. Glenn, M. D., of Ashland, Trustee for the Jacksonville Hospital for the Insane, was born on a farm in Ashland Co., O., Dec. 13, 1850, and received a literary education at Vermilion Institute, Hayesville, O., and graduated in medicine at the Medical College of Ohio in '75, the following winter taking a post graduate course at the medical department of the University of New York. Until '80 Dr. Glenn practiced in Ohio, when he

TRUSTEE GLENN.

moved to Tallula, Ill., where he not only practiced his profession, but engaged in the drug business and various successful enterprises. He sold the drug store in '90, and in the winter of '90-91 attended a post-graduate medical school. In the spring of '91 Dr. Glenn located at Ashland, and has had a very successful medical practice. He has been an active and influential republican in Central Illinois for years.

F. C. Winslow, of Jacksonville, Superintendent of the Jacksonville Hospital for the Insane, comes of hardy pioneer stock. His father was one of the early settlers of Northern Illinois. Dr. Winslow was born forty-six years ago and was raised in Freeport, Ill., where he received his early education. He completed his education by graduating from the literary and medical departments of the Northwestern University, and spent some time in the Cook County Hospital. Dr. Winslow perfected his professional studies in institutions in Vienna and Berlin, and in '75 was appointed assistant physician of the Jacksonville Hospital for the Insane. His appointment as super-

SUPERINTENDENT WINSLOW.

intendent was received with great favor by the friends of the institution. He is an active worker in the Masonic fraternity, and holds office in three of the grand bodies of the state. He is a member of the State Medical Society, the Tri-State Medical Society and the Morgan County Medical Society.

The Institution for the Blind.

N. W. Branson, of Petersburg, President of the Board of Trustees, Institution for the Education of the Blind, was born at Jacksonville, Ill., May 29, 1837, and graduated at Illinois College in June, 1857. He was admitted to the bar in '60, and settled at Petersburg and began practice in March, '60. Mr. Branson was married to Miss Fannie D. Regnier Feb. 21, '61. He was appointed Register in Bankruptcy by Chief Justice Chase in '67, and held the position until the repeal of the bankrupt act. Was a member of the House in '73 and Chairman of the Committee on State Institutions, re-

TRUSTEE BRANSON.

elected in '74. He was appointed trustee for Institution for the Blind in '77, and held the position until '93, when he resigned, and was again appointed in 1897. Mr. Branson was appointed special master in several of the most important railroad litigations by U. S. Circuit Courts of Southern and Northern Districts of Illinois in '82 and later. He was delegate to republican national convention, Cincinnati, '76, and was twice member of republican state committee.

Augustus Dow, of Pittsfield, Trustee of the Institution for the Education of the Blind, is one of the best known business men in western Illinois. He

TRUSTEE DOW.

served a term in the house of representatives with credit, and is a leading republican of the state. He is a flour manufacturer by occupation, and was born in South Coventry, Tolland county, Connecticut, Oct. 9, 1841, and in '58 moved to Pittsfield, where he has lived ever since. He received an academic education in his native town and from '62 to '65 was connected with the pay department of the United States army. After the war he returned to Pittsfield and engaged in the mercantile business, continuing it until '70, when he sold out and started the manufacture of flour on a large scale. Pittsfield is a democratic district, but he has been elected to the county board several times, and mayor of the city four years. Mr. Dow has been connected with all the improvements of a local nature, and is regarded as one of the foremost and most liberal citizens. He is an uncompromising republican, is a director in the First National Bank and is married.

Edward W. Rew, of Chicago, Trustee of the Institution for the Education of the Blind, was born in Chi-

TRUSTEE REW.

cago, Dec. 31, 1854, and attended the public schools until he was 12 years old, when he went to Dyrenfurths School of Trade, after which he learned the trade of bookbinder and paper ruler. For nineteen years he worked for the Western Bank Note and Engraving Co., and from there he entered the employ of Tom N. Donnelly & Co., one of the largest diamond brokerage firms in the west, as bookkeeper and financial man. He has been with this firm for the past six years. Mr. Rew has never been an office seeker.

Frank H. Hall, of Waukegan, superintendent of the Institution for the Education of the Blind, was born at Mechanics Falls, Me., Feb. 9, 1841, and entered the union army in the fall of '62 as corporal of Co. D, 23d Me. Inf., and afterwards was acting hospital steward. Mr. Hall was educated at Bates College, and before the close of his first year was elected principal of Towle Academy, Winthrop, Me. In '66 he moved to Illinois, and taught school for over two years at Earlville, receiving during that time a Life Teacher's Certificate. From '68-75 and '88-90 he was principal of the West Aurora Public Schools. In '75 Mr. Hall established the Sugar Grove "Farm School," and excepting one year was its principal and manager until '87. In '87-88 he was principal of the Petersburg schools. In '90 he was appointed superintendent of the Institution for the Blind, and held the office until '93, when he was removed by the democratic administration for political reasons. Mr. Hall was immediatetly tendered the Waukegan public schools, and superintended them until April, '97, when his old place as superintendent of the Blind Institution was offered him. He is inventor of the Braille writer, and co-inventor with Harrison & Seifried of the Stereotype maker. He is author

SUPERINTENDENT HALL.

of a number of school text books, embodying the advanced thought of modern times.

The State Board of Arbitration.

Daniel J. Keefe, of Chicago, Chairman State Board of Arbitration, was born in Cook county Sept. 27, 1853, and has been a laboring man all his life. He has been connected with the Chicago Lumber Vessel Unloaders Union as president since '82, and still holds the office, which is a salaried one. The union embraces about 1,100 men. He is now and has been for two years President of the International Longshoreman's Union, and is arbitrator for the Lake Carrier's association, the Longshoremen and the Lumber Dealers, representing the three elements on the arbitration board. He has been a delegate to the conventions of the American Federation of Labor since '92. All these things indicate that Mr. Keefe possesses the confidence of diverse elements—capital and labor, and that

ARBITRATOR KEEFE.

Gov. Tanner in selecting him to represent the labor element on the State Board of Arbitration certainly pleased everybody. He is married and has six children. This is his first political office. He always has been a conservative trade-unionist, and has been a staunch republican all his life.

Horace R. Calef, of Monticello, member State Board of Arbitration, was born in Piatt Co., Ill., Nov. 12, 1854. He was the oldest son of Rufus Calef, who came to Illinois in '52 and settled on a tract of 5,000 acres of magnificent land, and who in his day was one of the greatest cattle kings in the country. In '77 Horace Calef mar-

ARBITRATOR CALEF.

ried. He continued to live on the farm for several years, and at the age of 22 was elected supervisor. He proved so acceptable and valuable that he was reëlected several times filling four terms—until he moved out of the township. Mr. Calef turned his attention from cattle to horses, breeding a fine line of draft and roadsters. He brought the famous trotting stallion Walsingham to Piatt county, which was the start of a large business in roadsters in that county. He has done more than any other man to encourage the turning out of speed stock in central Illinois. He has a son and two daughters. Mr. Calef is one of the shrewdest political workers, and is an active and enterprising citizen. He has been a member of the Piatt County Agricultural Board for eight years.

Edward Ridgely, of Springfield, member State Board of Arbitration, vice Jos. B. Gill, resigned, was the candidate of the Gold-Standard Democrats of Illinois for state treasurer in '96, and has been an influential factor in politics and business in Springfield and Central Illinois since he attained his majority. He was born in Springfield, Nov. 3, 1859, and graduated from the Springfield High school in '76; Adams Academy, Quincy, Mass., in '77, and Harvard College in '81. In '81 he entered the Ridgely National bank as clerk, and in '84 was made assistant cashier and four years later was promoted to be cashier, a position he now holds. He is secretary of the Gas Light Co., the Wilmington and Springfield Coal Co., and treasurer of the Coal Operators' Mutual Fire Insurance Co. He is the son of Charles, and the grandson of Nicholas H. Ridgely, and therefore is the third generation of that family of bankers, widely known throughout the west as sound, conservative business men.

ARBITRATOR RIDGELY.

Mr. Ridgely was opposed to the free silver ideas of his party in '96 and was one of the leaders in the gold-standard democratic movement. He is married and has three children.

Joseph B. Gill, of Murphysboro, democratic member State Board of Arbitration, was lieutenant-governor '93-97, and probably stands closer to the laborers of the state at large than

ARBITRATOR GILL.

any other man. He served two terms in the house—'89-91, and his earnest efforts in behalf of the laboring population were evident in every measure in their interest that came before those two general assemblies. Among others Gov. Gill was instrumental in securing the passage of the truck store bill, the gross weight coal bill, and the weekly pay bill. He also did all he could to advance the arbitration bill. He was nominated for lieut-gov. in the democratic state convention of '92 on the first ballot, and presided with dignity and to the eminent satisfaction of senators of all parties over the senate for two sessions. In the spring of '94 while acting governor a demand came for troops from Toluca. Gov. Gill went to the scene in person and so powerful an influence did he exert that the trouble was settled without the militia. He was arbitrator between the M. & O. R. R. and its men in a labor dispute, the men winning. Shortly afterwards he was chosen arbitrator by the State Miners' convention between them and the operators in the troubles which resulted in the great strike of '95. The operators declined to arbitrate. Gov. Gill's selection as a member of the Board of Arbitration seems peculiarly appropriate. He was born near Marion, Ill., Feb. 17, 1862, and graduated from the Southern Normal and Ann Arbor Law School. He bought and published for several years the Murphysboro "Independent," selling it when he became lieutenant-governor. He is married and has one son.

Note—Owing to ill health, Gov. Gill was compelled to resign his place on the board, and go to California in May, '97.

The Illinois State Penitentiary.

John H. Pierce, of Kewanee, President of the Joliet Penitentiary Board, was born in Aurora, Ill., in January, 1843, and received a high school and commercial college education. He has been in the manufacturing business all his life, and is now president of the Western Tube Co., at Kewanee, one of the largest plants in the country, employing 1,600 to 1,800 persons. He has been connected with these works for 25 years. At first he was chosen secretary and afterwards president. It was formerly the Haxtun Steam Heater Co. Mr. Pierce served one term in the state senate—1886-90. After his term in the senate for six years he was assistant manager of the National Tube Works at McKeesport, Pa., the largest in the world, and had actual management of the works. He is married and has three children. Mr. Pierce is a Knight Templar. He

COMMISSIONER PIERCE.

has been an active and influential republican in northwestern Illinois for many years, but never has been an office seeker. His present office was tendered him without solicitation on his part.

Hamer H. Green, of Bloomington, Commissioner for the Joliet Penitentiary, was born in Crawford county, Ill., Dec. 31, 1854. Received a high school education. He went into the drug business in Anna and in Cairo in '73. In '76 he entered the law department of the Ann Arbor University, graduating in '79. He located in Bloomington and practiced law for about three years. Then he reëntered the drug business in that city, continuing until February, '97, when he sold out. He was appointed member of the State Board of Pharmacy by Gov. Fifer, and served for five years. Mr. Green is president and business director of the Pantagraph Printing and Stationery Co., one of the largest establishments of its kind in Illinois. He is also actively interested in a number of business enterprises in Bloomington and McLean county. He is an active and influential republican, and

COMMISSIONER GREEN.

although never an office seeker he has done all he could to advance the interests and principles of republicanism. He has been a staunch republican all his life. He is married and has one child—a daughter. Mr. Green is a prominent Mason and is an officer of the Grand Commandery of Knights Templar of Illinois.

Thomas O'Shaughnessy, of Chicago, Commissioner for the Joliet Penitentiary, was born in London, March 24, 1842, and three years later with the family came to America. He received a good education in New York city and Boston. He has been in the ready-made clothing business for the past 40

COMMISSIONER O'SHAUGHNESSY.

years, and in that long time has been connected with only two firms. The first was Bliss, Whiting, Pearce & McKinney, of Boston, Mass., which retired from business long ago. He has been with Clement, Bane & Co., Chicago, for the past 29 years. In '61 he enlisted in Co. I, 44th Mass. Vol. Inf., Col. F. L. Lee, commanding. Mr. O'Shaughnessy is married and has nine children. He has lived in Chicago ever since he first became connected with Clement, Bane & Co., 29 years, and never before held a political office and never wanted one. He has taken an active interest in politics, and has always been a staunch republican.

WARDEN McCLAUGHRY.

Maj. Robert Wilson McClaughry, Warden of the State Penitentiary, Joliet, was born in Hancock Co., Ill., June 22, 1839, and raised on a farm by strict old Presbyterian parents. He graduated when 21 from Monmouth College. His college life was a severe struggle for existence and education because of the straitened circumstances of his parents. One year as tutor in the college and another as editor of a democratic paper in Hancock county and then he enlisted in the 118th Reg., Ill. Vol. He was elected captain of Co. B, and a few months later major of the regiment. As major he entered the Vicksburg campaign. After Vicksburg fell he served in the department of the gulf, but his health failing, his superior officers secured his appointment as additional paymaster, U. S. A., at Springfield, where he remained until '65. Then followed a term as county clerk, several years of business, failure and poor health. In '74 came the unsolicited offer of wardenship of the Joliet prison. The ten years preceding his appointment had seen as many different wardens in charge and the final demoralization of the institution. No one can describe his methods—his success is well known. The prisoner soon found himself surrounded by temperate, gentlemanly guards and officers. He awoke to the realization that he was not only a human being but a man. Good conduct secured for him opportunities for reform and privileges, and bad conduct brought him face to face with prompt, severe, but humane punishment. Fourteen years of able management placed Warden McClaughry among the expert scientific prison men of the nation, and made Joliet prison famous as a model modern institution. In '88 he resigned to accept a call to Pennsylvania, where he organized and placed upon a firm foundation, the Pennsylvania State Industrial Reformatory. The health of his family requiring a change to a dryer climate, he resigned solely on this account, intending to accept a position at the head of the famous Allegheny County Workhouse near Pittsburgh. The news of his intended change reached the ears of Mayor-elect Washburne, when, in May, '91, the call to the superintendency of the Chicago police department came unsolicited from that gentleman. For two years and a half he was busily engaged organizing perfecting and divorcing from politics this department of public safety. Sept., '93, he was called by Gov. Altgeld to the superintendency of the Illinois State Reformatory, and remained in charge until March 1, '97, when he was requested by Gov. Tanner to again take charge of the Illinois State Penitentiary.

The Elgin Hospital for the Insane.

Walter S. Frazier, of Aurora, President Board of Trustees, Northern Illinois Hospital for the Insane, was born in New York state in 1835, and

TRUSTEE FRAZIER.

moved to Illinois in '57. He is one of the best known men in Kane county and has held many offices of honor during the past third of a century. In '65 he was clerk of the house of representatives in Springfield, and for several years was chairman of the republican congressional committee of his district. In '88, '90 and '92 Mr. Frazier was chosen member of the republican state committee, and in '91 was elected mayor of Aurora. Mr. Frazier is a director of the Merchants' National Bank, of Aurora, and founder of the firm of W. S. Frazier & Co., of road cart fame. At present he is owner and publisher of the Aurora Daily News, a newspaper of considerable influence. Mr. Frazier's long experience in Illinois politics has given him a wide acquaintance and standing among his party's leaders.

A. S. Wright, of Woodstock, Trustee Elgin Hospital for the Insane, was born Feb., 1847, in Pompey, N. Y. At an early age his parents died, leaving him dependent on his own resources. He enlisted at the age of 15 in the 22d N. Y. Cav., and was mustered out in Aug., '65. He came west in Jan., '66, and clerked in a drugstore until '70, at which time he embarked in the drug business for himself. Mr. Wright is well known for his work as secretary of the fair in his section and securing Gen. Longstreet and many other famous men as attractions during the nine years of his secretaryship. In politics there is no more energetic or astute worker in the state, and no man stands higher in the estimation of the men who lead the republican party of Illinois. One prominent feature of Mr. Wright's success is that he is ever true to his friends. As a partial recognition of his political services, in '89 Gov. Fifer appointed Mr. Wright a commissioner for the Joliet penitentiary, and he was elected secretary of the board. Mr. Wright is a self-made man, and never had the advantages of a college education. He is married, and has four children, one, Verne A., a prominent attorney of Chicago.

TRUSTEE WRIGHT.

Winfield Scott Cowen, of Shannon, Trustee Elgin Hospital for the Insane, was born Dec. 13, 1849, at Altoona, Pa. His father was a farmer of Scotch-Irish ancestry and moved to Illinois in '56. Mr. Cowen received a common school education and then returned to the farm. He moved to Shannon in '76 where he engaged in the grain and stock shipping business. He was elected to the town council in '80 and reëlected each year up to '84, when he was elected president of the town council. In '89 he was appointed postmaster of Shannon by President Harrison. In '92 he was a delegate to the republican national convention and voted for Blaine for president. He was frequently a delegate to state republican conventions and in '96 was chairman of his county delegation. He was elected mayor of Shannon in April, '97. In '72 he was married to Miss Lucy Hileman, of Carroll county. Mr. Cowen is a genial, companionable man. He is a 32d degree Mason.

TRUSTEE COWEN.

The State Fish Commission.

Nat H. Cohen, of Urbana, President State Fish Commission, is one of the most energetic young business men and staunchest republicans in eastern Illinois. He was born in Philadelphia in 1851, moved to Urbana in '77 and

COMMISSIONER COHEN.

the following year commenced business and now is the largest dealer in manufactured tobacco in central Illinois. He early associated himself with the republican party, and for nearly twenty years has spared neither time nor money for the success of its candidates and principles. He has a fine tenor voice and no night was too stormy for him to participate in campaign meetings, with glee clubs. Mr. Cohen for years has taken a deep interest in fishing, and has studied the habits and varieties of fish and their propagation. He has an extensive library on the subject, and his selection meets with the approbation of everybody.

S. P. Bartlett, Member and Superintendent of the State Fish Commission, was born in Quincy, Ill., January 2, 1842, and learned the printer's trade early in life in the office of the Quincy Whig. He was in commercial business for a number of years and in '70 took up with fish work. He was a member of the State Fish Commission continuously from the date of its organization until '93, when the democrats took charge of the administration, and Mr. Bartlett, a stalwart republican, was let out. The democrats couldn't get along without his assistance, and he was acting superintendent of the board from '93 until '97. Mr. Bartlett is one of the best known men in Illinois public life and knows more about fish than anybody else.

COMMISSIONER BARTLETT.

August Lenke, of Chicago, Member of the State Fish Commission, was born in Luedge, Prussia, March 16, 1844, and in '64 left his native land for Chicago, which has ever since been his home. At first he was in the grain business, but in '73 entered the wholesale coal business, and for the last 19 years has been a member of the firm of O.S. Richardson & Co., which is composed of himself and Mr. Richardson. By their energy and thrift they have acquired an enviable position in the commercial world. They are now the largest receivers in Chicago of anthracite coal by lake, controlling and operating five of the best equipped and largest coal docks in the city, from which they distribute to local merchants 250,000 tons annually. Socially Mr. Lenke is very popular, and is a substantial member of leading societies and orders, particularly on the West Side, where he resides. Mr. Lenke is one of the most substantial business men in the great western metropolis. He is too good a business man to mix much in politics and never sought an office in his life.

COMMISSIONER LENKE.

The Commission of Claims.

Judge William C. Jones, of Robinson, member State Commission of Claims, was born in Hutsonville, July 15, 1848. He received a literary education at the Ohio Wesleyan University, Delaware, O., and attended law school at the University of Michigan. He was admitted to the practice of law, May 9, '68, and immediately formed a law

COMMISSIONER JONES.

partnership with Hon. E. Callahan, his step-father, who made him an equal partner. He was elected as a democrat to the 27th General Assembly in '71; as county judge in '77; as circuit judge in '79, and was reëlected in '85. At the expiration of his term he formed a law partnership with Mr. E. E. Newlin. Later on Judge John C. Eagleton was taken into the firm, which is now Jones, Newlin & Eagleton. He married in '69, Miss Mary H. Steel, of Robinson, and they have two sons and a daughter. Judge Jones has been a successful financier. He is Vice President of the First National Bank of Robinson, and, also, largely interested in farming and fruit growing. He is a member of Gorin Commandery No. 14, K. T. He was appointetd as the minority member of the commission of claims by Governor Tanner, in April, '97.

ERRORS NOTED.

The compiler and publisher of this book is not responsible for the errors in the Official Vote in "Appendix B." Some of the mistakes are inexcusable. Comparison with the official tables in the secretary of state's office has not been made, and there may be errors in the tables. The following mistakes in names are noted:

Page 3—"Sewell" should be Sewall.

Page 19—"Mabery" should be Mabry.

Page 20—"Thomas W. Jamison" should be Thomas N. Jamieson.

Page 23—"Cook" should be Cooke.

Page 42—"McConnell" should be McConnel.

Page 43—Pemberton's second initial is "C."

Page 48—"Shannahan" should be Shanahan.

Page 48—"Andrews" should be Andrus.

Page 48—"Bissell" should be Busell.

Page 49—"Nicholle" should be Nicholls.

Page 50—"Salmons" should be Salmans.

Page 50—"Quanstrom" should be Quanstrum.

Page 51—"Dennis" should be Denis —E. Sullivan.

Page 51—"Dougherty" should be Daugherty.

Page 51—"Koldstedt" should be Kohlstedt.

Page 52—"Throwbridge" should be Trowbridge.

Page 54—"Murdock" should be Murdoch.

Page 58—"Flanagan" should be Flannigan.

Page 58—"Shappard" should be Shephard.

Page 59—Should be "Louis" Perrottet.

Page 59—"Dickon" should be Dickson.

Page59—"Parrish"should be Parish.

OTHER ERRORS.

In compiling such a work as this, which extends from the organization of the Territory of Illinois, and embraces nearly ninety years of the State's history, it is almost impossible to prevent small errors. The publisher will consider it a favor if any reader will notify him of errors that he may discover, so that succeeding editions may be corrected.

Were it possible, a complete "Blue Book" would be incorporated in this volume, but the recent change in administration and the many resignations and discharges in state offices, as well as state institutions, are a bar to a "Blue Book" of value. The edition two years hence it is expected will contain the names, salaries and addresses of every officer and employe of Illinois on the first day of January, 1899.

J. L. Pickering,

Compiler and Publisher.

ILLINOIS' COMMISSIONS AND BOARDS.

COMPLETE LIST, WITH DATES, TAKEN FROM THE OFFICIAL RECORD IN THE GOVERNOR'S OFFICE, MAY 11, 1897.

The University of Illinois.

TRUSTEES—Elected. No pay.

Ex-officio—The Governor; President State Board of Agriculture; Superintendent Public Instruction.

Name.	Postoffice.	Term Expires.
Thomas J. Smith	Champaign	1903
Mary T. Carriel	Jacksonville	1903
Francis M. McKay	Chicago	1903
Napoleon B. Morrison	Odin	1899
James E. Armstrong	Chicago	1899
Isaac S. Raymond	Sidney	1899
Lucy L. Flower	Chicago	1901
Alexander McLean	Macomb	1901
Samuel A. Bullard	Springfield	1901

Northern Illinois Normal.

TRUSTEES—App. March 18, '97. No pay.

A. A. Goodrich	Chicago	1899
Isaac L. Ellwood	DeKalb	1899
R. S. Farrand	Dixon	1899
W. C. Garrard	Springfield	1897
Charles H. Deere	Moline	1897

Eastern Illinois Normal.

TRUSTEES—Appointed April 14, '97. No pay.

Henry A. Neal	Charleston	1897
L. Ph. Wulff	Peoria	1897
A. H. Jones	Robinson	1899
W. H. Hainline	Macomb	1899
F. M. Youngblood	Carbondale	1899

State Normal.

TRUSTEES—No Appointments '97. No pay.

Charles I. Parker	Chicago	1899
Forrest F. Cook	Galesburg	1899
M. E. Plain	Aurora	1899
Clinton Rosette	DeKalb	1899
Jacob J. Bailey	Macomb	1899
Edward Doocy	Pittsfield	1897
Lyon Karr	Eureka	1895
E. R. E. Kimbrough	Danville	1897
Charles L. Capen	Bloomington	1897

Southern Normal.

TRUSTEES—Appointed April 14, '97. No pay.

Thomas S. Ridgeway	Shawneetown	1899
F. A. Prickett	Carbondale	1903
Douglas Helm	Metropolis	1903
S. P. Wheeler	Springfield	1901
A. C. Brookings	DuQuoin	1901

May 7—T. O. Johnson, Omaha, vice Ridgeway, resigned.

The State Penitentiary.

COMMISSIONERS—App. Feb. 17, '97; $1,500.

Thos. O'Shaughnessy	Chicago	1898
John H. Pierce	Kewanee	1900
Hamer H. Green	Bloomington	1902

WARDEN—R. W. McClaughry; $5,000.

Railroad and Warehouse Commission.

COMMISSIONERS—$3,500; app. Feb. 3, '97.

Cicero J. Lindly	Greenville	1899
Charles S. Rannells	Jacksonville	1899
Joseph E. Bidwell	Chicago	1899

The Southern Penitentiary.

COMMISSIONERS—App. Feb. 3, '97; $1,500.

Thomas W. Scott	Fairfield	1898
Joseph B. Messick	East St. Louis	1902
James E. Jobe	Harrisburg	1900

WARDEN—J. Mack Tanner; $2,500.

State Reformatory.

BOARD MANAGERS—App. Feb. 18, '97; $1,200.

William Jackson	Rock Island	The term is 10 years, and managers draw lots for long term.
Charles E. Felton	Chicago	
Francis Gilbert	Chicago	
Valentine Jobst	Peoria	
Samuel Fallows	Chicago	

WARDEN—George Torrence; $4,000.

Home for Juvenile Female Offenders.

STATE GUARDIANS FOR GIRLS—App. April 14, '97. No pay.

A. K. Perry	Aurora	1898
Vic. M. Richardson	Princeton	1898
Mrs. J. D. Harvey	Geneva	1897
Henry Whittemore	Sycamore	1899
Mrs. F. H. Blackman	Geneva	1896

SUPERINTENDENT—Ophelia L. Amigh; $1,000.

Soldiers' and Sailors' Home.

TRUSTEES—App. March 17, '97. No pay.

Wm. O. Wright	Freeport	1899
John W. Niles	Sterling	1903
James A. Sexton	Chicago	1901

SUPERINTENDENT—Wm. Somerville; $2,500.

Soldiers' Orphans' Home.

TRUSTEES—App. April 12, '97. No pay.

Edwin Harlan	Marshall	1899
John B. Wolf	Bloomington	1901
W. R. Page	Chicago	1903

SUPERINTENDENT—J. H. Magner; $2,500.

Soldiers' Widows' Home.

TRUSTEES—App. April 21, '97. No pay.

M. N. Stewart	Wilmington	1899
Mrs. Flo J. Miller	Monticello	1899
W. C. Newbery	Chicago	1899
Mrs. C. Erickson	Chicago	1899
Derella Johnson	Chicago	1899

MATRON—Mrs. Margaret R. Wickins; $800.

Fish Commission.

COMMISSIONERS—App. April 12, '97. No pay.

S. P. Bartlett	Quincy	1899
Nathan H. Cohen	Urbana	1898
August Lenke	Chicago	1897

State Board of Charities.

MEMBERS—App. March 23, '97. No pay.
J. C. Corbus...... .. Mendota.......... 1898
Julia C. Lathrop...... Rockford.......... 1900
R. D. Lawrence........ Springfield........ 1899
Wm. J. Calhoun........ Danville.......... 1901
Ephraim Banning...... Chicago.... 1897
SECRETARY—F. H. Wines; $3,000.

Institution for the Blind.

TRUSTEES—App. April 12, '97. No pay.
N. W. Branson......... Petersburg....... 1901
Augustus Dow......... Pittsfield... 1903
Edward W. Rew........ Chicago........ .. 1899
SUPERINTENDENT—Frank H. Hall; $1,800.

Deaf and Dumb Institution.

TRUSTEES—App. March 17, '97. No pay.
James R. Smith........ Taylorville....... 1899
Gates Strawn.......... Jacksonville 1903
George W. Harper..... Robinson......... 1901
SUPERINTENDENT—$2,500; no app't for '97.

Eye and Ear Infirmary.

TRUSTEES—App. March 25, '97. No. pay.
J. W. Pettit........... Ottawa. 1901
Frances B. Phillips... Bloomington..... 1903
L. S. Lambert.......... Galesburg 1899
SUPERINTENDENT—W. C. Butterworth; $1,500.

Asylum for Feeble-Minded Children.

TRUSTEES—App. March 16, '97. No pay.
Zeno K. Wood......... Mt. Pulaski 1899
Clarence R. Gittings.. Terre Haute...... 1903
Samuel C. Smiley .... O'Fallon.......... 1901
SUPERINTENDENT—W. L. Athon; $2,400.

Central Hospital for Insane.

TRUSTEES—App. March 23, '97. No pay.
Morris Emmerson..... Mt. Vernon 1899
F. L. Sharp............ Jacksonville..... 1903
James A. Glenn.. ..... Ashland.......... 1901
SUPERINTENDENT—F. H. Winslow; $3,500.

Asylum for Incurable Insane.

TRUSTEES—App. March 17, '97. No pay.
R. F. Bennett.......... Litchfield ....
Henry Alexander. . . Joliet. ....
Morrow P. Reed .... Peoria ....
SUPERINTENDENT—

Western Hospital for Insane.

TRUSTEES—App. March 17, '97. No pay.
Frank W. Gould. ..... Moline............ 1903
John I. McCauley ..... Clay City.......... 1901
Allen M. Clement...... Chicago......... 1899
SUPERINTENDENT—W. F. Taylor; ———

Southern Hospital for Insane.

TRUSTEES—App. Feb. 16, '97. No pay.
James C. Mitchell..... Marion 1899
L. Krughoff............ Nashville......... 1903
Samuel Hastings ... Cairo............. 1901
SUPERINTENDENT—W. A. Stoker; $3,000.

Eastern Hospital for Insane.

TRUSTEES—App. March 11, '97. No pay.
Geo. T. Buckingham.. Danville....... 1899
Len Small............. Kankakee 1901
John J. Magee.......... Chicago 1903
SUPERINTENDENT—Wm. G. Stearns; $3,500.

Industrial Home for Blind.

TRUSTEES—App. May 4, '97. No pay.
L. L. Smith............ Evanston 1899
William Ludewing.... Chicago 1899
William Barclay ...... Chicago 1899
Francis S. Peabody ... Chicago 1899
Jacob H. Hopkins..... Chicago 1899
SUPERINTENDENT—

Northern Hospital for Insane.

TRUSTEES—App. March 16, '97. No pay.
A. S. Wright .. . . Woodstock....... 1899
Walter S. Frazier...... Aurora........... 1903
W. Scott Cowen........ Shannon 1901
SUPERINTENDENT—John B. Hamilton; $3,500.

Illinois and Michigan Canal.

COMMISSIONERS—App. Feb. 11, '97. $5.
Clarence E. Snively... Canton 1899
Howard O. Hilton..... Rockford......... 1899
Frank M. Ryon.... .. Streator 1899
SECRETARY—W. L. Sackett; $1,900.
SUPERINTENDENT—Leon McDonald; $2,100.

Commission of Claims.

COMMISSIONERS—App. April 6, '97; $15 per diem, for not exceeding 90 days.
Walter L. Louden..... Carlyle........... 1901
Wm. C. Jones .... Robinson... ... 1901
John C. McKenzie.... Elizabeth.... 1901

Bureau of Labor.

COMMISSIONERS—App. Feb. 17, '95; $5 per diem for 30 days.
P. H. Donnelly .... Springfield....... 1897
James Alexander ..... Murphysboro ... 1897
S. M. Dalzell. .... Spring Valley.... 1897
Andrew Jaeger....... Alton............. 1897
T. D. Kelligar .... Pana............... 1897
SECRETARY—David Ross; $3,000.

State Board of Arbitration.

MEMBERS—App. March 23, '97; $1,500.
Daniel J. Keefe........ Chicago 1899
Horace R. Calef .... Monticello 1899
Joseph B. Gill.......... Murphysboro.... 1899
May 11—Edward Ridgely, Springfield, *vice* Gill, resigned.
SECRETARY—J. McCan Davis; $1,200.

Inspectors of Coal Mines.

James A. Keating..... Streator.. 1897
*Thomas Hudson...... Galva............ 1897
Robert Pickett .... Canton 1897
Henry Malloy .... Danville.......... 1897
*Walton Rutledge..... Alton. 1897
Thos. S. Cummings... Belleville......... 1897
*Evan D. John.......... Carbondale 1897
*Appointed by Gov. Tanner.

State Factory Inspectors.

No appointments by Gov. Tanner.
Mrs. Florence Kelly, Inspector $1,500.. 1897
Mrs. A. P. Stevens, assistant, $1,000...... 1897
Mrs. Belle M. Powell, deputy, $750....... 1897
Fannie Jones, deputy, $750.............. 1897
Abraham Bisno, deputy, $750 1897
P. E. Jensen, deputy, $750 1897
John Merz, deputy, $750 1897
Mary Moran, deputy, $750................ 1897
Mrs. Sarah Cunningham, deputy, $750.. 1897
Mrs. Emma Jameson, deputy, $750 1897
John Martin, deputy, $750................ 1897
All of Chicago.

State Historical Library.

TRUSTEES—App. May 7, '97. No pay.
Hiram W. Beckwith... Danville...... .. 1899
Edmund J. James..... Chicago. 1899
George N. Black....... Springfield. 1899
LIBRARIAN—Josephine Cleveland; $1,000.

Examiners of Mine Inspectors.

MEMBERS—App. March, '97; $3 per diem for ten days.
Richard Ramsay ...... Braceville 1899
Hugh Murray.......... Sparta........ ... 1899
J. R. Thomas.......... Ladd 1899
Thomas Haddon....... Pana........... ... 1899
Wm. Cruikshank ...... Middle Grove.... 1899

State Board of Health.

MEMBERS—App. April 21, '97. No pay.
Julius Kohl............Belleville............1897
Z. D. French...........Lawrenceville...1898
M. Meyerovitz.........Chicago...........1899
P. H. Wessel...........Moline.............1900
Florence Hunt.........Chicago............1901
L. Adelsberger.........Waterloo.........1902
C. B. Johnson..........Champaign........1903
SECRETARY—No appointment for '97; $3,000.

Live Stock Commission.

COMMISSIONERS—App. March 17, '97; $5.
James R. Goddard....Galesburg........1899
James P. Lott.........Chicago...........1898
James H. Paddock....Springfield.......1897
SECRETARY—Clarence P. Johnson; $1,800.

Dental Examiners.

BOARD—No appointments for '97; $5 a day.
G. A. McMillian........Alton..............1895
Letcher Irons..........Mt. Vernon.......1896
A. W. Harlan...........Chicago...........1897
L. L. Davis, Sec'y......Chicago...........1898
Joseph W. Wassall....Chicago...........1899

State Board of Education.

MEMBERS—No appointm'ts for '97. No pay.
William H. Green.....Cairo..............1897
E. A. Gastman.........Decatur............1897
E. R. E. Kimbrough...Danville...........1897
Charles L. Capen.....Bloomington......1897
Edward Doocy.........Pittsfield..........1897
Ella F. Young.........Chicago.............1901
Matthew Brady.......Chicago.............1901
Charles S. Thornton...Chicago.............1901
P. R. Walker...........Rockford............1901
Charles I. Parker.....Chicago.............1899
Forest F. Cook.........Galesburg..........1899
M. E. Plain.............Aurora..............1899
Wm. H. Fitzgerald....Chicago.............1899
Jacob J. Bailey........Macomb.............1899
S. M. Inglis (*ex-officio*).Springfield.........1899

Board of Pharmacy.

MEMBERS—Appointed for five years; $5.
Fred M Schmidt.......Chicago.............1898
Anson A. Culver......Momence............1900
H. Lee Hatch...........Jacksonville.......1900
William C. Simpson...Vienna..............1902
Albert Zimmerman...Peoria...............1898
SECRETARY—Frank Fleury; $2,000.

Lincoln Park Commission.

COMMISSIONERS—App. April 11, '97. No pay.
William Stewart, resigned; Horatio N. May, Peter Hand, F. K. Winston, Wm. Penn Nixon.

West Park Commission.

COMMISSIONERS—App. Feb. 2, '97. No pay.
Anton Petersen, Joseph W. Suddard, Chas. J. Pavlicek, Andrew J. Graham, Fred M. Blount, Wm. C. Eggert, Wm. J. Wilson.

Miscellaneous Appointments.

Adjutant General—Gen. J. N. Reece... $3,000
Insurance Supt.—J. R. B. Van Cleave... 3,500
State Geologist—C. H. Crantz........... 2,500
State Veterinarian—C. P. Lovejoy...... 3,000
Printer Expert—John H. Barton, per diem $6
Humane Agents:
Chicago.. $1,500
East. St. Louis—S. E. Nichols............ 1,500
Peoria—Samuel S. Smith.................. 1,500
Grain Inspectors:
Joliet—Thos. Stevenson......................Fees
Quincy...Fees
Decatur...Fees
Savanna—F. E. Lewis..........................Fees
Kankakee...Fees

EX-OFFICIO.

Commissioners of State Library.

Governor.
Secretary of State.
Superintendent of Public Instruction.

Commissioners of State Contracts.

Secretary of State.
Auditor of Public Accounts.
State Treasurer.
Attorney General.

Trustees Geological Museum.

Governor.
Secretary of State.
Superintendent of Public Instruction.

Lincoln Homestead Trustees.

Governor.
Secretary of State.
Auditor of Public Accounts.
State Treasurer.
Superintendent of Public Instruction.

STATISTICS REGARDING STATE INSTITUTIONS.

The following tables from the biennial report of the Board of Public Charities, shows the ordinary expenses of each institution for each fiscal year since the year 1875; the net cost to the State of Illinois; the average number of inmates during each year, and the per capita rate per annum, gross and net. The date of closing the fiscal year has been changed twice during the past eighteen years. Before 1875 the fiscal year closed on the 30th of November, but, in 1875, it closed on the 1st of October, so that the expenses for 1875 cover only ten calendar months. Since 1888 the fiscal year has closed on the 1st of July, so that the expenses for that year cover only nine calendar months. In calculating the rate per capita, however, these changes have been taken into account, and the rate is stated at the figure which it would have reached if the fiscal year had consisted of twelve full months. The fact that the three months taken off from the fiscal year 1888 were those in which the educational institutions have a vacation tended to increase the average number of inmates for that particular year, and correspondingly to diminish the per capita cost. This applies to the Institutions for the Deaf and Dumb and for the Blind, the Asylum for Feeble-Minded Children and the Soldiers' Orphans' Home.

An examination of the tables will satisfy an attentive reader that there has been, on the whole, a decided and steady improvement in the financial management of the State institutions.

NORTHERN HOSPITAL FOR THE INSANE, ELGIN.

YEAR.	Gross ordinary expenses.	Income not from State.	Cost to State.	Average number.	PER CAPITA COST.	
					Gross.	Net.
1875	$77,601 50	$9,154 90	$68,446 60	307	$303 32	$222 02
1876	105,348 85	22,250 78	83,098 07	466	227 53	178 32
1877	107,713 62	12,032 44	95,581 18	464	232 14	206 21
1878	104,080 09	7,906 88	96,173 21	498	208 99	193 12
1879	110,667 56	7,470 59	103,196 97	521	212 39	198 07
1880	104,167 16	11,260 99	92,906 17	521	200 10	178 32
1881	117,547 66	11,799 91	105,747 75	522	225 01	202 58
1882	110,465 96	11,003 27	99,462 69	519	212 81	191 64
1883	106,257 21	10,157 46	96,099 75	526	202 15	182 70
1884	109,549 44	14,616 91	94,932 53	526	208 45	180 48
1885	107,487 06	12,408 50	95,078 56	528	203 57	180 64
1886	115,021 90	19,916 79	95,105 11	533	216 00	178 43
1887	96,457 70	6,580 36	89,877 34	534	180 56	168 24
1888	73,124 43	9,653 55	63,470 88	527	185 00	160 57
1889	101,272 04	6,901 18	94,372 86	531	190 60	177 61
1890	90,224 81	8,681 98	81,542 83	513	175 73	158 82
1891	105,427 72	8,142 43	97,285 29	509	176 05	162 46
1892	143,778 84	9,210 58	134,568 26	905	158 79	148 62
1893	160,797 37	14,921 48	145,875 89	1,051	153 06	138 85
1894	154,275 47	16,707 17	137,568 30	1,095	140 86	125 61
1895	158,409 17	10,268 92	148,140 25	1,114	142 15	139 93
1896	160,539 45	10,930 28	149,609 17	1,206	140 30	130 75
Total	$2,520,205 01	$251,977 35	$2,268,227 66	640	$178 78	$160 91

ASYLUM FOR INSANE CRIMINALS, CHESTER.

YEAR.	Gross ordinary expenses.	Income not from State.	Cost to State.	Average number.	Per capita Gross.	Per capita Net.
1892	$16,448 17	$87 26	$16,330 91	51	$320 86	$319 10
1893	30,257 18	1,050 79	29,206 39	111	270 68	261 45
1894	25,709 99	1,615 18	24,094 81	112	227 95	213 63
1895	24,680 42	1,736 68	22,943 74	125	196 20	182 39
1896	24,567 04	2,307 00	22,262 04	124	198 02	177 42
Total	$121,704 80	$6,796 91	$114,837 89	104	$232 70	$219 57

ASYLUM FOR FEEBLE-MINDED CHILDREN, LINCOLN.

Year.	Gross ordinary expenses.	Income not from State.	Cost to State.	Average number.	Per Capita Cost.	
					Gross.	Net.
1875	$20,901 76	$2,423 01	$18,478 75	81	$309 65	$279 74
1876	28,812 87	2,630 56	26,182 31	80	300 16	327 28
1877	31,639 52	2,140 14	29,490 38	77	410 90	383 11
1878	53,062 88	3,686 80	49,376 08	168	315 35	293 91
1879	47,381 69	2,816 66	44,565 03	224	210 97	198 95
1880	59,502 70	5,132 65	54,370 05	274	217 57	198 42
1881	56,710 94	6,383 79	50,327 15	286	198 21	175 97
1882	63,284 23	7,885 66	55,398 57	279	226 69	198 56
1883	61,782 06	6,271 96	55,510 10	293	210 74	188 70
1884	54,372 82	4,817 29	49,555 53	292	186 41	169 71
1885	61,306 37	3,766 55	57,539 82	312	196 38	184 42
1886	65,600 72	4,115 33	61,485 39	341	192 33	180 31
1887	66,961 51	4,456 87	62,504 64	362	185 08	172 76
1888	51,292 42	5,046 59	46,245 83	387	176 95	159 53
1889	68,607 07	7,547 95	61,059 12	382	179 75	159 97
1890	72,809 83	6,325 08	66,484 75	410	177 49	162 07
1891	77,232 99	9,188 18	68,044 81	414	186 65	164 45
1892	89,534 55	8,802 24	80,732 31	485	184 61	166 46
1893	91,156 51	11,972 13	79,184 38	543	167 58	145 57
1894	83,046 35	9,405 27	73,641 08	546	151 97	134 76
1895	93,307 75	13,158 66	80,149 09	569	163 73	140 63
1896	94,048 31	14,280 55	79,767 76	587	160 19	135 86
Total	$1,392,355 85	$142,253 92	$1,250,101 93	336	$188 35	$169 11

SOLDIERS' ORPHANS' HOME, NORMAL.

Year.	Gross ordinary expenses.	Income not from State.	Cost to State.	Average number.	Per Capita Cost, Gross.	Per Capita Cost, Net.
1875	$43,426 43	$463 12	$42,963 31	297	$175 45	$153 70
1876	46,776 72	681 79	46,094 93	310	150 89	148 70
1877	42,498 83	84 26	42,414 57	275	154 54	154 50
1878	44,890 35	738 92	44,151 43	291	154 56	151 72
1879	41,859 79	237 22	41,622 57	302	138 78	137 82
1880	47,533 66	1,233 66	46,300 00	308	154 33	150 32
1881	43,461 52	664 96	42,796 56	301	144 50	142 18
1882	45,848 54	321 58	45,526 96	266	172 07	171 15
1883	45,071 93	353 16	44,708 77	273	165 07	163 77
1884	54,077 85	428 10	53,649 75	317	170 58	169 24
1885	50,537 68	157 62	50,380 06	328	153 83	153 60
1886	52,694 22	382 72	52,311 50	326	161 56	160 43
1887	49,687 61	653 41	49,034 20	341	145 88	143 96
1888	38,813 71	237 47	38,576 24	359	144 21	143 33
1889	50,960 08	549 68	50,410 40	344	148 33	146 73
1890	54,088 97	460 83	53,628 14	313	172 58	171 11
1891	53,200 11	812 69	52,387 42	399	133 41	131 38
1892	53,844 54	259 07	53,585 47	397	135 59	134 94
1893	51,176 56	293 42	50,883 14	388	131 89	130 85
1894	46,126 05	107 00	46,019 05	373	123 38	123 00
1895	51,274 46	264 32	51,010 14	419	122 24	121 61
1896	46,265 46	176 54	46,088 92	393	117 58	117 13
Total	$1,056,800 35	$9,571 54	$1,047,228 81	332	$144 37	$143 06

STATE HOME FOR JUVENILE FEMALE OFFENDERS.

Year.	Gross ordinary expenses.	Income not from State.	Cost to State.	Average number.	Per Capita Cost, Gross.	Per Capita Cost, Net.
1895	$19,722 18	$28 03	$19,694 15	27	$713 79	$712 78
1896	19,774 56	29 75	19,744 81	47	420 73	420 10
Total	$39,496 74	$57 78	$39,438 96	37	$533 74	$532 05

EASTERN HOSPITAL FOR THE INSANE, KANKAKEE.

Year.	Gross ordinary expenses.	Income not from State.	Cost to State.	Average number.	Per Capita Cost.	
					Gross.	Net.
1879	$2,286 60	$491 00	$1,795 60	....	....	....
1880	35,419 86	690 19	34,729 67	63	$558 14	$551 27
1881	62,071 38	3,072 93	58,998 45	185	335 63	318 91
1882	76,825 36	5,103 88	71,722 48	308	249 08	232 87
1883	93,017 96	5,350 04	87,667 92	399	233 14	219 72
1884	103,053 73	5,432 48	97,621 25	515	200 25	189 56
1885	207,425 18	8,985 02	198,440 16	1,119	185 42	177 34
1886	248,621 30	22,726 12	225,895 18	1,471	169 07	153 57
1887	246,952 50	22,068 29	224,084 21	1,518	162 65	148 11
1888	203,616 20	20,568 74	183,047 46	1,577	172 20	154 80
1889	260,350 37	18,234 28	242,116 09	1,633	159 44	148 27
1890	257,403 49	24,684 60	232,718 89	1,675	153 63	138 90
1891	272,303 25	25,191 78	247,111 47	1,707	159 53	144 77
1892	275,134 84	22,657 69	252,477 15	1,703	161 56	148 26
1893	288,836 80	29,659 91	259,176 89	1,877	153 88	138 07
1894	308,745 32	25,089 38	283,655 94	2,018	152 97	140 54
1895	322,702 86	32,027 43	290,675 43	2,095	153 99	138 71
1896	333,810 94	44,631 67	289,179 27	2,086	160 02	138 62
Total	$3,508,577 94	$316,664 43	$3,291,913 51	1,219	$163 93	$149 98

CENTRAL HOSPITAL FOR THE INSANE, JACKSONVILLE.

Year.	Gross ordinary expenses.	Income not from State.	Cost to State.	Average number.	Per Capita Cost. Gross.	Per Capita Cost. Net.
1875	$78,636 35	$18,399 26	$60,237 09	470	$200 77	$161 63
1876	109,248 90	20,843 92	88,404 98	467	234 15	189 30
1877	96,835 16	18,780 64	78,054 52	487	198 84	160 27
1878	106,905 73	11,538 96	95,366 77	496	215 51	192 27
1879	105,075 30	10,782 95	94,292 35	566	185 52	166 59
1880	116,955 06	9,287 70	107,667 36	625	187 29	172 27
1881	113,638 17	11,325 85	102,285 32	639	177 91	160 07
1882	120,643 77	12,727 41	107,916 36	639	188 90	169 04
1883	114,291 84	9,892 61	104,399 23	630	181 42	165 71
1884	121,902 78	10,764 37	111,138 41	629	193 74	175 69
1885	118,768 30	9,653 72	109,114 58	641	185 31	170 23
1886	153,146 73	10,986 69	142,160 04	856	178 94	166 08
1887	149,669 35	11,976 89	137,692 55	918	163 03	149 98
1888	114,974 46	7,177 52	107,796 94	907	169 00	158 45
1889	149,429 86	13,470 25	135,959 61	911	164 03	149 25
1890	147,812 21	13,517 89	134,294 32	900	164 25	149 23
1891	151,716 89	13,353 26	138,363 63	913	166 16	151 54
1892	178,703 20	13,171 01	165,532 19	1,079	165 62	153 42
1893	178,953 49	14,265 54	164,687 95	1,181	151 52	139 45
1894	169,967 75	13,251 61	156,716 14	1,198	141 87	130 81
1895	156,141 76	12,203 15	143,938 61	1,223	127 67	117 60
1896	158,694 39	20,044 73	138,649 66	1,290	123 00	107 48
Total	$2,912,111 45	$287,442 84	$2,624,668 61	803	$164 85	$148 58

INSTITUTION FOR EDUCATION OF THE BLIND, JACKSONVILLE.

Year.	Gross ordinary expenses.	Income not from State.	Cost to State.	Average number.	Per Capita Cost. Gross.	Per Capita Cost. Net.
1875	$24,763 77	$1,292 15	$23,471 62	62	$479 29	$458 46
1876	25,730 15	1,749 25	23,980 90	55	467 82	436 02
1877	24,979 22	1,280 30	23,698 92	57	438 18	415 78
1878	27,779 31	2,220 04	25,559 27	72	385 82	354 99
1879	27,913 51	1,697 54	26,215 97	75	370 84	349 55
1880	25,599 61	1,497 91	24,101 70	78	325 77	321 82
1881	28,348 73	1,323 57	27,025 16	77	369 94	350 98
1882	25,447 01	2,582 43	22,864 08	64	400 49	357 25
1883	27,852 06	1,627 21	26,224 85	79	352 53	331 96
1884	31,157 69	1,966 82	29,190 87	93	334 88	313 86
1885	33,388 69	1,826 24	31,562 45	98	339 52	325 13
1886	33,583 47	3,895 76	29,687 71	109	307 65	272 37
1887	39,709 80	3,091 67	36,618 13	124	320 40	295 45
1888	26,445 35	3 274 71	23,170 64	146	241 03	211 19
1889	37,318 70	4,652 80	32,665 90	111	335 78	293 92
1890	41,662 47	3,898 95	37,763 52	121	345 21	312 15
1891	41,863 13	5,077 73	36,785 40	136	307 59	270 28
1892	47,631 51	6,495 00	41,136 51	164	295 68	256 36
1893	48,203 55	8,188 46	40,015 09	148	324 25	269 17
1894	50,597 82	6,974 28	43,623 54	167	302 11	260 41
1895	50,090 97	7,822 51	42,268 46	165	301 84	254 70
1896	43,640 00	3,054 51	40,585 49	142	306 11	284 68
Total	$763,706 52	$75,400 34	$688,216 18	106	$325 95	$293 73

SOUTHERN HOSPITAL FOR THE INSANE, ANNA.

Year.	Gross ordinary expenses.	Income not from State.	Cost to State.	Average number.	Per Capita Cost.	
					Gross.	Net.
1875	$38,876 73	$4,063 50	$34,913 23	148	$315 22	$287 76
1876	51,011 68	6,078 74	44,932 94	204	250 05	220 20
1877	57,176 73	7,845 66	49,331 07	246	231 48	200 53
1878	80,040 41	4,807 83	75,232 58	394	203 15	190 94
1879	82,721 55	9,172 52	73,549 03	466	77 66	157 83
1880	92,990 70	8,394 06	84,596 04	498	186 64	169 87
1881	88,552 45	10,031 61	78,520 84	496	177 83	157 67
1882	98,180 77	9,249 22	88,931 55	498	199 18	180 39
1883	103,993 35	9,048 45	94,944 90	526	197 57	180 50
1884	102,689 20	10,424 78	92,264 42	576	178 18	160 18
1885	109,497 83	10,165 98	99,331 85	636	172 29	156 18
1886	111,968 91	11,524 83	100,444 08	655	170 99	153 35
1887	121,102 44	13,060 44	108,042 00	646	187 61	167 38
1888	87,512 21	10,682 87	76,829 34	630	185 35	162 72
1889	108,813 73	11,283 57	97,530 16	640	170 05	152 41
1890	103,498 42	11,918 82	91,579 60	612	169 07	149 60
1891	112,567 98	8,484 79	104,083 19	619	181 99	168 27
1892	133,663 70	12,015 64	121,648 06	802	166 63	151 65
1893	122,993 12	12,896 88	110,096 24	880	139 70	125 01
1894	117,376 07	14,793 01	102,583 06	847	138 49	121 03
1885	122,732 60	10,202 66	112,529 94	841	145 88	133 76
1896	111,566 30	15,271 27	96,205 03	837	133 25	115 00
Total	$2,150,502 88	$221,417 73	$1,938,019 15	577	$170 12	$152 75

INSTITUTION FOR EDUCATION OF THE DEAF AND DUMB, JACKSONVILLE.

Year.	Gross ordinary expenses.	Income not from State.	Cost to State.	Average number.	Per Capita Cost.	
					Gross.	Net.
1875	$55,260 86	$8,971 15	$46,289 71	210	$302 80	$231 84
1876	79,805 53	4,193 15	75,612 38	257	310 53	294 21
1877	77,804 92	4,974 47	72,830 45	263	295 88	276 92
1878	87,774 33	8,242 04	79,532 29	304	286 84	261 62
1879	82,723 73	5,124 83	77,598 90	301	274 91	257 80
1880	88,124 61	12,369 82	75,754 79	307	286 67	252 77
1881	96,776 55	9,519 16	87,257 39	359	269 58	243 06
1882	94,651 73	9,391 83	85,259 90	340	278 56	250 77
1883	102,180 97	9,352 08	92,828 90	374	273 55	248 21
1884	100,067 72	10,137 51	98,930 21	368	271 83	244 38
1885	105,242 76	9,640 51	95,602 25	369	285 37	259 08
1886	107,950 59	8,741 00	99,209 59	373	289 52	265 07
1887	105,977 49	8,879 40	97,098 09	362	292 57	268 00
1888	82,828 01	10,315 30	72,512 71	467	236 23	206 81
1889	105,915 80	9,712 81	96,202 99	365	290 47	263 84
1890	111,527 32	13,244 91	98,282 41	364	306 29	269 92
1891	114,860 33	12,342 39	102,517 94	371	309 64	276 37
1892	121,470 12	13,926 56	107,543 56	373	325 84	288 48
1893	114,112 48	12,862 62	101,249 86	368	310 09	275 14
1894	106,883 68	12,286 47	94,597 21	351	304 07	269 11
1895	106,335 86	9,756 73	96,579 13	361	291 42	267 41
1896	98,512 26	9,614 48	88,897 78	301	326 97	295 06
Total	$2,146,787 65	$213,599 22	$1,933,188 43	341	$239 58	$257 17

SOLDIERS' AND SAILORS' HOME, QUINCY.

Year.	Gross ordinary expenses.	Income not from State.	Cost to State.	Average number.	Per Capita Cost.	
					Gross.	Net.
1887	$69,085 27	$238 19	$68,847 08	270	$255 93	$255 05
1888	73,258 02	1,041 41	72,216 61	480	203 81	200 93
1889	121,774 05	3,533 73	118,240 32	653	186 30	180 98
1890	125,575 42	2,014 83	123,560 59	789	159 24	156 68
1891	134,209 07	1,339 52	132,869 55	882	152 19	150 67
1892	136,301 85	2,835 16	133,466 69	846	161 15	157 80
1893	144,142 39	5,156 53	138,985 86	860	167 56	161 57
1894	127,422 82	4,233 42	123,189 40	987	128 99	124 71
1895	131,692 54	2,615 40	129,077 08	1,050	124 95	122 46
1896	121,969 12	2,195 75	119,773 37	1,112	109 68	107 70
Total	$1,185,430 55	$25,204 00	$1,160,226 55	793	$149 50	$146 32

CHARITABLE EYE AND EAR INFIRMARY, CHICAGO.

YEAR.	Gross ordinary expenses.	Income not from State.	Cost to State.	Average number.	PER CAPITA COST.	
					Gross.	Net.
1875	$9,386 45	$1,870 87	$7,515 58	38	$341 20	$284 63
1876	12,653 51	2,265 80	10,387 62	45	281 19	230 84
1877	12,840 40	1,308 50	11,531 90	41	313 18	281 27
1878	18,478 23	100 00	18,378 23	77	239 98	238 68
1879	15,785 97	80 00	15,705 97	69	229 56	227 62
1880	15,624 92	....	15,624 92	62	250 96	250 96
1881	16,279 42	555 65	15,723 77	71	227 43	221 46
1882	18,001 55	....	18,001 55	72	248 64	248 64
1883	17,793 46	433 00	17,360 46	86	206 21	201 87
1884	17,586 87	212 50	17,374 37	78	224 41	222 75
1885	17,626 80	....	17,626 80	90	195 38	195 38
1886	20,045 05	352 58	19,692 47	117	170 77	168 31
1887	20,012 07	....	20,012 07	121	165 14	165 14
1888	16,661 38	....	16,661 38	127	174 65	174 65
1889	24,902 14	....	24,902 14	137	182 27	182 27
1890	24,206 68	....	24,206 68	139	174 53	174 53
1891	27,666 69	....	27,666 69	130	212 20	212 20
1892	25,051 24	....	25,051 24	132	189 69	189 69
1893	24,459 88	....	24,459 88	111	219 78	219 78
1894	23,087 52	....	23,087 52	112	205 66	205 66
1895	25,369 24	....	25,369 24	130	193 76	193 76
1896	24,759 39	60 95	24,698 44	133	186 12	185 66
Total	$428,278 86	$7,239 94	$421,038 92	96	202 68	199 20

TWELVE INSTITUTIONS—CONSOLIDATED.

1875	$373,998 79	$52 026 29	$321,972 50	1,795	$250 02	$215 25
1876	488,791 01	65,019 45	424,771 56	2,064	237 16	205 80
1877	482,071 39	51,940 72	430,130 67	2,074	231 78	207 39
1878	557,558 00	44,450 03	513,107 97	2,482	224 37	206 85
1879	551,214 66	43,498 90	507,715 76	2,707	202 75	187 56
1880	617,075 95	53,877 25	563,198 70	2,926	210 88	192 48
1881	655,861 79	58,694 99	597,166 80	3,135	209 21	190 48
1882	687,155 81	66,169 63	620,986 18	3,209	214 15	193 50
1883	714,421 85	62,552 33	651,869 52	3,471	205 81	187 80
1884	741,040 90	68,473 31	672,567 59	3,702	200 06	181 68
1885	864,329 12	65,137 57	799,191 55	4,444	193 71	179 85
1886	960,705 63	93,010 27	867,695 36	5,093	188 64	170 37
1887	1,014,018 40	78,739 27	935,279 13	5,230	180 66	165 65
1888	808,550 12	68,025 45	740,524 67	5,930	181 81	166 52
1889	1,081,773 50	76,156 00	1,005,617 59	6,024	179 58	166 94
1890	1,081,651 74	85,050 69	996,601 05	6,196	174 56	160 84
1891	1,147,673 23	84,719 72	1,062,953 51	6,552	175 17	162 24
1892	1,221,532 56	89,460 21	1,132,072 35	6,935	176 15	163 25
1893	1,255,089 33	111,267 76	1,143,821 57	7,520	166 88	152 09
1894	1,213,238 84	104,462 79	1,108,776 05	7,811	155 32	141 95
1895	1,262,459 81	100,084 55	1,162,375 26	8,129	155 28	142 97
1896	1,238,149 22	122,597 48	1,115,151 74	8,331	148 20	133 57
Total	$19,918,361 74	$1,644,414 66	$17,373,947 08	4,807	$188 33	$164 27

NOTE.—The Asylum for the Incurable Insane at Peoria, the Northwestern Hospital for the Insane at Rock Island, and the Industrial Home for the Blind at Chicago are not included in these tables. None of them are ready for occupancy and probably will not be occupied until the fall or winter of 1897. At this writing the General Assembly has not made appropriations for their completion and furnishing.

FIRST ILLINOIS CAPITOL, KASKASKIA. IT STILL STANDS.

SECOND ILLINOIS CAPITOL, VANDALIA, NOW FAYETTE COUNTY COURT HOUSE.

THIRD ILLINOIS CAPITOL, SPRINGFIELD, NOW SANGAMON COUNTY COURT HOUSE.

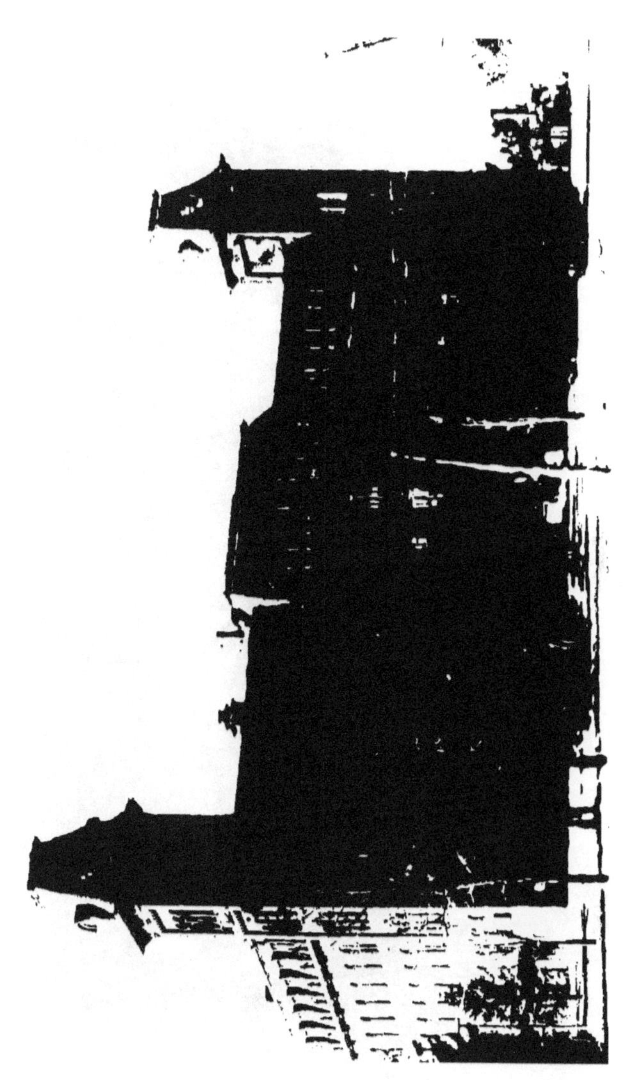

ENGINEERING HALL, UNIVERSITY OF ILLINOIS, CHAMPAIGN.

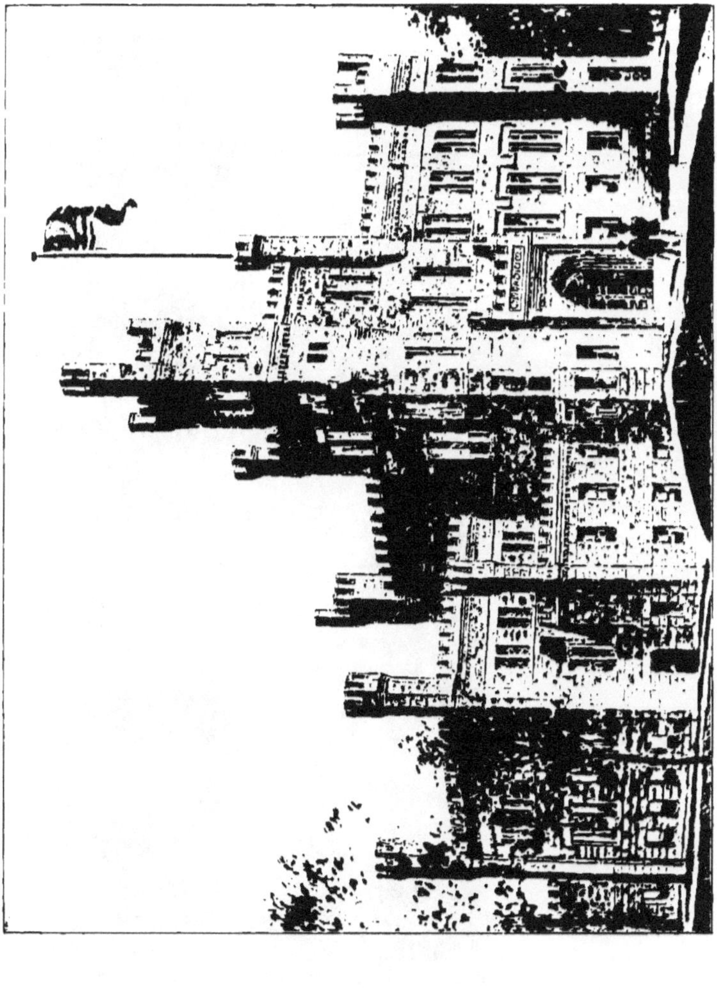

LIBRARY AND GYMNASIUM, NORMAL UNIVERSITY, NORMAL.

SOUTHERN NORMAL UNIVERSITY, CARBONDALE.

LIBRARY AND GYMNASIUM, NORMAL UNIVERSITY, CARBONDALE.

EASTERN NORMAL UNIVERSITY, CHARLESTON.

NORTHERN NORMAL UNIVERSITY, DEKALB.

ASYLUM FOR INCURABLE INSANE, PEORIA.

WESTERN HOSPITAL FOR INSANE, ROCK ISLAND.

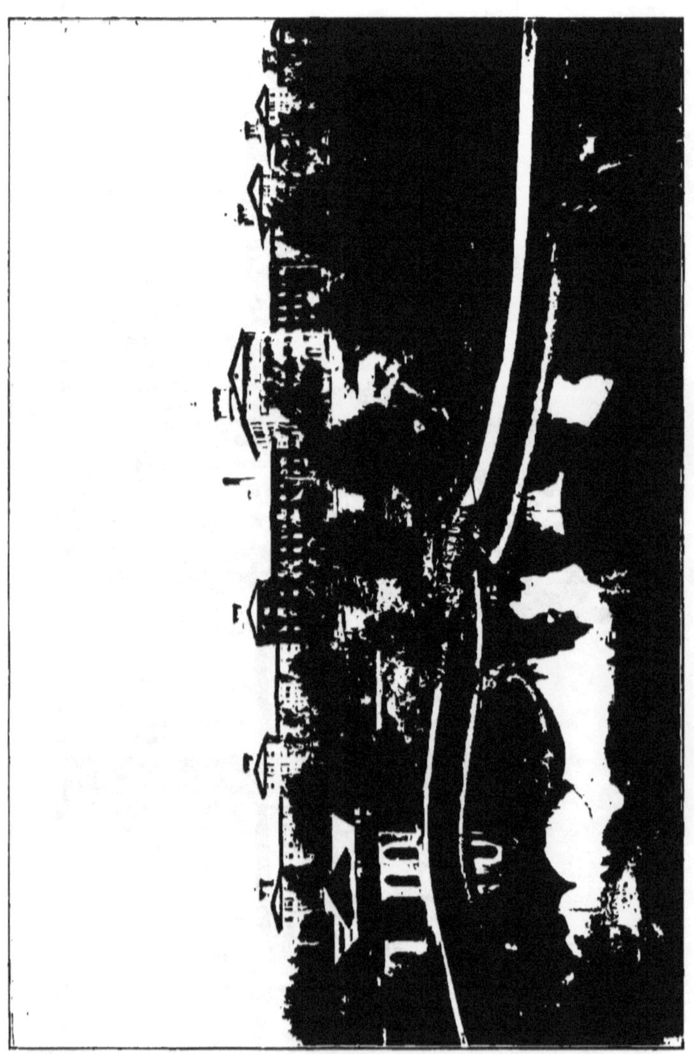

NORTHERN HOSPITAL FOR INSANE, ELGIN

ANNEX, NORTHERN HOSPITAL FOR INSANE, ELGIN.

JONATHAN BURR CONSERVATORY, NORTHERN HOSPITAL FOR INSANE, ELGIN.

ADMINISTRATION BUILDING, EASTERN HOSPITAL FOR INSANE, KANKAKEE.

NORTH WING, EASTERN HOSPITAL FOR INSANE, KANKAKEE.

SOUTH WING, "A" WARD, EASTERN HOSPITAL FOR INSANE, KANKAKEE.

WOMEN'S COTTAGES, EASTERN HOSPITAL FOR INSANE, KANKAKEE.

MAIN BUILDING, SOLDIERS' ORPHANS' HOME, NORMAL.

CENTRAL HOSPITAL FOR INSANE, JACKSONVILLE.

MAIN BUILDING ILLINOIS SOUTHERN HOSPITAL. ANNA, ILL.

ANNEX, SOUTHERN HOSPITAL FOR INSANE, ANNA.

NEW ADMINISTRATION BUILDING AND SOUTH WING, ILLINOIS SOUTHERN HOSPITAL FOR THE INSANE.

School and Chapel Building. Little Girls' Cottage. Main Building.

KINDERGARTEN ANNEX, DEAF AND DUMB, JACKSONVILLE.

SCHOOL BUILDING ASYLUM FOR FEEBLE-MINDED CHILDREN, LINCOLN.

ASYLUM FOR FEEBLE-MINDED CHILDREN, LINCOLN.

SOLDIERS' AND SAILORS' HOME, QUINCY.

ILLINOIS EYE AND EAR INFIRMARY, CHICAGO.

ILLINOIS STATE PENITENTIARY, JOLIET.

PRISON FOR FEMALE CONVICTS, ILLINOIS PENITENTIARY, JOLIET.

BIRD'S EYE VIEW STATE REFORMATORY, PONTIAC

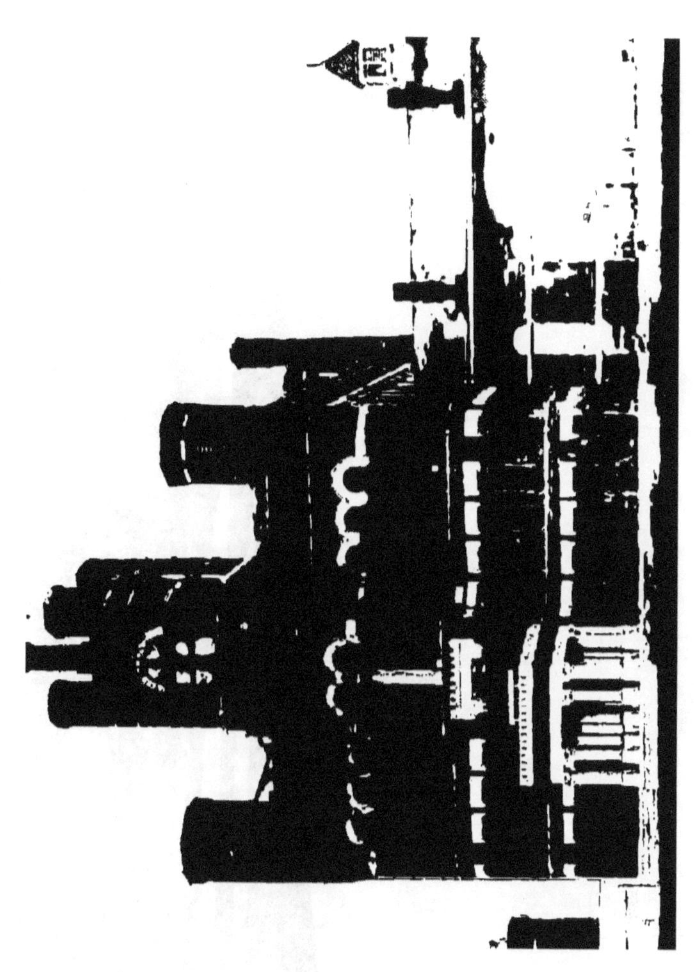

SOUTHERN ILLINOIS PENITENTIARY, CHESTER. (VIEW FROM MISSISSIPPI RIVER.)

(South End Southern Pen.)

PENITENTIARY FOR INSANE CRIMINALS (ON BLUFF), CHESTER.

LELAND HOTEL, SPRINGFIELD, SHOWING ANNEX BUILT IN '96.

ST. NICHOLAS HOTEL, SPRINGFIELD, SHOWING ANNEX BUILT IN '96.

MAIN OFFICE, ST. NICHOLAS HOTEL.

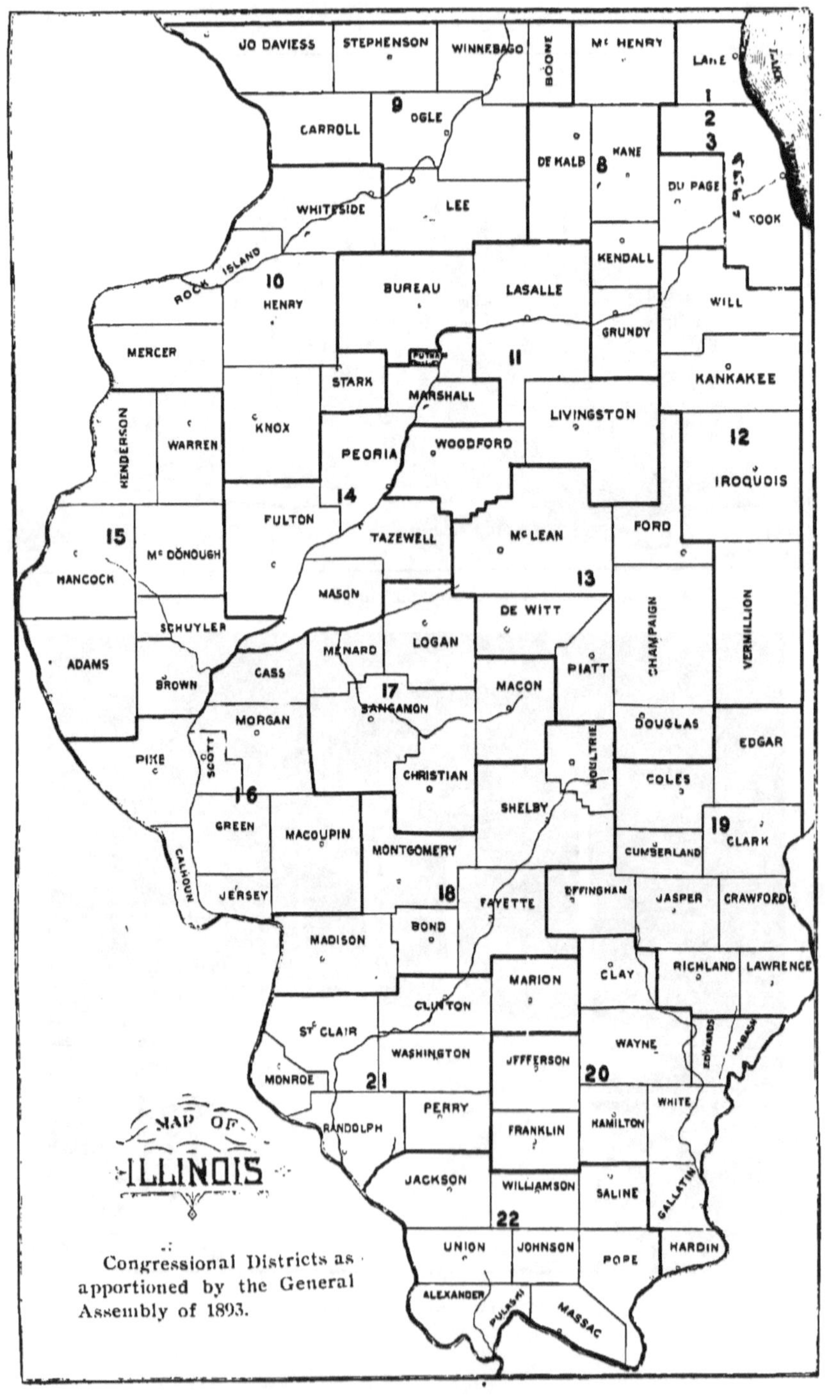

Congressional Districts as apportioned by the General Assembly of 1893.

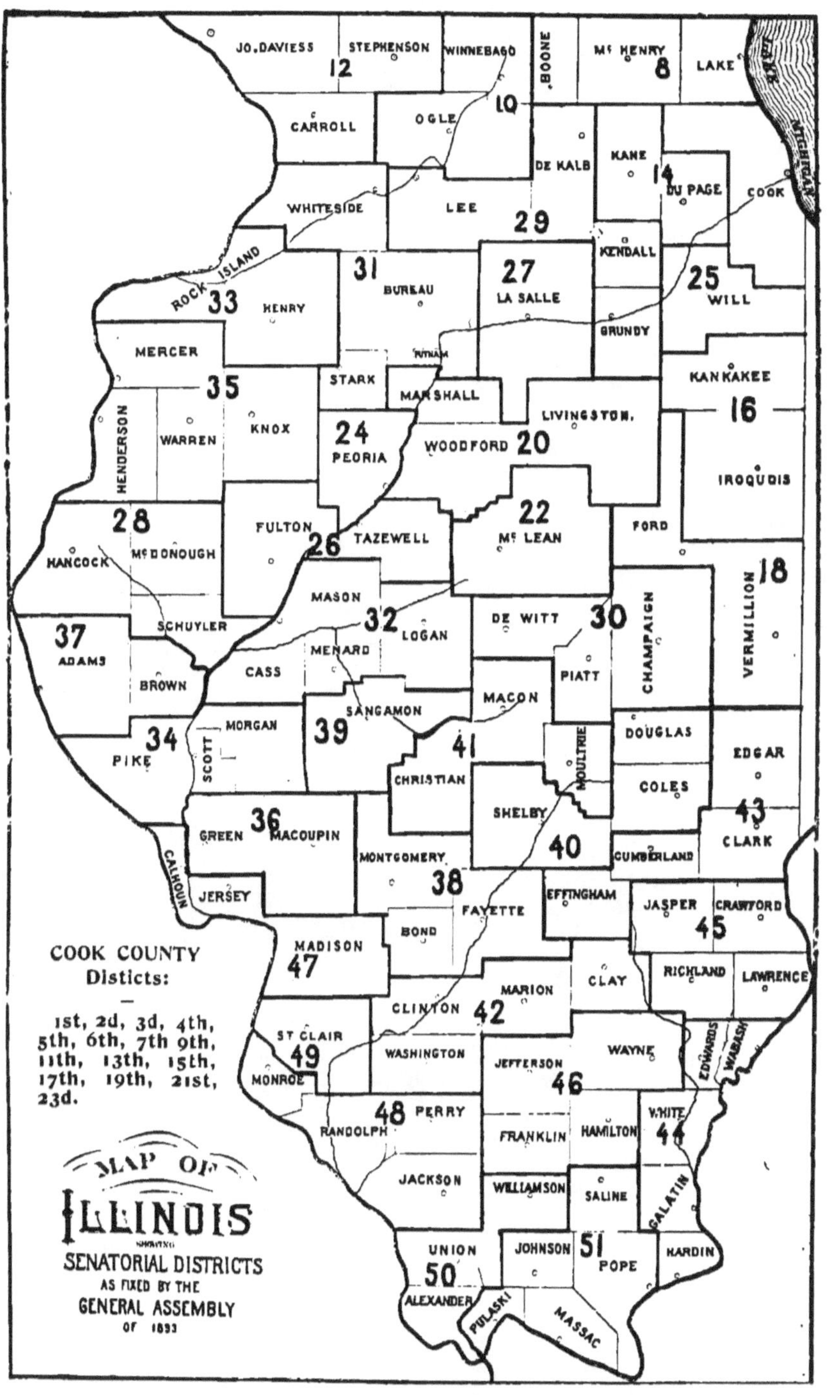

MAP OF
ILLINOIS
SHOWING
SENATORIAL DISTRICTS
AS FIXED BY THE
GENERAL ASSEMBLY
OF 1893
COOK COUNTY
Disticts:
1st, 2d, 3d, 4th, 5th, 6th, 7th 9th, 11th, 13th, 15th, 17th, 19th, 21st, 23d.
JO. DAVIESS
STEPHENSON
12
WINNEBAGO
BOONE
MC HENRY
8
LAKE
LAKE
10
CARROLL
OGLE
DE KALB
KANE
14
DU PAGE
COOK
MICHIGAN
WHITESIDE
LEE
29
ROCK ISLAND
KENDALL
31
27
25
33
HENRY
BUREAU
LA SALLE
WILL
GRUNDY
MERCER
PUTNAM
STARK
KANKAKEE
35
MARSHALL
LIVINGSTON.
16
HENDERSON
WARREN
KNOX
24
PEORIA
WOODFORD
20
IROQUOIS
22
28
FULTON
MC LEAN
FORD
HANCOCK
MC DONOUGH
26
TAZEWELL
18
MASON
VERMILLION
32
DE WITT
30
37
SCHUYLER
LOGAN
CHAMPAIGN
ADAMS
MENARD
CASS
PIATT
BROWN
MACON
SANGAMON
MORGAN
39
41
DOUGLAS
EDGAR
34
PIKE
SCOTT
CHRISTIAN
MOULTRIE
COLES
43
SHELBY
36
GREEN
MACOUPIN
CLARK
40
CALHOUN
MONTGOMERY
CUMBERLAND
38
JERSEY
EFFINGHAM
JASPER
CRAWFORD
FAYETTE
45
BOND
MADISON
47
RICHLAND
LAWRENCE
CLAY
MARION
CLINTON
42
ST CLAIR
EDWARDS
WABASH
49
WASHINGTON
WAYNE
JEFFERSON
MONROE
46
48
PERRY
WHITE
RANDOLPH
44
FRANKLIN
HAMILTON
JACKSON
WILLIAMSON
SALINE
GALATIN
UNION
JOHNSON
51
POPE
HARDIN
50
ALEXANDER
PULASKI
MASSAC

VOTE FOR PRESIDENT.

Counties.	Dem. and Peo.	Rep.	Pro.	S. Lab.	Nat. Party.	Ind. Dem.	M. of the R.
	Bryan and Sewell......	McKinley and Hobart......	Levering and Johnson......	Matchett and Maguire......	Bentley and Southgate......	Palmer and Buckner......	Bryan and Watson......
Adams	8,009	8,447	183	17	23	113	16
Alexander	1,791	2,802	4	1	2	21	22
Bond	1,662	1,967	66	....	9	8	2
Boone	653	3,111	58	3	2	15	4
Brown	2,060	1,024	21	....	1	8	3
Bureau	3,931	5,474	124	28	11	124	30
Calhoun	1,162	795	9	....	1	5	14
Carroll	1,473	3,314	53	5	9	19	7
Cass	2,462	1,946	31	2	1	14	8
Champaign	4,639	6,780	249	1	5	80	4
Christian	4,633	3,857	72	8	14	30	6
Clark	3,099	2,888	40	3	11	15	4
Clay	2,266	2,155	59	4	2	8	6
Clinton	2,570	1,863	12	1	2	12	2
Coles	3,963	4,534	54	5	7	51	19
Cook	151,910	221,823	2,149	727	163	2,600	236
Crawford	2,339	2,172	22	2	4	15	3
Cumberland	2,097	1,856	23	2	4	7	1
DeKalb	1,868	5,508	189	2	5	59	13
DeWitt	2,365	2,587	44	....	....	27	5
Douglas	2,135	2,666	48	....	1	12	5
DuPage	1,574	4,115	139	5	2	122	14
Edgar	3,726	3,822	51	3	6	63	3
Edwards	848	1,572	27	2	3	2	4
Effingham	2,953	1,895	39	4	1	21	....
Fayette	3,616	2,769	70	3	21	32	11
Ford	1,504	2,832	46	2	2	17	3
Franklin	2,227	2,038	16	3	1	6	6
Fulton	5,964	6,195	88	3	6	32	15
Gallatin	2,062	1,468	30	2	2	10	5
Greene	3,977	2,365	45	3	3	14	6
Grundy	2,056	3,246	89	8	2	20	18
Hamilton	2,406	1,767	35	1	1	3	2
Hancock	4,575	4,250	133	3	....	41	6
Hardin	899	780	7	....	....	3	1
Henderson	957	1,756	47	1	2	28	5
Henry	2,968	6,177	134	1	5	67	3
Iroquois	3,649	5,325	127	3	8	58	9
Jackson	3,619	3,879	45	9	31	25	12
Jasper	2,715	1,867	57	3	....	2	9
Jefferson	3,561	2,603	88	1	8	19	27
Jersey	2,373	1,641	49	3	4	6	4
Jo Daviess	2,383	3,594	90	2	1	80	8
Johnson	1,423	2,027	13	1	5	9	6
Kane	4,839	12,133	197	5	16	144	13
Kankakee	2,357	5,471	89	6	8	78	13
Kendall	772	2,128	51	2	3	18	2
Knox	3,464	7,681	144	6	....	86	16
Lake	1,756	5,027	87	4	7	35	21
LaSalle	8,088	11,548	181	26	14	170	20
Lawrence	1,945	1,972	52	1	7	11	3
Lee	2,465	4,797	56	5	3	75	4
Livingston	4,045	5,436	143	1	6	58	23
Logan	3,384	3,430	88	....	4	46	5
Macon	4,746	6,216	89	3	13	77	10
Macoupin	5,568	4,970	109	4	16	35	6

Official Vote—Continued.

Counties.	Dem. and Peo.	Rep.	Pro.	S. Lab.	Nat. Party.	Ind. Dem.	M. of the R.
	Bryan and Sewall	McKinley and Hobart	Levering and Johnson	Matchett and Maguire	Bentley and Southgate	Palmer and Buckner	Bryan and Watson ......
Madison	6,323	7,431	85	4	5	83	21
Marion	3,825	2,870	54	2	11	10	10
Marshall	1,885	2,216	36	3	2	16	3
Mason	2,405	2 100	54	1	4	16	2
Massac	869	2,046	12	3	1	7	....
McDonough	3,678	4,036	106	5	13	45	6
McHenry	1,910	5,047	102	2	2	51	3
McLean	6,320	9,964	307	10	9	94	8
Menard	2,012	1,642	29	....	1	18	6
Mercer	2,324	3,120	53	....	3	19	5
Monroe	1,651	1,446	6	7	2	18	1
Montgomery	4,104	3,622	105	3	5	19	13
Morgan	4,313	4,317	84	7	2	28	10
Moultrie	2,073	1,711	15	3	1	13	4
Ogle	2,134	5,210	95	2	3	77	8
Peoria	9,042	10,486	185	18	12	129	26
Perry	2,366	2,342	81	1	7	21	4
Piatt	1,951	2,579	33	3	5	22	7
Pike	5,315	3,111	97	3	21	18	14
Pope	1,069	1,852	8	....	....	8	5
Pulaski	1,152	2,081	4	2	2	12	....
Putnam	478	706	18	....	1	12	1
Randolph	3,074	3,024	80	4	12	28	7
Richland	2,062	1,693	20	1	17	7	....
Rock Island	4,658	7,323	63	14	12	87	34
Saline	2,292	2,605	22	4	1	5	4
Sangamon	8,566	8,998	243	2	11	98	16
Schuyler	2,325	1,848	63	2	3	11	9
Scott	1,598	1,261	19	....	1	11	....
Shelby	4,698	3,071	117	....	12	16	11
Stark	1,020	1,636	39	2	1	17	10
St. Clair	8,333	8,960	111	55	7	105	12
Stephenson	3,773	4,728	168	6	2	49	3
Tazewell	3,736	3,703	86	1	4	64	7
Union	2,989	1,842	35	4	2	11	9
Vermilion	5,737	8,767	192	6	20	91	12
Wabash	1,736	1,321	57	4	6	2	3
Warren	2,602	3,394	101	1	10	34	2
Washington	1,979	2,351	34	....	4	43	....
Wayne	3,094	2,906	24	1	40	6	8
White	3,409	2,771	33	....	2	8	12
Whiteside	2,777	5,577	88	1	7	63	11
Will	6,857	9,249	56	7	9	48	16
Williamson	2,573	3,027	9	....	2	17	9
Winnebago	2,438	8,242	219	9	7	51	9
Woodford	2,447	2,447	87	4	1	26	6
Total	464,523	607,130	9,796	1,147	793	6,390	1,090

"FOR" AND "AGAINST" THE PROPOSITION TO AMEND SEC. 2, ART. 14, OF THE CONSTITUTION.

COUNTIES.	Total Vote.	For Amendment.	Against Amendment.
Adams	16,808	1,515	526
Alexander	4,643	243	131
Bond	3,714	852	1,367
Boone	3,846	449	88
Brown	3,119	188	135
Bureau	9,722	1,370	180
Calhoun	1,986	110	134
Carroll	4,880	514	152
Cass	4,464	248	186
Champaign	11,758	1,232	573
Christian	8,620	792	390
Clark	6,060	601	1,106
Clay	4,500	214	171
Clinton	4,462	543	494
Coles	8,633	810	313
Cook	379,608	85,166	24,026
Crawford	4,557	931	516
Cumberland	3,990	260	257
DeKalb	7,734	1,098	131
DeWitt	5,028	548	185
Douglas	4,867	1,125	186
DuPage	5,971	1,054	149
Edgar	7,674	377	196
Edwards	2,458	144	157
Effingham	4,913	332	304
Fayette	6,522	353	229
Ford	4,406	799	224
Franklin	4,297	70	178
Fulton	12,303	2,677	2,393
Gallatin	3,579	223	418
Greene	6,413	509	381
Grundy	5,439	985	109
Hamilton	4,215	350	1,023
Hancock	9,008	777	385
Hardin	1,690	17	96
Henderson	2,796	231	100
Henry	9,355	1,352	559
Iroquois	9,179	774	272
Jackson	7,620	329	367
Jasper	4,653	349	146
Jefferson	6,307	468	560
Jersey	4,080	321	153
JoDaviess	6,158	773	158
Johnson	3,484	173	195
Kane	17,347	2,857	447
Kankakee	8,022	1,088	157
Kendall	2,976	429	105
Knox	11,397	962	389
Lake	6,937	1,196	148
LaSalle	20,047	3,171	444
Lawrence	3,991	162	261
Lee	7,405	1,039	218
Livingston	9,712	1,073	133
Logan	6,957	658	284
Macon	11,154	1,138	735
Macoupin	10,708	790	652
Madison	13,952	1,551	920
Marion	6,782	478	212
Marshall	4,161	345	59
Mason	4,582	522	316
Massac	2,938	229	162

"For" and "Against" the Proposition to Amend Sec. 2, Art. 14, of the Constitution—Concluded.

COUNTIES.	Total Vote.	For Amendment.	Against Amendment.
McDonough	7,889	836	304
McHenry	7,117	672	87
McLean	16,712	1,970	1,560
Menard	3,708	226	149
Mercer	5,524	609	313
Monroe	3,131	179	303
Montgomery	7,871	619	528
Morgan	8,761	1,010	1,686
Moultrie	3,820	253	129
Ogle	7,529	1,133	117
Peoria	19,808	2,610	1,645
Perry	4,822	847	246
Piatt	4,600	669	211
Pike	8,579	1,000	1,231
Pope	2,942	293	726
Pulaski	3,253	102	338
Putnam	1,216	175	42
Randolph	6,229	455	491
Richland	3,800	170	163
Rock Island	12,191	2,685	1,228
Saline	4,933	201	549
Sangamon	17,934	1,802	1,272
Schuyler	4,261	407	120
Scott	2,890	141	341
Shelby	7,925	723	305
Stark	2,725	627	186
St. Clair	17,583	1,728	866
Stephenson	8,729	689	454
Tazewell	7,601	1,049	515
Union	4,892	102	239
Vermilion	14,825	911	257
Wabash	3,129	312	112
Warren	6,144	856	355
Washington	4,411	314	386
Wayne	6,079	268	567
White	6,235	483	1,289
Whiteside	8,524	989	184
Will	16,242	2,164	515
Williamson	5,637	224	299
Winnebago	10,975	1,990	309
Woodford	5,018	540	181
Totals	1,090,869	163,057	66,519

VOTE FOR STATE OFFICERS.

Counties.	Governor.							Lieutenant-Governor.								
	John P. Altgeld	John R. Tanner	George W. Gere	Charles A. Baustian	Isaac W. Higgs	Wm. S. Forman	Scattering	Monroe C. Crawford	Wm. A. Northcott	Henry B. Kepley	Chas. R. Davis	Jno. A. Kirkpatrick	Chester A. Babcock	Henry D. Lloyd	Robert C. Allen	Scattering
Adams	7,997	8,341	219	11	23	125		8,015	8,320	190	12	28	152	16		
Alexander	1,788	2,774	4	1		19		1,817	2,757	4	1	2	17	22		
Bond	1,632	1,969	84		6	9		1,605	2,030	70		6	6	1		
Boone	641	3,070	74	3	1	17		637	3,105	61	3	2	14	4		
Brown	2,035	1,034	28		1	7		2,045	1,036	21			7	3		
Bureau	3,813	5,386	206	26	12	136		3,865	5,397	150	26	11	121	27		
Calhoun	1,153	792	10		1	4		1,153	793	8		1	5	6		
Carroll	1,417	3,313	80	5	9	19		1,428	3,308	60	5	11	16	7	5	
Cass	2,420	1,913	53	2	1	12		2,445	1,902	39	2	1	11	6		
Champaign	4,601	6,624	457	1	4	63		4,626	6,734	314	1	5	73	3		
Christian	4,605	3,855	86	8	9	32		4,606	3,864	71	8	14	31	5		
Clark	3,116	2,908	51	3	6	12		3,129	2,890	47	3	11	12	2		
Clay	2,221	2,167	66	6	5	14		2,245	2,155	62	4	2	13	6		
Clinton	2,532	1,868	16	1	1	10		2,531	1,876	16	1		10	1		
Coles	3,924	4,499	59	5	7	49		3,930	4,549	51	5	7	47	19		
Cook	164,078	205,960	3,709	595	139	3,880		153,661	218,260	2,636	689	137	3,425	287		2
Crawford	2,323	2,175	25	2	6	16		2,329	2,168	24	2	4	15	3		
Cumberland	2,062	1,864	29	2	7	9		2,076	1,860	24	2	7	7	3		
DeKalb	1,870	5,522	243	2	7	68		1,842	5,580	210	2	5	62	13		
DeWitt	2,349	2,554	88			20		2,364	2,580	47			20	6		
Douglas	2,097	2,669	65	1	1	22		2,125	2,657	54			25	5		
DuPage	1,571	4,013	210	4	2	117		1,553	4,074	169	5	2	112	9		
Edgar	3,674	3,810	66	2	6	66		3,692	3,805	59	3	6	62	3		
Edwards	824	1,565	44	2	3	10		839	1,572	33	2	2	3	3		
Effingham	2,945	1,882	43	5	1	18		2,940	1,885	48	5	2	17	1		
Fayette	3,573	2,728	80	3	20	35		3,579	2,795	75	3	18	31			
Ford	1,465	2,786	97	2	2	21		1,481	2,807	63	2	2	18	3		
Franklin	2,180	2,062	21	3	2	8		2,197	2,054	20	3		6	6		
Fulton	5,867	6,183	129	3	8	47		5,924	6,181	98	3	8	31	14		
Gallatin	2,047	1,474	26		2	8		2,065	1,467	26		2	8			
Greene	3,936	2,372	43	2	2	15		3,947	2,374	44	2	4	10			
Grundy	2,038	3,227	108	8	2	21		2,038	3,238	100	8	2	18	18		

Official Vote—Continued.

Counties.	Governor.							Lieutenant-Governor.								
	John P. Altgeld	John R. Tanner	George W. Gere	Charles A. Baustian	Isaac W. Higgs	Wm. S. Forman	Scattering	Monroe C. Crawford	Wm. A. Northcott	Henry B. Kepley	Chas. R. Davis	Jno. A. Kirkpatrick	Chester A. Babcock	Henry D. Lloyd	Robert C. Allen	Scattering
Hamilton	2,389	1,766	40	1	1	3	....	2,397	1,758	38	1	1	3	1	....	....
Hancock	4,499	4,277	178	3	1	38	....	4.549	4,248	150	3	1	37	6	....	....
Hardin	809	779	8	....	....	3	....	900	780	7	....	....	3	1	....	....
Henderson	931	1,753	63	1	2	32	....	945	1,758	49	1	3	30	5	....	....
Henry	2,969	6,080	205	....	6	83	1	2,946	6,149	163	....	5	72	2	....	....
Iroquois	3,562	5,283	200	5	9	67	....	3,594	5,308	154	4	10	54	6	....	....
Jackson	3,542	3,915	48	8	30	27	1	3,598	3,878	46	8	31	22	15	....	....
Jasper	2,692	1,884	56	3	....	1	....	2,701	1,871	57	3	....	1	9	....	....
Jefferson	3,543	2,599	97	1	6	22	....	3,548	2,606	90	1	....	18	24	....	....
Jersey	2,345	1,644	56	3	....	6	....	2,359	1,634	56	3	2	6	4	....	....
Jo Daviess	2,326	3,593	125	1	4	89	....	2,357	3,575	110	1	2	85	....	....	....
Johnson	1,408	2,029	17	1	....	11	....	1,417	2,024	14	1	5	9	6	....	....
Kane	5,069	11,656	292	6	19	186	....	4,802	11,941	237	5	20	162	15	....	....
Kankakee	2,368	5,414	94	6	1	73	....	2,361	5,416	94	5	7	74	13	....	....
Kendall	743	2,122	84	1	2	24	....	758	2,122	73	2	2	18	....	....	....
Knox	3,441	7,642	197	5	1	88	....	3,450	7,647	176	6	....	84	16	....	....
Lake	1,757	4,882	176	4	2	57	1	1,739	4,960	112	4	6	46	20	....	....
LaSalle	8,124	11,344	251	24	18	186	....	8,090	11,447	193	26	15	167	20	....	....
Lawrence	1,924	1,989	52	1	5	12	1	1,927	1,987	53	1	....	11	....	....	....
Lee	2,468	4,717	92	5	3	78	....	2,458	4,759	70	5	3	78	4	....	....
Livingston	3,974	5,411	202	1	6	78	....	4,030	5,416	157	1	5	54	12	....	....
Logan	3,337	3,430	131	....	7	35	....	3,385	3,409	101	....	4	36	4	....	....
Macon	4,692	6,171	175	4	11	105	2	4,757	6,193	129	4	15	81	10	....	....
Macoupin	5,511	4,976	148	3	16	31	....	5,533	4,984	123	3	19	29	6	....	....
Madison	6,295	7,374	99	5	4	104	....	6,258	7,439	86	5	5	76	18	....	....
Marion	3,781	2,890	70	2	12	12	....	3,794	2,886	58	2	12	11	6	....	....
Marshall	1,864	2,189	57	12	2	15	....	1,880	2,197	36	3	2	13	2	....	....
Mason	2,304	2,128	117	1	1	18	....	2,371	2,112	73	1	2	13	1	....	....
Massac	864	2,035	13	3	1	8	....	862	2,035	12	3	....	7	....	....	....
McDonough	3,598	4,025	161	4	12	63	....	3,643	4,032	121	4	13	46	6	....	....
McHenry	1,916	4,992	129	2	2	53	....	1,888	5,032	111	2	2	49	2	....	....
McLean	6,271	9,824	444	11	13	106	....	6.312	9,881	363	11	11	96	7	....	....

Menard	2,002	1,645	30		1	15		2,015	1,626	30		1	18	6		
Mercer	2,269	3,100	92		1	22		2,297	3,109	62		1	20	5		
Monroe	1,618	1,479	5	6	2	12		1,639	1,457	5	7	1	14	1		
Montgomery	4,077	3,592	123	3	5	24		4,078	3,603	17	3	5	16	11		
Morgan	4,183	4,371	141	7	3	33		4,274	4,335	97	7	3	25	10		
Moultrie	2,049	1,731	17	2	3	11		2,063	1,714	15	2	3	13			
Ogle	2,046	5,198	135	1	3	91		2,080	5,187	119	1	3	78	1		
Peoria	9,459	9,886	307	13	10	152	1	9,182	10,240	221	18	10	131	27		
Perry	2,330	2,363	77	1	8	21		2,342	2,351	77	1	7	19			
Platt	1,931	2,566	53	3	3	23		1,944	2,573	35	3	5	22	6		
Pike	5,236	3,147	121	3	22	17		5,267	3,145	98	3	25	14	6		
Pope	1,047	1,864	10			9		1,059	1,858	9			8	4		
Pulaski	1,155	2,074	6	2	2	11		1,155	2,074	4	2	2	11			
Putnam	465	698	32		1	10		468	701	27		1	10			
Randolph	3,011	3,043	94	4	10	29		3,049	3,014	83	4	8	28	7		
Richland	2,037	1,700	27		19	12		2,037	1,692	23		19	8			
Rock Island	4,839	7,081	99	11	11	94		4,694	7,246	80	12	11	84	27		
Saline	2,268	2,610	26	4	1	4		2,280	2,605	22	4		4	2		
Sangamon	8,563	8,836	279	2	11	93		8,442	8,942	254	2	11	87	14		
Schuyler	2,288	1,855	81	2	4	9		2,304	1,852	65	2	3	9	9		
Scott	1,550	1,289	23	2		8		1,583	1,264	22	1		8	3		
Shelby	4,609	3,084	153		10	16		4,670	3,075	140			16	9	10	
Stark	980	1,621	87	1		23		1,006	1,632	52	1	1	19	10		
St. Clair	8,374	8,881	125	39	3	115		8,324	8,951	122	48	5	97	11		
Stephenson	3,621	4,723	250	8		84		3,780	4,687	181	6	2	47	3		
Tazewell	3,717	3,060	127	2	2	51		3,737	3,682	90	1	1	48	7		
Union	2,976	1,840	38	4	2	11		2,991	1,823	40	5	2	11	9		
Vermilion	5,672	8,732	237	6	17	90	3	5,695	8,741	204	6	19	90	12		
Wabash	1,726	1,312	71	1	3	2		1,730	1,315	60	2	5	1	3		
Warren	2,506	3,395	167	1	11	47		2,564	3,381	130	1	11	34	2		
Washington	1,973	2,329	44		2	58		1,973	2,352	39		2	37			
Wayne	3,073	2,905	27	1	38	12		3,078	2,905	19	1	42	8	8		
White	3,385	2,781	41			7		3,400	2,774	37		2	6	12		
Whiteside	2,711	5,537	141	2	8	81		2,728	5,549	110	1	8	77	10		
Will	6,916	9,042	101	7	9	77		6,821	9,159	79	8	9	50	16		
Williamson	2,536	3,045	7		2	16		2,555	3,035	7			17	4		
Winnebago	2,504	8,010	414	7	1	63		2,432	8,225	302	7	4	54	11		
Woodford	2,354	2,440	155	4	2	26		2,412	2,428	107	4	2	23	4		
Totals	474,256	587,637	14,559	985	723	8,102	10	464,475	601,829	11,390	1,084	739	7,158	1,003	15	2

VOTE OF SECRETARY OF STATE AND AUDITOR OF PUBLIC ACCOUNTS.

Counties.	Secretary of State.							Auditor of Public Accounts.						
	Finis E. Downing...	James A. Rose......	Alonzo E. Wilson...	John Raymond Pepin..............	Lloyd G. Spencer...	Charles S. Wiley....	L. A. Quelmalz	Andrew L. Maxwell...........	James S. McCullough.......	Arthur J. Bassett...	Fred Heintz.........	John A. Hooper.....	Frederick E. W. Brink..............	Grant Dunbar.......
Adams.....................	8,035	8,318	189	12	27	102	14	8,025	8,317	190	12	28	107	15
Alexander..................	1,797	2,768	5	1	2	17	22	1,798	2,766	5	1	2	17	22
Bond.......................	1,627	1,978	72	....	7	7	1	1,634	1,974	71	....	7	7	1
Boone......................	639	3,103	61	3	1	14	4	640	3,101	60	3	2	14	4
Brown......................	2,054	1,030	21	....	1	7	3	2,057	1,023	21	....	1	7	3
Bureau.....................	3,857	5.406	145	26	11	118	27	3,851	5,406	145	26	11	118	27
Calhoun....................	1,155	793	9	....	1	5	6	1,155	793	9	....	1	5	6
Carroll....................	1,446	3,304	64	5	11	16	7	1,449	3,305	59	5	11	16	7
Cass.......................	2,455	1,899	39	2	1	7	6	2,450	1,899	39	2	1	12	6
Champaign..................	4,624	6,736	294	1	5	74	3	4,576	6,820	286	1	5	64	3
Christian..................	4,606	3,859	68	9	13	33	6	4,606	3,861	72	8	13	29	6
Clark......................	3,127	2,891	47	3	12	10	2	3,132	2,891	45	3	12	10	2
Clay.......................	2,243	2,156	62	4	2	13	6	2,242	2,159	62	4	2	12	6
Clinton....................	2,542	1,864	16	1	2	10	1	2,541	1,864	16	1	2	10	1
Coles......................	3,931	4,518	54	6	7	49	19	3,931	4,520	54	5	7	43	19
Cook.......................	152,542	218,117	2,578	757	143	3,306	199	152,411	218,227	2,523	776	130	3,312	203
Crawford...................	2,328	2,165	22	2	5	15	2	2,360	2,152	17	2	4	14	3
Cumberland.................	2,074	1,860	22	2	7	7	3	2,074	1,862	22	2	7	7	3
DeKalb.....................	1,843	5,580	209	2	5	58	13	1,843	5,580	209	2	5	58	13
DeWitt.....................	2,366	2,575	51	....	....	22	5	2,370	2,574	50	....	....	21	5
Douglas....................	2,120	2,648	52	....	1	21	5	2,121	2,664	52	1	1	21	5
DuPage.....................	1,559	4,083	163	5	2	109	11	1,554	4,087	161	5	2	109	11
Edgar......................	3,695	3,805	57	2	6	61	3	3,689	3,809	56	2	6	62	3
Edwards....................	839	1,574	30	2	2	3	3	839	1,573	31	2	2	3	3
Effingham..................	2,944	1,885	45	5	2	17	....	2,944	1,885	44	5	2	17	....
Fayette....................	3,581	2,795	74	3	21	29	7	3,581	2,794	75	3	21	29	7
Ford.......................	1,484	2,806	59	2	2	17	3	1,485	2,801	59	2	2	17	3
Franklin...................	2,200	2,052	18	3	1	6	5	2,198	2,063	16	3	1	5	5
Fulton.....................	5,928	6,180	97	3	7	31	14	5,927	6,177	97	3	9	31	14
Gallatin...................	2,056	1,464	26	....	2	8	2	2,055	1,464	26	....	2	8	2
Greene.....................	3,948	2,361	46	1	3	11	4	3,949	2,362	46	2	2	11	4

Grundy	2,045	3,236	100	8	2	18	18	2,041	3,235	99	8	2	18	18
Hamilton	2,399	1,759	37	1	1	3	1	2,399	1,758	37	1	1	3	1
Hancock	4,565	4,242	150	3	1	32	4	4,559	4,248	149	3	1	33	4
Hardin	901	779	7			3	1	901	779	7			3	1
Henderson	947	1,755	50	1	3	30	5	946	1,757	50	1	3	30	5
Henry	3,957	6,147	159	1	6	70	2	2,957	6,146	159	1	6	69	2
Iroquois	3,605	5,301	153	4	10	55	6	3,607	5,300	152	4	10	56	6
Jackson	3,585	3,876	47	8	34	22	15	3,586	3,883	46	8	34	22	15
Jasper	2,707	1,866	57	3		1	9	2,707	1,867	57	3		1	9
Jefferson	3,551	2,621	91	2	9	17	24	3.551	2,603	91	1	10	17	24
Jersey	2,365	1,629	56	3	2	5	4	2,367	1,629	56	3	2	5	4
JoDaviess	2,375	3,561	107	1	2	85	7	2,375	3,558	107	1	2	85	7
Johnson	1,416	2,025	14	1	5	9	6	1,416	2,024	14	1	5	9	6
Kane	4,797	11,961	228	4	20	153	13	4,800	11,959	226	4	20	151	13
Kankakee	2,355	5,421	94	5	8	75	13	2,354	5,415	94	5	8	73	13
Kendall	761	2,019	72	2	2	17	2	760	2,121	73	2	2	17	2
Knox	3,452	7,640	173	6		82	16	3,446	7,641	174	6		82	16
Lake	1,734	4,961	110	5	6	41	20	1,733	4,967	108	5	6	41	20
LaSalle	8,094	11,439	193	26	16	164	20	8,087	11,421	194	26	16	166	23
Lawrence	1,929	1,984	42	1	5	10	3	1,932	1,981	52	1	6	12	3
Lee	2,460	4,756	68	5	3	77	4	2,457	4,764	70	5	3	78	4
Livingston	4,033	5,418	156	1	6	52	12	4,034	5,420	154	1	6	52	12
Logan	3,381	3,404	99		3	34	4	3.391	3,406	100		4	35	4
Macon	4,757	6,190	123	3	16	80	10	4,763	6,192	126	3	15	80	10
Macoupin	5,535	4,979	120	4	20	29	6	5,539	4,979	118	4	20	29	6
Madison	6,305	7,410	92	5	5	73	18	6,305	7.411	89	5	6	74	17
Marion	3,797	2,884	55	2	12	10	7	3,797	2,882	56	2	12	10	7
Marshall	1,884	2,198	40	3	3	12	2	1,884	2,198	40	3	3	13	2
Massac	2,389	2,099	72	1	2	11	2	2,385	2,104	70	1	2	13	2
Mason	861	2,037	12	3	1	7		861	2,036	12	3	1	7	
McDonough	3,648	4,036	117	6	13	42	4	3,650	4,032	116	4	12	41	6
McHenry	1,888	5,029	111	2	2	49	2	1,891	5,029	111	1	2	49	2
McLean	6,305	9,882	359	11	11	95	7	6,300	9,885	357	9	11	94	7
Menard	2,016	1,634	30		1	18	6	2,016	1,626	31		1	18	6
Mercer	2,300	3,106	64		2	20	5	2,303	3,105	63		2	20	5
Monroe	1,652	1,445	4	7	2	13		1,652	1,442	4	7	2	13	1
Montgomery	4,081	3,597	118	3	5	18	11	4,078	3,598	119	3	5	18	11
Morgan	4,296	4,312	93	7	3	23	10	4,288	4,325	96	7	3	23	10
Moultrie	2,064	1,713	14	2	3	12		2,062	1,714	14	2	3	12	
Ogle	2,089	5,186	120	1	3	77	1	2,085	5,184	120	1	3	76	1
Peoria	9,196	10,247	211	19	10	124	26	9,157	10,198	209	18	10	123	26
Perry	2,347	2,350	75	1	7	19		2,364	2,349	75	1	7	20	
Piatt	1,947	2,572	35	3	5	21	6	1,947	2,572	35	3	5	21	6
Pike	5,270	3,143	97	3	23	13	6	5,264	3,144	97	3	23	14	7
Pope	1,050	1,873	7			8	5	1,060	1,859	8			8	5
Pulaski	1,152	2,074	6	2	2	11		1,150	2,076	4	2	2	11	
Putnam	467	702	27		1	10	1	468	702	26		1	10	1
Randolph	3,059	3,008	84	4	10	25	7	3,057	3,009	84	4	10	26	7
Richland	2,039	1,680	22		22	8		2,040	1,761	23		22	8	
Rock Island	4,693	7,247	77	13	13	81	26	4,681	7,242	79	13	12	81	26

Official Vote—Continued.

Counties.	Secretary of State.							Auditor of Public Accounts.						
	Finis E. Downing...	James A. Rose......	Alonzo E. Wilson...	John Raymond Pepin.............	Lloyd G. Spencer...	Charles S. Wiley....	L. A. Quelmalz.....	Andrew L. Maxwell...........	James S. McCullough.......	Arthur J. Bassett...	Fred Heintz.........	John A. Hooper.....	Frederick E. W. Brink.............	Grant Dunbar.......
Saline..........................	2,280	2,604	22	4	1	4	2	2,280	2,604	22	4	1	4	2
Sangamon........................	8,541	8,941	254	2	10	85	14	8,535	8,939	250	2	11	88	14
Schuyler........................	2,309	1,851	63	2	3	9	9	2,308	1,852	63	2	3	9	9
Scott...........................	1,585	1,258	20	2	....	9	3	1,588	1,257	20	1	....	8	....
Shelby..........................	4,632	3,068	144	....	10	16	9	4,635	3,063	144	....	10	16	9
Stark...........................	1,007	1,631	50	1	1	18	10	1,007	1,631	51	1	1	18	10
St. Clair.......................	8,330	8,936	120	48	6	92	11	8,336	8,939	120	48	6	92	11
Stephenson......................	3,796	4,666	179	7	2	46	2	3,793	4,671	179	7	2	45	2
Tazewell........................	3,740	3,678	88	1	3	46	7	3,743	3,677	89	1	3	47	7
Union...........................	2,985	1,830	35	2	1	10	8	2,987	1,831	35	4	1	10	9
Vermilion.......................	5,704	8,728	199	6	23	91	12	5,705	8,726	196	6	22	92	12
Wabash..........................	1,730	1,318	59	3	7	1	2	1,728	1,317	57	3	7	1	3
Warren..........................	2,556	3,385	122	1	11	34	2	2,569	3,384	122	1	11	33	2
Washington......................	1,976	2,348	37	....	4	38	....	1,972	2,342	37	....	4	49	....
Wayne...........................	3,080	2,907	23	1	38	5	8	3,079	2,908	22	1	42	5	8
White...........................	3,403	2,773	37	....	2	5	12	3,404	2,773	37	....	2	5	12
Whiteside.......................	2,731	5,553	108	1	8	77	11	2,731	5,556	108	1	8	73	10
Will............................	6,813	9,167	72	9	8	48	16	6,817	9,165	73	9	8	48	16
Williamson......................	2,546	3,040	7	....	2	16	4	2,550	3,039	6	....	2	16	4
Winnebago.......................	2,422	8,232	310	7	5	53	8	2,433	8,171	296	7	5	51	9
Woodford........................	2,423	2,428	101	4	2	22	4	2,421	2,430	101	4	2	22	4
Total.......................	463,746	601,357	11,193	1,159	800	6,892	937	463,561	601,574	11,096	1,172	794	6,898	948

VOTE FOR STATE TREASURER AND ATTORNEY GENERAL.

Counties.	State Treasurer.							Attorney General.						
	Edward C. Pace...	Henry L. Hertz...	Eugenio K. Hayes.	Fritz Hintze	Jodn A. L. Scott ..	Edward Ridgely..	Scattering.........	George A Trude ..	Edward C. Akin ..	Robert H. Patton..	Paul Ehman	George A. Gordon.	Daniel V. Samuels	Edwin I. Burdick.
Adams	8,029	8,309	192	12	28	111		8,030	8,310	188	12	25	108	16
Alexander	1,819	2,749	5	1	1	16		1,794	2,765	5	1	1	17	22
Bond	1,628	1,973	71		7	7		1,633	1,975	71		7	7	1
Boone	640	3,099	62	3	2	15		639	3,103	59	3	2	14	4
Brown	2,058	1,023	21		1	7		2,067	1,022	21		1	5	3
Bureau	3,865	5,387	145	26	11	123		3,858	5,397	144	26	13	121	27
Calhoun	1,155	793	9		1	5		1,155	793	9		1	5	6
Carroll	1,454	3,298	59	5	11	17		1,454	3,303	59	5	11	16	7
Cass	2,451	1,898	39	2	1	13		2,453	1,893	39	2	1	11	6
Champaign	4,635	6,732	296	1	5	77		4,629	6,736	292	1	6	73	3
Christian	4,612	3,853	73	7	13	28		4,604	3,877	71	8	12	28	6
Clark	3,130	2,891	46	3	12	10		3,331	2,891	45	3	12	10	2
Clay	2,242	2,157	61	5	3	12		2,243	2,156	62	4	3	12	6
Clinton	2,544	1,864	16	1	2	10		2,542	1,865	15	1	2	10	1
Coles	3,930	4,522	39	6	7	46		3,933	4,522	51	5	7	47	19
Cook	161,228	207,708	3,081	761	148	4,477		154,471	216,021	2,500	775	159	3,335	179
Crawford	2,336	2,165	23	2	5	14		2,336	2,167	22	2	5	15	3
Cumberland	2,075	1,859	23	4	8	7		2,076	1,859	21	2	7	7	3
DeKalb	1,850	5,564	214	2	5	63		1,848	5,577	210	2	5	57	11
DeWitt	2,374	2,569	51			21		2,370	2,574	51			21	5
Douglas	2,128	2,656	52	1	1	23		2,128	2,656	52		1	23	5
DuPage	1,581	4,037	173	5	2	117		1,568	4,085	164	5	2	109	11
Edgar	3,697	3,803	56	2	6	62		3,696	3,803	56	2	6	61	3
Edwards	843	1,570	31	2	2	3		839	1,574	31	2	2	2	3
Effingham	2,944	1,884	45	5	2	17		2,943	1,886	45	5	2	17	
Fayette	3,580	2,791	76	3	21	29		3,580	2,794	76	3	21	28	7
Ford	1,497	2,789	59	2	2	20		1,485	2,803	59	2	2	17	2
Franklin	2,199	2,052	17	3	1	6		2,197	2,053	15	3	1	5	5
Fulton	5,938	6,160	98	3	8	35		5,928	6,174	98	3	8	30	13
Gallatin	2,055	1,464	26		2	8		2,055	1,464	26		2	8	2
Greene	3,948	2,361	44	2	3	12		3,950	2,362	47	2	2	11	4
Grundy	2,047	3,230	99	8	2	18		2,040	3,235	100	8	2	18	18
Hamilton	2,400	1,757	37	1	1	3		2,400	1,756	37	1	1	3	

Official Vote—Continued

Counties.	Edward C. Pace...	Henry L. Hertz ...	Eugenio K. Hayes.	Fritz Hintze.......	John A. L. Scott...	Edward Ridgely..	Scattering.........	George A. Trude..	Edward C. Akin ..	Robert L. Patton..	Paul Ehman.......	George A. Gordon.	Daniel V. Samuels	Edwin I. Burdick.
	State Treasurer.							Attorney General.						
Hancock	4,569	4,233	150	3	1	33	......	4,567	4,239	150	3	1	31	5
Hardin	901	779	7	......	......	3	......	901	779	7	......	......	3	1
Henderson	946	1,755	52	1	4	30	......	947	1,755	50	1	3	30	5
Henry	2,964	6,125	169	1	6	71	......	2,971	6,133	157	1	6	68	2
Iroquois	3,611	5,295	150	5	9	57	......	3,613	5,299	151	4	9	57	6
Jackson	3,587	3,876	46	8	37	22	......	3,582	3,882	47	8	37	22	15
Jasper	2,704	1,867	58	3	......	1	......	2,704	1,866	58	3	......	1	9
Jefferson	3,559	2,590	91	1	9	17	......	3,548	2,602	92	1	9	17	26
Jersey	2,370	1,627	56	3	2	5	......	2,367	1,629	56	3	2	5	4
Jo Daviess	2,389	3,540	106	1	2	90	......	2,375	3,559	107	1	2	85	7
Johnson	1,416	2,023	14	1	5	9	......	1,416	2,023	14	1	5	9	6
Kane	4,833	11,896	237	3	20	168	......	4,826	11,948	222	3	21	149	13
Kankakee	2,358	5,415	96	5	8	76	......	2,355	5,417	96	5	8	75	13
Kendall	762	2,115	74	2	2	19	......	760	2,120	72	2	2	18	2
Knox	3,456	7,625	175	6	......	85	......	3,453	7,643	170	5	......	83	16
Lake	1,749	4,931	114	5	6	51	......	1,735	4,962	108	5	6	41	20
LaSalle	8,129	11,371	197	26	16	168	......	8,124	11,408	194	26	16	165	19
Lawrence	1,929	1,984	52	1	6	11	......	1,928	1,985	52	1	6	11	3
Lee	2,466	4,735	73	5	3	81	......	2,459	4,752	70	5	3	78	4
Livingston	4,043	5,407	155	1	6	53	......	4,038	5,416	152	1	6	51	12
Logan	3,421	3,401	100	......	6	31	......	3,392	3,405	92	......	4	34	3
Macon	4,772	6,181	127	3	15	82	......	4,773	6,185	121	3	15	80	11
Macoupin	5,535	4,981	120	4	20	29	......	5,537	4,977	121	4	20	29	6
Madison	6,307	7,405	90	5	5	75	......	6,304	7,405	90	5	6	74	19
Marion	3,807	2,869	57	2	12	9	......	3,793	2,883	56	2	12	10	6
Marshall	1,890	2,184	40	1	3	13	......	1,892	2,190	38	3	3	13	2
Mason	2,396	2,086	76	1	2	13	......	2,375	2,102	71	2	2	12	2
Massac	806	2,036	12	......	1	7	......	860	2,037	13	3	1	7	......
McDonough	3,652	4,023	120	4	13	43	......	3,653	4,030	117	4	13	46	6
McHenry	1,889	5,020	115	2	2	50	......	1,894	5,025	112	1	2	49	2
McLean	6,305	9,864	364	9	13	96	......	6,311	9,874	356	10	12	93	7
Menard	2,016	1,623	30	......	1	20	......	2,017	1,623	32	......	1	19	6
Mercer	2,307	3,095	67	......	2	20	......	2,300	3,104	65	......	2	20	

Monroe	1,653	1,443	4	6	2	13		1,652	1,444	4	6	2	13	1
Montgomery	4,078	3,595	119	3	5	21		4,079	3,597	120	3	5	18	11
Morgan	4,302	4,306	99	7	3	22		4,315	4,292	92	7	3	21	10
Moultrie	2,069	1,712	14	2	3	12		2,065	1,713	14	2	3	12	
Ogle	2,091	5,182	122	1	3	76		2,085	5,181	121	1	3	78	2
Peoria	9,299	10,122	225	18	10	139		9,340	10,107	214	18	11	118	26
Perry	2,353	2,341	73	1	7	20		2,366	2,348	75	1	7	20	
Piatt	1,946	2,571	36	3	5	22		1,946	2,572	35	3	5	22	6
Pike	5,269	3,140	98	4	25	14		5,267	3,141	97	3	23	14	7
Pope	1,062	1,857	9	1		8		1,063	1,858	8			8	4
Pulaski	1,147	2,075	9	2	2	12		1,148	2,080	4	2	2	11	
Putnam	468	700	28		1	10		468	701	27		1	10	1
Randolph	3,056	3,006	84	4	11	25		3,057	3,009	84	3	11	25	7
Richland	2,040	1,691	22		22	8		2,039	1,691	21		21	9	
Rock Island	4,720	7,199	87	13	12	87		4,697	7,243	77	13	12	80	26
Saline	2,280	2,604	22	4	1	4		2,280	2,603	22	4	1	4	2
Sangamon	8,483	8,774	255	2	11	303		8,535	8,917	272	2	11	90	14
Schuyler	2,307	1,851	64	2	3	9		2,308	1,851	65	2	3	9	9
Scott	1,586	1,248	21	3		8		1,597	1,248	22			5	2
Shelby	4,633	3,062	146		10	16		4,634	3,062	146		10	16	8
Stark	1,007	1,625	56	1	1	17		1,005	1,633	51	1	1	17	10
St. Clair	8,343	8,929	120	49	6	92		8,346	8,932	123	48	6	92	12
Stephenson	3,811	4,645	184	7	2	47		3,799	4,664	178	7	2	44	2
Tazewell	3,746	3,671	90	1	3	48		3,744	3,677	88		3	47	7
Union	2,989	1,828	35	4	1	10		2,988	1,830	35	4	1	10	10
Vermilion	5,710	8,716	203	6	23	92		5,712	8,721	203	6	23	95	12
Wabash	1,731	1,317	61	2	7	1	1	1,731	1,317	59	2	7	1	3
Warren	2,577	3,372	125	1	11	34		2,568	3,383	123	1	11	33	2
Washington	1,998	2,328	37		4	38		1,976	2,349	37		4	38	
Wayne	3,023	2,845	19	2	175	6		3,077	2,907	22	1	44	5	8
White	3,403	2,770	37		2	6		3,404	2,772	37		2	5	12
Whiteside	2,739	5,557	108	1	8	75		2,733	5,555	108	1	8	74	10
Will	6,847	9,125	78	9	8	54		6,823	9,173	76	7	8	43	16
Williamson	2,551	3,038	6		2	16		2,549	3,038	6		2	15	4
Winnebago	2,493	8,128	328	7	6	56		2,448	8,224	296	7	5	52	8
Woodford	2,424	2,417	106	4	2	22		2,427	2,424	103	4	2	22	4
Total	473,050	589,714	11,859	1,160	958	8,413	1	466,306	598,965	11,115	1,163	830	6,912	922

VOTE FOR TRUSTEES OF THE UNIVERSITY OF ILLINOIS.

Counties.	Richard P. Morgan	Julia Holmes Smith	Nelson W. Graham	Mary Turner Carriel	Thomas J. Smith	Francis M. McKay	Lucy P. Gaston	Carrie L. Grout	Ella M. Orr	Mrs. Belle Sales	Mrs. Emma Timblin	Mrs. Fany Cavanaugh	Mary E. Metzgar	Martha J. Adams	Martha C. Collins	Simon H. Busey	Charles F. Babcock	August Niehaus
Adams	8,070	7,917	8,050	8,499	8,492	8,490	277	277	291	15	14	14	54	59	47	108	107	103
Alexander	1,794	1,791	1,805	2,769	2,769	2,769	5	5	5	2	2	2	2	2	2	17	17	16
Bond	1,655	1,653	1,652	2,045	2,045	2,045	88	89	87				34	27	35	9	9	9
Boone	641	642	640	3,170	3,164	3,165	77	78	76	3	3	3	2	1	1	14	14	14
Brown	2,057	2,057	2,055	1,029	1,023	1,022	21	21	21				1	1	1	7	7	7
Bureau	3,868	3,876	3,870	5,549	5,543	5,544	185	177	177	26	26	26	15	13	13	119	120	121
Calhoun	1,172	1,171	1,172	805	805	805	14	14	14				1	1		5	5	5
Carroll	1,455	1,455	1,454	3,311	3,309	3,314	66	66	64	5	5	5	12	11	10	16	16	16
Cass	2,501	2,503	2,504	2,019	2,014	2,013	65	65	68	2	2	2	1	1	1	11	11	11
Champaign	5,190	5,225	5,176	7,740	7,699	7,723	521	503	501	2	3	2	27	10	15	109	80	81
Christian	4,717	4,718	4,717	4,045	4,043	4,041	88	87	88	10	10	10	14	14	14	29	28	28
Clark	3,136	3,132	3,131	2,942	2,943	2,943	67	62	65	4	4	4	16	16	16	11	12	11
Clay	2,293	2,292	2,294	2,295	2,294	2,294	84	83	81	5	5	5	2	2	2	12	12	12
Clinton	2,549	2,544	2,544	1,857	1,865	1,862	16	17	15	1	1	1	2	2	2	10	10	10
Coles	3,930	3,928	3,929	4,551	4,551	4,551	72	72	72	5	5	5	7	7	7	43	43	44
Cook	152,935	153,005	152,637	220,581	220,268	220,193	3,166	3,074	3,024	891	890	1,078	243	182	176	3,317	3,322	3,292
Crawford	2,345	2,345	2,343	2,184	2,183	2,185	36	34	34	2	2	2	6	6	7	14	14	14
Cumberland	2,096	2,097	2,096	1,883	1,880	1,880	24	25	24	2	2	2	10	9	10	7	7	7
DeKalb	1,844	1,850	1,844	5,612	5,609	5,612	233	235	233	2	2	2	7	6	6	59	59	59
DeWitt	2,386	2,382	2,381	2,602	2,604	2,603	62	62	62							22	22	22
Douglas	2,132	2,136	2,134	2,697	2,696	2,695	79	79	76	1	1	1	2	1	1	21	21	21
DuPage	1,578	1,568	1,561	4,085	4,087	4,099	170	169	169	5	5	6	3	3	3	110	110	108
Edgar	3,699	3,700	3,698	3,828	3,825	3,826	77	78	79	2	2	3	6	6	6	60	60	60
Edwards	850	850	850	1,652	1,653	1,653	37	37	37	2	2	2	2	2	2	3	3	2
Effingham	2,978	2,974	2,976	1,926	1,924	1,925	51	53	53	5	6	5	2	2	3	17	17	17
Fayette	3,618	3,622	3,612	2,902	2,905	2,905	129	133	106	3	3	6	66	57	91	31	31	30
Ford	1,493	1,495	1,492	2,868	2,869	2,867	75	74	73	2	2	2	6	5	5	19	17	17
Franklin	2,200	2,200	2,199	2,052	2,052	2,052	17	17	17	3	3	3	1	1	1	6	6	6
Fulton	6,009	6,018	6,006	6,548	6,531	6,533	169	165	177	5	5	5	18	14	13	29	28	30
Gallatin	2,055	2,055	2,055	1,465	1,465	1,465	26	26	26				2	2	2	8	8	8
Greene	4,014	4,017	4,023	2,462	2,448	2,451	72	75	72	2	2	2	3	3	3	11	11	11
Grundy	2,061	2,060	2,061	3,366	3,366	3,365	144	144	144	8	8	8	2	2	2	20	20	20
Hamilton	2,398	2,394	2,398	1,755	1,757	1,756	38	41	38	1	1	1	1	1	1	3	3	3

Hancock	4,575	4,582	4,577	4,289	4,285	4,286	166	168	165	3	3	3	3	3	3	31	31	31
Hardin	901	901	900	779	779	779	7	7	7	......	......	......	......	......	......	3	3	3
Henderson	956	957	957	1,834	1,833	1,832	71	70	70	1	1	1	9	7	7	32	31	31
Henry	2,986	2,999	2,984	6,201	6,198	6,195	185	177	179	3	3	3	27	10	12	70	69	68
Iroquois	3,677	3,687	3,676	5,514	5,507	5,514	234	228	225	3	3	3	18	13	16	56	53	53
Jackson	3,609	3,606	3,617	3,999	4,002	3,996	57	57	57	8	8	8	41	40	41	22	22	20
Jasper	2,718	2,720	2,718	1,898	1,897	1,897	75	75	75	3	3	3	......	......	......	1	1	1
Jefferson	3,596	3,597	3,596	2,641	2,641	2,641	108	110	108	1	1	1	9	9	9	17	18	16
Jersey	2,376	2,374	2,376	1,655	1,655	1,654	76	75	75	3	3	3	5	5	5	5	5	5
JoDaviess	2,380	2,376	2,377	3,562	3,565	3,566	123	125	122	1	1	1	3	3	3	85	85	85
Johnson	1,436	1,438	1,437	2,063	2,061	2,061	15	15	15	3	3	3	5	6	5	9	9	9
Kane	4,823	4,845	4,819	[1]2,282	[1]2,240	[1]2,241	302	299	294	5	4	6	32	26	26	143	141	141
Kankakee	2,360	2,359	2,360	5,656	5,652	5,651	119	116	116	5	5	5	9	9	9	78	77	75
Kendall	758	758	759	2,182	2,181	2,178	105	106	103	2	2	2	5	3	3	16	16	16
Knox	3,459	3,467	3,459	7,726	7,732	7,733	171	167	166	5	5	5	27	20	19	84	83	81
Lake	1,739	1,745	1,740	4,990	4,978	4,985	139	141	139	4	4	4	7	7	7	38	38	38
LaSalle	8,130	8,136	8,120	[1]1,656	[1]1,650	[1]1,651	252	244	242	28	29	29	22	19	20	156	157	156
Lawrence	1,927	1,928	1,927	1,984	1,988	1,986	54	55	55	1	1	1	9	9	9	11	11	11
Lee	2,481	2,477	2,477	4,866	4,856	4,857	80	83	82	5	5	5	3	3	3	78	78	77
Livingston	4,126	4,066	4,105	5,646	5,644	5,648	229	226	216	1	1	1	20	18	16	57	58	55
Logan	3,420	3,420	3,396	3,477	3,464	3,474	124	130	124	1	1	1	5	5	5	32	34	34
Macon	4,842	4,853	4,846	6,770	6,741	6,737	185	186	180	5	6	5	20	19	20	80	79	77
Macoupin	5,839	5,846	5,836	5,450	5,438	5,437	184	188	184	4	3	3	16	16	16	30	29	29
Madison	6,311	6,298	6,307	7,415	7,423	7,419	125	127	126	6	5	5	5	6	6	78	72	74
Marion	3,956	3,963	3,954	3,063	3,067	3,061	72	69	69	2	2	2	19	19	19	9	10	9
Marshall	1,887	1,895	1,891	2,230	2,224	2,223	62	52	47	3	3	3	3	3	3	12	14	16
Mason	2,473	2,470	2,465	2,206	2,200	2,202	96	103	92	1	1	1	5	5	5	15	13	14
Massac	863	862	857	2,106	2,104	2,104	22	22	11	3	3	3	1	1	1	7	7	7
McDonough	3,677	3,674	3,674	4,101	4,101	4,102	155	157	152	4	4	4	40	32	30	41	41	40
McHenry	1,902	1,899	1,899	5,051	5,052	5,053	134	134	134	1	1	1	4	3	3	50	51	50
McLean	6,329	6,321	6,319	10,105	10,105	10,105	524	518	508	10	10	10	11	11	11	93	91	91
Menard	2,014	2,015	2,015	1,626	1,626	1,625	28	28	28	......	......	......	1	1	1	20	20	20
Mercer	2,341	2,343	2,339	3,529	3,531	3,531	100	101	93	......	......	......	10	4	5	21	21	21
Monroe	1,674	1,660	1,670	1,439	1,449	1,442	6	6	6	7	7	7	1	1	1	14	14	14
Montgomery	4,101	4,104	4,104	3,700	3,687	3,685	149	151	143	3	4	3	7	7	11	18	18	18
Morgan	4,506	4,553	4,515	5,682	5,538	5,525	135	148	152	8	9	8	4	4	4	20	18	18
Moultrie	2,083	2,088	2,086	1,726	1,726	1,725	17	17	17	3	3	3	3	3	3	13	12	12
Ogle	2,083	2,083	2,082	5,189	5,180	5,178	120	121	119	1	1	1	3	3	3	78	79	79
Peoria	9,214	9,194	9,175	10,462	10,461	10,433	280	274	258	18	18	18	19	11	16	130	131	167
Perry	2,361	2,362	2,358	2,410	2,412	2,411	88	88	88	1	1	1	8	8	8	20	20	20
Piatt[1]	2,003	2,001	2,005	2,818	2,814	2,814	77	74	75	4	3	3	15	15	14	23	21	21
Pike	5,422	5,432	5,417	3,426	3,411	3,411	176	182	192	4	3	3	25	35	22	16	15	15
Pope	1,057	1,058	1,057	1,856	1,856	1,856	8	8	8	......	1	......	......	1	......	8	8	7
Pulaski	1,161	1,159	1,160	2,074	2,077	2,074	4	4	4	2	2	2	2	2	2	11	11	11
Putnam	475	475	474	740	739	740	42	42	39	......	......	......	3	......	......	11	10	10
Randolph	3,065	3,065	3,063	3,023	3,025	3,024	24	24	23	5	4	4	12	11	13	25	25	25
Richland	2,041	2,044	2,040	1,681	1,682	1,681	25	25	26	......	......	......	30	30	29	10	9	1[illegible]
Rock Island	4,707	4,706	4,701	7,376	7,385	7,372	111	119	106	13	13	15	80	38	35	82	82	8[illegible]
Saline[1]	2,281	2,281	2,281	2,602	2,602	2,602	22	22	22	4	4	4	1	1	1	4	4	[illegible]
Sangamon	8,580	8,567	8,568	9,124	9,129	9,119	306	306	307	4	4	3	16	16	16	102	101	10[illegible]

Official Vote—Continued.

Counties.	Richard P. Morgan	Julia Holmes Smith	Nelson W. Graham	Mary Turner Carriel	Thomas. J. Smith	Francis M. McKay	Lucy P. Gaston	Carrie L. Grout	Ella M. Orr	Mrs. Belle Sales	Mrs. Emma Timblin	Mrs. Fann Cavanaugh	Mary E. Metzgar	Martha J. Adams	Martha Collins	Simon H. Busey	Charles F. Babcock	August Niehaus
Schuyler	2,312	2,309	2,312	1,860	1,860	1,858	65	66	66	2	2	2	4	4	4	9	9	9
Scott	1,694	1,696	1,689	1,498	1,463	1,462	27	29	40	3	2	2	1	......	1	8	8	8
Shelby	4,644	4,644	4,644	3,122	3,119	3,114	171	193	179	......	......	......	14	14	14	15	15	15
Stark	1,019	1,021	1,019	1,670	1,667	1,667	71	68	68	1	1	1	3	2	2	17	16	16
St. Clair	8,350	8,326	8,330	8,952	8,965	8,958	143	141	141	52	52	52	6	6	6	98	97	96
Stephenson	3,817	3,834	3,794	4,683	4,691	4,687	212	232	207	8	8	7	18	4	3	43	45	43
Tazewell	3,752	3,759	3,754	3,720	3,714	3,711	107	111	107	2	2	2	8	6	6	50	48	48
Union	3,021	3,020	3,019	1,865	1,857	1,864	35	30	34	4	4	4	1	1	1	10	10	10
Vermilion	5,724	5,731	5,719	8,812	8,802	8,807	242	240	248	6	6	6	29	23	23	91	95	92
Wabash	1,719	1,718	1,718	1,316	1,316	1,315	61	61	61	3	3	3	12	11	10	1	1	1
Warren	2,664	2,668	2,664	4,323	4,307	4,302	227	225	214	4	4	4	29	17	19	36	35	35
Washington	1,986	1,979	1,982	2,398	2,409	2,405	39	39	40	......	......	......	4	4	4	37	38	38
Wayne	3,091	3,092	3,092	2,998	2,998	2,997	26	26	26	1	1	1	50	49	47	6	6	6
White	3,442	3,442	3,442	2,819	2,817	2,817	49	49	49	......	......	......	3	3	3	6	7	7
Whiteside	2,752	2,756	2,758	5,620	5,617	5,617	156	154	143	4	2	1	58	24	24	75	76	75
Will	6,834	6,836	6,818	9,273	9,264	9,262	102	99	101	7	7	7	13	10	10	49	49	48
Williamson	2,555	2,555	2,553	3,040	3,045	3,045	......	......	......	......	......	......	......	......	......	......	......	......
Winnebago	2,449	2,465	2,436	8,302	8,260	8,293	406	522	399	8	8	8	9	11	10	52	48	49
Woodford	2,440	2,432	2,433	2,449	2,455	2,456	144	141	140	5	5	5	3	2	2	20	20	20
Total	467,665	467,664	467,070	615,694	614,900	614,799	14,506	14,533	14,182	1,328	1,324	1,512	1,458	1,181	1,203	6,965	6,919	6,901

FOR CLERKS OF THE SUPREME COURT.

Southern Grand Division.

Counties.	Jacob O. Chance.	Robert E. Mabery.
Alexander	1,760	2,635
Bond	1,640	1,977
Clay	2,251	2,157
Clinton	2,546	1,869
Crawford	2,336	2,165
Edwards	851	1,573
Effingham	2,948	1,888
Fayette	3,585	2,797
Franklin	2,199	2,052
Gallatin	2,064	1,465
Hamilton	2,392	1,759
Hardin	900	779
Jackson	3,598	3,878
Jasper	2,739	1,873
Jefferson	3,581	2,603
Johnson	1,417	2,024
Lawrence	1,929	1,987
Madison	6,315	7,420
Marion	3,810	2,888
Massac	859	2,039
Monroe	1,655	1,445
Perry	2,362	2,375
Pope	1,058	1,859
Pulaski	1,158	2,075
Randolph	3,063	3,024
Richland	2,044	1,695
Saline	2,286	2,601
St. Clair	8,390	8,958
Union	2,990	1,835
Wabash	1,744	1,325
Washington	1,984	2,357
Wayne	3,081	2,905
White	3,408	2,773
Williamson	2,550	3,038
Total	87,463	86,093

Central Grand Division.

Counties.	Ethan A. Snively.	Albert D. Cadwallader.	John Gill.	George E. Ayers.
Adams	8,073	8,336		
Brown	2,058	1,028		
Calhoun	1,155	792		
Cass	2,462	1,902		
Champaign	4,653	6,744		
Christian	4,614	3,868		
Clark	3,099	2,898		
Coles	3,945	4,523		
Cumberland	2,078	1,856		
DeWitt	2,356	2,579		
Douglas	2,134	2,695		
Edgar	3,696	3,806		
Ford	1,494	2,803		
Fulton	5,965	6,174	1	
Greene	3,956	2,364		
Hancock	4,595	4,244		
Jersey	2,377	1,632		
Logan	3,306	3,538		
Macon	4,785	6,197		
Macoupin	5,554	4,986		
Mason	2,399	2,031		
McDonough	3,666	4,045		
McLean	6,318	9,903		
Menard	2,029	1,625		
Montgomery	4,078	3,603		1
Morgan	4,300	4,335		
Moultrie	2,070	1,721		
Piatt	1,949	2,580		
Pike	5,288	3,150		
Sangamon	8,667	8,881		
Schuyler	2,321	1,858		
Scott	1,589	1,258		
Shelby	4,652	3,061		
Tazewell	3,768	3,691		
Vermilion	5,715	8,743		
Total	131,164	133,450	1	1

Northern Grand Division.

Counties.	Christopher Mamer.	Robert B. Mitchell.	Scattering
Boone	3,099	615	
Bureau	5,397	3,522	
Carroll	3,315	1,424	
Cook	217,560	150,655	
DeKalb	5,593	1,821	
DuPage	4,099	1,577	
Grundy	3,235	1,990	
Henderson	1,755	930	
Henry	6,141	2,833	
Iroquois	5,318	3,592	
JoDaviess	3,572	2,359	
Kane	11,971	4,799	
Kankakee	5,424	2,324	
Kendall	2,123	751	
Knox	7,671	2,984	
Lake	4,950	1,701	
LaSalle	11,444	7,953	
Lee	4,734	2,422	
Livingston	5,425	4,011	
Marshall	2,191	1,882	
McHenry	5,027	1,885	
Mercer	3,108	2,153	
Ogle	5,183	2,072	
Peoria	10,208	9,165	1
Putnam	707	456	
Rock Island	7,268	4,503	
Stark	1,631	896	
Stephenson	4,599	3,904	
Warren	3,392	2,525	
Whiteside	5,564	2,676	
Will	9,186	6,597	
Winnebago	8,219	2,202	
Woodford	2,447	2,373	
Total	381,556	241,552	1

FOR CLERKS OF THE APPELLATE COURTS.

Counties.	First Appellate District.							
Cook	Thomas W. Jamison	218,853	Thomas G. McElligott	153,272	Charles L. Saylor	2,468	Emanuel Donziger	3,338

Second Appellate District.				Third Appellate District.				Fourth Appellate District.		
Counties.	Christopher C. Duffy	William D. Stewart	Scattering.	Counties.	George W. Jones	William C. Hippard	Scattering.	Counties.	Frank W. Havill	Morris Emmerson
Boone	3,102	613		Adams	8,091	8,335		Alexander	1,751	2,635
Bureau	5,421	3,499		Brown	2,058	1,028		Bond	1,638	1,982
Carroll	3,310	1,420		Calhoun	1,155	792		Clay	2,250	2,158
DeKalb	5,589	1,828		Cass	2,459	1,905		Clinton	2,545	1,871
DuPage	4,122	1,570	1	Champaign	4,652	6,747		Crawford	2,336	2,163
Grundy	3,240	1,985		Christian	4,615	3,867		Edwards	841	1,587
Henderson	1,756	929		Clark	3,070	2,932		Effingham	2,947	1,887
Henry	6,159	2,814		Coles	3,945	4,523		Fayette	3,584	2,798
Iroquois	5,319	3,593		Cumberland	2,081	1,857		Franklin	2,204	2,051
JoDaviess	3,577	2,356		DeWitt	2,369	2,577		Gallatin	2,065	1,466
Kane	11,991	4,773		Douglas	2,139	2,663		Hamilton	2,403	1,758
Kankakee	5,420	2,323		Edgar	3,695	3,807		Hardin	900	779
Kendall	2,131	752		Ford	1,491	2,806		Jackson	3,599	3,877
Knox	7,674	2,985		Fulton	5,950	6,190		Jasper	2,709	1,875
Lake	4,959	1,696		Greene	3,958	2,361		Jefferson	3,570	2,622
LaSalle	11,489	7,937		Hancock	4,603	4,242		Johnson	1,417	2,025
Lee	4,760	2,394		Jersey	2,375	1,632		Lawrence	1,935	1,986
Livingston	5,433	4,008		Logan	3,425	3,400		Madison	6,329	7,407
Marshall	2,200	1,873		Macon	4,781	6,195		Marion	3,807	2,885
McHenry	5,033	1,876		Macoupin	5,554	4,987		Massac	858	2,040
Mercer	3,111	2,155		Mason	2,405	2,108		Monroe	1,661	1,438

Ogle	5,189	2,056		McDonough	3,666	4,046		Perry	2,356	2,381
Peoria	10,303	9,080		McLean	6,318	9,905		Pope	1,057	1,858
Putman	705	456		Menard	2,029	1,627		Pulaski	1,155	2,078
Rock Island	7,272	4,496		Montgomery	4,081	3,600	1	Randolph	3,067	3,018
Stark	1,636	889		Morgan	4,306	4,325		Richland	2,044	1,608
Stephenson	4,676	3,814		Moultrie	2,070	1,713		Saline	2,286	2,604
Warren	3,398	2,522		Piatt	1,947	2,582		St. Clair	8,406	8,948
Whiteside	5,572	2,672		Pike	5,300	3,133		Union	2,988	1,837
Will	9,183	6,597		Sangamon	8,684	8,855		Wabash	1,777	1,297
Winnebago	8,263	2,130		Schuyler	2,318	1,858		Washington	1,992	2,348
Woodford	2,450	2,368		Scott	1,594	1,257		Wayne	3,077	2,917
				Shelby	4,649	3,060		White	3,404	2,779
				Tazewell	3,768	3,692		Williamson	2,548	3,037
				Vermilion	5,717	8,739				
Total	164,443	90,459	1	Total	131,318	133,346	1	Total	87,506	86,090

VOTE FOR REPRESENTATIVES IN CONGRESS BY DISTRICTS.

FIRST DISTRICT.

Counties.	James R. Mann.	James H. Teller.	Thomas R. Strobridge.	Benjamin J. Werthermer.				
Cook	51,582	23,123	595	957				

SECOND DISTRICT.

Counties.	William Lorimer.	John Z. White.	James Craigmile.	William P. Crenshaw.				
Cook	35,045	28,309	594	561				

THIRD DISTRICT.

Counties.	Hugh R. Belknap.	Clarence S. Darrow.	Solomon Ebersoll.	John Krebs.	Michael L. Morris.	John J. Fanning		
Cook	22,075	21,485	182	255	109	21		

FOURTH DISTRICT.

Counties.	Daniel W. Mills.	James McAndrews.	Archibald Sprott.	James E. Gillis.	J. Augustus Weaver.	Charles W. Woodman.		
Cook	22,364	20,454	236	419	129	375		

FIFTH DISTRICT.

Counties.	George E. White	Edward T. Noonan.	Thomas L. Haines.	Thomas E. Courtney.	John A. McDonell.
Cook	23,053	19,975	257	233	1,813

SIXTH DISTRICT.

Counties.	Edward D. Cook	Joseph S. Martin.	Ira J. Mason.	Sigmund Zeisler.
Cook	25,723	19,144	269	537

SEVENTH DISTRICT.

Counties.	George Edmund Foss	Olaf E. Ray.	James Clement Ambrose.	Michael W. Robinson.	L. P. Quinn.	Scattering.
Cook	36,550	19,471	379	508	24	3
Lake	4,960	1,742	99	33	16	......
Total	41,510	21,213	478	541	40	3

EIGHTH DISTRICT.

Counties.	Albert J. Hopkins.	Simeon N. Hoover.	Augustus R. Dodd.
McHenry	5,037	1,874	108
DeKalb	5,599	1,821	197
Kane	11,944	4,848	219
DuPage	4,140	1,561	143
Kendall	2,114	766	54
Grundy	3,239	1,991	97
Total	32,073	12,861	818

NINTH DISTRICT.

Counties.	Robert R. Hitt.	Charles O. Knudson.	James Lamont.					
Boone	3,104	638	61					
Winnebago	8,243	2,424	309					
Stephenson	4,691	3,815	160					
JoDaviess	3,587	2,376	106					
Carroll	3,322	1,453	56					
Ogle	5,227	2,080	119					
Lee	4,775	2,455	64					
Total	32,949	15,241	866					

TENTH DISTRICT.

Counties.	George W. Prince.	William R. Moore.	William Goldsworthy.	William C. Holden.	Dan Keheler.			
Whiteside	5,568	2,668	102	72	......			
Rock Island	7,301	4,409	77	245	......			
Mercer	3,108	2,132	50	170	......			
Henry	6,165	2,736	125	236	1			
Knox	7,678	2,921	143	543	......			
Stark	1,639	875	39	135	......			
Total	31,459	15,741	536	1,401	1			

ELEVENTH DISTRICT.

Counties.	Charles M. Golden.	Walter Reeves.	John W. Hosier.					
Bureau	3,920	5,375	148					
LaSalle	8,101	11,535	176					
Livingston	4,048	5,433	140					
Woodford	2,445	2,422	93					
Total	18,514	24,765	557					

TWELFTH DISTRICT.

Counties.	Joseph G. Cannon.	George L. Vance.	J. J. Hales.	J. E. McMahon.
Will	9,116	6,900	54	......
Kankakee	5,423	2,360	85	......
Iroquois	5,308	3.629	138	1
Vermilion	8,719	5,724	201	......
Total	28,566	18,613	478	1

THIRTEENTH DISTRICT.

Counties.	Vespasian Warner.	Frank M. Palmer.	Thomas J. Scott
Ford	2,801	1,497	53
McLean	9,896	6,319	349
DeWitt	2,629	2,314	58
Piatt	2.578	1,944	36
Champaign	6,751	4,639	288
Douglas	2,669	2,098	49
Total	27,334	18,811	833

FOURTEENTH DISTRICT.

Counties.	Joseph V. Graff.	Nicholas E. Worthington.	Daniel R. Sheen	Theodore Holly.
Putnam	701	461	21	18
Marshall	2,206	1,875	35	20
Peoria	10,191	9,222	200	139
Fulton	6,199	5.790	89	153
Tazewell	3.727	3,680	72	53
Mason	2,120	2,385	54	9
Total	25,144	23,413	471	392

FIFTEENTH DISTRICT.

Counties.	William H. Neece.	Benjamin F. Marsh.	E. Lawrence Grosh.					
Henderson	962	1,758	39					
Warren	2,594	3,406	100					
Hancock	4,562	4,290	136					
McDonough	3,745	3,979	96					
Adams	8,032	8,317	175					
Brown	2,058	1,026	18					
Schuyler	2,343	1,829	54					
Total	24,296	24,605	618					

SIXTEENTH DISTRICT.

Counties.	William H. Hinrichsen.	John I. Rinaker.	M. M. Cooper.					
Cass	2,450	1,908	35					
Morgan	4,319	4,327	88					
Scott	1,588	1,263	17					
Pike	5,287	3,140	101					
Greene	3,951	2,364	47					
Macoupin	5,497	5,041	116					
Calhoun	1,155	794	9					
Jersey	2,368	1,638	50					
Total	26,615	20,472	463					

SEVENTEENTH DISTRICT.

Counties.	James A. Connolly.	Ben F. Caldwell.	Edmund Miller.	Edward G. King.				
Menard	1,630	2,022	23	14				
Logan	3,388	3,428	74	41				
Sangamon	8,740	8,827	224	62				
Macon	6,195	4,808	103	76				
Christian	3,860	4,629	60	24				
Total	23,813	23,714	484	217				

EIGHTEENTH DISTRICT.

Counties.	Thomas M. Jett.	William F. L. Hadley.	Frank H. Ashcraft.					
Madison	6,274	7,480	74					
Bond	1,651	1,971	71					
Montgomery	4,114	3,576	114					
Fayette	3,596	2,782	75					
Shelby	4,651	3,074	123					
Moultrie	2,071	1,717	14					
Total	22,358	20,599	471					

NINETEENTH DISTRICT.

Counties.	Benson Wood.	Andrew J. Hunter.	Cains C. Griffith	John J. Sewell.				
Coles	4,543	3,847	51	78				
Edgar	3,801	3,549	52	134				
Clark	2,910	2,992	41	143				
Cumberland	1,867	2,007	19	79				
Effingham	1,932	2,873	33	51				
Jasper	1,882	2,573	51	129				
Crawford	2,169	2,288	22	55				
Richland	1,701	1,916	14	131				
Lawrence	1,988	1,915	41	10				
Total	22,793	23,960	324	810				

TWENTIETH DISTRICT.

Counties.	Orlando Burrell	James R. Campbell.	Thomas Riley.
Clay	2,158	2,248	11
Jefferson	2,619	3,560	12
Wayne	2,922	3,076	5
Hamilton	1,767	2,380	12
Edwards	1,575	850	1
Wabash	1,334	1,735	1
Franklin	2,053	2,202	4
White	2,832	3,350	5
Gallatin	1,469	2,058	......
Hardin	779	900	3
Total	19,508	22,359	54

TWENTY-FIRST DISTRICT.

Counties.	Everett J. Murphy.	Jehu Baker.
Marion	2,905	3,797
Clinton	1,879	2,541
Washington	2,363	1,986
St. Clair	9,108	8,239
Monroe	1,503	1,597
Randolph	3,045	3,054
Perry	2,376	2,367
Total	23,179	23,581

TWENTY-SECOND DISTRICT.

Counties.	John J. Hall.	George W. Smith.					
Jackson	3,685	3,906					
Union	2,989	1,839					
Alexander	1,783	2,685					
Pulaski	1,152	2,065					
Johnson	1,429	2,015					
Williamson	2,561	3.033					
Saline	2,295	2,599					
Pope	1,058	1,858					
Massac	859	2,046					
Total	17,811	22,066					

VOTE FOR MEMBERS OF THE STATE BOARD OE EQUALIZATION.

FIRST DISTRICT.

Counties.	George F. McKnight.	Frank R. Bagley.	Albert H. Sherman.	Robert L. Henry.				
Cook	51,693	23,024	605	974				

SECOND DISTRICT.

Counties.	John J. McKenna.	Charles C. Schumacher.	E. L. Kletzing.	Henry E. Hansen.				
Cook	34,205	29,010	593	566				

THIRD DISTRICT.

Counties.	Solomon Simon.	Patrick J. Wall.	Oscar Odelius.	John Morris.	Patrick J. Dunning.			
Cook	22,329	20,923	204	244	50			

FOURTH DISTRICT.

Counties.	Andrew McAnsh.	Patrick E. Canfield.	Barnett H. Veeder.	Victor I. Ohreustein.				
Cook	23,150	20,163	239	277				

FIFTH DISTRICT.

Counties.	Albert Oberndorf.	August J. Kowalski.	Arthur Ferris.	Dominick P. Kivilin.	Eli Brandt.	John Gilbert.
Cook	24,402	19,055	270	463	255	56

SIXTH DISTRICT.

Counties.	Henry Severin.	Emil Hoechster	George Foster.	John Schoen.
Cook	25,667	19,307	247	506

SEVENTH DISTRICT.

Counties.	Edward S. Taylor.	Daniel A. Grady.	George W. Shanber.	Joseph Reardon
Cook	36,698	19,102	404	532
Lake	4,973	1,733	113	36
Total	41,671	20,835	517	568

EIGHTH DISTRICT.

Counties.	Theodore S. Rogers.	Edward W. Kines.	Sylvester H. Dewey.
McHenry	5,032	1,876	109
DeKalb	5,586	1,820	203
Kane	12,006	4,736	222
DuPage	4,129	1,545	152
Kendall	2,126	746	67
Grundy	3,237	1,982	102
Total	32,116	12,705	855

NINTH DISTRICT.

Counties.	Charles A. Works.	George W. Curtis.	T. D. Wilcoxen.
Boone	3,102	641	58
Winnebago	8,087	2,448	292
Stephenson	4,651	3,831	171
JoDaviess	3,567	2,392	106
Carroll	3,303	1,460	57
Ogle	5,186	2,093	110
Lee	4,758	2,471	69
Total	32,654	15,336	862

TENTH DISTRICT.

Counties.	Thomas P. Pierce.	John Miller.	Martin Boyd.	William Mellor.	James H. Andrews.	George R. Hill.	A. B. Cook.	Scattering.
Whiteside	5,588	......	......	......	......	......	......	......
Rock Island	7,270	4,688	......	......	......	......	......	......
Mercer	3,121	......	40	......	......	......	......	......
Henry	6,174	11	......	1	1	1	1	......
Knox	7,690	3	......	......	......	......	......	2
Stark	1,642	......	......	......	......	......	......	2
Total	31,485	4,702	40	1	1	1	1	4

ELEVENTH DISTRICT.

Counties.	M. A. Bronson.	Samuel M. Barnes.	Edward P. McMurray.
Bureau	3,869	5,415	141
LaSalle	8,130	11,435	182
Livingston	3,992	5,507	151
Woodford	2,431	2,438	96
Total	18,422	24,795	570

TWELFTH DISTRICT.

Counties.	Frank P. Martin.	C. M. Briggs.	L. B. Cobb.					
Will	9,179	6,819	61					
Kankakee	5,423	2,311	88					
Iroquois	5,303	3,624	145					
Vermilion	8,719	5,716	199					
Total	28,624	18,470	493					

THIRTEENTH DISTRICT.

Counties.	Frank K. Robeson.	Abel S. Scott.	John McDonald					
Ford	2,803	1,491	54					
McLean	9,894	6,311	351					
DeWitt	2,572	2,361	65					
Piatt	2,576	1,948	33					
Champaign	6,705	4,681	289					
Douglas	2,664	2,099	49					
Total	27,214	18,891	841					

FOURTEENTH DISTRICT.

Counties.	William O. Cadwallader.	Thomas Cooper	James M. Winn.	N. E. Worthington.				
Putnam	702	456	22	......				
Marshall	2,199	1,875	38	......				
Peoria	10,110	9,166	197	1				
Fulton	6,167	5,749	94	......				
Tazewell	3,644	3,717	85	......				
Mason	2,107	2,388	61	......				
Total	24,929	23,351	497	1				

FIFTEENTH DISTRICT.

Counties.	John S. Cruttenden.	T. F. Manning.	Thomas Barton.					
Henderson	1,757	929	30					
Warren	3,396	2,518	73					
Hancock	4,252	4,457	128					
McDonough	4,039	3,544	128					
Adams	8,550	7,823	104					
Brown	1,020	1,843	228					
Schuyler	1,859	2,219	105					
Total	24,873	23,333	796					

SIXTEENTH DISTRICT.

Counties.	Louis D. Hirsheimer.	James H. Hackett.	Marcellus C. Petefish.					
Cass	2,465	1,892	35					
Morgan	4,345	4,270	99					
Scott	1,591	1,255	18					
Pike	5,439	2,989	97					
Greene	3,954	2,362	44					
Macoupin	5,556	4,976	122					
Calhoun	1,158	784	9					
Jersey	2,380	1,629	50					
Total	26,888	20,157	474					

SEVENTEENTH DISTRICT.

Counties.	Thomas N. Leavitt.	John P. Faris.	Enoch Payne.	Joseph Wallace				
Menard	1,628	2,027	26	13				
Logan	3,403	3,396	93	32				
Sangamon	8,912	8,557	251	75				
Macon	6,233	4,794	98	74				
Christian	3,866	4,610	64	25				
Total	24,042	23,384	532	219				

EIGHTEENTH DISTRICT.

Counties.	Joseph F. Long.	John A. Bingham.	Ishmael L. Clayton.
Madison	6,315	7,408	88
Bond	1,640	1,974	73
Montgomery	4,073	3,607	121
Fayette	3,592	2,768	88
Shelby	4,642	3,060	124
Moultrie	2,070	1,717	14
Total	22,332	20,534	508

NINTEENTH DISTRICT.

Counties.	John D. Mitchell.	Richard Cadle.	Jefferson P. Hobart.
Coles	4,526	3,937	51
Edgar	3,805	3,700	54
Clark	2,921	3,105	43
Cumberland	1,860	2,082	17
Effingham	1,888	2,951	41
Jasper	1,869	2,697	57
Crawford	2,165	2,321	22
Richland	1,694	2,046	17
Lawrence	1,985	1,931	42
Total	22,713	24,770	344

TWENTIETH DISTRICT.

Counties.	Andy Hall.	John R. Boyd.						
Clay	2,128	2,249						
Jefferion	2,652	3,526						
Wayne	2,910	3,084						
Hamilton	1,764	2,395						
Edwards	1,578	845						
Wabash	1,323	1,742						
Franklin	2,052	2,205						
White	2,777	3,402						
Gallatin	1,464	2,066						
Hardin	779	900						
Total	19,427	22,414						

TWENTY-FIRST DISTRICT.

Counties.	Charles H. Roe.	John W. Larimer.						
Marion	2,876	3,824						
Clinton	1,867	2,547						
Washington	2,356	1,986						
St. Clair	8,982	8,372						
Monroe	1,457	1,652						
Randolph	3,014	3,068						
Perry	2,402	2,340						
Total	22,954	23,789						

TWENTY-SECOND DISTRICT.

Counties.	Robert W. Watson.	William A. Wall.						
Jackson	3,641	3,843						
Union	2,990	1,833						
Alexander	1,793	2,773						
Pulaski	1,161	2,074						
Johnson	1,417	2,025						
Williamson	2,557	3,043						
Saline	2,290	2,601						
Pope	1,057	1,861						
Massac	858	2,039						
Total	17,764	22,092						

VOTE FOR SENATORS IN THE EVEN NUMBERED DISTRICTS.

SECOND DISTRICT.

Counties.	Selon H. Case.	Moses Salomon.	Thos. J. Canty.				
Cook	17,223	12,168	263				

FOURTH DISTRICT.

Counties.	William C. Eakins.	Daniel F. Curley	Christopher Anderson.	William H. Overton.	Harry P. Fleming.		
Cook	13,363	14,702	245	379	312		

SIXTH DISTRICT.

Counties.	William Sullivan.	Bernard J. Mahoney.	Ulysses G. Reynolds.	Henry Thwing.			
Cook	13,974	11,254	160	232			

EIGHTH DISTRICT.

Counties.	Flavil K. Granger.	Samuel F. Knox.	John Corlett.				
Lake	4,969	1,693	103				
McHenry	5,053	1,854	111				
Boone	3,104	615	59				
Total	13,126	4,162	273				

TENTH DISTRICT.

Counties.	M.L. Ettinger.	DelosW.Baxter.	F. B. Rolph.	B. F. Sheets.
Winnebago	2,425	8,200	294	......
Ogle	2,123	5,141	132	2
Total	4,548	13,341	426	2

TWELFTH DISTRICT.

Counties.	Homer F. Aspinwall.	William A. Barber.	George H. Smith.
JoDaviess	3,574	2,367	107
Stephenson	4,690	3,786	156
Carroll	3,309	1,414	56
Total	11,573	7,567	319

FOURTEENTH DISTRICT.

Counties.	Henry H. Evans.	George S. Bowen.	Herman A. Fischer.
Kane	11,957	4,772	245
DuPage	4,088	1,561	172
Total	16,045	6,333	417

SIXTEENTH DISTRICT.

Counties.	Isaac Miller Hamilton.	Alexis L. Granger.	Robert Wilkinson.				
Kankakee	5,318	2,487	90				
Iroquois	5,248	3,650	149				
Total	10,566	6,137	239				

EIGHTEENTH DISTRICT.

Counties.	Charles Bogardus.	J. A. Pence.	John M. McCabe.				
Vermilion	8,752	5,712	......				
Ford	2,828	1,491	3				
Total	11,580	7,203	3				

TWENTIETH DISTRICT.

Counties.	Robert B. Fort.	R. R. Wallace.	Benjamin R. Johnson.				
Marshall	2,243	1,856	36				
Woodford	2,437	2,431	97				
Livingston	5,418	4,089	132				
Total	10,098	8,376	265				

TWENTY-SECOND DISTRICT.

TWENTY-FOURTH DISTRICT.

Counties.	James D. Putnam.	Henry Mansfield.	Stephen Martin.	John A. Vandeventer.
Peoria	10,146	9,218	209	154

TWENTY-SIXTH DISTRICT.

Counties.	W. Scott Edwards.	William A. Moore.
Fulton	6,214	5,937
Tazewell	3,675	3,795
Total	9,889	9,732

TWENTY-EIGHTH DISTRICT.

Counties.	Orville F. Berry.	Wm. E. Manifold.	John C. McCabe.
Hancock	4,380	4,472	114
McDonough	4,045	3,661	108
Schuyler	1,855	2,311	62
Total	10,280	10,444	284

THIRTIETH DISTRICT.

Counties.	Henry M. Dunlap.	J. R. Scott.	J. D. Mandeville.
Champaign	6,761	4,567	296
Piatt	2,578	1,927	31
DeWitt	2,577	2,302	53
Total	11,916	8,796	380

THIRTY-SECOND DISTRICT.

Counties.	C. C. Judy.	A. A. Leeper.
Cass	1,918	2,415
Menard	1,722	1,860
Mason	2,128	2,371
Logan	3,429	3,360
Total	9,197	10,006

THIRTY-FOURTH DISTRICT.

Counties.	Melville D. Massie.	Edward McConnell.	Thomas Hembrough.	Anderson Foreman.
Pike	3,144	4,564	107	736
Scott	1,259	1,501	18	88
Morgan	4,300	4,222	90	97
Total	8,703	10,287	215	921

THIRTY-SIXTH DISTRICT.

Counties.	William F. Burgdorff.	William L. Mounts.	B. F. Waggoner.
Greene	2,358	3,870	45
Macoupin	4,966	5,489	131
Total	7,324	9,359	176

THIRTY-EIGHTH DISTRICT.

Counties.	William M. Fogler.	Nathaniel S. Dresser.	John D. Collins.				
Montgomery	3,601	4,073	121				
Bond	1,944	1,676	68				
Fayette	2,791	3,586	74				
Total	8,336	9,335	263				

FORTIETH DISTRICT.

Counties.	Stanton Pemberton.	Wm. H. Ragan.	Frank Montgomery.				
Douglas	2,687	2,075	40				
Coles	4,572	3,882	77				
Shelby	3,088	4,335	324				
Total	10,347	10,237	441				

FORTY-SECOND DISTRICT.

Counties.	W. Rollin Smith.	Charles E. Hull.	J. L. Black.				
Clay	2,159	2,242	2				
Marion	2,941	3,761	......				
Clinton	1,875	2,539	......				
Washington	2,357	1,983	......				
Total	9,332	10,525	2				

FORTY-FOURTH DISTRICT.

Counties.	Ross Graham.	John Landrigan.					
Wabash	1,324	1,730					
Edwards	1,567	856					
White	2,795	3,386					
Gallatin	1,466	2,052					
Hardin	780	899					
Total	7,932	8,923					

FORTY-SIXTH DISTRICT.

Counties.	S. H. Watson.	Joseph T. Payne.					
Franklin	2,046	2,207					
Jefferson	2,631	3,552					
Wayne	2,946	3,050					
Hamilton	1,764	2,387					
Total	9,387	11,196					

FORTY-EIGHTH DISTRICT.

Counties.	Albert C. Bollinger.	Harmon P. Burroughs.					
Monroe	1,516	1,589					
Randolph	3,018	3,067					
Jackson	3,876	3,610					
Perry	2,375	2,368					
Total	10,785	10,634					

FIFTIETH DISTRICT.

Counties.	Walter Warder.	A. Ney Sessions.					
Williamson	3,043	2,552					
Union	1,832	2,994					
Alexander	2,753	1,821					
Total	7,628	7,367					

VOTE FOR REPRESENTATIVES IN THE 40TH GENERAL ASSEMBLY BY DISTRICTS.

FIRST DISTRICT.

Counties.	William G. Laub.	Charles A. Wathier.	John C. Sterchie.	John Budinger.	Henry J. Brubaker.	John E. Mulloy.	Joseph Friedman.	S. Levinson.	Mathias Kiedinger.	George Stephens.
Cook	18,628½	18,249½	15,268½	14,781	347	1,291	3,356½	180	216	1,360

SECOND DISTRICT.

Counties.	Peter A. Rowe.	Augustus W. Nohe.	Peter J. McGinnis.	William W. Clark.	W. F. MacLachlan	Sherman P. Cody.	Rudolph Mulac.
Cook	24,472½	25,404½	32,171½	1,090	1,272	3,319½	1,354

THIRD DISTRICT.

Counties.	George W. Miller.	Charles W. Nothnagel.	John P. McGoorty.	Walter D. Hawk.	L. K. Davis.	David M. Henderson.	Henry J. Bourke.	Scattering.
Cook	35,295½	35,225½	36,622½	1,104	1,956	2,140½	261	3

FOURTH DISTRICT.

Counties	Timothy Hogan.	Charles F. Weidmaier.	Michael J. Butler.	John Staudacher.	Dana A. Mitchell.	Michael A. Cogley.	Lee F. English.	Charles D. Harrison.
Cook	19,026½	20,150½	21,677	20,431½	997	713	1,307	1,626

FIFTH DISTRICT.

Counties.	John C. Buckner.	William O. La Monte.	Frank R. Cain.	Samuel B. Lingle.	Richard E. Corigan.	Joseph Powell.
Cook	24,956½	23,422½	22,351½	331	3,491½	25,930½

SIXTH DISTRICT.

Counties.	George M. Boyd.	Charles M. Eldredge.	Henry C. Bartling.	George E. Beckwith.	Howard T. Wilcoxen.	Charles J. Flick.
Cook	20,303½	20,417	17,642	16,206½	408½	1,301

SEVENTH DISTRICT.

Counties.	William Thiemann.	Clark J. Tisdel.	Ross C. Hall.	Joseph L. Whitlock.	Richard M. Springer.	John H. Essen.
Cook	28,148	27,922½	19,604½	1,232½	1,322	6,524

EIGHTH DISTRICT.

Counties.	Du Fay A. Fuller.	George R. Lyon.	Jacob S. Edelstien...	George C. Rogers.	Mervin Andrews.
Lake	7,389½	7,416½	4,270½	1,412	282½
McHenry	7,525½	7,526½	5.478	219	311½
Boone	4,218	4,199	1,629	1,133½	201½
Total	19,133	19,142	11,377½	2,764½	795½

NINTH DISTRICT.

Counties.	David E. Shannahan.	John Oshea.	Christian R. Walleck.	Henry G. Franz.	Arthur Gourley.	S. F. Adalia Satalecki.	Edward F. Cullerton.	Patrick F. Carney.
Cook	22,667½	10,196	11,778½	9,642	231	1,382	1,307	3,473

TENTH DISTRICT.

Counties.	Joseph W. Bacharach.	Lars M. Noling.	Victor H. Bovey.	Henry Andrews.	Charles M. Whipple.	John Budlong.
Winnebago	6,481½	9,194	7,406½	7,934½	851½	884
Ogle	6,025½	5,119	3,431½	5,123	313	89
Total	12,507	14,313	12,838	13,057½	1,164½	973

ELEVENTH DISTRICT.

Counties.	Ernest G. Schubert.	Walter Sayler.	Joseph S. Schwab.	Larned E. Meacham.	William D. Wilcox.	Mark J. McKamara.
Cook	28,056½	27,201	30,384	887	3,969	832

TWELFTH DISTRICT.

Counties.	James R. Berryman.	David C. Bissell	Theodore F. Ellis.	Michael Stoskopf.	Richard A. Oliver.
JoDaviess	5,553½	5,077½	324	3,609½	3,596½
Stephenson	6,683	6,665	430	6,587½	5,400½
Carroll	4,904½	4,995	149½	2,175½	2,186
Total	17,141	16,737½	903½	12,372½	11,183

THIRTEENTH DISTRICT.

Counties.	James P. Cavanaugh.	William Carmody.	Edward J. Novak.	Niles Johnson.	Michael E. Clare.	Harry Goldstine.	Isaac Levin.	Simon Shaeffer.	James Kozisek.
Cook	15,328	7,420	10,890	139	1,243	715	523	6,897	1,111

FOURTEENTH DISTRICT.

Counties.	Charles P. Bryan.	William F. Hunter.	Samuel Alschuler.	James L. Backus.
Kane	17,669½	17,638	14,513	658
DuPage	6,389	5,978½	4,780	473½
Total	24,058½	23,616½	19,293	1,131½

FIFTEENTH DISTRICT.

Counties.	Patrick J. Meaney.	Henry D. Nicholle.	Peter F. Galligar.	George L. McConnell.	Herman L. Parmalla.	William Schrieder.	John F. Murray.	Thomas Oneil Jones.
Cook	15,301	14,614½	15,649	12,657½	260½	468	1,114½	277

SIXTEENTH DISTRICT.

Counties.	Ed. C. Curtis.	Almet Powell.	Freeman P. Morris.	David Lowery.	John W. Stokes.
Kankakee	8,061½	7,978	2,800	4,632½	263
Iroquois	7,782½	7,865	7,152½	3,792½	404½
Total	15,844	15,843	9,952½	8,425	667½

SEVENTEENTH DISTRICT.

Counties.	Albert Glade.	Daniel V. McDonough	Frank J. Brignadello	Timothy Ryan.	John McDonnell.	William Burke.	D. F. Ford.
Cook	22,801½	11,494	11,491½	231	683½	3,198	240

EIGHTEENTH DISTRICT.

Counties.	Charles A. Allen.	Martin B. Bailey.	G. W. Salmons.	John M. McCabe.	William M. Bines.
Vermilion	13,062	13,054	15,709	1,497	......
Ford	4,147½	4,056	4,089½	279	15
Total	17,209½	17,110	19,798½	1,776	15

NINETEENTH DISTRICT.

Counties.	John F. Quanstrom.	Robert C. Busse.	Joseph S. Geshkewick	Benjamin M. Mitchell.	Ira Blanchard.	James N. Fitzsimons.
Cook	15,825½	15,571½	13,413	14,655	385½	1,716½

TWENTIETH DISTRICT.

Counties.	John L. McGuire.	Chas. Fosbender.	Oscar F. Avery.	Isaac B. Hammers.	William R. Thorpe.
Marshall	2,889½	3,002	3,274	3,264½	95
Woodford	3,924	3,425¼	3,570	3,664½	277
Livingston	6,081½	6,019½	8,212½	8,119	417
Total	12,895	12,447	15,056½	15,048	789

TWENTY-FIRST DISTRICT.

Counties.	Fred A. Busse.	David Revell.	James H. Farrell.	Rebert J. Reed.	Paul K. Dealy.	William A. Stiles.	Carl A. Oman.
Cook	21,671½	20,726	24,861	331	959½	2,103½	3,793½

TWENTY-SECOND DISTRICT.

Counties.	Duncan M. Funk.	Arthur J. Scrogin.	James F. O'Donnell.	James VanShoick.
McLean	14,512	14,596½	18,363½	1,001½

TWENTY-THIRD DISTRICT.

Counties.	Lawrence Kilcourse.	Albert J. Olson.	Dennis E. Sullivan.	George A. Landgren.	Leonard H. Wood.	Thomas J. Loftus.
Cook	15,828	16,262	11,552½	10,619½	319½	1,521½

TWENTY-FOURTH DISTRICT.

Counties.	Aquilla J. Dougherty.	Alva Merrill.	Peter Cahill.	Almon H. Bristol.	John G. Spicer.	James E. Wilson.	Henry Mansfield.
Peoria..................	15,058½	14,965½	12,900½	13,169	437	341	1

TWENTY-FIFTH DISTRICT.

Counties.	John Koldstedt.	William H. Steen.	Robert B. Graves.	Joseph Kain.
Will......................	13,781	13.822	9,419½	10,938

TWENTY-SIXTH DISTRICT.

Counties.	Jonathan Merriam.	John W. Johnson.	Lute C. Breeden.	Simon B. Beer.
Fulton	8,994	9,492	8,917	9,005
Tazewell	5,670½	5,512	5,617	5,628
Total	14,664½	15,004	14,534	14,633

TWENTY-SEVENTH DISTRICT.

Counties.	John Wylie.	Irving H. Throw-bridge.	John McLauchlan	Albert C. Croswell.	Fred W. Eados.	George Poundstone.
LaSalle	17,003	16,910	12,046½	11,927½	728½	11½

TWENTY-EIGHTH DISTRICT.

Counties.	Lawrence Y. Sherman.	Ulyses A. Wilson.	Wm. A. Compton.	Jas. A. Teel.	John W. Gray.
Hancock	6,336	6,297	6,737½	6,627½	421
McDonough	6,198	5,989	6,424	4,507	294
Schuyler	2,757	2,772½	3,255	3,752	144
Total	15,271	15,058½	16,416½	14,886½	859

TWENTY-NINTH DISTRICT.

Counties.	Washington I. Guffin.	John K. Ely.	James Branen.	J. N. Bed-ford.
Lee	7,097½	7,110½	7,102½	202
DeKalb	8,163½	8,194	5,652½	630½
Kendall	3,166½	3,165	2,224	195
Grundy	5,110½	5,114	5,956½	285
Total	23,538	23,583½	20,935½	1,312½

THIRTIETH DISTRICT.

Counties.	Samuel B. Garver.	Seymour Marquiss.	Henry C. Suttle.	E. H. Robb.	N. M. Barnett.
Champaign	10,125½	10,119½	13,752	522	......
Piatt	3,865½	3,869½	5,752	73	......
DeWitt	3,928½	3,859½	6,880	195	3
Total	17,919½	17,848½	16,384	790	3

THIRTY-FIRST DISTRICT.

Counties.	George Murray.	Jerry W. Dinneen.	Caleb C. Johnson.	Jas. W. Fletcher.	Jas. E. Barnard.
Whiteside	8,243	8,254	7,892½	307	197
Bureau	8,129¾	8,124¼	10,398	323	1,193
Putnam	1,051½	1,049	1,331	64	93
Stark	2,432	2,373½	2,466½	90	359
Total	19,856¼	19,800¾	22,088	784	1,842

THIRTY-SECOND DISTRICT.

Counties.	David C. White.	John S. Nicholson.	Joseph A. Horn.	James M. Large.
Cass	2,663	3,149	3,679½	3,677
Menard	2,448	2,438½	3,005	3,085½
Mason	3,624½	2,926	3,494	3,507
Logan	5,124	5,125½	5,134½	5,003
Total	13,859½	13,639	15,313	15,272½

THIRTY-THIRD DISTRICT.

Counties.	William Payne.	Edwin W. Houghton.	William McEniry ...	Thomas H. Ellis.	Daniel L. Keleher.
Rock Island	10,921½	10,901½	13,188	880	211½
Henry	9,064½	9,120½	8,290	369½	505
Total	19,986	20,022	21,478	1,249½	716½

THIRTY-FOURTH DISTRICT.

Counties.	Frederick L. Sharpe.	John B. Joy.	John D. Huffman.	Frank L. Hall.	Robert T. Hicks.	James Rough.
Pike	4,709	4,651	6,811	6,872	273	2,001½
Scott	1,740	1,746½	1,909½	1,807½	52	957
Morgan	6,340½	6,655½	6,119½	6,093	178	240½
Total	12,789½	13,053	14,930	14,862½	503	3,199

THIRTY-FIFTH DISTRICT.

Counties.	Frank A. Murdock.	James O. Anderson.	James R. Barnett.	Marvin McKim.	John Harpman.
Knox	11,455	11,410	8,699½	347	1,509½
Henderson..............	2,649½	2,648	3,389	138	49
Warren	5,089½	5,089½	7,390½	261	355
Mercer	4,677½	4,659½	6,412½	127½	271
Total	23,871½	23,807	25,891½	873½	2,184½

THIRTY-SIXTH DISTRICT.

Counties.	George B. Metcalf.	William V. Rhodes.	William T. Conlee.	Howard C. Bliss.
Greene	5,956	5,775	5,728	313½
Macoupin	14,767	8,024½	7,843½	723
Total	20,723	13,799½	13,571½	1,036½

THIRTY-SEVENTH DISTRICT.

Counties.	George W. Montgomery.	Elmer A. Perry.	Charles F. Kincheloe.	John C. Rickey.	John T. Simmons.	Charles L. Koch.	Eugene McPhail.
Adams	11,704	11,434	14,639	10,014	564	502	......
Brown	2,569½	2,938½	1,218½	2,147½	38	14	5
Total	14,273½	14,372½	15,857½	12,161½	602	516	5

THIRTY-EIGHTH DISTRICT.

Counties.	Thomas P. Morey.	Abram Brokaw.	Obed E. Lovett.	Joseph P. Price.	David K. Barber.
Montgomery	5,318½	5,424	6,000½	6,260½	333
Bond	3,173	2,850½	2,356½	2,351½	131
Fayette	4,215½	4,180½	5,403½	5,340	210
Total	12,707	12,455	13,760½	13,952	674

THIRTY-NINTH DISTRICT.

Counties.	Charles E. Selby.	Abner G. Murray.	Edward L. Merritt.	George L. Harnsberger.	C. E. Vigal.	S. P. V. Arnold.
Sangamon	13,247½	13,273½	12,679	12,912½	618	22

FORTIETH DISTRICT.

Counties.	Stroder M. Long.	Caleb R. Torrence.	Joseph P. Barricklow.	Isaac B. Craig.	Julius F. Christman.					
Douglas	4,213½	3,826	3,221½	3,047	95					
Coles	6,743½	6,732½	5,732	5,891	140½					
Shelby	4,218½	5,045	6,270½	6,334	1,138½					
Total	15,175½	15,603½	15,224	15,272	1,374					

FORTY-FIRST DISTRICT.

Counties.	Oliver T. Atchison.	Vincent E. Foy.	James E. Sharrock.	William G. Cochran.	Henry C. White.					
Macon	7,063½	7,008½	9,320	9,335	275½					
Christian	6,286½	6,656	5,995	5,696½	905½					
Moultrie	3,292½	2,698	2,394	2,669	325½					
Total	16,642½	16,362½	17,709	17,700½	1,506½					

FORTY-SECOND DISTRICT.

Counties.	Thomas B. Needles.	Morris J. O'Harnett.	John A. Barnes.	Hugh V. Murray.						
Clay	3,198½	3,075	3,320	3,378½						
Marion	4,370½	4,340½	5,691	5,725						
Clinton	2,765	2,856	3,665½	3,919						
Washington	3,840	3,255½	2,979	2,978						
Total	14,174	13,527	15,655½	16,030½						

FORTY-THIRD DISTRICT.

Counties.	Fenton W. Booth.	Barney L. Hussman.	Eb. Stewart.	Hamlin Rippetoe.	Thomas Radcliff.	William Dewero.
Edgar	11,411	5,284½	5,284½	165	600	....
Clark	8,636	4,020	4,018	111½	1,369½	....
Cumberland	5,521	2,696	2,823½	65	807½	3
Effingham	5,493½	4,314	4,289	142	264½	....
Total	31,061½	16,314½	16,415	483½	3,040½	3

FORTY-FOURTH DISTRICT.

Counties.	Samuel A. Williams.	David T. Warford.	B. S. Organ.	Nathan D. Bryant.
Wabash	2,058	1,913½	2,637	2,592
Edwards	2,372	2,366	1,276	1,268
White	4,082	4,078	5,086	5,131
Gallatin	2,199½	2,203	3,091½	3,100½
Hardin	1,160	1,183½	1,348½	1,350½
Total	11,871½	11,744	13,439	13,442

FORTY-FIFTH DISTRICT.

Counties.	Jesse P. Jones.	William H. Lathrop.	Duane Gaines.	William Hart.	Perry A. Lambird.
Jasper	2,668½	2,987½	3,649½	3,540	965½
Crawford	3,207½	3,284½	3,397½	3,399½	191
Richland	2,351½	2,613½	2,836	2,814½	574½
Lawrence	3,033	2,657	2,726	2,708½	74½
Total	11,260½	11,542½	12,609	12,462½	1,805½

FORTY-SIXTH DISTRICT.

Counties.	Oberton R. Mallory.	Wallace B. Flanagan.	Daniel R. Webb.	F. G. Blood.
Franklin	3,139	3,019½	3,291½	3,308½
Jefferson	3,921	3,934½	5,339	5,345½
Wayne	4,319½	4,407	4,606½	4,640
Hamilton	2,225½	3,141½	3,561½	3,558½
Total	13,605	14,502½	16,798½	16,852½

FORTY-SEVENTH DISTRICT.

Counties.	John A. Sheppard.	Robert B. English.	Jett A. Kirby.	Charles L. Wood.	E. C. Giberson.
Madison	9,468½	9,459½	11,142	11,134	
Jersey	3,593	3,473	2,378	2,335	1½
Calhoun	1,688	1,764	1,098	1,292½	
Total	14,749½	14,696½	14,618	14,761½	1½

FORTY-EIGHTH DISTRICT.

Counties.	Robert C. Brown.	Harry B. Ward.	Joseph W. Drury.	Robert H. Allen.
Monroe	2,151½	2,170½	2,489	2,465½
Randolph	4,793½	4,412	4,533	4,570½
Perry	3,508½	3,650	3,538½	3,540½
Jackson	5,824½	5,826	5,381	5,388
Total	16,278	16,058½	15,941½	15,964½

FORTY-NINTH DISTRICT.

Counties.	John E. Thomas.	Lewis Perrottet.	Jule C. Jarvis.	George F. Wombacher	John Owens
St. Clair	14,069	12,513½	12,239	12,000	830½

FIFTIETH DISTRICT.

Counties.	William D. Dewoody.	Elbert H. Dickon.	William H. Warder.	William Q. McGee.
Williamson	4,544½	4,517	3,864	3,838½
Union	2,632½	2,876½	4,468½	4,469½
Alexander	4,087	4,144½	2,684	2,805
Total	11,264	11,538	11,016½	11,113

FIFTY-FIRST DISTRICT.

Counties.	Joseph W. King.	William H. Parrish.	Fletcher A. Trousdale.
Pulaski	3,105½	3,109	3,411
Massac	3,054½	3,054½	2,383
Johnson	3,039	3,033	3,169
Pope	2,793½	2,786	2,450
Saline	3,904½	3,896½	6,483
Total	15,897	15,879	17,896

ABSTRACT OF VOTES

Given at a special election held on the third day of November, A. D. 1896, in the counties comprising the Forty-seventh Senatorial District of the State of Illinois, for senator to the XL General Assembly, to fill the vacancy caused by the death of the Hon. Charles A. Herb:

Counties.	Louis F. Lumaghi.	David R. Sparks.
Madison	6,263	7,468
Jersey	2,371	1,641
Calhoun	1,156	793
Total	9,790	9,902

GENERAL INDEX.

Legislative Directory '97; Appendix A: Statistical History, Governors, Boards, Commissions, Portraits of State Buildings; Appendix B: Official Vote for '96.

CAPITOLS, STATE INSTITUTION BUILDINGS, ETC.

All in Appendix A.

The Hall of the House and Senate Chamber interiors will be found in the Legislative Directory.

ENGRAVINGS IN THIS BOOK BY BLOMGREN, CHICAGO; PHOTOS BY BURLEIGH AND ANDERSON, SPRINGFIELD.

www.ingramcontent.com/pod-product-compliance
Lightning Source LLC
Chambersburg PA
CBHW020317240426
43673CB00039B/832

* 9 7 8 3 7 4 4 6 9 2 4 4 1 *